Mr. & Mrs. David E. Johnson
Colonia Juarez
Chih. , Mexico

# Commentary
## on the
# Book of Mormon

# Commentary on the Book of Mormon

## By

### GEORGE REYNOLDS

A Member of the First Council of the Seventy, 1890-1909

*Author of*

A COMPLETE CONCORDANCE OF THE BOOK OF MORMON
A DICTIONARY OF THE BOOK OF MORMON
THE MYTH OF THE MANUSCRIPT FOUND
THE STORY OF THE BOOK OF MORMON

## and

### JANNE M. SJODAHL

Editor and Associate-Editor of *Deseret News*, 1890-1913

*Author of*

AN INTRODUCTION TO THE STUDY OF THE BOOK OF MORMON
THE REIGN OF ANTI-CHRIST

*Co-Author of*

DOCTRINE AND COVENANTS COMMENTARY

### VOLUME I—THE SMALL PLATES OF NEPHI

*Edited and arranged by* PHILIP C. REYNOLDS
Salt Lake City, Utah
1955

DESERET NEWS PRESS

# PREFACE

To add to the knowledge concerning the Book of Mormon that has accumulated since it was first introduced and declared to be, like the Bible, the inspired and revealed "Word of God," the authors of these volumes, after unending study, herewith present their findings.

After reading and re-reading and reading again, its sacred pages, they turned to writing about them. Each time they did, new and more beautiful concepts presented themselves to their always active minds. But *it* was only a beginning. There was much to learn. Their thoughts were, undoubtedly, like those of Sir Isaac Newton, who, when near the end of a life crowded with the truths he had helped unfold said, "I am but as a child playing on the sands by the sea. I have found a few pretty pebbles, *washed by the spray,* but beyond me, unfathomed and unexplored, lies the great ocean of whose depths and mysteries I know nothing."

The thoughts expressed in this *Commentary* are given only as "an introduction to the study of the Book of Mormon" and are intended merely as a guide to its perusal. As the reader progresses in the consideration of this divine and glorious revelation, new vistas and fresh horizons are sure to enter his scope and soon he will find himself worshiping with a strange but delightsome people who testify of their Israelitic ancestry, of the Law of Moses, of Isaiah, and of the Messiah, Jesus Chirst, who brought and placed before them his Gospel as he previously had to the Jews.

Every book has, or should have an objective. It may be to impart knowledge of religion, of history, of pedigree, or whatnot; it may be to edify by meditation and essays; or it may be to instruct with poetry and by parable. The Book of Mormon, indeed, includes all these objectives and more, but its principal purpose, throughout, is similar to that of the Bible — to bring God and man together through the one great Mediator, Jesus Christ.

To quote some words spoken by the first and the last writers in the sacred record and make them a living part of this preface, we refer the reader to II Nephi 4:15 and Moroni 10:27.

The Prophet Nephi said,

And upon these [the Small Plates] I write the things of my soul, and many of the scriptures which are engraven upon the plates of brass. For my soul delighteth in the scriptures, and my heart pondereth them, and writeth them for the learning and the profit of my children.

A millennium later Moroni wrote,

And I exhort you to remember these things; for the time speedily cometh that ye shall know that I lie not, for ye shall see me at the bar of God; and the Lord God will say unto you: Did I not declare my words unto you, which were written by this man, like as one crying from the dead, yea, even as one speaking out of the dust.

In the ages that came and went between their times, many holy prophets of the Nephites added and recorded their prophecies and their wisdom upon the plates from which the Book of Mormon was translated. We offer the following comments, which is *our* understanding of and *our* testimony to the great truths they unfold.

To the late Elders George Reynolds and Janne M. Sjodahl, who spent much of their time and abilities ferreting out the accumulated evidence herewith presented, we owe the credit for the comments and biographical notes.

In humility, we offer them, praying our Heavenly Father, by his Spirit, to render them most for our good and greatest for his glory. With full purpose of heart, we dedicate them to all who desire to know the "mind and will of God."

P. C. R.

# FOREWORD

For many centuries prior to the ruthless invasion by the Spanish Conquerors, Cortes and Pizarro, in the Sixteenth Century, there flourished at various times in both North and South America, several distinct civilizations, the very remains of which are today the wonder and admiration of the world.

The land of America, known to geographers and early voyagers as the New World, is constantly yielding abundant evidence of ancient cultural enlightenment.

Almost daily, announcement is made of the discovery of objects of ancient art or utility; a temple, a pyramid, a sculptured vase or a finely-woven woolen garment; handiwork of the goldsmith's craft; evidence of the surgeon's skill; objects of reverence and adoration; great cities and highways; altogether prophesing of the past, of a beauty and a culture, of such as, perhaps, we at this time have very little idea.

From the Isthmus of Panama both to the north and also to the south, throughout the uplands and valleys of the great Cordillera, are the remains of great nations and peoples, whose influence and dominion extended to the far-flung shores of both continents and even to the islands of the sea. Of them it has been said that the old and perhaps contemporary nations of the Near-East, i.e. Egypt, Chaldea, and Babylonia, were insignificant when compared with the vast empires which extended over the Americas.

At the time the great armies of the Roman Empire had brought, what was thought to be, all the people of the earth into submission to their imperial master, a civilization in America reached a peak of excellence unprecedented by any people of antiquity. This period is known in history as the "Golden Age of the Maya." Here the fine arts, architecture, astronomy, government, and religion reached a perfection and an originality which make them to America, what the classic creations of Greece and Rome are to Europe.

The question is very often asked "Who were these strange people, and from whence did they come?" Very little is known of the history of these civilizations. Their rise and progress, their millions of people present an enigma which science has been unable to explain. Who they were and where at was the land of their genesis we do not know; we cannot tell. Science has formulated very little knowledge to assist us in this dilemma. Indeed, it is one of the most perplexing sections in the history of the world. It is a mystery. Like the rising sun, they suddenly appeared upon the horizon of civilization; almost as suddenly they departed. One sentence may give the experience of a thousand years — "They came; they prospered, and, at the very meridian of their glory, they vanished. It was as the event of a day."

Many attempts have been made to answer the foregoing riddle. Most of them have been merely guesses, though, some of course, have bases of fact. LePlongeon, the eminent student of the Maya, in a desperate effort to explain the many relationships between the New and Old World cultures, declares that Egypt, itself, was peopled by wanderers from "Mayapan." Some declare that Asia-Minor or Egypt is the probable answer. Lord Kingsborough energetically defends the idea of Israelitic ancestry. Others suggest the fabled *Atlantis* of Plato.

There are reasons to support each and perhaps all of these conclusions. Few will deny that much of the learning of ancient America resembles Egyptian and Semitic cultures. Few will deny that its myths and legends are replete with form and ritual, the existence of which had been thought to be only of the "kingdom of Pharaoh and the lands of the prophets." The definite influence of Asiatic forebears may be seen in the numerous writings and the physical characteristics of the wretched remnant which still survives.

Which of all these theories is correct, science has not yet established.

A new group has advanced the theory of American origin, principally on a purely political basis of loyalty to a geographic mass. This group insists that it is not patriotic to attribute to any foreign land the "home-land" of this culture. This unscientific theory appeals to a few.

The real truth is that these civilizations are not indigenous in America. For their beginnings we must seek elsewhere. The several stages of the stone age, followed by the copper or bronze age, upon which archeologists build the pre-historic story of Europe and Asia are missing here. No parallel periods are found here. The beginnings are more abrupt. The earliest evidences of enlightenment are among the civilizations showing the highest development. The first expressions of culture reveal the borrowed customs and learning and experience of ages.

The chronology of man in America, is a sequence of generations of highly social beings. Their legends evince a rich and priestly heritage. They built great cities, improved roads connected remote parts of their empire; government was largely by consent of those governed; their laws were based on their religious conceptions; their ideas of God, with whom they believed they dwelt in close relationship, influenced their art and gave shape and form to many of their conclusions.

Yet, whence they came and when, no man knows. However, nothing is being left undone, no stone untouched or unturned, which like the *Rosetta Stone* of the Nile, might unlock the vast stores of knowledge and information hidden behind the inscrutable faces of innumerable and incomprehensible glyphs.

This is a work for science to perform. Each season new evidences are being added, yet, students of archeology, like players of chess, are as yet stalemated—they have the kings and the pawns but they cannot move. They have the records, but they cannot read them. Like workmen on a building they constantly increase its size and dimensions, but they know little of the mystery surrounding each stone with which they build.

Science lingers, here, in the lap of abundance; its methods are so slow; its findings of fact are so belated, that impatiently, many have come to regard the problem as the great American Riddle, a puzzle, the parts of which, it is hoped, may eventually be put together and the story of American antiquity be reconstructed.

## Book of Mormon Geography

The Book of Mormon is not a geography. The writers of the sacred record gave little space and did not make much of an effort to describe, in so many words, the physical features of the regions, wherein took place, the events they recorded. It is not a record of borders and boundary lines, of rivers and highways, of areas of population and industry but as will be repeatedly shown, the Book of Mormon is a book of doctrine.

In the Book of Alma many find what they consider to be the key to Book of Mormon geography. (Alma 22:27-34) That passage was written to furnish important information concerning the missionary travels of the elders and priests and also to indicate the vast territory over which the Nephites and the Lamanites had spread, as far as knowledge of countries, rivers, and cities can be conveyed without drawings or maps. But the attempts that are constantly being made to identify the cities and lands of the Book of Mormon with the old and obscure ruins found in Mexico and points further south, will end in failure; this is the opinion of many who have made it an object of search and research. Certainly, such attempts will produce little good. It is folly to associate oneself with any peculiar notion and say of some particular ruin, "This is the City of Zarahelma" or, "There is the Land of Bountiful." Such ventures in thought are merely guesses, and such speculation leads to confusion.

In this connection a statement made in 1890 by George Q. Cannon will be sufficient; Elder Cannon said,

There is a tendency, strongly manifested at the present time among some of the brethren, to study the geography of the Book of Mormon. We have heard of numerous lectures, illustrated by suggestive maps, being delivered on this subject during the present winter, generally under the auspices of the Improvement Societies and Sunday Schools. We are greatly pleased to notice the increasing interest taken by the Saints in this holy book. It contains the fullness of the Gospel of Christ, and those who prayerfully study its sacred pages can be made wise unto salvation. It also unravels many mysteries connected with the history of the ancient world, more particularly of this Western Continent, mysteries which no other book explains. But valuable as is the Book of Mormon both in doctrine and history, yet it is possible to put this sacred volume to uses for which it was never intended, uses which are detrimental rather than advantageous to the cause of truth, and consequently to the work of the Lord.

We have been led to these thoughts from the fact that the brethren who lecture on the lands of the Nephites or the geography of the Book of Mormon are not united in their conclusions. No two of them, so far as we have learned, are agreed on all points, and in many cases the variations amount to . . . thousands of miles. These differences of views lead to discussion, contention, and perplexity; and we believe more confusion is caused by these divergences than good is done by the truths elicited.

How is it that there is such a variety of ideas on this subject? Simply because the Book of Mormon is not a geographical primer. It was not written to teach geographical truths. What is told us of the situation of the various lands or cities of the ancient Jaredites, Nephites, and Lamanites is usually simply an incidental remark connected with the doctrinal or historical portions of the work; and almost invariably only extends to a statement of the relative position of some land or city to contiguous or surrounding places, and nowhere gives us the exact situation or boundaries so that it can be definitely located without fear of error.

It must be remembered that geography as a science, like chronology and other branches of education, was not understood or taught after the manner or by the methods of the moderns. It could not be amongst those peoples who were not acquainted with the size and form of the earth, as was the case with most of the nations of antiquity, though not with the Nephites. Their seers and prophets appear to have received divine light on this subject.

The First Presidency have often been asked to prepare some suggestive map illustrative of Nephite geography, but have never consented to do so. Nor are we acquainted with any of the Twelve Apostles who would undertake such a task. The reason is, that without further information they are not prepared even to suggest. The word of the Lord or the translation of other ancient records is required to clear up many points now so obscure that, as we have said, no two original investigators agree with regard to them. When, as in the case, one student places a certain city at the Isthmus of Panama, a second in Venezuela, and a third in Guiana or northern Brazil, it is obvious that suggestive maps prepared by these brethren would confuse instead of enlighten; and they cannot be thus far apart in this one important point without relative positions being also widely separate.

For these reasons we have strong objections to the introduction of maps and their circulation among our people which profess to give the location of the Nephite cities and settlements. As we have said, they have a tendency to mislead, instead of enlighten, and they give rise to discussions which will lead to division of sentiment and be very unprofitable. We see no necessity for maps of this character, because, at least, much would be left to the imagination of those who prepare them; and we hope that there will be no attempt made to introduce them or give them general circulation. Of course, there can be no harm result from the study of the geography of this continent at the time it was settled by the Nephites, drawing all the information possible from the record which has been translated for our benefit But beyond this we do not think it necessary, at the present time, to go, because it is plain to be seen, we think, that evils may result therefrom.*

From this we may feel sure that if, ever, the time comes, or that it is expedient for the Saints to have this information, it will come to them through the regularly established source, the prophet, seer, and revelator, the Presiding High Priest of the Church and no one else.

\* \* \*

One cannot get a testimony of the Book of Mormon by studying its geography!

There is one way, only, one may attain that end.

That end is once more pointed to by one who was a Lutheran minister and who first heard the Gospel plan preached in Stockholm, Sweden. He came to Utah and joined the Church of Jesus Christ of Latter-day Saints; among its members he became a prominent writer and editor. He compiled, with the late Hyrum M. Smith of the Council of the Twelve Apostles, the Doctrine and Covenants *Commentary* and who, with George Reynolds, is the author of the comments and biographical notes which follow in this volume.

In an impersonal letter, this same convert, many years ago, wrote,

Dear Reader:

In the Book of Mormon is the Gospel in its fulness. You belong to a church. You probably have a confession of faith. If there is the least shadow of doubt in your mind as to the truth of what you believe, the origin of your ordinances, or the divine approbation of your worship, you would do well if you compare your faith and practices with the teachings of our Lord, as recorded in this Sacred Record. If they do not correspond with these teachings, they are not his and remember the promise is given:—

"And when ye shall receive these things, I would exhort you that ye would ask God, the Eternal Father, in the name of Christ, if these things are not true; and if ye shall ask with a sincere heart, with real intent, having faith in Christ, he will manifest the truth of it unto you, by the power of the Holy Ghost."

(Moroni 10:4)

(Signed)—Janne M. Sjodahl.

## "Plates of Gold"—Statement by Padre Gay

In a small, but immensely interesting brochure, published by the Museum of the American Indian, Heye Foundation, New York City, 1920, entitled, *"Goldsmith's Art in Ancient Mexico,"* by Marshall H. Saville and one of a Series coming under the heading, *"Indian Notes*

*An editorial published in *The Juvenile Instructor*, Jan. 1, 1890. President Cannon was then a member of the First Presidency.

*and Monographs,"* a statement made by Padre Gay in his *"Historia de Oaxaca"* (1521) is included in his work by the above mentioned author.

Father Gay was one of those self-sacrificing and unselfish Catholic Priests who sought to carry Christianity to the native races of America in the early part of the Sixteenth Century. He was among the first to explore the vast extent of territory over which the Spaniards later became the complete rulers.

Father Gay is the author of *"Historia de Oaxaca;"* on the Sixty-second page of Volume I, is the statement referred to here. We reproduce, herewith, word for word, Page 175 of the first mentioned treatise, *"Goldsmith's Art in Ancient Mexico,"* in which the statement is used.

The declaration made by Padre Gay is remarkable in that one could barely prepare, in so few words, a description of similar plates, more consistent with what the Latter-day Saints know of the Plates from which the Book of Mormon was translated.

OAXACA JEWELS          175

found at the same time, were formerly in possession of Don Francisco Leon of Oaxaca.

An interesting specimen in the Sologuren collection is a gold disc, 13 cm. 1mm. in diameter, recently found in a grave at San Pablo Huitzo. It is a breast ornament, with faint incised lines around the edge, representing the hieroglyph of the sun, *tonatiuh.* In the center is the hieroglyph *ollin,* the seventeenth of the twenty day-signs of the Nahuan calendar, and means motion or movement. Hence the meaning of the combined glyphs would be "the movement of the sun," referring to the four seasons of the year. Padre Gay mentions that the Mixtecan Indians *"sold to some European antiquarians, very thin plates of gold, evidently worked with the hammer, which their ancestors had been able to preserve, and on which were engraved ancient hieroglyphs."**

Mrs. William Stuart, during her residence in San Geronimo, in the Tehuantepec region of Oaxaca, was much interested in archeology and accumulated a small collec-

AND MONOGRAPHS

*Italics are this Editor's.

## Plates

The word *plates* (not *breastplates* or *headplates*) appears 141 times in the Book of Mormon. Two of these can be found in the translation of the inspired *Preface*. There were the "brass *plates*" or the "*plates* of brass" which are sometimes called the "*plates* of Laban" and on which were engraved a genealogy of Lehi, the "Book of Moses," many of the prophecies of the holy prophets, and a history of the Jews down to the reign of King Zedekiah.

There were the "*plates* of Nephi," which included a set of "Large *Plates*" and a set of smaller ones. The "large" *plates,* Nephi tells us,

"Contain an account of the reign of the kings and the wars and contentions of my people."

Upon the smaller ones he engraved a record of the,

"Ministry of my people."

A part of the smaller plates was known as the "Plates of Jacob." Nephi says of the "Small Plates,"

"Wherefore the Lord hath commanded me to make these plates for a wise purpose in him, which purpose I know not."

There were, also, the twenty-four gold plates found by the followers of King Limhi, who were sent out to find Zarahemla. From the place where they started, the Land of Lehi-Nephi, they wandered far to the north and there came upon the remains of a great people, among whose relics were these "*plates* of gold." King Mosiah was a seer and translated them with the help of the *Interpreters* and found thereon a story of a people who left the Tower of Babel at the time of the "confusion of tongues." That story follows them from the time mentioned to the time they destroyed each other in civil warfare about nineteen centuries later. A condensed account of their history, taken from those plates by Moroni, is found in the Book of Ether.

It is to be remembered that Mormon made, or caused to be made, a set of plates upon which he recorded the abridgment of the Large Plates as he made it. After he "had made an abridgment from the plates of Nephi, down to the reign of this king Benjamin, of whom Amaleki spake," he found, upon examination of the many plates in his possession, the Small Plates. He was so struck by the things he read on them — prophecies concerning the coming of Christ and many of the words of Nephi—that he was constrained, by the Spirit of the Lord that was in him, to put them with his own work. For, he says,

"And now, I do not know all things; but the Lord knoweth all things that are to come; wherefore, he worketh in me to do according to his will."

The wisdom and foreknowledge of the Lord was manifest in the early part of his latter-day work. Martin Harris, than whom, perhaps, there was none other more ready and willing to help the cause than he, in his anxiety to prove to his friends and his relatives that Joseph Smith had the plates, the possession of which he claimed and the work was of God, prevailed upon the Prophet to let him show the first 116 pages of the manuscript to them. These pages, were lost. Were it not for the wisdom of him, "who knoweth all things," an insurmountable difficulty may have arisen. The pages lost covered the same period of time as was covered by the Small Plates. In other words, a double record was had of these times. Can we conceive of anything more wise or more "foreknowing" than this?

It is this set of "Small Plates" that this volume will hereafter consider.

## In Conclusion

One day the disciples of Jesus were about to despair. They had been thrown out of the synagogue, and some of them had been arrested and scourged and placed in irons. The Savior, seeing their distress, comforted them and said,

"If the world hate you, ye know it hated me before it hated you."

And,

"If they have persecuted me, they will also persecute you."

When we remember those who first presented the Book of Mormon and advocated its acceptance as the revealed word of God, we can easily recall the scene presented here. We, also, think of that most beautiful portion of sacred literature, the Sermon on the Mount:

"And blessed are all they who are persecuted for my name's sake, for theirs is the kingdom of heaven.

"And blessed are ye when men shall revile you and persecute, and shall say all manner of evil against you falsely, for my sake;

"For ye shall have great joy and be exceeding glad, for great shall be your reward in heaven; for so persecuted they the prophets who were before you."

(III Nephi 12:10-12)

The ancient Midianite Prophet Balaam was taken to the top of a mountain by Balak, who was king of the Moabites. Below where they stood were the "numbers" of Israel; their thousands and tens of thousands, their flocks and herds and all they possessed. Balak feared the Children of Israel because they had destroyed his neighbors, the Amorites and besides, he had heard much of the strength and fierceness of their armies. The king had sent messengers to the prophet saying,

"Behold, there is a people come out from Egypt: behold, they cover the face of the earth, and they abide over against me:

"Come now therefore, I pray thee, curse me this people; for they are too mighty for me: . . ." (Numbers 22:5-6)

Balak offered Balaam rich reward and high honor if he would comply. Three times the king importuned the prophet, who, at length, instead of cursing them, blessed them and said something like this,

"How can I curse that which the Lord is pleased to bless?"

Indeed, the Book of Mormon has been cursed by a multitude of Balaams and Balaks in every part of this earth, but the complete answer is the same as the conclusion of Balaam's,

"How can I curse that which the Lord is pleased to bless?"

The preaching of the Book of Mormon brought together many who believed and who took upon themselves the hated name, *Mormon*. Others became more bitter and malignant. To ridicule the Book of Mormon was a daily pastime and to deny and deride *Mormonism* was a piety. Any excuse and every pretext was ample in the attempt to exterminate the "Mormons." Their enemies kindled fires, they thought would consume "Mormonism." With their own hands, they dug pits into which they hoped "Mormonism" would fall. But when they saw their fires illumine the paths of those who sought Eternal Life, when they saw that the more they dug the more they tilled the soil, wherein, had been cast, the seeds of everlasting truth, the more bitter became their hate and the more unlimited their spite. They left no stone untouched or unturned that they might throw at the bulwarks and the battlements of the Restored Church of Christ.

To destroy the Book of Mormon, they argued amongst themselves, would be to get rid of the very idea of *"Mormonism."* To this end they lost no time or left a thing undone. Soon they reached that point where, it has been said, "The last effort of human wickedness cannot pass,"—they sought the life of God's Prophet. As it is written of the Apostle Paul, so it may be said of the Prophet Joseph Smith: "They hired assassins to put him to death; he was brought before their courts and accused of false crimes by witnesses suborned for that purpose. He was arrested, tried, beaten, scourged, imprisoned" and at length, "He died as a martyr." He sealed his testimony with his own blood.

"Now," they said, "Mormonism will surely die." They thought that the heart beats in the Prophet's breast were the great "heart-throbs" of Mormonism. But, in this they were mistaken. Mormonism is immortal. The Book of Mormon is immortal, because it has

"God for its author, Omnipotence for its shield, and Eternity for its glorious life."

Clothed in the beautiful garment of priesthood and sustained by its power, members of the Church of Jesus Christ of Latter-day Saints will proclaim the Gospel's truths and shall not cease until the last enemy of truth and righteousness is subdued. They will not rest from their labors or slacken their zeal until the blessings of the Gospel of Jesus Christ are spread among all the inhabitants of this earth, and not until his *will*, done in heaven, shall be done upon earth.

There is no power that can destroy the virtue and vitality of these books, the Holy Bible and the Book of Mormon. There is no darkness that can extinguish their light. But far beyond that point in men's lives, where all human understanding ceases and all worldly glory fades, the Bible and the Book of Mormon will go on to help the helpless and, indeed, help all those who have no other helper but the Lord.

Thanks be to God, this book is written. The Bible now has a companion. Both testify of the other, and together, they will live on forever, the inspired and revealed "Word of God," the Mind and Will of our Father, the Advice and Counsel of our Savior and our King.

Twenty centuries ago, the Risen Redeemer said to his Disciples among the Nephites,

"No weapon that is formed against you shall prosper; and every tongue that shall rise against thee in judgment, thou shalt condemn."

(III Nephi 22:17)

May I, in humility, apply these words to the Bible and the Book of Mormon.

Now, in conclusion, may I read, in the spirit of prayer, the last verse of the Sixty-fifth Section of the Book of Doctrine and Covenants,

"Wherefore, may the kingdom of God go forth, that the kingdom of heaven may come, that thou, O God, mayest be glorified in heaven so on earth, that thine enemies may be subdued; for thine is the honor, power and glory, for ever and ever. Amen."

—P. C. R.

## ACKNOWLEDGEMENTS

To many persons I express appreciation for their encouragement — with particular mention to Harold Lundstrom for editorial assistance and to Thomas S. Monson for printing and publication advice and help.

—P. C. R.

THE

## BOOK OF MORMON

An Account Written by

### THE HAND OF MORMON

UPON PLATES

TAKEN FROM THE PLATES OF NEPHI

Wherefore, it is an abridgment of the record of the people of Nephi, and also of the Lamanites—Written to the Lamanites, who are a remnant of the house of Israel; and also to Jew and Gentile— Written by way of commandment, and also by the spirit of prophecy and of revelation—Written and sealed up, and hid up unto the Lord, that they might not be destroyed—To come forth by the gift and power of God unto the interpretation thereof — Sealed by the hand of Moroni, and hid up unto the Lord, to come forth in due time by way of the Gentile—The interpretation thereof by the gift of God.

An abridgment taken from the Book of Ether also, which is a record of the people of Jared, who were scattered at the time the Lord confounded the language of the people, when they were building a tower to get to heaven—Which is to show unto the remnant of the House of Israel what great things the Lord hath done for their fathers; and that they may know the covenants of the Lord, that they are not cast off forever—And also to the convincing of the Jew and Gentile that JESUS is the CHRIST, the ETERNAL GOD, manifesting himself unto all nations—And now, if there are faults they are the mistakes of men; wherefore, condemn not the things of God, that ye may be found spotless at the judgment-seat of Christ.

TRANSLATED BY JOSEPH SMITH, JUN.

---

### THE TITLE PAGE OF THE BOOK OF MORMON

We may consider this to be what we now call a Preface. It was written by Moroni, who was the last to engrave his experiences and admonitions upon the sacred plates whereon his father, Mormon, had made an abridgment of the Large Plates of Nephi,

It appeared upon the last plate thereof and was translated by the Prophet Joseph Smith. On page 71 of Volume 1, History of the Church, is a statement by the Prophet concerning this Title Page or Preface, we read,

"I wish to mention here that the title page of the *Book of Mormon* is a literal translation, taken from the last leaf on the left hand side of the collection or book of plates, which contained the record which has been translated, the language of the whole running the same as all Hebrew writing in general; and that said title page is not by any means a modern composition, either of mine or any other man who has lived or does live in this generation.

Joseph Smith, Jun."

# THE FIRST BOOK OF NEPHI

## HIS REIGN AND MINISTRY

*An account of Lehi and his wife Sariah, and his four sons, being called, (beginning at the eldest) Laman, Lemuel, Sam, and Nephi. The Lord warns Lehi to depart out of the land of Jerusalem, because he prophesieth unto the people concerning their iniquity and they seek to destroy his life. He taketh three days' journey into the wilderness with his family. Nephi taketh his brethren and returneth to the land of Jerusalem after the record of the Jews. The account of their sufferings. They take the daughters of Ishmael to wife. They take their families and depart into the wilderness. Their sufferings and afflictions in the wilderness. The course of their travels. They come to the large waters. Nephi's brethren rebel against him. He confoundeth them, and buildeth a ship. They call the place Bountiful. They cross the large waters into the promised land, &c. This is according to the account of Nephi; or in other words, I, Nephi, wrote this record.*

## CHAPTER 1

*Nephi's Statement Concerning Himself, 1—Language and Authenticity of the Record, 2-3—Calling of Lehi to the Prophetic Office and His Vision, 4-15—Nephi's Writing an Abridgment of His Father's Record, 16-17—Lehi Delivers His Message to the People, 18-19—Is Persecuted, 20.*

### 1. *Nephi's statement concerning himself.*

1. I, Nephi, having been born of goodly parents, therefore I was taught somewhat in all the learning of my father; and having seen many afflictions in the course of may days, nevertheless, having been highly favored of the Lord in all my days; yea, having had a great knowledge of the goodness and the mysteries of God, therefore I make a record of my proceedings in my days.

---

VERSE 1. Nephi, the youngest of four sons of Lehi and Sariah, the others being Laman, Lemuel, and Sam; all born in Palestine. "Nephi" means "prophet," one who speaks for God. That name, the Hebrew "nebi," the Egyptian "Kneph" and "Noub," and the Uto-Astecan "Nahua," seem to be closely related. The word is still found in "Napo," the name of one of the affluents of the Amazon River; also, in such Indian names as "Nepas," "Nahuapos" and "Napotas." There is a city and a river in Colombia, S. A., named "Nechi." This is almost the same as Nephi. If you compare "Nechi" with the Egyptian "Necho" (Pharaoh) which is the same as

Nephi, it is evident they are alike. The vowels mean little or nothing. When we consider that the original inhabitants of America were a people who were versed "in the learning of the Jews and the language of the Egyptians" it is not surprising to find the name "Nephi," or that name in a different form, in an amazing number of geographic instances.

Elder George Reynolds traces this celebrated name to an Egyptian root. He says, "Its roots are Egyptian; meaning, good, excellent, benevolent. . . . One of the names given to the god (Osiris), expressive of his attributes, was Nephi, or Dnephi . . . and the chief city dedicated to him was called N-ph, translated into Hebrew as Noph, in which form it appears in Hosea, Isaiah and Jeremiah, its modern English name is Memphis."

This agrees with a statement credited to Eusebius, to the effect that the Egyptians called the Creator *Kneph. Noub* or *Nouv,* according to Champollion, was the *Knouphis* of Strabo, and the same as the *Kneph* of Plutarch and Eusebius. *Naba,* according to Gesenius, in Niphil, means "To speak under divine influence," as a prophet, (Naba, in Kal, means "to boil up," as a fountain; hence to pour forth words, as those who speak under divine influence.)

It is necessary to note that all forms of Nephi, such as Dnephi, Kneph, Noub, Nouv, Knouphis, Nebo, Naba, Nechi, and Necho, with many others, are variants of the same name.

How expressive is the name Nephi, when we understand its meaning. How well it corresponds with the character and mission of this great son of Lehi!

*Goodly parents.* Nephi, in introducing himself, calls attention to the noble character of his parents. He recognizes the advantages that may come to a child through father and mother, both by means of heredity and superior home environments. He knew the value of parental teaching when coupled with a life worthy of emulation. It is characteristically Jewish to honor the parents in this manner. Jewish autobiographers, in beginning their life story, almost always, pay tribute to their lineage. In doing this, Nephi continued a custom that had become a mark of all faithful writers among the Jews. We may consider the fact that Nephi did this, to be a strong bit of evidence supporting the claims made by the Book of Mormon.

Josephus starts the story of his life by stating that he was a descendant of a long line of priests and nobles. Of his father, Matthias, he states that he "was considerable for his extraction but more for his justice and authority in Jerusalem." He then says that he was raised by his brother, Matthias, and was instructed in the sciences. He was, he adds, so precocious, as a child of fourteen years of age that "I was praised by all men in regard to the good affection I had to learning; and priests and the noblest citizens vouchsafed to ask my opinion of things that concerned our laws and our ordinances." Josephus, like Nephi, notes the piety of his ancestors and the knowledge he had received in his childhood.

The author of "Ecclesiasticus" says of his grandfather, a man named Jesus, that he "was a man of great diligence and wisdom among the Hebrews," and the author of "The History of Susanna" says of the heroine that "her parents were righteous and taught their daughter according to the law of Moses."

*The learning of my father.* Hebrew learning, also called, "the learning of the Jews," (v. 2), consisted, at this time, chiefly in a knowledge of the Law (Torah), now known as the Pentateuch; the Prophets down to and including Isaiah and some books now no longer extant, some of which are mentioned in the Scriptures, as for instance, the Book of Nathan, (2 Chron. 2:29), the Book of Enoch (Jude 14), the Book of Memorial (Ex. 17:14), the Book of Jasher (Josh. 10:13), and the Book of Records (Ez. 4:15).

In the Law the Jews were taught the divine origin of the heavens and the earth, through acts of creation; the beginning of the human race, the "fall" and its consequences and the promise of redemption. They were taught the lesson of sin and destruction in the flood, but also the renewal of the covenants of God and the re-peopling of the earth by the descendants of Noah. They were further shown the beginning of the Hebrew people, their history and development, by which they became, notwithstanding human frailties and stubbornness, the foundation of the Messianic kingdom of God on earth. They were taught a moral law that surpasses anything ever conceived by man, and a civil law and ritualistic service, exactly suited to their conditions and calculated to educate them in righteousness and holiness.

This "learning of the Jews" was meant to be applied to every day affairs. It was to be their very life, and not only something to discuss. The Jew had to become familiar with the words of the Law. He was told: "Bind them for a sign upon thy hand"; "they shall be as frontlets between thy eyes," "thou shalt write them upon the posts of thy house" and on thy gates (Deut. 6:8-9); "ye shall teach them diligently to thy children, speaking of them when thou sittest in thy house and when thou walkest by the way, when thou liest down and when thou risest up (Deut. 11:19). Joshua was commanded to meditate on the Law day and night (Josh. 1:8-9), and one of the duties of the king was to have a copy of the Law made and to read it every day (Deut. 17:19).

The following quotations illustrate the importance which the Jews attach to the reading of the Law:

"Rabbi Chananya, the son of Teradyon, said, 'That if two sit together and interchange no words of Torah, they are a meeting of scorners, concerning whom it is said, The godly man sitteth not in the seat of the scorners (Ps. 1:1); but if two sit together and interchange words of Torah, the divine Presence abides between them. . . . R. Simeon said, If three have eaten at a table and have spoken no words there of Torah, it is as if they had eaten of sacrifices to dead idols. . . . R. Chalafta, the son of Dosa, of the village of Chananya, said, When ten persons sit together and occupy themselves with the Torah, the Sheschina (the glory of the Lord) abides among them."

Other sacred books were called "Prophets." Some of these were historical, as the Books of Samuel, the Kings, the Chronicles, etc. Others were didactic and prophetic. The Psalms, the Proverbs, the Song of Solomon and Ecclesiastes were known as "the Writings."

Besides the written word, the Jews had a venerable tradition by means of which the historical background of the records was preserved, and opinions, rulings, judgments, judicial decisions, customs and important incidents were transmitted by word of mouth from one generation to another generation. The Levites, who had charge of the sacred buildings and the objects consecrated for the divine services, also were the educators of the people.

Sometime after the destruction of the temple by Titus and the dispersion of the people, the tradition was committed to writing. This literary composition is known as the "Mishna," meaning "repetition." Later, notes or commentaries were written on this text. These explanations are known as the "Gemara," or "complement." The Mishna and Gemara together constitute the Talmud ("instruction"), of which there are two versions: one composed at Jerusalem (about 390 A.D.), and one at Babylon (about 420 A.D.). The Talmud is by far the most important literary work of the adherents of the Mosiac faith, next after the inspired writings of the Old Testament.

As an illustration of the peculiar, deductive explanations of the Scriptures in the Talmud, the following may be referred to. In the Law (Deut. 27:5) it is for-

## 2. *Language and authenticity of the record.*

2. Yea, I make a record in the language of my father, which consists of the learning of the Jews and the language of the Egyptians.

3. And I know that the record which I make is true; and I make it with mine own hand; and I make it according to my knowledge.

---

bidden to use iron tools in building an altar to the Lord. Why? Rabbi Johannan explains it thus. He says that iron signifies war and strife. The altar is atonement and peace. Therefore the two of them must not come together. "Thus we are taught the value of peace in the home, peace between city and city, nation and nation." (Prof. Graetz, History of the Jews, Vol. 2, p. 329)

The following sentiments are illustrative of the philosophy of the Talmud:

"Love peace and pursue it at any cost." . . . "Remember it is better to be persecuted than to persecute." . . . "Be not prone to anger." . . . "He who giveth alms in secret is greater than Moses himself." . . . "It is better to utter a short prayer with devotion than a long one without fervor." . . . "He who having but one piece of bread in his basket, and says, What shall I eat tomorrow? is a man of little faith." (Farrar, The Life of Christ, p. 680.)

Curiously enough, some modern critics have belittled the Talmud, very much in the same spirit as that by certain readers of the Book of Mormon. They have found it "uncouth," "unintelligible," "tedious," and "unprofitable." But that only proves that the literary taste and fashions of the world have changed since the composition of these works. It proves nothing against the truths that may be contained in the Talmud, and nothing against the revelations in the Book of Mormon. Truth is truth, no matter how presented, and gold is gold, whether offered on a silver tray or wrapped in rags.

Nephi could, of course, not be familiar with the Talmud, as known in modern times, but the essence of that volume is much older than the books containing it. It gives us an idea of "the learning of the Jews."

*Favored of the Lord.* To Nephi the most valued favor was his knowledge of the goodness and the mysteries of God. Are we, perhaps, prone to look upon afflictions as evidence of divine disapproval and upon temporal advantages, such as wealth, health, pleasures, power, etc., as "favors"? Well, they may be blessings, but they are not the most valuable possessions of man. Knowledge is worth more than riches; the goodness of God is often manifest in the midst of affliction. We note that Nephi says that it was his knowledge of the goodness and the mysteries of God that inspired him to write. No book is of any real value that is not founded on knowledge and experience.

*The Mysteries of God.* These are truths known only by divine revelation. The preaching of the gospel to the Gentiles is a "mystery" (Romans 16:25). The doctrines of the incarnation, the birth, the death, the resurrection of Christ and, we may add, the salvation for the dead, are mysteries.

VERSE 2. The language of my father was, undoubtedly, Hebrew, since Lehi had "dwelt in Jerusalem all his days." (v. 4)

*Learning of the Jews.* See notes under verse 1.

*Language of the Egyptians.* Lehi had mastered the difficult Egyptian language, in addition to the learning of the Jews. This is noted as one of his great accomplish-

## 3. *Calling of Lehi to the prophetic office, and his vision.*

4. For it came to pass in the commencement of the first year of the reign of Zedekiah, king of Judah, (my father, Lehi, having dwelt at Jerusalem in all his days); and in that same year there came many prophets, prophesying unto the people that they must repent, or the great city of Jerusalem must be destroyed.

5. Wherefore it came to pass that my father, Lehi, as he went forth prayed unto the Lord, yea, even with all his heart, in behalf of his people.

6. And it came to pass as he prayed unto the Lord, there came a pillar of fire and dwelt upon a rock before him; and he saw and heard much; and because of the things which he saw and heard

ments. Of Moses, too, it was said that he was learned in all the wisdom of the Egyptians (Acts 7:22), which, of course, included the language of and their writing.

The Egyptians had no less than three different kinds of characters. The oldest was the *hieroglyphs*. They had about a thousand of these, and some of these were pictures of the celestial bodies, human figures, limbs, animals, such as quadrupeds, birds, fishes, insects, reptiles, houses, furniture, tools, etc., all symbolic of some object, some quality or some action. The *Hieratic* characters were less elaborate, but still too numerous for practical purposes. The *Demotic* characters were the simplest. Clement of Alexandria is quoted as having said: "Those who are educated among the Egyptians learn first that mode of writing which is called epistolographic (demotic or common); secondly Hieratic, which the sacred scribers use, and lastly, the Hieroglyphic."

Those who had mastered the difficulties of the language of Egypt, spoken and written, could study the entire civilization of the country. And, be it remembered, the Egyptians excelled in architecture, in sculpture, painting, navigation, metallurgy. They knew how to work in gold, silver, copper, iron and lead. They had musical instruments and were skilled in the art of weaving and dyeing. They had a law code for which they claimed divine origin. They were great agriculturists and prosperous merchants. As for religion, they believed in One God—the only living Substance, "the only existence in heaven and on earth that is not begotten." They, further, believed in two divine Beings, whose unity was expressed in the name, "UA-EN-UA," which is said to mean, "One of One." But they had, further, so great a number of gods that someone said it was easier to find a god in Egypt than a man. The principal gods were eight in number. Amun was the chief of these, and Maut or Mut was the mother of all. They had a priesthood and a number of consecrated women who assisted in the temple service. The presiding high priest was called *Sam.* They also had a system of "mysteries" into which only a few were initiated. They had altars and sacrifices, and above all, an elaborate ritual for the dead. One of their great myths was the "story" as we should call it, of Osiris and Isis, in which the resurrection of the body and the appearance of man before the judgment seat of the gods, as undertsood in Egypt, are set forth.

VERSE 3. *The record is true.* It is not a romance; it is not fiction. It is founded on "knowledge."

VERSE 4. *The first year of the reign of Zedekiah.* That is the time in which the great story of Nephi begins. Zedekiah reigned between 597 and 586 B.C., and

he did quake and tremble exceedingly.

7. And it came to pass that he returned to his own house at Jerusalem; and he cast himself upon his bed, being overcome with the Spirit and the things which he had seen.

8. And being thus overcome with the Spirit, he was carried away in a vision, even that he saw the heavens open, and he

according to 2 Chronicles 36:11, he was twenty-one years of age, when Nebuchadnezzar, who had extended the Babylonian Empire to the coast of the Mediterranean, appointed him king over Judah. It was a time of political turmoil all over the world. From the very beginning of his reign, some of the priests and princes of Judah urged Zedekiah to revolt and strike for liberty from the Babylonian rule. The Egyptians, who had been beaten back from Asia-Minor, since their crushing defeat at Carchemish (600 B.C.) also urged Zedekiah to break his oath of allegiance to the Babylonians. Ambassadors from Edom, Moab, Ammon, Tyre and Sidon promised support, and even exiles in Babylon agitated for revolt.

It was under such circumstances that the Lord sent many prophets to the people, who warned them of impending disaster, unless they would repent.

One of these prophets was Jeremiah. He told the people that the Lord had given all the surrounding countries to Nebuchadnezzar, "the king of Babylon, my servant," (Jer. 27:6) and to the exiles in Babylon he wrote a special letter, imploring them to be loyal to the king. He promised them that if they would build and plant and live in peace, they would be permitted to return home in 70 years. (Jer. 29:4-10)

Another great prophet, according to the Book of Mormon, was Lehi. His special message is recorded in verse 13.

The Lord sent these messengers because he had "compassion on his people and on his dwelling place: But they mocked the messengers of God, and despised his words, and misused his prophets, until the wrath of the Lord arose against his people, till there was no remedy." (Chron. 36:15, 16)

But all warnings were in vain. Zedekiah revolted. Then, in 587 B.C., Nebuchadnezzar came and besieged Jerusalem. Too late did the Egyptians attempt to rescue the city. Zedekiah was captured, as he fled toward Jericho. His sons, who fell into the hands of the Babylonians, were slain. He, himself, after having been blinded, was carried in chains to Babylon. Nebuchadnezzar also took the treasures of the temple and the palace and carried them to his own capital, and thus the words of the prophets of the Lord came true, notwithstanding the efforts of the politicians.

VERSE 8. *Lehi's calling and vision.* During the first year of the reign of Zedekiah, Lehi was prompted to pray for his people. While thus engaged, a pillar of fire, resting on a rock, appeared before him. While gazing upon this wonder, he heard and saw many things, undoubtedly referring to the history of the people which made him tremble exceedingly. Returning to the house exhausted, he "cast himself upon his bed" (v. 7). It was then he saw God sitting upon his throne, surrounded with angels and praising their God.

*Numberless concourses of angels.* This expression reminds us, perhaps, of Daniel who saw "the Ancient of Days" on his throne: "Thousand thousands ministered to him, and ten thousand times ten thousands stood before him." All ready to carry out his commandments. Daniel says, "the judgment was set and the books were opened." Or, as we should say, the court was in session. Judgment was about to

thought he saw God sitting upon his throne, surrounded with numberless concourses of angels in the attitude of singing and praising their God.

9. And it came to pass that he saw one descending out of the midst of heaven, and he beheld that his luster was above that of the sun at noon-day.

10. And he also saw twelve others following him, and their brightness did exceed that of the stars in the firmament.

11. And they came down and went forth upon the face of the earth; and the first came and stood before my father, and gave unto him a book, and bade him that he should read.

12. And it came to pass that as he read, he was filled with the Spirit of the Lord.

13. And he read, saying: Wo, wo, unto Jerusalem, for I have seen thine abominations! Yea, and many things did my father read concerning Jerusalem—that it should be destroyed, and the inhabitants thereof; many should perish by the sword, and many should be carried away captive into Babylon.

14. And it came to pass that when my father had read and seen many great and marvelous things, he did exclaim many things unto the Lord; such as: Great and marvelous are thy works, O Lord God Almighty! Thy throne is high in the heavens, and thy power, and goodness, and mercy are over all the inhabitants of the earth; and, because thou art merciful, thou wilt not suffer those who come unto thee that they shall perish!

15. And after this manner was the language of my father in the praising of his God; for his soul did rejoice, and his whole heart was filled, because of the things which he had seen, yea, which the Lord had shown unto him.

be pronounced upon the "four beasts," that is, the Babylonian, the Medo-Persian, the Macedonian and the Roman Empires.

The vision of Lehi was analogous to this. But the impending judgment in his vision was upon Judah and Jerusalem, and not upon pagan empires.

VERSE 9. *One descending out of the midst of heaven.* In the vision of Daniel, "One like the Son of man" — or rather *a* son of man — "came with the clouds of heaven."

VERSE 11. *Gave him a book.* This contained the decision of the court. It was the judgment of that great court.

VERSE 15. *He did exclaim many things.* Lehi, after having read the book, exclaimed, "Great and marvelous are thy works, O Lord God Almighty!" He realized the power of God. But also his justice, goodness and mercy. And therefore his heart was filled with joy, notwithstanding his sympathy with the people. In the vision it became clear to him, as it would be to all who can see "the end from the beginning" that the goodness and mercy of God are best served by his justice. And therefore his heart was filled with joy. (See 2 Samuel 24:14 and Rev. 19:1-3)

#### 4. *Nephi makes an abridgment of his father's record.*

16. And now I, Nephi, do not make a full account of the things which my father hath written, for he hath written many things which he saw in visions and in dreams; and he also hath written many things which he prophesied and spake unto his children, of which I shall not make a full account.

17. But I shall make an account of my proceedings, in my days. Behold, I make an abridgment of the record of my father, upon plates which I have made with mine own hands; wherefore, after I have abridged the record of my father then will I make an account of mine own life.

#### 5. *Lehi delivers his message to the people.*

18. Therefore, I would that ye should know, that after the Lord had shown so many marvelous things unto my father, Lehi, yea, concerning the destruction of Jerusalem, behold he went forth among the people, and began to prophesy and to declare unto them concerning the things which he had both seen and heard.

19. And it came to pass that the Jews did mock him because of the things which he testified of them; for he truly testified of their wickedness and their abominations; and he testified that the things which he saw and heard, and also the things which he read in the book, manifested plainly of the coming of a Messiah, and also the redemption of the world.

#### 6. *Is Persecuted.*

20. And when the Jews heard these things they were angry with him; yea, even as with the prophets of old, whom they had cast

---

VERSE 16. *I, Nephi, do not make a full account.* Lehi, as Jeremiah and other phophets, kept a record of his visions, dreams and prophecies, his public discourses and his talks to his children; Nephi does not intend or propose to copy his record in full. He gives part of it in an abridged form, as an introduction to his own story. 1 Nephi 1:18 to the end of chapter 8 seems to be a synopsis of the record of Lehi. His own record would then begin with chapter 9.

VERSE 17. *Which I have made with mine own hands.* Not only the writing, but also the plates. The childen of Lehi were well educated and skilful laborers.

VERSE 19. *The coming of a Messiah.* The message of Lehi included a promise of the coming of the Redeemer of the world. Redemption means deliverance from guilt, from sin, from death and from all evil. (See Eph. 1:7; Col. 1:14; 1 Pet. 1:18; Rom. 8:23; Eph. 1:14; Eph. 4:30; 1 Cor. 1:30; Titus 2:14)

VERSE 20. Here the very mission of the Book of Mormon is stated. The apostate rulers of the people planned the death of Lehi, because of his faithfulness. The Book of Mormon shows that God is mighty "even unto the power of deliverance."

out, and destroyed, and slain; and they also sought his life, that they might take it away. But behold, I, Nephi, will show unto you that the tender mercies of the Lord are over all those whom he hath chosen, because of their faith, to make them mighty even unto the power of deliverance.

---

*Concourses of Angels.* The word "angel" means "messenger"; generally a bearer of a message from God. According to Hebrew writers of old, God makes even winds, his angels and flaming fires his ministers. (Psalm 104:4, literal translation.) Some apply the term to Spiritual forces, as when they tell us that the Almighty sent five angels to punish the idolators that worshiped the golden calf at Mt. Sinai, viz., "indignation, anger, fury, ruin, wrath." But generally angels are regarded as persons of a higher order than human beings. In the apocryphal Book of Enoch the "sons of God", in Gen. 6:2, who begat "giants" with "the daughters of men", are called "angels," (Enoch 7:2). They are, however, fallen angels, sworn to do evil. Their number is given as 200. In other ancient writings angels are represented as innumerable. According to some, 600,000 angels descended on Mt. Sinai, when the Law was given.

The angels were supposed to be organized into classes or divisions, called "thrones, dominions, virtues (meaning, strength, efficacy, as the Latin 'virtus'), princedoms, powers," etc. All these, with their commanders, the archangels, were supposed to act as mediators between God and man. Paul, in his letter to the Colossians refutes this conception, which seems to have entered the churches in Asia Minor. He does not deny the existence of angels, or their organization; but he denies that they are the intermediaries between God and man. His argument is: Christ is the very image of God; all things were created by him; whether they be thrones, or dominions, or principalities, or powers, they were created by him and for him; he has preeminence in all things; he is, therefore, the Mediator, and the angels are his servants. (Col. 1:14-20)

In the Book of Enoch the following names and offices of the chief angels are given:

*Uriel* is said to preside over clamor and terror.
*Raphael* presides over the spirits of men.
*Raguel,* inflicts punishment over the world.
*Michael* presides over human virtues and commands the nations.
*Sarakiel* presides over spirits of men that have transgressed.
*Gabriel* presides over Isiat (an unknown region), Paradise and cherubim.
*Phanuel* is the seventh.

Michael and Gabriel, Raphael and Phanuel, it seems, have the special mission of casting spirits (hosts) of Zazeel (Satan) into a fiery, blazing furnace. (Book of Enoch, 35:6)

All this is, of course, fanciful, but we must not forget that in the Prophet Daniel, Michael is said to be "the great prince which standeth for the children of thy people," or that there is a "Prince of the kingdom of Persia," as well as a Michael and a Gabriel. (Daniel 8:16; 9:21; 10:12 and 13)

According to the "Word of God," the angels are ministering spirits (Heb. 1:14; Ps. 68:17; 91:11; Dan. 7:10; Luke 2:13), and in the Doctrine and Covenants, Moroni, John the Baptist, Peter, James and John, as well as Michael and Gabriel and Raphael are called angels, and the important information is added that, "There are no angels who minister to this earth but those who belong or have belonged to it." We are also informed that the angels reside in the presence of God, "where all things for their glory are manifest—past, present and future." Keys are also given whereby angels of light may be distinguished from the messengers of darkness. (See D. and C., Secs. 129 and 130:5-7; 128:20, 21; Sec. 13; Sec. 17:5-16)

---

## ADDITIONAL INFORMATION REGARDING THE PERSONS REFERRED TO IN FIRST NEPHI

Where Italics are used in writing a name it indicates that a biographical sketch of that person is herewith included.

### Lehi

A Hebrew prophet of the tribe of Manasseh, whom the Lord called to warn the Jews of their coming captivity in Babylon. Lehi was a man of considerable means and of good repute among the Jews. He had dwelt in Jerusalem all his life, though, from the influence that the language of the Egyptians appears to have had on him, it is not improbable that he was brought, in some way, in intimate contact with that people. In the first year of the reign of Zedekiah, king of Judah (B. C. 600) the Lord gave Lehi a number of prophetic dreams and visions and in compliance with the admonitions of those manifestations he went forth among the Jews proclaiming the sorrows that would inevitably be theirs if they did not repent and return to the Lord. But the Jews treated Lehi just as they were treating all the rest of the prophets who came to them. They paid no heed to the message he bore. When he reproved them for their wickedness and abominations they grew angry with him and when he talked of the coming of the Messiah and the redemption of the world they mocked him. But he did not cease to labor in their midst until their anger grew so intense that they sought his life and they would have slain him if the Lord had not protected him; for it was not to be that Lehi should fall a victim to their hatred. The Lord had designed him for a greater work—he was to be the father of a multitude of people and to this end God delivered him from the fury of the Jews. When it became impossible for him to remain longer and minister unto them he was instructed to gather up such things as he could carry and take them into the wilderness with his family where the Lord would teach him what more he required at his hands.

When Lehi received the command to depart he immediately set about fulfilling it, and taking with him his family and such goods and food as he could carry, he left the doomed city where he had so long dwelt, leaving behind him his house and property, his gold, his silver, and other precious things all of which he willingly gave up that he might be obedient to the heavenly message.

Lehi's family consisted of his wife, *Sariah*, and his four sons Laman, Lemuel, Sam and Nephi. Lehi had also daughters but whether they were born at this time is not evident from the record. We have no account in the Book of Mormon of the precise road which Lehi and his family took when they left Jerusalem. Undoubtedly they traveled through the wilderness of Judea southward till they reached the eastern arm of the Red Sea. They journeyed along the Arabian shore of that sea for some little distance till they came to a valley through which a small stream flowed. To the river Lehi gave the name of Laman after his eldest son and the valley he called Lemuel. Here they pitched their tents and rested for some time. While tarrying in this valley, Lehi, by divine direction, twice sent his sons to Jerusalem: the first time to obtain certain most precious records, the second, to bring a family to join them in their journey. The head of this family was named Ishmael. In both undertakings the young men were successful and the company was strengthened by the addition of *Zoram* and Ishmael and his family. Soon after, five marriages took place; Zoram married Ishmael's eldest daughter and the four sons of Lehi espoused four younger ones.

While Lehi and his party dwelt in the valley of Lemuel he received many glorious manifestations from the Lord. Like Enoch, John the Revelator and others, he had the world's future history mapped out before him and he not only saw things that related to his own posterity but the scene widened until he appears to have been shown all that would happen to the sons and daughters of mankind to the very last generation. (See I Nephi, chap. 8) Nephi, his son, was favored of the Lord with similar manifestations.

Before long Lehi was directed to resume his journey and a wonderful instrument, prepared by divine condescension which he called "*Liahona*," was given him to guide the wandering feet of the company in their travels.

So particular was the Lord that Lehi's party should not come in contact with the people of Arabia, through which land they passed, that he gave them the command that they should not cook their meat lest the flames or smoke from their fires should draw attention towards them but he promised that he would make their meat sweet to them, that they could eat it with pleasure and satisfaction without it being cooked with fire. Probably it was dried after the manner that the people in this region often dry beef and other meats.

To their next tarrying place, which they reached in four days, they gave the name Shazer. After a short rest, during which time they killed game for food, they again took up their line of march, keeping in the most fertile parts of the wilderness which were near the borders of the Red Sea. Thus they continued journeying for some time, when by direction of the Liahona they changed the course of their travels and moved almost directly east across the Arabian peninsula until they reached the waters on its eastern coast. There they found a very fruitful land which they called *Bountiful* because of the abundance of its natural productions. To the sea which washed its shores they gave the name of Irreantum, which being interpreted, means many waters. If we understand correctly these waters were a portion of the gulf of Oman, or Arabian sea. The journey thus far occupied eight years from the time they left Jerusalem.

When the people of Lehi reached the seashore they rejoiced that their tedious wanderings on land were over. *Nephi*, by divine direction, built a ship to carry them across these great waters. When the vessel was finished the voice of the Lord came to Lehi commanding that he and his people should arise and go aboard the ship. The next day they embarked, every one according to his age, taking with them their provisions, seeds and such other things as it was desirable they should carry across the ocean to their new home, far away on its opposite shores.

During Lehi's travels in the wilderness two sons were born to him whom he named Jacob and Joseph, respectively. The patriarch and his wife were now advancing in years and their peace was much disturbed on the ocean by the cruel conduct of Laman and others towards Nephi. In fact the miseries induced by this conduct nearly resulted in the death of the aged couple.

After many days the vessel with its precious freight reached the shores of this continent, at a place we are told by the Prophet Joseph Smith near where the city of Valparaiso, Chili now stands. Then, with hearts full of rejoicing, they left the vessel that had carried them safely across the wide ocean and went forth upon the land which God had given to them and to their generations after them. And they pitched their tents and began to make a new home. They put the seeds into the earth, which they had brought from Jerusalem. To their great joy these seeds grew exceedingly and they were blessed with abundance. Upon the land they found many beasts of the forest, also cows, asses, horses, goats and other animals that are for the use of man and in the earth they found precious ores of gold, silver and copper. Then they erected an altar and to show their thankfulness to God they offered sacrifices and burnt offerings according to the law of Moses, as was their wont under such circumstances.

The course taken by Lehi and his people has been revealed with some detail. We are told by the Prophet Joseph Smith that Lehi and his company traveled in nearly a southeast direction until they came to the nineteenth degree of north latitude then nearly east to the sea of Arabia, then sailed in a southeast direction and landed on the continent of South America, in Chili, thirty degrees south latitude. This voyage would take them across the Indian and South Pacific Oceans.

Some time, we know not how long, after Lehi's arrival, believing that his end was approaching, he gathered his children together as did his forefathers before him and being inspired by the spirit of prophecy he blessed them, foretelling many things that should occur to them to their latest generations.

Soon after Lehi had uttered these blessings the Lord took him from this earth to dwell with him in eternity.

## SARIAH

The wife of Lehi. She was the mother of six sons and some daughters, the number of the latter is not given in the Book of Mormon. But very little is said of Sariah in the sacred record; she is only mentioned by name five times but we are of the opinion, from the incidental references made to her, that she did not possess very great faith in the mission of her husband, or in the fulfillment of his prophecies; she rather regarded him as a visionary man, who was leading her and her children into trouble and danger by his dreams and revelations and consequently was prone to murmur when any difficulty arose. Four of her sons were grown to manhood when she left Jerusalem (B.C. 600); the other two were born during the little company's eight years' journey in the wilderness. When Sariah's daughters were born is very uncertain; they are not spoken of at the time their parents left Jerusalem; nor is their birth afterwards mentioned. We are told nine or ten years after the company's departure from the Holy City, when it was on the ocean, that Lehi and Sariah were well stricken with years, so we think it is quite possible that Lehi's daughters were born at Jerusalem. This is made more probable when we remember that Nephi, the youngest of four sons, would probably be about twenty years old when his younger brothers were born. It seems reasonable, when we consider the ag of Sariah, that it was during this lapse of twenty years and not later, that his sisters came into the world.

Of Sariah's birth and death we have no record nor to what tribe of Israel she belonged. She lived to reach the promised land and being then aged and worn out by the difficulties and privations of the journey through the Arabian wilderness very probably passed into her grave before her husband.

*Sariah* is obviously Hebrew. It is a name of extreme beauty and force. Its roots are in Sara, a princess, and Jah or Iah, Jehovah, thus meaning a princess of Jehovah; a most fitting name for the mother of a multitude of nations.

## LAMAN

The eldest son of Lehi and Sariah. From the fact that his father dwelt in Jerusalem all his days, it is presumable that Laman was born in that famed city and during the reign of King Josiah. Laman was a stubborn, willful, unbelieving and desperate man. He had no faith in the revelations given to his father and was the leader in all the troubles and contentions in the wilderness, going so far as to propose the murder of his brother Nephi and also of his father. Placing no credence in the prophecies that Jerusalem would be destroyed, he unwillingly left that city and as unwillingly journeyed in the wilderness, every difficulty, every hardship encountered by the party being a fresh pretext for murmurs against God and his father and for renewed assaults upon Nephi. Giving way to this spirit of rebellion and cruelty he grew more hardened as he advanced in years. One of his great complaints was that Nephi had usurped the position properly belonging to his elder brothers as the active leader of the company, though Lehi was recognized as their head as long as he lived and the Lord appears to have so honored him. Laman and Lemuel where not unaware that God had chosen Nephi for the position he occupied; they well knew that the expedition under their guidance would be a failure, as their desires were continually to return to Judea and that, therefore, they would be most unsuitable to carry the purposes of their father to a successful issue. Laman, with his brothers, returned twice to Jerusalem, the first time to obtain the plates of brass from Laban, the second time to bring *Ishmael* and his family.

Soon after their return this second time, Laman married one of the daughters of Ishmael and from this marriage appears to have sprung the royal house of the Lamanites and the leading spirits of that race, until the times when Nephite apostates gained the supremacy in the Lamanite nation and became the kings, rulers, commanders and teachers of that people. For details of the journey in the Arabian wilderness and across the ocean, see *Nephi, Lehi*. Laman lived to witness the death of his father and no sooner had this occurred than he entered into a conspiracy with those who sympathized with him to kill Nephi and take charge of the colony. So embittered was their hate, so determined their purpose, that Nephi's friends deemed it advisable to separate; and this left Laman and his followers to the quiet possession of the first home of the race on the land of promise. Those who remained with Laman were his own family, Lemuel and his family and the sons of Ishmael and their families. If there were any others they are not mentioned. No sooner had the division taken place than the Lamanites began to sink into barbarism. The nomadic habits which they had acquired in their wanderings in the wilderness remained with them and dominated their lives; they were shut out from the presence of God, as they were left without the priesthood when Nephi withdrew; the other party had also the possession of the records, which in itself was regarded as a great grievance by the children of Laman. In the next generation, when those who were familiar with the civilization of the Jews had passed away their descent became more rapid and we read of them as a cruel, degraded, dark-skinned race, living by the chase, feeding on raw meat, idle and ignorant and exceedingly loathsome in their habits.

### LEMUEL

The second son of *Lehi* and *Sariah*, born in Jerusalem about B.C. 620 or 625. He appears in history as the shadow of his elder brother *Laman;* where the latter led he followed but lacked, to some extent, the active, aggressive malignity of Laman's turbulent and vindictive character. In all the rebellions in the Arabian wilderness, in all the murmurings against the providences of the Lord, in all the inhuman assaults upon *Nephi,* Lemuel sided with and sustained Laman and when, after the death of Lehi, the colony divided, Lemuel and his family joined their fortunes to that of his elder brother. Of Lemuel's domestic life we only know that he married a daughter of Ishmael. Of the time and place of his death we are told nothing. The descendants of Lemuel appear to have inherited the characteristics of their progenitor—they took a secondary place in the Lamanite nation and we do not read of one prominent character in Nephite or Lamanite history, who was descended from him.

### SAM

An Israelite of the tribe of Manasseh. He was the third son of *Lehi* and Sariah and was born and brought up in Jerusalem. He accompanied his parents in their exodus from that city (B.C. 600) and was privileged, with them, to reach the promised land. He does not appear to have been a leading spirit but was obedient and faithful and in almost every case sided with the right and followed the teachings of his father and the counsels of his more fervent brother, Nephi. For this he suffered the anger and abuse of his elder brothers who sometimes resorted to personal violence when matters did not go to suit them. When the colony divided, after the death of Lehi, Sam and his family joined their fortunes to those of Nephi. Of Sam's birth and death we have no record. He married one of the daughters of Ishmael while the party was encamped in the valley of Lemuel on the borders of the Red Sea.

*Sam* is a name which some shallow-pated opponents of the Book of Mormon have been disposed to ridicule. But it is pure Egyptian. It was the distinctive name of one of the highest orders of their priesthood. The great Rameses himself belonged to the order of Sam. The fact that Lehi gave to two of his sons such peculiarly Egyptian names shows how great an influence the literature of that country must have had on his life. (Sam and Nephi)

### NEPHI, THE SON OF LEHI

One of the greatest prophets whose presence ever dignified this earth. He was one of the most lovable of men, true as steel, never wavering, full of integrity, faith and zeal. He loved the Lord with all his heart. It is seldom we find a character in the history of this fallen world that was as perfect or as complete as that of Nephi. He was naturally a leader, his faith and courage made him so, while his devout humility gave him strength with heaven. In many respects he resembled Moses, not only was he their law-giver but a practical teacher of his people in the every-day concerns of life. Like Enoch, he was a prophet, seer and revelator, one in whom were deposited the mysteries of God's dealings with future generations; like Abraham, he was a father to his people; like Melchizedek, he was their king and high priest; like Noah, he was a ship-builder by which he delivered his family and like Tubalcain "an instructor of every artificer in brass and iron." In one respect he was like almost all the prophets, for he was derided, mocked, abused and persecuted by those who should have loved him most, those whose welfare he made his constant labor.

Nephi was the son of Lehi, a devout Israelite, of the tribe of Manasseh, who resided in Jerusalem. He was born probably about B.C. 617, was married B.C. 600 in the valley of Lemuel on the borders of the Red Sea. He lived to a ripe old age and had a numerous posterity, though of his immediate sons and daughters the Book of Mormon is entirely silent. It is presumable that one of his sons succeeded him under the title of Nephi II as king of the Nephites.

When, on account of the persecution of the Jews, Lehi was commanded by the Lord to leave Jerusalem, Nephi gladly seconded all his efforts and became a help and a stay to his father during the many troubles and perplexities of the toilsome journey through the Arabian wilderness. Early in that journey they rested for a time in a little valley bordering on the Red Sea, to which Lehi gave the name of Lemuel. Twice while they tarried there the sons of Lehi were commanded to return to Jerusalem. The first time they went to obtain certain records relating to the tribe and God's dealings with his people (See *Zoram*); the second time to invite Ishmael and his family to join them in their migration. When they had accomplished the purpose of their stay in the valley of Lemuel the Lord commanded them to depart and provided a guide for their travels in the shape of a divinely prepared compass which they called *"Liahona."* During the whole of the journey, its peace was marred by the rebellious and violent conduct of Lehi's unbelieving and unrepentant sons, of whom *Laman* was the leader. The first serious outbreak was during the return of Lehi's sons from Jerusalem to the tents of their father with Ishmael and his family. Some of the sons of Ishmael seem to have regretted the step which their father had taken. Possibly, like Laman and Lemuel, they had no faith in the prophecies of the servants of God, who declared that yet a little while and Jerusalem should be destroyed and Laman and Lemuel soon impregnated them with that spirit of malice and discontent that they themselves had already so prominently shown. Two of the daughters of Ishmael also manifested this spirit. As usual, the way in which they showed their feelings was by abusing and ill-treating Nephi. He was the special object of their dislike, by reason of his faithfulness to the commandments of God and because the Lord had shown to him that he should be their ruler.

When the spirit of rebellion first manifested itself, as they journeyed in the wilderness, Nephi rebuked the malcontents in somewhat severe terms. Angry with his words of reproof and entreaty the rebellious portion of the camp took Nephi and bound him with cords, their intention being to leave him in the wilderness to be devoured by the wild beasts. But Nephi in mighty faith prayed to the Lord to deliver him and that the cords that bound him might be burst. His petitions were answered. No sooner had he offered this prayer than the bands were loosed and he stood a free man before his brethren.

Again, in the love of his heart, he pleaded with his tormentors. But they were still filled with the spirit of malice and murder and once more sought to lay violent hands upon him. However, the wife of Ishmael and one of her daughters and also one son begged so earnestly for them to desist that at last their hearts were softened and in sorrow and humility they sought Nephi's forgiveness. This he freely granted without a moment's hesitation, he was but too glad to have them turn from their cruel and wicked course. Still, as they had offended God as well as injured their brother, Nephi exhorted them to pray unto the Lord for forgiveness, which they did.

This outbreak was but the precursor and type of many others that afterwards troubled the little company. Another, which occurred shortly after, originated in so apparently trivial an incident as the breaking of Nephi's bow while in the Arabian desert. It appears that in one of their expeditions for food Nephi, who was their most expert hunter, broke his bow which was made of fine steel. Because of this misfortune they obtained no food and as a result they became very hungry. Being hungry, they grew quarrelsome and rebellious. To such an extent did this spirit prevail in the camp that even Lehi so far forgot himself as to murmur against the providences of God. Nephi, ever faithful, alone refrained from complaining against the Lord, he exhorted his brethren, as was his custom in times of trouble and sorrow, to put away the hardness of their hearts and humble themselves before the Lord and then all would be well with them. His words had their effect. Lehi felt truly chastened and was brought down into the depths of sorrow. When in this condition the word of the Lord came to him and he was instructed to look upon the Liahona and read the things that were written thereon. The reproof that was written on the ball was such as to make Lehi tremble exceedingly but it also brought relief to the party, as the writing instructed them where food could be obtained. Nephi, having made a bow out of wood, went with it and a sling and stones and found the game in the place that the writing had indicated. He slew enough food for all the company. When he returned to the tents of his people, bearing the beasts he had slain, there was great rejoicing in the hearts of all and they humbled themselves before the Lord and gave thanks to him.

When the people of Lehi reached the sea shore they rejoiced greatly that their tedious wanderings were over; for they had not traveled in a straight line from coast to coast but had wandered around and about as the Liahona directed them, which worked according to their faith and faithfulness. Eight years had been spent in taking a journey which, had they been as faithful as they should have been, would only have occupied a few weeks or months.

They pitched their tents by the sea shore and after many days, the voice of the Lord came unto Nephi, saying, "Arise, and get thee into the mountains." As ever, Nephi obeyed the heavenly word. He went up into the mountain and there cried unto the Lord. Then the Lord spoke unto him and commanded him to build a ship after a manner and pattern that he would show him, that the people might be carried across the great waters that lay before them.

Here a difficulty presented itself to the mind of Nephi. He had no tools and how was it possible to build a ship without the proper instruments. So he laid the matter before the Lord who in answer to his prayers told him where he could find ore with which he might make the tools he needed.

Nephi at once proceeded to carry out the commands of the Lord. With the skins of beasts he made a bellows to blow the fire but fire he yet had none, as the Lord had not permitted a fire to be lighted in the wilderness. So he smote two stones together and their first fire was lighted since the company left the borders of the Red Sea. When his forge was made and his fire was lit, Nephi began to melt the ore that he had obtained to make the tools that he needed.

When his brothers saw that Nephi was about to build a ship they began to ridicule him. They would give him no help for they did not believe he was instructed of the Lord. Nephi became very sorrowful because of the hardness of their hearts. When they saw this they were glad and tauntingly told him they knew that he was lacking in judgment and could not accomplish so great a work as to build a ship. Then Nephi recounted many things wherein the power of God had been manifested in the deliverance of their fathers. All of which he impressed upon them as a lesson that when God commanded men should obey without doubt or without question. Said he, "If God had commanded me to do all things, I could do them. If he should command me that I should say to this water, Be thou earth, it would be earth. Then how much less is it to build one ship than to do the marvelous works of which I have told you."

At first when Nephi held out these great truths to his brethren they were angry and threatened to throw him into the sea but the Spirit of God was so powerfully upon him that they dared not touch him lest they wither, even if he but held out his hand towards them they received a shock.

After a time the Lord told him to stretch forth his hand again toward his brethren and that they should not wither; but the power of God should smite them and this he was commanded to do that they might know that the Lord was their God. So Nephi stretched forth his hand as he was commanded and the Lord shook them as he had promised. Then they fell down to worship their younger brother, whom in times past they had so much abused, but he would not permit them. He said, "I am thy brother, even thy younger brother, wherefore worship the Lord thy God and honor thy father and thy mother."

Then the brothers of Nephi worshiped the Lord and showed their repentance by helping Nephi to build the ship; while he, from time to time, received the word of the Lord as to how he should work its timbers; for he did not work after the manner of the ship-builders of that time nor after any mannner that men were accustomed to. But he built the ship just as the Lord had shown it to him and he often went up into the mount and prayed to the Lord and God showed him many great things.

Now, when the vessel was finished Nephi's brothers saw that it was good and its workmanship exceedingly fine therefore they again humbled themselves before heaven. Then the voice of the Lord came to them and commanded them to go on board which words they willingly obeyed and at once put forth to sea. The vessel was then driven by the winds towards the promised land. After they had been sailing prosperously for a number of days the hearts of Nephi's brothers and of the sons of Ishmael and others grew merry and in their merriment they forgot the Lord. They danced and sang and became very boisterous and rude. This conduct pained Nephi exceedingly. He feared lest God should be angry with them and smite them. Therefore he began to protest with much seriousness against the course they were taking but they grew angry with him and his two elder brothers, Laman and Lemuel, took him and bound him. So furious were they that they treated him with great harshness, binding the cords so tightly around his limbs that they caused him much suffering.

Then the Liahona ceased to work. It had been directing the course of the ship thus far but now that they had rebelled against the Lord it would no longer point the way that they should sail. They were in a dilemma, for not one of them knew which way the ship should be steered. To add to their trouble and perplexity there arose a great and terrible tempest and the ship was driven back upon the waters for three days and though they were afraid that the raging waters would ungulf their little vessel yet so hardened were they that they would not loose Nephi.

On the fourth day matters were still worse. There appeared to be no hope but that they would be swallowed up in the sea. Then, and not till then, did they seem to understand that the judgments of God were upon them and that they must unavoidably perish unless they repented. Then they reluctantly loosened the bands which bound Nephi's wrists and ankles, and let him go free. But his limbs by reason of the way in which he had been bound were swollen and he tells us great was the soreness thereof. Nevertheless, in all his afflictions he never murmured.

During the time that Nephi had been thus bound his father Lehi had begged most earnestly for the release of his son but the rebels had threatened everyone who sought Nephi's release and his parents, who had now grown aged, were brought down to sick beds by reason of their afflictions and came very near to being cast into a watery grave.

When Nephi was freed he took the "Liahona" and it commenced to work as before. He prayed to the Lord after which the winds ceased to blow, the storm passed away and there was a great calm. Then Nephi took charge of the ship and guided it in its course towards the promised land, which, after many days it reached in safety.

Arrived on the land of promise they found it rich in minerals and fruitful. The little colony at once proceeded to sow the seeds they had brought with them and were delighted to find that they fruitified and brought forth abundantly and all might have been peace and happiness in their midst had it not been for the murderous jealousy of Laman and his associates. After a time, Lehi called his posterity and others together and blessed them. Many and glorious were the promises made by the patriarch to Nephi. Soon after this Lehi passed away to his eternal reward.

No sooner was Lehi dead than the hatred that rankled in the hearts of Laman and those who sympathized with him seemed to have become intensified. It became evident that the two peoples could not live together in peace. They had nothing in common except that they belonged to the same family. Laman's vindictiveness grew so cruel that Nephi's life was in danger and as the easiest way out of the difficulty Nephi was instructed of the Lord to take those who would listen to his teachings and obey the commandments of God into some other part of the land. Therefore he gathered together those people who would hearken to him and taking that portion of the property that belonged to them, as also the sacred records, the sword of Laban, the Liahona and other treasures they departed into the wilderness. Those who listened to Nephi and accompanied him on this journey were, besides his own family, his brothers Sam, Jacob and Joseph, his sisters, whose names are not given and Zoram, with their families. There might have been, possibly, some others, as we are led to infer from the statement in the Book of Mormon but who they were we are not told.

The distance which Nephi and his people traveled was not, probably, very great; that is, it is not to be measured by thousands of miles, for we find that in a very few years the Lamanites had found out their place of retreat and were harassing and making war upon them.

The Nephites desired that the land they now possessed should be called the land of Nephi and this was the name by which it was always afterward known. The people of Nephi made yet another request. It was that Nephi should be their king. This desire did not altogether please him but for the safety of his people he consented. The kingly power in his hands partook much of the nature of fatherhood. His people were few in numbers and he looked after their individual interests, guided them in their undertakings, directed them in their labors and when he found that there was danger of an attack from the embittered adherents of Laman, he took the sword of Laban and using is as a pattern, fashioned other swords for their defense. Being thus prepared for the attacks of their enemies the Nephites repulsed them every time they came to battle.

Nephi also taught his people to be industrious. They were a lonely people, cut off from communication with all the rest of the world, without excitements and with very few amusements that are common to most peoples. He knew that nothing would be so dangerous to their spiritual welfare, as well as to their health, as to permit them to spend their days in idleness. He, therefore, taught them many kinds of work, the women to take the wool of the sheep and the hair of the llamas and make clothes thereof; while upon the men devolved the labor of building a temple. Holding the Holy Priesthood himself he consecrated his brothers Jacob and Joseph to be priests also.

Shortly after the arrival of Lehi and his little party on this continent Nephi received a commandment from the Lord to make certain plates of ore on which to engrave the doings of his people. And a few years later Nephi received further instructions wherein he was commanded to make other plates upon which also were to be engraven the history of the Nephite people. By them both these plates were called the plates of Nephi but they were not used for identically the same purpose. Upon one set of plates was inscribed the religious history of the people, upon the other was given in greater detail the history of their wars, contentions, development and other secular matters.

Some years later, how long we are not told, Nephi anointed another man to be king over his people and then, having grown old, he died. So greatly was he beloved by his subjects that the people called the next king, Nephi the second, the next, Nephi the third and so on. He had been their prophet, priest and king; father, friend and guide; protector, teacher and leader; next to God, their all in all.

### Laban

A rich, unscrupulous and powerful Israelite of the tribe of Joseph though a dweller in Jerusalem (B.C. 600). While Lehi and his little company were resting in the valley of Lemuel that patriarch was commanded of the Lord to send his sons back to Jerusalem to obtain certain records that were in the possession of Laban. The records, which were engraven on plates of brass, being intimately associated with Lehi's ancestors, were highly necessary for the welfare of his descendants when they established themselves in a new home, far from communication with any other people.

When the elder sons of Lehi were informed of the Lord's wishes they entered many objections to returning to Jerusalem. They claimed to be afraid of Laban, who was a man of considerable influence, having much wealth and many servants at his command. It was not until Nephi had pleaded with them that they would consent to go. Though young, he had learned an exceedingly valuable lesson, that the Lord does not require his children to do impossible things but that when he gives them a command he opens up the way for them to accomplish his requirements. Nephi felt at this time that if the Lord desired that they should have the records, then in the possession of Laban, he would control circumstances in such a way that they could obtain them.

The young men accordingly returned to Jerusalem. When they reached the holy city it was decided that Laman, being the eldest, should first go to Laban and endeavor to obtain the records. Laman had no faith in his mission and consequently was unsuccessful. He was much abused by Laban for asking for the records and returned to his brothers feeling very down-hearted. The young men then decided that they would endeavor to purchase the records from Laban, so they went to their father's house and gathered up some of the valuables that they had left therein when they deserted their home for the journey into the wilderness. Taking these precious things to Laban they offered them in exchange for the plates. He, seeing how great was the value of the property offered him, desired to obtain it without giving up the records in return. He, therefore, with the aid of his servants, drove the young men from his house and sent his retainers to slay them but he did not permit them to carry back the valuables they had brought. These he kept for himself.

After this second unsuccessful effort, Laman and Lemuel were very angry and they went so far as to beat their younger brothers Sam and Nephi with a rod. While doing so an angel appeared before them and upbraided them for their evil conduct. This rebuke for a time quieted them but the effects of this heavenly visitation were short lived.

Laman and Lemuel were now very anxious to return to the wilderness but Nephi would not consent. He was determined that, by the the help of the Lord, he would not go back without the records. Accordingly, he resolved to make the next attempt himself; so when night came he walked towards the city, being followed at some distance by his brothers. They do not appear to have had the courage to enter the gates but stood without the walls, while Nephi entered the city not knowing exactly where he should go or what he should do. He relied wholly on the Spirit of the Lord to guide him. As he approached the house of Laban he perceived a man lying on the ground in a drunken stupor. The Spirit of the Lord directed Nephi to slay Laban, for he was a robber and at heart, a murderer. He had robbed the sons of Lehi of the property they had taken to him in their effort to exchange it for the records and had afterwards sought their lives. But, though fully justified, Nephi shrank from taking the life of a fellow being. Never before had he shed human blood. But the Spirit of the Lord whispered to him that it was better that one man should be slain than that a whole people should perish in ignorance. If Lehi's company and their descendants should go to the new land, which would afterwards be their home, without any account of the dealings of God with their forefathers, the mighty works he had done for their preservation and the laws which he had given that they might please him, they would gradually grow in darkness in all these respects and by and by lose sight of their Creator and become a wicked, degraded and unbelieving people.

Nerved by this monition, Nephi drew Laban's sword from its scabbard and cut off his head. He then quickly disrobed the body and placed the dead man's armor on his own person. Thus attired, he entered the house of Laban, and it being dark, it was not easy to recognize him. Assuming the voice of Laban he called to a servant named Zoram, who had the keys of the treasury, and told him to bring the plates which he needed. Zoram, deceived by the voice and the armor of his master, at once obeyed.

## ZORAM

The servant of *Laban* (B.C. 600), afterwards the friend of Nephi. When Nephi had slain Laban near his house at Jerusalem, he went into the dead man's residence and assuming the voice of Laban, commanded Zoram, who had the keys of the treasury, to bring the records he needed. It being night Zoram was deceived and quickly obeyed. Then Nephi commanded Zoram to follow him with the records to his brethren. This Zoram did supposing that the brethren to whom Nephi alluded were the elders of the Jews.

The name Zoram, is probably from the Hebrew "Zur," a rock,[1] signifying a trustworthy, reliable character. It is perpetuated throughout Book of Mormon history.

Nephi and Zoram took their course to the place where Nephi's brothers had secreted themselves outside the walls of Jerusalem. When the latter saw them coming they were greatly afraid, for they did not recognize their brother, dressed in the armor of Laban. They thought that he had been killed and that these men were coming to slay them also, so they fled before them. Nephi, perceiving the difficulty, called to them in his own voice. While this arrested their flight, on the other hand it alarmed Zoram. He would have returned in terror to Jerusalem and no doubt have spread the alarm if Nephi had not caught hold of him, given him assurances of good will and made a covenant with him that if he would be faithful to Nephi and his brethren he should be a free man like unto them; for it appears that Zoram was a bond-servant, most probably an Israelite who had fallen into debt and as provided by the law of Moses, was serving Laban till that debt was paid by his services. This covenant Zoram faithfully kept. He went down with the sons of Lehi into the wilderness and he and his posterity were numbered with the people of Nephi ever afterward.

In the valley of Lemuel, Zoram married the eldest daughter of Ishmael. When Lehi, previous to his death, blessed his posterity he also extended his blessings to Zoram. Nothing is said of Zoram's children, though some conspicuous men of later Nephite history—*Amalickiah, Ammoron, Tubaloth,* for instance — were his descendants, neither have we any record of his death.

## ISHMAEL

A righteous Israelite of the tribe of Ephraim, who with his family, which was large, lived in Jerusalem, B.C. 600. At this time Ishmael must have been advanced in years for he had five marriageable daughters besides several grown up sons. By the commandment of the Lord, the sons of *Lehi* returned from their encampment

---

[1] "Lo khezuranu Zuram." (Not as our rock is their rock. Deut. 32:31.)

on the borders of the Red Sea to Jerusalem and invited Ishmael and his family to join them in their journey to a promised land. The Lord softened their hearts and they accepted the invitation, left their home and went with the young men into the wilderness; though from the oft-repeated rebellious conduct of some of Ishmael's sons it appears that they never had much faith, if any at all, in the prophetic mission of Lehi or in the woes pronounced upon Jerusalem by the servants of the Most High. Soon after the arrival of the party at the tents of Lehi, the eldest daughter of Ishmael was married to Zoram and four others wedded the sons of Lehi. In the vicissitudes of the toilsome journey in the Arabian desert Ishmael appears to have been faithful to the Lord but when the company reached a place to which was given the name of Nahom, Ishmael died and was there buried. His demise was the cause of much sorrow to his family and was made the pretext, by its rebellious portions, for renewed murmuring and fresh outbreaks.

### Jacob

See biographical sketch after Book of Jacob.

### Joseph

The younger son of Lehi and Sariah, born to them during the difficulties and sorrows of their journey across the Arabian Peninsula (about 595 B.C.). We are told very little of his life or character but he appears to have been an upright man and a faithful servant of the Lord. At the time of his father's death he was still small but was blessed by that patriarch with the rest of the family shortly before Lehi's departure from this earth. Joseph with his elder brother Jacob was ordained, by Nephi, a priest to minister to the Nephites, after the separation of that people from the adherents of Laman. Of his private history or death we are told nothing. Jacob, speaking of himself and Joseph, says: We did magnify our office [of priests] unto the Lord, taking upon us the responsibility, answering the sins of the people upon our own heads, if we did not teach them the word of God with all diligence.

### Joseph

The son of the patriarch Jacob, and the ancestor of the Nephites and Lamanites. Lehi was descended from his son Manasseh and Ishmael from Ephraim. He is referred to with great affection by a number of the Nephite worthies. Lehi quotes (II Nephi, 3) some very important prophecies of Joseph which do not appear in the Bible. The Nephites are frequently called, by their teachers, the seed or house of Joseph.

### Irreantum

The name given by Lehi's colony to an arm of the Indian Ocean on the eastern coast of Arabia. On its shores Nephi and his brethren built the ship that carried them to this continent. It was either the Persian Gulf or Gulf of Oman, the which does not clearly appear from the records. Nephi informs us that the meaning of the word Irreantum is many waters.

## CHAPTER 2

*Lehi departs from Jerusalem and pitches his tents in the Valley of Lemuel,*
*1-10—Laman and Lemuel murmur against their father, 11-15—Nephi and*
*Sam believe, 16-17—Nephi's prayer and the Lord's answer, 18-24.*

### 1. *Lehi departs from Jerusalem and pitches his tents in the Valley of Lemuel.*

1. For behold, it came to pass that the Lord spake unto my father, yea, even in a dream, and said unto him: Blessed art thou Lehi, because of the things which thou hast done; and because thou hast been faithful and declared unto this people the things which I commanded thee, behold, they seek to take away thy life.

2. And it came to pass that the Lord commanded my father, even in a dream, that he should take his family and depart into the wilderness.

3. And it came to pass that he was obedient unto the word

VERSE 1. *In a dream.* What are dreams, and what causes them? These are questions not yet fully answered. But it is certain that divine messages have often been communicated to man by means of dreams. In all probability, the command of God to Abraham to depart from Haran came to him in a dream. (Gen. 12:1) At least, the remarkable vision of which we find an account in Gen. 15, ended in the dream in which the Patriarch saw the oppression of his descendants in Egypt for a period of four generations. (Gen. 15:12-16) The dreams of Abimelech (Gen. 20:1-15), of Joseph (Gen. 37:5-11), of Pharaoh (Gen. 41:1-32) are all well known. It was in a dream that the Lord appeared to Solomon and gave that young king the privilege of asking for a special favor, which the king accepted, by expressing a desire for wisdom and understanding to judge the people. (1 Kings 3:5-12) The dreams of Nebuchadnezzar (Dan. 2:1-28) are important parts of the word of the Lord to all the world. The Prophet Joel promises dreams as one of the manifestations of the Spirit of the Lord: "And it shall come to pass afterward [in the last days, Acts 2:17] that I will pour out my spirit upon all flesh; and your sons and your daughters shall prophesy, your old men shall dream dreams, your young men shall see visions." (Joel 2:28)

It has been demonstrated that a person asleep may receive impressions from extraneous sources, although the reflective or reasoning organs are at rest. The smell of flowers may cause him to dream that he is walking in a garden. Sleeping in a smoky room may create the impression of a conflagration and a hot water bottle at his feet may cause him to dream that he is standing on a volcano. This being the case, we may not deny the power of heavenly messengers to produce certain impressions upon the mind, during sleep, for the purpose of conveying important messages. Only to be thus favored, we must have faith. One who doubts is not in a fit or proper condition to receive a message by that means. We must also have the Holy Spirit to interpret.

There are false, as well as true dreams. Jeremiah says on behalf of the Lord, "I have heard what the prophets said, that prophesy lies in my name, saying, I have dreamed, I have dreamed." (Jer. 23:25) And Zechariah (10:2) utters this

of the Lord, wherefore he did as the Lord commanded him.

4. And it came to pass that he departed into the wilderness. And he left his house, and the land of his inheritance, and his gold, and his silver, and his precious things, and took nothing with him, save it were his family, and provisions, and tents, and departed into the wilderness.

5. And he came down by the borders near the shore of the Red Sea; and he traveled in the wilderness in the borders which are nearer the Red Sea; and he did travel in the wilderness with his family, which consisted of my mother, Sariah, and my elder brothers, who were Laman, Lemuel, and Sam.

6. And it came to pass that when he had traveled three days in the wilderness, he pitched his tent in a valley by the side of a river of water.

---

solemn warning, "For the idols have spoken vanity, and the diviners have seen a lie, and have told false dreams."

*They seek to take away thy life.* Persecutors, because inspired by the archenemy, are always murderous. But it was not the mission of Lehi to seal his testimony with his blood. The Lord had other work for him. He was to break new ground and lay the foundations of the great latter-day work, which the Prophet Joseph Smith, as an instrument in the hand of God, established, preparatory to the coming of the Son of Man, to reign over all the earth in power and glory. For that reason, and not merely to save his life, he was commanded to depart.

VERSE 4. *Into the Wilderness.* Students of the Book of Mormon should note that the Hebrews gave the name of wilderness or desert to places that were suitable for pastures for sheep and cattle even though they were not cultivated. The desert of Judea, south of Jerusalem, which is referred to in this chapter, was the place in which John the Baptist first preached repentance (Matt. 3:1; Luke 1:80), and it was, probably, the wilderness into which Jesus was "led up of the spirit," to be tempted. (Matt. 4:1) At the time of Joshua it had six cities. (Jos. 15:61, 62) It is now, or was a few years ago when the writer (J. M. Sjodahl) was a missionary there for the Latter-day Saints, one of the most dreary and desolate regions of the country.

VERSE 5. *The Borders of the Red Sea.* May have been near the head of the Gulf of Akabah, the eastern arm of the Red Sea, which is separated from the western arm by the Sinai Peninsula, where the children of Israel wandered for forty years. Anciently Akabah was connected with Suez and Cairo by means of a Roman road. During the Mohammedan reign it has always been an important stopping place for pilgrims on their way to Mekka, the holy city of Islam.

*Sariah.* The wife of Lehi. The name is derived from the Babylonian, "Sarratu," which, in the city of Ur, where Abraham lived, was the title of a goddess, the consort of the moon god. In the language of Abraham, "Sarratu" became "Sarai." (Gen. 11:28) Later when the Lord made a covenant with the Patriarch and changed his name from "Abram" to "Abraham," his wife's name was changed from "Sarai" to "Sarah." (Gen. 17:15) The name means "Princess." In the Book of Mormon the form of the name is somewhat different. I venture the suggestion that "Sariah" is an abbreviation of "Sarah-Jah," and that means "Princess of the Lord" (Jehovah).

*Laman.* The oldest son of Lehi. The letter "m" frequently takes the place of "b." "Laman" may, therefore, be regarded as the same as "Laban," which was

7. And it came to pass that he built an altar of stones, and made an offering unto the Lord, and gave thanks unto the Lord our God.

8. And it came to pass that he called the name of the river, Laman, and it emptied into the Red Sea; and the valley was in the borders near the mouth thereof.

9. And when my father saw that the waters of the river emptied into the fountain of the Red Sea, he spake unto Laman, saying: O that thou mightest be like unto this river, continually running into the fountain of all righteousness!

10. And he also spake unto Lemuel: O that thou mightest be like unto this valley, firm and steadfast, and immovable in keeping the commandments of the Lord!

---

the name of the father of Jacob's two wives, Leah and Rachel. The word means, "white."

This name is found in various forms all over America. According to Dr. Brinton the Yameos Indians on the Maranon River are also called, Llameos, Lamas and Lamistas. In the Lama linguistic stock he places the Alabonos, in which we easily recognize "Laban" (A-labon-o). Near Truxillo, in South America, there are the Lamanos or Lamistas, of the Quichua linguistic stock. According to Reclus, quoted by Dr. Cyrus Thomas, there is or was a tribe of Indians of the Ulva stock, near Blewfields River, also called the Lama River, called Lamans. Dr. Brinton mentions the Rama Indians as living on a small island in the Blewfields lagoon. "Lama" and "Rama" are the same word.

The word "laban" in the Indian language means the same as in the Hebrew, "white." Rafinesque says the Lenape "laban-ibi" means "white water." The word "Lumonaki" is interesting. According to the same authority, it means "white land." In "abnaki" the initial "l" seems to have been dropped. Dr. Brinton says that the Algonquins used to refer to their eastern kindred as Abnakis, meaning their "white ancestors." But if we read Labnakis (from Laban-aki) it means the inhabitants of the "white land" or lamanite (white) ancestors. Lumonaki would be the same as the Book of Mormon "land of Lamoni," and, curious enough, also the "Hvitra-mannaland" or "white man's land" of the Icelanders who visited America during the Eleventh Century of our era.

*Lemuel.* The second son of Lehi, probably named after Lemuel mentioned in Prov. 31:1, 4, who is supposed to be Solomon, the king. The name means either "Godward" or "God is bright."

*Sam.* The third son of Lehi. The name is Egyptian. "It was the distinctive name of one of the highest orders of the priesthood. The great Rameses, himself, belonged to the order of Sam." (George Reynolds)

VERSE 7. *An altar of stones.* According to the Mosaic law, an altar was to be built either of earth or of stones not "polluted" by any tools. (Ex. 20:24, 25) This injunction seems to have been necessary in order to save Israel from a tendency to make images, like those of the Egyptians, to worship. Their altars were not to be ornamented with heads of apes or dogs or snakes; they were to be built entirely of stones, as formed by nature, lest the worshiper might get the impression that he offered sacrifices to an image instead of Jehovah. The altar of Lehi was built of stones probably because he anticipated an extended sojourn in the Valley of Lemuel, by the River Laman.

## 2. *Laman and Lemuel murmur.*

11. Now this he spake because of the stiffneckedness of Laman and Lemuel; for behold they did murmur in many things against their father, because he was a visionary man, and had led them out of the land of Jerusalem, to leave the land of their inheritance, and their gold, and their silver, and their precious things, to perish in the wilderness. And this they said he had done because of the foolish imaginations of his heart.

12. And thus Laman and Lemuel, being the eldest, did murmur against their father. And they did murmur because they knew not the dealings of that God who had created them.

13. Neither did they believe that Jerusalem, that great city, could be destroyed according to the words of the prophets. And they were like unto the Jews who were at Jerusalem, who sought to take away the life of my father.

14. And it came to pass that my father did speak unto them in the valley of Lemuel, with power, being filled with the Spirit, until their frames did shake before him. And he did confound them, that they durst not utter against him; wherefore, they did as he commanded them.

15. And my father dwelt in a tent.

## 3. *Nephi and Sam believe.*

16. And it came to pass that I, Nephi, being exceeding young, nevertheless being large in stature, and also having great desires to know of the mysteries of God, wherefore, I did cry unto the Lord; and behold he did visit me, and did soften my heart that I did believe all the words which had been spoken by my father; wherefore, I did not rebel against him like unto my brothers.

---

VERSE 11. *Murmured in many things against their father.* Here begins a tragic story of the rebellion of children against their parents. The future history of Nephites and Lamanites, with its wars and contentions, bloodshed and destruction, is here seen, as it were in the embryo from which it was developed.

Note the character of the rebellious sons. Their stubbornness (they were "stiff-necked" v. 11); their love of money (they regretted the treasure that had been left behind, v. 11); their lack of faith (they were sure they would perish in the wilderness, v. 11); their ignorance (they knew not the dealings of God, v. 12 and they rejected his word through the prophets, v. 13); and finally, their weakness in the presence of the manifestations of the Spirit of the Lord, (v. 14).

VERSE 16. *Nephi.* In Nephi we meet an entirely different character. He was young and strong, and yet possessing that humility which made him hunger and thirst after knowledge. He sought knowledge by means of prayer. And because of the knowledge he received, he also had faith. Where humility, knowledge and faith

17. And I spake unto Sam, making known unto him the things which the Lord had mani-fested unto me by his Holy Spirit. And it came to pass that he believed in my words.

### 4. Nephi's prayer and the Lord's answer.

18. But, behold, Laman and Lemuel would not hearken unto my words; and being grieved because of the hardness of their hearts I cried unto the Lord for them.

19. And it came to pass that the Lord spake unto me, saying: Blessed art thou, Nephi, because of thy faith, for thou hast sought me diligently, with lowliness of heart.

20. And insomuch as ye shall keep my commandments, ye shall prosper, and shall be led to a land of promise; yea, even a land which I have prepared for you; yea, a land which is choice above all other lands.

21. And inasmuch as thy brethren shall rebel against thee, they shall be cut off from the presence of the Lord.

22. And inasmuch as thou shalt keep my commandments, thou shalt be made a ruler and a teacher over thy brethren.

23. For behold, in that day that they shall rebel against me, I will curse them even with a sore curse, and they shall have no power over thy seed except they shall rebel against me also.

24. And if it so be that they rebel against me, they shall be a scourge unto thy seed, to stir them up in the ways of remembrance.

---

dwell, there can be no rebellion, neither against parental authority, nor against God, whom the parents represent in the home.

VERSE 17. *Sam.* Sam also believed, and the two brothers are notable illustrations of obedience to the great commandment, "Honor thy father and thy mother; that thy days may be long upon the land which the Lord thy God giveth thee." (Ex. 20:12)

VERSE 18. *Hardness of heart,* means unyielding, stubborn, "stiffnecked" (v. 11). Those were the weaknesses that caused the failure of Laman and Lemuel. In the kingdom of God, obedience is the condition of success. When Saul tried to justify his disobedience by the magnitude of his sacrifices, Samuel replied, "Hath the Lord as great delight in burnt offerings and sacrifices, as in obeying the voice of the Lord? Behold to obey is better than sacrifice, and to hearken than the fat of rams. For rebellion is as the sin of witchcraft, and stubbornness is as iniquity and idolatry."[1] Stubbornness is contrasted to obedience to the voice of the Lord.

VERSE 20. *Ye shall prosper.* The lesson taught in this verse is that the Lord takes an interest in the affairs of nations as well as individuals, and that national pros-

---

[1]A better translation of these last lines would be: "The sin of necromancy, rebellion and even idolatry and wrongdoing (come from) stubbornness."

perity is the result of loyalty to God, while godlessness certainly brings disasters upon nations.

How strikingly this great truth is illustrated in the history of the American natives!

In North America, in Central and South America we find evidences of great culture—ruins of a civilization long ago forgotten. The Pueblo type with its center in upper Rio Grande Valley, the Aztec type in the stretch of country between the Rio Grande and Lake Nicaragua, the Maya type in Yucatan, the Nahua type in Mexico, the Panama and Colombia types in those countries, the Inca type in Peru and the Bolivia type further south—all these, with their achievements in architecture, sculpture, agriculture, spinning, weaving, their skill in forming stone implements and pottery, their rudimentary writing, their ingenious calendars, and their social and religious institutions, testify to prosperity and progression. But degeneration followed in the footsteps of idolatry, sensuality and autocracy and wars and bloodshed completed the destruction.

VERSES 18-24 of this chapter are a very important part of the the Book of Mormon. They are a record of the divine appointment of Nephi to the position of leadership: "Thou shalt be made a ruler and a teacher over thy brethren. (v. 22)

There comes a time in the experience of every servant of the Lord when he, often after an intense spiritual struggle, becomes conscious of his special mission in mortality and his relationship to God. The crisis is sometimes described as a "new birth." It is a complete and actual change in the conditions and circumstances of the person involved. It is as if one were passing from death to life. It is an unconditional surrender to God. Such an experience was that of Jacob at Bethel, where, after the dream of the ladder, he dedicated himself to the service of Jehovah: "The Lord shall be my God . . . and I will surely give the tenth unto thee." (Gen. 28:10-22) It was the experience of the boy Samuel, that caused him to exclaim before the Lord: "Speak, for thy servant heareth." (Sam. 3:2-14) See also the vision of Isaiah, who said: "Here am I, send me" (Is. 6:1-8); and Jeremiah, when he was installed in his office by divine authority (Jer. 1:4-10); and Saul, who, trembling and astonished, in perfect submission, asked: "Lord, what wilt thou have me to do?" (Acts 9:1-8) The boy Joseph Smith passed through a similar crisis in the "sacred grove," where he had the glorious theophany of the Father and the Son. From that day he was another boy, with a new outlook upon the present and the future. It was such experience the boy Nephi had. And he returned to his father's tent with new responsibilities.

## CHAPTER 3

*The sons of Lehi return to Jerusalem for certain records in the possession of Laban, 1-12—Laban refuses to deliver them, 13-14—Nephi exhorts his brethren, 15-21—Laban robs the brothers of their property, 22-27—Another conflict between Laman and Nephi and the appearance of an angel, 28-31.*

This chapter and the following contain the account of the first mission of Nephi, after his divine appointment to the position of leadership. (2:18-24) His call came in the form of a dream had by his father Lehi, in which he and his brothers were directed to go and get certain important records. The account shows how Nephi, by the power of the Spirit of the Lord, overcame opposition and obstacles, and returned to his father after a successful mission. Success was the reward of faith and intelligently directed energy.

The chapter may be divided as follows:

## 1. *The sons of Lehi return to Jerusalem.*

1. And it came to pass that I, Nephi, returned from speaking with the Lord, to the tent of my father.

2. And it came to pass that he spake unto me, saying: Behold I have dreamed a dream, in the which the Lord hath commanded me that thou and thy brethren shall return to Jerusalem.

3. For behold, Laban hath the record of the Jews and also a genealogy of thy forefathers, and they are engraven upon plates of brass.

4. Wherefore, the Lord hath

VERSE 1. *I Nephi, returned from speaking with the Lord, to the tent of my father.* Nephi, grief-stricken, had, evidently, retired to some solitary place where he could pour out his soul in prayer, undisturbed, on behalf of his rebellious brothers, and where the Lord answered him, as recorded in the previous chapter, vv. 19-24. Then he returned to the tent. This was the turning point in the life of young Nephi. (See note, chapter 2)

VERSE 3. *Brass.* The Hebrew word (nekhoshet), which the Bible translators have rendered "brass" should rather be "copper," as is clear from Deuteronomy 8:9, where we read: "a land out of whose hills thou mayest dig brass," meaning "copper." For what we call "brass" is an alloy of copper and zinc, and is not mined as such. It is not known that the Hebrews in early days were acquainted with "brass," but they knew the alloy of copper and tin, which we call bronze. Anciently any alloy of copper was called "brass." The Hebrews used copper quite extensively for cups, pots, knives, etc. (Ex. 38:3; Num. 16:39; Jer. 52:18) It was used for helmets, coats of mail, shields, chains and mirrors. (1 Sam. 17:5, 38; 2 Sam. 21:16, 22:15) The altar and its network, the basins, the "sea" that rested on the oxen, and the oxen themselves, and also the two pillars, Boaz and Jachin, that stood before the temple,—all were of "brass." (Chron. 4:1-15)

The records of the Jews and the genealogy of Lehi were both absolutely necessary to the development of the colony in the new land. Without sacred literature a people is liable to become lost in darkness. Without genealogical data, the links that join individuals to their ancestors are unknown. There must be weighty reasons why the Lord has caused the records of the Jews, as well as those of the first apostles

commanded me that thou and thy brothers should go unto the house of Laban, and seek the records, and bring them down hither into the wilderness.

5. And now, behold thy brothers murmur, saying it is a hard thing which I have required of them; but behold I have not required it of them, but it is a commandment of the Lord.

6. Therefore go, my son, and thou shalt be favored of the Lord, because thou hast not murmured.

7. And it came to pass that I, Nephi, said unto my father: I will go and do the things which the Lord hath commanded, for I know that the Lord giveth no commandments unto the children of men, save he shall prepare a way for them that they may accomplish the thing which he commandeth them.

8. And it came to pass that when my father had heard these words he was exceeding glad, for he knew that I had been blessed of the Lord.

9. And I, Nephi, and my brethren took our journey in the wilderness, with our tents, to go up to the land of Jerusalem.

10. And it came to pass that when we had come up to the land of Jerusalem, I and my brethren did consult one with another.

11. And we cast lots—who of us should go in unto the house of Laban. And it came to pass that the lot fell upon Laman; and Laman went in unto the house of Laban, and he talked with him as he sat in his house.

12. And he desired of Laban the records which were engraven upon the plates of brass, which contained the genealogy of my father.

## 2. *Laban refuses to deliver the records.*

13. And behold, it came to pass that Laban was angry, and thrust him out from his presence; and he would not that he should

---

of the Savior, and the descendants of Lehi, to be preserved for the benefit of this generation.

VERSE 4. *Go and seek the records and bring them down hither.* The commandments of God are definite. Not, Try to find the records and bring them hither, but, Find them and bring them here. Not, Do your best, but Do as commanded. The mission of Nephi and his brothers was not merely something that possibly could be done, but something they could and *must* do.

VERSE 7. *I will go.* Nephi so understood it. He consented to go, because his faith told him that when the Lord gives a commandment, he also prepares the way for its fulfillment. The Apostle Paul, in his letter to the Philippians (2:13), expresses this doctrine thus, "For it is God which worketh in you both to will and to do of his good pleasure." There is, therefore, no excuse for disobedience, or for failure.

have the records. Wherefore, he said unto him: Behold thou art a robber, and I will slay thee.

14. But Laman fled out of his presence, and told the things which Laban had done, unto us. And we began to be exceeding sorrowful, and my brethren were about to return unto my father in the wilderness.

### 3. Nephi exhorts his brethren.

15. But behold I said unto them that: As the Lord liveth, and as we live, we will not go down unto our father in the wilderness until we have accomplished the thing which the Lord hath commanded us.

16. Wherefore, let us be faithful in keeping the commandments of the Lord; therefore let us go down to the land of our father's inheritance, for behold he left gold and silver, and all manner of riches. And all this he hath done because of the commandments of the Lord.

17. For he knew that Jerusalem must be destroyed, because of the wickedness of the people.

18. For behold, they have rejected the words of the prophets. Wherefore, if my father should dwell in the land after he hath been commanded to flee out of the land, behold, he would also perish. Wherefore, it must needs be that he flee out of the land.

19. And behold, it is wisdom in God that we should obtain these records, that we may preserve unto our children the language of our fathers;

20. And also that we may preserve unto them the words which have been spoken by the mouth of all the holy prophets, which have been delivered unto them by the Spirit and power of God, since the world began, even down unto this present time.

21. And it came to pass that after this manner of language did I persuade my brethren, that they might be faithful in keeping the commandments of God.

---

VERSE 14. *Were about to return.* After the first feeble attempt to obtain the records, Laman was determined to return and report failure.

VERSES 15-21. *As the Lord liveth.* The four brothers, evidently, held a council meeting in which Laman made his proposition to return. Nephi opposed the motion in a speech that is well worth studying.

He begins his argument with a solemn assertion that there would be no return before the mission had been fulfilled. Then he proposes a plan whereby, Laman being willing, they might purchase the records. Lastly, he shows why it was necessary for them to obtain possession of them—That we may preserve unto our children the language of our fathers, and the prophetic word spoken since the world began. Those records were really a question of life and death to the descendants of Lehi. Nephi's eloquent plea won the day.

*The land of our father's inheritance.* v. 16. This was the homestead of Lehi, which he had inherited. Generally, the land, which in Palestine always was con-

## 4. *Laban robs the sons of Lehi.*

22. And it came to pass that we went down to the land of our inheritance, and we did gather together our gold, and our silver, and our precious things.

23. And after we had gathered these things together, we went up again unto the house of Laban.

24. And it came to pass that we went in unto Laban, and de-

sidered as the property of the Lord, went, by the right of inheritance, to the sons, the firstborn receiving a double portion. If a man left no sons, the inheritance passed to his daughters; if there were no daughters, it went to his brothers; in case there were no brothers, it went to his father's brother; the nearest kinsman was the heir. (Num. 37:8) But every fiftieth year, land that had been sold went to the first owner. The same rule was observed regarding houses in villages and unwalled towns. They reverted to the former owner at the jubilee. Houses in walled cities, could be redeemed any time during a full year after they had been sold. But if they were not redeemed during that time, they belonged to the purchaser and his heirs forever. (Lev. 25:8, 23)

Such was the law in Palestine. It was a good foundation for a United Order.

Is it a mere accident that similar rules were observed by many of the inhabitants of America at the time of the arrival of the Spaniards?

Among the Zapotecs and Mixtecs, for instance, no one had a right to sell his land in perpetuity; the law forbade transfer out of a family either by marriage or otherwise; and if a proprietor was compelled by the force of necessity to dispose of his real estate, it returned after a lapse of some years to his son or to his nearest relative, who paid the holder the consideration for which it was pledged, or its equivalent. (Bancroft, Native Races, vol. 2, p. 228)

Down in South America, among the Peruvians, similar regulations were in force. "The whole territory of the empire," Prescott says, "was divided into three parts, one for the Sun, another for the Inca and the last for the people. . . . The lands assigned to the Sun furnished a revenue to support the temples and maintain the costly ceremonial of the Peruvian worship and the multitudinous priesthood. Those reserved for the Inca went to support the royal state, as well as the numerous members of his household and his kindred, and supplied the various exigencies of government. The remainder of the lands was divided per capita, in equal shares among the people. . . . The division of the soil was renewed every year, and the possessions of the tenant were increased or diminished according to the numbers in the family. . . . The nearest approach to the Peruvian constitution was probably in Judea, where, on the recurrence of the great national jubilee, at the close of every half-century, estates reverted to their original proprietors." (Prescott, Peru, vol. 1, p. 56)

The existence of such laws and regulations in America at that time suggests the probability that the original law makers were familiar with the Law of Moses and the history of the Palestine of the Hebrew patriarchs and the Egypt at the time of Joseph.

VERSE 22. *Gold and silver and precious things.* The plan of Nephi, reluctantly accepted by Laman, was to gather up the abandoned valuables and offer Laban an exhorbitant price for the records. A well-to-do Hebrew at that time may have had considerable property, accumulated perhaps for several generations. In the negotiations between Abraham and Ephron, the son of Zohar, for a burial ground, the sum of 400 shekels of silver ($300) was considered a mere bagatelle. Abraham

sired him that he would give unto us the records which were engraven upon the plates of brass, for which we would give unto him our gold, and our silver, and all our precious things.

25. And it came to pass that when Laban saw our property, and that it was exceeding great, he did lust after it, insomuch that he thrust us out, and sent his servants to slay us, that he might obtain our property.

26. And it came to pass that we did flee before the servants of Laban, and we were obliged to leave behind our property, and it fell into the hands of Laban.

27. And it came to pass that we fled into the wilderness, and the servants of Laban did not overtake us, and we hid ourselves in the cavity of a rock.

## 5. Another conflict and the appearance of an angel.

28. And it came to pass that Laman was angry with me, and also with my father; and also was Lemuel, for he hearkened unto the words of Laman. Wherefore Laman and Lemuel did speak many hard words unto us, their younger brothers, and they did smite us even with a rod.

29. And it came to pass as they smote us with a rod, behold, an angel of the Lord came and stood before them, and he spake unto them, saying: Why do ye smite your younger brother with a rod? Know ye not that the Lord hath chosen him to be a ruler over you, and this because of your iniquities? Behold ye shall go up to Jerusalem again, and the Lord will deliver Laban into your hands.

30. And after the angel had spoken unto us, he departed.

31. And after the angel had departed, Laman and Lemuel again began to murmur, saying: How is it possible that the Lord will deliver Laban into our hands? Behold, he is a mighty man, and he can command fifty, yea, even he can slay fifty; then why not us?

---

insisted on paying for the lot. Very well, Ephron says, it is worth 400 shekels, "What is that betwixt me and thee?" As much as to say, That is a mere trifle.

Lehi had left in his abandoned house, gold and silver and precious objects, and the brothers offered it all for the records.

VERSE 27. *In vain.* Laban secured the valuable property for himself and compelled the brothers to flee for their lives. He had murder in his heart.

VERSES 28-31. *The conflict in the cave.* Nephi and his brothers had now found refuge in a cave. Possibly the very sepulcher which Abraham had bought of Ephron (Gen. 23:3-16), situated at Hebron, about eighteen miles south of Jerusalem. Here Sarah, Abraham, Isaac, Rebekah, Jacob and Leah were buried. It is to this day one of the very sacred places of the Mohammedan world.

The predicament in which Nephi now found himself was perplexing and must have caused him great anxiety. Laman, always angrily brooding upon the supposed injustice he had suffered in the appointment of Nephi to the leadership, now could excuse his opposition by the apparent failure of the plan of his brother to get the records. Moreover, they had lost their property and their lives were in danger. Was not Nephi, clearly, a false prophet? Lemuel soon joined Laman in opposition. Nephi was silent. But, no doubt, he was pouring out his soul in prayer. The older brothers, unable to control their vulgar and brutal anger, resorted to physical violence, the argument of the beast. Still, Nephi was silent. But, suddenly, an angel of the Lord appeared on the scene. All was changed. We can imagine Laman and Lemuel trembling, when from the lips of the heavenly messenger the rebuke came: "Know ye not that the Lord hath chosen him to be a ruler over you, and this because of your iniquities? Behold ye shall go up to Jesusalem again."

The Lord vindicated his faithful servant. He always does.

## NOTES

Kingsborough, Volume 8, page 358, states that copper plates were found with hieroglyphical engravings. One is described as being a foot and a half long, and 7 inches wide; others shorter and narrower. An old Indian chief stated that he was told by his forefathers that these plates were given them by a man called God; that there had been many more of other shapes and had writing upon them."

In the British Museum, London, England, there is a set of from 15 to 18 very thin silver plates, 15 inches by 5 inches, on which is engraved Buddha's first prayer and other writings sacred to the followers of Buddha. There is also a gold plate, 10 inches by 3 inches, exceedingly thin, yet engraved on both sides. It appears to be, according to the legend, a letter from one native prince to another.—Bishop David A. Smith.

## CHAPTER 4

*Nephi and his brothers go up to Jerusalem, 1-5—Laban slain with his own sword, 6-18—Nephi secures the records, 19-29—Zoram joins the brothers, 30-38.*

### 1. Nephi and his brothers go up again.

1. And it came to pass that I spake unto my brethren, saying: Let us go up again unto Jerusalem, and let us be faithful in keeping the commandments of the Lord; for behold he is mightier than all the earth, then why not mightier than Laban and his fifty, yea, or even than his tens of thousands?

2. Therefore let us go up; let us be strong like unto Moses; for he truly spake unto the waters of the Red Sea and they divided hither and thither, and our fathers came through, out of captivity, on dry ground, and the armies of Pharaoh did follow and were drowned in the waters of the Red Sea.

3. Now behold ye know that this is true; and ye also know that an angel hath spoken unto you; wherefore can ye doubt? Let us go up; the Lord is able to deliver us, even as our fathers, and to destroy Laban, even as the Egyptians.

4. Now when I had spoken these words, they were yet wroth, and did still continue to murmur; nevertheless they did follow me up until we came without the walls of Jerusalem.

5. And it was by night; and I caused that they should hide themselves without the walls. And after they had hid themselves, I, Nephi, crept into the city and went forth towards the house of Laban.

---

VERSES 1-3. We have here another masterly discourse by Nephi. He urges his brothers to carry out the commandment of the Lord, given through the angel, and he argues that the Lord who destroyed the Egyptians in the Red Sea, could destroy Laban, if necessary. His brothers were still angry and murmuring. Even the angel had not been able to change the hearts of Laman and Lemuel. However they went along.

VERSE 5. *And it was night.* This seems to indicate that the cave in which they had been camping was one day's journey from Jerusalem. That would answer the question of Machpelah at Hebron. A day's journey was 16-20 miles.

*Crept into the city.* Nephi left his brothers outside the city wall. He himself got into the city. Just how is not explained. In the large gates of a walled city, there was a small door or rather window, through which those who were entitled to enter might do so, when the gate was closed for the night. He might have literally "crept" in through such an aperture, by the grace of the watchman. It was always a small opening, sometimes only two feet square.

Nephi, the son of a prominent, well-to-do citizen, coming alone to the gate, a belated wanderer, unfortunately overtaken by the shadows of the night, might readily obtain an entrance through what some have called "the needle's eye," par-

## 2. Laban slain.

6. And I was led by the Spirit, not knowing beforehand the things which I should do.

7. Nevertheless I went forth, and as I came near unto the house of Laban I beheld a man, and he had fallen to the earth before me, for he was drunken with wine.

8. And when I came to him I found that it was Laban.

9. And I beheld his sword, and I drew it forth from the sheath thereof; and the hilt thereof was of pure gold, and the workmanship thereof was exceeding fine, and I saw that the blade thereof was of the most precious steel.

10. And it came to pass that I was constrained by the Spirit that I should kill Laban; but I

---

ticularly if he had a piece of money with which to make his account of himself plausible; whereas, if the brothers had come together at that hour, suspicions might have been aroused. The wisdom that inspired Nephi is seen in his conduct, and his account is so simple, so natural, as to make a perfect impression of its authenticity on the mind of the careful reader.

VERSE 8. *It was Laban.* We note that the youthful leader of his brothers, at the time did not follow a plan previously prepared. He proceeded as the Spirit led the way. Soon he found himself outside the house of Laban. Lying on the ground, was a human form. It was the dreaded enemy. And on closer inspection, Nephi found that he was unconscious, under the influence of wine.

The Hebrews were not, generally speaking, an intemperate people, but they enjoyed festivals. Besides the yearly occasions prescribed by law, they celebrated birthdays, marriages, harvest, vintage, and special occasions, as, for instance the return of the Prodigal. On such occasions great quantities of food and wine were consumed. Even at funerals, they feasted.

It is not improbable that Laban had celebrated, in the midst of convivial friends, his acquisition of the property of Lehi. For that was an unexpected "harvest."

There are some notable instances of intemperate drinking on record in the Hebrew Scriptures.

The case of Belshazzar, king of Babylon, is well known. It was his last debauch. For, "In that night was Belshazzar, the king of the Chaldeans, slain." (Dan. 5:30)

Another but less known instance is that of Nabal, a wealthy sheep owner. On one occasion, when he made a feast for his shearers, David sent word to him and asked for a tribute, as a recognition of the protection he had enjoyed for his flocks. Nabal refused. David then prepared for a raid on his property. But Abigail, the wife of Nabal, saved the situation by sending to David, without the knowledge of her husband, a handsome gift of provisions. In the meantime, Nabal feasted and drank. The next day, when he heard what his wife had done, he suffered a heart attack: "His heart died within him, and he became as a stone." About ten days afterwards he died. (Sam. 25:36-38)

Now here was Laban. Already dead to the world.

VERSE 9. *His sword.* This weapon was destined to play an important part in the history of the Nephites. It served Nephi as a pattern when he found it necessary to arm his people for defense against Lamanite marauders. (2 Ne. 5:14) He,

said in my heart: Never at any time have I shed the blood of man. And I shrunk and would that I might not slay him.

11. And the Spirit said unto me again: Behold the Lord hath delivered him into thy hands. Yea, and I also knew that he had sought to take away mine own

life; yea, and he would not hearken unto the commandments of the Lord; and he also had taken away our property.

12. And it came to pass that the Spirit said unto me again: Slay him, for the Lord hath delivered him into thy hands;

13. Behold the Lord slayeth

himself, wielded it in many a sanguinary combat. (Jac. 1:10) King Benjamin won victories with it (Words of Mormon 13), and, toward the end of his reign in Zarahemla, he turned it over to his son Mosiah. (Mos. 1:16) In a revelation dated New York, June, 1829, the Three Witnesses, Oliver Cowdery, David Whitmer and Martin Harris were given the promise, conditioned on their faith and faithfulness, that they would obtain a view of the sword of Laban, as well as the plates, the breastplate, the Urim and Thummim and the miraculous directors. (D. & C. 17:1) A short time after the revelation was given, the promise was fulfilled.

David Whitmer, on Sept. 7, 1878, in a conversation with Elders Orson Pratt and Joseph F. Smith, said, in part:

"Joseph, Oliver and myself were together when I saw them [the plates]. We not only saw the plates of the Book of Mormon, but also the brass plates, the plates of the Book of Ether . . . and many other plates . . . there appeared as it were, a table with many records, or plates upon it, besides the plates of the Book of Mormon, also the sword of Laban, the directors [i.e., the ball which Lehi had], and the interpreters. I saw them as plainly as I see this bed [striking it beside him with his hand], and I heard the voice of the Lord as distinctly as I ever heard anything in my life, declaring that the records of the plates of the Book of Mormon were translated by the gift and power of God." (Andrew Jensen, Historical Record, p. 217)

Nephi took this sword from Laban and examined it. Its hilt was of pure gold and the blade of precious steel. There is no reason for doubting the accuracy of this statement.

It is true enough that in most, if not in all, of the passages in the Old Testament where the English version has "steel" the original has a word that means "copper." But in Jeremiah 15:12, where the Prophet asks: "Shall iron break the northern iron and the steel?" scholars have suggested that "the northern iron" may mean steel, while the "steel" mentioned is copper. In Nahum 2:4, where the prophet speaks of raging chariots that seem like "torches," the word translated "torches" (paldah) should be rendered "steel." And weapons of "steel" are said to be found in ancient tombs in Egypt, which statement can well be credited, for steel is not a new invention or discovery. Only the modern way of making it is new. Ancient ironmasters, we are told, obtained iron and steel by simply a hearth or fireplace in which the ore and the charcoal were mixed and a blast applied to obtain the necessary high temperature. According to Diodorus Siculus,[2] some of the ancients buried sheets of iron in the earth and left them there till what he calls the "weak parts" was consumed by rust. What remained was "steel." This was used for weapons and objects of various kinds.

[2]A Greek historian who lived during the times of Julius Caesar and Augustus, author of a work on the history of the world from creation to the wars of Julius Caesar.

the wicked to bring forth his righteous purposes. It is better that one man should perish than that a nation should dwindle and perish in unbelief.

14. And now, when I, Nephi, had heard these words, I remembered the words of the Lord which he spake unto me in the wilderness, saying that: Inasmuch as thy seed shall keep my commandments, they shall prosper in the land of promise.

15. Yea, and I also thought that they could not keep the commandments of the Lord ac-cording to the law of Moses, save they should have the law.

16. And I also knew that the law was engraven upon the plates of brass.

17. And again, I knew that the Lord had delivered Laban into my hands for this cause—that I might obtain the records according to his commandments.

18. Therefore I did obey the voice of the Spirit, and took Laban by the hair of the head, and I smote off his head with his own sword.

### 3. *Nephi secures the records.*

19. And after I had smitten off his head with his own sword, I took the garments of Laban and put them upon mine own body; yea, even every whit; and I did gird on his armor about my loins.

20. And after I had done this, I went forth unto the treasury of Laban. And as I went forth towards the treasury of Laban, behold, I saw the servant of Laban who had the keys of the treasury. And I commanded him in the voice of Laban, that he should go with me into the treasury.

21. And he supposed me to be his master, Laban, for he beheld the garments and also the sword girded about my loins.

22. And he spake unto me concerning the elders of the Jews, he

---

VERSES 10-18. *The death of Laban.* Nephi stood there with the sword of Laban in his hand. Presently the voice of the Spirit urged him to destroy his enemy. But he shrunk from the thought. He had never shed the blood of man. The inner voice came again: "Behold the Lord hath delivered him into thy hands." The commandment was from God.

The indictments against Laban were grave. (1) He had refused to deliver up the records peacefully; (2) he had robbed the sons of Lehi of their property; (3) he had decided to kill the brothers; (4) humanly speaking, there was no possibility of obtaining the records as long as Laban lived. Nephi obeyed the inner voice. "It is better that one man should perish than that a nation should dwindle and perish in unbelief." This was a Jewish proverb, equivalent to: "Of two evils choose the lesser." And so, after a great deal of hesitation, Nephi destroyed Laban with his own sword (v. 18).

VERSE 22. *The elders of the Jews.* This verse and v. 27 gives us, by inference, some interesting information concerning Laban.

The Jews had certain officials they called *shoterim.* In the English version

knowing that his master, Laban, had been out by night among them.

23. And I spake unto him as if it had been Laban.

24. And I also spake unto him that I should carry the engravings, which were upon the plates of brass, to my elder brethren, who were without the walls.

25. And I also bade him that he should follow me.

26. And he, supposing that I spake of the brethren of the church, and that I was truly that Laban whom I had slain, wherefore he did follow me.

27. And he spake unto me many times concerning the elders of the Jews, as I went forth unto my brethren, who were without the walls.

28. And it came to pass that when Laman saw me he was exceeding frightened, and also Lemuel and Sam. And they fled from before my presence; for they supposed it was Laban, and that he had slain me and had sought to take away their lives also.

---

that word is translated officers, or assistants or Scribes. That is more correct. They were probably, "secretaries." They are mentioned in the following texts:

Deut. 16:18: "Judges and officers shalt thou make thee in all thy gates."

Here the "officers" (*shoterim*) were associated with the judges in the exercise of their judicial functions in the gates where the courts were held.

Josh. 8:33: "And all Israel, and their elders, and officers, and their judges stood on this side of the ark."

Here their presence was required when the people made a covenant with the Lord at Mt. Ebal. See Deut. 29:10, where we have the account of a covenant made in the land of Moab.

Numb. 11:16: "Gather unto me 70 men of the elders of Israel, whom thou knowest to be elders of the people, and officers over them."

Here the duties of the "officers" (*shoterim*) called them to be present at the appointment of seventies, who were to "bear the burden of the people with Moses."

But the shoterim also had special duties during time of war. In the first place, they were to explain to the conscripts that certain conditions exempted them from service: (1) Those who had a new house not yet dedicated; (2) those that just planted a vineyard; (3) those who were about to be married; (4) and, finally, those who were fearful and fainthearted (probably physically unfit), all these were exempt from service. (Deut. 20:5-8) When the army was ready for organization, the "officers" appointed captains to lead them. (20:9) It was further, the duty of these "officers" to take messages from the commander-in-chief to the people. (Josh. 1:10; 3:2-4) They might be compared to the modern adjutant generals.

Considering the fact that Laban had charge of the genealogy—necessary for religious services and for census taking, in case of war; and also that he was the possessor of a sword, such as only a man of high military rank would be likely to own, we may safely conclude that his position was that of a shoterim (an "officer") in Jerusalem.

29. And it came to pass that I called after them, and they did hear me; wherefore they did cease to flee from my presence.

4. *Zoram joins the brothers.*

30. And it came to pass that when the servant of Laban beheld my brethren he began to tremble, and was about to flee from before me and return to the city of Jerusalem.

31. And now I, Nephi, being a man large in stature, and also having received much strength of the Lord, therefore I did seize upon the servant of Laban, and held him, that he should not flee.

32. And it came to pass that I spake with him, that if he would hearken unto my words, as the Lord liveth, and as I live, even so that if he would hearken unto our words, we would spare his life.

33. And I spake unto him, even with an oath, that he need not fear; that he should be a free man like unto us if he would go down in the wilderness with us.

34. And I also spake unto him, saying: Surely the Lord hath commanded us to do this thing; and shall we not be diligent in keeping the commandments of the Lord? Therefore, if thou wilt go down into the wilderness to my father thou shalt have place with us.

35. And it came to pass that Zoram did take courage at the words which I spake. Now Zoram was the name of the servant; and he promised that he would go down into the wilderness unto my father. And he also made an oath unto us that he would tarry with us from that time forth.

36. Now we were desirous that he should tarry with us for this cause, that the Jews might not know concerning our flight into the wilderness, lest they should pursue us and destroy us.

37. And it came to pass that when Zoram had made an oath unto us, our fears did cease concerning him.

38. And it came to pass that we took the plates of brass and the servant of Laban, and departed into the wilderness, and journeyed unto the tent of our father.

VERSE 35. *Zoram was the name.* Zoram, a servant of Laban, now a captive in the hands of Nephi, evidently became converted by the kind yet powerful address of his captor, who testified that the Lord had commanded him to do "this thing." He made a covenant with the sons of Lehi and accompanied them to the tent of their father. During the journey in the wilderness Zoram married the eldest daughter of Ishmael. (2 Ne. 16-7)

One of their descendants was Ammoron, brother of Amalickiah, who waged war with the Nephites, in the years 26-9 of the reign of the Judges. (Alma 52:3) It is not improbable that the Aymaras in the Andean mountains, from south latitude 15 to 20, and through about 6 degrees longitude (Dr. Brinton) derive their name from this descendant of Zoram. Dr. Brinton estimates the number of Aymaras in this region at about a half million souls.

There is, as far as I know, no certain clue to the meaning of the name Zoram. The Hebrews called the city of Tyre, "Zor," or "Zur," which means a "rock." It was also called, "Zor em Sidonim," meaning, "Tyre, the Capitol of the Sidonians." A natural abbreviation of this descriptive name would be, "Zor-am." If this derivation is correct, the servant of Laban may have been a Tyrian.

Since the days of David and Solomon, there was a lively traffic between Tyre and Jerusalem. Hiram, king of Tyre, sent messengers to David, with timber of cedars, and masons and carpenters, to build him a house (1 Chron. 7:1), and Solomon sent for one Hiram of Tyre, who was the son of a "man of Tyre" and a woman of the tribe of Naphtali. This Hiram was a skilful worker in all "works of brass," and he made the various costly metal ornaments and objects for which the temple of Solomon became famous.

Zoram may have been a descendant of one of these laborers, or some other Tyrian, and therefore known in the house of Laban as Zoram, the man of Tyre.

## CHAPTER 5

The return of the sons, an occasion of great joy, 1-9.—Contents of the brass plates, 10-16—Lehi's prophecy, 17-22.

### 1. *The return of the sons, an occasion of great joy.*

1. And it came to pass that after we had come down into the wilderness unto our father, behold, he was filled with joy, and also my mother, Sariah, was exceeding glad, for she truly had mourned because of us.

2. For she had supposed that we had perished in the wilderness; and she also had com-

---

VERSES 1-9. *Sariah as wife and mother.* Consider the loyalty of this Hebrew lady, the consort of Lehi. Without full assurance in her heart of the divine mission of her husband, she had, without murmuring, given up her comfortable home in the city and accompanied him out into the dreary wilderness. She was a true and faithful wife.

The Hebrew ideal of a wife is stated by the Creator himself: "It is not good that the man should be alone; I will make him an help meet for him." (Gen. 2:18) "A help meet for him." That means a companion, really, his counterpart. And the nature of the "help" is set forth in Proverbs, in a poem by the mother of King Lemuel. (Prov. 31:10-29) I beg to offer the following paraphrase of this great composition:

### THE WORDS OF KING LEMUEL

#### THE PROPHECY THAT HIS MOTHER TAUGHT TO HIM

A worthy wife, if you can find,
her price is far above pearls.
In his heart her husband safely trusts in her,
and he shall have no lack of gain.
She brings him good, but never harm
as long as days and life shall last.
She sorts the wool, she sorts the flax
and works it, as she pleases, with her hands.
She's like the merchantmen,—
brings her provisions from afar.
She rises while it is yet night and gives her household rations for the day,
her maids their daily tasks.
She sees a field and buys it—
and with the labor of her hands, a vineyard plants.
She girds her loins with strength,
and strong are e'en her arms.
She finds that prosp'rous is her work—
her lamp does not go out at night.[1]
She turns the spindle well,
and works the distaff, too.
Her hand she holds out to the poor,
her arms to those in need.

---

[1]*See Notes.*

plained against my father, telling him that he was a visionary man; saying: Behold thou hast led us forth from the land of our inheritance, and my sons are no more, and we perish in the wilderness.

3. And after this manner of language had my mother complained against my father.

4. And it had come to pass that my father spake unto her, saying: I know that I am a visionary man; for if I had not seen the things of God in a vision I should not have known the goodness of God, but had tarried at Jerusalem, and had perished with my brethren.

> She fears not chilling snow,
> her household double garments wear.
> She makes blankets for herself of tapestry,
> clothing of fine linen and purple.
> Known is her husband at the gate,
> upon his seat among the elders of the land.
> Fine linen garments she makes and sells,
> supplies the Canaanites [merchants] with girdles.
> With strength and honor clothed, she
> rejoices at the day to come.
> For wisdom openeth her mouth—
> the Law of Kindness on her tongue.
> She watches o'er her household well,
> and none eat bread in idleness.
> Her children stand and call her blessed,
> her husband also praiseth her.
> True, many daughters have done well,
> but you, among them all, excel.
> All favor is deceitful, beauty vain,
> a wife that feareth God, great praise shall gain.
> O give her of the fruit that she has raised,
> and let her in the gates by all be praised.

That is to say, the perfect ideal of a wife, according to the Hebrew idea, was one who had both wisdom and strength to manage a household successfully in all its diversified requirements, in the house and without, while her husband attended to the equally arduous and exacting duties of public office. And to her many other gifts and qualifications she added the fear of the Lord, which sanctified her whole being and activity.

The ideal woman is faithful and loyal; she is a laborer, active and industrious; she is wide awake and prudent; she is strong, in body as well as in character; she is tender and benevolent; provident and refined; a credit to her husband and the glory of her children.

Perhaps there never was such a perfect woman, any more than there ever was a perfect man, except the One; but such was the pattern. Such was the ideal. And it is safe to say, that Mother Sariah, the wife of Lehi, came as near this ideal as any woman ever did. She had to, in order to be the mother of such a son as Nephi, and the ancestress of a race, such as that of which we read in the Book of Mormon. That great mission required great qualifications, in the woman, as in the man.

*But Sariah was also a Mother.* There is no human emotion stronger than the love of a mother. For that reason, when our Heavenly Father undertakes to impress

5. But behold, I have obtained a land of promise, in the which things I do rejoice; yea, and I know that the Lord will deliver my sons out of the hands of Laban, and bring them down again unto us in the wilderness.

6. And after this manner of language did my father, Lehi, comfort my mother, Sariah, concerning us, while we journeyed in the wilderness up to the land of Jerusalem, to obtain the record of the Jews.

7. And when we had returned to the tent of my father, behold their joy was full, and my mother was comforted.

---

upon his people the comforting thought that they are not forgotten by him, he appeals to their experience of a mother's constancy in her affections. "Can a woman," he asks through the Prophet Isaiah, "forget her sucking child, that she should not have compassion on her first born son?"

Can she?

Not if she is a normal mother.

But the suffering at the time of trial, when the hour of Crucifixion has come —when the sword pierces the very soul (Luke 2:35)—that anguish is in proportion to the intensity of the emotion. Such an hour had now come to Sariah. She felt certain that her four sons had perished in the wilderness. And as this conviction grew stronger, she became a doubter and an accuser. "Behold," she said to her husband, "*thou* hast led us forth from our home, and my sons are no more."

We note that great love, whether a mother's or a father's, often is pessimistic. It is inclined to see the worst side of a case, rather than the favorable one. Love, says the Apostle, "beareth all things, hopeth all things." (1 Cor. 13:7) But he is speaking of brotherly love in the church. A mother's love is inclined to fear, rather than hope. Hagar, in her hour of great trial, cast her firstborn under a shrub and cried in agony, "Let me not see him die." Through her blinding tears she imagined that the angel of life, approaching to bless her and her boy, was none other than the angel of death. Similarly, Jacob, listening to the voice of his parental love, exclaimed, "Joseph is not, and Simeon is not, and ye will take Benjamin, too." (Gen. 42:36); while, as a matter of fact, Joseph, at that very moment, was, virtually, the mighty ruler of Egypt, and Simeon was his guest. Sariah, as a mother, would gladly have fought lions, or gone through fire or swum the deep, without fear, for her children; for, in the actual presence of danger, "There is no fear in love; but perfect love casteth out fear." (John 4:18) But under the circumstances she felt helpless. It was another case of "Rahel weeping for her children refused to be comforted . . . because they were not." (Jer. 31:15)

*Lehi's faith.* Lehi was wise. He did not contradict his wife. He did not meet accusation with accusation. Perhaps deep down in his heart he felt very much as his wife felt. If he did, he gave no indication of it. True to his calling and duty, he stood up and spoke the language of faith instead of surmises of emotion. By *faith* he knew that their sons were safe and would return to them. That was his testimony. Undoubtedly, that was what Sariah wanted to hear. She needed assurance. She would have been very much disappointed if Lehi had admitted that she, perhaps, was right. She wanted to be contradicted. His faith was her comfort (v. 6).

*Their joy was full.* And now the boys arrive. They have fulfilled their mission successfully. There is indescribable joy in the tent. Joy over the reunion. But also because the experience of Sariah had left, as an after effect, the sweet assurance

8. And she spake, saying: Now I know of a surety that the Lord hath commanded my husband to flee into the wilderness; yea, and I also know of a surety that the Lord hath protected my sons, and delivered them out of the hands of Laban, and given them power whereby they could accomplish the thing which the Lord hath commanded them. And after this manner of language did she speak.

9. And it came to pass that they did rejoice exceedingly, and did offer sacrifice and burnt offerings unto the Lord; and they gave thanks unto the God of Israel.

## 2. Contents of the plates.

10. And after they had given thanks unto the God of Israel, my father, Lehi, took the records which were engraven upon the plates of brass, and he did search them from the beginning.

11. And he beheld that they did contain the five books of Moses, which gave an account of the creation of the world, and also of Adam and Eve, who were our first parents;

---

that they were engagd in the work of the Lord. Her sorrow had been turned into gladness, her doubt into faith (v. 8).

Note that the gratitude of this family was expressed not only in testimony but in sacrifice and burnt offerings to the Lord (v. 9). That is the only acceptable form of gratitude. Fervent words may be pleasant and desirable, at times, but as a rule, unless they are accompanied by something tangible, they are as shots with blank cartridges. They may produce smoke but do not bring down the game. The Lord instructed Israel, "None shall appear before me empty." (Ex. 23:15; 34:20; Deut. 16:16 and 17) That was, properly, the law of the Hebrews.

*The burnt offering.* This consisted of an animal without blemish. The officiating priest laid his hands on its head, signifying that an atonement for sin was about to be made. The animal, symbolically carrying the sins and guilt of the owner, was slain and its body consumed by the fire on the altar. (Lev. 1) The act was symbolical of the death of our Lord as the Lamb of God.

The *Sacrifice* mentioned was perhaps a meat offering, which consisted of fine flour, oil and frankincense. Some of this was burnt upon the altar; the rest was eaten. (Lev. 2)

We may conclude from this, that the return of the sons was the occasion of a solemn divine service and a genuine feast.

VERSE 11. *The five Books of Moses.* This title should be noted. The books referred to are in our day generally known as the Pentateuch, a word meaning literally, five-fifths, i.e., in this case, five books. Greek translators of the Old Testament are supposed to have introduced that title. It was not used at the time of Lehi.

Josephus, in his *Jewish Antiquities,* calls this part of the Old Testament, the "Holy Books of Moses," and in his treatise against Apion, in enumerating the sacred books of the Jews, he says, "five of them belong to Moses." In the New Testament this section is merely called the "Law." (Matt. 12:5; 22:36-40) Ezra and Nehe-

THE FIRST BOOK OF NEPHI

12. And also a record of the Jews from the beginning, even down to the commencement of the reign of Zedekiah, king of Judah;

13. And also the prophecies of the holy prophets, from the be-ginning, even down to the commencement of the reign of Zedekiah; and also many prophecies which have been spoken by the mouth of Jeremiah.

14. And it came to pass that my father, Lehi, also found upon

---

miah refer to the same section as the "Law of Moses," (Ezr. 7:6) and the "Book of the Law of Moses" (Neh. 8:1) sometimes only the "Book of Moses" (Ezr. 6:18; Neh. 13:1; 2 Chron. 25:4). When they speak of the "Book of Moses," singular, they do so consistently, because in all ancient Hebrew manuscripts, what we know as five books was one single roll. The division into books is a later arrangement. The Jews generally call the entire book, or books, the *Torah*, which means the "Law;" or, the "Torah of Moses." Some Jewish writers call them the "Five-fifths of the Law."

From all this we may conclude that, if the Book of Mormon were a modern composition, as some suppose, the author would, in this verse, have made use of the comparatively modern designation, "Pentateuch," rather than the more ancient "Five Books of Moses."

When Nephi gives us the information that the metal plates of Laban contained the Five Books of Moses, he ends, as far as the Latter-day Saints are concerned, a controversy still dividing Bible scholars of the world. He tells us, first, that Moses is the responsible author of those books; and, secondly, that there are only five "Books of Moses," not six, as those exceedingly learned men assure us, who throw the Book of Joshua in the Pentateuch, for good measure. Nephi is right. And that is proved by the fact that the Samaritan Pentateuch, which in all probability came into existence at the time of the separation of Israel and Judah, during the reign of Rehoboam, does not include the Book of Joshua, although the Samaritans also had a copy of the latter book.

That Nephi is right also in ascribing the authorship to Moses is as certain.

As is well known, there is a class of critics who claim to have discovered that the Pentateuch is a mixtum composition, consisting of a number of literary fragments, no less than four, probably many more, all of which belong to a post-Mosaic time, and some to a time as late as Ezekiel. They surmise that, centuries after Moses, an author arose in the kingdom of Judah, who in his historic compositions referred to the Deity as Jehovah, while another historian in the kingdom of Israel used the name Elohim. Some time after these authors, an editor cut these histories to pieces and put the fragments together in an abbreviated form, in order to make a continuous story of the two. Then, they claim, there is a priestly code which came into existence during the time of Ezekiel and was woven into the story of the two other documents. Finally, the Deuteronomy was written by someone during the time of King Josiah.

There was a time when the many arguments needed to support this theory were regarded as the very quintessence of erudition, particularly among young atheists and rationalists. But they have been weighed and found wanting.

For instance, Professor George Frederick Wright, D.D., LL.D., Oberlin College, Ohio, has pointed out that:

"On consulting the evidence it appears that in Genesis and the first three chapters of Exodus [where this — the *Jehovah-Elohim* — clue was supposed to be

the plates of brass a genealogy of his fathers; wherefore he knew that he was a descendant of Joseph; yea, even that Joseph who was the son of Jacob, who was sold into Egypt, and who was preserved by the hand of the Lord, that he might preserve his father, Jacob, and all his household from perishing with famine.

---

most decisive] Jehovah occurs in the Hebrew text 148 times, but in 118 of these places other texts[1] have either Elohim or Jehovah Elohim. In the same section, while Elohim alone occurs 179 times in the Hebrew, in 49 of the passages one or the other designation takes its place; and in the second and third chapters of Genesis where the Hebrew text has Jehovah Elohim (Lord God) 23 times, there is only one passage in which all the texts are unanimous on this point."

It requires no great learning to see that, unless the critics can furnish an infallibly correct Hebrew text—one that will stand the test of real textual criticism —their argument from words or names is the flimsiest of fallacies.

That Moses had access to many records and documents now lost is certain. Noah must have left some records to his descendants. We know that Abraham wrote books. And so did Joseph. Even in Egypt, the Israelites had their recorders (shoterim, badly translated "officers"), and they, naturally, would preserve in writing such judicial decisions as were rendered by their magistrates, especially by Joseph. Moses would, of course, have access to these records. Then there were Egyptian, Assyrian and Babylonian tablets by the hundreds. There was the law of Hammurabi, and many other documents. And Moses would certainly avail himself of all literary helps within his reach, treasuring up the pearls and consigning the remainder to the shell heap.

A theory that deserves some consideration may be stated somewhat like this: Moses may have compiled the Book of the Covenants which occupies the section from Exodus 20:22 to 24:7, from records written in Egypt, under divine guidance, as indicated in the opening sentence, "And the Lord said unto Moses, Thus thou shalt say unto the children of Israel." The rest of the books may have been given to the people in the wilderness, first verbally and then in copies written by the recorders (officers). See Deut. 17:11; 24:8; and Lev. 10:11. The final codification may have been done after the death of Moses, perhaps under the supervision of Eleazar, the son of Aaron, (Num. 3:32) or by Joshua. The Deuteronomy must be accredited to Moses, except of course, the account of his death, which was added thereafter. That the books, under the hands of copyists and collectors may have suffered modifications and even textual errors is not denied. But that does not effect the original authorship. It has been suggested that Moses may have composed a great part of Genesis, while he was an exile in Median. (Ex. 2:15-25)

There are some peculiarities connected with the Pentateuch, which the critics have ignored. One is the absence of the name *Jerusalem* from that part of the Bible. If it were true that a great part of it was written by an author in the capital of Judah, that city would have been given a prominent place in the document. Mr. Andrew Craig Robinson, M.A., Ballineen, Ireland, argues:

"It seems strange then to find the Yahvist [document] supposed to have been written in the southern kingdom, and to have been imbued with all its prejudices, consecrating Bethel by a notable theophany (Gen. 28:16-19), whilst in all that he is supposed to have written in the Pentateuch he never once makes mention of his own Jerusalem. And so the 'priestly' writer also, to whom a shrine like Bethel

---

[1]The other texts are, the Septuagint, the Samaritan, the translation of Aquila, the early Syriac and the Latin Vulgate.

15. And they were also led out of captivity and out of the land of Egypt, by that same God who had preserved them.

16. And thus my father, Lehi, did discover the genealogy of his fathers. And Laban also was a descendant of Joseph, wherefore he and his fathers had kept the records.

---

ought to be anathema, is found nevertheless consecrating Bethel with another theophany: 'Jacob called the name of the place where God spoke to him Bethel' (Gen. 35:14, 15), and he never mentions Jerusalem. What is the explanation of all this? What is the inner meaning of this absence of the name Jerusalem from the Pentateuch? Is it not this: that at the time the Pentateuch was written, Jerusalem, with all her sacred glories, *had not entered yet into the life of Israel?*"

In other words, the Pentateuch must have been composed before Israel had become settled in Canaan.

Another notable fact, which justifies the same conclusion, is the absence in the Pentateuch of all reference to ritual song and music, such as constituted part of the divine service in Judah at the time when the critics suppose the "priestly" code was written. At that time, the people had harps, timbrels, cymbals, psalteries, songs and singers, but no such instruments and no sweet vocalists, are mentioned in the Books of Moses as belonging to the Tabernacle and the sacred ritual. That proves that they must have been composed long before the date assigned to them by the critics.

There is another omission. The title "Lord of Hosts" is not found in the Pentateuch, for the simple reason that the book was composed before the time of Samuel, when that appellation was first applied as a title of the Almighty.

*The creation of the world and Adam and Eve.* This is the beginning of Genesis, the First Book of Moses. It is the first authoritative information given to the race concerning the origin of the universe and man, the fall and the promise of redemption.

Some regard this wonderful story as myth. But from the Pearl of Great Price we learn that God himself, in a vision on a high mountain revealed to Moses what he afterwards wrote concerning a new heaven and earth, man and the plan of salavation. (See the "Writings of Moses," as revealed to Joseph Smith in June and December, 1830). That is how he got his information. There is no more important part of the Bible than this.

Somebody has said:

"The Bible as a whole is like a chain hanging upon two staples. The Book of Genesis is the one staple, the Book of Revelation the other. Take away either staple, the chain falls in confusion. If the first chapters of Genesis are unreliable, the revelation of the beginning of the universe, the origin of the race, and the reason of its redemption is gone. If the last chapters of Revelation are displaced the consummation of all things is unknown."

Except, of course, it is revealed again by the source of all truth.

The importance of this "chain" in the plan of salvation is evidenced by the fact that God again revealed both the first and the last link of it to the Prophet Joseph Smith—both the visions of Moses and the visions of John the Revelator. (D. & C., Sec. 77)

VERSE 13. *Zedekiah and Jeremiah.* Both were contemporary with Lehi. Zedekiah, the king, ended his days in Babylon, a captive. Jeremiah, the prophet, loved his people and country and refused to accept favors of the Babylonian monarch.

## 3. *Lehi's prophecy.*

17. And now when my father saw all these things, he was filled with the Spirit, and began to prophesy concerning his seed —

18. That these plates of brass should go forth unto all nations, kindreds, tongues, and people who were of his seed.

19. Wherefore, he said that these plates of brass should never perish; neither should they be dimmed any more by time. And he prophesied many things concerning his seed.

20. And it came to pass that thus far I and my father had kept the commandments wherewith the Lord had commanded us.

21. And we had obtained the records which the Lord had commanded us, and searched them and found that they were desirable; yea, even of great worth unto us, insomuch that we could preserve the commandments of the Lord unto our children.

22. Wherefore, it was wisdom in the Lord that we should carry them with us, as we journeyed in the wilderness towards the land of promise.

---

The panic-stricken politicians who fled to Egypt, in order to escape the vengeance of the Babylonians, carried Jeremiah with them, fearing, no doubt, his influence with the foreign rulers in Jerusalem.

VERSE 14. *Genealogy of his Fathers.* This personal record must have been considered of the greatest importance, since it was kept with the costly metal plates. In the days, when large family Bibles were cherished possessions, there generally were leaves for genealogical data in those venerable volumes. They became valuable when kept for generations. This must have been some such record. (v. 16)

VERSE 18. *These Plates . . . unto all Nations.* It appears that after the sacrifice and offerings, and when the repast had been finished and the plates examined, Lehi gathered his family and, filled with the Holy Spirit, addressed them on the nature and value of the records. During the course of his address he prophesied that these plates "should go forth unto all nations"—not the plates, surely, but their contents.

The one set of plates could not go to all nations, but copies of the contents, written and printed could, and have been widely distributed.

VERSE 19. *Never Perish; neither . . . dimmed any more by Time.* May we conclude from this that Laban had not taken proper care of the records? That they had lost their brightness, become dim, and, perhaps, begun to evince signs of corrosion? If so, that would be another strong reason why they should be taken from him and handed over to Lehi.

At all events, they shall never perish; never be dimmed any more by time.

### NOTES

*King Lemuel* is by most commentators considered as referring to Solomon, but recent Bible scholars suppose it to be a fictitious name through which the maxims enunciated are made applicable to all.

*Her lamp does not go out at night.* It is said that to sleep in the dark, without a night lamp, was regarded as an evidence of poverty in the Orient.

*The Hebrews* had a keen appreciation of the hereditary influence of the mother upon her children. Among the blessings of the Almighty on Joseph, his father enumerates the blessings derived from the physical unity of the child with its mother, (Gen. 49:25) And when the women of Jerusalem heard the sermons of our Lord and saw his miracles, they thought of the mother that bore and nursed him. (Luke 11:27) There is a great lesson in this.

*The Five Books of Moses, see* "Pentateuch" on page 450.

## CHAPTER 6

*Nephi explains the purpose of his writings — The salvation of men.*

1. And now I, Nephi, do not give the genealogy of my fathers in this part of my record; neither at any time shall I give it after upon these plates which I am writing; for it is given in the record which has been kept by my father; wherefore, I do not write it in this work.

2. For it sufficeth me to say that we are a descendent of Joseph.

3. And it mattereth not to me that I am particular to give a full account of all the things of my father, for they cannot be written upon these plates, for I desire the room that I may write of the things of God.

4. For the fulness of mine intent is that I may persuade men to come unto the God of Abraham, and the God of Isaac, and the God of Jacob, and be saved.

5. Wherefore, the things which are pleasing unto the world I do not write, but the things which are pleasing unto God and unto those who are not of the world.

6. Wherefore, I shall give commandment unto my seed, that they shall not occupy these plates with things which are not of worth unto the children of men.

---

VERSES 1-6. *The Purpose of this Volume.* Nephi states that his only aim in writing is to persuade men to come to God for salvation. Consequently, he does not copy the genealogy of his fathers, beyond stating that they are descendants of Joseph. There is then nothing superfluous in this volume. Its contents are sifted and preserved because they are essential in the divine plan of salvation.

*God of Abraham, Isaac and Jacob.* (v. 4) That is the only true and living God; God, in whose image man was made; God, the Creator, Ruler and Redeemer of the world, to whom we "honor and glory for ever and ever."

In the story of the call of Moses to undertake the mission of liberating Israel from Egyptian bondage, we are told that the "angel of the Lord" manifest himself as a flame, and that when Moses approached, the angel speaking as the representative of the Deity, said, "I am the God of thy fathers, the God of Abraham, the God of Isaac, and the God of Jacob." (Ex. 3:6; Acts 7:32)

Moses replied (Ex. 3:13), "Behold, when I come to the children of Israel, and shall say unto them, The God of your fathers hath sent me to you; and they shall say to me, What is his name? What shall I say unto them?"

This may appear to us a peculiar question. But the Egyptians (and the Israelites in Egypt were very tainted with Egyptian ideas) had a great many gods and goddesses besides the one great, self-existant, immortal and inscrutable Creator. They had Osiris, Isis, Anubis, Nephys, Horus, Set, Hator, Tefnut, Apis, etc. A great leader among the Egyptians had to know these deities, and their secret names, whereby they were supposed to exist and rule in the world. Hence, the question of Moses was perfectly natural. What name shall I give?"

The angel, again speaking on behalf of God whose messenger he was, said, "Thus shalt thou say to the children of Israel, I AM hath sent me unto you. . . .

The Lord God of your fathers, the God of Abraham, the God of Isaac, and the God of Jacob, hath sent me unto you: this is my name for ever, and this is my memorial unto all generations." (Ex. 3:14, 15)

In some of the revelations to Joseph Smith, our Savior introduces himself as "The Great I AM," (D. & C. 29:1), or "the Great I AM, Alpha and Omega, the beginning and the end." (D. & C. 38:1)

In Exodus (Ex. 6:2 and 3) the Lord, further, speaks to Moses: "and I appeared unto Abraham, unto Isaac, and unto Jacob by the name of God Almighty, but by my name Jehovah was I not known to them."

Some have understood this to mean that the author, or "editor" of Exodus did not know that the patriarchs had heard the sacred name, wherefore he concluded that it was first revealed to Moses. But the mistake should not be charged to the author of Exodus but to his critics.

As early as Enos, the son of Seth and grandson of Adam, men "began to call upon the name of Jehovah." (Gen. 4:26) Or, rather, they began to call themselves after the name of Jehovah, just as the followers of Jesus, the Christ, at Antioch (Acts 11:26), at an early day, were called Christians. (Compare Alma 46:12-16)

Noah knew the sacred name, for he "builded an altar unto Jehovah." (Gen. 8:20) It was known to Abraham, for after the battle of Amraphel and his allies, he told Melchizedek, "I have lifted up my hand to Jehovah, the most high God," and made a promise not to touch anything of the spoils. But if it was known to Abraham, it was known to the other patriarchs. It was, in fact, known in Babylonia, in Egypt, and all over the world. And this is but natural. For the entire human race and all religions originated after the flood, in the family of Noah.

But although the name was known, the full meaning of it was not understood. That was what God revealed to Moses for the first time, when he said, "I AM THAT I AM," and, "Say unto the children of Israel, I AM hath sent me." (Ex. 3:14) This is the same as the "One Who Exists."

When God sent Moses to the Pharaoh of Egypt with a demand for the liberation of Israel, he manifested himself for the first time in the act of fulfilling his covenants with the patriarchs, by placing himself at the head of their enslaved descendants and making them his people, in a special sense. This was new.

The great religious teacher, John Calvin, realizes, that it was not the name, the letters, that were unknown before the time of Moses, but the deep significance of the name, and Hengstenberg says:

"Hitherto that Being, who in one aspect was Jehovah, in another had always been Elohim. The great crisis now drew nigh in which Jehovah Elohim would be changed into Jehovah. In prospect of this event God solemnly announced himself as Jehovah."

The pronunciation of the sacred name is not known now, because the Hebrews long ago discontinued giving audible utterance to it, fearing that they might commit blasphemy by so doing. (Ex. 20:7; Lev. 24:11) Josephus might, perhaps, have told us something of the correct spelling, but he merely says,

"Moses having no cause to distrust that which God had promised him, and being confirmed by these things whereof he was both an eyewitness and hearer, he prayed to God, that if there were any occasion to express the like power in Egypt, he would vouchsafe to further the effect beseeching him further that he would not conceal his name, to the end that when he should offer sacrifice to him, he might call upon the name. God declared unto him his name, which beforetime had been concealed amongst men, and of which also it is not lawful for me to speak."

Scholars generally agree that "Jehovah" is not the correct spelling. Many prefer Jahweh or Yahweh. Many other forms are suggested. But as long as the subject is under discussion, the accepted form need not be rejected.

Dr. Clark, in his Commentary, has the following suggestion:

"Abraham was the father of the Ishmaelites, and with him was the covenant first made. Isaac was the father of the Edomites, as well as the Israelites, and with him was the covenant renewed. Jacob was the father of the twelve patriarchs, who were the founders of the Jewish nation, and to him were the promises particularly confirmed. Hence we see that the Arabs and the Turks in general, who are descendants of Ishmael; the Edomites, now absorbed among the Jews, who are the descendants of Esau; and the Jewish people wheresoever scattered, who are the descendants of Jacob, are all heirs of the promises included in this primitive covenant, and their gathering-in with the destiny of the gentiles may be confidently expected."

## CHAPTER 7

*Nephi and his brethren go to Jerusalem again, this time to get wives, 1-5—Ishmael and his family converted, some become disaffected, 6-7—Nephi's pleadings arouse anger, 8-16—Nephi's prayer answered, 17-22.*

### 1. Nephi and his brethren on a second mission to Jerusalem.

1. And now I would that ye might know, that after my father, Lehi, had made an end of prophesying concerning his seed, it came to pass that the Lord spake unto him again, saying that it was not meet for him, Lehi, that he should take his family into the wilderness alone; but that his sons should take daughters to wife, that they might raise up seed unto the Lord in the land of promise.

2. And it came to pass that the Lord commanded him that I, Nephi, and my brethren, should again return unto the land of Jerusalem, and bring down Ishmael and his family into the wilderness.

3. And it came to pass that I, Nephi, did again, with my brethren, go forth into the wilderness to go up to Jerusalem.

4. And it came to pass that we went up unto the house of Ishmael, and we did gain favor in the sight of Ishmael, insomuch that we did speak unto him the words of the Lord.

---

VERSE 1. *Raise up seed unto the Lord.* The first divine commandment to men, created in God's image, was: "Be fruitful, and multiply and replenish the earth, and subdue it." (Gen. 1:28) In order to enable Adam to keep this divine law, God formed a woman of a "rib" taken from the side of Adam, wherefore he, on seeing this new, glorious creation, said, "This is now bone of my bones and flesh of my flesh: She shall be called Woman, because she was taken out of man." The Creator added to this: "Therefore shall a man leave his father and mother, and shall cleave unto his wife; and they shall be one flesh." (Gen. 2:22-24; 19:4-5) The commandment to replenish the earth has not been canceled; it will be in force until the entire earth is filled with the children of God.

The entire population of the earth is estimated at about 2,500,000,000 (two and one-half billion) souls, of which one-half or 1,250,000,000 live in Asia 450,000,000 in Europe, 198,000,000 in Africa, 350,000,000 in North and South America, and about 9,000,000 in Australia. The increase is rapid in modern times. In 1814 the population of the earth was estimated at about 700,000,000. Since then there has been an increase of a billion, or more, owing to a better understanding of the laws of hygiene. If the increase continues at the present rate, the mission of the human race in mortality will before long, of necessity, be one of intelligent cooperation, for the preservation of life, instead of one of destructive competition, for the simple reason that the earth will be too small for billions to be at war with each other.

God commands the sons of Lehi to go to Jerusalem and bring Ishmael and his family down to the Valley. He must have been a friend of the family. Both he and Lehi were the descendants of Joseph, Ishmael through Ephraim and Lehi through Manasseh. His family consisted of his wife, two sons with their families, and five daughters. (v. 6)

5. And it came to pass that the Lord did soften the heart of Ishmael, and also his household, insomuch that they took their journey with us down into the wilderness to the tent of our father.

## 2. Ishmael and his family converted, some become disaffected.

6. And it came to pass that as we journeyed in the wilderness, behold Laman and Lemuel, and two of the daughters of Ishmael, and the two sons of Ishmael and their families, did rebel against us; yea, against me, Nephi, and Sam, and their father, Ishmael, and his wife and his three other daughters.

7. And it came to pass in the which rebellion, they were desirous to return unto the land of Jerusalem.

## 3. Nephi's pleadings arouse anger.

8. And now, I, Nephi, being grieved for the hardness of their hearts, therefore I spake unto them, saying, yea, even unto Laman and unto Lemuel: Behold ye are mine elder brethren, and how is it that ye are so hard in your hearts, and so blind in your minds, that ye have need that I, your younger brother, should speak unto you, yea, and set an example for you?

9. How is it that ye have not hearkened unto the word of the Lord?

10. How is it that ye have forgotten that ye have seen an angel of the Lord?

VERSE 4. *A successful mission.* Nephi and his brothers spoke to Ishmael, the word of the Lord. They had a message for him. That was the secret of their influence as missionaries.

VERSE 5. *The Lord did soften their hearts.* That was the cause of their success. There is no successful missionary labor, unless the missionary is the humble instrument of the Lord—His mouthpiece.

VERSE 6. *Did rebel against us.* Shortly after the little company had left Jerusalem, the question of returning to the city or continuing the journey seems to have been brought up for discussion, possibly at one of their meetings. The difficulties of the trail may have been greater than some of them at first anticipated; under the circumstances, the wilful doubt of Laman and Lemuel was catching. At all events, the little company faced destruction as a consequence of dissension. Laman, Lemuel, the two sons of Ishmael with their families and two daughters of Ishmael, joined in opposition to Nephi, Sam, Ishmael, his wife and three daughters, who were in favor of continuing the journey. The opposition was in the majority.

VERSES 8-16. *Nephi pleads with his brethren.* Nephi, in this, from every point of view, masterly address, reminds his two brothers, Laman and Lemuel, of some indisputable facts: (1) They had seen an angel; (2) they had been miraculously delivered from death at the hands of Laban; (3) they had obtained the records.

After these facts had been placed before them, he promised them that if they would be faithful, they would obtain a better land, and they would receive knowledge, at some future time, of the destruction of Jerusalem.

11. Yea, and how is it that ye have forgotten what great things the Lord hath done for us, in delivering us out of the hands of Laban, and also that we should obtain the record?

12. Yea, and how is it that ye have forgotten that the Lord is able to do all things according to his will, for the children of men, if it so be that they exercise faith in him? Wherefore, let us be faithful to him.

13. And if it so be that we are faithful to him, we shall obtain the land of promise; and ye shall

know at some future period that the word of the Lord shall be fulfilled concerning the destruction of Jerusalem; for all things which the Lord hath spoken concerning the destruction of Jeruslaem must be fulfilled.

14. For behold, the Spirit of the Lord ceaseth soon to strive with them; for behold, they have rejected the prophets, and Jeremiah have they cast into prison. And they have sought to take away the life of my father, insomuch that they have driven him out of the land.

---

If, however, notwithstanding all this, they would return, very well, he exclaimed, "go up to the land," but remember—and this is the word of the Spirit of the Lord—"if ye go, ye will also perish."

I doubt whether even a Lincoln could improve this speech a great deal.

VERSE 14. *Jeremiah have they cast into prison.* This may be considered an important historical clue, confirming the authenticity of the record. Let us turn for a moment to the pages of history.

In the year 608 B.C., Josiah, king of Judah, fell at Megiddo, in an attempt to prevent the Egyptian army from marching through Palestine on its way north against Assyria. Jehoahaz succeeded him. But he was deposed by the Egyptian ruler, Pharaoh Necho, who placed Jehoiakim on the throne instead.

At the battle of Carchemish, in the year 605 B.C., the Egyptians were defeated and, as a consequence, driven out of Syria. Jehoiakim was then forced to swear allegiance to the Babylonian ruler.

In the same year, Jeremiah directed his secretary, Baruch, to commit his prophecies to writing. The king heard part of the sacred roll and ordered it all destroyed, whereupon he sent his officers to apprehend the two servants of the Lord. But they could not be found, then.

Jehoiakim, shortly before the exodus of Lehi, made an alliance with Egypt, but his death saved him from the vengeance of Nebuchadnezzar. Jehoiachin succeeded him, and in 596 B.C., he and his household and thousands of citizens were carried captive to Babylon. That was the first deportation.

If we suppose that Nephi and his brethren came to Jerusalem on their mission to the house of Ishmael, at the time when Jehoiakim broke with Babylon and made a treaty of alliance with Egypt, we can understand why Laman, who without doubt was leaning toward the Egyptian party, again rebelled against his father and his brother, and why some of the members of the household of Ishmael sided with him. For, had not the king thrown off the Babylonian yoke, and was not Egypt going to save Jerusalem? It looked, indeed, as if the prophecies of Lehi would be proved false. Jeremiah was gone—imprisoned, for aught he knew, and his prophecies concerning the destruction of Jerusalem would not be fulfilled.

15. Now behold, I say unto you that if ye will return unto Jerusalem ye shall also perish with them. And now, if ye have choice, go up to the land, and remember the words which I speak unto you, that if ye go ye will also perish; for thus the Spirit of the Lord constraineth me that I should speak.

16. And it came to pass that

when I, Nephi, had spoken these words unto my brethren, they were angry with me. And it came to pass that they did lay their hands upon me, for behold, they were exceeding wroth, and they did bind me with cords, for they sought to take away my life, that they might leave me in the wilderness to be devoured by wild beasts.

## 4. Nephi's prayer answered.

17. But it came to pass that I prayed unto the Lord, saying: O Lord, according to my faith which is in thee, wilt thou deliver me from the hands of my brethren; yea, even give me strength that I may burst these bands with which I am bound.

18. And it came to pass that when I had said these words, behold, the bands were loosed

from off my hands and feet, and I stood before my brethren, and I spake unto them again.

19. And it came to pass that they were angry with me again, and sought to lay hands upon me; but behold, one of the daughters of Ishmael, yea, and also her mother, and one of the sons of Ishmael did plead with my brethren, insomuch that they

It was to some such blind reasoning that Nephi replied: "Ye shall know at some future time that the word of the Lord shall be fulfilled concerning the destruction of Jerusalem." That event was now so near that Nephi, led by the spirit of prophecy, could state positively that they would hear about it before they were much older. The news reached them perhaps before they left the Valley of Lemuel; or at all events, before they embarked on the sea voyage.

VERSE 16. *They were angry.* The immediate effect of the great argument of Nephi was to arouse anger against him. The brute passion soon turned into brutal actions. The opponents, unable to justify their position, seized him, bound him, and doomed him to death.

VERSE 18. *The bands were loosed.* Jeremiah was cast into a deep dungeon, a water cistern in which the water had nearly all evaporated and left a residue of mud and slime. He was rescued by an Ethiopian eunuch by the name of Ebed-Melech, who acted on secret instructions from the king, Zedekiah, but he was kept in prison until the fall of the city.

Nephi was rescued by direct intervention of the Lord, in answer to prayer. The cords fell from his hands and from his feet, and he could once more stand forth and plead with his brothers. They were still angry. But a daughter of Ishmael and also one of his sons who had formerly opposed Nephi, changed their attitude, when they saw his miraculous deliverance. Nephi now had a majority on his side, and his brethren humbly apologized for their wickedness. Thus the

did soften their hearts; and they did cease striving to take away my life.

20. And it came to pass that they were sorrowful, because of their wickedness, insomuch that they did bow down before me, and did plead with me that I would forgive them of the thing that they had done against me.

21. And it came to pass that I did frankly forgive them all that they had done, and I did exhort them that they would pray unto the Lord their God for forgiveness. And it came to pass that they did so. And after they had done praying unto the Lord we did again travel on our journey towards the tent of our father.

22. And it came to pass that we did come down unto the tent of our father. And after I and my brethren and all the house of Ishmael had come down unto the tent of my father, they did give thanks unto the Lord their God; and they did offer sacrifice and burnt offerings unto him.

---

incident ended. The little company soon reached the Valley of Lemuel and celebrated its homecoming, as on a former occasion, with sacrifice and burnt offerings. (1 Ne. 5:9)

### NOTES

*The meaning of the First Command.* This doctrine makes clear the meaning of the first great command, to multiply and replenish the earth. It is not only for the joy and satisfaction of humanity that the sex relation, with the possibility of begetting offspring, prevails on earth, but as much for the fulfilment of the eternal great Plan. It becomes a necessary duty, for all wedded persons who dwell on earth, to bring children into the world. This is the greatest and holiest and most necessary mission of man, with respect to the waiting spirits. Fatherhood and motherhood become glorified in the light of the eternal plan of salvation.

Women enjoy all the endowments and blessings of the Priesthood in connection with their husbands. The family is the basis of society on earth, and as there must be organization amongst all intelligent beings, someone must be spokesman for the family. In the family, the man is the spokesman and presiding authority, and, therefore, the Priesthood is bestowed upon him.—*Rational Theology,* John A. Widtsoe, "The Apostle," p. 97.

The word which in the story of the creation of man is translated "rib," (Hebrew *zelah*) occurs 38 times in the Old Testament. Nowhere, except in that account, is it rendered "rib." In a number of passages it is translated "side," (Ex. 25:12, 14; 26:20; 27:7; 36:25, 31; 37:35; 38:7) In 2 Samuel 16:13 it is rendered, "hillside." And in Ezekiel 41 it occurs ten times and is rendered, "side chambers." Why the translators of Genesis should have preferred "rib" to "side" is a mystery. "Chamber" would, in my opinion or judgment be preferable. The side chambers of the temple were used for sacred purposes. In some of them the sacred utensils and the vast treasures of the sanctuary were, no doubt, stored. But the body of Adam was a temple of God, with its side chambers, as well as main chambers, in which the main springs of life were stored. From these chambers it pleased God to draw his material for the second sacred structure, to be joined to the first. And so Adam, who was perfectly conscious of what the Lord had done during his sleep, exclaimed, as soon as he saw the new creation, "This is now bone of my bones, and flesh of my flesh."

### CHAPTER 8

*Lehi's dream in the Valley of Lemuel, 1-35—His fear for his two elder sons, 36-38.*

## 1. Lehi's dream.

1. And it came to pass that we had gathered together all manner of seeds of every kind, both of grain of every kind, and also of the seeds of fruit of every kind.

2. And it came to pass that while my father tarried in the wilderness he spake unto us, saying: Behold, I have dreamed a dream; or, in other words, I have seen a vision.

3. And behold, because of the thing which I have seen, I have reason to rejoice in the Lord because of Nephi and also of Sam; for I have reason to suppose that they, and also many of their seed, will be saved.

4. But behold, Laman and Lemuel, I fear exceedingly because of you; for behold, methought I saw in my dream, a dark and dreary wilderness.

5. And it came to pass that I saw a man, and he was dressed in a white robe; and he came and stood before me.

6. And it came to pass that he

VERSE 1. *All manner of seeds . . . and also of the seeds of fruit.* Indicates a long stay in the Valley of Lemuel.

VERSE 2. *I have had a dream.* (See note Chap. 2:1) Dreams and visions are often mentioned together, as here, indicating their close relationship, although belonging to different sections of the mental field. The famous manifestations of Nebuchadnezzar concerning the golden image (Dan. 2) was a dream, but the interpretation of it was revealed to Daniel in a night "vision" (v. 10), and the prophet refers to it as "thy dream and the visions of thy head" (v. 28). On the other hand, the appearance of the Father and the Son to Joseph Smith in the sacred grove was not a dream but a vision. The appearance of our Lord, of Moses, of Elias and Elijah in the Kirtland Temple in 1836 were so many visions. The Prophet explains: "The veil was taken from our minds, and the eyes of our understanding were opened. We saw the Lord standing upon the breastwork of the pulpit." (D. & C. 110:1, 2)

VERSE 4. *Lehi feared exceedingly.* Lehi did not dismiss the dream as an illusion. He accepted it as a message from God. It brought him joy because of Nephi and Sam, but he feared because of Laman and Lemuel. In olden days dreams were often accepted as revelations. Eliphas, one of the friends of Job, said, "Now a thing was secretly brought to me, and mine ear received a little thereof. In thoughts from the visions of the night, when deep sleep falleth on men, fear came upon me, and trembling, which made all my bones to shake." (Job 4:13, 15) Job, in his sufferings, exclaims, "When I say, My bed shall comfort me, my couch shall ease my complaint; then thou scarest me with dreams, and terrifiest me through visions," (Job 1:13, 14), an experience which many sufferers have had. Elihu, another of the friends of Job, argues: "For God speaketh once, yea twice, yet man perceiveth it not. In a dream, in a vision of the night, when deep sleep falleth upon men, in slumberings upon the bed; then he openeth the ears of men, and

spake unto me, and bade me follow him.

7. And it came to pass that as I followed him I beheld myself that I was in a dark and dreary waste.

8. And after I had traveled for the space of many hours in darkness, I began to pray unto the Lord that he would have mercy on me, according to the multitude of his tender mercies.

9. And it came to pass after I had prayed unto the Lord I beheld a large and spacious field.

10. And it came to pass that I beheld a tree, whose fruit was desirable to make one happy.

11. And it came to pass that I did go forth and partake of the fruit thereof; and I beheld that it was most sweet, above all that I ever before tasted. Yea, and I beheld that the fruit thereof was white, to exceed all the whiteness that I had ever seen.

12. And as I partook of the fruit thereof it filled my soul with exceeding great joy; wherefore, I began to be desirous that my family should partake of it also; for I knew that it was desirable above all other fruit.

13. And as I cast my eyes round about, that perhaps I might discover my family also, I beheld a river of water; and it ran along, and it was near the tree of which I was partaking the fruit.

14. And I looked to behold from whence it came; and I saw the head thereof a little way off; and at the head thereof I beheld your mother, Sariah, and Sam, and Nephi; and they stood as if they knew not whither they should go.

15. And it came to pass that I beckoned unto them; and I also did say unto them with a loud voice that they should come unto me, and partake of the fruit, which was desirable above all other fruit.

16. And it came to pass that they did come unto me and partake of the fruit also.

17. And it came to pass that I was desirous that Laman and Lemuel should come and partake

sealeth their instruction." (Job 33:14-16) Lehi was seized with fear; not for himself, but for his two sons. One of the objects of this dream was to acquaint Lehi with the condition of his sons, in order that he might warn them, and bring them to repentance. America might have had a different history, if Laman and Lemuel had accepted the sweet fruit of the tree and acknowledged Nephi as their divinely appointed leader.

### A Synopsis of the Dream

1. A man robed in white, a messenger from our Heavenly Father, takes Lehi, in a dream, through a dark and dreary wilderness, to a large and spacious field. (1 Ne. 8:5-9)

This, probably, is a representation of the long journey and voyage of Lehi from the Valley of Lemuel to the new, promised land.

2. In this spacious field he sees a tree, bearing sweet and delicious fruit, the eating of which filled his soul with joy. (vv. 10-12)

of the fruit also; wherefore, I cast mine eyes towards the head of the river, that perhaps I might see them.

18. And it came to pass that I saw them, but they would not come unto me and partake of the fruit.

19. And I beheld a rod of iron, and it extended along the bank of the river, and led to the tree by which I stood.

20. And I also beheld a straight and narrow path, which came along by the rod of iron; even to the tree by which I stood; and it also led by the head of the fountain, unto a large and spacious field, as if it had been a world.

21. And I saw numberless concourses of people, many of whom were pressing forward, that they might obtain the path which led unto the tree by which I stood.

22. And it came to pass that they did come forth, and commence in the path which led to the tree.

23. And it came to pass that there arose a mist of darkness; yea, even an exceeding great mist of darkness, insomuch that they who had commenced in the path did lose their way, that they wandered off and were lost.

24. And it came to pass that I beheld others pressing forward, and they came forth and caught hold of the end of the rod of iron; and they did press forward through the mist of darkness, clinging to the rod of iron, even until they did come forth and partake of the fruit of the tree.

25. And after they had partaken of the fruit of the tree they did cast their eyes about as if they were ashamed.

The tree we are told, represents the love of God in the hearts of men (1 Ne. 11:22, 25 and 15:22), and, we may perhaps presume, especially as manifested in the many blessings, both temporal and spiritual, which God was about to bestow upon Lehi and his descendants in the new land, in accordance with the promises which Joseph received of his father Jacob. (Gen. 49:22-26) That was the fruit Laman and Lemuel rejected.

3. In looking about for his family, Lehi sees a "river of water" running close to the tree. At the head of this water, Sariah, Sam and Nephi were standing, uncertain where to go. He called them, and they came to him. Soon he discovered Laman and Lemuel, and called them too; but "they would not come." (vv. 12-18)

Concerning the water in the river, Nephi explains it was "filthiness." But his father was occupied with other things, looking for his family, and he did not notice the filthy condition of the water. (1 Ne. 15:27) The angel who explains the dream to Nephi places before him a fearful picture of war between his descendants and those of his brethren, and then he says, pointing to that battle array, "Behold the fountain of filthy water which thy father saw; yea, even the river of which he spake; and the depths thereof are the depths of hell." Which is about the same as to say that the conditions in which wars originate are the same as those in which all hell has its origin. The "depths" of both are the same. (1 Ne. 12:16)

4. Lehi, next, sees a "rod of iron" extending along the banks of the river; also a straight and narrow path, both of which led to the tree. The path also led

26. And I also cast my eyes round about, and beheld, on the other side of the river of water, a great and spacious building; and it stood as it were in the air, high above the earth.

27. And it was filled with people, both old and young, both male and female; and their manner of dress was exceeding fine; and they were in the attitude of mocking and pointing their fingers towards those who had come at and were partaking of the fruit.

28. And after they had tasted of the fruit they were ashamed, because of those that were scoffing at them; and they fell way into forbidden paths and were lost.

29. And now I, Nephi, do not speak all the words of my father.

30. But, to be short in writing, behold, he saw other multitudes pressing forward; and they came and caught hold of the end of the rod of iron; and they did press their way forward, continually holding fast to the rod of iron, until they came forth and fell down and partook of the fruit of the tree.

31. And he also saw other multitudes feeling their way towards that great and spacious building.

32. And it came to pass that many were drowned in the depths of the fountain; and many were lost from his view, wandering in strange roads.

33. And great was the multitude that did enter into that strange building. And after they did enter into that building they did point the finger of scorn at me and those that were partaking of the fruit also; but we heeded them not.

past the head of the fountain to a large field, "as if it had been a world." Multitudes pressed forward in order to gain the path, and many reached it. But a dark mist falls, and some are lost, while others take hold of the iron rod and find the tree. (vv. 19-24)

The rod of iron is the word of God, and more especially the prophetic word concerning the new land of promise and the establishment of the kingdom of God in the latter-days. (See 1 Ne. 11:25 and 15:23-25) The "fountain" in verse 20, must refer to the source from which the tree had its life-giving moisture, for it represented "the love of God," as did the tree. (1 Ne. 11:25) It could not have been the fountain from which the filthy water in the river had its origin. The mists of darkness are the temptations of the devil. (1 Ne. 12:17)

5. Lehi, next, sees a great, spacious building, standing in the air. It is filled with human beings—fools and scoffers—who, with their ribaldry succeed in making apostates and transgressors of some of those who had tasted of the fruit of the tree. (vv. 25-28)

This building represents "vain imaginations and the pride of the children of men." (1 Ne. 12:18) A building of such intangible material and without a foundation cannot stand. Our age needs to be reminded of the fact that mockery is a sin, and that scoffers are far from the kingdom of God. Blessed is the man that does not sit in "the seat of the scornful." (Psalm 1:1) "Be not deceived; God is not mocked: for whatsoever a man soweth, that shall he also reap." (Gal. 6:7) We

34. These are the words of my father: For as many as heeded them, had fallen away.

35. And Laman and Lemuel partook not of the fruit, said my father.

## 2. *Lehi fears for Laman and Lemuel.*

36. And it came to pass after my father had spoken all the words of his dream or vision, which were many, he said unto us, because of these things which he saw in a vision, he exceedingly

---

are living in an age in which even sacred things are made the objects of jests and ridicule.

That such conduct is displeasing in the sight of the Almighty is strikingly illustrated by the story of Elisha and the scoffers of Bethel. (2 Kings 2:23, 24) The Prophet Elisha was going to Bethel, and was nearing the city when he was surrounded by a crowd of young scoffers. Our common Bible translations says, "little children," but the words so translated should in this place be rendered, "young men," or "youths," as, for instance, in 1 Kings 20:15. These young men, in all probability, were pupils in some idolatrous school of prophets at Bethel, where a golden calf had been set up by Jeroboam, in defiance of the temple service at Jerusalem. Having heard of the miraculous ascent of Elijah and the appointment of Elisha as his successor, they took occasion to ridicule the prophet. "Go up, thou baldhead," they cried, meaning, "Why don't you ascend, thou baldhead! Go on, ascend!" Like Elijah! They were mocking God in his representatives. Then Elisha turned toward them and gave them a searching look whereupon he "cursed" or rebuked them in the name of the Lord. "And there came out two she bears out of the wood, tore forty and two children of them."

I am aware that critics have aimed their arrows at this Biblical story, as against many others. They have charged the prophet with unnecessary cruelty. But the fact is that the prophet was no more responsible for the fate of these mockers, than was Noah for the flood, or Jonah for the destruction of Nineveh.

But the bears? Well, they did not belong to Elisha. Dr. Clarke, in his Commentary, asks: "Is it not possible that these young men had been destroying the whelps of the she bears that now pursued them? The statement that they were she bears gives color to this conjecture." Also the fact so many pupils were gathered together. Most likely, they had been on some kind of an excursion. Children do not accidentally get together in large numbers. Only when they go in the capacity of a school, or a Sunday school, or some organization. They may have been out in the woods for the purpose of ridding the country of predatory animals, to save the sheep. They may have destroyed, or even captured, cubs belonging to these bear mothers, and if they had not stopped to insult the prophet, they might have reached their homes in safety. The fury of a bear mother was proverbial in Israel. When Hushai advised Absalom not to pursue David, he said, "Thou knowest thy father and his men, that they be mighty men, and they be chafed in their minds, as a bear, robbed of her whelps in the field." (2 Sam. 17:8)

The story is a striking illustration of the sinfulness of levity regarding sacred things and persons.

VERSE 36. *The Presence of the Lord.* Lehi feared that Laman and Lemuel might be cast off from the Presence of the Lord. This Presence is what in older Jewish writings is called the *Shekinah,* referring to the indwelling of the Lord in his Sanctuary. It was the Shekinah, or indwelling, also called "the Glory of the Lord" that rested on Mt. Sinai, for the Lord "called Moses out of the midst of a cloud, and the sight of the Glory of the Lord was like devouring fire on the top of the

feared for Laman and Lemuel; yea, he feared lest they should be cast off from the presence of the Lord.

37. And he did exhort them then with all the feeling of a tender parent, that they would hearken to his words, that perhaps the Lord would be merciful to them, and not cast them off; yea, my father did preach unto them.

38. And after he had preached unto them, and also prophesied unto them of many things, he bade them to keep the commandments of the Lord; and he did cease speaking unto them.

---

mountain in the eyes of the children of Israel." (Ex. 24:15-17) It was a manifestation of Light in the pillar of cloud that guided Israel through the wilderness. (Ex. 40:34-38) "My Presence shall go with thee, and I will give thee rest." (Ex. 33:14) It was the Shekinah that filled the Temple of Solomon. (2 Chron. 7:1-3) The Prophet Ezekiel in his vision, sees the Shekinah departing from the temple. (Ez. 10:19; 11:22) and then again entering into the new temple. (Ez. 43:2-5) We can understand from this that to be cast out from "the Presence of the Lord" is to become spiritually lost.

What Lehi feared came, alas! to pass. (2 Ne. 5:20)

## NOTES

*Visions.* "God never bestows upon his people, or upon an individual, superior blessings without a severe trial to prove them, to prove that individual, or that people to see whether they will keep their covenants with him, and keep in remembrance what he has shown them. Then the greater the vision, the greater the display of the enemy. So when individuals are blessed with visions, revelations or manifestations, look out, then the Devil is nigh you, and you will be tempted in proportion to the visions, revelations, or manifestations you have received.—President Brigham Young.

"If the Lord Almighty should reveal to a high priest or to any other than the head, things that are true, or that have been and will be, and show him the destiny of this people twenty-five years from now, or a new doctrine that will in five, ten, or twenty years from now become a doctrine of this Church and Kingdom, but which has not yet been revealed to this people, and reveal it by the same spirit, the same messenger, the same voice, the same power that gave revelations to Joseph when he was living, it would be a blessing to that high priest or individual; but he must rarely divulge it to a second person on the face of the earth, until God reveals it through the proper source to become the property of the people at large. Therefore when you hear Elders say that God does not reveal through the president of the Church that which they know, and tell wonderful things, you may generally set it down as a God's truth that the revelation they have had is . . . not from God."—President Brigham Young.

## CHAPTER 9

*Two Sets of Plates, 1-4—For a Wise Purpose in Him, 5, 6.*

1. And all these things did my father see, and hear, and speak, as he dwelt in a tent, in the valley of Lemuel, and also a great many more things, which cannot be written upon these plates.

2. And now, as I have spoken concerning these plates, behold they are not the plates upon which I make a full account of the history of my people; for the plates upon which I make a full account of my people I have given the name of Nephi; wherefore, they are called the plates of Nephi, after mine own name; and these plates also are called the plates of Nephi.

3. Nevertheless, I have received a commandment of the Lord that I should make these plates, for the special purpose that there should be an account engraven of the ministry of my people.

4. Upon the other plates should be engraven an account of the reign of the kings, and the wars and contentions of my people; wherefore these plates are for the more part of the ministry; and the other plates are for the more part of the reign of kings and the wars and contentions of my people.

5. Wherefore, the Lord hath commanded me to make these plates for a wise purpose in him, which purpose I know not.

6. But the Lord knoweth all things from the beginning; wherefore, he prepareth a way to accomplish all his works among the children of men; for behold, he hath all power unto the fulfilling of all his words. And thus it is. Amen.

---

VERSE 2. *The Plates of Nephi.* Nephi, in this chapter, closes the abridgment of the record of his father (1 Ne. 1:17) with the statement that he has made two sets of plates, each set being called the "Plates of Nephi." One set contains the record of the "ministry of my people," the other, an account of the reign of kings, wars and contentions; in other words, one is an ecclesiastical, the other a political history.

VERSE 5. *For a wise purpose.* This arrangement was made in obedience to a divine commandment, for a wise purpose, which, however, was hidden from Nephi. God does not always—perhaps seldom—explain the reason why he gives a commandment. A loving child does not ask for reasons, when God speaks.

When Mormon had finished his abridgment from the political history of Nephi, down to the reign of King Benjamin, he found, after research, the other plates of Nephi, "which contained this small account of the prophets, from Jacob down to the reign of King Benjamin, and also many of the words of Nephi." Being much impressed with the contents of this record, he put the plates with his own work. "And I do this," he says, "for a wise purpose; for thus it whispereth me, according to the workings of the Spirit of the Lord which is in me." ("Words of Mormon, 3-7.)

This purpose did not become perfectly clear until during the summer of 1828. About that time Martin Harris had copied 116 pages of the translation, as slowly dictated by the Prophet Joseph, and, in his anxiety to convince his friends of the divinity of the work in which he and the prophet were engaged, he persuaded the latter to permit him to show them these pages. This part of the manuscript was lost. The loss would have been irreparable, but for the existence of the second set of plates of Nephi, which could be translated instead. (See D. & C. 3:12-14; 10:3-13)

## NOTES

A second translation of the text represented by the missing manuscript would, except for a special miracle, have been characterized by literary differences which, no matter how unessential, would have furnished enemies an excuse for doubting and rejecting the entire work. The double record obviated that difficulty by providing independent accounts covering the same period of time.

A good translator, it may be observed, does not merely transform mechanically words from one language into the words of another. It is the sentiment, the vision, the inspiration of the author he endeavors to communicate through the new vehicle which we call a "translation." That is one reason why two or more independent translators of the same paragraph never use identically the same words or sentences. Each necessarily leaves some of his own personality in his work, even when it is inspired by the divine Spirit. There is always a marked difference in style in the writings of, for instance, Paul and Peter and John, and, we may add, Joseph Smith, Brigham Young and David O. McKay, because they are not mechanical implements without intelligence. On the contrary, it is their intelligence, their individuality, their will, their free agency as well as their other gifts and accomplishments, that the Spirit of the Lord makes use of. The Spirit is the same, but "there are diversities of gifts." (I Cor. 12:4)

Furthermore, a good translator must be familiar with the subject he deals with. One absolutely ignorant of farming could not translate a work on agriculture. Only a poet can translate Shakespeare, and only a philosopher can give us an idea of Einstein's "Relativity." One who has never left the ground could give us only a poor description, even in a translation, of Lindbergh's flight across the Atlantic. By the same rule, only one who has the Spirit of the Lord can understand and translate the inspired writings, correctly. No philosopher, no school of philosophy can give us a correct understanding of either the Bible or the Book of Mormon, except by the aid of the divine Spirit.

Nephi made two sets of plates. That Nephi made use of metal for writing material, when the intention was to produce a record that could be moved from place to place and yet be durable enough to be preserved for centuries, is very probable. Speaking of the Mayas, Dr. Sylvanus G. Morley says: "The material upon which the Maya glyphs are presented are stone, wood, stucco, bone, shell, metal, plaster, pottery and fiber paper. . . . Texts have been found carved on the wooden lintels of Tikal, molded in the stucco reliefs of Palenque, scratched on shells from Copan and Belize, etched on a bone from Wild Cane Key, British Honduras, engraved on metal from Chichen Itza, drawn on the plaster-covered walls of Kabah, Chichen Itza and Uxmal, and painted in fiber-paper books." (An Introduction to the Study of Maya Hieroglyphics, p. 22)

Stone and paper are the most common kind of material used but metal would, naturally, be the best material for the purposes Nephi had in view.

Concerning writing and writing materials in South America little is known. The following from the pens of Rivero and von Tschudi is quoted as being in accordance with the generally reliable information they had:

"The ancient Peruvians had two kinds of writings: one, and certainly the most ancient, consisted in a species of hieroglyphic characters; the other, in knots made of threads of divers colors.

"The hieroglyphics of the Mexicans were very distinct and graved on stone or metal. In southern Peru there has not yet been discovered any vestige of hieroglyphics painted on paper."

In North America, on the Lenape records of the creation, the flood and the crossing of the waters by their ancestors, see, "An Introduction to the Study of the Book of Mormon," Sjodahl, pp. 460-470.

## CHAPTER 10

*The beginning of Nephi's account of his own reign, 1-2—Lehi's prophecy in the Valley of Lemuel: Concerning the destruction of Jerusalem and the Babylonian captivity, 3—Concerning the Messiah, a Savior of the world, 4-6—Concerning John the Baptist, 7-10—The Gospel among the Jews, 11—Israel scattered and gathered, 12-14—Nephi desires to see, to hear and to know, 15-22.*

### 1. *The beginning of Nephi's account.*

1. And now I, Nephi, proceed to give an account upon these plates of my proceedings, and my reign and ministry; wherefore, to proceed with mine account, I must speak somewhat of the things of my father, and also of my brethren.

2. For behold, it came to pass after my father had made an end of speaking the words of his dream, and also of exhorting them to all diligence, he spake unto them concerning the Jews—

### 2. *Prophecy concerning the destruction of Jerusalem.*

3. That after they should be destroyed, even that great city Jerusalem, and many be carried away captive into Babylon, according to the own due time of the Lord, they should return again, yea, even be brought back out of captivity; and after they should be brought back out of captivity they should possess again the land of their inheritance.

VERSES 1-2. Here Nephi begins the story of his own reign and ministry by a synopsis of a prophecy by his father, following the account of the dream of the tree in the field. (Chap. 8) Undoubtedly, the dream and the subsequent prophetic discourse influenced the entire life of Nephi. Fathers too often neglect giving the children the benefit of their experiences and mature judgment. Lehi did not neglect his duty in this respect.

VERSE 3. *They should be destroyed . . . carried away captive.* This would indicate that, at the time this prophecy was delivered, Jerusalem had not yet been destroyed, or, if it had, that word of it had not yet reached the Valley of Lemuel. It was in the year 596 B.C., according to the calculation of scholars, that Jehoiachin and thousands of prominent citizens with him, were carried away to Babylon. Among others was the prophet Ezekiel. The temple was also plundered of its costly treasures. Zedekiah was appointed king. It was not until ten years later that Jerusalem, because of the treachery of Zedekiah, was destroyed and the temple and other public buildings were demolished by fire. (2 Kings 24 and 25 ch.) This was in the year 586 B.C.

Then the doom of the kingdom of Judah was complete. The captivity was a separation not only from house and home and the land of inheritance, but also from the worship of Jehovah, the God of their fathers, because to the faithful Jew, worship was intimately connected with the temple in Jerusalem. By the rivers of Babylon the captives wept and hung their harps upon the willows, for, "How

### 3. *Concerning the Messiah, a Savior of the world.*

4. Yea, even six hundred years from the time that my father left Jerusalem, a prophet would the Lord God raise up among the Jews — even a Messiah, or, in other words, a Savior of the world.

5. And he also spake concerning the prophets, how great a number had testified of these

---

shall we sing the Lord's song in a strange land?" (Psalm 137:4) Jeremiah wrote to the captives and tried to arouse them to faith and hope by assuring them that their captivity would be ended in seventy years. (Jer. 29:1-14) Ezekiel, who was in Babylon, also promised them in the name of the Lord that they would be permitted to return and build a new temple.

*Destroyed.* This word does not mean "annihilated." Jerusalem was "destroyed" when its houses were laid in ashes, its walls broken down and many of its inhabitants carried away into captivity; that was destruction, but the city always remained, even if in ruins. Nephi (2 Ne. 25:9) says the Jews were "destroyed" from generation to generation, but he explains what he means (v. 16), viz., The Lord hath "scourged them from generation to generation." It is well to remember that destruction does not always mean complete extermination.

VERSE 4. *Six hundred years.* If, as is quite commonly supposed, our Lord was born four years before the beginning of our era, the exodus of Lehi from Jerusalem would have taken place in what in our chronology would be the year 604 B.C., or the year after the battle at Carchemish, where the Egyptians were defeated by the Chaldeans. That would, from an historical point of view, have been the logical time for the laying of the foundations of a new dispensation, in another part of the world, because from now on Palestine was to be the battle ground of the great world powers for supremacy.

*A Messiah.* Dr. Klausner, in his "Jesus of Nazareth," asks what Jesus is to the Jew. His book is written specially for the Jews. He answers the question by saying that, to the Jew, he is neither God nor the Son of God; neither the Messiah, nor even a prophet; but that, if his teachings were stripped of certain objectionable features, they would form the most admirable code of ethics, and he would be the greatest author of parables that ever lived.

Some Christian theologians have taken a similar view. According to them, all that man needs is a consciousness of his oneness with God. The life of Christ was completely dominated by that consciousness, and his work as a Savior is to arouse his consciousness in us. There is no need of expiation or sacrifice. As we share Christ's consciousness of the divine, our lives are transformed, and we are saved, and that is all there is to it.

Lately, theologians have even gone farther. They have suggested that a new religion is needed, stripped of everything supernatural; they propose substituting "humanism" for the Gospel, and to form a society in which all cooperate for the common good, and call that their church. In that society, there will be no place for the Messiah.

The Book of Mormon does not speak in uncertain terms on such subjects. It does not leave us in doubt. Here, in this discourse, Father Lehi states four positive facts: (1) that the Lord God (Jehovah Elohim), at a stated time, would raise up a prophet among the Jews; (2) that this prophet would be the promised Messiah,

things, concerning this Messiah, of whom he had spoken, or this Redeemer of the world.

6. Wherefore, all mankind were in a lost and in a fallen state, and ever would be save they should rely on this Redeemer.

---

or the Savior of the world; (3) that his mission of salvation would be in the nature of "redemption"; (4) that man, in his fallen state, would be lost without a Redeemer. All this refers to Jesus. He is the Prophet, the Messiah, the Savior, the Redeemer.

As the Prophet, he declares the plan of salvation to God's children, for a prophet is one who speaks "for God." As the Messiah, the "Anointed One," the "Christ," he is the Mediator between God and man and the Ruler of God's kingdom. As the Savior, his mission is to save his people—which means all who acknowledge him as their Savior — from their sins. That is the meaning of the blessed name, JESUS, the Greek form of the Hebrew, Jehoshuah, or, Joshuah. As the Redeemer he delivers his people, from guilt, by means of pardon; (Eph. 1:7); from the power and dominion of sin, by means of holiness (1 Pet. 1:16-19); from the grave, by means of the resurrection (Rom. 8:21-23); and from all evil (Eph. 1:14; 4:30; 1 Cor. 1:30; Tit. 2:14).

VERSE 6. *A fallen state.* The statement that mankind, without a divine Redeemer, would be lost is borne out by history and also by individual experience. Without constant aid and guidance from a higher source, nations degenerate morally, even if they maintain physical superiority, until they lose themselves in superstition on the one hand and atheism on the other, and life becomes very much of a case of "dog eat dog." Consider the human race before the flood, when the wickedness became so great that the Lord actually was sorry "that he had made man on earth." (Gen. 6:1-7) Read David's estimate of the moral status of mankind at his time, when the Lord looked down from heaven to see "if there were any that did understand and seek God," but found that "they are all gone aside, they are all together become filthy." Then look at the picture drawn by Paul in his letter to the Romans, of the moral status of the Greek and Roman civilizations:

"Their throat is an open sepulchre; with their tongues they have used deceit; the poison of asps is under their lips . . . their feet are swift to shed blood; destruction and misery are in their ways and the way of peace they have not known. (Rom. 3:9-18)

Read also his picture of the last days:

"Perilous times shall come. For men shall be lovers of their own selves, covetous, boasters, proud, blasphemers, disobedient to parents, unthankful, unholy, without natural affection, truce-breakers, false accusers, incontinent, fierce, despisers of those that are good, traitors, heady, highminded, lovers of pleasures more than of God; having a form of godliness but denying the power thereof." (2 Tim. 3:1-5. See also Rev. chap. 18)

The natural tendency of the race, if the Spirit of God withdraws, is toward degeneracy. And that is true of the individual, too. Unless a man constantly studies the word of God, attends to his prayers, partakes of the Sacrament, joins in public worship whenever possible, and attends to his duties, as given him by our heavenly Father, he will gradually sink lower and lower, until he becomes, as far as spiritual things are concerned—a corpse.

Without a divine Redeemer, man would be lost.

## 4. *Concerning John the Baptist.*

7. And he spake also concerning a prophet who should come before the Messiah, to prepare the way of the Lord—

8. Yea, even he should go forth and cry in the wilderness: Prepare ye the way of the Lord, and make his paths straight; for there standeth one among you whom ye know not; and he is mightier than I, whose shoe's latchet I am not worthy to unloose. And much spake my father concerning this thing.

---

VERSE 7. *A prophet . . . before the Messiah.* This refers to John the Baptist, whose mission it was to "prepare the way of the Lord." John was the son of Zacharias, a priest and temple worker, and his wife Elizabeth, a cousin of Mary, the mother of Jesus. He was six months the senior of our Lord. His mission was to be the herald, or forerunner, of the Messiah, and as such prepare the way for him. In pursuance of this mission, he appeared in the wilderness, in the fifteenth year of the reign of the emperor Tiberius, and preached: "Prepare ye the way of the Lord;" the Messiah had already come; he was standing among them, unknown. (John 1:26)

The fact that Jesus had a forerunner, a herald, to proclaim his advent and command that the way be prepared for him, proves that he was more than a common mortal, more than a teacher and reformer. When kings and potentates in those days were about to travel, they notified their subjects that they were coming, and that they wanted the roads repaired and straightened so that there should be no unnecessary delay. A notable illustration of this Oriental custom was furnished by the sultan of Turkey, Abdul-Hamid II, when he, having received word that the German emperor desired to visit Jerusalem, issued an order that the road between Jaffa and Jerusalem be prepared for the imperial visitor. This was done. Hundreds of men and women were drafted for work on the road. Now, the very mission of John proves that the advent of Jesus was the coming of a King to his kingdom.

John appeared in the garb of a prophet. He was clad in a loose garment of camel hair, held together by a leather girdle. His food was wild honey and locusts —probably the pods of the locust tree, known as "Carob," or "Saint John's Bread."

John baptized those who repented and believed his message. For baptism belongs to all dispensations. Adam was baptized. (Pearl of Gr. Pr., Mos., 6:52, 64, 65) There is evidence that baptism was practiced by the Patriarchs. When Jacob received the divine command to go to Bethel and build an altar there "unto God," he ordered his household, and all that were with him, to put away "the strange gods," and to "be clean," and to "change your garments." This cleaning process was not a common washing, but a religious rite connected with the altar service that was to be observed. (Gen. 35:1-7) The washing of clothes, mentioned in Ex. 19:10, is best understood in the same way, since it was part of the "sanctification" of the people, preparatory to the manifestations of God on the mountain. The Jews, at the time of our Lord, understood the principle of baptism, for they asked John, "Why baptizest thou then, if thou be not that Christ, nor Elias, neither that prophet?"

The question is sometimes asked, whether those who were baptized by John had to be baptized again, in order to become members of the Church of Christ. Probably not. The baptism of John was performed with divine authority and had, we may say, legal force until our Lord, after the resurrection, authorized his Apostles to baptize in his name.

9. And my father said he should baptize in Bethabara, beyond Jordan; and he also said he should baptize with water; even that he should baptize the Messiah with water.

10. And after he had baptized the Messiah with water, he should behold and bear record that he had baptized the Lamb of God, who should take away the sins of the world.

VERSE 9. *Baptism of the Messiah.* Jesus was baptized by John. That was, in his case, the fulfilment of all righteousness. (Matt. 3:15) He was not baptized again. Nor were his apostles, as far as we know. Twelve disciples at Ephesus were re-baptized. (Acts 19:1) In all probability, they had been baptized with the baptism of John after the Christian baptism had been instituted and substituted for that of John, in which case their first baptism would have been invalid.

*John the Baptist a great prophet.* "The question arose from the saying of Jesus, 'Among those that are born of women there is not a greater prophet than John the Baptist; but he that is least in the kingdom of God is greater than he' (Matt. 11:11). How is it that John was considered the greatest of prophets?
"First. He was entrusted with the important mission of preparing the way before the face of the Lord. Whoever had such a trust committed to him before or since? No man.
"Secondly. He was entrusted with the important mission, and it was required at his hands, to baptize the Son of man.
"Thirdly. John, at that time, was the only administrator in the affairs of the kingdom there was then on earth, and holding the keys of power. The Jews had to obey his instructions or be damned, by their own law which he had given to Moses on the mount, and thereby magnified it and made honorable, instead of destroying it. The son of Zacharias wrested the keys, the kingdom, the power, the glory from the Jews, by the holy anointing and decree of heaven, and these three reasons constitute him the greatest born of a woman. . . .
"Jesus was looked upon as having the least claim in God's kingdom, and, seemingly, was the least entitled to their acceptance of him as a prophet; as if he had said, 'He that is considered the least among you is greater than John—that is I, myself." (Hist. of the Church, vol. 5, p. 260-1)

To this we may be permitted to add that, according to the D. & C. (Sec. 84:28) John was ordained, when eight days old, "unto this power, to overthrow the kingdom of the Jews," as well as to prepare them for the coming of the Lord. What a tremendous power and authority were his! And he exercised them, too. For with him the Mosaic dispensation came to an end.

VERSE 10. *The Lamb of God.* Our Lord is the Lamb of God which taketh away the sin of the world. (John 1:29, 36) He was typified by the paschal lamb and by the sacrifices offered from the beginning. (Is. 53:7; Luke 23:25; Acts 8:32; 1 Pet. 2:21-3; Rev. 5:6, 8, 12; 13:8) In Rev. 5, the Lamb has seven horns and eyes, "which are the seven spirits of God sent forth into all the earth," i.e., invested with the attributes of God, power and omniscience, and receiving the homage of the universe.

*Bethabara.* The place where John baptized. The meaning of that word is "house" or "place of passing over," supposed to refer to the place where the Israelites passed over Jordan: "Beth-Abarah." It is also called "Bethany" from a word which is said to mean, "place of ships" (boats). It was a place "beyond Jordan," and is not the Bethany on the Mount of Olives, the name of which comes from a word meaning "place of dates."

## 5. *The Gospel among the Jews.*

11. And it came to pass after my father had spoken these words he spake unto my brethren concerning the gospel which should be preached among the Jews, and also concerning the dwindling of the Jews in unbelief. And after they had slain the Messiah, who should come, and after he had been slain he should rise from the dead, and should make himself manifest, by the Holy Ghost, unto the Gentiles.

## 6. *Israel scattered and gathered.*

12. Yea, even my father spake much concerning the Gentiles, and also concerning the house of Israel, that they should be compared like unto an olive-tree, whose branches should be broken off and should be scattered upon all the face of the earth.

---

VERSE 11. *The Gospel.* Lehi, in his discourses in the Valley of Lemuel, made his little colony acquainted with the Gospel of Jesus. It was necessary for them to know this so that they could take its truth with them over to the new home land. For, after all, there is no knowledge, within the whole range of human thought and research, that is of greater importance. It is his Gospel that has, even in its diluted condition, been an incentive to such progress as has been made. Who has taught men unselfishness? Who has taught us to pray to God, as children to their Father? Who has inspired men to acts of mercy, as evidenced in innumerable institutions? Is there anything that is good, or wise, or noble, that has not come from Jesus? What would song and music and art and architecture be without the inspiration of Jesus? "Take Jesus from civilization and you change its history, its poetry, its art, its literature, its government, its morals, its religion, and its hope of the great hereafter. Since his death art is purer, prose holier, poetry sweeter; man enjoys more, lives better, dies happier; truth has new significance; life better objects, hope better prospects, and death new revelations." (The Church of Christ, by A. Layman)

VERSE 12. In the preceding verse we are informed that Lehi spoke of the Jews and the Gentiles. The Jews were to reject the Gospel of Jesus and then "dwindle in unbelief." Here we are told that he also prophesied concerning the house of Israel, to which he, as a descendant of Manasseh, belonged.

*The House of Israel.* He compares Israel to an olive-tree, whose branches, i.e., the various tribes, would be broken off and scattered "upon the face of the earth." The ten tribes revolted, in 975 B.C., under Jeroboam, who introduced idolatry, notwithstanding the protests of such mighty prophets as Elijah and Elisha, and others. The kingdom attained to its greatest political prominence under Jeroboam II, (823-772 B.C.), who added Hamath and Damascus to the territory of Israel. But during the last king, Hoshea, (730-721 B.C.) Tiglath-Pileaser, the Assyrian king, desolated the territory east of the Jordan. Hoshea became tributary to the Assyrians. But, in an evil hour he revolted and entered into an alliance with Egypt. Shalmaneser then came and besieged Samaria, and after three years of hostilities and sufferings on the part of the Israelites, made an end of the independence of the kingdom. A great many of the people were transported to the provinces of Assyria, and people from Media, Babylonia, and neighboring countries were sent to Pales-

13. Wherefore, he said it must needs be that we should be led with one accord into the land of promise, unto the fulfilling of the word of the Lord, that we should be scattered upon all the face of the earth.

14. And after the house of Israel should be scattered they should be gathered together again; or, in fine, after the Gentiles had received the fulness of the Gospel, the natural branches of the olive-tree, or the remnants of the house of Israel, should be grafted in, or come to the knowledge of the true Messiah, their Lord and their Redeemer.

---

tine, to inhabit the abandoned cities and waste places. Thus the branches of the olive-tree were broken off and scattered. (2 Kings 17:1-18)

Very little is known for certain about the fate of the Israelites that were removed to Assyria. But in the II Book of Esdras (apocryphal), chap. 13, a vision is related, in which the seer sees a great multitude gathered against the Messiah, who, from his holy mountain (Zion), overcomes his adversaries. Then he calls to him another multitude, which is said to be the ten tribes. Concerning these, we read:

"Those are the ten tribes, which were carried away prisoners out of their own land in the time of Osea, the king, whom Shalmaneser the king of Assyria led away captive, and he carried them over the waters [the great rivers], and so came they into another land. But they took this counsel among themselves, that they would leave the multitude of the heathen, and go forth into a further country, where never mankind dwelt, that they might there keep their statutes, which they never kept in their own land. And they entered into Euphrates by the narrow passage of the river. For the Most High then shewed signs for them, and held still the flood, till they were passed over. For through that country there was a great way to go, namely, of a year and half: and the same region is called Arsareth. Then they dwelt there until the latter time; and now when they shall begin to come, the Highest shall stay the springs of the stream again, that they may go through: therefore sawest thou the multitude with peace. But those that be left behind of thy people are they that are found within my borders. Now when he destroyeth the multitude of the nations that are gathered together, he shall defend his people that remain. And then shall he show them great wonders."

We do not quote this as authoritative history. It is merely the record of a tradition extant at the time the book was written, and undoubtedly long before that time. That it has some historical value cannot be denied. At any rate, we know that Israel has been scattered among the nations, and more particularly among the nations of northern Europe and the islands of the sea, including particularly the British Isles, Iceland, and the Scandinavian and Teutonic countries, all of which were "islands" because they were reached by crossing the water.

VERSE 13. *We should be scattered.* Lehi argues that, he, since the Lord had decided that Israel should be distributed among all the nations, would willingly go to the land of promise, when called upon to do so. How could, otherwise, the blessing of Jacob upon Joseph (Gen. 49:22-6) "His branches [literally, "daughters"] run over the wall," have been fulfilled? He was to have the blessings of his father "unto the utmost bound of the everlasting hills."

VERSE 14. *The remnants . . . should be grafted in.* This is a promise that the house of Israel, wherever the remnants may be, shall come to the knowledge of the true Messiah, after the Gentiles have received the Gospel.

## 7. *Nephi desires to see, to hear and to know.*

15. And after this manner of language did my father prophesy and speak unto my brethren, and also many more things which I do not write in this book; for I have written as many of them as were expedient for me in mine other book.

16. And all these things, of which I have spoken, were done as my father dwelt in a tent, in the valley of Lemuel.

17. And it came to pass after I, Nephi, having heard all the words of my father, concerning the things which he saw in a vision, and also the things which he spake by the power of the Holy Ghost, which power he received by faith on the Son of God — and the Son of God was the Messiah who should come—I, Nephi, was desirous also that I might see, and hear, and know of these things, by the power of the Holy Ghost, which is the gift of God unto all those who diligently seek him, as well in times of old as in the time that he should manifest himself unto the children of men.

18. For he is the same yesterday, to-day, and forever; and the way is prepared for all men from the foundation of the world, if it so be that they repent and come unto him.

19. For he that diligently seek-

---

On April 3, 1836, at the Kirtland temple, the prophet Joseph Smith and Oliver Cowdery had, as will be remembered, four glorious visions. They saw the Lord and received from him the assurance that he had accepted the temple, built to his name. Then "the heavens were again opened unto us; and Moses appeared before us, and committed unto us the keys of the gathering of Israel from the four parts of the earth, and the leading of the ten tribes from the land of the north." (D. & C. 110:11) And thus began the fulfilment of this part of the prediction of Lehi in the Valley of Lemuel.

VERSE 17. *Desirous . . . to know.* When Nephi had heard his father's account of his vision and his subsequent discourse (vv. 11-16), he was desirous of obtaining knowledge for himself, by the power of the Holy Ghost, of the great truths revealed to his father. Having strong faith, he felt sure that the Messiah, the Son of God, could, and would, impart that knowledge to him.

VERSE 18. *For he is the same . . . forever.* He, the Messiah, and the way is prepared for all, from the foundation of the world. It was through the Messiah that the Saints in the *past* obtained knowledge of the truth. It is through the Messiah that the Saints *now* can receive knowledge, and through him it will come *forever,* to those who diligently seek him.

"God lives. We are his children. He has given back to earth his priesthood. He has spoken and is speaking through his prophets. To each of us he gives spiritual light just in the measure we are ready and willing to take it, and his blessings are ours, not for sinning disobedience to the truth already given, but through the righteous keeping thereof. We may not rightfully expect that God will flash either to our minds or to our spirits new knowledge for which we are not ready and for which we have no need. We may rightfully expect only that God will give new

eth shall find; and the mysteries of God shall be unfolded unto them, by the power of the Holy Ghost, as well in these times as in times of old, and as well in times of old as in times to come; wherefore, the course of the Lord is one eternal round.

20. Therefore remember, O man, for all thy doings thou shalt be brought into judgment.

21. Wherefore, if ye have sought to do wickedly in the days of your probation, then ye are found unclean before the judgment-seat of God; and no unclean thing can dwell with God; wherefore, ye must be cast off forever.

22. And the Holy Ghost giveth authority that I should speak these things, and deny them not.

---

lessons when we have learned the old ones and they no longer serve our wants. (Pres. J. Reuben Clark, Jr., Conference Sermon, April 9, 1933)

VERSE 20. *Thou shalt be brought into judgment.* Because the way to obtain knowledge has been prepared, and because the Lord is willing to impart it to those who seek, therefore, those who neglect to avail themselves of the means provided, will justly be brought into judgment. Ignorance, under the circumstances, is condemnable.

VERSE 22. *The Holy Ghost giveth authority.* Nephi, having obtained a testimony "by the power of the Holy Ghost," could speak by the authority given by the same divine Person.. Learning does not give authority to speak for God. Nor is a blameless life the same as divine authority. Nor a desire to speak. One of the early revelations through the Prophet Joseph Smith was addressed to his brother Hyrum on this subject. The Lord said:

"Behold, I command you, that you need not suppose that you are called to preach until you are called. Wait a little longer, until you shall have my word, my rock, my church, and my gospel, that you may know of a surety my doctrine. . . . Seek not to declare my word, but first seek to obtain my word, and then shall your tongue be loosed. . . . But now hold your peace, study my word which hath gone forth among the children of men [the Bible], and also study my word which shall come forth among the children of men, or that which is now translating," [the Book of Mormon], (D. & C. 11:15-22).

In this revelation, the Lord says (v. 21) that when his tongue is loosed, "Then, if you desire, you shall have my Spirit and my word, yea, the power of God unto the convincing of men." Here, too, we learn that it is the Holy Spirit that giveth authority to speak.

### NOTES

"As to the question of authority, nearly everything depends upon it. No ordinance can be performed to the acceptance of God without divine authority. No matter how fervently men may believe or pray, unless they are endowed with divine authority they can only act in their own name, and not legally nor acceptably in the name of Jesus Christ, in whose name all these things must be done. Some suppose this authority may be derived from the Bible, but nothing could be more absurd. . . . If by reading and believing the Bible this authority could be obtained, all who read the Bible and believed it would have it—one equally with another." (Pres. Joseph F. Smith, "Gospel Doctrine")

To speak in the name of Jesus without authority is both idle and dangerous. God will not be mocked. We remember the incident related in Acts 19. Certain "vagabond" Jews at Ephesus, professional exorcists, undertook to rebuke evil spirits in the name of Jesus, as the Apostle Paul did. They said, "We adjure you by Jesus whom Paul preacheth." There were seven of them. But the demoniac cried, "Jesus I know, and Paul I know, but who are ye?" Whereupon he leaped upon them and overcame all of them, although they were seven, and they fled naked and wounded. (Acts 19:13-17)

Josephus is authority for the information that some Jews formerly traveled from place to place and performed exorcisms, alleging that the secrets of rebuking evil spirits in the name of the Messiah had been handed down to them from King Solomon. Josephus says he had seen a man by the name of Eleasar adjure a demoniac. And he describes the performance thus, "He put a ring that had a root of those sorts mentioned by Solomon to the nostrils of the demoniac, after which he drew out the demon through his nostrils; and when the man fell down, immediately he adjured him to return into him no more." From this description of a fake performance, we can imagine what kind of "vagabonds" these Jews at Ephesus were. They may have thought that they could effect a genuine cure by merely mentioning the name of Jesus. But, alas! They had no divine authority. They knew that. And the evil spirit knew it too. The result was disastrous to them.

*"Vagabonds."* The Hebrew word so translated is, "nod." Its fundamental meaning is to wave as reeds in the wind, or to flap like a bird with the wings. Hence Cain is said to be a fugitive and a "vagabond,"—one moving back and forth. The Jews who practiced exorcism in all probability moved their bodies back and forth, or perhaps they swung their arms or swayed their heads while they were performing, and therefore were called "vagabonds," in the meaning suggested by the Hebrew root of the word. When our Lord, referring to John the Baptist, asked the multitude, "What went ye out into the wilderness to see? A reed shaken with the wind?" It is not impossible that he had this class of "vagabonds" in mind. Did ye come to consult one of your professional exorcists? Well, John was not one of them. He was more than a prophet. He was "Elias, which was for to come." (Matt. 11:7-15)

## CHAPTER 11

*Nephi's Vision on the Mount: Nephi and the Spirit of the Lord, 1-7—*
*Meaning of the tree in Lehi's vision, 8-11—The Virgin, the Mother of the Son*
*of God, 12-23—The rod of iron, 24, 25—The baptism and ministry of Jesus,*
*26-31—The crucifixion, 32, 33—The large and spacious building, 34-6.*

## 1. Nephi and the Spirit of the Lord.

1. For it came to pass after I had desired to know the things that my father had seen, and believing that the Lord was able to make them known unto me, as I sat pondering in mine heart I was caught away in the Spirit of the Lord, yea, into an exceeding high mountain, which I never had before seen, and upon which I never had before set my foot.

2. And the Spirit said unto me: Behold, what desirest thou?

3. And I said: I desire to behold the thing which my father saw.

4. And the Spirit said unto me: Believest thou that thy father saw the tree of which he hath spoken?

5. And I said: Yea, thou knowest that I believe all the words of my father.

6. And when I had spoken these words, the Spirit cried with a loud voice, saying: Hosanna to the Lord, the most high God; for he is God over all the earth, yea, even above all. And blessed art thou, Nephi, because thou believest in the Son of the most high God; wherefore, thou shalt behold the things which thou hast desired.

---

VERSE 1. *Caught away in the Spirit of the Lord.* Ezekiel had a similar experience He says the Spirit lifted him up, and he heard the voice of a great "rushing" when the glory of the Lord arose from his place. The Spirit "lifted him up," and took him away. That is, he fell into a trance, after which he went to Tel-Abib, by the river Chebar, where many of the captives of Israel dwelt. And there, after seven days, the word of the Lord came to him. (Ezek. 3:12-27) On another occasion the same prophet says, "The Spirit lifted me up between the earth and the heaven, and brought me in the visions of God to Jerusalem." (Ezek. 8:3) Again, speaking of his vision of the valley of the dead, he says, "The hand of the Lord was upon me, and he carried me out in the Spirit of the Lord, and set me down in the valley." (Ezek. 37:1) Moses was "caught up into an exceedingly high mountain" (P. of Gr. Price, Mos. 1:1), and our Lord himself, in his controversy with the Tempter, was shown the glory of the world (Matt. 4:8) from the summit of an exceeding high mountain. Paul was caught up "to the third heaven," which he also calls "paradise," where he heard "unspeakable words," "which it is not lawful for a man to utter." (2 Cor. 12:2-4) The Apostle John, too, was "in the Spirit," when he heard and saw the great visions recorded in his Revelations. Nephi was similarly favored with visions and supernatural manifestations.

VERSE 6. *Hosanna.* The Spirit of the Lord, contemplating the great faith of Nephi, and his desire for knowledge, cries with a loud voice, "Hosanna to the Lord!" The Hebrew, "hoshiah-na" is an acclamatory prayer for the well-being of somebody,

7. And behold this thing shall be given unto thee for a sign, that after thou hast beheld the tree which bore the fruit which thy father tasted, thou shalt also be-hold a man descending out of heaven, and him shall ye witness; and after ye have witnessed him ye shall bear record that it is the Son of God.

### 2. *Meaning of he tree in Lehi's vision.*

8. And it came to pass that the Spirit said unto me: Look! And I looked and beheld a tree; and it was like unto the tree which my father had seen; and the beauty thereof was far beyond, yea, exceeding of all beauty; and the whiteness thereof did exceed the whiteness of the driven snow.

9. And it came to pass after I had seen the tree, I said unto the Spirit: I behold thou hast shown unto me the tree which is precious above all.

10. And he said unto me: What desirest thou?

11. And I said unto him: To

---

and it means, literally, "save now!" In this connection it is a prayer to the Lord by the Spirit for the preservation of the young prophet in his faith. It is a remarkable illustration of the truth stated thus by St. Paul: "The Spirit itself maketh intercession for us . . . according to the will of God." (Rom. 8:26, 27)

We note that this prayer (or, is it a song?) of the Spirit has the form of Hebrew poetry:

> Hosanna to the Lord,
> the Most High God;
>
> For he is God over all the earth,
> yea, even above all.
>
> And blessed art thou, Nephi,
> because thou believest in the
> Son of the Most High God.

The chief characteristic of Hebrew poetry is, as is well known, "parallelism," which means the rhythm of thought, rather than sound, and the arrangement of the words in such a manner that their full meaning comes out first in the second or third line.

VERSE 7. *A man descending out of heaven.* The Scriptures tell us that the Lord is able to do exceeding abundantly above all that we ask or think (Eph. 3:30), and that "he giveth to all men liberally" (James 1:5). This is true in the case of Nephi. He asked to know the things his father had seen. That prayer was granted. And in addition he was accorded the privilege of visions far beyond his expectations. That is always the case when we ask in faith and let the Holy Spirit dictate our prayers.

VERSE 8. *I looked and beheld a tree.* The prayer of Nephi is heard, and he is shown the very tree which his father had seen (v. 21); it was a tree of dazzling beauty, "white as driven snow." There can be no more striking symbol of purity than that.

know the interpretation thereof —for I spake unto him as a man speaketh; for I beheld that he was in the form of a man; yet nevertheless, I knew that it was the Spirit of the Lord; and he spake unto me as a man speaketh with another.

## 3. *The Virgin, the Mother of the Son of God.*

12. And it came to pass that he said unto me: Look! And I looked as if to look upon him, and I saw him not; for he had gone from before my presence.

13. And it came to pass that I looked and beheld the great city of Jerusalem, and also other cities. And I beheld the city of Nazareth; and in the city of Nazareth I beheld a virgin, and she was exceedingly fair and white.

14. And it came to pass that I saw the heavens open; and an angel came down and stood be-fore me; and he said unto me: Nephi, what beholdest thou?

15. And I said unto him: A virgin, most beautiful and fair above all other virgins.

16. And he said unto me: Knowest thou the condescension of God?

17. And I said unto him: I know that he loveth his children; nevertheless, I do not know the meaning of all things.

18. And he said unto me: Behold, the virgin whom thou seest is the mother of the Son of God, after the manner of the flesh.

---

VERSE 11. *The interpretation.* Having seen the tree, in the vision, Nephi was desirous, more than ever, to know the interpretation.

VERSE 12. *He had gone.* The Spirit of the Lord did not answer the question concerning the interpretation of the symbol directly. He withdrew his visible presence, but the manifestation continued. Nephi saw first the City of Jerusalem, and then the City of Nazareth. And in this city he saw a beautiful Virgin. (v. 13)

And then the heavens were opened to him, and he saw an angel come down and stand before him. From now on, it is this heavenly messenger who acts as interpreter. "What beholdest thou?" he asks. (v. 14) The answer is, "A Virgin, most beautiful and fair." (v. 15)

VERSE 16. *The condescension of God.* The next question of the angel is: "Knowest thou the condescension of God?"

To "condescend" is to descend, voluntarily, from a superior rank, or position, to one that is inferior. The Apostle Paul uses the word in that sense, in his admonition, "Mind not high things, but condescend to men of low estate." (Rom. 12:16) But how did the vision of the Virgin suggest the question of the condescension of God? That Nephi did not understand. His answer, therefore, was somewhat hesitating: "I know that God loves his children; nevertheless, I do not know all things." (v. 17)

VERSE 18. *The Virgin.* The angel recognized that here was a mystery, too deep for Nephi, wherefore he hastened with the explanation that, "Behold the Virgin whom thou seest is the Mother of the Son of God, *after the flesh.*" As Nephi accepted

19. And it came to pass that I beheld that she was carried away in the Spirit; and after she had been carried away in the Spirit for the space of a time the angel spake unto me, saying: Look!

20. And I looked and beheld the virgin again, bearing a child in her arms.

21. And the angel said unto me: Behold the Lamb of God, yea, even the Son of the Eternal Father! Knowest thou the meaning of the tree which thy father saw?

22. And I answered him, saying: Yea, it is the love of God, which sheddeth itself abroad in

---

this tremendous revelation by faith, he needed no further explanation of the significance of the term, "condescension of God," used by the angel.

VERSE 19. *The Virgin carried away in the Spirit.* Now the vision of the Virgin is, for a time, blotted out, and when she again appears, she has a lovely child, whom the angel introduces by the joyful message: "Behold the Lamb of God, yea, even the Son of the Eternal Father!"

That was the end of this part of the vision. The angel, therefore, asked Nephi, "Knowest thou [now] the meaning of the tree which thy father saw?" He had asked for an explanation of the symbol of the tree. The vision had been given in answer to that request. He understood.

VERSE 22. *The love of God.* He could truthfully reply, as he did, "Yea, it is the love of God, which sheddeth itself abroad in the hearts of the children of men."

In other words, the tree symbolized the same eternal truth, which our Lord taught Nicodemus: "For God so loved the world, that he gave his only begotten Son, that whosoever believeth in him should not perish, but have everlasting life." (John 3:16) That also explains the vision of the Virgin and the blessed Child, Jesus.

*Kenosis.* Bible students have a special term, "K e n o s i s," for the voluntary condescension, or humiliation, of our Lord, in coming to this world as its Redeemer. This word means that he gave up his divine attributes completely and became a man, like other sons of Adam. Paul states this clearly. (Phil. 2:5-8) See the accounts of the birth of our Savior, Matt. 1:18-24; Luke 1:26-38; 2:1-14. St. Paul says, "When the fulness of time was come, God sent forth his Son, made of a woman, made under the law, to redeem them that were under the law, that we might receive the adoption of sons." (Gal. 4:4-5)

Such are the historical facts. Our Lord came. The Eternal Father sent him. It was divine love that caused him to come.

"That the Son of God, in becoming the Son of man, should submit himself to the regular human method of coming into the world is one of the most sublime proofs of his loving condescension to us. Yet one thing we must not forget,—that this family into which he was born was, on both sides, of royal stock, both Joseph and Mary being descendants of King David." (The Popular and Critical Bible Encyclopedia, vol. 2, p. 1017, under, "Kenosis.")

The condescension of our Lord in coming to fulfil his mission in mortality was also the condescension of God, the Eternal Father, in sending him forth on this mission.

*The Virgin.* That is the title given to the Mother of Jesus in the prophecy of his birth. (Is. 7:14; Matt. 1:23) There is very little information in the New Testament concerning Mary. But from what is written about her, it is evident that she was a woman of the highest mental and spiritual culture. That she was a regular visitor in the temple, well known by the officials in the sacred edifice, is also indicated by

the hearts of the children of men; wherefore, it is the most desirable above all things.

23. And he spake unto me, saying: Yea, and the most joyous to the soul.

---

the story of the appearance of her divine Son there at the age of twelve years. A boy of obscure parentage would not have had a chance to remain among the learned doctors for several days, as he did.

Early traditions, recorded in the Protevangelium and some other apocrypha, relate that Mary was born at Nazareth, the daughter of Joachim and his wife, Anna. The father is said to have been a very wealthy citizen, known for his generosity and observance of the law. For many years the worthy couple lived together childless. But, finally, they promised the Lord that a child of theirs would be dedicated to the Lord, i.e. to the temple service. Then, in due time, the baby girl, to whom they gave the name of Mary, came. She was the answer to their prayers, the reward for their faithfulness.

When the little girl was three years old—so the tradition avers—she was taken to the temple and, in accordance with the promise made, dedicated to the service of the Lord. From now on, she was raised and educated under the direction of the authorities of the temple. The summer months, it is said, she spent at Nazareth, the rest of the year she served in the Sanctuary.

Now, it seems to have been customary, as regards the young ladies raised for the temple service, to give them an opportunity, when they arrived at the marriagable age, to choose for themselves whether they would continue to remain the virgins of the Lord for ever, or become wives and mothers. Mary's choice was to continue the temple service, but, guided by a special revelation, the high priest selected Joseph of Nazareth to be her legal guardian and husband. (Protev. Chapt. 8 ) She was then twelve years old.

After the wonderful story of the birth of the Savior of the world the evangelists say little of Mary. She is mentioned in the account of the marriage feast at Cana (John 2), and as one attending a gathering outside a synogogue where Jesus had been preaching (Mark 3:31), and then as standing near the cross, when her crucified Son commended her to the care of John (John 19:25-7). She is, finally, mentioned as one of the women present in the "upper room" in Jerusalem, after the ascension of Jesus from the Mount of Olives. (Acts 1:13, 14)

Tradition has it that she died in Jerusalem in the year 48 A.D., and that her body also was taken to heaven. The latter "assumption" is based on the story that the apostles, three days after her interment, found the tomb empty.

All this, except the accounts given by the evangelists, is tradition. That the story has an historic foundation is not denied. But to separate the historic element from what is mere fiction, is not always possible at this late day.

Before leaving this subject, a word should be said of Anna, the prophetess, mentioned by Luke. She, too, must have been one of the virgins of the Lord, dedicated to the temple service. She was of the tribe of Asher. This may be accounted for by the fact that when Hezekiah, king of Judah, sent a call to Israel, as well as Judah, to come to Jerusalem to celebrate the passover, some people of the tribe of Asher, and also of the tribes of Manasseh, Issachar, and Zebulon, humbled themselves and came to Jerusalem. The forefathers of Anna may have come to Jerusalem at that time. The forebears of Lehi, of the tribe of Manasseh, may also have come at the invitation of Hezekiah. (2 Chron. 30:1-12, 16, 19 ) The Evangelist says of Anna, that she was a prophetess. Like Mary, she had been given to a husband, when grown up. She had lived with him only seven years. Now she was eighty-four years old, a widow, but

## 4. The Rod of Iron.

24. And after he had said these words, he said unto me: Look! And I looked, and I beheld the Son of God going forth among the children of men; and I saw many fall down at his feet and worship him.

25. And it came to pass that I beheld that the rod of iron, which my father had seen, was the word of God, which led to the fountain of living waters, or to the tree of life; which waters are a representation of the love of God; and I also beheld that the tree of life was a representation of the love of God.

---

"she departed not from the temple, but served God with fastings and prayers night and day." Furthermore, she preached the gospel of the Redeemer "to all them that looked for redemption in Jerusalem." (Luke 2:36-8 )

The regular hours of prayer were "the third hour of the day" (Acts 2:15), corresponding to 9 o'clock a.m.; "the sixth hour" (Acts 10:9), 12 o'clock noon; and the "ninth hour" Acts 3:1), 3 o'clock p.m.

Fasting seems to have been required twice a week. (Luke 18:12)

Verse 25. *The Rod of Iron.* In this remarkable vision, there are several parts which all call for serious thought.

There is the "mist of darkness" (1 Ne. 8:23), which is so thick that people lose their way in it. That is the actual condition of the world, as regards moral and spiritual truths. Notwithstanding the numerous institutes of learning, and the marvelous progress in material and mechanical fields, people are lost, as in a fog, when confronted by the social problems of the day.

Then, there is the iron rod, which represents the word of God (I Ne. 15:24) and is so placed that those who are lost can seize it, and, by following it, will reach safety.

There is, further, the fountain of living water, symbolizing the love of God, as manifested in the outpouring of the Holy Spirit; for we read,

"In the last day, that great day of the feast, Jesus stood and cried, saying, If any man thirst, let him come unto me, and drink. He that believeth on me, as the Scripture hath said, out of his belly shall flow rivers of living water. But this he spake of the Spirit, which they that believeth on him should receive." (John 7:37-9)

Finally, there is the tree of life, which symbolizes the love of God, as manifested in the gift of life eternal.

The great lesson of the vision of the iron rod is, therefore, that the word of God—and by this we mean the Bible, the Book of Mormon, the Doctrine and Covenants, the Pearl of Great Price, and whatever else the Lord graciously reveals through the channels selected by him—has been given, or will be given, in order that his children may not get lost in the dark mists, but find the truth, and the way to temporal salvation and life eternal, through the Holy Spirit.

Well may we then ask ourselves, Do we study the Word of God? In our homes and our meetings of worship? Are we teaching our children the word of God? Do we believe the word of God? Are we practicing its precepts? These are questions of life and death.

## 5. *The baptism and ministry of Jesus.*

26. And the angel said unto me again: Look and behold the condescension of God!

27. And I looked and beheld the Redeemer of the world, of whom my father had spoken; and I also beheld the prophet who should prepare the way before him. And the Lamb of God went forth and was baptized of him; and after he was baptized, I beheld the heavens open, and the

---

VERSE 26. *Look . . . the condescension of God.* Another manifestation in the great vision begins here. It is another revelation of the condescension of God.

VERSE 27. *The Lamb of God was baptized.* The evangelists tell us that John the Baptist, at the time of the maturity of Jesus, appeared in the wilderness of Judea and proclaimed that the kingdom of God, of which the prophets of old had spoken (Is. 40:3-5; Dan. 7:13, 14) was at hand. His appearance caused a tremendous sensation. Large crowds from Jerusalem and Judea, and especially from the region round about Jordan, came to hear John, who urged them to repent and prepare themselves to receive the Messiah. Many believed, confessed their sins and received baptism for the remission of sins.

Even some Pharisees and Sadducees came to his baptism. There is reason to believe that they came privately (like Nicodemus to Jesus, because they did not wish to mingle with the common herd of sinners), wherefore John rebuked them with words that must have penetrated their very souls:

"O generation of vipers, who hath warned you to flee from the wrath to come? Bring forth therefore fruits of repentance . . . And now also the ax is laid unto the root of the trees: therefore every tree which bringeth not forth good fruit is hewn down, and cast into the fire." (Matt. 3:1-12; Mark 1:3-8; Luke 3:4-18; John 1:19-28)

The main topics of the discourses of John were repentance, confession of sin, forgiveness, and the coming of the kingdom of God. But those were also the chief subjects that occupied the thoughts of the Jews when they were preparing themselves for the new year, the ten days of repentance between New Year's day and the day of atonement ("yom kippur"), and that great fast day, itself, wherefore it has been thought probable that John began his ministry during that time of preparation.

To this day, the Jews, in their synagogues, as part of their services on the day of atonement, confess their sins and pray, in unison:

"Thou hast chosen us from all peoples, thou hast loved us and taken pleasure in us, and hast exalted us above all tongues; thou hast sanctified us by thy commandments, and brought us near unto thy service, O our King, and hast called us by thy great and holy Name. . . . And thou hast given us in love, O Lord our God, this day of atonement for pardon, forgiveness and atonement . . . We have trespassed, we have been faithless, we have robbed, we have spoken basely, we have committed iniquity, we have wrought unrighteousness," etc. . . . "Our God and God of our fathers, pardon our iniquities on this day of atonement; blot out our transgressions and our sins, and make them pass away from before thine eyes; as it is said, I, even I, am he that blotteth out thy transgressions for mine own sake; and I will not remember thy sins."

Some such confessions and prayers were undoubtedly said by the multitudes

Holy Ghost come down out of heaven and abide upon him in the form of a dove.

28. And I beheld that he went forth ministering unto the people, in power and great glory; and the multitudes were gathered together to hear him; and I beheld that they cast him out from among them.

---

by the Jordan, who came to be baptized, as a preparation for the coming of the kingdom of the Messiah. And now, the Messiah, himself, came and prayed. Not secretly, but openly, among the people. That is clear from John's reply to the Pharisees, "There standeth one among you, whom ye know not" (John 1:26), and also from the record of Luke, "Now when all the people were baptized, it came to pass, that Jesus also being baptized and praying, the heaven was opened." (Luke 3:21)

Now we understand why the angel calls attention to the condescension of God as manifested in the baptism of his beloved Son. For Jesus actually took part, with the people, in the services of John. It "becometh us," he said, "to fulfil all righteousness." That is, all the ordinances instituted for the furtherance of righteousness. He had been circumcized, and became an heir to all the promises to Abraham. He observed the passover and the other festivals. He fasted and prayed, and now he accepted the initial rite of John, in the same spirit.

He had no sins of his own to confess, but, as the Lamb of God, the sin of the world had been laid upon him. It was for the entire world he acted, when he confessed and prayed for forgiveness, and then was baptized. That is clear from what John says on that occasion: "Behold the Lamb of God, which taketh away the sin of the world." (John 1:29) That is what baptism was to Jesus.

*In the form of a dove.* Different opinions have been held regarding this phrase. Did the Holy Spirit descend in the form of a dove, literally speaking, or is that only a figure of speech? Matthew, Mark and John say that he descended "like a dove," which may mean in the manner of that beautiful bird, but Luke seems to give ground for the opinion that the Spirit had assumed the form of a dove, for he says, "descended in a bodily shape like a dove upon him." But there is really no contradiction in the inspired accounts. The Prophet Joseph explains that the meaning is that the Spirit descended "in the sign of the dove." The Prophet says:

"The sign of the dove was instituted before the creation of the world, a witness for the Holy Ghost, and the devil cannot come in the sign of a dove. The Holy Ghost is a personage, and is in the form of a personage. It does not confine itself to the form of a dove, but in sign of the dove. The Holy Ghost cannot be transformed into a dove; but the sign of a dove was given to John to signify the truth of the deed, as the dove is an emblem, or token, of truth and innocence." (Hist. of the Church, vol. V, p. 261).

In all probability the Spirit appeared to our Lord "in bodily form" as he appeared to Nephi at the beginning of this vision (v. 11), but invisible to the multitude and even to John. However, John and the people, probably, saw a dove, as it descended and hovered over Jesus. The people paid little or no attention to the incident, but to John it was the sign by which he recognized that Jesus was the Messiah, the Son of God.

The additional manifestation, the voice: "Thou art my beloved Son; in thee I am well pleased" (Luke 3:22), was heard, probably, only by Jesus. He needed

29. And I also beheld twelve others following him. And it came to pass that they were carried away in the Spirit from before my face, and I saw them not.

30. And it came to pass that the angel spake unto me again, saying: Look! And I looked, and I beheld the heavens open again, and I saw angels descending upon the children of men; and they did minister unto them.

31. And he spake unto me again, saying: Look! And I looked, and I beheld the Lamb of God going forth among the children of men. And I beheld multitudes of people who were sick, and who were afflicted with all manner of diseases, and with devils and unclean spirits; and the angel spake and showed all these things unto me. And they were healed by the power of the Lamb of God; and the devils and the unclean spirits were cast out.

that very assurance, before the Spirit "led," or as Mark says, "drove" him out into the wilderness, to be tempted "of the devil." (Matt. 4:1-11; Mark 1:12, 13)

VERSES 27-31. In this section, Nephi is shown in vision the administration of our Lord, including the selection of twelve apostles. It is a peculiarity of this part of the vision that the twelve, during the time of the ministry of the Master, are eliminated; they are "carried away in the Spirit from before my face," (v. 29) and then, after a while, they appear as "angels descending upon the children of men; and they did minister unto them." The word "angel," means "messenger," especially from God to man, and that is what the apostles are. The word "apostle" also means "messenger."

VERSE 31. *Healed by the power of the Lamb of God.* Nephi now sees Jesus as the great Physician, surrounded by multitudes who were afflicted with all manner of diseases. "And they were healed by the power of the Lamb of God."

According to the Scriptures, God has in all ages manifested his power by means of miraculous healing. David sings:

"Bless the Lord, O my soul;
and all that is within me, bless his holy name.
"Bless the Lord, O my soul,
and forget not all his benefits:
"Who forgiveth all thy iniquities;
who healeth all thy diseases;
"Who redeemeth thy life from destruction,
who crowneth thee with loving-kindness and mercies."
(Ps. 103:1-4)

Here, the forgiveness of sins, the healing of infirmities, and the redemption of life itself from destruction are said to be the "benefits" which God confers upon his children.

Our Lord began his ministry on earth by preaching and healing (Mark 1:21-3:11). And when, on one occasion, some officers (scribes) charged him with blasphemy, because he said to one afflicted with palsy, "Son, thy sins be forgiven thee," he refuted the charge by asking them "whether it is easier to say to the sick person, Thy sins be forgiven thee; or to say, Arise, and take up thy bed and walk." When no one answered, he continued, "But that ye may know that the Son of

## 6. The Crucifixion.

32. And it came to pass that the angel spake unto me again, saying: Look! And I looked and beheld the Lamb of God, that he was taken by the people; yea, the Son of the everlasting God

---

man hath power on earth to forgive sins (he saith to the sick of palsy), I say unto thee, Arise, and take up thy bed and go thy way into thy house." (Mark 2:6-11) The power to heal the sick was the evidence of the authority to forgive sins. The apostles were endowed with the same power. (Mark 3:14, 15) And so were the Seventy. (Luke 10:1-9, 17)

Furthermore, power to heal is one of the spiritual gifts promised to those who believe. (I Cor. 12:28-31; Acts 5:12-15)

The Biblical miracles have been the subject of controversy among students of theology. Nature study, in the opinion of many, has seemed to justify the conclusion that the so-called laws of nature are absolutely unchangeable, and that a miracle in defiance of any such law is an impossibility.

The obvious reply to this view is that no one knows all the laws of nature, and that a miracle may be as much in accordance with some law of nature as the most common occurrence. In other words, healing by faith, or by the power of the priesthood, may be as scientifically possible as cure by any of the remedies known to *materia medica*. Leibnitz, for one, is an exponent of this view.

The laws of nature are unchangeable. That is to say, as far as we know, a given cause always has the same effect. If it were not so, rational beings would have no incentive to effort, since effects could not be calculated from cause. You might sow, but there would be no reason to expect a harvest. You might build, but would your building stand the next day? Possibly. Possibly not, if there is no link between cause and effect. The world would then be chaos.

But, if God sees fit, in any particular case, to deviate from the uniformity which we call natural law, he certainly has the power to do so, whether with or without any human instrumentality, and then we have a miracle. "Whatsoever the Lord pleased, that did he in heaven, and in earth, in the seas, and all deep places." (Ps. 135:6) "But our God is in the heavens: he hath done whatsoever he hath pleased." (Ps. 115:3) That is the only rational explanation of the miracles, ever offered.

*The devils and the unclean spirits were cast out.* Attention is called to the fact that the Jewish people, at the time of the beginning of our era, suffered oppression under a foreign government. Nature added calamities to the trying situation. An earthquake is mentioned, in which 30,000 people perished. Hostile Arabs made incursions from time to time. Scarcity of food and diseases went hand in hand. The whole country, and particularly Galilee, had an unusual number of sick persons. Many were epileptics; others suffered from mental disorders. Even educated persons at that time regarded epilepsy and insanity as "possession." The sufferer, it was thought, had a demon, an unclean spirit, and sometimes several such spirits in his body, besides his own. The disciples of our Lord, who wrote the New Testament, believed in the terrible reality of "possession." And so did our Lord, himself.

Let us consider one instance. It happened in the synagogue at Capernaum. A pitiable sufferer, who had "a spirit of an unclean demon" (literal translation), had managed to enter the house of worship with the multitude. The very presence of Jesus seemed to be a torment to the spirit, for he cried with a loud voice, and

was judged of the world; and I | was lifted up upon the cross and
saw and bear record. | slain for the sins of the world.
33. And I, Nephi, saw that he |

demanded not to be destroyed. Jesus, rebuked him and commanded him to leave
the sufferer. Immediately the latter fell into a paroxysm which must have been
fearful to witness, but as soon as it was over, the patient arose, unharmed and
cured. Whereupon the people were amazed and said to each other, "What a word
is this! For with authority and power he commandeth the unclean spirits, and
they come out." Here was no sorcery, no incantations, no herbs with magic power.
Here was, clearly, divine authority. And the fame of him went out . . . round
about. (Mark 1:23-27; Luke 4:33-37) There can be no doubt that both our Lord
and the people generally regarded this as a reality.

In all probability, popular opinion went too far at times, in attributing all
cases of certain maladies to the direct interference of the devil and his servants.
But it is equally probable that the so-called scientific view of our day also goes
too far, in branding all explanations that accept the reality of spiritual evil forces
in connection with diseases, as superstition. That is not scientific. With the Scriptures before us we cannot reject the belief in spirits, good and bad, as a delusion.
Futhermore, in the experience of some of our missionaries, cases of "possession" are
not entirely unknown in our own age. (D. and C. Commentary, Sec. 76, notes; see
also "History of the Scandinavian Mission," Andrew Jenson, pp. 30, 50, 82)

VERSE 33. *Lifted up upon the cross.* Nephi now sees the Lamb of God "taken
by the people," "judged of the world," "lifted up upon the cross and slain for the
sins of the world."

"Taken by the people" is a remarkably accurate statement of what actually
happened in Gethsemane. For all the evangelists relate that Judas came with a
great multitude, really a mob, sent by the chief priests and elders of the people,
and armed with swords and staves, just like a rabble. John adds that they were
led by "officers from the chief priests and Pharisees," and Luke notes that there
were "chief priests, captains of the temple and elders" in the crowd. (Matt. 26:47, 48;
Mark 14:43, 44; Luke 22:52; John 18:3, 12-14)

"Judged of [or by] the world" is also a notable expression.

The word "world" in the New Testament has different meanings. For instance,
it stands for an "age," an era, as in Matt. 28:20. (Aionos) But another word (kosmos)
is also used, which stands either for the entire universe, as an organized arrangement,
or for the people on earth, mankind. It means also, in a narrower sense, the government of a dispensation, as for instance the old Mosaic rule, which placed itself in
opposition to the kingdom of God, as represented by our Lord and his Council of
Twelve. In this sense it is found in John 14:19 and 15:18, 19, and other places.

Jesus was actually judged by the representatives and rulers of the old dispensation,
the old "world" as seen by Nephi, in his vision.

Jesus, having been apprehended in Gethsemane, was first taken to Annas, the
father-in-law of Caiaphas and formerly president of the Sanhedrin, whom Josephus
refers to as Ananus, the son of Seth. (John 18:12, 13 and 19-25) Annas sent him,
bound, to Caiaphas, the president of the Sanhedrin. (John 18:24) As soon as this
council could be summoned for a session, Jesus was arraigned and witnesses were
introduced to testify against him. But it soon developed that it was not easy to
establish guilt where no guilt existed. Witnesses had heard him say this or that,
but nothing he had said or done could be construed as blasphemy against God, or
profanation of the sanctuary. He had, it is true, cleansed the temple ground, but

## 7. *The large and spacious building.*

| 34. And after he was slain I saw the multitudes of the earth, | that they were gathered together to fight against the apostles of |
|---|---|

they could not urge that against him, although that was the actual "offense" which the priests could not forgive him. It is possible that he had interfered with their filthy business of cattle selling and shady money transactions in the close proximity of the temple on two different occasions, (Matt. 21:12, 13; John 2:13-17) but, as stated, they could not demand a death sentence on that ground, because they, themselves, not he, were the offenders. Finally Caiaphas, fearing that the victim might escape him rose and said, "I adjure thee by the living God, that thou tell us whether thou be the Christ, the Son of God."

There is silence in the hall. Every eye is focused on the prisoner. And in the stillness of death, turning toward the persecutor and, with a voice that must have penetrated the very soul of the old sinner, he replied, "Thou hast said!" which is the same as, "Yes, I am!" And then he added, "Hereafter shall ye see the Son of Man sitting on the right hand of Power, and coming in the clouds of heaven." (Matt. 26:57-68)

Now they did not, according to the high priest, need any witnesses. He himself had said that he was the Messiah, and the Son of God, and he asserted that he would some day be their judge. "What think ye?" The Sanhedrin thus appealed to, answered, "He is guilty of death." That was the sentence of that Jewish council.

If there had been any feelings of humanity in that assembly, they might have executed the sentence by stoning, as in the case of Stephen, the martyr. (Acts 7:54-60) In fact, they threatened to take his life in accordance with their own law. (John 19:7) And Pilate urged them to do just that. (John 19:6) But stoning would have been a comparatively speaking, humane death. Their plan was to deliver him up to the Roman governor as a traitor and a rebel, and to demand crucifixion, the most agonizing, the most degrading mode of death ever conceived either on earth or in hell. Consequently, they immediately delivered Jesus to Pontius Pilate. (Matt. 27:2) The accusation before the governor was that he claimed to be the Messiah, which to the Roman could mean only one thing, "the king of the Jews," a pretender in opposition to Caesar. On that charge, Pilate, after tremendous pressure had been brought to bear, condemned him to the cross. And thus he was judged by the representatives of the entire world, Jewish and Roman, as stated in the vision of Nephi.

Crucifixion was an indescribably cruel and loathsome mode of death. It is supposed to have come from Persia, and that it was adopted by the Romans as a fitting punishment of rebellious slaves. It was always preceded by scourging, which reduced the naked body to a bleeding, quivering mass, and when the victim, after this unnecessary cruelty, was tied, or nailed, to the cross, where he suffered all the torments of the damned—burning fever, thirst, the sting of insects, utter helplessness as regards all the elementary functions of nature—the spectacle presented was one of extreme horror. No wonder that Nature shrouded Calvary in a thick veil of darkness, while the Son of God suffered and expired on the cross. "Now from the sixth hour there was darkness over all the land unto the ninth hour." (Matt. 27:45) From noon till 3 o'clock, the time for the evening sacrifice. And thus the "Lamb of God" died for us.

VERSE 34. *Against the apostles of the Lamb.* In his vision, Nephi sees the multitudes of the earth" arrayed against the Apostles of the Lamb. The war between the two opposing forces did not end with Calvary. The apostles represented the kingdom the Lamb; for thus were the twelve called by the angel of the Lord.

35. And the multitude of the earth was gathered together; and I beheld that they were in a large and spacious building, like unto the building which my father saw. And the angel of the Lord spake unto me again, saying: Behold the world and the wisdom thereof; yea, behold the house of Israel hath gathered together to fight against the twelve apostles of the Lamb.

---

of God on earth. For did not our Lord, at his last meeting with his disciples before his death, assure them that he had "appointed" (bequeathed) them the kingdom as the Father had appointed him (Luke 22:29; see also 12:31, 32)? Hence the war upon the apostles, who represented that kingdom, and who had at their service all authority in heaven and on earth (Matt. 28:18-29), through the exercise of the Priesthood, in righteousness. (D. and C. 107:18, 19; 121:35-37)

VERSE 35. *A large and spacious building.* This war was carried on by the "multitudes of the earth," whose headquarters was some large structure "like unto the building which my father saw."

*The world and the wisdom thereof.* This large building, the angel explains, is, or represents, the world and its wisdom. It represents the world as marshaling and mobilizing the forces of its institutes of learning, all its philosophy (wisdom), against the apostles of the Lord.

What is, then, the nature of this wisdom?

The "wisdom of the world," for one thing, is not, like divine truth, an unchangeable, eternal rock; rather, it resembles the waves that beat against the cliff, now rising, now falling, now raging, now gently rolling, according to the winds that blow. It is constantly changing.

The "wisdom of the world" today is different to that of yesterday; tomorrow it will be different to that of today. But no matter what form or color it may assume in the marvelous kaleidoscope of history, it offers no clue today, and will offer none tomorrow, any more than it did in the past, to the solution of the vital problems, the true answer to which it has pleased God to reveal only in the gospel of the Crucified One—"Unto the Jews a stumbling block, and unto the Greeks foolishness; but unto them which are called, both Jews and Greeks, Christ the power of God, and the wisdom of God." (1 Cor. 1:21-4) And this is as true now as it ever was. That "the world by wisdom knew not God" was never more evident than it is in our day.

The so-called "Enlightenment" in the 18th century, which was a natural but radical re-action against the then prevalent orthodoxy, is an illustration of the futility of trusting to the wisdom of the world for guidance in matters of eternal values.

During this "Enlightenment" it was discovered that man was not the miserable earth worm of the old theology, to be trampled in the dust, but that he is a being exalted above other creatures, possessing intelligence, entitled to certain inalienable rights on earth as well as an eternal destiny.

An estimate of the world different from that of the old orthodoxy followed. The absurd view that matter itself is evil and that the earth is at best a prison, the kingdom of satan, an abode of torment from which to escape by death, was discarded. By and by the sciences made themselves heard. The telescope, the microscope, the appliances of the various laboratories, unveiled ever more and greater wonders and constructed a marvelously beautiful universe of which previous centuries did not even dream.

36. And it came to pass that I saw and bear record, that the great and spacious building was the pride of the world; and it fell, and the fall thereof was exceeding great. And the angel of the Lord spake unto me again, saying: Thus shall be the destruction of all nations, kindreds, tongues, and people, that shall fight against the twelve apostles of the Lamb.

---

During this period of Enlightenment human reason was awakened from a long slumber and placed in a seat of honor.

The Enlightenment freed man from the serfdom of feudalism, if not entirely from the curse of its degrading militarism; it paved the way for the great ideals of democracy which are the cornerstones of the government of the United States and all free governments. It was the beginning of an industrialism which, if rightly guided, would have ennobled the human race and made every home a divine abode. It blazed the way for liberty, equality and fraternity—the very goal of human existence.

With these achievements to its credit, it appeared for a while as if human philosophy might have found God and a restored paradise, independently of divine revelation. Especially since the most brilliant minds of the age, freed from fear and "prejudices," engaged in the endless search. With philosophers, such as Bacon, Descartes, Locke, Spinoza, Kant, Fichte, Schopenhauer, Hegel, Leibnitz; with scientists, among whom we need only mention Galileo, Kepler, Newton, Lamarck, Darwin, Spencer, Lyell, Laplace, Huxley; with theologians, such as De Wette, Schleiermacher, Wellhausen, Driver, and with a host of others including poets, historians, dramatists, biographers, and even revivalists, all devoting their resources of knowledge and powers of reasoning to the search, one would seem justified in expecting success.

And the results?

One result is that the world quite generally has come to regard the sacred Scriptures as nothing but fragmentary remnants of an ancient literature. It is hardly ever consulted as a guide to correct conduct in the affairs of daily life.

Human reason has been exalted to the position of highest authority on questions of truth and morals, a position it cannot fill, now or ever.

Another result is that the 19th century democracy has broken down in war, revolution, economic disorder and crime. Wise men of the present day admit that what they call the "old order" is irrevocably gone and is about to be replaced by a new form of government.

And it is not only religion that is under attack. Scientific research and application are also in danger. Over a large part of the world, censorship is threatening to enslave the sciences. This generation has lived to see students in great institutes of learning take the lead in a crusade against free speech, and a free press. The prevalence of that spirit would be the end of learning. It would mean death to all sciences.

*The Godhead.* The doctrine of the Deity is by far the most important of all. On a correct knowledge of God depends life eternal. (John 17:3) And our life on earth, our personal conduct, our relations with our fellowmen and with society are governed by our belief in, or rejection of, God as our Father, our Ruler, our final Judge. Godlessness is a menace to a family, a community, a nation, as well as the individual.

According to the revelations—the only reliable source of information on that subject—three Divine Persons constitute the Council of the Godhead.

1. *The Father.* That there is a Divine Father we learn from innumerable revelations, former as well as recent. Consider the following:

"Do ye thus requite the Lord? . . . Is not he thy Father that hath brought thee?" (Deut. 32:6)

"Now therefore thus shalt thou say unto my servant David . . . and when thy days shall be fulfilled, and thou shalt sleep with thy fathers, I will set up thy seed after thee . . . I will be his father, and he shall be my son." (2 Sam. 7:8-14)

"Doubtless thou art our Father, though Abraham be ignorant of us, and Israel acknowledge us not; Thou O Lord, art our Father, our Redeemer; thy name is from everlasting." (Is. 63:16)

"Ye have received the spirit of adoption, whereby we cry, Abba, Father. The Spirit itself beareth witness with our spirit that we are the children of God. (Rom. 8:15, 16)

(See also Alma 11:44; Hela. 14:12; Mor. 5:77)

(Christ) "glorifies the Father, and saves all the works of his hands, except those sons of perdition who deny the Son after the Father has revealed him." (D. and C. 76:43)

2. *The Son.* There is also a Son in the Godhead. Jesus Christ is called the Father's "beloved Son." (Ps. 2:7; Matt. 3:17) In the view of the Apostle Paul, God raised Jesus from the dead because he is his Son:

"And we declare unto you glad tidings, how that the promise which was made unto the fathers, God hath fulfilled the same unto us their children, in that he hath raised us Jesus again; as it is also written in the second psalm, Thou art my Son, this day have I begotten thee." (Acts 13:32, 33)

Jesus Christ is "the Great I AM." (D. and C. 29:1; 38:1; 39:1; 110:1-3) Compare the vision of Moses as related in Ex. 3:1-14. Here we learn that the Great I AM is none other than the God of Abraham, the God of Isaac, and the God of Jacob (v. 6), whose name is Jehovah, or Yahveh.

Jesus Christ is also called, God's "Holy Child":

"The kings of the earth stood up, and the rulers were gathered together against the Lord, and against his Christ. For of truth against thy holy child Jesus, whom thou hast anointed, both Herod, and Pontius Pilate, with the gentiles, and the people of Israel, were gathered together." (Acts 4:26, 27)

See also John 1:34; 5:25; 19:7; Acts 9:20; Rev. 2:18.

Jesus speaks of his angels. (Matt. 13:41; 16:27; 24:31) He makes the claim that the Father has delivered "all things" to him, and that knowledge of the Father can be obtained only through him. (Matt. 11:27) He claims, furthermore, that prayers offered in his name will receive special attention by the Father:

"Verily, verily, I say unto you, Whatsoever ye shall ask the Father in my name, he will give it you. Hitherto have ye asked nothing in my name: Ask, and ye shall receive, that your joy may be full." (John 16:23, 24)

No mere human being could make such a claim, truthfully.

3. *The Holy Ghost.* In this Divine Council there is also a third member, a Person, sometimes called, The Holy Ghost, and sometimes, The Holy Spirit. He has all the divine characteristics. He is infinitely wise, holy, good and tender. Our Lord, immediately before his death, explained the special mission of the Holy Spirit. He told his disciples that he was about to leave them, but would return. However, they were not to be left "comfortless" (rather, "orphans") while waiting for him (John 14:18). They would have the Spirit of Truth abiding with them. Our Lord says:

"When the Spirit of Truth is come, he will guide you into all truth: for he shall not speak of himself; but whatsoever he shall hear, that shall he speak; and he will show you things to come. . . . He shall glorify me; for he shall receive of mine, and shall show it unto you." (John 16:13-15; comp. 14:15-18)

That the Holy Spirit is a Divine Person is further evident from the instructions of our Lord concerning baptism. He said to the Twelve:

"Go ye therefore and teach all nations, baptizing them in the name of the Father, and of the Son, and of the Holy Ghost. (Matt. 28:19)

Here both the personality and equality of the three members of the Godhead are clearly taught.

The same truth is conveyed in the Apostolic blessing:

"The grace of the Lord Jesus Christ, and the love of God, and the communion of the Holy Ghost, be with you all." (2 Cor. 13:14)

The enumeration of the three is the recognition of three distinct Personalities, and each has, moreover, his own characteristic—"grace," "love," and "communion."

Distinct personal acts are attributes to the Holy Spirit. He speaks. (Acts 28:25) He prophesies. (I Tim. 4:1-3) He makes intercession for the Saints. (Rom. 8:25, 27) He can be grieved. (Eph. 4:30) He can be sinned against. (Matt. 12:31)

All these are attributes of a person. (See also I Ne. 11:11)

*A Divine Power.* But there is also a "Spirit of Jehovah," a "Spirit of God" (Ps. 51:13; Is. 63:11-14) which is not a person, but that divine force, or power, that, like the wind, cannot be seen, and yet is the element by which all animate creatures live. (Job 27:3; 33:4; Ps. 104:29, 30) By which the whole universe is animated, filled with life, and governed. It was this spirit that "moved upon" (might be translated, "was brooding upon") the face of the waters (Gen. 1:2) as a bird broods over its nest (Deut. 32:11). It is a regenerating principle which "bloweth where it listeth, but [thou] canst not tell whence it cometh and whither it goeth. (John 3:8) It is an element in which we "live, move, and have our being" (Acts 17:28), a true light which "lighteth every man that cometh into the world. (John 1:9) It can be imparted and received. (John 20:29; Acts 2:4) It is an element in which the believer is baptized. (Acts 1:5; 2:16-18; Joel 2:28) It is the light of Christ

". . . and the light of the sun, and the power thereof by which it was made. As also he [Christ] is in the moon, and is the light of the moon, and the power thereof by which it was made; and also the light of the stars, and the power thereof by which they were made; and the earth also, and the power thereof, even the earth upon which you stand. And the light which shineth, which giveth you light, is through him who enlighteneth your eyes, which is the same light that quickeneth your understandings; which light proceedeth forth from the presence of God to fill the immensity of space—the light which is in all things, which giveth life to all things, which is the law by which all things are governed, even the power of God who sitteth upon his throne, who is in the bosom of eternity, who is in the midst of all things." (D. and C. 88:7-13)

It is through this Light, this Power, that God

"Comprehendeth all things, and all things are before him, and all things are round about him; and he is above all things, and in all things, and is through all things, and is round about all things; and all things are by him, and of him, even God, forever and ever." (D. and C. 88:41)

*Immanence.* Some exponents of the wisdom of the world—philosophers, we may call them—who reject the revelations concerning the personal Godhead, yet claim to be believers in the divine element, or force, which they conceive of as "immanent" in the matter of which the universe is composed. By "immanence" they mean the indwelling of something divine in the material world as its soul, or "the spirit that animates it and which takes various forms, such as heat, light, gravitation, electricity, and the like; the all-embracing substance of which men and things are but differentiations; the principle of unity underlying all multiplicity; the infinite consciousness in which all things have their existence; the indwelling personality with whom we commune when we contemplate nature or look into our own souls." (Arthur C. McGiffert, "The Rise of Modern Religious Ideas, p. 201)

It will be seen from this that the philosophy referred to and revelation come quite close to a perfect agreement on recognizing the existence of a divine element that permeates the universe. But there is a noteable difference. Revelation says that, transcending this force, directing and controlling it, there is a Godhead, consisting of three divine Persons, infinite in majesty and glory, the Creators and Rulers of heaven and earth and all that is in them; while the philosophy boldly asserts that there are no such Persons. The force directs itself. It *is* God. That is the philosophy of immanence. But is that real philosophy?

We are told that the indwelling divine force manifests itself as electricity. Very well. Can that force send a message without a person who thinks and writes and operates the keys according to certain rules? Has the force itself personality enough to act without a person on the outside of it in control? Or, we hear a sermon over the radio. Is there no person somewhere who speaks? Worldly wisdom says, Certainly not. Revelation says, Yes, indeed.

VERSE 36. *The pride of the world.* The large and spacious building also represents the pride of the world. The world, just now, is very proud of its wisdom, although it is a building standing "as it were in the air," doomed to fall.

"Pride goeth before destruction, and a haughty spirit before a fall." (Prov. 16:18) "A man's pride shall bring him low, and honor shall uphold the humble in spirit." (Prov. 29:23)

Pride was the downfall of Lucifer. It was manifested, first, in his exaggerated estimate of himself. Did he not come before the Lord God and in a boastful spirit asserted his ability to redeem all mankind? "One soul shall not be lost." It was secondly, manifested in his demand for reward: "I will be thy Son." "Give me thine honor." It was, finally, manifested in his rebellion against the allwise decision of God. Then he was cast out. (Book of Moses, Pearl of Great Price, 4:1-4; B. of Abr. 3:26-27; D. and C. 29:36, 37; 76:25-29. Compare Is. 14:3-23, where the destruction of Babylon is depicted under the imagery of the fall of Lucifer.)

Korah, Dalthan and Abiram rose up against Moses, and were swallowed by the earth. (Num. 16:1-3, 32, 33) Miriam spoke against Moses, and became leprous. (Num. 12:1, 2, 10) Absalom lied about his father David, and ended his days hanging in an oak. (2 Sam. 15:3-11; 18:9, 14) Nebuchadnezzar became boastful and lost his reason for some time. (Dan. 4:29-34) Herod (Agrippa), the murderer of the Apostle James, the brother of John, accepted divine honor by his flatterers, and was eaten by loathsome worms. (Acts 12:21-23)

Surely, "God resisteth the proud, but giveth grace unto the humble." (James 4:6)

## GENERAL NOTES

*The Holy Spirit.* Last spring, when we visited Walker, the Indian Chief, he was dull and sulky, and lay in his tent, and the first thing he said was, 'Brother Brigham, lay your hands upon me, for my spirit has gone away from me, and I want it to come back again! He was full of anger, for his people had been fighting, and he did not know whether to turn to the side of peace or war. We laid hands upon him, and he felt better. At his request we sang some Mormon hymns, and as we left his tent, he was full of the good Spirit and would not injure this people, no not one particle. He was full of kindness and love of God, and all his works. He traveled with us to Iron County and had dreams which amounted to revelations. If I could have kept him with me all the time, do you suppose he would have had an evil spirit? No, he would have been filled with the Spirit of the Lord." (Brigham Young, Jour. of Dis., vol. 2, p. 143-4)

*Jesus and the Jews.* Among the educated Hebrews of our day a change of attitude toward Jesus of Nazareth has taken place. Several publications on his life and teachings prove this. "A Jewish View of Jesus," by H. G. Enelow, published by the Bloch Publ. Co., New York, is an illustration of this fact. This author arrives at the conclusion that the love Jesus has inspired, the solace he has given, the good he has engendered, the hope and joy he has kindled are unequaled in human history, and he expresses the hope that Jesus may yet serve as a bond of union between Jew and Christian, when his teaching is better known. Mr. Enelow also says, "Of course, the modern Jew deplores the tragic death of Jesus. Yet, if it was not inevitable—which perhaps it was—it certainly is irrevocable."

Without, at this time, discussing the question whether the crucifixion was, or was not, inevitable, I venture one suggestion. The adherents of the Mosaic faith in our day have various representative organizations. One of these might, even at this late day, sincerely review the proceedings against Jesus before the Sanhedrin, and if he is found to be innocent, as he certainly would be, then proclaim that fact before all the world. That would go far toward restoring the ancient covenant people to the favor of God and men.

In a revelation to the Prophet Joseph, the Lord has provided that if "the children shall repent, or the children's children, and turn to the Lord their God." and make restitution for their own trespasses or those of their fathers, or fathers' fathers, "then thine indignation shall be turned away; and vengeance shall no more come upon them, saith the Lord thy God, and their trespasses shall never be brought any more as a testimony before the Lord against them. (D. and C. 98:47-48)

*The Jews and the Saints.* "Some of you may be familiar with the agitation that is going on at the present time, in the publications, against the Jewish people. There should be no ill-will, and I am sure there is none, in the heart of any true Latter-day Saint, toward the Jewish people. By the authority of the holy Priesthood of God, that has again been restored to the earth, and by the ministration, under the direction of the prophet of God, apostles of the Lord Jesus Christ have been to the Holy Land and have dedicated that country for the return of the Jews, and we believe that in the due time of the Lord they shall be in the favor of God again. And let no Latter-day Saint be guilty of taking any part in any crusade against these people. I believe in no other part of the world is there as good feeling in the hearts of mankind towards the Jewish people as among the Latter-day Saints." (President Heber J.Grant, Improvement Era, vol. 24, p. 747)

## CHAPTER 12

*Nephi's vision of the Land of Promise, 1-5—The coming of the Lord to the people of Nephi and his kingdom among them, 6-12—War between Nephites and Lamanites, 13-20 — Lamanites dwindle in unbelief and become dark, 21-23.*

## 1. *Nephi's vision of the land of promise.*

1. And it came to pass that the angel said unto me: Look, and behold thy seed, and also the seed of thy brethren. And I looked and beheld the land of promise; and I behold multitudes of people, yea, even as it were in number as many as the sand of the sea.

---

VERSE 1. *And I looked and beheld the land of promise.* The "land of promise," evidently, refers to America, and, since both North and South America, according to President Brigham Young, are the land of Zion (see Doctrine and Covenants Commentary, p. 792), we may infer that what he saw was the entire America. Undoubtedly, he saw the place where he was to land; probably he saw the general configurations of the two continents, their mountains, their snow-capped peaks, the plains, the rivers, the lakes; in all probability he obtained an idea of the climate, the resources, etc. When he arrived here, he was, therefore, not an entire stranger. He had the knowledge needed by a leader of the colony, the chief, as he became later, of mighty tribes and nations.

President Brigham Young had a similar pre-vision of Salt Lake valley, and more particularly of the temple, before he ever came here and could exclaim, "This is the place." At the general conference of the Church, April 6, 1853, he said in his conference address:

"I scarcely ever say much about revelations, or visions, but suffice it to say, five years ago last July I was here and saw in the spirit the temple, not ten feet from where we have laid the cornerstone. I have not inquired what kind of a temple we should build. Why? Because it was represented before me. I have never looked upon that ground, but the vision of it was there. I see it as plainly as if it was in reality before me. . . . I will say, however, that it will have six towers instead of one." (Jour. of Dis., vol. 1, p. 132)

The great prophet Ezekiel furnishes another illustration of pre-vision. In the 25th year of the Babylonian captivity, while he was living in Babylon, the hand of the Lord was upon him and brought him to Palestine. There he was shown a new temple. He says:

"In the visions of God brought he me into the land of Israel, and set me upon a very high mountain, by which was the frame of a city on the south [Jerusalem]. And he brought me thither, and, behold, there was a man, whose appearance was like the appearance of brass, with a line of flax in his hand, and a measuring reed; and he stood in the gate. And the man said unto me, Son of man, behold with thine eyes, and hear with thine ears, and set thine heart upon all that I shall shew thee; for to the intent that I might shew them unto thee art thou brought hither; declare all that thou seest to the house of Israel." (Ez. 40:2-4)

The prophet is then led through the gateway of the outer court of the temple into the court itself; then he passes to a gateway opposite him, and is led into the inner court; the structure of the temple is then revealed to him, as well as the buildings connected with it; and lastly he is shown other buildings in the inner court, and learns their dimensions. The prophet describes the vision with remarkable minuteness, as he was commanded to do. We may feel sure that the vision of Nephi concerning the land of promise was no less clear and minute than the vision of Ezekiel concerning the temple, which is yet to be built in the holy city.

Nephi learned a great deal about the history of America—multitudes at war, convulsions of nature, the coming of Christ, etc. and, we may feel sure, he saw the rise of the United States and understood its mission and destiny. One of the apostles appointed under the direction of the Prophet Joseph, viz., Parley P. Pratt, in a patriotic address in Salt Lake City, July 4, 1853, said in part, concerning this mission:

"When we contemplate the designs of the country and its influence, we contemplate not merely our own liberty, happiness and progress, nationally and individually, but we contemplate the emancipation of the world, the flowing of the nations to this fountain, and to the occupation of these elements blending together in one common brotherhood. They will thus seek deliverance from oppression, not in the style of revolution but by voluntarily emerging into freedom, and the free occupation of the free elements of life. . . .

"Do you mean that we shall return again to our fathers' land and compel them to be American citizens?

"No. But to two hundred millions of people on the American continent, dignified by the principles of American freedom, Europe must bow. . . .

"Suffice it to say, the continent is discovered, the elements of life and happiness are known to exist, and are partly developed, and constitutions and governments formed, and principles beginning to be instituted and developed, and influences are at work of such magnitude and greatness, that language is inadequate to express the probable results; we can only borrow the language of the prophets, which is also insufficient to convey the idea properly, that is, The earth shall be full of knowledge, light, liberty, brotherly kindness and friendship; none will have need to teach his neighbor to know the Lord, but all will know him from the least to the greatest; darkness will flee away, oppression will be known no more, and men will employ blacksmiths to beat up their old weapons of war into ploughshares and pruning-hooks . . . the world will be renovated both politically and religiously." (Jour. of Disc., vol. 1, pp. 142-3)

Nephi must have had some such impressions from his vision of the promised land.

—*Multitudes of people.* After having viewed the land of promise, Nephi saw, in the vision, that his descendants and the descendants of his brethren became "multitudes of people"—"as many as the sand of the sea"; that is, an exceedingly great number.

Just how numerous the descendants of Lehi were in America at the time of the discovery by Columbus, or how many there are now, is not known, but there must be several millions of them, at the present time.

According to one estimate, there were in the territory now constituting the United States about 850,000 Indians, at the time of the discovery by Columbus in 1492. But the number dwindled, and in 1930 the census registered only 340,541. There are, however, a great many Indians in Mexico, Central and South America.

It is now pretty well recognized that the most advanced traits of character and culture developed in two special centers, viz., in South America in the Andean region, and in Central America, and that arts and industries spread from these centers to other areas, north and south.

Does not this harmonize with the history of the Book of Mormon, according to which we might expect a nucleus of Nephite culture somewhere with its development, and a Lamanite nucleus somewhere else with its development?

Dr. Daniel G. Brinton, possibly the greatest Americanist of his day, came to the conclusion that "the culture of the native Americans strongly attest the ethnic unity of the race. This applies equally to the ruins and relics of its vanished nations, as to the institutions of existing tribes." (The American Race, p. 43)

This appears to me to be one more confirmation of Book of Mormon history, according to which the common origin of the two principal nations of that history is clearly set forth.

As to the languages, Dr. Brinton says they, too, give evidence of "psychic identity." There are, indeed, he says, indefinite discrepancies in lexicography and in morphology; but in their logical substructure they are strikingly alike. (Ibid. p. 55)

However, where he cannot find sufficient coincidences of words and grammar in two languages to classify them as related, he regards them as independent "stocks," or "families." There are, he finds, about eighty such in North America, and as many in South America.

Here again, the history of the Book of Mormon is corroborated, since that history deals with at least three different immigrations, The Jaredite, the Mulekite and the Lehite, from which, naturally, various linguistic "stocks," or "families," might have developed in the course of centuries.

These stocks, Dr. Brinton says, offer us our best basis for the ethnic classification of American tribes; the only basis, indeed, which is of any value. (Ibid. pp. 56-57) On this basis he divides the entire race into the following five groups:—

1. The North Atlantic
2. The North Pacific
3. The Central
4. The South Pacific, and
5. The South Atlantic Group.

"There is," Dr. Brinton says, "a distinct resemblance between the two Atlantic groups, and an equally distinct contrast between them and the Pacific groups, extending to temperament, cultural and physical traits." (Ibid. p. 58)

1. *The North Atlantic Group.* To this group belong the Eskimos, the Athabaskans or Jinne, and the Algonkins, who, at the time of the discovery of America, occupied the Atlantic coast from Cape Fear to Cape Hatteras, and the entire area of New England. Related to the Algonkins are the Crees, the Blackfeet, the Abnakis, the Lenapis, and others, and they are all supposed to have come from a locality north of the St. Lawrence River and east of Lake Ontario.

In this group we have, further, the Iroquois, who, at the time of the first French explorations in North America lived in the State of New York and parts of Canada. The Cherokees, the Mohawks, the Hurons, the Oneidas, the Onandagas, the Senecas, the Susquehannocks, etc., are all members of the same linguistic stock. They are supposed to have come from some region between the lower St. Lawrence and Hudson Bay. We have the word of the Prophet Joseph, received by revelation, for the statement that Onandagus, from whom the Onandagas presumably derive their name, was a great prophet, "known from the eastern sea to the Rocky Mountains." (Introduction to the Study of the Book of Mormon, Sjodahl, p. 266)

In this North Atlantic group we have, further, the Muskokis, who occupied the lowlands between the Appalachian mountains and the Gulf of Mexico, and from the Atlantic to the Mississippi. Their near relatives were the Choctaws, the Creeks, the Chickasaws, the Seminoles, etc. Choctaw legends point to a mound in Winston County, Mississippi, as the locality where their ancestors once lived, or where the Choctaws and Chickasaws were separated. The Creeks had a religious festival which they called BUSK (from *puskita*, meaning "fast"), which was observed at the time of the year when the ears of corn became edible. This word reminds us of the Hebrew festival called *pesach* (passover), which was observed in the month of Nisan, a name which means *the Month of the Green Ears*.

In this group we have also the Pawnees, who have a tradition that they came from the south to their homes in the area between the middle Missouri river and the Gulf of Mexico; also the Dakotas or Sioux, who occupied the entire Missouri valley as far up as the Yellowstone, and who are supposed to have formed part of a migration from the East, which seems to have been going on for centuries before the discovery by Columbus. It was Sioux warriors who annihilated General Custer's command in 1876. Among their related tribes were the Mandans and Minnetarees.

To this group the Kioways are also counted. They lived in the upper basin of the Missouri river, the life of wild hunters. They have, in fact, been called the "Arabs of the Great American Desert." To a student of the Book of Mormon, this designation might suggest a comparison between the Kioways and the Gadianton bands. (Hel. 2:4, 11, 12)

2. *The North Pacific Group.* To this group the following belong, — A number of tribes on the northwest coast and California; the Yumas, and the Pueblos.

As for the Indians on the northwest coast, the Tlinkits live in good wooden houses and display skill in carving and painting. Their chiefs, or some of them, have totem poles of which there are specimens 50 feet high, elaborately carved and painted. The first explorers that visited them, in 1741, found that they had seaworthy canoes, dressed leather, utensils of stone, and ornaments or silver and copper. They had articles of iron imported from the south, and money, consisting of shells. They also had slaves.

The Yumas lived in the valley of the Colorado river, Arizona, and in southern California. They were found there, in 1540, by Coronado. They called themselves Apaches, which is said to mean "fighters," a cognomen also bestowed upon the Tinnes, the Mojaves, and others. The Yumas and the Maricopas cultivated corn and beans on irrigated fields.

The Pueblo tribes, at one time, had their characteristic dwellings in Arizona and adjacent territory, dotting an area estimated at two hundred thousand square miles. Their houses were built of adobes, as a rule, and each house was large enough to accommodate an entire community. The Casas Grandes ("big houses") in northern Chihuahua are among the best known of these structures.

The remains of so-called cliff houses are also found in the canyons and gorges of the Colorado and its affluents. They are often located in seemingly inaccessible places, near the edge of precipices hundreds of feet above the level land below. Round or square towers are frequently found near the cliff dwellings in places convenient for observation.

The Pueblo Indians, according to Dr. Brinton, are not all of one stock, or lineage. The Moqui Pueblos belonged to the Uto-Aztecan branch, and the Pimas to some other branch of the stock. The other Pueblos are divided into three stocks —the Kera, the Tehua, and the Zuni.

Recent research by an expedition under the direction of Mr. Albert B. Reagan of Ouray, Ohio, is said to have convinced him that the cliff houses of that region, and the caves, were occupied about 570 A.D., and that they were not permanent residences, but used during the farming season. Mr. Reagan explored twenty-six cliff houses and granaries in the Florence canyon, and twenty-eight in the Chandler canyon.

3. *The Central Group.* The most important stock in this group is the Uto-Aztecan, which, according to Dr. Brinton's classification, comprises the Ute, or Shoshonian, the Sonoran, and the Nahuatl branches. These three, he holds, are offshoots from some one ancestral stem. The Utes, the Shoshones and the Comanches

in the north; various tribes in Sonora, Chihuahua, Sinaloa and Durango in the center, and the Nahuas, also called Aztecs, in the south. All these are one stock. The Nahuatl language and culture were the highest developed. The lower level of the Utes is accounted for by the lack of nutritious food in sufficient quantity; by their inadequate protection by means of suitable clothing, winter and summer, and by the unsanitary dwellings, which sometimes were merely holes in the ground.

The Comanches were also called "Snake Indians," and the sign representing their tribe was the same, in the sign language, as that which signified a snake.

The Otomis are said to have been the earliest settlers of Central Mexico. At the time of the arrival of the Spaniards, their language was the most widely distributed. They were agriculturists. They had ornaments of gold, copper and hard stones, and they were noted for musical ability.

The Tarascos were the inhabitants of the present state of Michoacan. Their capital city was Tzintzuan, and they had buildings of cut stone laid in mortar. They had cotton, gold, and copper. Their armor consisted of helmet, body pieces, and greaves, all covered with copper or gold plates. They had a form of picture-writing, but no specimen of this has been preserved. Their supreme God was Tucah-Pacha. They also worshiped the sun.

The Totonacos were the Indians whom Cortez first met. They inhabited a territory in the present state of Vera Cruz. They said they had lived there eight hundred years, and that they had come from the northwest. They had attained a high degree of culture, and were almost white in color. They, too, were sun worshipers, and their priests wore long, black gowns. Their cities were surrounded with fruit trees and grain fields, and presented the vista of a paradise.

The Zapotecs occupied the present state of Oaxaca, where there are still said to be 265,000 of them. They formed at one time a great state. They were living in villages and constructed houses of stone and mortar. The ruins of Mitla are an evidence of their culture. Recent explorations there have yielded important results.

The Mixtecs adjoined the Zapotecs on the west. In culture they were the equals of their neighbors. The Zapotecs and the Mixtecs had a calendar, similar to that of the Aztecs. They called their language the "language of the noble people" (ticha za).

The Zoques, Mixes, and some other tribes inhabited the mountain regions of the isthmus of Tehuantepec. The Spaniards found them a savage, valorous race, but they are the very opposite today. Their traditions indicate that they came from the south.

The Chinantecs who inhabited Chinantla, a part of Oaxaca, are said to have lived in secluded valleys and on rough mountain sides. Their language is said to be different from any tongue of the surrounding tribes. Dr. Berendt, quoted by Dr. Brinton. (The American Race, p. 144), says: "Spoken in the midst of a diversity of languages connected more or less among themselves, it is itself unconnected with them, and is rich in peculiar features both as to its roots and its grammatical structure. It is probable that we have in it one of the original languages spoken before the advent of the Nahuas on Mexican soil, perhaps the mythical Olmecan."

The Chapanecs had a tradition that they had come to Chiapas from Nicaragua, from the south. Another tradition said they had reached their territory from the north, following the Pacific coast as far as Soconusco, where they divided, some entering the mountains of Chiapas, and others proceeding southward to Nicaragua, where they settled on the shores of Lake Managua.

The traditions do not necessarily contradict each other. There may have been a northward trek, and also a southward. One may have preceded the other. Centuries may have intervened between the two migratory movements.

The Chapanecs are described as lighter in color than most Indians. They knew a hieroglyphic system of writing and had books. A small band is said to have wandered as far south as the Chiriqui Lagoon.

The Mayas of Yucatan, around Lake Peten and the affluents of the Usumacinta, and the Lacandones of Chiapas, Mexico, and the upper basin of the Usumacinta river, belong to the same branch of the Maya-Quiche stock. Related branches were the Quiches, the Cakchiquels and the Mams in Guatemala, and the Tzendals (or Tzeltals) and Tzotzils in Tabasco. Traditions tell of two migrations into Yucatan, one from the southeast and another from the southwest. If we accept the idea of two migrations, says Dr. Alfred M. Tozzer ("A Comparative Study of the Mayas and the Lacandones," p. 7) we can assume that they were composed of people of the same stock, possessing the same language, customs and religion. There is a line of ruined cities stretching southeast into Honduras and another to the southwest toward the river Champoton. The chronicles of the Mayas go back to the beginning of our era. They were great builders. The very old ruins of Copan, Palenque, T-Ho and other cities, no less than the more recent remains of Uxmal, Chicken-Itza, etc., are evidence of their wonderful art. Dr. Brinton states that the Mayas had seaworthy canoes at the time of Columbus, and that they had commercial dealings with Cuba at that time. They also maintained commerce with the people of Southern Mexico and used beans, shells, precious stones, and flat pieces of copper as media of exchange. The Maya hieroglyphs are an evidence of a high degree of intelligence, and the Maya calendar is a marvel of ingenuity.

*Dividing Line Between the North and South.* According to Dr. Brinton, the mountain chain between Nicaragua and Costa Rica and between the Rio Frio and the southern and eastern streams, forms the ethnographic boundary of North America. South of this line, the linguistic characteristics indicate affinity with South America.

There are many tribes in Central America. We mention the Huaves on the isthmus of Tehuantepec; the Lencas in central Honduras, and the Xicaques, also in Honduras. These are said to speak a language related to the Nahuatl. The Ulvas, the Lacandones and some others are sometimes called "Caribs," but only to denote their supposedly lower degree of culture. The Mosquito Indians occupied a territory near the Bluefield lagoon. The Ramas lived on an island in this lake. "Rama," it will be observed, is a familiar name in Book of Mormon history.

4. *The South Pacific Group* comprises two regions: The Colombian and the Peruvian.

The Colombian region comprises Northwestern South America, north of the equator and west of the Orinoco. At the time of the discovery by the Spaniards, the Cunas lived on the Isthmus of Panama, a territory, ethnographically, regarded as part of South America, as it was, politically, a part of Colombia until 1903.

The Chocos occupied the eastern shore of the Gulf of Uraba and the lower valley of the Atrato. Some of them inhabited the Pacific coast, where a remnant of them still is found. They are called Sambos, a name that reminds us of the Book of Mormon name, Sam. The Chocos were at one time merchants and skilful metal workers.

In the mountain districts of Merida, Venezuela, south of Lake Maracaibo, there is a linguistic stock known as the Timotes. They were agriculturists. They buried their dead in specially made vaults, the entrances to which were closed with large stones.

The Mariches lived in the highlands near the City of Caracas. They are said to be extinct now.

The Chibchas, or Muyscas, were at the time of the conquest located on the upper Magdalena river in the vicinity of Bogota, Colombia. They were a cultured people. Detached tribes of this stock were found all along the Isthmus and in Costa Rica. They had an extensive system of irrigation; they weaved cotton and worked gold with great skill. They were represented in both North and South America. Dr. Brinton makes this significant observation:

"As to the course of migration, I do not think that the discussion of the dialectic changes leaves any room for doubt. They all indicate attrition and loss of the original form as we trace them from South into North America; evidently the wandering hordes moved into the latter from the southern continent. So far, there is no evidence that any North American tribe migrated into South America." (The American Race, p. 185)

In the Peruvian region we note, first, the Kechuas, or Quichuas.

Judging from the extent of the country in which their language is spoken they must have occupied a territory nearly 2,000 miles in length, from 3 degrees north of the equator to at least 32 (some say 35) degrees south. They occupied part of this vast area even before the Incas rose to prominence. It was the opinion of von Tschudi (Organismus der Khetsua Sprache, p. 64) that wherever the Kechua was spoken at the time of the conquest, it had been spoken thousands of years before the Inca dynasty began. According to one tradition of the Incas, the original home of the Kechua was in the Lake Titicaca basin, on the boundary between Peru and Bolivia. Some modern scholars, Sir Clement Markham, among others, doubt this. They believe that the Kechuas first appeared in South America in the region of Quito, in the north, and that they gradually worked their way south until they were stopped at the northern shore of Lake Titicaca, by warlike tribes. But how did they happen to "appear" in Quito, if they had not come from North America, nor from the South? And who were the warlike tribes that halted them at Lake Titicaca? Is it not easier to believe that the currents of migration at one time were from the south to north, and at some other time from north to south? According to one tradition, two Kechua-speaking tribes. the Mantas and the Caras, occupied the coast from the Gulf of Guayaquil to the Esmeraldas river. The ancestors of the Caras had, it is said, come there in rafts and canoes from some northern settlement. The Macas on the eastern slope of the Andes, near the equator, have been referred to as part of the Scyra stock.[1] The southern limit of the Kechua language has been put at latitude 30 south, where Coquimbo now is situated. But it was also spoken in colonies farther south.

Among the tribes of the Kechua stock were the Casamarcas, on the headwaters of the Maranon; the Incas between Rio Apurimac and Paucartampa; the Lamanos or Lamistas, about Truxillo, and the Mantas on the northern coast of the Gulf of Guayaquil.

The Aymaras form another member of the Kechua stock. They occupied a location to the south of the Kechuas, from latitude 15 degrees to 20 degrees, approximately 300 miles from north to south, and 400 from east to west. The total population of this area today is said to be 600,000, of which two-thirds are pure-blood Indians, and the rest are a mixture of races. Lake Titicaca is situated in Aymara territory, and some consider them the originators of the culture which the Kechuas under the Incas extended over a considerable part of the Pacific coast. According to tradition, Manco Capac, the founder of the Inca dynasty, came from the shores of Lake Titicaca, and from the foam of the Lake, the great Viracocha arose, who taught the people such useful arts as they knew, and the principles of their religion. The ruins of Tiahuanaco, in Aymara territory, are still among the mysteries of American archaeology.

---

[1] Scyri means "chiefs"; probably related to, "Sarai" and "czar."

5. *The South Atlantic Group* is divided into two regions, The Amazonian, and The Pampean.

In the Amazonian region, the Tupis are mentioned first. At the time of discovery they lived on the coast of Brazil from the mouth of the La Plata to the Amazon river, and far up that mighty river. They are said to have wandered up the coast from some southern region. The population of Uruguay today has a large percent of Tupi blood in their veins, perhaps 90 percent. Some of the Tupis, in order to escape the European invaders, fled as far as to the highlands of Bolivia, which proves that even before the days of steam and electricity, the Indians could and did migrate large distances. The Tupis are described as tall, light in color, and athletic. They knew how to make hammocks, cultivate the ground, and make beautiful ornaments of feathers.

The Tapuyas are another linguistic stock in this region. They are said to be the most ancient and the most widely distributed native people in Brazil. The name, which was applied to them by the Tupis, means, "strangers," or "enemies," and is indicative of hostility. They are supposed to have been the early constructors of the numerous shell-heaps along the Atlantic coast, and these are supposed to be at least two thousand years old, probably more. When first discovered, the Tapuyas were low in the scale of culture. They did not, as a rule, wear clothes. They lived in huts made of branches and leaves of trees. They had no tribal organization. But they were skilful hunters, and they made bows, arrows, stone axes, baskets, and —something out of the ordinary for Indians—tapers.

The Arawaks were widely disseminated throughout South America. They were found from the head waters of the Paraguay river to the highlands of southern Bolivia. They had also found their way to the Antilles and the Bahama islands. The Antis, a member of this stock, is thought to have occupied the original home, between the rivers Ucayali, Pachita, and Perene. The Antis inhabited the slopes of the Cordilleras, being a mountain people, while the Campas lived in the plains. Some of the Arawaks bred and trained hunting dogs, and made fine pottery. They hammered native gold into ornaments, carved masks of wood, and made canoes.

The Caribs, at the time of the discovery, were found in the Lesser Antilles, the Caribby Islands, and on the mainland from the mouth of the Essequibo river to the Gulf of Maracaibo. Dr. Brinton traces this stock to the mainland of northern Venezuela, the province of Cumana or New Andalusia. The Caribs in the hills of French Guiana are said to be light in color, and at birth almost white. Concerning their original location Dr. Brinton says:

"The lower Orinoco basin was for a long time the center of distribution of the stock; they probably had driven from it nations of Arawak lineage, some of whom, as the Goajiros, they pushed to the west, where they were in contact with the Carib Motilones, and others to the islands and the shores to the east. The Carijonas and Guaques on the headwaters of the Yapura or Caqueta are now their most western hordes, and the Pimenteras on the Rio Paruahyba are their most eastern. We can thus trace their scattered bands over thirty-five degrees of latitude and thirty of longitude. The earliest center of distribution which best satisfies all the conditions of the problem would be located in the Bolivian highlands, not remote from that I have assigned to the Arawaks." (The American Race, p. 255)

Among some of the Caribs marriage of a daughter to her father, or a sister to her brother, was not uncommon. Like some other ancient peoples, they were cannibals. But in some respects they were ahead of their neighbors in culture. They had fine canoes, and they used sails. Their pottery was of a fine quality, and they had picture writing.

The Zaparos should also be mentioned. That name is sometimes spelled Xeberos,

2. And it came to pass that I beheld multitudes gathered together to battle, one against the other; and I beheld wars, and rumors of wars, and great slaughters with the sword among my people.

---

sometimes Jeberos (pronounced, "Heberos," which, accidentally, or otherwise, bears a strong resemblance to the Old Testament name, Heber, the father of Peleg and Joktan; which name according to Gesenius, means something on or from the other side of a river, a valley, a sea, etc.) At present their main body is found between the rivers Pastaza and Napo and along the Maronon. Among the members of the stock are the Moronas, the Napotoas, and the Nepas.

The Antipas, of the Jivaro linguistic stock, are located above the Pongo de Manseriche.

In the Pampean region there are the Chaco stocks, the Pampeans and Aracaunians, and the Patagonians and Fuegians.

---

This attempt at a review of the Indian linguistic stocks and tribes, although far from complete, illustrates the accuracy of the vision in which "multitudes of people" pass before the spiritual eyes of the youthful seer, Nephi. These "multitudes" were his descendants, and the descendants of his brothers, in the Book of Mormon called Nephites and Lamanites, respectively.

We do not regard all the American natives as the children of these two ancestral sources. The Book of Mormon tells us something of two more immigrations, that of the Jaredites shortly after the dispersion of the human family from the land of Shinar; and that of the attendants of Mulek, who came from Jerusalem about the same time as Lehi. Both these left an indelible impress on the American race. And there are reasons to believe, if the testimony of American archaeology is not misleading, that other elements have been added through migration. But these two, the descendants of Lehi, the Nephites and Lamanites, form a most important part of the material of which the American race is composed. There is no other known and satisfactory explanation of some of its physical traits, linguistic affinities, myths, legends, religious observances, and social institutions.

VERSE 2. *Multitudes gathered to battle . . . wars and rumors of wars.* The history of man on earth is largely a story of strife, war and bloodshed. The ancient fable has it that Zeus, pitying the earth on account of the multitudes she has to sustain, resolved to send discord among men, and thus cause them to destroy each other. Whatever truth this fable may be intended to convey is applicable to the American aborigines. They certainly have tried to exterminate each other in mortal combats.

Speaking first of North America, explorers point out that the entire area between the Alleghanies and the Rocky Mountains was at one time dotted with entrenched camps and fortifications, generally made of earth. There were ramparts, stockades and trenches. These bear witness of the intelligence of the builders, but also of the conditions of hostility that made such structures necessary. They must have been a race of warriors.

Fort Hill in Ohio furnishes an example of the forts of the ancient Moundbuilders. It rises, according to Marquis de Nadaillac, (Prehistoric America, p. 89), from an eminence overlooking the little river of Paint Creek. The walls enclose an area of 111 acres. Above the stream, which formed a natural defense, they are hardly four feet high, but everywhere else the height is six feet, and there are some thirty-five

3. And it came to pass that I beheld many generations pass away, after the manner of wars and contentions in the land; and I beheld many cities, yea, even that I did not number them.

---

feet thick. Several openings made entrance easy. One of them leads to a second enclosure, the walls of which have been destroyed, evidently by fire. Squires suggests that the dwellings of the inhabitants were in this square, and that two other enclosures, one circular and one semicircular, may have been used for meetings of the chiefs and for the performance of sacred rites. There are many others. Squires thinks that there was a continuous chain of fortifications, arranged with great intelligence and stretching diagonally across the state of Ohio from the sources of the Alleghany and of the Susquehanna in the State of New York to the Wabash river. Fort Ancien, forty-two miles from Cincinnati, is on the left bank of the Little Miami, and forms a central citadel behind a line of fortifications. It has been estimated that 628,000 cubic yards of earth were used in its construction. Nadaillac mentions that an observation has often been made "that the outline of these walls made a rough sketch of the continents of America." "A purely accidental coincidence," the Marquis exclaims, but to him the very existence of the Indians in America is probably merely an accidental coincidence. Autochthonous? Just like "Topsy."

South of Tehuantepec the Nahuas, of which the Aztecs were the most representative and best known tribe, occupied the Mexican table-land, generally called, Anahuac. Mr. Bancroft considers that their traditions take us back to the sixth century, and that they held sway until the 16th century. He says further:

"During the course of these ten centuries we may follow now definitely now vaguely the social, religious and political convulsions through these aborigines were doomed to pass. From small beginnings we see mighty political powers evolved, and these overturned and thrown into obscurity by other and rival unfoldings. Religious sects we see in like manner succeed each other, coloring their progress with frequent persecutions and reformations, not unworthy of old-world mediaeval fanaticism, as partisans of rival deities shape the popular superstition in conformity with their deeds. Wars long and bloody, are waged for plunder, for territory, and for souls; now to quell the insurrection of tributary princes, now to repel the invasion of outer barbarian hordes. Leaders, political and religious, rising to power with their nation, faction, city, or sect, are driven at their fall into exile, and thereby forced to seek their fortunes and introduce their culture among distant tribes. Outside bands, more or less barbarous, but brave and powerful, come to settle in Anahuac, and to receive, voluntarily or involuntarily, the benefits of its arts and sciences." (Native Races, vol. 2, p. 96)

The same may be said, in general terms, of the Mayas in Yucatan and the Central and South American stocks. The history of all of them is a tale of strife and war.

Verse 3. *After the manner of wars.* Nephi sees, in his vision, that many generations pass away "after the manner of wars"; that is, their time on earth was shortened by such conditions as wars necessarily bring about, viz., famine, pestilence, and general anarchy.

About the time when Nephi had this vision, Ezekiel, who was in Babylon, also had a vision concerning war, or rather the nations that made war, Egypt, Elam, Ashur, Meshech, Tubal, and others. He sees their end in the realm of the dead. They shall not lie with the mighty ones, "which are gone down to hell with their weapons of war." They may have been buried as heroes, with their swords under

4. And it came to pass that I saw a mist of darkness on the face of the land of promise; and I saw lightnings, and I heard thunderings, and earthquakes, and all manner of tumultuous noises; and I saw the earth and the rocks, that they rent; and I saw mountains tumbling into pieces; and I saw the plains of the earth, that they were broken up; and I saw many cities that they were sunk; and I saw many that they were burned with fire; and I saw many that did tumble to the earth, because of the quaking thereof.

5. And it came to pass after I saw these things, I saw the vapor of darkness, that it passed from off the face of the earth; and behold, I saw multitudes who had fallen because of the great and terrible judgments of the Lord.

2. *The coming of the Lord to the people of Nephi and his kingdom among them.*

6. And I saw the heavens open, and the Lamb of God descending out of heaven; and he came down and showed himself unto them.

7. And I also saw and bear record that the Holy Ghost fell upon twelve others; and they were ordained of God, and chosen.

---

their heads, but, Ezekiel says, "their iniquities shall be upon their bones, though they were the terror of the mighty in the land of the living." (Ez. 32:17-32) The ancient warrior nations cannot find a place of honor—not even in hell; that is, in the realm of the dead!

*I beheld many cities.* Nephi saw, notwithstanding wars and slaughter, many cities, in fact, so many that he did not number them. The vision cannot have been limited to a small area of the land of promise. It must have included the entire continents.

VERSES 4-5. In these verses the signs preceding the appearance of the Lord to his people in America are predicted. For the fulfillment see 3 Nephi, chapters 8-10.

VERSE 6. *Lamb of God descending.* See 3 Nephi 11:1-10.

VERSE 7. *Holy Ghost fell upon twelve others.* The word "others" calls attention to the fact that they are not the same as the twelve referred to in verse 9. For their names see 3 Nephi 19:4.

*Ordained of God, and chosen.* In his last discourse to the Twelve, our Lord said, in part, as recorded by John, "Ye have not chosen me, but I have chosen you, and ordained you." (John 15:16) "Chosen" (exelexamen) means selected after careful consideration. "Ordained" (ethaeka) means, to put someone into a condition to do a certain thing, as, for instance, when a ruler of a nation selects somebody and empowers him to represent the nation at home or abroad. They were "to go and bring forth fruit," relying on the promise that, "Whatsoever ye shall ask of the Father in my name, he may give it you." In Mark (3:14, 15) the mission of the Twelve is expressed thus: "And he ordained twelve, that they should be with him, and that he might send them forth to preach, and to have power to heal sicknesses, and to cast out devils [demons]." That was bringing forth "fruit."

8. And the angel spake unto me, saying: Behold the twelve disciples of the Lamb, who are chosen to minister unto thy seed.

9. And he said unto me: Thou rememberest the twelve apostles of the Lamb? Behold they are they who shall judge the twelve tribes of Israel; wherefore, the twelve ministers of thy seed shall be judged of them; for ye are of the house of Israel.

10. And these twelve ministers whom thou beholdest shall judge thy seed. And, behold, they are righteous forever; for because of

---

VERSE 8. *Disciples of the Lamb.* The twelve chosen here are called "disciples of the Lamb"; the twelve ordained in Palestine are called, "apostles of the Lamb."

VERSE 9. *They are they who shall judge.* The Twelve chosen in Palestine have been given authority to judge the twelve tribes of Israel, including the twelve ministers selected by our Lord to administer to the descendants of Lehi. "For," the angel says, "ye are of the house of Israel." Peter, it will be remembered on one occasion, desired to know what special reward the Twelve could expect. Our Lord replied: "Verily I say unto you, That ye which have followed me, in the regeneration when the Son of man shall sit in the throne of his glory, ye also shall sit upon twelve thrones, judging the twelve tribes of Israel." (Matt. 19:28; Luke 22:30. See also Luke 22:30 and Rev. 2:26)

VERSE 10. *And these twelve ministers . . . shall judge thy seed.* That is, the descendants of Nephi. These remarkable passages of the Scriptures give us some faint idea of the intended plan of government our Lord has in mind for his kingdom that is to come.

*They are righteous forever.* Our Lord, who knows the hearts of men, knew that these twelve disciples would remain faithful.

*Their garments are made white in his blood.* He knew that their faith in the atoning blood of the Lamb of God was of such a nature that the purity of their garments would not be sacrificed by them for the things of the world.

The expressions, "Their garments are made white in his blood"; and, "In the blood of the Lamb" (v. 11) are also found in the Revelation of John (7:14), where the angel explains that the multitudes standing before the throne, and before the Lamb, arrayed in white robes, are they which came out of great tribulation and now are serving God day and night in his temple. They, too, "have washed their robes and made them white in the blood of the Lamb." Therefore are they before the throne of God.

This exceedingly solemn imagery recalls to our minds the sacrifices of the pre-Christian dispensations, and particularly the sacrificial rite on the day of atonement under the Mosaic law. That was a day of fasting, confession of sins and atonement, followed by rejoicing.

On that day Aaron, or whoever held the office of high priest, clean and attired in priestly robes, came to the sanctuary with a young bullock for a sin offering and a ram for burnt offering. These he offered and thus made atonement for himself and his house. Some of the blood he sprinkled upon the mercyseat, i.e. the covering of the ark in the Holy of Holies. He was now prepared to officiate as mediator between God and the people.

In this office he presented two goats before the Lord at the door of the tabernacle of the congregation. By lot one was selected to be the Lord's; the other to be the "scapegoat." The high priest now laid his hands on the scapegoat and

THE FIRST BOOK OF NEPHI 109

their faith in the Lamb of God their garments are made white in his blood.

11. And the angel said unto me: Look! And I looked, and beheld three generations pass away in righteousness; and their garments were white even like unto the Lamb of God. And the angel said unto me: These are made white in the blood of the Lamb, because of their faith in him.

12. And I, Nephi, also saw many of the fourth generation who passed away in righteousness.

## 3. War between Nephites and Lamanites.

13. And it came to pass that I saw the multitudes of the earth gathered together.

14. And the angel said unto

---

thereby transferred symbolically the sins of the people upon him. The animal dedicated to the Lord was slain as a sin offering. The scapegoat was led into the wilderness and set free. And thus an atonement was made for the Priest and the sanctuary and for the entire people. According to the Talmud, in the evening the maidens all went forth arrayed in white garments, into the vineyards, where they rejoiced, singing and dancing, and inviting the young men to come and select their brides. They had, figuratively speaking, washed their clothes and made them white in the blood of the lamb, the prototype of our Lord, the Lamb of God. Their sins had been confessed, atoned for and forgiven.

It is sometimes said that the white robes are the righteousness of Christ, which is imputed to the believer in him, because of his faith. But that does not make good sense. The righteousness of our Lord cannot by any figure of speech be said to be washed clean in his blood. His blood was shed for us, not for himself. In Rev. 19:8 we read that the fine linen, clean and white, in which the bride of the Lamb is arrayed, "is the righteousness of the saints."

The "bride" is the Church (Eph. 5:23, 27, 32), and the "fine linen" in which she is arrayed is the individual righteousness of the members, acquired through the obedience of faith, while the adornment of the church of the world consists of purple and scarlet, gold, precious stones and pearls—all objects without any spiritual value. (Rev. 17:4; 18:16)

VERSES 11-12. *Three generations; the fourth generation.* Having seen, in his vision, the administration of our Lord and his disciples, Nephi now sees that the result of their work was that righteousness prevailed among the people for a period of three generations, but that in the fourth generation, i.e. in the fourth century after the manifestation of our Lord, unbelief and iniquity again predominated to such an extent that war, pestilence, famine and other calamities swept the land, until the Nephites became extinct. (Alma 45:9-12; Hel. 13:5-10; Morm. 6)

VERSE 13. *Multitudes of the earth,* are in this part of the vision, the descendants of Lehi. (Vs. 14, 15)

"Earth" in this verse stands for America. The Hebrews sometimes employed this word to denote their own country. (Compare Is. 28:22, quoted in Rom. 9:28; Ps. 72:8; James 5:17)

VERSES 14-15. *Gathered together to battle.* Nephi first sees the descendants of Lehi as multitudes developing in the land. Then he sees them divided into two

me: Behold thy seed, and also the seed of thy brethren.

15. And it came to pass that I looked and beheld the people of my seed gathered together in multitudes against the seed of my brethren; and they were gathered together to battle.

16. And the angel spake unto me, saying: Behold the fountain of filthy water which thy father saw; yea, even the river of which he spake; and the depths thereof are the depths of hell.

17. And the mists of darkness are the temptations of the devil, which blindeth the eyes, and hardeneth the hearts of the children of men, and leadeth them away into broad roads, that they perish and are lost.

18. And the large and spacious building, which thy father saw, is vain imaginations and the pride of the children of men. And a great and a terrible gulf divideth them; yea, even the word of the justice of the Eternal God, and the Messiah who is the Lamb of God, of whom the Holy Ghost beareth record, from the beginning of the world until this time, and from this time henceforth and forever.

---

main branches, later called Nephites and Lamanites. Finally he sees them at war, in battle array against each other.

VERSE 16. *The depths of hell.* The angel explains that this course of events is represented by the river which Lehi saw (I Ne. 8:13). This river was a filthy stream, originating in the depths of hell. (1 Ne. 15:26-29; Rev. 16:13, 14)

VERSE 17. *Mists of darkness.* The results of war are here set forth. They are, temptations, spiritual blindness, hardness of heart, deviation from the narrow path of righteousness and, finally, ruin.

VERSE 18. *Imagination and pride.* The angel once more calls the attention of Nephi to the large and spacious building. (I Ne. 8:26, 28) He is again reminded of the fact that it represents the "vain imaginations" ("wisdom") and the pride of the world.

The author of the Apocryphal book generally known as Ecclesiasticus, but also called, "The Wisdom of Jesus, the Son of Sirach," has something to say of both pride and humility. For instance:

"Pride is hateful before God and man: and by both [hatred and pride] doth one commit iniquity."

"Why is earth and ashes proud? . . . And he that is today a king tomorrow shall die."

"The beginning of pride is when one departeth from God, and his heart is turned away from his maker."

"For pride is the beginning of sin, and he that hath it shall pour out abomination." (Eccl. 10:7-13)

Concerning humility:

"My son, go on with thy business in meekness; so shalt thou be beloved of him that is approved."

"The greater thou art, the more humble thyself, and thou shalt find favor before the Lord."

"Mysteries are revealed unto the meek." (3:17-19)

19. And while the angel spake these words, I beheld and saw that the seed of my brethren did contend against my seed, according to the word of the angel; and because of the pride of my seed, and the temptations of the devil, I beheld that the seed of my brethren did overpower the people of my seed.

20. And it came to pass that I beheld, and saw the people of the seed of my brethren that they had overcome my seed; and they went forth in multitudes upon the face of the land.

## 4. Lamanites dwindle in unbelief and become dark.

21. And I saw them gathered together in multitudes; and I saw wars and rumors of wars among them; and in wars and rumors of wars I saw many generations pass away.

22. And the angel said unto me: Behold these shall dwindle in unbelief.

23. And it came to pass that I beheld, after they had dwindled in unbelief they became a dark, and loathsome, and a filthy people, full of idleness and all manner of abominations.

---

St. Paul cautions Timothy against appointing novices, that is, young converts, to responsible positions, "lest being lifted up with pride he fall into the condemnation of the devil." (1 Tim. 3:6) From which it is inferred that pride was the beginning of the fall of Lucifer.

> "Th' infernal serpent, he it was whose guile . . . deceived
> The mother of mankind, what time his pride
> Has cast him out from heaven with all his host
> Of rebel angels: by whose aid aspiring
> To set himself in glory 'bove his peers
> He trusted to have equalled the Most High,
> If he opposed: and with ambitious aim
> Against the throne and monarchy of God,
> Raised impious war in heaven, and battle proud,
> With vain attempt. Him th' Almighty Power
> Hurled headlong flaming from th' eternal sky,
> With hideous ruin and combustion, down
> To bottomless perdition."—Milton, Paradise Lost.

VERSES 19-20. In these two verses, Nephi sees the victory of the Lamanites over the Nephites, and the dispersion of the Lamanites throughout the land.

VERSE 21. *Multitudes.* These "multitudes" are the Lamanites after the battle of Cumorah. (Comp. Morm. 8:7, 8; Moroni 1:2)

VERSE 23. *They became dark.* The information given here, that moral degeneration, unbelief, etc., has some connection with the color of the skin, is important. It proves that so-called racial differences, although they may be due to deep-seated physiological processes and heredity, are not incompatible with the proposition that God "hath made of one blood all nations of men." (Acts 17:26)

## GENERAL NOTES

The Lamanites or Indians are just as much the children of our Father and God as we are. . . . They are of the house of Israel; they once had the Gospel delivered to them, they had the oracles of truth; Jesus came and administered to them after his resurrection, and they received and delighted in the gospel until the fourth generation when they turned away and became so wicked that God cursed them with this dark and benighted and loathsome condition. (Brigham Young, J. of D., vol. 14, p. 86)

## CHAPTER 13

*Many nations and kingdoms of the Gentiles, 1-3—A great and abominable church, 4-9—The wrath of God upon the descendants of Lehi, 10-11—Columbus and the history of America, 12-19—The Bible, 20-29—The Book of Mormon, 30-39—The first and the last, 40-42.*

## 1. *Many nations and kingdoms of the Gentiles.*

1. And it came to pass that the angel spake unto me, saying: Look! And I looked and beheld many nations and kingdoms.

2. And the angel said unto me: What beholdest thou? And I said: I behold many nations and kingdoms.

3. And he said unto me: These are the nations and kingdoms of the Gentiles.

---

Nephi, in the preceding chapter, has given an account of his vision of the Land of Promise, the manifestation of our Lord, and the degeneration of the descendants of Lehi. In this chapter he sees, in visions, the restoration of divine revelation to all men, Jews and Gentiles.

VERSE 1. *Many nations and kingdoms.* The angel first shows him the Gentile nations and governments, as they existed, probably, at the time when the Roman Catholic church began to become a world power, after the end of the western Roman empire. This is generally regarded as having come in 476 A.D., when Romulus Augustus was deprived of his office as the representative of the Emperor Zenis, who resided in Constantinople, and Odoager assumed the place of ruler over Italy. That was one of the great epochs in history. For the removal of the imperial power from Rome paved the way for the assumption of worldly sovereignty by the popes, as the Apostle Paul says would happen: "For the mystery of iniquity doth already work: only he who now letteth will let, until he be taken out of the way. And then shall that Wicked be revealed." (2 Thess. 2:7, 8) It came about gradually. In 607 Pope Boniface III was recognized as the spiritual ruler of the world, by Emperor Phocas. Later the ruling descendants of Charles Martel and the popes exchanged courtesies and gifts. The popes bestowed divine blessings and titles on the Carolingians, and these gave the popes large sections of Italy, which really were not theirs to give. Finally, in the year 800 A.D., Pope Leo III put a crown on the head of Charlemagne and proclaimed him the emperor of a new holy Roman empire, a proclamation which must have been in the nature of high treason, since the actual emperor still lived in Constantinople.

Gibbon says of these times: "The world beheld for the first time a Christian bishop invested with the prerogatives of a temporal prince: the choice of magistrates, the exercise of justice, the imposition of taxes and the wealth of the palace of Ravenna."

Nephi saw the condition of the gentile nations and governments during this critical time of history.

The kingdoms of the world being spread out, in this vision, as a map, before the eyes of the prophet, he sees a great and abominable church taking form. Its characteristics are given.

## 2. The foundation of a Church.

4. And it came to pass that I saw among the nations of the Gentiles the foundation of a great church.

5. And the angel said unto me: Behold the foundation of a church which is most abominable above all other churches, which slayeth the saints of God, yea, and tortureth them and bindeth them down, and yoketh them with a yoke of iron, and bringeth them down into captivity.

6. And it came to pass that I beheld this great and abominable church; and I saw the devil that he was the foundation of it.

7. And I also saw gold, and silver, and silks, and scarlets, and fine-twined linen, and all manner of precious clothing; and I saw many harlots.

8. And the angel spake unto me, saying: Behold the gold, and the silver, and the silks, and scarlets, and the fine-twined linen, and the precious clothing, and the harlots, are the desires of this great and abominable church.

9. And also for the praise of the world do they destroy the saints of God, and bring them down into captivity.

---

VERSE 4. *Among the Gentiles.* (1) He notes that the foundations are being laid among the Gentiles, not among the Jews.

VERSE 5. *Slayeth the Saints of God.* (2) He notes that it is a persecuting church, which brings thralldom, instead of liberty, into the world.

VERSE 6. *The devil the foundation of it.* (3) He notes that the organizer is no other than the devil.

VERSE 7-8. *Wealth and harlots, its possessions.* (4) He notes her wealth in gold and silver; her gorgeous apparel, silks and scarlets and fine-twined linen and all manner of precious clothing, and, in addition, a multitude of harlots.

VERSE 9. *For the praise of the world.* (5) He notes, finally, that this church occupies such a position relative to the world, that, by destroying the Saints of God and bringing them into captivity, she gains the praise of the world.

"*Saints.*" This refers, probably, to the Jews. The Jews, as a people, chosen by God and consecrated to his service, are called "saints." (See Psalms 16:3; 34:9; 89:5, 7; 106:16; and possibly Dan. 7:18, 21, 27.) The word has the same meaning of men and women consecrated to the service of the Lord, in the New Testament and the revelations given in our day, and is, therefore, applied to the members of the Church of our Lord. The persecuting church in the vision was to be the enemy of all the Saints of God, beginning with the children of Israel.

This persecuting church is identical with the "woman" in the Revelation by John (18:14), which is arrayed in purple and scarlet, and keeping a golden cup full of filthiness. She is also called "Babylon," from an inscription on her forehead.

It is an organization characterized by that condition of spiritual degeneracy described by St. Paul as a "falling away," the "man of sin," "perilous times," or, the reign of antichrist. (2 Thess. 2:3, 4; 1 Tim. 4:1-5; 2 Tim. 3:1-5)

From the early days of the Christian church, these prophecies have been understood to refer to the Roman Catholic church and papacy.

The reformers generally so understood them. In the dedication of the authorized version of King James, the translators say that the writings of that monarch "in defense of the Truth" "hath given such a blow unto that man of sin, as will not be healed," and in the Westminster Confession it is expressly stated that, the head of the Roman church is "that antichrist, that man of sin and son of perdition, that exalteth himself in the church against Christ and all that is called god." This is the view of Cranmer, Ridley, Latimer, Hooper, Luther, Calvin, Melancthon, Beza and many others; and of later writers, Hooker, Newton, Bengal, Doddridge, Michaelis, and others.

According to this school of interpreters of the prophecies, all the marks of the apostasy, all the characteristics of the man of sin, are found in the Roman church and the papal institution. The man of sin is represented as opposing and exalting himself above all that is called god, and this is considered fulfilled in the papal office, the incumbents of which exalt themselves above all authority, human and divine, claiming the title of "king of kings and lord of lords," and applying to themselves the words of the psalm: "All kings shall bow down before thee." The man of sin is seated in the "temple of God," showing himself as God, and this, they claim, is fulfilled in the papal office, where the popes assume divine attributes and prerogatives, such as infallibility and authority to forgive sins.

Even some Catholic writers agree with the interpretation here outlined. Hear, for instance Abbot Joachim, founder of a Catholic monastery, Giovanni del Fiore, in Calabria. He wrote toward the end of the 12th century:

"The church of Peter, the church of Christ which was full, is now empty. For, although she now seems full of people, yet they are not her people but strangers. They are not her sons, the citizens of the heavenly Jerusalem, but the sons of Babylon. What profits the name of Christ, where the power is wanting? The church is, as it were, widowed; there are but few or no bishops, who, to save the flock, expose themselves a prey to the wolves. Every man seeks his own, and not the things of Jesus Christ." . . .

"Where is there more contention, more fraud, more vice and ambition than among the clergy of our Lord? Therefore must judgment begin from the house of the Lord, and the fire go forth from his sanctuary, to consume it, in order that others may perceive what will be done with them, when he spares not even his sinning children." . . .

The abbot characterizes Pope Pascal II as a traitor of the church, who has reduced her to servitude. He says:

"Although the secular princes have wrested many things by violence from the church, as for example, the kingdoms of the Sicilies . . . yet, even the popes themselves have wrested many things from the princes . . . and the pope will not only long after temporal things, as belonging to him, but also after spiritual things [such] as do not belong to him, Thus will it come to pass, that he will seat himself in the temple of God, and, as a god, exalt himself above all that is called god, that is, above the authority of all prelates."

"Gold was brought to Christ, that he might have the means of fleeing to Egypt; myrrh, was offered him as if in allusion to his death; incense, that he might praise God; not that he might rise up against Herod, or fall as a burden upon Pharaoh; not that he might give himself up to sensual delights, or reward benefits received with gratitude. The vicegerents of Christ in these latter times care nothing for the incense; they seek only the gold, in order that they, with great Babylon, may mingle the goblets, and pollute their followers with their own uncleanliness."

Abbot Joachim held the view that antichrist would be a king in alliance with a pope. Such a pope, he thought, might come from the heretics and, armed seemingly, with power to perform miracles, ally himself with the antichristian secular power and stir up persecution, as Simon Magus is said to have incited Nero to kindle the fires of hatred against the Christians.

Robert Grosshead, an English, Catholic bishop, in 1250, A.D., wrote:

"To be sure, the pope, being the vicegerent of Christ, must be obeyed. But when a pope allows himself to be moved by motives of consanguinity, or any other secular interest, to do anything contrary to the precepts and will of Christ, then he who obeys him, manifestly separates himself from Christ and his body, the church, and from him who fills the apostolic chair as the representative of Christ. But, whenever universal obedience is paid him in such things, then comes the true, and complete apostasy—the time of antichrist." (See the History of the Church by Neander, vol. 4, pp. 185 and 222-26)

VERSES 7-8. *Many harlots.* In the Scriptures this word generally denotes a woman who is unfaithful to her husband. But it also means a nation, pledged to serve Jehovah, that turns away from him to worship other gods. (Hos. 1 and 2; Ez. 16 and 23) It also means an apostate church. (Rev. 17:1; 19:2; and perhaps Nah. 3) Sometimes the term is applied to a community that excels in commercial activities, as, for instance, Tyre. (Is. 23:17, 18) That city is said to be committing fornication with all the kingdoms of the world, referring to its far-flung commerce and shipping. Rahab, the woman in Jericho who befriended the two scouts of Joshua and who became one of the maternal ancestors of Jesus, is called a "harlot." (Josh. 2:1; Heb. 11:31) But it is possible that this is a misunderstanding of a word in the original which many mean a "hostess," an "inn-keeper." Some scholars favor this interpretation of it. It is highly improbable that the two spies of Joshua would have resorted to a house of ill-fame in order to obtain the information desired by the commanding general. It is also improbable that a common woman would have had the religious faith in God which Rahab had, who said: 'For the Lord your God, he is God in heaven above, and in earth beneath." Those are hardly the words of an outcast.

What does the word stand for in the vision of Nephi? Is it a literal or a figurative expression? If we interpret it at all, we must understand it literally. During the days of the apostate church, "harlots" were a merchandise, as were gold, silver, purple, scarlet, linen and precious clothing. That is according to the text.

Let us remember that the moral condition in the pagan world during the early centuries of our era was anything but one of purity. St. Paul describes it as it was in his day. (Rom. 1:21-32) Not only did immorality in its various revolting forms flourish privately, but it was legalized in some countries. Christianity tried to extirpate it, but, it stands to reason that when entire nations were incorporated in the church, individual immorality went in with the crowd. The efforts of the church were, therefore, not successful. And during the Middle ages deplorable conditions prevailed. It is claimed that during the crusades thousands of women accompanied the armies who went to fight for the holy places in Palestine. Prostitution came to be regarded as an indispensable social institution, and even high clergymen are said to have derived incomes from it. When all the facts are considered, it is clear that the vision of Nephi is literally true. "Harlots" were actually considered a desirable merchandise.

No aspersion against the Roman Catholic church, as she is today, is intended by these paragraphs. The vision of Nephi concerns the conditions of several centuries ago. The laws of today are aiming at suppression, and in this work the Roman Catholics are collaborating with other religious organizations.

### 3. *The wrath of God upon the descendants of Lehi.*

| | |
|---|---|
| 10. And it came to pass that I looked and beheld many waters; and they divided the Gentiles from the seed of my brethren. | 11. And it came to pass that the angel said unto me: Behold the wrath of God is upon the seed of thy brethren. |

VERSE 11. *The wrath of God upon the seed of thy brethren.* That explains the condition of the native communities in America at the time immediately preceding the incursion of the Spaniards. These came as the executors of divine judgment, just as the Babylonians at one time overran Palestine as the messengers of divine wrath. The descendants of Lehi had been given to understand repeatedly that they could prosper here only if they would keep the commandments of God. This they failed to do. As communities, they destroyed each other. By bloodshed they polluted the country that ought to have been dedicated to the Lord. They dwindled in unbelief. That caused darkness, both in body and soul. Mr. Bancroft, speaking of some of the Indians. observes:

"From the frozen, wind-swept plains of Alaska to the malaria-haunted swamps of Darien, there is not a fairer land than California; it is the neutral ground, as it were, of the elements, where hyperboreal cold, stripped of its rugged aspect, and equatorial heat, tamed to a genial warmth, meet as friends, inviting, all blustering laid aside. Yet if we travel northward from the Isthmus, we must pass by ruined cities and temples, traces of mighty peoples, who there flourished before a foreign civilization extirpated them. On the arid deserts of Arizona and New Mexico is found an incipient civilization. Descending from the Arctic sea we meet races of hunters and traders, which can be called neither primitive nor primordial, living after their fashion as men, not as brutes. It is not until we reach the Golden Mean in Central California that we find whole tribes subsisting on roots, herbs and insects; having no boats, no clothing, no laws, no God; yielding submissively to the first touch of the invader; held in awe by a few priests and soldiers." —(Native Races, vol. 1, p. 339)

That is strange. But from the wrath of the Lord, neither a congenial climate nor a bounteous soil can furnish man protection.

However, the Lamanites were by no means all bad. Compared to their conquerors, they were rather a superior race, if Las Casas, the great bishop of Chiapas, does not exaggerate. He writes:

"I was one of the first who went to America. Neither curiosity nor interest prompted me to undertake so long and so dangerous a voyage. The saving of souls of the heathen was my sole object. It was said that barbarous executions were necessary to punish or check the rebellion of the Americans. But to whom was this owing? Did not this people receive the Spaniards who first came among them with gentleness and humanity? Did they not show more joy in proportion, in lavishing treasure upon them, than the Spaniards did greediness in receiving it? Though they gave up to us their lands and riches, we would also take from them their wives and children and their liberty. To blacken the character of this unhappy people, their enemies assert that they are scarcely human beings. But it is we who ought to blush for having been less men and more barbarous than they . . . The Indians still remain untainted by many vices usual among Europeans, such as ambition, blasphemy, swearing, treachery, which have not taken place among them. They have scarcely an idea of these. (Quoted by Israel Worsley in, A View of the American Indian, p. 35)

Bancroft, too, finds much to admire in the natives. Speaking of the Nahuas, for instance, he describes them as frugal, kind to children and slaves, possessing

## 4. *Columbus and the history of America.*

12. And I looked and beheld a man among the Gentiles, who was separated from the seed of my brethren by the many waters; and I beheld the Spirit of God, that it came down and wrought upon the man; and he went forth upon the many waters, even unto the seed of my brethren, who were in the promised land.

---

a degree of civilization, ingenuity and aptitude for learning. And yet, with these and other redeeming qualities, they were vain as regards gorgeous clothing and costly feasts; they were ferocious in war and cruel in inflicting punishments. Thus, for instance, they would kill a couple of women who happened to quarrel in a public place. They were superstitious. They practiced human sacrifices. In fact, prisoners of war were often disposed of on the altar of some deity. On occasions, they ate human flesh, possibly as a religious rite.

By incessant warfare and acts of violence, they dimmed the light of revelation and polluted the land dedicated to the cause of God and liberty.

Therefore, the wrath of God was poured out upon them. But the wrath of God, was as always, intended for their salvation from total destruction.

VERSE 12. *A man among the Gentiles.* This man, who was separated from the Lamanites by many waters and who was prompted to cross those waters, was Columbus.

Christopher Columbus, or, as his name is written in Spanish, Cristóbal Cólon, was born in Genoa (or vicinity), Italy in the year 1436. Neither birth place nor birth date is known with absolute certainty. The parents were Domenico and Susanna Fontanarossa Colombo, both belonging to families of weavers.

Christopher Columbus, at a very early age went to sea. He became familiar with the routes followed by the merchantmen in the Mediterranean and the Atlantic. In 1477 he went to Iceland and Frisland (supposed to be the Faeroislands), and a few years later he spent some time on the Gold Coast, in Africa.

Notwithstanding his life as a sailor, Columbus found time to study languages, astronomy, and the science of navigation. He became also an expert map maker —all necessary accomplishments for the fulfilment of his mission.

In 1470, Columbus, after a battle with pirates, escaped to Lisbon, where many prominent geographers and navigators lived. Here, at a religious service, he saw a young, noble lady, Philippa, the daughter of the governor of Porto Santo, then deceased. They were married, and for some time they lived with her mother on the estate. This was situated on a little island three hundred miles out in the ocean. The governor had left a number of maps and valuable notes on navigation, and Columbus studied these thoroughly. In this quiet resort, the thought of going out west on the mysterious expanse of water may well have ripened in the mind of the young adventurer.

At this time, Genoa, Florence and Venice commanded the commerce of the Mediterranean. They brought silks, and other costly fabrics, and spices from Persia and India. These were carried by camels across the deserts to the Red Sea and the Nile, and then by ships over the Mediterranean to Europe. Those who commanded the trade routes became wealthy and powerful. The great question of the age was, therefore, how to reach the East by some cheaper and more convenient route than by the sea. Columbus was one of the few at that time, who believed that the East, with its fabulous wealth of gold, perfumes and spices, could be found by sailing west. Consequently, he laid his plan before the king of Portugal. This monarch seems to have looked upon the daring scheme with favor. But he could not afford to invest large sums on a problematic enterprise, the country being impoverished by war. He submitted the question to learned men who, as usual, did not agree. A trial expedition was sent out secretly, and the leaders of this dishonest attempt to rob Columbus of the fruit of his labors, returned after a few days and reported that you might as well expect to find land in the sky as in that waste of waters. Columbus, on learning that the Portugese king had played a trick, decided to appeal to the rulers of Spain.

During seven long years Columbus importuned King Ferdinand for a hearing. But he was generally regarded as a visionary. Even the children in the streets knew him as one mentally unsound. When, at last, the learned council condescended to make a report, it was to the effect that the plan was too foolish to merit attention. "It is absurd," they said, "to believe that there are people on the other side of the world, walking with their heels upward, and their heads hanging down. And then, how can a ship get there? The torrid zone through which they must pass, is a region of fire, where the very waves boil. And even if a ship could perchance get around there safely, how could it ever get back? Can a ship sail uphill?"

With such arguments the wise men of Spain were about to drive Columbus out of the country. In fact, he decided to go to France. But, fortunately, the queen, Isabella, had as much to say in such matters as her royal consort. And she listened to friends of Columbus. She was even willing to raise money on her jewels to defray the expenses of a voyage. But this was not required of her. Luis de Santangel, who held the keys to the treasury of Aragon, looked after the finances. The agreement between the regents and Columbus was signed on April 17, 1492. Columbus shed tears of joy. He had reached the goal, after eighteen long years of labor, disappointments and heartache.

Columbus is described as a man of commanding presence, tall and powerful, fair, ruddy complexion, and blue-grey eyes. By the time he sailed for the new world, his hair had turned white. His bearing was courteous and his conversation was captivating. Notwithstanding all discouragement, he never lost faith in his divine calling and mission.

It was on August 3, 1492, that Columbus with three vessels—the Santa Maria, the Pinta, and the Niña, with 90 souls on board—set out from Palos, Spain. It was on October 12, the same year that Columbus with a retinue of officers and men set foot on the beach of an island which he named San Salvador. Columbus was dressed in a gorgeous military suit of scarlet, embroidered with gold, for how did he know whether he was not to meet some splendidly arrayed potentate in this land? Had he not arrived in India, of which country Marco Polo and others had told such wonderful tales? At all events, he was prepared. But as soon as he landed, he prostrated himself and on bended knees kissed the ground. Then he planted a cross and took possession of the country in the name of Ferdinand and Isabella. The natives who witnessed these to them incomprehensible ceremonies, he called Indians, because he supposed that he had reached an island off the coast of India.

The nationality and birthplace of Columbus have frequently been discussed. A few years ago, on January 14, 1922, to be exact, an Associated Press dispatch from Lisbon, Portugal, announced that a member of the Portuguese Academy of Science, Senor Patrocinio Ribeiro, in an address to the academy, had maintained that he was born in Portugal.

That announcement came shortly after a prelate, the Right Rev. Mgr. Rey Soto, during a visit in New York, had stated that Columbus was of Jewish lineage. He claimed that this had been proved by documents at the home of ancestors of the great sailor, in Spain. He said Columbus knew this but concealed it because of the persecution that raged against the Jews at that time.

13. And it came to pass that I beheld the Spirit of God, that it wrought upon other Gentiles; and they went forth out of captivity, upon the many waters.

---

There is nothing in itself improbable in the assumption that Columbus had the blood of Israel in his veins. On the contrary, his character and his mission were of such nature as to lend some color to that assumption. Nephi saw him "among" the Gentiles, but that does not necessarily mean that he was a Gentile. I am inclined to the view that Nephi, when stating that he was "separated from the seed of my brethren by the many waters," in reality says that they were brethren and that was the main element that separated them from each other. But, be that as it may, the following lines are of interest in this connection:

"The story of the Jews in America begins with Christopher Columbus. On Aug. 2, 1492, more than 300,000 Jews were expelled from Spain . . . and on Aug. 3, the next day, Columbus set sail for the west, taking a group of Jews with him . . . Columbus himself tells us that he consorted much with Jews. The first letter he wrote detailing his discoveries was to a Jew. Indeed, the eventful voyage itself which added to men's knowledge and wealth 'the other half of the earth,' was made possible by Jews.

"The pleasant story that it was Queen Isabella's jewels which financed the voyage has disappeared under cool research. There were three Maranos or 'secret Jews' who wielded great influence at the Spanish Court: Luis de Santangel, who was an important merchant of Valencia and a 'farmer' of the royal taxes; his relative Gabriel Sanchez, who was the royal treasurer; and their friend, the royal chamberlin, Juan Cabrero . . . Santangel craved permission to advance the money himself, which he did, 17,000 ducats in all, about $20,000, perhaps equal to $160,000 today.

"Associated with Columbus in the voyage were at least five Jews: Luis de Torres, interpreter; Marco, the surgeon; Bernal, the physician; Alonzo de la Calle, and Gabriel Sanchez . . . Luis de Torres was the first man ashore . . . He settled in Cuba." (The International Jew, Dearborn, Mich., 1920, p. 33)

On January 4, 1493, Columbus set sail on the Nina for Spain, having left 40 men at Fort Nativity, as a beginning of a colony. He reached the harbor of Palos, in Spain, on March 15. His first voyage ended in a blaze of glory. The story of his return and achievements flew from mouth to mouth. Bells were ringing, and torches were blazing in the streets at night. Their royal majesties wept for joy, when thinking of the palaces and riches that would be theirs, as their reward for having beaten the Moors at Granada and driven the Jews out of Spain.

Columbus made three more voyages. He cruised in the Caribbean, discovered the island of Trinidad and the South American coast at the delta of the Orinoco, and he coasted along the coast of Honduras. But the vision of Nephi does not include the later experiences of Columbus. In opening the way across the deep between the Gentiles in the Old World and the descendants of Lehi in the New, his mission was fulfilled.

VERSE 13. *Other Gentiles.* Other than those with whom the lot of Columbus had been cast, others than the Latin race. Others were also to be urged by the Spirit to go forth on the waters. This calls our attention to the Cabots, whose discoveries were as momentous as those of Columbus.

John Cabot, an Italian navigator who had moved to Bristol, England, came to the conclusion that since the degrees of longitude are shorter towards the pole than at the equator, the shortest route to India would be in a north-westerly direction. King Henry VII authorized him to try. He reached the coast of Labrador, and supposed that he had come to the kingdom of Tartary, just as Columbus imagined he had reached India. This was in 1497.

Sebastian Cabot, son of John, had accompanied his father on this voyage. He continued the explorations after him. The same year in which Columbus found the coast of South America and Vasco de Gama rounded the Cape of Good Hope, on the way to India, Sebastian Cabot discovered New Foundland and coasted as far south as Chesapeake Bay. He gave England a continent, but no one, at that time, considered his achievement worth while. Nobody now knows even his burial place.

*Spirit of God.* According to the vision of Nephi, it was the Spirit of God that prompted first Columbus and then the Gentiles to go forth upon the waters.

That Columbus considered himself inspired is well authenticated history. The following from an enlightening article by Mark Petersen on, "American History and Nephi's Vision," published in the Deseret News, March 25, 1933, proves that he was very much conscious of his divine calling:

"Many biographies have been written concerning Columbus. We take one at random, and quote from 'Columbus, Don Quixote of the Seas,' by Jacob Wasserman, translated into English from the German by Eric Sutton and published in Boston:

"On page 18 of this book, Columbus is directly quoted as follows:

" 'From my first youth onward, I was a seaman, and have so continued until this day. Wherever ship has been I have been. I have spoken and treated with learned men, priests and laymen, Latin and Greeks, Jews and Moors, and with many men of other faiths. The Lord was well disposed to my desire, and he bestowed upon me courage and understanding; knowledge of seafaring he gave me in abundance; of astrology as much as was needed, and of geometry and astronomy likewise. Further, he gave me joy and cunning in drawing maps and thereon cities, mountains, rivers, islands and the harbors, each one in its place. I have seen and truly I have studied all books, cosmographies, histories, chronicles and philosophies, and other arts, for which our Lord with provident hand unlocked my mind, sent me upon the seas, and gave me fire for the deed. Those who heard of my emprise called it foolish, mocked me, and laughed. But who can doubt but that the HOLY GHOST INSPIRED ME?' "

"On page 46 of the same book, we read that in the year of his success, Columbus wrote upon one occasion to King Ferdinand: 'I CAME TO YOUR MAJESTY AS THE EMISSARY OF THE HOLY GHOST.' "

John Fiske has this to say: "It was no doubt the symptom of a reaction against his misfortunes that he grew more and more mystical in these days, consoling himself with the belief that he was a chosen instrument in the hands of Providence for enlarging the bounds of Christendom." In this mood, Columbus, the historian says, studied the prophecies and attributed his discoveries to miraculous inspiration.

VERSE 13. *Out of captivity.* The "other" Gentiles are here referred to as captives, and their going forth is their liberation. On this subject, Mr. Petersen, in the article just quoted, says:

"The history of the Pilgrims and Puritans gives ample evidence of the type of captivity they left to come to a land of freedom and liberty. However, we quote herein a story published in the 1933 manual for deacons quorums of the Church to illustrate that the captivity was literal—even a captivity behind jail doors."

The story follows:

"If one were to search among all the Prophet Joseph Smith's progenitors for one who best typified his righteous zeal for true freedom and his dauntless devotion to

14. And it came to pass that I beheld many multitudes of the Gentiles upon the land of promise; and I beheld the wrath of God, that it was upon the seed of my brethren; and they were scattered before the Gentiles and were smitten.

---

truth, perhaps no finer exemplification could be found than his fifth great-grandfather, the Rev. John Lathrop.

"He was a young minister of the Church of England, happily married, with a family of beautiful children. He labored faithfully until in his conscience he felt he could no longer approve the things he must teach. He resigned his position, left the church, and in 1623 became pastor of the First Independent Church of London.

"Persecution raged against him and his little band of devoted followers. They were forced to meet secretly, to escape the anger of the opposing bishop. One day, as they met in worship, they were discovered by agents of the bishop, who suddenly invaded their meeting place, seized forty-two of their number, and sent them in fetters to the old Clink Prison, in Newgate. Finally all but Mr. Lathrop were released on bail, but he was deemed too dangerous to be set at liberty.

"During these months of his imprisonment a fatal sickness had seized upon his wife, and she was about to die. Upon his urgent entreaty the bishop consented for him to visit his dying wife, if he would promise to return. He reached home in time, gave her his blessing, and she passed away. True to his promise, he returned to prison. His poor, orphaned children wandered about in helpless misery, until some one suggested that they appeal to the bishop at Lambeth. One can picture the mournful procession as they came before him, and made known their sorrowful plight.

" 'Please, sir,' they cried piteously, 'release our father or we too shall die.' The bishop's heart was softened and touched with pity, and he granted to John Lathrop his freedom, if he would promise to leave the country and never return.

"Gathering around him his children and 32 of his congregation, he sailed to America, settling in New England, where he was warmly welcomed and soon became one of the leaders among the Puritans of his day."

The literal fulfilment in all its details of this prophetic vision is a marvelous feature of it.

VERSE 14. *Multitudes of the Gentiles upon the Land of Promise.* With this paragraph the story of the vision of Nephi is focused more particularly on the United States. The prophet sees multitudes gathered here.

*The First Settlers.* The explorations of the Cabots proved the beginning of the colonization of North America. Before the close of the 17th century, the French had explored the Great Lakes, the Fox, Maumee, Wabash, Wisconsin, and Illinois rivers, and the Mississippi from the Falls of St. Anthony to the Gulf. They had traversed a vast region from New Foundland to Texas. In 1688, the population of this "New France" was estimated at 11,000.

British sailors and colonists were also moved upon to settle in the new country. Sir Martin Frobisher, in 1576, entered Baffin Bay and declared the country in that region to be the possession of the British crown. Sir Francis Drake, from a mountain top in Panama, gazed upon the Pacific, and decided that he would sail on that ocean. He went through the straits of Magellan and then coasted north as far as Oregon. Sir Humphry Gilbert and his half-brother Sir Walter Raleigh planted colonies here and hunted for gold and pearls, and learned to use tobacco. At that time England was threatened by the Spanish Armada, and when Sir Walter returned to America, after an absence of three years, he found that his family and colony had perished. How, history does not say. In 1607, the London Company sent a colony to South Virginia, where Captain Newport founded the first permanent English

15. And I beheld the Spirit of the Lord, that it was upon the Gentiles, and they did prosper and obtain the land for their inheritance; and I beheld that they were white, and exceeding fair and beautiful, like unto my people before they were slain.

16. And it came to pass that I, Nephi, beheld that the Gentiles who had gone forth out of captivity did humble themselves be-

---

settlement in the United States. It was called Jamestown in honor of the King of England. Another trading concern, the Plymouth Company, sent settlers to North Virginia.

In 1609, Captain Henry Hudson, an English navigator in Dutch service, entered the Hudson River. The Hollanders claimed the territory called New Netherland, where the foundations of the city of New York were laid, in 1613.

The first permanent settlement in Delaware was made near Wilmington by Swedish colonists, in 1638, on a tract of land called New Sweden. Swedes also established the first settlement in Pennsylvania, but these settlements were soon absorbed by the Hollanders and then by the English.

The period between 1607 and 1775 saw the English settlements expand and become thirteen prosperous colonies. They were: Virginia, Massachusetts, New Hampshire, Connecticut, Rhode Island, New York, New Jersey, Pennsylvania, Delaware, Maryland, South Carolina, North Carolina and Georgia. They had little in common. Each colony had its own problems, its own struggles. But this seeming disorder was but transitory. The Divine Architect was assembling his material for a new nation, destined to raise the Ensign of liberty to all the world.

VERSE 15. *The Gentiles did prosper and obtain the land.* According to the vision of Nephi, the wrath of God was upon the descendants of his brothers, wherefore they were scattered, while the Spirit of the Lord was upon the Gentiles, and they obtained the land as their inheritance. The title is therefore of divine origin. It is indisputable.

—*White, fair, and beautiful.* Those characteristics seem to point to the Anglo-Saxon race. In this connection a few statistics may be of interest. The entire population of the United States in 1950 was, according to the census, 150,697,361. Of these, 343,410 were Indians. Consequently, 150,353,951 were immigrants or descendants of immigrants.

In 1950 there were in the United States 33,750,653 persons born in foreign countries, some as follows:

| | | | |
|---|---|---|---|
| England and Wales | 2,027,845 | Netherlands | 374,668 |
| North Ireland | 45,228 | Belgium | 138,391 |
| Ireland (Eire) | 2,396,456 | Switzerland | 287,175 |
| Norway | 854,674 | France | 361,589 |
| Sweden | 1,189,639 | Germany | 4,726,946 |
| Denmark | 426,607 | Canada | 2,982,318 |

This is an index to the origin of a majority of the population in the United States, counting both foreign born and their descendants.

—*Like unto my people.* Nephi saw the resemblance between this race and the Children of Israel. We know that the blood of Israel is flowing in the veins of a great many of these immigrants.

fore the Lord; and the power of the Lord was with them.

17. And I beheld that their mother Gentiles were gathered together upon the waters, and upon the land also, to battle against them.

18. And I beheld that the power of God was with them, and also that the wrath of God was upon all those that were gathered together against them to battle.

19. And I, Nephi, beheld that the Gentiles that had gone out of captivity were delivered by the power of God out of the hands of all other nations.

VERSES 16-19. The discovery and settlement of America, and more particularly, the United States, was the work of the Lord.

"Our fathers, under His inspiration, gave us the constitution of our country, the bill of rights which defines our privileges and places limitations beyond which we may not go. Liberty, when carried to the extreme, results in license. I want to impress upon this congregation, my brethren and sisters who are here, that the Lord our God has been the author of it all. It was he who led you from your native lands. You people from the green fields and lanes of England, you did not leave your homes because you did not love your native land. You had fought for it, defended it, and were ready to fight for it again. You people from Scotland, you people from Ireland and Wales, from Germany and the islands of the sea, oh, if I only had the time to go back and tell you I could show you that the whole story of your lives had been written by the finger of God. So we are here; here, thank the Lord, citizens of the best government in the world. We are here, members of the Church of Christ our Lord which has been restored through the medium of heavenly messengers who had authority to give to men upon earth, the keys of the holy priesthood. What for? For the redemption of the human family. Whether men believe it or not these things are true, and ultimately they will believe it, and there is no power either in earth or hell that can stay the progress of the Church, unless its people prove recreant to the covenants that they have entered into with our Father who is in heaven. Just so, there is no power that can wreck the government that God has established in this country unless it be the people themselves, and that I do not expect nor believe can occur.

"The Lord in his scripture tells us that no one can come to this land unless he be brought or directed by the Spirit of the Lord, and so he has brought this people here. He brought the faith of the devoted Puritans of New England; he brought the patriotism of the Dutch at New York; he brought the gallantry of the cavaliers of Virginia; the light-hearted energy of the French of New Orleans. Just the kind of composite body of men to establish a government that could not be dominated by any particular race or tongue, but made composite, that all men might be welcomed to it, live under and enjoy its privileges." (President Anthony W. Ivins, Conference Sermon, Oct. 1932, pp. 107-108)

George Washington acknowledged the sovereignty of the Lord and the importance of religion as a condition of national success. In his Farewell Address he expresses this as follows:

"Of all the dispositions and habits which lead to political prosperity, religion and morality are indispensable supports. In vain would that man claim the tribute of patriotism who should labor to subvert these great pillars of human happiness, these firmest props of the duties of men and citizens. The mere politician, equally with the pious man, ought to respect and cherish them. A volume could not trace all their connections with private and public felicity. Let it simply be asked—and I ask it of you—Where is the security for property, for reputation, for life, if the sense of religious obligation desert the oaths, which are the instruments of investigation in

## 5. *The Bible.*

20. And it came to pass that I, Nephi, beheld that they did prosper in the land; and I beheld a book, and it was carried forth among them.

21. And the angel said unto me: Knowest thou the meaning of the book?

22. And I said unto him: I know not.

23. And he said: Behold it proceedeth out of the mouth of

---

courts of justice? And let us with caution indulge the supposition that morality can be maintained without religion. Whatever may be conceded to the influence of refined education on minds of peculiar structure, reason and experience both forbid us to expect that national morality can prevail in exclusion of religious principle."

VERSE 17. *Mother Gentiles . . . to battle against them.* In verses 17-19 the prophet beholds in his vision the war by which the independence of the United States was established: (1) The Gentile immigrants humbled themselves before the Lord. (2) The "mother gentiles" were defeated, because the wrath of God was upon them. (3) The Gentile immigrants were delivered by the power of God "out of the hands of all nations."

The conflict known as the American War of Independence was precipitated (April 19, 1775) when General Gage sent a force from Boston to seize provisions at Concord, Mass., and to capture the two prominent leaders, Samuel Adams and John Hancock. On June 15, George Washington was appointed Commander of the Colonial forces, and on July 4, 1776, the Declaration of Independence dissolved allegiance to the British crown. In July 1778, the Americans were strengthened by the presence of a French fleet outside New York, and a considerable land force. Cornwallis, trapped in the Yorktown peninsula, where LaFayette's forces were joined by Washington's, and by 4,000 under Rochambeau, and 3,000 from De Grasse's fleet in the West Indies, surrendered on October 19, 1781. The treaty of peace was signed in Paris, September 3, 1783. By this treaty the independence of the United States was recognized, and the colonies received an addition of all the territory between the Alleghanies and the Mississippi. New York was evacuated by the British on November 25, 1783. The battles on the waters were mostly confined to privateering. John Paul Jones, with a few vessels, made important captures in British waters.

It was thus that the land was "redeemed by the shedding of blood." (D. and C. 101:79, 80; 77: 2 N. 1:7)

VERSE 20. *And I beheld a book.* A book appears in notable visions of other prophets of old. Daniel is instructed regarding the contents of the "Scripture of Truth," containing a prophetic history of the world to the last days. (Dan. 10 and 11) Ezekiel was shown a book, which he was commanded to "eat," or, as we should say, "digest," containing a message to the house of Israel. (Ez. 5:1) Zechariah (5:1) saw a "flying roll," which contained a "curse" upon the land because of the transgressions of the inhabitants. And John the Revelator mentions the "Book of Life" (3:5; 13:8; 20:12); also a sealed book (5:1), containing the history of the world in prophetic symbols, and a "little book" (a codicil, as it were). (Rev. 10:2, 8:11)

VERSE 23. *It proceedeth out of the mouth of a Jew.* The book which Nephi saw was the Old Testament, and more especially the Law, also called the "Torah," as given to the world by Ezra.

a Jew. And I, Nephi, beheld it; and he said unto me: The book that thou beholdest is a record of the Jews, which contains the covenants of the Lord, which he hath made unto the house of Israel; and it also containeth many of the prophecies of the holy prophets; and it is a record like unto the engravings which are upon the plates of brass, save there are not so many nevertheless, they contain the covenants of the Lord, which he hath made unto the house of Israel; where-

fore, they are of great worth unto the Gentiles.

24. And the angel of the Lord said unto me: Thou hast beheld that the book proceedeth forth from the mouth of a Jew; and when it proceeded forth from the mouth of a Jew it contained the plainness of the gospel of the Lord, of whom the twelve apostles bear record; and they bear record according to the truth which is in the Lamb of God.

25. Wherefore, these things go forth from the Jews in purity

Ezra was one of the most prominent Jews in the Babylonian captivity, a descendant of Aaron and in all probability born in Babylon. It was through his influence, humanly speaking, that the return of the exiles was accomplished. (Ez. 7:6 and 28) He led, personally, the second great company to Jerusalem.

Jews and Christians alike regard Ezra as one of the great prophets of the Lord. Among the Jews there is a saying, something like this, "If the Law had not been given by Moses, Ezra was worthy, and by him it would have been given. And Christian authors, such as Irenaeus, Tertullian, Clement of Alexandria, and others actually thought that the Old Testament had become lost during the Babylonian captivity, and that it was restored through Ezra, by divine revelation. Modern scholars do not accept that view, but it is thought that he collected copies of the sacred manuscripts extant, and that he, and other learned men, by scholarly criticism, determined the text and the canon. They accepted twenty-two books as divine. They divided them into three parts, the Law, the Prophets and the Hagiographa or Psalms, a division to which our Lord refers as follows, "All things must be fulfilled, which were written in the law of Moses, and in the prophets, and in the psalms, concerning me." (Luke 24:44) It is also thought probable that Ezra and the other members of the governing council, such as Haggai and Zechariah, edited the manuscripts, and added such passages as could not have been written by the authors of the sacred books themselves, as for instance the account of the death of Moses, etc.

In the book of Nehemiah there is a very impressive account of the acceptance of the Word of God by the people, that may be compared to a similar scene at Sinai, when the Law was given through Moses. (Ex. 24:3-8) In the Book of Nehemiah we read that the people asked Ezra to bring the Book of the Law. He did so. The people were gathered at the water gate (on the east). Ezra and a number of the priesthood occupied a platform. From this, Ezra, after a fervent prayer, read "in the book of the law of God distinctly and gave the sense, and caused them to understand the reading. (Neh. 8:1-8) The reading occupied several hours every day for seven days (v. 18). And on another occasion, "And they stood up in their place, and read in the book of the Law of the Lord their God one fourth part of the day; and another fourth part they confessed and worshiped the Lord their God." (Neh. 9:3)

This was the beginning, as far as known, of the Jewish divine services, with prayer, Bible reading and preaching from Scripture texts, a form that has been

unto the Gentiles, according to the truth which is in God.

26. And after they go forth by the hand of the twelve apostles of the Lamb, from the Jews unto the Gentiles, thou seest the foundation of a great and abominable church, which is most abominable above all other churches; for behold, they have taken away from the gospel of the Lamb many parts which are plain and most precious; and also many covenants of the Lord have they taken away.

27. And all this have they done that they might pervert the right ways of the Lord, that they might blind the eyes and harden the hearts of the children of men.

28. Wherefore, thou seest that after the book hath gone forth through the hands of the great and abominable church, that

perpetuated in Christian churches, and which should never be abandoned, for the obvious reason that it is the word of God that is the life of the Church.

We can now understand why the Prophet Nephi sees the ancient Scriptures proceeding from the "mouth of a Jew." His prophetic vision was fulfilled in the year 444 B.C.

VERSE 26. *Many parts taken away.* We are here informed that this book, as it came from the mouth of the Jew, contained the same gospel of the Lord of which the Apostles bear record. That is to say, the prophecies and the rites, the clothes, the buildings, the sacrifices, all were typical of the plan of salvation which became a reality in the life, the teachings, the death, and glorification of our Lord, as recorded in the New Testament. The Apostle Paul, in the letter to the Hebrews, makes this very clear.

But after this book, together with the record of the Apostles, goes forth "by the hand [not mouth] of the Apostles" (v. 26), then the ecclesiastical organization comes into existence, which has "taken away from the gospel of the Lamb many parts which are plain and most precious." (v. 26) The object of this mutilation is stated in verse 27.

VERSE 28. *Many plain and precious things taken away from the book.* This, as I understand it, refers to books and, perhaps, parts of books, that have been destroyed, rather than to the corruption of the texts in the books extant.

Many modern scholars are changing their attitude toward the Bible. They admit, for instance, that the books of the New Testament almost without exception belong to the first century, although they were not gathered together in a volume, as we know them, until a couple of centuries later. Archeological finds prove that the grammar, the vocabulary, the form of the letters, the diction and the historical background stamp them as products of that early age. They also admit that in all essential particulars the text we have is identical with the original writings. They consider these conclusions established by the scientific methods of criticism applied to thousands of manuscripts.[1]

There are discrepancies. And even apparent contradictions. In the Old Testament, and particularly in the Chronicles, dates and names are sometimes hopelessly changed. In fact, the entire chronology of the Old Testament, before the Temple of Solomon, is guesswork. Usher calculates the time from the creation to the flood

[1]Dr. Kennicott collated 630 MSS for his critical edition of the Hebrew Bible. De Rossi collated 734 more. And upwards of 1600, 26 complete, have been examined for modern editions of the New Testament and 1364 for the Old. These figures are given by Dr. Joseph Angus, but since that time many more manuscripts have come to light.

there are many plain and pre- | book, which is the book of the
cious things taken away from the | Lamb of God.

---

to be, 1656 years; the Septuagint makes it, 2262 years; Josephus, 2256 years. Similar discrepancies appear in the following periods. From the flood to the call of Abraham, Usher, 427 years; Sept., 1207; Josephus, 1062. From the call of Abraham to the exodus, Usher, 430, Sept. 425, Josephus, 445. From the exodus to the foundation of the temple of Solomon, Usher, 479, Sept. 601, Josephus, 621. From the temple of Solomon, to the restoration of Cyrus, Usher, 476, Sept. 476, Josephus, 493. From the restoration by Cyrus to our Lord, Usher, 536, Sept. 537, and Josephus, 534 years. That is, the entire time from the creation to the beginning of our era appears thus:

> Usher ..................................................4004 years
> Septuagint ........................................5508 years
> Josephus ..........................................5411 years

To this may be added that the Samaritan text makes the period between the creation and the exodus 2809 years.[2]

In the New Testament, too, there are numerous variations. A few of these will have to suffice for illustrations. In Matthew 19:17: "Why callest thou me good?" Griesbach notes another reading: "Why asketh thou me concerning the good?" The doxology in the Lord's prayer, "For thine is the kingdom, and the power, and the glory, for ever. Amen," is lacking in some MSS. Matt. 16:2, 3 is omitted in some MSS. The last 12 verses of Mark are missing in some MSS. The story of an

---

[2]A very ingenious hypothesis has been suggested by Victor Rydberg, a Swedish scholar. He believed that the translators of the Septuagint, who were working in Egypt by order of an Egyptian ruler, endeavored to bring their chronology to some extent in harmony with the Egyptian calculations, in order to make the Hebrew Bible more acceptable to Egyptian historians. He draws the following tables:

| Egyptian: | | Septuagint: | |
|---|---|---|---|
| First dynasty | 263 years | Adam | 230 years |
| Second dynasty | 302 years | Seth | 205 years |
| Third dynasty | 214 years | Enos | 190 years |
| Fourth dynasty | 284 years | Kenan | 170 years |
| Fifth dynasty | 165 years | Mahalaleel | 165 years |
| Sixth dynasty | 198 years | Jared | 162 years |
| Seventh dynasty | 53(?) years | Enoch | 165 years |
| Eighth dynasty | 146 years | Methuselah | 187 years |
| Ninth dynasty | 409 years | Lamech | 188 years |
| Tenth dynasty | 185 years | Noah | 600 years |
| Eleventh dynasty | 43 years | | |
| Total | 2262 years | Total | 2262 years |
| Twelfth dynasty | 160 years | Shem | 102 years |
| Thirteenth dynasty | 453 years | Arphaxad | 135 years |
| Fourteenth dynasty | 184 years | Kenan | 130 years |
| Fifteenth dynasty | 284 years | Selah | 130 years |
| Sixteenth dynasty | 511 years | Heber | 134 years |
| Seventeenth dynasty | 151 years | Peleg | 130 years |
| Eighteenth dynasty | 34 years | Regu | 132 years |
| | | Serug | 130 years |
| | | Nahor | 179 years |
| | | Terah | 70 years |
| | | Till Exodus of Abraham | 75 years |
| | | Till Jacob goes to Egypt | 215 years |
| | | Till Exodus | 215 years |
| Total | 1777 years | Total | 1777 years |

These tables illustrate, I believe, the futility of solving the problem of the Hebrew chronological data, even with the aid of Egyptian time tables.

29. And after these plain and | it goeth forth unto all the nations
precious things were taken away | of the Gentiles; and after it goeth

---

angel "moving" the water of Bethesda (John 5:4) is absent from some MSS. Many omit the story of the woman in John 8:1-11. Peter's visit to the grave (Luke 24:12) is omitted in some MSS, but Griesbach considers the verse genuine.

Such are the variations in the text. Dr. Joseph Angus remarks: "In the 7959 verses of the New Testament there are not more than ten or twelve various readings of great importance, and these affect not the doctrines of the Scriptures, but only the number of proof passages in which they are revealed."

Such variations are easily accounted for. Many of them are accidental. A copyist can accidentally mistake one letter for another. He can happen to leave out words or lines, or repeat sentences. Sometimes the changes are made deliberately, in order to correct grammar, or perhaps establish proof of a doctrine. Sometimes owners of a manuscript would make marginal notes, and a copyist may have incorporated them in the text, thinking that they belonged to it originally. An Armenian translation of St. Mark has been found in which the last 12 verses of Mark are said to have been written by a church father, Aristion. If that is correct, he, no doubt, added it to the gospel because it was an accepted tradition at that time in his part of the church. They may have been part of the original, for the end leaf of a papyrus might easily get lost.

Nephi, in his wonderful vision, sees that many precious things had been taken away from the book. For the reasons here given I believe this was fulfilled in the destruction of books that originally belonged to the collection of inspired literature.

People have a wrong idea of the civilization of the early ages. They are apt to think of the people as ignorant, unable to read and write. But not so. In all probability, while the slaves were ignorant, a majority of the citizens could both read and write. Letters, written even by school children, have been unearthed in later years.

It is not maintained that every one could write like the artists whose manuscripts have been preserved. On the contrary, experts in penmanship were probably few, as they still are. For that reason, even the apostles engaged writers, as we may gather from the statement of St. Paul in his letter to the Colossians, that only the salutation was by his own hand. (Col. 4:18; 1 Cor. 16:21; 2 Thess. 3:17) This is important. For, if the writers of the books of the Bible engaged amanuensis, as they certainly did, then the discrepancies in "style" which have caused "higher critics" to dissect the writings, may be due to different secretaries instead of different authors, since the learned scribes certainly had some latitude in the choice of words or construction of sentences.

Books were numerous. In the famous Alexandrian library, there were at one time circa 700,000 volumes. During the siege of the city by Julius Caesar, part of the library was destroyed by fire, but the loss was somewhat repaired by the turning over of the collection at Pergamos to Cleopatra by Mark Anthony. It remained for the so-called Christian Roman emperor, Theodosius the Great, to destroy that precious collection of literature, in the interest of the church, in the year A.D. 389. Similar acts of vandalism have occurred again and again. Precious books were given to the flames. The same policy was resurrected in America by the first Spanish missionaries who made bonfires of the literature of the Mayas. The vision of Nephi was fulfilled literally.

VERSE 29. *Goeth forth unto all the nations.* The collection of sacred books, thus limited, is given to all nations as the "Bible."

forth unto all the nations of the Gentiles, yea, even across the many waters which thou hast seen with the Gentiles which have gone forth out of captivity, thou seest—because of the many plain and precious things which have been taken out of the book, which were plain unto the understand-

ing of the children of men, according to the plainness which is in the Lamb of God—because of these things which are taken away out of the gospel of the Lamb, an exceeding great many do stumble, yea, insomuch that Satan hath great power over them.

## 6. *The Book of Mormon.*

30. Nevertheless, thou beholdest that the Gentiles who have gone forth out of captivity, and have been lifted up by the power of God above all other nations, upon the face of the land which is choice above all other lands, which is the land that the Lord God hath covenanted with thy father that his seed should have for the land of their inheritance; wherefore, thou seest that the Lord God will not suffer that the Gentiles will utterly destroy the mixture of thy seed, which are among thy brethren.

31. Neither will he suffer that the Gentiles shall destroy the seed of thy brethren.

32. Neither will the Lord God

suffer that the Gentiles shall forever remain in that awful state of blindness, which thou beholdest they are in, because of the plain and most precious parts of the gospel of the Lamb which have been kept back by that abominable church, whose formation thou hast seen.

33. Wherefore saith the Lamb of God: I will be merciful unto the Gentiles, unto the visiting of the remnant of the house of Israel in great judgment.

34. And it came to pass that the angel of the Lord spake unto me, saying: Behold, saith the Lamb of God, after I have visited the remnant of the house of Israel —and this remnant of whom I

---

The first Bible society for the purpose of distributing Bibles was formed in 1710 by Baron Karl Hildebrand von Canstein, Halle, Germany, and by the year 1834 this institute had distributed 2,754,350 copies of the Bible, and about two million copies of the New Testament. The American Bible Society, founded in 1816, in 1930, had distributed in all, 216,189,915 copies of the Bible. The British and Foreign Bible Society alone has distributed the sacred volume in 450 different languages and dialects, and altogether, the Scriptures are now available in more than 500 tongues. Thus, the vision of Nephi has come true.

VERSE 30. *The mixture of thy seed, which are among thy brethren.* The Indians, whom we usually call Lamanites, are a mixed race. Some are the descendants of Nephi, some of the brothers of Nephi. That is evident from the divine promise: "God will not suffer that the Gentiles will utterly destroy the mixture of *thy* seed (v. 30), which are among thy brethren. Neither will he suffer that the Gentiles shall destroy the seed of thy brethren" (v. 31). See also 4 Ne. 17.

speak is the seed of thy father—wherefore, after I have visited them in judgment, and smitten them by the hand of the Gentiles, and after the Gentiles do stumble exceedingly, because of the most plain and precious parts of the gospel of the Lamb which have been kept back by that abominable church, which is the mother of harlots, saith the Lamb—I will be merciful unto the Gentiles in that day, insomuch that I will bring forth unto them, in mine own power, much of my gospel, which shall be plain and precious, saith the Lamb.

35. For, behold, saith the Lamb: I will manifest myself unto thy seed, that they shall write many things which I shall minister unto them, which shall be plain and precious; and after thy seed shall be destroyed, and dwindle in unbelief, and also the seed of thy brethren, behold, these things shall be hid up, to come forth unto the Gentiles, by the gift and power of the Lamb.

36. And in them shall be written my gospel, saith the Lamb, and my rock and my salvation.

37. And blessed are they who shall seek to bring forth my Zion at that day, for they shall have the gift and the power of the Holy Ghost; and if they endure unto the end they shall be lifted up at the last day, and shall be saved in the everlasting kingdom of the Lamb; and whoso shall publish peace, yea, tidings of great joy, how beautiful upon the mountains shall they be.

38. And it came to pass that I beheld the remnant of the seed of my brethren, and also the book of the Lamb of God, which had proceeded forth from the mouth of the Jew, that it came forth from the Gentiles unto the remnant of the seed of my brethren.

---

VERSE 34. *The remnant of the house of Israel.* This "remnant," is the "seed of thy father;" that is, the descendants of Lehi, both Nephites and Lamanites.

*Smitten by the Gentiles.* From the very first advent of the European conquerors, the Indians have been the victims of cruelty. Las Casas, who came to America with Columbus in his third voyage, and who from the year 1530 traveled as a missionary in various parts of Central America, reports what he saw in Hispaniola. Indians were distributed in lots of 50 or 100 or 500, with the understanding that they were to be taught "the things of our holy faith." They became slaves and were simply worked and flogged to death. Sometimes they attempted mutiny with disastrous consequences to themselves. They were slaughtered, impaled on stakes, burned at the stake. Indians were hung up in rows and slowly tortured to death with sword points. Some were broiled over a slow fire and children were drowned without compunction. Mr. John Fiske says, "This tyranny went on until the effect was like that of a pestilence. The native population rapidly diminished until labour grew scarce, and it was found necessary in Hispaniola to send and kidnap Indians from other islands, and to import from Seville, negroes that had been caught in Portuguese Africa." (John Fiske, The Discovery of America, vol. 2, p. 445)

The remnant was indeed "smitten." The Indians were "visited in judgment,"

39. And after it had come forth unto them I beheld other books, which came forth by the power of the Lamb, from the Gentiles unto them, unto the convincing of the Gentiles and the remnant of the seed of my brethren, and also the Jews who were scattered upon all the face of the earth, that the records of the twelve apostles of the Lamb are true.

## 7. *The last and the first.*

40. And the angel spake unto me, saying: These last records, which thou hast seen among the Gentiles, shall establish the truth of the first, which are of the twelve apostles of the Lamb, and shall make known the plain and precious things which have been taken away from them; and shall make known to all kindreds, tongues, and people, that the Lamb of God is the Son of the Eternal Father, and the Savior of the world; and that all men must come unto him, or they cannot be saved.

41. And they must come according to the words which shall be established by the mouth of the Lamb; and the words of the Lamb shall be made known in the records of thy seed, as well as in the records of the twelve apostles of the Lamb; wherefore they both shall be established in one; for there is one God and one Shepherd over all the earth.

42. And the time cometh that he shall manifest himself unto all nations, both unto the Jews and also unto the Gentiles; and after he has manifested himself unto the Jews and also unto the Gentiles, then he shall manifest himself unto the Gentiles and also unto the Jews, and the last shall be first, and the first shall be last.

---

but their day of judgment in this probation is passed, and the day of salvation has come, with the coming forth of the Book of Mormon (v. 36), and the proclamation of the gospel from the mountains (v. 37).

VERSE 39. *I beheld other books.* The Book of Mormon. Its mission is to convince Gentiles, Lamanites and Jews of the truth of the Bible.

VERSE 40. *These last records.* The Book of Mormon confirms the Bible. It makes known "plain and precious things," once a part of the Bible but now missing. The lost records may, or may not, be recovered, but the truths they contained are not lost. They are found in the Book of Mormon. This volume also testifies to all the world that Jesus is the Son of God, and the Redeemer of the world.

VERSE 42. *Shall manifest himself.* Two epochal manifestations are here mentioned. In the first he appears to both Jews and Gentiles. The New Testament is a record of this manifestation. In the second he appears to the Gentiles and also to the Jews. "The last shall be the first, and the first shall be the last." We now seem to be in the second manifestation, at the beginning of its last phase, the manifestation to the Jews.

For a comprehensive account of the origin, contents and authenticity of the

Book of Mormon, see "The Articles of Faith" by Dr. James E. Talmage and "An Introduction to the Study of the Book of Mormon," by Elder J. M. Sjodahl.

## GENERAL NOTES

*The Book of Mormon, the book which the world today needs.* No apology for the Book of Mormon is offered. None is needed. It is the very book the world today needs.

It is a witness for God—a "new witness," as the late President B. H. Roberts put it. It testifies to the divinity of Jesus, and the relationship of man to God.

It shows, moreover, the only road there is to universal peace and prosperity, two conditions that have eluded human wisdom for centuries. It proves that the children of God can live together in brotherly love and economic independence, if they will cleanse their hearts of sinful selfishness, be just in all their dealings and live in accordance with the laws of God. The descendants of Lehi lived in Millennial conditions for a century and a half, until class distinction again arose, which, as always, resulted in religious strife, civil war, and, finally, a war of extermination. If the Book of Mormon had no other message to the world than this, it would, even so, be a pearl of great price. It is a book for our statesmen, our sociologists and jurists, as well as for theologians and philosophers.

*Remarkable evidence.* The following remarkable incident was told by President Heber J. Grant in his sermon in the Tabernacle, Salt Lake City, April 8, 1932:

I have often mentioned it in public, that while I was being entertained at a dinner in London by one of the managers of the great New York Life Insurance Company I met a gentleman who had been connected with the British Legation in Constantinople and who had spent years in the Holy Land. He had been to America a number of times. I spent the evening, after dinner, chatting with him because of his remarkable experiences and the interesting things he had to say. Finally he said to me:

"Mr. Grant, do you know that I ran across the most inexplicable thing of my life the last time I visited Canada. I went way up into the northern wilds of Canada, beyond all civilization, visiting with those heathen Indians. I found among them the exact pattern, woven in colored beads, of Holy Land rugs, and in no other part of the world that I have visited have I seen rugs of the same pattern as those oriental rugs in the Holy Land, and in some sections certain patterns have come down for hundreds, almost thousands of years, in one family. They have no fabrics up among those Indians with which to do weaving, but they had the exact patterns, yet they had never heard of Jerusalem, and it is the most inexplicable thing of my life."

I said: "That is very easy to a Mormon. Have you ever heard of the Book of Mormon?"

"No."

"I will send you a copy. It is the Bible, so to speak, of the American Indians, their sacred history, and you will find that the forefathers of the American Indians and other peoples who have been in this continent came from Jerusalem."

He said: "What! That explains the inexplicable."

Now that may not be counted by some as much as a straw of evidence, but to my mind it is a very great evidence regarding the divine authenticity of the Book of Mormon.

## CHAPTER 14

*Gentiles who accept the gospel numbered among the House of Israel, 1-8—Only two churches, 9-16—The time set for the fulfilling of the Covenants with Israel, 17—John the Revelator, 18-20—End of the vision, 30.*

### 1. *Gentiles who accept the gospel numbered among the Israelites.*

1. And it shall come to pass, that if the Gentiles shall hearken unto the Lamb of God in that day that he shall manifest himself unto them in word, and also in power, in very deed, unto the taking away of their stumbling blocks—

2. And harden not their hearts against the Lamb of God, they shall be numbered among the seed of thy father; yea, they shall be numbered among the house of Israel; and they shall be a blessed people upon the promised land forever; they shall be no more brought down into captivity; and the house of Israel shall no more be confounded.

3. And that great pit, which hath been digged for them by that great and abominable

VERSE 1. *Stumbling blocks.* The destruction of some parts of the collection of the sacred books made it more difficult to understand God's plan of salvation, in some particulars, and the difficulties caused many to stumble and fall (1 Ne. 13:29). They became stumbling blocks. But these will be removed when the Lord manifests himself. The Gospel will be revealed and made plain. Every principle will be seen to be part of one complete and perfect plan.

VERSE 2. *They shall be numbered among . . . the house of Israel.* The promise here given is that those who do not harden their hearts but accept the Gospel will be counted among the descendants of Lehi, and, consequently, as children of the House of Israel. As members of the church, they are not Americans, Englishmen, Germans, Scandinavians, etc., but Israelites. The church, as a spiritual organization is not circumscribed by political boundaries. It is destined to fill the earth and to unite the human family into one great brotherhood.

This is also the doctrine of St. Paul: "Know ye therefore that they which are of faith, the same are the children or Abraham. . . . In thee shall all nations be blessed." (Gal. 3:7, 8) See also Rom. 10:12; Gal. 3:27, 28.

VERSE 3. *That hell which hath no end.* Hell is endless. (See I Ne. 15:29, 34, 35; 2 Ne. 1:13; Jac. 6:10; D. and C. Commentary, pp. 81, 131, 209, 564, 577)

In the religious conceptions of the Hebrews, from the early ages, there was a world, or kingdom, of the dead, as well as of the living. That world they called "Sheol."

The meaning of this word is not clear. Some derive it from "sha-al," to ask, to seek, and suggest that it means the land about which so many questions are asked, as for instance, "Man giveth up the ghost, and where is he?" (Job 15:10) Others reject that explanation.

According to the Old Testament, Sheol, the domain of the dead, is situated under the surface of the earth. "The Lord . . . bringeth down to the grave, and bringeth up." (1 Sam. 2:6) "Hell from beneath is moved for thee to meet thee

church, which was founded by
the devil and his children, that
he might lead away the souls of

men down to hell—yea, that
great pit which hath been digged
for the destruction of men shall

---

at thy coming." (Is. 14:9) "When I shall bring thee down with them that descend
into the pit." (Ezek. 26:20) Such are the expressions used.

It is a land of darkness and the shadow of death: "Before I go whence I shall
not return, even to the land of darkness and the shadow of death; a land of darkness, as darkness itself; and of the shadow of death, without any order, and where
the light is as darkness." (Job 10:21, 22) It is not only dark but also chaotic
("without any order").

Sometimes "Sheol" stands for the grave, where the body rests. This is the
meaning of the word when Sheol is represented as a place in which there is no
remembrance, no knowledge. "For in death there is no remembrance of thee:
in the grave who shall give thee thanks?" (Ps. 6:5) "For the living know that
they shall die: but the dead know not anything." (Ecclesiastes 9:5) This is fully
explained in verse 10: "For there is no work, nor device, nor knowledge, nor wisdom, in the grave, whither thou goest." "For the grave cannot praise thee, death
can not celebrate thee: they that go down into the pit cannot hope for thy truth."
(Is. 38:18) In these and many similar passages, where the inspired authors seem
to teach that the dead are in a state of unconsciousness, they refer only to the grave.

But Sheol also stands for that part of the land of the dead where the spirits
dwell after death. And these spirits are not unconscious. The remarkable story
of Saul and the woman of Endor (1 Sam. 28:7-20) shows the Hebrew conception
of the state of the dead. Saul, cut off from divine revelation through the regular
channels, and being threatened by the Philistines, went to a woman reputed
to be in communication with the spirits beyond the veil. He asked her to call
up Samuel, the prophet. According to the account, Samuel did appear and foretold
the death of Saul: "Tomorrow shalt thou and thy sons be with me." (v. 19) No
matter what view we may take of the historical substance of this account, we
perceive that the Hebrews at an early day believed that the spirits of the dead
were alive in Sheol, that they retained an outward resemblance to their former
selves, and that they were interested in earthly affairs. The Prophet Isaiah
(14:9-23) predicts the fall and utter destruction of Babylon under the grand
imagery of a general commotion in hell. Hell arouses the kings of the nations,
whose bodies lie in "glory," each in his own grave, (v. 18). They speak to the
king of Babylon and express their contempt for him. They will not even accord
him an honorable burial. He is to be cast out of the grave as a "carcass trodden
under feet." (v. 19) Here again we see the Hebrew idea of the status of the
human spirits in Sheol.

In the New Testament we learn more about the realm of the dead, which in
those writings is called Hades. The departed ones are in Hades, but not all in
the same part of it. The "rich man" (Luke 16:19-31) after death, lifted up his
eyes in Hades and saw Abraham afar off, and Lazarus "in his bosom," a position
of great honor. To his request that Abraham would send Lazarus for a drop of
water, Abraham replied that it could not be done. "Between us and you there
is a great gulf fixed: so that they which would pass from hence to you cannot;
neither can they pass to us, that would come from thence." Our Lord, in this
parable certainly endorses the belief of the Hebrews in separate abodes in Hades
for the departed spirits. From the well known word of our Lord on the cross, we
learn that the name of that part of the world of the dead where the righteous
dead first go is called Paradise. (Luke 23:43) St. Paul was permitted to see some-

be filled by those who digged it, unto their utter destruction, saith the Lamb of God; not the de- | struction of the soul, save it be the casting of it into that hell which hath no end.

---

thing of this region and hear words "not lawful," or perhaps not possible, to utter. (2 Cor. 12:4) The "tree of life" is in this part, and they who overcome have the promise that they will be permitted to eat of its fruit. (Rev. 2:7)

In Sheol, or Hades, as understood by the Hebrews, there is also a place of torment. David says: The wicked shall be turned into hell, and all the nations that forget God." (Ps. 19:17) This part of Sheol is referred to as a place of "fire." "For a fire is kindled in mine anger, and shall burn unto the lowest hell . . . and set on fire the foundations of the mountains." (Deut. 32:22) It is an "everlasting fire, prepared for the devil and his angels" (Matt. 25:41); wherefore the evil spirits, on one occasion, challenged our Lord with the question, whether he had come to torment them before the time (Matt. 8:31). Jesus is to be revealed from heaven with his mighty angels "in flaming fire taking vengeance on them that know not God . . . who shall be punished with everlasting destruction (2 Thess. 1:7-9). The place is compared to a "lake of fire" burning with "brimstone"; and the "beast" and the "false prophet"—the antichristian powers, both political and religious—are to be cast into it. (Rev. 19:20) Also the "devil that deceiveth them" (Rev. 20:10), and death hell (Hades) and whosoever "is not found written in the Book of Life" (vv. 14, 15). Further, "the fearful and unbelieving, and the abominable, and murderers, and whoremongers, and sorcerers, and idolaters, and all liars, shall have their part in the lake which burneth with fire and brimstone: which is the second death." (Rev. 21:8)

We have seen now that Sheol, or Hades, in the Scriptures, sometimes means the entire realm of the dead, sometimes only a part of it, as the grave, paradise, the lake of fire, etc. For a correct understanding of the subject, this distinction is important.

This is an exceedingly solemn subject. It calls for serious consideration. And the thought must never be lost sight of that if a soul is finally lost, it is not because God does not want that soul. The plan of salvation is for both living and dead. And none that can be saved will perish. Destruction is only for those who, in the pride of their hearts, refuse to be saved on the conditions of the Son of God.

Some hold that the Hebrews received their religious concepts from Babylonian, or Egyptian, or other pagan sources. Delitzsch, the eminent German Assyriologist, did much to popularize this view.[1]

The fact, probably, is that all the people of the near Orient drew their wisdom from the same original sources. They were all one family of peoples. Assyrians, Chaldeans, Arameans and Syrians were really one nation. And the Hebrews belonged to the same group, as is clear from the fact that Bethuel, the son of Abraham's brother Nahor, and the father of Laban and Rebecca, who became the wife of Isaac, is called a Syrian (Gen. 25:20). In Deut. 26, the Israelite, who came to the altar of God with a gift consisting of the products of the earth, was directed to say, "A Syrian ready to perish was my father, and he went down into Egypt" (v. 5), so that the Israelites, if the race is considered, was one with the Syrians, or Arameans. The distinction between these nations was one of geography, rather than race. Consequently we may accept it as natural that their civilizations had a common origin.

---

[1]His lecture entitled, "Der babylonische Ursprung Hebraischer Ideen" was attended by the then Emperor William II, who was a large contributor to the funds for Babylonian research, and the prestige of the Emperor helped to make the theory of the learned lecturer acceptable.

4. For behold, this is according to the captivity of the devil, and also according to the justice of God, upon all those who will work wickedness and abomination before him.

5. And it came to pass that the angel spake unto me, Nephi, saying: Thou hast beheld that if the Gentiles repent it shall be well with them; and thou also knowest concerning the covenants of the Lord unto the house of Israel; and thou also hast heard that whoso repenteth not must perish.

6. Therefore, wo be unto the Gentiles if it so be that they harden their hearts against the Lamb of God.

7. For the time cometh, saith the Lamb of God, that I will work a great and a marvelous work among the children of men; a work which shall be everlasting, either on the one hand or on the other—either to the convincing of them unto peace and life eternal, or unto the deliverance of them to the hardness of their hearts and the blindness of their minds unto their being brought down into captivity, and also into destruction, both temporally and spiritually, according to the captivity of the devil, of which I have spoken.

8. And it came to pass that when the angel had spoken these words, he said unto me: Rememberest thou the covenants of the Father unto the house of Israel? I said unto him, Yea.

## 2. Only two churches.

9. And it came to pass that he said unto me: Look, and behold that great and abominable church, which is the mother of

---

But they did not all preserve the traditions of their fathers with equal care. In this respect the Jews predominated. Their religion was pure, as long as they followed the leadership of their inspired prophets.

VERSE 4. *According to the captivity of the devil, and . . . the justice of God.* The thought seems to be expressed here that the justice of God is a saving principle even in Sheol, where souls are the captives of the adversary.

VERSE 7. *A great and a marvelous work.* The coming forth of the Book of Mormon is here referred to, as the beginning of the proclamation of the gospel and the foundation of the latter-day church. The effects of this upon the children of men will be, either peace and life eternal, or a further hardening of the hearts and mental blindness, followed by both temporal and spiritual destruction.

VERSE 8. *Rememberest thou the covenants?* These covenants may refer, in the first place, to the blessings which Jacob gave his sons before his death, and more particularly those bestowed upon Joseph, Ephraim and Judah, as representatives of the people. (Gen. 48:15-21; 49:1-27) These were divine promises, to be fulfilled in due time. Or, they may, secondly, refer to the covenant made with Israel at Mt. Sinai. (Ex. 24:7, 8) These referred more especially to the inheritance of Canaan and blessings connected therewith. The angel reminds Nephi of the covenants. It is always well to remember God's promises and our obligations.

VERSE 9. *Great and abominable church.* The angel again calls attention to the church seen in the previous chapter (vv. 4-9).

abominations, whose foundation is the devil.

10. And he said unto me: Behold there are save two churches only; the one is the church of the Lamb of God, and the other is the church of the devil; wherefore, whoso belongeth not to the church of the Lamb of God belongeth to that great church, which is the mother of abominations; and she is the whore of all the earth.

11. And it came to pass that I looked and beheld the whore of all the earth, and she sat upon many waters; and she had dominion over all the earth, among all nations, kindreds, tongues, and people.

12. And it came to pass that I beheld the church of the Lamb of God, and its numbers were few, because of the wickedness and abominations of the whore who sat upon many waters; nevertheless, I beheld that the church of the Lamb, who were the saints of God, were also upon all the face of the earth; and their dominions upon the face of the earth were small, because of the wickedness of the great whore whom I saw.

13. And it came to pass that I beheld that the great mother of abominations did gather together multitudes upon the face of all the earth, among all the nations of the Gentiles, to fight against the Lamb of God.

14. And it came to pass that I, Nephi, beheld the power of the Lamb of God, that it descended upon the saints of the church of the Lamb, and upon the covenant people of the Lord, who were scattered upon all the face of the earth; and they were armed with righteousness and with the power of God in great glory.

15. And it came to pass that I beheld that the wrath of God was poured out upon the great and abominable church, insomuch that there were wars and rumors of wars among all the nations and kindreds of the earth.

16. And as there began to be wars and rumors of wars among all the nations which belonged to the mother of abominations, the angel spake unto me, saying: Behold, the wrath of God is upon the mother of harlots; and behold, thou seest all these things—

---

VERSE 10. In this vision there are only two churches, one a large, influential church, and one a small church as regards membership, but nevertheless diffused throughout the world. (vv. 11, 12)

VERSES 13-16. The thought presented in these paragraphs seems to be this: The great church is gathering the forces of the various nations for war upon the Lamb of God (v. 13). Then the power of the Lamb of God descends upon the Saints of the Church and upon the Children of Israel (the covenant people), and they are armed with "righteousness and with the power of God in great glory," not with armaments of war. (v. 14) The situation now develops to one of hostilities among the nations of the great church themselves. Instead of being united in a war upon the Lamb, they are fighting each other. (v. 16)

## 3. *The time for the fulfilling of the covenants.*

17. And when the day cometh that the wrath of God is poured out upon the mother of harlots, which is the great and abominable church of all the earth, whose foundation is the devil, then, at that day, the work of the Father shall commence, in preparing the way for the fulfilling of his covenants, which he hath made to his people who are of the house of Israel.

---

VERSE 17. If we assume that the expression, "the work of the Father shall commence," refers to the famous Balfour Declaration which pledged the British government to the "establishment in Palestine of a national home for the Jewish people," then, the "wrath of God" would represent World War I and II. The prediction in this paragraph is, then, the same as the prophecy on war in the D. and C., section 87:3, where it is stated that when Great Britain calls upon other nations in order to defend herself against other nations, then "war shall be poured out upon all nations." The result will be "sword and bloodshed," mourning on earth, famine, plague, earthquakes, thunder and lightning, "until the consumption decreed hath made a full end of all nations"—an expression which can mean nothing less than the end of the old social or political order and the beginning of a new, all of which is a necessary preparation for the coming of the "day of the Lord." (D. and C. 87:6-8)

The World War I was, humanly speaking, perhaps the greatest calamity in the history of the human race since the flood. Just why and how it started has not, so far, been made perfectly clear. In a general way it must be considered as the natural outcome of a policy of which Prince Bismarck, in his day, was the most able apostle. It began in a controversy between Austria and Serbia, on July 28, 1914, after the assassination in Bosnian territory of the Austrian Archduke Francis Ferdinand, and lasted until November 11, 1918, a period of four years, three months and fourteen days. The peace treaty between the allies and Germany was signed at Versailles, June 28, 1919. The treaty between the United States and Germany was signed on July 2, 1921. Twenty-nine nations had been involved in the hostilities against Germany, Austria-Hungary, Turkey and Bulgaria. The loss of life was simply appalling. The total number of men mobilized was, 65,264,810. Of these, Russia had 12,000,000; Germany, 11,000,000; France, 8,410,000; the United States, 4,800,000. The grand total of dead, wounded, prisoners and missing was, 36,415,258. The number of killed in battle, 7,449,087. Of these 4,699,087 were mourned by the United States and the Allies, and 2,750,000 by the central powers. The United States had a list of total casualties numbering, 283,509, in-including killed in battle, 48,909. The direct war expenses of all the belligerents are estimated at $186,000,000,000. Like totals of World War II have not yet been assessed. They are greater and in some places, still go on.

As far as human eye can see, this tremendous upheaval was unavoidable, if the plans of the Father were to be carried out as regards the promised land. That country had to be set free, if the Jews were to gather there; it had to be protected from a world-embracing militarism that was closing in around it. These objects were accomplished by the war. It cleared the way for Zionism.

*The growth of Zionism.* In 1840, Moses Mess, a German socialist, wrote, referring to the Jews:

"We shall always remain strangers among the nations . . . They will never respect us so long as we place our great memories in the second rank, but in the first, [the] principle, 'ubi bene ibi patria.'"

He formulated a complete plan for the colonization of the Holy Land. But very few regarded any such plans at that time as anything but imagination.

The Prophet Joseph Smith was one of the few persons in the world at that time who believed in Zionism, and in 1840 he sent Apostle Orson Hyde to dedicate the land for the gathering of the Jews. Orson Hyde fulfilled this mission, and the dedicatory prayer was offered up on the Mount of Olives, October 24, 1841.

In 1864, the historian, Heinrich Graetz, recognized that an awakening had taken place among the Jews, comparable to that which preceded the return of the exiles from Babylonia under the leadership of Nehemiah and Ezra.

In 1895, Theodore Herzl wrote his famous book, "Der Judenstaat" (the Jewish State). The idea embodied in this treatise was at once grasped by Israel Zangwill, who invited Mr. Herzl to give a lecture on the subject in London before a Jewish society. The lecture was given in 1896. The same year, the Turkish sultan offered the Jews a charter authorizing them to colonize Palestine, in return for an agreement not to continue the agitation against him on account of the Armenian massacres —a proposition which they, of course, could not even consider, as they did not control the European press.

A call for a general Jewish congress was issued in 1897. This congress convened the following year in Basel, Switzerland. It declared the object of Zionism to be, "To establish for the Jewish people a home in Palestine." This is the so-called Basel Program. From the year 1901 the Zionists have held biannual sessions of their congress.

In 1903 the Marquis of Landsdown suggested that the Zionists settle some place in Africa. He wrote:

"If a site can be found suitable to the Jewish Colonial Trust, Ltd., and agreeable to the government, he would be prepared to entertain favorable proposals for the establishment of a Jewish colony or settlement on conditions which will enable the members to observe their national customs."

The suggestion was rejected by the sixth Zionist congress. It was Palestine, not Africa, that the Jews had in view as a national home.

The World War began, as stated, on July 28, 1914. Among the early steps of the conflict was the severance of Egypt from Turkish rule and the establishment of a British protectorate. This was done on December 18, 1914, but the arrangement was terminated on February 28, 1922, and March 15, that year, Egypt was recognized as an independent kingdom.

The primary object of Turkey in joining the belligerents on the German side was to deprive England of her line of communication with India by way of the Suez canal. This led to a rather spectacular campaign in the near East. The Turks were driven away from the Sinai peninsula and made to retreat northward. Beersheba fell into the hands of General Sir E. N. Allenby on October 31, 1917. Shortly afterwards Gaza was taken, and then Jaffa. Two British columns were now moving northward, sweeping the Turkish forces before them. By November 25, Jerusalem was surrounded. Not a shot was fired against the Holy City. On December 10, 1917, the Mayor, under the protection of a white, improvised flag, went out to find an officer of high enough rank to accept the city, and when he found one, Jerusalem was turned over to the British. No blood was shed in the transfer, this time, of the venerable, war-battered city of David. The Balfour declaration had been issued previously, viz., on November 2, 1917.

We note that Palestine, on July 22, 1922, shortly after the British protectorate over Egypt was terminated and the independence of that country was recognized, was by the League of Nations assigned to Great Britain. This seems to me to be a remarkable fulfillment of the following prophecy of Isaiah:

### 4. *John the Revelator.*

18. And it came to pass that the angel spake unto me, saying: Look!

19. And I looked and beheld a man, and he was dressed in a white robe.

20. And the angel said unto me: Behold one of the twelve apostles of the Lamb.

---

"But now thus saith the Lord that created thee, O Jacob, and he that formed thee, O Israel, Fear not: for I have redeemed thee, I have called thee by thy name; thou art mine. . . . For I am the Lord thy God, the Holy One of Israel, thy Savior: I gave Egypt for thy ransom, Ethiopia and Seba for thee. Since thou wast precious in my sight, thou hast been honorable and I have loved thee: therefore will I give men for thee, and people for thy life." (Is. 43:1-4)

Humanly speaking, it was Great Britain that gave up Egypt and Ethiopia for Palestine, and it was Great Britain that lost 60,000 men in the campaign against Turkey in this war, but from the viewpoint of the prophet, it was God who brought about the liberation of Palestine. God was the redeemer, and the ransom paid was as stated.

That this prophecy refers to the last gathering of Israel is clear from the 5th verse of the chapter quoted:

"Fear not: for I am with thee: I will bring thy seed from the east, and gather thee from the west; I will say to the north, Give up; and to the south, Keep not back; bring my sons from far, and my daughters from the ends of the earth."

The 18th World Zionist congress was held at Praha (Prague), Czecho-Slovakia, August 21, 1933, with 332 delegates present. At that congress the President urged the Jews to make Palestine a "land of fulfillment rather than a land of promise."

At the time of the congress (1933) there were about 200,000 Jews and circa 800,000 Arabs in Palestine. In Transjordania, a country double the size of Palestine, there are only about 300,000 inhabitants. The Zionists are therefore asking for an opening for immigrants into Transjordania as well as Palestine.

The work of the Father has, indeed, begun, as regards the gathering of his covenant people in the land of their fathers. At the present time (1955) there are 1,850,000 Jews in the state of Israel, part of Palestine.

VERSE 20. *Behold one of the twelve apostles of the Lamb.* This Apostle was John (v. 27), the "disciple whom Jesus loved." (John 21:20), the author of the fourth Gospel (John 21:24), the Revelation (Rev. 1:19) and three epistles, all of which books are a part of the New Testament.

John was the younger brother of James. They were two sons of Zebedee and Salome, whose home was in Bethsaida, in Galilee. The father was a fisherman. He seems to have been well to do, because he had "hired servants" in his employ (Mark 1:20), and Salome was among the women who "ministered" to Jesus during his mission in mortality. (Matt. 27:56) He is supposed to have been one of the two disciples of John the Baptist, who became the disciples of Jesus, as related in John 1:35-40. Andrew, Simon Peter's brother, is mentioned as one of the two. John was fervently devoted to his Master. He was present during the trial and crucifixion of our Lord, and Jesus committed his mother to his care. (John 19:26, 27) He is said to have remained in Jerusalem till the death of Mary, about the year 48 A.D.

According to Gal. 2:3-9, Paul and Barnabas, while in Jerusalem, were given the "right hands of fellowship" by James, Cephas (Peter) and John, with the

21. Behold, he shall see and write the remainder of these things; yea, and also many things which have been.

22. And he shall also write concerning the end of the world.

23. Wherefore, the things which he shall write are just and true; and behold they are written in the book which thou beheld proceeding out of the mouth of the Jew; and at the time they proceeded out of the mouth of the Jew, or, at the time the book proceeded out of the mouth of the Jew, the things which were written were plain and pure, and most precious and easy to the understanding of all men.

24. And behold, the things

---

understanding that they were to labor among the Gentiles, while the older apostles would continue their labor among the Jews. This took place probably about the year A.D. 52. The leadership of the church, at that time centered in Jerusalem. When Paul left Ephesus, about the year A.D. 65, John succeeded him. Tertullian (Adv. Haer.) relates that John, during the reign of Domitian, was taken to Rome and thrown into a cask of oil, but that he was miraculously saved from death and exiled to Patmos. Domitian died in the year A.D. 65, and the exile must have taken place before that year. On the accession of Emperor Nerva he was liberated, and returned to Ephesus. The last years of John, as far as recorded history goes, are lost in obscurity, but all agree that he lived for many years. It was not till the end of the first century, possibly, that this majestic figure—as it were—fades out of the picture.

These events and dates are all important. As is well known, the great Roman hierarchy claims that the government of the church, by the appointment of the Apostle Peter, was established in Rome. Their list of popes contains no less than four names—Linus, Anacletus, Clement I and Evaristus—all representing alleged successors of the Apostle Peter during the last half of the first century, while the Apostle John, whom even the Apostle Paul recognized as one of the three "pillars" of the church (Gal. 2:3-9), was still active. The claim is incredible on the face of it.

VERSE 21. *Behold, he shall see and write.* We are here told that John was to write about that which Nephi saw: "The remainder of these things;" and also many things "which have been;" may refer particularly to his Gospel, which begins with the story of the "Word," the "Logos," the Son of God. He was also to write of the "end of the world" (v. 22). This refers undoubtedly to the book of Revelation. These writings were to be added to the Bible: "the book which proceeded out of the mouth of a Jew" (v. 23). See also 1 Ne. 13:20-23, 38, 40.

VERSES 22-29. *Concerning the end of the world.* It certainly is in accordance with the mind and will of the Lord that the people of his church should read and understand the book known as the Revelation by John, to which reference is made here. In the very beginning of that remarkable literary production we are informed that it contains the revelation which God gave unto Jesus Christ, for the purpose of making future events known to his servants (Rev. 1:1). To this information is added this assurance: "Blessed is he that readeth, and they that hear the words of this prophecy, and keep the things that are written therein: for the time is at hand" (v. 3). Then, at the close of the book, the author warns against adding to, or taking away from it (22:18, 19). Any change would destroy the symbolism. Now, here Nephi is shown the sacred writing long before the time of John, and in our own day and age, in the month of March, 1832, the Prophet Joseph received a

which this apostle of the Lamb shall write are many things which thou hast seen; and behold, the remainder shalt thou see.

25. But the things which thou shalt see hereafter thou shalt not write; for the Lord God hath ordained the apostle of the Lamb of God that he should write them.

26. And also others who have been, to them hath he shown all things, and they have written them; and they are sealed up to come forth in their purity, according to the truth which is in the Lamb, in the own due time of the Lord, unto the house of Israel.

27. And I, Nephi, heard and bear record, that the name of the apostle of the Lamb was John, according to the word of the angel.

28. And behold, I, Nephi, am forbidden that I should write the remainder of the things which I saw and heard; wherefore the things which I have written sufficeth me; and I have written but a small part of the things which I saw.

---

special revelation, containing a "key" to the first eleven chapters of the book. Not a detailed explanation, but a key that lets the reader in, as it were, and gives him an opportunity to study the details for himself, under the guidance of the Spirit of Truth. God wants us to study this book.

And no wonder. In the letters to the seven churches in Asia Minor, it contains the most solemn warnings against sin, false doctrines and lukewarmness in the faith. (Rev. 2:1-4:21) In the rest of the book is shown the gradual progress and development of the great apostasy, but also the final victory of the Lamb of God—the progress of the world through wars, famine, pestilence, earthquakes, etc., to the Millennial reign of peace, truth and righteousness. It is, we may say, the time-piece of the church, showing the hour of the day. It is a compass to consult on the stormy Main of human history.

*The Apostle John is the author.* This is clear from this vision of Nephi. Scholars now recognize that this is the unanimous testimony of the first and second centuries of our era, too. It is the view of Justin Martyr, Irenaeus, Tertullian, Clement of Alexandria and Origen. But in the third century Dionysius, a disciple of Origen, asserted that its author was a presbyter, or Elder, by the name of John. Some even maintained that it was forged by Cerinthus, the notorious heretic against whom, according to Irenaeus, the Gospel of John was written. However, the book was finally accepted by the majority of the members of the church, as the work of the Apostle John.

At the time of the reformation the question of authenticity was again discussed. Martin Luther revived the controversy by asserting that the book was neither apostolic nor prophetic. But then, Luther, as a "higher critic," also characterized the Epistle of James as "straw." He even questioned the propriety of the conduct of our Lord in purifying the temple, as related by John in the Gospel. Referring to the expression, "And when he had made a scourge of small cords [or rather rushes], he drove them all out," etc., Luther asks whether that is not an act of rebellion, and then he argues apologetically, as it were, that this act of our Lord is not to serve as something for others to imitate in as much as he made himself this time a servant, not of the New, but the Old Testament, and the

## 5. *End of the vision.*

29. And I bear record that I saw the things which my father saw, and the angel of the Lord did make them known unto me.

30. And now I make an end of speaking concerning the things which I saw while I was carried away in the spirit; and if all the things which I saw are not written, the things which I have written are true. And thus it is. Amen.

---

disciples of Moses.[2] Luther was a mighty preacher and a masterful organizer, but not an authority on either textual or "higher" critcism. The Revelation has been accepted as authentic, notwithstanding the dictum of the great reformer. Scholarship has in this respect, as in others, vindicated the Book of Mormon.

The main objection to the same authorship of the Revelation and the Gospel is the alleged difference in style. But if the books were written at different times, and different secretaries were employed in the purely literary composition, the differences in style present no difficulty.

VERSE 30. *And thus it is. Amen.* The closing words may indicate that the foregoing, from the beginning of chapter 11, was intended as a sermon and was delivered as such. Undoubtedly, the family of Lehi held regular services on the Sabbath, and the vision, as related, would naturally form a fruitful subject for discourses.

The word "Amen," as a substantive, means "truth," as in Isaiah 65:16: "He who blesseth himself in the earth shall bless himself in the God of Truth (Amen); and he that sweareth in the earth shall swear by the God of Truth (Amen)." In the letter which John was directed to write to the bishop in Laodicea, Jesus calls himself, "Amen, the faithful and true witness, the beginning of the creation of God." (Rev. 3:14. See also Rev. 19:11) As part of the Mosaic ritual it was a strong confirmation, as in Num. 5:22, or Deut. 27:14-26. At the close of a prayer, as in Psalm 106:48, (Compare 1 Cor. 14:16) it means, "May it so be." Our Lord frequently uses the word as a solemn affirmation, as for instance in John 3:3, "Amen, amen, I say unto thee, Except a man be born again, he cannot see the kingdom of God," where, however, the English version has, "Verily, verily."

The ancient Egyptians had a god, Amen, whom the priests at Thebes endeavored

---

[2]"Ist das nicht aufruhrisch?" Luther asks. "Diese That Christi ist nicht zum Exempel zu ziehen; er hat sie nicht als Diener des Neuen, sondern des Alten Testament und Mosis Schuler gethan." (Quoted by Dean Farrar in "Life of Christ," p. 134.) This is a strange misunderstanding of the incident, as related in the fourth Gospel. It assumes that Jesus, overcome by wrath, makes a whip and unmercifully swings it on the heads and bodies of the numerous merchants and money changers on the temple ground. If Jesus had done that, he would have committed assault and battery, for he had no legal authority to use the lash on anybody. But Jesus was not one to take the law in his own hands. He was, first of all, a law-abiding citizen. He could, without fear of contradiction, ask his opponents, Which of you convinceth me of sin? (Joh. 8:46.) Scourging, or beating, more or less severely, was a penalty regulated by law and custom, but whether inflicted in the community, the synagogue, the home, or elsewhere, to be legal, it must have legal authority behind it. Jesus did not assault the people on the temple ground. John could not mean to say that he did. We must compare John 2:13-17 with Matt. 21:12, Mark 11:15 and Luke 19:45. If we do, we find that our Lord, "cast out them that sold and bought; saying unto them, 'It is written, My house is the house of prayer: but ye have made it a den of thieves.' That was how he cast them out. And in that rebuke, he was fully supported by public opinion. The small cords, or rushes, he naturally used in helping the caretakers of the cattle and sheep to drive the animals out of the sacred precincts.

to introduce as superior to Osiris, but not successfully. Dr. E. A. Wallis Budge has preserved the following prayer to him:

"Homage to thee, O thou God, holy one, great in beneficent deeds, thou Prince of Eternity, who presideth over his place in the Sektet Boat, thou mighty one of risings in the Atet Boat! Praises are ascribed to thee both in heaven and upon earth. * * * Thou placest thy souls in Tettet (Busiris or Mendes) and thine awe is in Suten-henen. * * * Grant thou that I may have my existence among the living, and that I may float down and sail up the river among thy followers." (Osiris and the Egyptian Resurrection," p. 74)

The name of this divinity is one evidence among many of the close association between the Hebrews and the Egyptians.

## GENERAL NOTES

*America, a Christian nation.* Our government, in its beginning, recognized the power of prayer, for in the first gathering of Congress, the senate and the house, prayer was offered before a thing was undertaken in the way of legislation. Among those wonderful men who met at Carpenter Hall on September 5, 1774, were some of the greatest Americans. They bowed in prayer and more than half of them knelt when the prayer was being offered. (Senator Reed Smoot, of the Council of the Apostles, in a sermon in the Tabernacle, Salt Lake City, October 9, 1932.)

*Bible and Babel.* The Babylonian account of the creation begins thus: "When the heavens above were not (yet) named; below, the solid (earth) bore no name; Apsu (the ocean) the First of all, who begat them, and the Prototype Tamat, who caused them all to be born, mingled together their waters . . . trees did not unite a thicket of reeds . . . when not one of the gods (as) yet arisen, no destiny (had been determined) then were the gods formed, then arose first Lakhmu and Lakhamu. Until they had grown up," etc.

Compare this with the opening statement of the Hebrew Genesis: "In the beginning God created the heaven and the earth."

"We see therefore that the Babylonians made the origin of the divine nature an event in the creation, but the Old Testament resounds with a nobler strain, telling us that the divine Spiritual Being existed before matter, and that it was just He who designed the Universe, and with sovereign impulses brought it to fulfillment." (Professor Koenig, "Bibel und Babel").

*The Bible a Book without an equal.* In one respect at least the Bible of Christianity is unique. It is a compound scripture, so to speak, embracing the canonic writings of two of the world's great religions. And the point is one of importance. Whatever may be said of either collection separately, taken together the Old and New Testaments constitute a sacred book unusually rich in contents and balanced in outlook. The Christians have great reason to be thankful that when the church got out into the gentile world and became independent of the synagogue it still kept the Jewish Bible. To have failed to retain and hold in higher regard the unique treasures of religious poetry in the Psalms, the literary remains of the great reforming prophets, and the wealth of didactic stories in the narrative books, would have been a loss indeed; and it may be added that the practical sense so generally manifested in the Old Testament — concerned with the present world—serves as a valuable offset. . . . On the other hand, Christianity has contributed to the joint Scriptures the matchless figure of Jesus, the powerful and arresting personality of Paul, and a new spirit, a life which is felt even when it cannot be described or labeled, and which certainly has had much to do with the influence exerted by the Bible during the past eighteen centuries. (Dr. Frank Eakin, "Revaluing Scripture," pp. 208-9.)

## CHAPTER 15

*Nephi returns to the tent of his father, 1-12—The Olive tree, 13-20—*
*The tree of life, 21, 22—The rod of iron, 23-25—The river, 26-36.*

### 1. *Nephi returns to the tent of his father.*

1. And it came to pass that after I, Nephi, had been carried away in the spirit, and seen all these things, I returned to the tent of my father.

2. And it came to pass that I beheld my brethren, and they were disputing one with another concerning the things which my father had spoken unto them.

3. For he truly spake many great things unto them, which were hard to be understood, save a man should inquire of the Lord; and they being hard in their hearts, therefore they did not look unto the Lord as they ought.

4. And now I, Nephi, was grieved because of the hardness of their hearts, and also, because of the things which I had seen, and knew they must unavoidably come to pass because of the great wickedness of the children of men.

5. And it came to pass that I was overcome because of my afflictions, for I considered that mine afflictions were great above all, because of the destructions of my people, for I had beheld their fall.

6. And it came to pass that after I had received strength I spake unto my brethren, desiring to know of them the cause of their disputations.

7. And they said: Behold, we cannot understand the words which our father hath spoken concerning the natural branches of the olive-tree, and also concerning the Gentiles.

8. And I said unto them: Have ye inquired of the Lord?

---

VERSE 1. *I returned to the tent.* Nephi had been "caught away in the Spirit of the Lord" into an exceedingly high mountain. (Chap. 11:1) Now he returns. This expression may indicate that he had been absent in body as well as in spirit; or it may mean that he awoke from the special condition during which the impressions of the vision had been received. The Apostle Paul, speaking, no doubt, of his own experience, when he was "caught up to the third heaven," says, "Whether in the body, I cannot tell; or whether out of the body, I cannot tell: God knoweth," and this he repeats, as if for greater emphasis. (2 Cor. 12:2, 3)

VERSE 5. *I was overcome.* From this verse and the following, it is clear that what he had seen had overwhelmed him so completely that it took some time before he regained his physical strength.

If I understand the chapter correctly, it tells us that the family were gathered for devotion in the tent of Lehi, and that the vision of their father was the subject under discussion. Very soon the discussion became a dispute between the sons of Lehi, who had neglected to pray for light and guidance. Then Nephi, as soon as he was able to speak to them, gave his testimony and explained the points in dispute.

9. And they said unto me: We have not; for the Lord maketh no such thing known unto us.

10. Behold, I said unto them: How is it that ye do not keep the commandments of the Lord? How is it that ye will perish, because of the hardness of your hearts?

11. Do ye not remember the things which the Lord hath said? —If ye will not harden your hearts, and ask me in faith, believing that ye shall receive, with diligence in keeping my commandments, surely these things shall be made known unto you.

12. Behold, I say unto you, that the house of Israel was compared unto an olive-tree, by the Spirit of the Lord which was in our fathers; and behold are we not broken off from the house of Israel, and are we not a branch of the house of Israel?

## 2. The Olive Tree.

13. And now, the thing which our father meaneth concerning the grafting in of the natural branches through the fulness of the Gentiles, is, that in the latter days, when our seed shall have dwindled in unbelief, yea, for the space of many years, and many generations after the Messiah shall be manifested in body unto the children of men, then shall the fulness of the gospel of the Messiah come unto the Gentiles, and from the Gentiles unto the remnant of our seed—

14. And at that day shall the remnant of our seed know that they are of the house of Israel, and that they are the covenant people of the Lord; and then shall they know and come to the knowledge of their forefathers, and also to the knowledge of the gospel of their Redeemer, which was ministered unto their fathers by him; wherefore, they shall come to the knowledge of their Redeemer and the very points of his doctrine, that they may know how to come unto him and be saved.

15. And then at that day will they not rejoice and give praise unto their everlasting God, their

---

*The Olive Tree.* This was one of the subjects of dispute. The expression refers to the house of Israel (v. 12). The descendants of Lehi are of the house of Israel, and therefore a branch of the olive tree (v. 14). This branch was broken off when the people dwindled in unbelief (v. 13). It was grafted into the tree when, after many generations, the Gospel was revealed in its fulness and so far as it has been accepted by the remnant (v. 16). But the restoration applies not only to the descendants of Lehi but also to the Jews (v. 19). And it is the last. There will be no more dispersion (v. 20).

This sermon had the intended effect. The brothers of Nephi humbled themselves before the Lord. (v. 20) The only criterion of a successful sermon is its effects on the hearers. Nephi gained his object.

The olive tree is very beautiful. Its white flowers are produced in great abundance. They resemble those of the lilac. The aged olive tree is often surrounded by young and thrifty shoots (Ps. 128:3), like children. On festive occasions women

rock and their salvation? Yea, at that day, will they not receive the strength and nourishment from the true vine? Yea, will they not come unto the true fold of God?

16. Behold, I say unto you, Yea; they shall be remembered again among the house of Israel; they shall be grafted in, being a natural branch of the olive-tree, into the true olive-tree.

17. And this is what our father meaneth; and he meaneth that it will not come to pass until after they are scattered by the Gentiles; and he meaneth that it shall come by way of the Gentiles, that the Lord may show his power unto the Gentiles, for the very cause that he shall be rejected of the Jews, or of the house of Israel.

18. Wherefore, our father hath not spoken of our seed alone, but also of all the house of Israel, pointing to the covenant which should be fulfilled in the latter days; which covenant the Lord made to our father Abraham, saying: In thy seed shall all the kindreds of the earth be blessed.

19. And it came to pass that I, Nephi, spake much unto them concerning these things; yea, I spake unto them concerning the restoration of the Jews in the latter days.

20. And I did rehearse unto them the words of Isaiah, who spake concerning the restoration of the Jews, or of the house of Israel; and after they were restored they should no more be confounded, neither should they be scattered again. And it came to pass that I did speak many words unto my brethren, that they were pacified and did humble themselves before the Lord.

---

sometimes adorned themselves with garlands of olive leaves (Judith 15:13), which have a silvery, glistening sheen.

An olive branch was the emblem of peace. The door and posts of the entrance to the temple, and also to the holy of holies, were made of olive wood, to symbolize the access to God through peace as a result of the atonement. The two large cherubim on the ark were also made of olive wood. (1 Kings 6:23, 31, 33)

The Prophet Zechariah had a remarkable vision of two olive trees standing by a golden candlestick. He asked the angel who was his guide, for an explanation of the two trees. He answered, "These are the two anointed ones," [probably Joshua and Zerubbabel] "that stand by the Lord of the whole earth," as waiting for his commands in order to carry them out. Jehovah surveys the whole earth, and is cognizant of the disturbing events that are troubling his people, and his inspired servants are ready at all times to bring divine light to them, from the sanctuary. (Zech. 4:1-3, 11-14)

The Prophet Jeremiah compares Judah to a "green olive tree, fair and of goodly fruit" (11:16; Hos. 14:6). In Romans 11:17, 24, the Gentiles are "wild olives" grafted upon the the stock of a cultivated olive tree, while the "natural branches" are broken off. Wicked men are compared to olive trees that cast off their flowers and therefore bear no fruit. (Job 15:33) Children are compared to "olive plants" (Ps. 128:3). They are beautiful. They are a blessing. They are God's reward for righteousness.

### 3. *The Tree of Life.*

21. And it came to pass that they did speak unto me again, saying: What meaneth this thing which our father saw in a dream?

What meaneth the tree which he saw?

22. And I said unto them: It was a representation of the tree of life.

---

VERSE 21. *What meaneth this thing which our father saw?* There were three kinds of trees, or plants, in the garden which our heavenly Father planted eastward in the Land of Eden. There were plants beautiful to the eye, fragrant, and suitable for food. In the midst of the garden there was the tree of life, which seems to have had medicinal qualities. (See Gen. 3:22, and Rev. 2:7 and 22:2, where the tree is said to bear twelve manner of fruits and leaves "for the healing of the nations.") There was also the tree, the eating of which produced knowledge of good and evil, but also death. (Gen. 2:9 and 17; comp. Prov. 3:18, 11:30; Ezek. 47:12)

Lehi, in his vision had seen a beautiful tree with sweet fruit (1 Ne. 8:10, 11), and this tree, we are told, was a representation of the tree of life.

We may not fully understand all that the account in Genesis of the fall of man conveys to the reader, but we do realize that it is not a myth. It is history. "Adam fell that man might be; and men are that they might have joy." (Alma 2:25) "Adam did fall by the partaking of the forbidden fruit, according to the word of God; and thus we see, that by his fall, all mankind became a lost and fallen people." (Alma 12:22) "Now we see that the man had become as God, knowing good and evil; and lest he should put forth his hand and take also of the tree of life, and eat and live for ever, the lord God placed cherubim and the flaming sword, that he should not partake of the fruit—" (Alma 42:3)

From a moral point of view, we learn in this narrative that our first parents were free, moral agents, capable of choosing for themselves a course of action, and therefore responsible for their acts.

We also learn that sin is the transgression of the divine law, the result of which is death. From the very moment that man partook of the forbidden tree he was in the power of death.

The Scriptures refer to death in various terms, all very instructive. It is a return to dust (Gen. 2:7; 3:19). It is a withdrawal of the breath (Ps. 104:29, 30). It is being unclothed (2 Cor. 5:3, 4). It is a sleep (Ps. 76:5; John 11:13). It is a journey (Phil. 1:23; 2 Tim. 4:6, 7). It is also an enemy, to be destroyed by our Lord (1 Cor. 15:25, 26, 54-57).

The Mosaic story of the fall conveys another important truth. It shows us that man was not sent out upon the uninhabited wastes of the earth before he was fully equipped for the struggle before him. How long time he had developed in Paradise under divine tuition, we know not. But we know that in the garden, God had taught him the value of plants and trees, and how to take care of them. (Gen. 2:15) He had become so familiar with the animal kingdom that he could name the animals according to their characteristics. (v. 19) He was undoubtedly familiar with astronomy, for otherwise the sun, the planets, the stars could not have been to him for signs, and for seasons, and for days and for years. (Gen. 1:14)

The first man, according to the Mosaic account, appeared on earth with a remarkable degree of civilization. History confirms this view, for, no matter how far back the records go, they present us with evidences of civilization.

## 4. *The rod of iron.*

23. And they said unto me: What meaneth the rod of iron which our father saw, that led to the tree?

24. And I said unto them that it was the word of God; and whoso would hearken unto the word of God, and would hold fast unto it, they would never perish; neither could the temptations and the fiery darts of the adversary overpower them unto blind-ness, to lead them away to destruction.

25. Wherefore, I, Nephi, did exhort them to give heed unto the word of the Lord; yea, I did exhort them with all the energies of my soul, and with all the faculty which I possessed, that they would give heed to the word of God and remember to keep his commandments always in all things.

VERSE 24. *It was the Word of God.* In his vision, Lehi saw a rod of iron, by means of which the wanderers on Life's narrow path, surrounded by dark, delusive mists of error, could find their way to the tree of life. (I Ne. 8:19) This "rod," Nephi says, was the Word of God.

This term, as I understand it, comprehends all that God has revealed to man, and more especially that which belongs to the plan of salvation. Some of the revelations have been preserved in written volumes, of which we then can properly say that they contain the Word of God.

Among the ancient books so known are the Old and New Testaments, and, as we, as members of the Church of Jesus Christ of Latter-day Saints believe, the Book of Mormon, and the writings of Moses and Abraham, as preserved in the Pearl of Great Price. All these, we claim, are inspired, which means that they were written by "holy men of God," who spake [as they were] moved by the "Holy Ghost" (2 Pet. 1:21); they are given by "inspiration of God"[1] (2 Tim. 3:16).

Modern volumes, similarly inspired, are, The Doctrine and Covenants and the writings of Joseph, the Prophet, as preserved in the Pearl of Great Price.

Let us hear some testimonies concerning the Word of God, universally known as the "Bible."

"Here is a book whose ante-mundane voices had grown old, when voices spoke in Eden. A book which has survived not only with continued but increasing lustre, vitality, vivacity, popularity, rebound of influence. A book which comes through all the shocks without a wrench, and all the furnaces of all the ages—like an iron safe—with every document in every pigeon hole, without a warp upon it, or the smell of fire . . . a book dating from days as ancient as those of the Ancient of Days, and which, when all that makes up what we see and call the universe shall be dissolved, will still speak on in thunder-tones of majesty, and whisper-tones of love, for it is wrapping in itself the everlasting past, and opening and expanding from itself the everlasting future; and, like an all-irradiating sun, will roll on, while deathless ages roll, the one unchanging, unchangeable revelation of God." (The Rev. George S. Bishop, D.D., East Orange, N. J.)

"Young man, my advice to you is that you cultivate an acquaintance with and

[1]The original for "inspired of God" is "theopneustos," which may be rendered, "God-breathed." The Word of God may come to us with the force of the rock-rending storms of Sinai, or in the sweet music of the harp of the royal shepherd. It is, in either case, the wind, the breath, of God. It is his word.

firm belief in the Holy Scriptures, for this is your certain interest. I think Christ's system of morals and religion, as he left them with us, the best the world ever saw or is likely to see." (Benjamin Franklin)

"I have said and always will say that the studious perusal of the sacred volume will make better citizens, better fathers, and better husbands." (Thomas Jefferson)

"The Bible is the book of all others for lawyers as well as divines, and I pity the man who cannot find in it a rich supply of thought and rule of conduct." (Daniel Webster)

"The farther the ages advance in civilization the more will the Bible be used." (Goethe)

"All countries that refuse the cross wither, and the time will come, when the vast communities and countless myriads of America and Australia, looking upon Europe as Europe now looks upon Greece, and wondering how so small a space could have achieved such great deeds, will find music in the songs of Zion and solace in the parables of Galilee." (Benjamin Disraeli)

As Latter-day Saints we believe that such testimonies are applicable to all revelations of God to man.

## UNIVERSAL RELIGION

Since the human race has a common origin, all religions must have come from the one source. The covenant of God with Noah is the beginning, after the flood, of all religious systems. The Author of that covenant was God. And he made it binding upon Noah and all his descendants. It included "all flesh that is upon the earth." (Gen. 9-1-17) It was essentially the same as the covenant with our first parents in the garden of Eden (Comp. Gen. 1:22, 26-28), but it had two important additions. It prohibited the eating of flesh with the blood in it, because the blood, or rather the life, was the essential element in the atoning sacrifices. It also prohibited the shedding of human blood and fixed the penalty for the transgression of this law:

"Whoso sheddeth man's blood, by man shall his blood be shed: for in the image of God made he man."

The rainbow now became the visible symbol of this covenant. God so ordained it.

From this originally pure source all religions have come. As the descendants of Noah dispersed, the inhabitants of Mesopotamia, Arabia, Palestine, Syria, etc., received their religious traditions, customs and ideals through Shem, while those who occupied the shores of the Persian Gulf, Egypt, Ethiopia, Libya, etc., preserved the traditions of Ham, and the Aryan race, sometimes called the Japhetic or Indo-European group, perpetuated the religious ideals as handed down by the descendants of Japhet. Even the religions of the American Indians—the Peruvians, the Mayas, the Nahuas, and the North American tribes—are from the same source, through the Jaredites and the descendants of Lehi, and perhaps other immigrants from the Old World. The common origin accounts for the similarity that exists. The widely different conditions of life account for many of the differences in religious ideas and observances.

When speaking of the various races, it may be necessary to remember that there never was any well defined geographic line between them. They always intermingled, in some places more, in others less intimately, as Noah, in his patriarchal blessings foretold, when he said that Ham, through Canaan, would become a servant of servants "unto his brethren," and that Japhet would be enlarged and dwell "in the tents of Shem." (Gen. 9:25-27) This has been fulfilled. Various kindreds, tongues, peoples and nations have always occupied the same territory, in part. And as they mingled together, they borrowed from each other, they added their own philosophies, their own ceremonies, they made changes to suit new conditions, they formed, reformed, and reformed the reforms, and gradually a great number of religious systems were brought into existence, each different from the others, and all retaining a modicum of the original truth. The rod of iron is in evidence, even where the mists are thick.

Contrary to prevalent impressions perhaps, we must regard the various "pagan" religions and philosophies—the doctrines of Hinduism, Buddhism, Confucianism, etc., in Asia; the mythologies of the ancient Greeks, Romans, Anglo-Saxons, and Teutons in Europe; the elaborate observances and rites of the Egyptians in Africa, and the simpler religious legends and forms of worship of the Indians in America— all these, we say, must be regarded, historically considered, as the development in divergent directions of the one original patriarchal religion, precisely as we regard the Roman and Greek Catholicism and Protestantism, with all its sects, historically, as so many parts of the religion of Jesus of Nazareth.

This view of the nature of paganism is suggested by the argument of St. Paul at Lystra, when the priests of the Roman colonists there were about to offer sacrifices to him and Barnabas, thinking that they were Jupiter and Mercurius. Paul argued: They were not gods but men; they were the servants of the living God, which made heaven and earth—

"Who in times past suffered all nations to walk in their own ways, nevertheless he left not himself without witness, in that he did good, and gave us rain from heaven, and fruitful seasons, filling our hearts with food and gladness. (Acts 14:16, 17; comp. Rom. 1:19, 20)

The manifestation of the power and the goodness of God was a revelation that even the natural man could understand, and many did. There must have been men and women in many parts of the world, in all ages, who feared God and lived righteous lives, according to the light they had. The Apostle Peter learned that lesson by special revelation (Acts 10:9-16), in which he was warned not to call "common" (or unclean), that which God had cleansed.

In the Old Testament we read of Job. He was a native of the land of Uz, possibly in Arabia, and he lived before the Mosaic dispensation had been established. It is supposed that he was a contemporary of Isaac, the son of Abraham. He certainly was a servant of the Lord, and was recognized as such by the Lord (Job 1:8; Ezek. 14:14, 20; Jas. 5:11), although he was not, as far as now known, a Hebrew. We read of Jethro (also called, Hobab, Reuel and Raguel), the father-in-law of Moses, who was a priest in the land of Midian, presumably a descendant of Cush, the son of Ham, and not of the fourth son of Abraham and Kethurah. He was a servant of the Lord. (Ex. 18:1-23)

A strange character is Balaam. He was a resident of Pethor (probably in Mesopotamia) and he was widely known for his prophetic gift. (Numb. 22:5) He had communication with God, and he certainly received information concerning the future of Israel and its enemies. He fell, because he loved the wages of unrighteousness, and was slain in a battle against Israel (Numb. 31:8). But he did not sin through ignorance. (Comp. Deut. 23:4, 5; Josh. 24:9; Jude 11; Rev. 2:14)

In the prophetic book of Jonah we are taught that the Lord was concerned about the wicked, idolatrous city of Nineveh (Jonah 4:11), which was founded by Nimrod, a descendant of Ham, through Cush, (Gen. 10:8) and that he accepted the prayers and the repentance of the inhabitants.

Cyrus, the Persian ruler, is by the Lord himself accorded such titles as "my shepherd" (Isa. 44:28), his "Anointed"[2] (Isa. 45:28). According to 2 Chron. 36:22, the Lord inspired Cyrus to set the exiles free, and he acknowledged that, "The Lord God of heaven hath charged me to build him a house in Jerusalem."

The Ethiopian nobleman, the queen's secretary of the treasury, (Acts 8:27) and Cornelius, the Roman Centurian at Caesarea, are notable examples of the love of God of his children, without preference for race or nationality. (Acts 10:1, 2, 34, 35) Consider the following:

## SOME ANCIENT RELIGIONS

*Zoroastrianism.* At times men have arisen in the various nations who, like Moses or Elijah among the Jews, have endeavored to arouse the people from slumber and direct their spiritual life according to high ideals.

One of these mighty men of old was Zoroaster, or, Zarathustra, the founder of Zoroastrianism. He was born, as now generally accepted, in the northwestern part of Persia, near the Caspian sea, probably in the year 660 B.C. Tradition has it that when he was thirty years of age he received a revelation, whereupon he came forward as a reformer of the superstitions and falsehoods that had crept into the old religion.

Zoroastrianism teaches the existence of One, Supreme God, Ahura Mazda, a name generally abbreviated to, Ormadz. Over against this Deity the Zoroastrians place the personified evil principle, Angra Mainyu, which name appears in the abbreviated form, Ahriman. On the side of Ormadz there are a host of good angels, such as Good-mind, Right, Justice, Power, Dominion, Kingdom, Piety, Love, Immortality, etc. On the side of Ahriman there are evil spirits, such as Hunger, Thirst, Wrath, Lies, Harlots, etc. Between these two opposite hosts there is constant warfare, but the good will ultimately overcome the evil.

The Zoroastrians are generally classed as fireworshipers. But they deny this, and explain that they fix their eyes on the flame as the purest and most glorious element in existence, while they humble themselves before the Supreme Being and acknowledge their dependence on him.

The Medians and Persians had a tribe, or a caste, the Magi, who had charge of religion, arts, and the higher culture generally. They were highly honored, as was the tribe of Levi in Israel. Three of these Magi, as will be remembered, came to Bethlehem to pay homage to Jesus, whose star they had seen in the east. The followers of Zoroaster are still represented by the Ghebers in Persia and the Parsees in India.

*Manicheism.* This religious system is a modification of Zoroastrianism. Its founder was a Persian nobleman, Mani, or Manes, born in the year 216 A.D. In his youth he joined a sect in South Babylonia, known as Baptists. At the age of 25 he appeared at the coronation of the Persian ruler, Schapur I. Shortly afterwards he traveled through India and made a number of converts. His disciples proclaimed him to be a true prophet of the living God, and his philosophy was diffused throughout the then known world. During the reign of King Boram I over Persia, he suffered martyrdom by crucifixion.

Manicheism recognizes the existence of the two princples of good and evil and the constant conflict between them. Darkness, it holds, always aspires to light, and, at times, engulfs a portion of it. By such a process the world, including human nature with its conflicting impulses and desires, has come into existence.

The great church father, Augustine (b. 354, d. 430) bishop at Hippo, Africa,

---

[2]The Hebrew word for "anointed" is "mashiach," which in the New Testament is translated, "Christ."

was in his younger years associated with the Manicheans. Later he carried on a controversy against them, as well as the Donatists and the Pelagians, but, although he opposed them on behalf of the church, their philosophical speculations penetrated the whole church, and are still in evidence in the theology of Christian churches.[3]

*Greek and Roman myths.* According to the poets, the gods dwelt in a palace on Olympus, the highest peak of the mountain chain between Thessaly and Macedonia. Zeus was the chief of the gods. They were in appearance human in form; grander and more beautiful than men, but still human. They were inconceivably strong. When Zeus shook his locks the whole Olympus trembled. They moved with lightning speed from one place to another. In the twinkling of an eye, Athene, the goddess, drops from the heights of Olympus down to Ithaca. They see all; they hear all. Zeus, from his throne on Mount Ida, can follow the events of the battle before Troy in Asia Minor. As regards mental qualifications they are also far above men, and they visit impiety and injustice with punishment, but they are not above exhibiting deceit, hatred, cruelty and jealousy, themselves.

Tremendous battles were fought by the gods. After the conflict with the Titans, Zeus divided the government of the world between himself and his two brothers. He gave the oceans and the waters to Poseidon and the infernal regions to Hades. This did not suit the powerful goddess Gaea, wherefore she gave birth to the giant Typhoeus, a monster with a hundred flame-breathing dragons' heads, whom she sent to overthrow Zeus. A great battle followed which shook heaven and earth. Zeus, at length conquered and cast his adversary into Tartary, or, according to another version, into Mount Aetna, Sicily, whence he at times still breathes fire and flames towards heaven.

The most ancient legend concerning the origin of man derives the human race from trees and rocks. But some asserted that man was called into existence by Zeus and the other gods. Another account makes Prometheus, a Titan, the originator of men. Man, they say, was made of clay and water, and the goddess Athene breathed a spirit into him.

Various views were also held concerning the original condition of mankind. Some held that the race worked itself up from a state of barbarism, with the assistance of the gods. Others held that man was at first living in a state of innocent happiness, communicating with the gods, and that he lost this happiness by his presumption.

Prometheus helped man to become civilized. He stole fire from the gods and taught man how to use it. But because man polluted this pure element, Prometheus was seized and chained to a rock, where an eagle devours his liver in the daytime. But as it grows again during the night, there is a meal every day for the eagle.

Another legend accounts for the existence of evil in the world. Zeus ordered Hephaestus to make an image of a beautiful woman. The gods gave her life and named her Pandora. Aphrodite gave her the charms that kindle love. Athene instructed her in the arts. Hermes gave her a smooth tongue and a crafty disposition.

---

[3] A few years ago (1930) a German scientist, Professor Carl Smidth, visited Egypt when rumors reached him of a find by Arabian fellahin, while digging in the earth, of a wooden casket containing a number of papyri. The professor found them in the shop of a second-hand dealer. They were very much damaged, but the scientist succeeded in deciphering the word, "Kephalaion." This, he knew, was the title of one of Mani's lost books. Not having the necessary funds with which to buy the leaves, he went home and tried to interest others in them, but without success. On a second visit in Egypt, he found that a private collector in London had bought half of them. He bought the other half. These are now in Berlin. They contain Mani's Kephalaion, a collection of letters of Mani, and a biography of the founder of Manicheism. They will, when translated, give a complete picture of the life and teachings of Mani, from his own point of view. We shall then know how much modern Christianity has retained of Manicheism, once its greatest rival.

The seasons and the graces adorned her with flowers and fine raiment. Zeus then sent her to Epimetheus who made her his wife. In the house of Epimetheus there was a closed jar which contained all kinds of diseases and ills. No one was allowed to open this jar, but curiosity got the better of Pandora, and she removed the lid. Out came all kinds of diseases and troubles. They have been with us ever since. The only thing left is Hope.

According to another legend, the gods first created a golden age. Men lived in this age free from care and sorrow and disease. At last they sank into death peacefully; how, we do not know. But they live in the upper regions as good spirits, and they are guarding and protecting mortals. After this, the gods created a second race of men. They were inferior to the first. Their age was the silver age. By and by they became idle, effeminate and rebellious. Zeus then blotted out that race, and created a third, the race of bronze. This became headstrong and violent. They destroyed themselves in sanguinary strife, or, according to another version, they perished in the flood of Deucalion, the Greek Noah, who became the ancestor of a new race of men.

It is quite interesting to compare such myths and legends of paganism with the authentic accounts of the sacred Scriptures.

*Hinduism* is the oldest of the living religions of India. Its chief characteristic is the caste system. The name of the ruling caste is "Brahman," or "Brahmin." They are the priests, and their word is law. Even the shadow of a Brahman is sacred. The three chief gods of Hinduism are Brahma, the creator, Vishnu, the preserver, and Siva, the destroyer. The sacred books of the Hindus are the Vedas.

*Jainism* is an early reform movement in India, by which it was hoped to improve Hinduism. Soon after Jainism another reform movement arose, known as Buddhism. Some regard Buddhism not as a religion but as a system of morality and philosophy. Some have suggested that Buddha is none other than Noah.

*Sikhism* is another Indian religion. Its founder, Nanak, was born in 1469 at Lahore, and died in 1539. The aim of Nanak was to unite the Mohammendans and Hindus into one brotherhood. The Sikhs have been taught to worship God, to practice morality and to fight. They have had two wars with the British, and been defeated. In the World War they distinguished themselves on several occasions. There are now about three million Sikhs in India.

*Confucianism* can be referred to as proof of the divine sanction of the Command, "Honor thy father and thy mother," for the strength of China, notwithstanding her weakness, is obedience to that precept. Confucius lived 551-479 B.C. Late in life he was appointed minister of crime in the province of Lu, and it is said he was so successful, through his wisdom and justice, that he almost wiped out crime in that province. He held that acts in conformance with the five virtues of kindness, uprightness, decorum, wisdom and truth comprise the whole duty of man. He was a teacher of morals rather than religion. He considered that the history of China dates back to 2356 B.C.

*Taoism* is another religious, or philosophic, system of China. The founder, Laotse, is venerated throughout the empire. Its object is to give the greatest possible happiness to the individual.

*Shinto* is the official religion of Japan. It originated about 660 B.C. According to its sacred records Japan was the first divine work of creation, and the Mikado was the son of the Sun. The Japanese constitution starts with the declaration that the emperor occupies the throne of a lineal succession unbroken for eternities. The

## 5. *The River.*

26. And they said unto me: What meaneth the river of water which our father saw?

27. And I said unto them that the water which my father saw was filthiness; and so much was his mind swallowed up in other things that he beheld not the filthiness of the water.

28. And I said unto them that it was an awful gulf, which separated the wicked from the tree of life, and also from the saints of God.

29. And I said unto them that it was a representation of that awful hell, which the angel said unto me was prepared for the wicked.

30. And I said unto them that our father also saw that the justice of God did also divide the wicked from the righteous; and the brightness thereof was like unto the brightness of a flaming fire, which ascendeth up unto God forever and ever, and hath no end.

31. And they said unto me: Doth this thing mean the torment of the body in the days of probation, or doth it mean the final state of the soul after the death of the temporal body, or doth it speak of the things which are temporal?

32. And it came to pass that I said unto them that it was a representation of things both temporal and spiritual; for the day should come that they must be judged of their works, yea, even the works which were done by the temporal body in their days of probation.

---

emperor is, therefore, regarded as a person of divine origin, with divine authority. Shintoism, it is said, has no creed, no doctrinal system, no moral code, no priests, and no images, although it has about 14,000 gods, and is broken up into 13 sects.

VERSE 26. *What meaneth the river of water?* The brothers of Nephi asked this question. Nephi explains that the water in the river was filthy, but that the fact had escaped their father, because of other things that had occupied his mind. He also explains that the water represents the awful gulf that separates the wicked from the tree of life, and from the association with the saints (v. 28). The gulf that separates Dives from Lazarus in Hades is in existence already on this side of the grave. Saints and sinners never endure the company of each other.

The water also represents hell, prepared for the wicked (v. 29) by the devil (v. 35).

VERSE 30. *The Justice of God.* The gulf represented by the contaminated water is not the only separating obstacle between the righteous and the wicked, saints and sinners. The justice of God also stands between the two camps. In the vision of Lehi, this appeared like a flaming fire, ever ascending toward heaven. Note that the fountain of this contaminated river is the "depth of hell," and that the wars that ensued between the descendants of Lehi originated in those depths. (I Ne. 12:15, 16)

VERSE 32. *They must be judged by their works.* As a consequence of this justice of God, the day of judgment will come to each individual, and all will be judged according to the deeds done in the body.

33. Wherefore, if they should die in their wickedness they must be cast off also, as to the things which are spiritual, which are pertaining to righteousness; wherefore, they must be brought to stand before God, to be judged of their works; and if their works have been filthiness they must needs be filthy; and if they be filthy it must needs be that they cannot dwell in the kingdom of God; if so, the kingdom of God must be filthy also.

34. But behold, I say unto you, the kingdom of God is not filthy, and there cannot any unclean thing enter into the kingdom of God; wherefore there must needs be a place of filthiness prepared for that which is filthy.

35. And there is a place prepared, yea, even that awful hell of which I have spoken, and the devil is the foundation of it; wherefore the final state of the souls of men is to dwell in the kingdom of God, or to be cast out because of that justice of which I have spoken.

36. Wherefore, the wicked are rejected from the righteous, and also from that tree of life, whose fruit is most precious and most desirable above all other fruits; yea, and it is the greatest of all the gifts of God. And thus I spake unto my brethren. Amen.

VERSES 33-35. *If they be filthy . . . they cannot dwell in the kingdom of God.* The judgment of God is not the arbitrary dictum of an Autocrat; it is rather a careful selection, a classification and an assignment of each soul, to the place and condition for which he is best fitted, on the evidence of his own thoughts, words and acts in this life. It is an eminently just judgment. "Even so, Lord God Almighty, true and righteous are thy judgments." (Rev. 16:7)

"Does not the soul, then, when in this state, depart to that which resembles itself, the invisible, the divine, immortal, and wise? And on its arrival there, is it not its lot to be happy, free from error, ignorance, fears and the wild passions and all the other evils to which human nature is subject?" (Plato)

GENERAL NOTES

The student of the Book of Mormon may be interested in the following specimens of non-Christian literature.

Special attention is called to the Icelandic songs. They are interesting both on account of the language and the contents.

The Icelandic tongue was spoken, until the 13th century, not only in Iceland but in the Scandinavian countries. the Faeroe Islands, Shetland, the Orkneys, the Hebrides, and on the coasts of England, Scotland and Ireland. It was brought over to Iceland by the Norwegians who first settled there.

It is closely related to what is known as Old English, which was spoken in England till the time of William the Conqueror (1027-87).

We who believe that the blood of Israel is coursing in the veins of a large portion of the Anglo-Saxon race and its near kindred, also realize that these venerable compositions, together with the sagas, myths and biographies of the Icelanders must have been influenced by the Israelites who settled among them. That enhances their interest.

## ICELANDIC SONGS

## END OF THE WORLD

### (Ragnarok)

Brothers go to combat,
Cruel wounds inflicting.
Kindred tear asunder
Friendship's tender bonds.
Earth is full of evil:
Whoredom, fornication;
Swords and battle axes
Beat against the shields.

Wolves and mighty whirlwinds
Spread on earth destruction
Ere the world goes under,
Ere dread ragnarok.
Earth is quaking, trembling,
Female giants flying,
None regards another,
Each one for himself.

Mime's sons are playing,
Gjallarhorn is brought forth,
Aesir-god is well known
By the sounding blasts.
Hejmdal sounds the trumpet
Toward heaven pointing,
From the head of Mime
Odin counsel seeks.

Branches of the ash-tree,
Yggdrasil, the olden,
They are sighing, trembling
For the giant's free.
Wanderers to Helhjem

Move with fear and terror
Until death is swallowed
By a son of Surt.

What about the Aesir?
What about the Elfins?
Jotunhejm is shaking,
Aesir meet to plan,
Dwarfs, though wise, are helpless
At the rocky portals
Of the lofty mountains,
Know ye also that?

Garm, at Gnipehollow,
Barks, the world arousing;
Fenris' chains are breaking,
Soon the wolf is free.
Farther still I'm seeing,
Much more I could tell you
Of the gods, exalted,
And of Ragnarok.

* * * *

Darkened is the sungod,
Earth by water covered,
And the stars of heaven
Give no more their light.
Flames strike flames, like serpents,
Hissing, spitting, circling;
Towards heaven the dancing,
Lurid blazes flash.

But after this fiery consummation, there is a resurrection of the world:

Again I see the earth
Arising from the deep,
And on the mountain top
The eagle finds his prey.
The purling mountain streams
Are hast'ning to their goal,
And earth in green arrayed
Is fair as ne'er before.

* * * *

Fairer than the sun
Is a hall I see,
Covered all with gold,

G I M L E is its name.
There will all the good
Live and dwell in joy
In eternity.

Then the Mighty One,
He who rules the world,
Comes from Heaven down,
Takes the judgment seat.
All things he doeth judge,
Ending strife for ever,
Tells us what is holy
Here upon the earth.

## STANZAS from HAVAMAL

Better burden none can carry
On his way, than wisdom, knowledge;
Poorest baggage on the journey
Is intoxicating drink.

Mead is not for men to relish,
't is not good, as some folks tell us;
For the more we drink such nectar,
Sooner do we loose our minds.

Dullard is the bird, the heron,
Hov'ring round a drunkard's tables,
Robbing people of their senses.
By such feathers I was tied up
When I was at Gunlod's home.

Drunk I was, intoxicated,
At the home of Wise Man Fjalar.
Well it is when, after drinking,
Each one gets his senses back.

Wise let princes be, and silent,
Fearless, brave and strong in combat.
Glad let all men be and joyful
Till the last day's early dawn.

Craven, dumb is he who's thinking
That his life will last for ever
If he only shuns all danger.
Old age finds and ends him surely.
Though he may have dodged the spear.

Death takes herds and flocks and kindred,
Thou, thyself, wilt soon be lifeless;
But the praise you've been accorded,
That will never, never die.

Death takes herds and flocks and kindred,
Death thyself will soon make lifeless;
One thing lives, I know, for ever:
Judgment passed on him who died.

## PERSIAN

O Thou who existedst from eternity, and abidest for ever! Sight cannot bear thy light, praise cannot express Thy perfection. Thy light melts the understanding, and Thy glory baffles wisdom; to think of Thee bewilders reason; Thy essence confounds thought. Science is like blinding desert sand on the road to Thy perfection. The town of literature is a mere hamlet compared with the word of Thy knowledge.

\* \* \*

Human thought and knowledge combined can only spell the first letter of Thy love.

\* \* \*

The man who has constantly contended against evil, morally, physically, inwardly and outwardly, may fearlessly meet death; well assured that radiant spirits will lead him across the luminous bridge into a paradise of eternal happiness.

\* \* \*

Souls risen from the grave will know each other, and say: That is my father, or my mother, my wife or sister.

\* \* \*

The wicked will say to the good, Wherefore, when I was in the world, did you not teach me to act righteously? O ye pure ones, it is because you did not instruct me, that I am excluded from the assembly of the blessed.

\* \* \*

The best way of worshiping God is in allaying the distress of the times, and improving the condition of mankind.

\* \* \*

All good thoughts, words and actions are from the celestial world.

\* \* \*

Be very scrupulous to observe the truth in all things.

Once upon a time the fishes of a certain river took counsel together, and said: They tell us that our life and being is from the water; but we have never seen water, and we know not what it is. Then some among them, wiser than the rest, said, We have heard that there dwelleth in the sea a very wise and learned fish who knoweth all things. Let us journey to him and ask him to show us water, or explain to us what water is. So seven of them set out on their travels and came at last to the sea wherein the sage fish dwelleth. On hearing their question, he replied,—

O ye, who seek to solve the knot,
Ye live in God, yet know him not.

* * *

One night Gabriel from his seat in Paradise heard the voice of God sweetly responding to a human heart. The angel said, Surely this must be an eminent servant of the Most High, whose spirit is dead to lust and lives on high. The angel hastened over land and sea to find this man, but could not find him in the earth or heavens, At last he exclaimed, O Lord, show me the way to this object of thy love. God answered, Turn thy steps to yon village, and in the pagoda thou shalt behold him. The angel sped to the pagoda, and therein found a solitary man kneeling before an idol. Returning, he cried, O Master of the world! Hast thou looked with love on a man who invokes an idol in a pagoda? God said, I consider not the error of ignorance. This heart, amid its darkness, has the highest place.

## BUDDHIST TEACHINGS

The effect of water poured on the root of a tree, is seen in the branches and fruit; so in the next world are seen the effects of good deeds performed here.

* * *

There are treasures laid up in the heart—treasures of charity, piety, temperance and soberness. These treasures a man takes with him beyond death, when he leaves this world.

* * *

Man never dies. The soul inhabits the body for a time, and leaves it again. The soul is myself; the body is only my dwelling place.

* * *

Death is not death; the soul merely departs, and the body falls. It is because men see only their bodies that they love life and hate death.

* * *

O Thou Eternal One! Thou Perfection of Time! Thou Truest Truth! Thou Changeless Essence of all Change! Thou Most Excellent Radiance of Mercy, I take refuge in Thee.

As the great universe hath no boundary, and the light sections of heaven have no gateway, so the Supreme reason has no limits.

We do not suppose our prayers are the only prayers in the world. We ought to respect all prayer. Men of prayer belong to all countries; they are strangers nowhere. Such is the doctrine taught by our holy books.

The divine law is as a cloud which, with a garland of light, spreads joy on the earth.

The water falls on all creatures, on herbs, bushes and trees; and each pumps up to its own leaves and blossoms what it requires for its special need. So falls the rain of the law on the many-hearted world. The law is for millions; but it is one, and it is alike beautiful to all.

Only the religious man is good. And what is religion? It is the perfect agreement of the will with the conscience.

Alms and pious demonstrations are of no worth compared with the loving-kindness of religion. The festival that bears great fruit is the festival of duty.

A man may recite large portions of the law, but if he is not a doer of it, he is like a herdsman who counts the cattle of others.

One should seek for others the happiness one desires for one's self.

There is no higher duty than to work for the good of the whole world.

Practise not usury in thy lending. Thou shalt abstain from acquiring the property of another by fraud or violence.

Contract no friendships with the hope of gain.

Speak the truth; do not yield to anger; and when asked, give of the little thou hast. By those steps thou wilt approach the Immortals.

The good man, when reviled, reviles not again; when smitten, he is not angry; when treated violently, he returns love and good-will; when threatened with death, he returns no malice.

We should be deaf to hear evils of others and blind to perceive their imperfections.

## HINDU TEACHINGS

Shun wealth and pleasures repugnant to law; and avoid even lawful acts, if they may cause pain or offense to mankind.

* * *

No man can obtain knowledge of the soul without abstaining from evil actions and having control over his senses and his mind; nor can he attain it if he is actuated by desire for reward.

* * *

Labor makes known the true worth of man, as fire brings the perfume out of incense.

* * *

Religion is tenderness toward all creatures.

* * *

Large rivers, great trees, wholesome plants and wealthy persons are not created for themselves, but to be of service to others.

* * *

He who, to give himself pleasure, injures animals that are not injurious, adds nothing to his own happiness, either living or dead. But who never gives pain to any creature, by confinement or death, but seeks the good of all sentient beings, enjoys bliss without end.

## CHINESE WISDOM

God is the parent of men. He is compassionate and unwearied in blessing. He inspects kingdoms and makes no mistakes. Clear-seeing and intelligent, he dwells with men in all their actions. He is offended with wrong-doing.

* * *

What you would not like to have done to yourself, do it not unto others. When you labor for others, do it with the same zeal as if it were for yourself.

* * *

The mean man sows, that himself or his friends may reap; but the love of the perfect man is universal.

## EGYPTIAN WISDOM

God all in all.

I am that which has been, which is, and which will be; and no one has yet lifted the veil which covers me.

The world is not to be comprehended. God, who made it, has forbidden it.

What we say in secret is known to him who made our inner nature. He who made us is present with us, though we are alone.

Who can bless Thee or give thanks for Thee or to Thee? How shall I revere Thee? O Father! It is impossible to comprehend Thy hour or Thy time.

Shall I love Thee as if I were something of myself, or as if I had anything of my own, or rather as if I belonged to another?

Thou art what I am. Thou art what I do. Thou art what I say. Thou art all things, and there is nothing which thou art not.

Thou art all that is made and all that is not made.

Thou art the mind that understandeth all things; thou art the good that doest all things; Thou art the Father that makest all things; Thou art Thyself.

Of matter, the most subtle portion is the air; of air, the most subtle part is the soul; of the soul, the most subtle part is the mind; of the mind, the most subtle part is God.

What is truth, through me, praises Truth. What is good, through me, sings praises to the Good.

O All! receive a rational homage from all things. Thou art God.

Thy Messenger, by the fire, by the air, by the earth, by the water, by the spirit, by all things, proclaimeth these things concerning Thee.

## FOUND IN THE TALMUD

If you commit a sin twice, you will think it allowable.

He who marries for money, it shall be a curse to him.

The true reward is not of this world.

The world is saved by the breath of the school children.

Jerusalem was destroyed because the instruction of the young was neglected.

He who has more learning than good works, is like a tree with many branches but few roots. The first wind throws it on its face.

It is woman through whom God's blessings are vouchsafed to a house. She teaches the children, speeds the husband to the house of worship, and welcomes him when he returns.

These four shall not enter into Paradise: The scoffer, the liar, the hypocrite and the slanderer. To slander is to commit murder.

Says an idolator: If God hates idolatry, why does he not destroy it? And someone answered: Men worship the sun, the moon, the stars; would you ask him to destroy these because men are foolish?

If misfortune come upon a man, let him not cry to Michael or Gabriel, but unto Me let him cry, and I will answer him; as it is written, Everyone who calls upon the Lord shall be saved.

## What is Common to All

All religions believe in a Supreme Being, be he a person or a cosmic Force.

Divine incarnation is believed in by Hinduism, Buddhism, Christianity, and others.

Divine revelation is claimed by all.

All have sacred writings.

## An Arabian Rhyme

On parents' knees a naked, newborn child,
Weeping thou satst, while all around thee smiled;
So live that, sinking in thy long, last sleep,
Thou then mayest smile while all around thee weep.

## CHAPTER 16

*Effect of the discourses of Nephi on his brothers, 1-6—Intermarriages between the families of Lehi and Ishmael, 7-9—Lehi and his company continue their journey to Shazar, 10-13—The journey continued from Shazar, 14-17—An accident on the hunt is the cause of famine, 18-25—The warning on the Liahona, 26-32—The journey continued, 33—Death of Ishmael and subsequent events, 34-9.*

### 1. *Effects of the discourses of Nephi on his brothers.*

1. And now it came to pass that after I, Nephi, had made an end of speaking to my brethren, behold they said unto me: Thou hast declared unto us hard things, more than we are able to bear.

2. And it came to pass that I said unto them that I knew that I had spoken hard things against the wicked, according to the truth; and the righteous have I justified, and testified that they should be lifted up at the last day; wherefore, the guilty taketh the truth to be hard, for it cutteth them to the very center.

3. And now my brethren, if ye were righteous and were willing to hearken to the truth, and give heed unto it, that ye might walk uprightly before God, then ye would not murmur because of the truth, and say: Thou speakest hard things against us.

4. And it came to pass that I, Nephi, did exhort my brethren, with all diligence, to keep the commandments of the Lord.

5. And it came to pass that they did humble themselves before the Lord; insomuch that I had joy and great hopes of them, that they would walk in the paths of righteousness.

6. Now, all these things were said and done as my father dwelt in a tent in the valley which he called Lemuel.

---

VERSE 2. *The guilty taketh the truth to be hard.* Nephi here states a fact, amply confirmed. A sermon intended to arouse a slumberer out of his sleep, or to turn a sinner from his evil ways, never is "pleasant" to the offender. It stings and smarts and crushes. Those who heard John the Baptist address the people as a "generation of vipers," and telling them that, as chaff, they would be burned in unquenchable fire; or, those who heard the Apostle Peter, on the day of Pentecost, accuse his audience of being the murderers of Jesus of Nazareth, did not like the sermons. They did not exclaim, What beautiful discourses! They were, instead, "pricked in their hearts," and that hurt. It was in the agony of soul that they cried out, "What are we to do?" Such are the effects of the inspired word of God on guilty consciences, if it produces repentance.

VERSE 5. *They did humble themselves.* The brothers of Nephi humbled themselves this time. The chief trouble was that they could not, or would not, accept Nephi as their leader, although the Lord had called him to that position. That question had to be settled before they could continue their journey. It was settled, temporarily, and Nephi rejoiced, full of hope for the future.

## 2. *Intermarriages.*

7. And it came to pass that I, Nephi, took one of the daughters of Ishmael to wife; and also, my brethren took of the daughters of Ishmael to wife; and also Zoram took the eldest daughter of Ishmael to wife.

8. And thus my father had fulfilled all the commandments of the Lord which had been given unto him. And also, I, Nephi, had been blessed of the Lord exceedingly.

9. And it came to pass that the voice of the Lord spake unto my father by night, and commanded him that on the morrow he should take his journey into the wilderness.

## 3. *Lehi and his company . . . Shazer.*

10. And it came to pass that as my father arose in the morning, and went forth to the tent door, to his great astonishment he beheld upon the ground a round ball of curious workmanship; and it was of fine brass. And within the ball were two spindles; and the one pointed the way whither we should go into the wilderness.

VERSE 7. *Marriages in the Valley of Lemuel.* Ishmael and his family were brought down from Jerusalem by Nephi and his brothers, according to a divine command. (1 Ne. 7:2) Marriage for the purpose of raising up posterity "unto the Lord" was enjoined upon them as a sacred duty.

Ishmael had five daughters and two sons. During the journey from Jerusalem to the Valley of Lemuel, Laman and Lemuel opposed Nephi. They even bound him and plotted his death. Two of the daughters of Ishmael sided with Laman and his supporters. One daughter of Ishmael stood up valiantly for Nephi, and plead so sincerely for his righteous cause that he was set free. (1 Nephi 7:19) Thus a line of cleavage was already drawn. In all probability, the two girls who had sided with Laman and Lemuel became their wives, while the valiant little girl, possibly the youngest of them, joined her hero in the sacred relationship contemplated. There were two girls left. Zoram, the servant of Laban, married the oldest daughter, and Sam presumably the remaining girl.

VERSE 8. *All the commandments fulfilled.* Nephi says, that his father had thus fulfilled all the commandments of the Lord. He had now set his house in order. He was ready to continue the long journey. The wives were not an encumbrance on the road, but their greatest help.

*And also I, Nephi had been blessed . . . exceedingly.* Nephi, undoubtedly refers to his wife—an exceedingly delicate and fine compliment.

VERSE 10. *A round ball of curious workmanship.* Lehi had received a command to start on his journey on the morrow. Naturally, his great concern was how to find the road through the wilderness, and how to avoid encounters with enemies. Ezra, in leading a large company of his countrymen from Babylonia to Jerusalem, was confronted with a similar problem. He could have obtained an armed escort from the king, but because he had told the ruler that the Lord would protect them, he was, as he says, ashamed to ask the king for a band of soldiers, thereby proving

11. And it came to pass that we did gather together whatsoever things we should carry into the wilderness, and all the remainder of our provisions which the Lord had given unto us; and we did take seed of every kind that we might carry into the wilderness.

12. And it came to pass that we did take our tents and depart into the wilderness, across the river Laman.

13. And it came to pass that we traveled for the space of four days, nearly a south-southeast direction, and we did pitch our tents again; and we did call the name of the place Shazer.

## 4. The journey continued from Shazer.

14. And it came to pass that we did take our bows and our arrows, and go forth into the wilderness to slay food for our families; and after we had slain food for our families we did return again to our families in the wilderness, to the place of Shazer. And we did go forth again in the wilderness, following the same direction, keeping in the most fertile parts of the wilderness, which were in the borders near the Red Sea.

that his faith in Jehovah had no practical value; he gathered his company, instead, at the river Ahavah, and for three days they fasted and prayed for guidance and protection. Then they set out on their perilous journey. "And the hand of our God," Ezra says, "was upon us, and he delivered us from the hand of the enemy, and of such as lay in wait by the way." (Ezra 9:15-23, 31, 32)

As for Lehi, the problem of guidance and protection from robbers was solved in a most remarkable way. He was up early in the morning. As he stood by the opening of the tent, undoubtedly wondering what course to take, he perceived a ball on the ground. He picked it up and found, on examining it, that it contained two spindles, one of which pointed the way "whither we should go." That solved the problem. The spindle indicated the general direction, and also where to go to find food and safety from robber bands. See, Liahona, p. 229.

Verse 11. Seed of every kind. Not of every kind that existed, but of every kind that they had on hand. They must have remained long enough in the Valley of Lemuel to raise crops and to accumulate various kinds of provisions.

Verse 13. Direction. Having crossed the river Laman, they traveled for four days in a south-southeast direction, to a place which they called Shazer.

Shazer. This name may have been, originally, the Hebrew chazer (or chazier), "grass" (Ps. 104:14). It must have been an inviting place to weary travelers. The little company remained there long enough to replenish their store of provisions. Then they continued their journey along the eastern shore of the Red Sea.

Verse 14. And we did go forth again in the wilderness. Following the sea shore, Lehi and his company, after "the space of many days," must have come to some place not very far from the present Medina, one of the sacred cities of Islam, in the kingdom of Hejaz. This part of Arabia was at one time settled by Israelites of the tribe of Simeon.

Simeon was the second son of Jacob and Leah. His sister was Dinah. (See Gen. 34:25-31; 35:23)

The tribe of Simeon, at the time of the exodus, had "fifty and nine thousand

15. And it came to pass that we did travel for the space of many days, slaying food by the way, with our bows and our arrows and our stones and our slings.

16. And we did follow the directions of the ball, which led us in the more fertile parts of the wilderness.

17. And after we had traveled for the space of many days, we did pitch our tents for the space of a time, that we might again rest ourselves and obtain food for our families.

---

and three hundred" men, able to bear arms. (Numb. 1:23) At the time of the entrance into Palestine, forty years afterwards, there were only "twenty and two thousand and two hundred." (Numb. 26:14) It was then the smallest tribe in Israel. Its inheritance was part of the territory of Judah, in the southern part of the country (Josh. 1:1-9), but after a while it seems that Judah took back part of the land allotted to Simeon. (I Kings 19:3) In I Chron. 4:24-31 several cities are enumerated and the information given that they were the cities of the sons of Simeon "unto the reign of David." In the same chapter we are told that 500 of the sons of Simeon, during the reign of Hezekiah, king of Judah, emigrated to Mt. Seir, the mountainous country of the Edomites, east of the Dead Sea, while others went "to the entrance of Gedor, even unto the east side of the valley," where Hamites had dwelt of old (vv. 39, 40). This is supposed to be the region in which Medina and Mekka are situated, and an Arab tradition has it that the very sanctuary at Mekka was founded by Israelites of the tribe of Simeon, at the time of King David.[1]

VERSE 16. *We did follow the directions of the ball.* Under ordinary circumstances Lehi would have had commercial dealings with the mixed population—Arabs, Ishmaelites, Simeonites, etc., through the countries of which they traveled. But the "director" led the company through the most fertile parts of the wilderness, instead of the more thickly populated regions. They had to forage for themselves. They were thus preserved from contact with the idolatrous tribes. Perhaps this was necessary because of the rebellious disposition of the brothers of Nephi.

VERSE 17. *Another resting place.* After having been on the road "for the space of many days"—how many we know not—the company found another suitable camping place. Here they remained for the "space of a time."

*Space of a time.* In the prophetic writings of the Hebrews the word "time" often stands for a "year." See Daniel 4:16 and 29; also 7:25, where "a time and times and the dividing of time" (for half a time) generally is understood to mean three years and a half, as in Dan. 12:7.[2] If, as I consider probable, the expression, "space of a time" is the same as Daniel's term, "the dividing of time," then, Nephi tells us in his idiomatic language that the company remained at this unnamed place for half a year, which is by no means improbable. (Comp. 1 Ne. 11:19 and perhaps Luke 1:26, 36) But "Time" may also mean "season;" that is, an appointed time. And as the Jews sometimes counted six seasons[3] in a year, of two months each, the "space of a time" may mean two months—an entire season.

[1] Victor Rydberg, in "Medeltiden's magi," p. 200, states this theory as advanced by Prof. R. Dozy in his, "Ein Beitrag zur alttestamentlichen Kritik und zur Erforschung des Ursprungs des Islams," Leipzig, 1864.

[2] However, "year" sometimes stands for the prophetic year of 360 days. Then 3½ years is equal to 1260 days, each day representing a common year. See Ezek. 4:5, 6; Dan. 9:24; Rev. 4:15 and 10:3.

[3] They were, beginning October 15, Seed time, winter, cold, harvest, heat and summer. "Seedtime and harvest, and cold and heat, and summer and winter . . . shall not cease." (Gen. 8:22.)

## 5. *An accident and famine.*

18. And it came to pass that as I, Nephi, went forth to slay food, behold, I did break my bow, which was made of fine steel; and after I did break my bow, behold, my brethren were angry with me because of the loss of my bow, for we did obtain no food.

19. And it came to pass that we did return without food to our families, and being much fatigued, because of their journeying, they did suffer much for the want of food.

20. And it came to pass that Laman and Lemuel and the sons of Ishmael did begin to murmur exceedingly, because of their sufferings and afflictions in the wilderness; and also my father began to murmur against the Lord his God; yea, and they were all exceeding sorrowful, even that they did murmur against the Lord.

21. Now it came to pass that I, Nephi, having been afflicted with my brethren because of the loss of my bow, and their bows having lost their springs, it began to be exceedingly difficult, yea, insomuch that we could obtain no food.

22. And it came to pass that I, Nephi, did speak much unto my brethren, because they had hardened their hearts again, even unto complaining against the Lord their God.

23. And it came to pass that I, Nephi, did make out of wood a bow, and out of a straight stick, an arrow; wherefore, I did arm myself with a bow and an arrow, with a sling and with stones. And I said unto my father: Whither shall I go to obtain food?

24. And it came to pass that he did inquire of the Lord, for they had humbled themselves because

---

This was the third station on the road, the Valley of Lemuel being the first and Shazer the second.

VERSE 18. *Fine steel.* See 1 Ne. 4:9.

*I did break my bow.* The serious result of this accident was scarcity of food, and famine. (v. 19)

VERSES 20-22. Presently, Laman and Lemuel begin another agitation against their brother. They are joined by the sons of Ishmael, and also by Father Lehi. Even a prophet of the Lord can make mistakes. The disaffection towards Nephi soon became open rebellion against God (v. 22). This brought Nephi out in defense of the Lord. "I, Nephi, spoke much *unto my brethren,* because they had hardened their hearts again." (v. 22 ) Note that he did not rebuke his father.

VERSE 23. *Nephi to the rescue.* The next step of Nephi was to make a bow and an arrow of wood, and to prepare a sling with suitable stones. Thus equipped, he asked his father for instructions as to where to go to find game. Nephi recognized the authority of his father as the head of the family.

VERSES 24-25. *Lehi inquired of the Lord.* But he came before his Maker in all humility, with sorrow in his heart.

of my word; for I did say many things unto them in the energy of my soul.

25. And it came to pass that the voice of the Lord came unto

my father; and he was truly chastened because of his murmuring against the Lord, insomuch that he was brought down into the depths of sorrow.

## 6. *The warning on the Liahona.*

26. And it came to pass that the voice of the Lord said unto him: Look upon the ball, and behold the things which are written.

27. And it came to pass that when my father beheld the things which were written upon the ball, he did fear and tremble exceedingly, and also my brethren and

the sons of Ishmael and our wives.

28. And it came to pass that I, Nephi, beheld the pointers which were in the ball, that they did work according to the faith and diligence and heed which we did give unto them.

29. And there was also written upon them a new writing, which

---

*Arrows and slings.* At the time of Lehi, the Jews were not, generally speaking, great hunters. In the early days, the pursuit of wild beasts either for the protection of the domestic animals and the cultivated fields, or for food, was a common occupation, both necessary and dangerous. We read of Nimrod, the "mighty hunter before the Lord" (Gen. 10:8, 9); Esau was a "cunning hunter," a man of the field (Gen. 25:27), skilled in the use of the bow (Gen. 27:3). But generally the Hebrews in later times did not practise archery either for hunting or for sport. The bow and the arrow became weapons of war, the play things of soldiers and rulers in times of peace. To use either the bow or the sling successfully, it was necessary to possess great strength and long practice.

These facts account for the predicament of Nephi and his brothers. They were not really skilled archers. Or, their bows may not have been of the best material, or make. Or, they may not have understood how to take good care of them, since they were out of commission at this early stage of the journey.

At all events, Nephi was inspired to come to the rescue. The Lord could use him as his instrument. The older brothers, who ought to have had the knowledge and experience necessary to overcome the difficulty, proved their weakness by their inactivity and grumbling. Nephi proved his strength by his activity.

*Slings.* These were also effective weapons in the hands of a youth, like Nephi. The story of David and Goliath was well known by these boys. (I Sam. 17:32-53)

At the time of the Judges, the men of the tribe of Benjamin were celebrated for their skill as stone slingers. "Among all this people there were seven hundred chosen men lefthanded; every one could sling stones at an hair breadth, and not miss." (Judges 20:16)

VERSES 26-32. *God's answer.* Nephi had asked his father for instructions as to where to go to find game. Lehi presented the matter before the Lord. God then directed him to look upon the ball (v. 26). Just what was written is not stated, but it had the effect of causing Lehi, his older sons, the sons of Ishmael and the women to fear exceedingly (v. 27). They were evidently unnerved by fear.

Nephi, then, looked and discovered (1) that the pointers worked according to the faith and diligence and heed which they gave unto them; (2) that the Lord would instruct them from time to time, by means of the pointers, concerning his

was plain to be read, which did give us understanding concerning the ways of the Lord; and it was written and changed from time to time, according to the faith and diligence which we gave unto it. And thus we see that by small means the Lord can bring about great things.

30. And it came to pass that I, Nephi, did go forth up into the top of the mountain, according to the directions which were given upon the ball.

31. And it came to pass that I did slay wild beasts, insomuch that I did obtain food for our families.

32. And it came to pass that I did return to our tents, bearing the beasts which I had slain; and now when they beheld that I had obtained food, how great was their joy? And it came to pass that they did humble themselves before the Lord, and did give thanks unto him.

## 7. The journey continued to Nahom.

33. And it came to pass that we did again take our journey, traveling nearly the same course as in the beginning; and after we had traveled for the space of many days we did pitch our tents again, that we might tarry for the space of a time.

## 8. Death of Ishmael.

34. And it came to pass that Ishmael died, and was buried in the place which was called Nahom.

---

ways; and (3) that the instructions asked for as to where to go to find food were given (vv. 28, 29).

Nephi did not linger now. He immediately follows the directions given. The result is that he obtains the needed provisions, and there is joy in the camp. (vv. 30-32)

VERSE 33. *We did again take our journey.* Peace being established and provisions obtained, the company continues its journey "for the space of many days," and rests "for the space of a time." See verse 17. This is the fourth station on the road, the others being, the Valley of Lemuel, Shazer, and a station not named.

VERSE 34. *Ishmael died and was buried.* "The righteous spirit that departs from this earth is assigned its place in the paradise of God; it has its privileges and honors which are in point of excellency, far above and beyond human comprehension; and in this sphere of action, enjoying this partial reward for its righteous conduct on the earth, it continues its labors, and in this respect is very different from the state of the body from which it is released. For while the body sleeps and decays, the spirit receives a new birth; to it the portals of life are opened. It is born again in the presence of God." (President Joseph F. Smith, "Gospel Doctrine," p. 554.)

*Nahom.* That was the name given to this place. Special attention is called to the word. According to Bible commentators, it means, "consolation." Was that a proper name for a place of death and burial?

"Nahom," or "nachum" (from the Hebrew "nacham") means "consolation,"

35. And it came to pass that the daughters of Ishmael did mourn exceedingly, because of the loss of their father, and because of their afflictions in the wilderness; and they did murmur against my father, because he had brought them out of the land of Jerusalem, saying: Our father is dead; yea, and we have wandered much in the wilderness, and we have suffered much affliction, hunger, thirst, and fatigue; and after all these sufferings we must perish in the wilderness with hunger.

36. And thus they did murmur against my father, and also against me; and they were desirous to return again to Jerusalem.

37. And Laman said unto Lemuel and also unto the sons of Ishmael: Behold, let us slay our father, and also our brother Nephi, who has taken it upon him to be our ruler and our teacher, who are his elder brethren.

38. Now, he says that the Lord has talked with him, and also that angels have ministered unto him. But behold, we know that he lies unto us; and he tells us these things, and he worketh many things by his cunning arts, that he may deceive our eyes, thinking, perhaps, that he may lead us away into some strange wilderness; and after he has led us away, he has thought to make himself a king and a ruler over

---

but it also means "vengeance," on the supposition that there is some consolation in retribution. Isaiah uses the word in that sense. (Is. 1:24) In view of what occurred at this place, the name, "Consolation," is peculiarly appropriate.

VERSE 35. *The daughters of Ishmael did mourn exceedingly.* Mourning was an elaborate ceremony among the Jews and other Orientals. When Job heard of his misfortunes he "rent his mantle and shaved his head and fell down upon the ground and worshiped." (Job 1:20) His friends, who by appointment, came to mourn with him, "lifted up their voice and wept; and they rent every one his mantle and sprinkled dust upon their heads toward heaven, and sat down by him upon the ground seven days and seven nights." (Job 2:12, 13) The mourning for Jacob in Egypt lasted seventy days (Gen. 50:3, 10). The Israelites wept for Moses thirty days (Deut. 34:8). Friends were expected to "weep with them that weep" (Rom. 12:15), but frequently mourners were hired to weep. (Eccl. 12:5; Jer. 9:17-20; Acts 9:39) The mourning was often conducted in a tumultuous manner (Mark 5:38). Friends provided the mourners with food, called the "bread of bitterness," and the "cup of consolation." In later times food was left at the grave for the benefit of the poor. The mourning for Ishmael must have been an elaborate function, according to the circumstances, since they "did mourn exceedingly."

VERSES 36-39. *They did murmur.* The ceremonial mourning being over, the slumbering rebellious disposition was awakened. They murmured. They began talking of returning to Jerusalem. (v. 36)

This was an opportunity for Laman. He promptly proposed to condemn both his father and his brother Nephi to death (v. 37), on the ground that they were plotting the destruction of the company (v. 38).

The Lord himself, in some miraculous manner interfered on behalf of his

us, that he may do with us according to his will and pleasure. And after this manner did my brother Laman stir up their hearts to anger.

39. And it came to pass that the Lord was with us, yea, even the voice of the Lord came and did speak many words unto them, and did chasten them exceedingly; and after they were chastened by the voice of the Lord they did turn away their anger, and did repent of their sins, insomuch that the Lord did bless us again with food, that we did not perish.

servants. Their lives were saved, the rebels were humbled, and the blessings of the Lord were again enjoyed. (v. 39)

## GENERAL NOTES

Ishmael is not an uncommon name among the descendants of Abraham. It means, "Whom God hears." Six persons having that name are mentioned in the Old Testament.

(1) Ishmael, the son of Abraham and Hagar, is the most famous of these. He was born at Mamre, but, together with his mother, he was separated from the household of Abraham, at the age of 16 years. He cast his lot with Arabs of the desert, and soon became a leader among them. Having married an Egyptian girl, he became the father of twelve sons, whom Arabian historians recognize as the ancestors of a considerable portion of the Arabian people, while the other part, supposed to be the descendants of Joktan, are called "pure Arabs." (Gen. 11:12-18)

(2) Another Ishmael was a prince of Judah, who treacherously murdered Gedaliah, whom the king of Babylon had appointed governor of Palestine, whereupon he fled and found refuge among the Ammonites. (2 Kings 25:23-25; Jer. 40:7; 41:15) This happened about the year 588 B.C.

Other persons named Ishmael are mentioned in Ezra 10:22; 1 Chron. 8:38; 9:44; 2 Chron. 19:11; 23:1.

*Arabia.* After the destruction of Jerusalem, a large number of Jews found refuge in this country and became influential. Christianity also was introduced there very early. Islam, the religious system of Mohammed (c. 570-632 A.D.), is conceded to be composed, at least partly, of both Jewish and Christian elements. With Mohammed, Arabian literature began to flourish. Under his successors schools were founded in Bagdad, Bokhara, and other places. Libraries were established in Alexandria, Bagdad and Cairo. During the tenth century, the Arabs were the standard bearers of knowledge. The Calif Hakem II is said to have collected 600,000 volumes for his library in Spain. They are credited with the creation of chemical pharmacy and great progress in the science of astronomy. They produced poets, philosophers, and historians. It is sad to contemplate the decline that came to that people, as compared with their former achievements.

Modern Arabia is divided into several principalities. Among these are Hejaz, Asir, Yemen, Nejd and Iraq. On Feb. 24, 1930, King Abdul Azis Ibn Saud of the Hejaz and of Nejd and King Feisal Ibn Hussein of Iraq met on board a British warship in the Persian gulf and recognized each other as independent rulers, whereupon ambassadors were exchanged and an end made of rivalry of long standing.

*Nahkum.* Mr. Thomas Gann, in his, "Maya Cities," (p. 161) mentions "Nahkum" as one of a group of ruined Maya cities, the others being, Naranjo, Tikal and Uaxactun. How is the frequent discovery of the identity of old American proper nouns with Book of Mormon names to be accounted for? It cannot always be coincidence.

## CHAPTER 17

*The journey from Nahom to Bountiful, 1-6—The Lord commands Nephi to build a ship, 7-16—Opposition of his brothers, 17-22—Nephi's great argument, 23-47—Opposition silenced, 48-52—A convincing miracle, 53-55.*

## 1. *From Nahom to Bountiful.*

1. And it came to pass that we did again take our journey in the wilderness; and we did travel nearly eastward from that time forth. And we did travel and wade through much affliction in the wilderness; and our women did bear children in the wilderness.

2. And so great were the blessings of the Lord upon us, that while we did live upon raw meat in the wilderness, our women did give plenty of suck for their children, and were strong, yea, even like unto the men; and they began to bear their journeyings without murmurings.

3. And thus we see that the commandments of God must be fulfilled. And if it so be that the children of men keep the commandments of God he doth nourish them, and strengthen them, and provide means whereby they can accomplish the thing which he has commanded them; wherefore, he did provide means for us while we did sojourn in the wilderness.

4. And we did sojourn for the space of many years, yea, even eight years in the wilderness.

5. And we did come to the land which we called Bountiful, because of its much fruit and also

VERSE 1. *We did travel nearly eastward.* From Jerusalem to Nahom, the course of the company of Lehi had been in a south-easterly direction. They had perhaps followed the mountain chain which runs parallel with the Sea. At Nahom, the direction was changed to "nearly eastward." They must have found a convenient mountain pass leading to the interior of the country.

VERSE 2. *Raw meat.* It was an exceedingly strenuous journey. Hunger, fatigue, thirst, hot winds, sand storms, dangers from poisonous insects and wild animals, were some of the difficulties they had to contend with.

Among the afflictions mentioned in the record of Nephi is the necessity of eating "raw meat." Just why the meat could not have been roasted does not appear. But there must have been some pressing reason for not making fires regularly, since the Mosaic law forbids the eating of blood and, particularly in the partaking of the Pascal lamb, the eating of raw flesh, lest they should consume blood with it.[1]

It may be that it was necessary for them not to betray their presence by smoke from fires, even although the country was only sparsely settled. At all events, they subsisted on raw food and thrived on it, by the blessing of God.

VERSE 4. *Eight years in the wilderness.* The sojourn in the wilderness lasted eight years. While traveling in a south-easterly direction, they may have reached some

---

[1]The blood, as the vehicle of life, was exempted for sacrificial service as an atonement for sin, and should therefore not be used for food.

wild honey; and all these things were prepared of the Lord that we might not perish. And we beheld the sea, which we called Irreantum, which, being interpreted, is many waters.

6. And it came to pass that we did pitch our tents by the sea-shore; and notwithstanding we had suffered many afflictions and much difficulty, yea, even so much that we cannot write them all, we were exceedingly rejoiced when we came to the seashore; and we called the place Bountiful, because of its much fruit.

## 2. Nephi commanded to build a ship.

7. And it came to pass that after I, Nephi, had been in the land of Bountiful for the space of many days, the voice of the Lord came unto me, saying: Arise, and get thee into the mountain. And it came to pass that I arose and went up into the mountain, and cried unto the Lord.

8. And it came to pass that the Lord spake unto me, saying: Thou shalt construct a ship, after

---

point in the present Yemen, a thousand miles from Jerusalem. Traveling in an easterly direction, another thousand miles would have taken them to the Arabian Sea, perhaps in the present country of Oman. They could have made that in eight years.[2]

Arabia is a large country, almost as large as one-fourth of Europe. Along the western part of the peninsula a mountain chain runs parallel with the Red Sea. From this mountain range the country slopes toward the east. It is sparsely watered, but has many oases. The province of Oman is mountainous, with majestic peaks which lift their heads as high as 10,000 feet above the sea.

VERSE 5. *Bountiful.* This name was given to the last station of the journey through the wilderness, on account of the abundance of fruit found there, as well as wild honey. (Vv. 5 and 6) The Hebrew name would probably be "Shaepha Rab," meaning, "great quantity" or, "great supply." That word is found as a proper name in 1 Chron. 4:37, where *Shiphi* is mentioned as one of the descendants of Simeon and father of one of the princes who, according to the records of Hezekiah, fled to Gedor, on the "east side of the valley."

*Irreantum.* All we know about this word is that it means, "many waters."

VERSE 7. *For the space of many days.* Probably months. Compare I Ne. 16:17.

*Into the mountain.* The meaning is, into the mountain region. The expression occurs in the Old Testament with that meaning, as for instance when Moses says that the Lord will plant the children of Israel "in the mountain of thy inheritance" (Ex. 15:17), and many other places. Or, it may refer to a mountain cave, as in Gen. 19:30, where Lot is said to have taken refuge in a cave which was "in the mountain." At all events, the land Bountiful was a mountainous country.

*Cried unto the Lord.* Earnest prayer in privacy was the preparation of Nephi for the mission he had been called to perform. Prayer is the best preparation for any work, be it either spiritual or material.

---

[2]See the adventures of Cabeza de Vaca and his companions in, "Introduction to the Study of the Book of Mormon," Sjodahl, p. 87.

the manner which I shall show thee, that I may carry thy people across these waters.

9. And I said: Lord, whither shall I go that I may find ore to molten, that I may make tools to construct the ship after the manner which thou hast shown unto me?

10. And it came to pass that the Lord told me whither I should go to find ore, that I might make tools.

11. And it came to pass that I, Nephi, did make a bellows where-with to blow the fire, of the skins of beasts; and after I had made a bellows, that I might have where-with to blow the fire, I did smite two stones together that I might make fire.

12. For the Lord had not hitherto suffered that we should make much fire, as we journeyed in the wilderness; for he said: I will make thy food become sweet, that ye cook it not;

13. And I will also be your light in the wilderness; and I will prepare the way before you, if it

---

VERSES 8-16. In this narrative the prominent feature is the partnership, or cooperative arrangement between our Lord and his young servant: "Thou shalt construct a ship," . . . "that I may carry thy people across the water" (v. 8). "The Lord told me whither I should go to find ore" . . . "that I may make tools to construct the ship" (vv. 9, 10). "Ye shall keep my commandments" . . . and then, "Ye shall be led towards the promised land" (vv. 13-16). This is God's own arrangement: You build the ship—I will carry the people across.

Such partnership is in perfect accord with a universal and immutable law pertaining to our very existence. For, if, as Paul expresses it (Acts 17:28), we live, and move, and have our being in God, as "we are also his offspring," then the same laws under which God operates must be applicable to us. Popularly, this law is expressed in the saying, "God helps those that help themselves," but it is better worded in Holy Writ. In one of the Psalms we read, "Except the Lord build the house, they labor in vain that build it." (Ps. 127:1) And the Apostle Paul, "It is God which worketh in you both to will and to do good of his good pleasure" (Phil. 2:13); and again, "I can do all things through Christ which strengtheneth me" (Phil. 4:13). The correct attitude of man in this blessed partnership is perfect co-ordination of all his efforts under the Divine guidance and power. That, in fact, is the very essence of faith in God.

This thought is well expressed by Mr. Basil King in his admirable discourse on "Faith and Success." He says that faith is moved by divine discontent. It seeks, it asks, it strives. Faith, according to St. James, is dead, if it is without works. It is not faith. It is nothing. To exist at all Faith must prove its force by doing. "And this doing must be linked with the Divine. It depends on the Divine. Its aim is to cooperate with God."

To this it can be added that even scientists are beginning to recognize faith as a force. According to an Associated Press dispatch dated December 26, 1933, Dr. Arthur H. Compton of the University of Chicago, a Nobel prize winner in physics in 1927, authorized the statement that although science does not prove the existence of a God to whom men are as his children, yet the evidence which it offers for an intelligent Power working in the world does make such a postulate plausible. He continues:

so be that ye shall keep my commandments; wherefore, inasmuch as ye shall keep my commandments ye shall be led towards the promised land; and ye shall know that it is by me that ye are led.

14. Yea, and the Lord said also that: After ye have arrived in the promised land, ye shall know that I, the Lord, am God; and that I, the Lord, did deliver you from destruction; yea, that I did bring you out of the land of Jerusalem.

15. Wherefore, I, Nephi, did strive to keep the commandments of the Lord, and I did exhort my brethren to faithfulness and diligence.

16. And it came to pass that I did make tools of the ore which I did molten out of the rock.

## 3. *The great controversy in the Land of Bountiful.*

17. And when my brethren saw that I was about to build a ship, they began to murmur against me, saying: Our brother is a fool, for he thinketh that he can build a ship; yea, and he also

"It is thus possible to see the whole great drama of evolution as moving toward the goal of personality, the making of persons, with free, intelligent wills, capable of learning nature's laws, of glimpsing God's purpose in nature and of sharing that purpose. It is an inspiring setting in which we thus find ourselves, as we recognize the greatness of the program of nature which is unfolding before us we feel that we are part of a great enterprise in which some mighty intelligence is working out a hidden plan. Indeed, God has placed us in a position to help in furthering his program. For do we not hold in our hands and control the conditions of vegetable and animal life on this planet and to some extent, human life?"

VERSE 11. *Bellows.* (Hebrew, "mappuach.") An implement well known to the Hebrews from olden times. (Jer. 6:29) As made in Egypt, they consisted of leather secured into a frame, from which a long pipe extended for carrying the wind to the fire. They were worked by the feet, the operator standing upon them, one under each foot, and pressing them alternately down and pulling the empty skin up by means of a string. They may also have had the smaller bellows, made of wood and skin, of the kind which still are in use in many countries.

VERSE 12. *No cooking.* See v. 2. The Mosaic law prohibited the making of fire on the Sabbath (Ex. 35:3), but the reason for that was that the people were not permitted to do any ordinary work of any kind on that day, such as gathering sticks, for instance, with which to make the fire. (Num. 15:32)

The Sabbath was instituted to be a sign between Jehovah and his people, in order that all the world might know that it is He who sanctifies his people, Israel. (See Ex. 31:12-17)

VERSE 16. *Molten out of the rock.* "Molten," or "melted," describes a substance reduced to a state of fusion by means of heat, as, for instance, "molten iron." Also an object formed by melting and casting, as, for instance, a "molten image."

The use of fire in metallurgy was well known to the Hebrews. (Ex. 32:24)

VERSES 17-22. *The accusation.* In reading this account of the great controversy in the land of Bountiful in Asia, we may assume that Nephi, having carried out the instructions of the Lord and made the tools necessary, laid the matter of the building of the ship before the members of the little colony, since the law of

thinketh that he can cross these great waters.

18. And thus my brethren did complain against me, and were desirous that they might not labor, for they did not believe that I could build a ship; neither would they believe that I was instructed of the Lord.

19. And now it came to pass that I, Nephi, was exceeding sorrowful because of the hardness of their hearts; and now when they saw that I began to be sorrowful they were glad in their hearts, insomuch that they did rejoice over me, saying: We knew that ye could not construct a ship, for we knew that ye were lacking in judgment; wherefore, thou canst not accomplish so great a work.

20. And thou art like unto our father, led away by the foolish imaginations of his heart; yea, he hath led us out of the land of Jerusalem, and we have wandered in the wilderness for these many years; and our women have toiled, being big with child; and they have borne children in the wilderness and suffered all things, save it were death; and it would have been better that they had died before they came out of Jerusalem than to have suffered these afflictions.

21. Behold, these many years we have suffered in the wilderness, which time we might have enjoyed our possessions and the land of our inheritance; yea, and we might have been happy.

22. And we know that the people who were in the land of Jerusalem were a righteous people; for they kept the statutes and judgments of the Lord, and all his commandments, according to the law of Moses; wherefore, we know that they are a righteous people; and our father hath judged them, and hath led us away because we would hearken unto his words; yea, and our brother is like unto him. And after this manner of language did my brethren murmur and complain against us.

23. And it came to pass that I, Nephi, spake unto them, saying: Do ye believe that our fathers, who were the children of Israel, would have been led away out of the hands of the Egyptians if they had not hearkened unto the words of the Lord?

24. Yea, do ye suppose that

---

common consent[3] undoubtedly applied to their important plans and decisions. We may assume that Nephi reported the divine commandments and instructions received, for their approval or rejection.

Then the brothers, or some of them, raised their objections. (1) They asserted emphatically that their brother, Nephi, was a "fool," if he thought that they could build a ship and cross the ocean (v. 17). (2) On that ground they refused to labor on the ship in question. (3) The representation of Nephi that he had only communicated to them the commandment of the Lord they pronounced a falsehood: "Neither would they believe that I was instructed of the Lord" (v. 18).

[3]Compare D. & C., Sec. 26.

they would have been led out of bondage, if the Lord had not commanded Moses that he should lead them out of bondage?

25. Now ye know that the children of Israel were in bondage; and ye know that they were laden with tasks, which were grievous to be borne; wherefore, ye know that it must needs be a good thing for them, that they should be brought out of bondage.

26. Now ye know that Moses was commanded of the Lord to do that great work; and ye know that by his word the waters of the Red Sea were divided hither and thither, and they passed through on dry ground.

27. But ye know that the Egyptians were drowned in the Red Sea, who were the armies of Pharaoh.

28. And ye also know that they were fed with manna in the wilderness.

29. Yea, and ye also know that Moses, by his word according to the power of God which was in him, smote the rock, and there came forth water, that the children of Israel might quench their thirst.

30. And notwithstanding they being led, the Lord their God, their Redeemer, going before them, leading them by day and giving light unto them by night, and doing all things for them which were expedient for man to receive, they hardened their hearts and blinded their minds, and reviled against Moses and against the true and living God.

31. And it came to pass that according to his word he did destroy them; and according to his word he did lead them; and according to his word he did do all things for them; and there was not any thing done save it were by his word.

32. And after they had crossed the river Jordan he did make them mighty unto the driving out of the children of the land, yea, unto the scattering them to destruction.

33. And now, do ye suppose that the children of this land, who were in the land of promise, who were driven out by our fathers, do ye suppose that they were righteous? Behold, I say unto you, Nay.

34. Do ye suppose that our fathers would have been more

This attitude of the brothers was a stunning blow to Nephi. He was grief-stricken. His opponents rejoiced thinking that they had won the day. "We knew," they said, "that you could not construct a ship." (v. 19)

(4) The next move of the brothers was to turn their accusations against their father. He, they said, it is who has led us out of Jerusalem to suffer for years, and perish, in the wilderness, when we might have stayed at home in comfort and ease (vv. 20, 21).

(5) Having gone to this extreme in their opposition,[4] they invented an excuse

[4]According to the law of Moses they had forfeited their lives, and Lehi might have been their judge. The law was: "He that curseth [or revileth] his father, or his mother, shall surely be put to death." (Ex. 21:17)

choice than they if they had been righteous? I say unto you, Nay.

35. Behold, the Lord esteemeth all flesh in one; he that is righteous is favored of God. But behold, this people had rejected every word of God, and they were ripe in iniquity; and the fulness of the wrath of God was upon them; and the Lord did curse the land against them, and bless it unto our fathers; yea, he did curse it against them unto their destruction, and he did bless it unto our fathers unto their obtaining power over it.

36. Behold, the Lord hath created the earth that it should be inhabited; and he hath created his children that they should possess it.

37. And he raiseth up a righteous nation, and destroyeth the nations of the wicked.

38. And he leadeth away the righteous into precious lands, and the wicked he destroyeth, and curseth the land unto them for their sakes.

39. He ruleth high in the heavens, for it is his throne, and this earth is his footstool.

40. And he loveth those who will have him to be their God.

Behold, he loved our fathers, and he covenanted with them, yea, even Abraham, Isaac, and Jacob; and he remembered the covenants which he had made; wherefore, he did bring them out of the land of Egypt.

41. And he did straiten them in the wilderness with his rod; for they hardened their hearts, even as ye have; and the Lord straitened them because of their iniquity. He sent fiery flying serpents among them; and after they were bitten he prepared a way that they might be healed; and the labor which they had to perform was to look; and because of the simpleness of the way, or the easiness of it, there were many who perished.

42. And they did harden their hearts from time to time, and they did revile against Moses, and also against God; nevertheless, ye know that they were led forth by his matchless power into the land of promise.

43. And now, after all these things, the time has come that they have become wicked, yea, nearly unto ripeness; and I know not but they are at this day about to be destroyed; for I know that

for their rebellion. They asserted that the Jews, their friends and neighbors, their fellow-citizens, were a righteous people whom their father had misjudged. And Nephi, they said, was just like him (v. 22).

VERSES 23-47. *The defense of Nephi.* Now Nephi was aroused. The brutal attack on Father Lehi made him realize the seriousness of the situation. And so, in the dignity and majesty of his office, he met their accusations. Their position was clear. They did not, they had said, believe that God had spoken to Lehi, or to their brother; nor that the Jews in Jerusalem were an unrighteous people, ripe for destruction. Nephi, therefore, began his defense by asking a penetrating question, Do you believe that the Children of Israel would have been led out of bondage in Egypt, if God had not spoken through his servant Moses (vv. 23, 24)? Then he

the day must surely come that they must be destroyed, save a few only, who shall be led away into captivity.

44. Wherefore, the Lord commanded my father that he should depart into the wilderness; and the Jews also sought to take away his life; yea, and ye also have sought to take away his life; wherefore, ye are murderers in your hearts and ye are like unto them.

45. Ye are swift to do iniquity but slow to remember the Lord your God. Ye have seen an angel, and he spake unto you; yea, ye have heard his voice from time to time; and he hath spoken unto you in a still small voice, but ye were past feeling, that ye could not feel his words; wherefore, he has spoken unto you like unto the voice of thunder, which did cause the earth to shake as if it were to divide asunder.

46. And ye also know that by the power of his almighty word he can cause the earth that it shall pass away; yea, and ye know that by his word he can cause the rough places to be made smooth, and smooth places shall be broken up. O, then, why is it, that ye can be so hard in your hearts?

47. Behold, my soul is rent with anguish because of you, and my heart is pained; I fear lest ye shall be cast off forever. Behold, I am full of the Spirit of God, insomuch that my frame has no strength.

4. *Opposition in the camp silenced.*

48. And now it came to pass that when I had spoken these words they were angry with me, and were desirous to throw me

---

asserted that they did know (1) That the children of Israel were in bondage (v. 25); (2) that Moses was commanded to lead them out of Egypt through the Red Sea (v. 26); (3) that the Egyptians were drowned in the pursuit (v. 27); (4) that the Israelites were miraculously supplied with manna to eat and with water to drink (vv. 28, 29). You know, Nephi said, all this, and you know also that, although they were led by their Redeemer, by day and by night, they hardened their hearts and reviled Moses and even God; wherefore he destroyed them in the wilderness (vv. 30-32). This was an obvious lesson of history applied upon their own case, and also a solemn warning of what the consequences of their own disobedience might be.

But he continues his argument: Do you suppose, he asks, that the Canaanites would have been driven out of their land if they had been a righteous people? Or, that the Jews under Joshua would have been more favored than the Canaanites, if the latter had been a righteous people (v. 33)?

No! he said. God is no respecter of persons. He favors the nations that are righteous and destroys those who are ripe in iniquity. He leads those that fear him to choice lands, and he curses the lands of the wicked. He rules in heaven and on earth (his throne and his footstool), and he fulfills his covenants with his children (vv. 34-46).

VERSE 47. *My frame has no strength.* Nephi closes his great defense, delivered under the powerful influence of the Holy Spirit, completely exhausted. (Comp. Dan. 10:16-18)

into the depths of the sea; and as they came forth to lay their hands upon me I spake unto them, saying: In the name of the Almighty God, I command you that ye touch me not, for I am filled with the power of God, even unto the consuming of my flesh; and whoso shall lay his hands upon me shall wither even as a dried reed; and he shall be as naught before the power of God, for God shall smite him.

49. And it came to pass that I, Nephi, said unto them that they should murmur no more against their father; neither should they withhold their labor from me, for God had commanded me that I should build a ship.

50. And I said unto them: If God had commanded me to do all things I could do them. If he should command me that I should say unto this water, be thou earth, it should be earth; and if I should say it, it would be done.

51. And now, if the Lord has such great power, and has wrought so many miracles among the children of men, how is it that he cannot instruct me, that I should build a ship?

52. And it came to pass that I, Nephi, said many things unto my brethren, insomuch that they were confounded and could not contend against me; neither durst they lay their hands upon me nor touch me with their fingers, even for the space of many days. Now they durst not do this lest they should wither before me, so powerful was the Spirit of God; and thus it had wrought upon them.

---

VERSE 48. *They were angry with me.* The first effect of the powerful defense of Nephi was to set the hearts of his brothers aflame with anger, and, in the heat of the passion, they decided to murder their younger brother by drowning. But, as they approached him, to carry out their evil design, he solemnly warned them, in the name of Almighty God, that whosoever should lay hand on him to hurt him, would be stricken by the divine power within him.

VERSES 49-51. *Another appeal.* Again he commanded them not to murmur against their father, and not to refuse to do the work which God expected of them (v. 49). He, finally showed them that it is entirely reasonable to expect divine instructions (vv. 50, 51).

VERSE 52. *Neither durst they lay hands on him . . . for the space of many days.* Their anger now turned into fear, and for many days they did not touch their brother. Perhaps they remembered Miriam, the sister of Moses, who was stricken with leprosy, when she engaged in a conspiracy against the prophet of the Lord.[5] (Num. 12:1-15) Or, Korah, Dathan and Abiram who, for their rebellion, were swallowed up by the earth (Num. 16:31-33).

---

[5]It appears that Moses had taken an Ethiopian (or Cushite) woman, not mentioned elsewhere for wife, in addition to Zipporah, the Midianite girl. (Ex. 2:20) Miriam objected to this marriage and concluded that Moses had forfeited his right to the place of the prophet of the Lord. She induced Aaron to side with her. Together they argued that the Lord did not need Moses. He could speak through them. Evidently, as the instigator of this rebellion, she became leprous and was excluded from the camp for seven days. And the journey of the entire people was delayed for that length of time, out of respect for the erring sister of the prophet of God.

## 5. *A convincing miracle.*

53. And it came to pass that the Lord said unto me: Stretch forth thine hand again unto thy brethren, and they shall not wither before thee, but I will shock them, saith the Lord, and this will I do, that they may know that I am the Lord their God.

54. And it came to pass that I stretched forth my hand unto my brethren, and they did not wither before me; but the Lord did shake them, even according to the word which he had spoken.

55. And now, they said: We know of a surety that the Lord is with thee, for we know that it is the power of the Lord that has shaken us. And they fell down before me, and were about to worship me, but I would not suffer them, saying: I am thy brother, yea, even thy younger brother; wherefore, worship the Lord thy God, and honor thy father and thy mother, that thy days may be long in the land which the Lord thy God shall give thee.

---

VERSE 53. *Stretch forth thine hand again.* The fear of the rebellious brothers gradually gave way to a sensation of freedom from all danger. In all probability they were about to carry out their murderous plan—or, rather, make another attempt —when the Lord commanded Nephi to stretch forth his hand against them a second time, because He—the Lord—was about to give them a manifestation of his power.

VERSE 54. *I stretched forth my hand.* Nephi instantly obeyed the divine commandment, whereupon the Lord, according to his word, caused them to "shake" in such a manner that they became convinced that God was on the side of Nephi. When God undertakes to manifest his power, be it in shaking "the powers of heaven" (Luke 21:26), or the "foundations of the hills" (Ps. 18:7), or "the nations" (Ezek. 31:16), or all things and all "men that are upon earth" (Ezek. 38:20), there is no doubt as to who is the Ruler of the universe.

VERSE 55. *The conversion.* This ended their opposition for the time being. The brothers fell down before Nephi and would have worshiped him, if he had permitted them to do so. (Comp. Rev. 19:10 and 22:9) He exhorted them to worship God and to honor father and mother, according to the law of God.

## CHAPTER 18

*The ship of Nephi, 1-4—The embarkation, 5-6—Children of the wilderness, 7—The voyage, 8-23—The journey continued on land, 24-25.*

## 1. *The ship of Nephi.*

1. And it came to pass that they did worship the Lord, and did go forth with me; and we did work timbers of curious workmanship. And the Lord did show me from time to time after what manner I should work the timbers of the ship.

2. Now I, Nephi, did not work the timbers after the manner which was learned by men, neither did I build the ship after the manner of men; but I did build it after the manner which the Lord had shown unto me;

wherefore, it was not after the manner of men.

3. And I, Nephi, did go into the mount oft, and I did pray oft unto the Lord; wherefore the Lord showed unto me great things.

4. And it came to pass that after I had finished the ship, according to the word of the Lord, my brethren beheld that it was good, and that the workmanship thereof was exceeding fine; wherefore, they did humble themselves again before the Lord.

VERSES 1-4. *The ship completed.* Nephi and his brethren and other members of the colony now applied themselves to the work of construction of the ship, in accordance with the instructions Nephi received from time to time of the Lord.

Like all Hebrews of that time, they were, no doubt, somewhat familiar with ships and ship building. There was a navigable lake in Palestine, the Sea of Galilee. Smaller boats and larger craft were constantly plying its sometimes turbulant waves. They were familiar with the extensive Phoenician shipping. Hiram, king of Tyre, delivered at the port of Jaffa the timber that was cut in the Lebanon mountains for the temple of Solomon. (2 Chron. 2:16) And it is on record that Solomon established stations at Ezion-geber and Elath, where he built ships for which the king of Tyre furnished navigators and crews, and that these ships were dispatched to the land of Ophir, whence they returned with costly cargoes, especially gold and precious stones.[1] (1 Kings 9:28, 10, 11)

[1]Just where Ophir was is not known. There are all kinds of conjectures on that subject. Ophir may be another name for Africa. The suggestion that Afr in the name Africa is the same root as Ophr in Ophir is perhaps not far-fetched. Mr. Cancroft has the following on Ophir:

"The Phoenicians were employed about a thousand years before the Christian era, by Solomon, king of the Jews, and Hiram, king of Tyre, to navigate their fleets to Ophir and Tarshish. They returned, by way of the Mediterranean, to the port of Joppa, after a three year's voyage, laden with gold, silver, precious stones, ivory, cedar, apes and peacocks. Several authors have believed that they had two distinct fleets, one of which went to a land since known as America, and the other to India. Huet, bishop of Avranches, and other authors, are persuaded that Ophir was the modern Sofala . . . According to Arius Montanus, Genebrardus, Vatable, and other writers, Ophir is the island of Hispaniola. It is said that Christopher Columbus was induced to adopt this idea by the immense caverns which he found there, from which he supposed that Solomon must have obtained his gold. Postel and others have believed that Ophir was Peru. Horn claims that the Phoenicians made three remark-

## 2. The embarkation.

5. And it came to pass that the voice of the Lord came unto my father, that we should arise and go down into the ship.

In the account by Luke of the voyage of St. Paul to Rome (Acts 27 and 28) there is some interesting information concerning ancient ships and navigation. Some ships must have been quite large. The vessel which was wrecked on the coast of Malta (Melite) had 276 souls on board, among whom Paul was one. It also had a cargo of wheat. It has been calculated that it must have been a ship of more than 500 tons' capacity. The large vessels had sails and were steered by means of an oar in the stern. On the prow stood the insignia by which the ship was known, as for instance, "Castor and Pollux," on the ship which carried Paul from Malta. The vessels were frail, at best. In stormy seas they were, therefore, girded with cables, called "helps" (Acts 27:17), to keep them from being broken up. They were equipped with anchors, and a boat for communication with the shore, when at anchor. Also with sounding lines. Navigation consisted mostly in following the shores, or, at night, the stars. The captain was the navigator, and the officer who had charge of the steering apparatus was called the "governor."

VERSE 2. *Not after the manner of men.* But the ship that Nephi built was different from the common types.

VERSE 3. *I did pray oft.* The ship was built according with instructions from heaven, and they were given in answer to prayer. It is the praying soul that hears God speak. Moses is an illustration of this truth: "And when Moses was gone into the Tabernacle of the congregation to speak with Him, then he heard the voice of One speaking unto him from off the mercy seat that was upon the ark of testimony from between the two cherubim, and He spake unto him." (Num. 7:89.) The life and work of the Prophet Joseph Smith is another illustration of the same truth.

VERSE 4. *It was good, and the workmanship . . . exceeding fine.* Even the brothers of Nephi acknowledged that. It was a good ship. In all probability they would not have to depend on cables to keep it together in a storm. It was exceedingly fine. It was so nicely put together that it did not leak. The men who had said that a ship in which to cross the ocean could not be built by them, now humbled themselves and acknowledged their error.

VERSE 5. *The voice of the Lord came to my father.* We notice that the communications from God came through Lehi, who was the head of the colony, whenever the entire community was concerned.

---

able voyages to America; the first, under the direction of Altas, son of Neptune; the second, when they were driven from the coast of Africa to the most remote parts of the Atlantic Ocean, and arrived at a large island to the west of Libya; and the third, in the time of Solomon, when the Tyrians went to Ophir to seek for gold.

"According to those who believe that there were two distinct fleets, that of Solomon and that of Hiram, the first set out from Ezion-geber, sailed down the Red Sea, doubled Cape Comorin, and went to Taproban (Ceylon), or some other part of India; this voyage occupied one year. The other fleet passed through the Mediterranean, stopping at the various ports along the coasts of Europe and Africa, and finally, passing out through the straits of Gades, continued its voyage as far as America and returned after three years to its starting place, laden with gold." (Native Races, vol. 5, pp. 64-65) This may not be considered as historic. It may be rejected as mere surmises. But the Mayas had a Votan tradition, similar to the Odin or Wuotan-saga of the Aesir. If there never was any communication anciently between Asia and America, that fact, as others, is an insolvable mystery.

6. And it came to pass that on the morrow, after we had prepared all things, much fruits and meat from the wilderness, and honey in abundance, and provisions according to that which the Lord had commanded us, we did go down into the ship, with all our loading and our seeds, and whatsoever thing we had brought with us, every one according to his age; wherefore, we did all go down into the ship, with our wives and our children.

### 3. Children of the wilderness.

7. And now, my father had begat two sons in the wilderness; the elder was called Jacob and the younger Joseph.

### 4. The voyage.

8. And it came to pass after we had all gone down into the ship, and had taken with us our provisions and things which had been commanded us, we did put forth into the sea and were driven forth before the wind towards the promised land.

---

VERSE 6. *Prepared all things.* This included fruit and meat from the wilderness, and honey, and other provisions.

Just what kind of fruits they had we are not told. Palestine, anciently, produced a great variety of trees, shrubs and vegetables. Among many others, these are mentioned in the Scriptures: Almonds, wild and cultivated; apple, probably the quince, or the lemon; calamus, a sweet cane; figs, "husks," (Luke 15), the pods of the carob-tree, also known as the St. John's tree, which pods were often fed to pigs; the mandrake, the mulberry, which was a kind of fig; nuts of many varieties; olives, pomegranates, sycamore, a kind of fig; beans, millet, a small grain; lentils, and the grapevine, known in history ever since the days of Noah; also, cucumbers, garlic, leeks, melons, onions, anise, or dill; bay-tree, cassia, a kind of cinnamon; coriander, yielding a fruit (called "seed"), the size of a pepper corn; mustard, saffron, and flax. All these are mentioned in the Scriptures. Lehi, undoubtedly, had been instructed to take with him in the ship whatever fruit and vegetables were needed for food during the voyage, and for agricultural purposes in the promised land.

The "honey in abundance" may have been both the product of the bee, and the syrup made of dates, which the Hebrews called "honey" ("debash," Gen. 43:11).

VERSE 7. *Two Sons.* We are here informed that two sons, Jacob and Joseph, were born to Lehi in the wilderness. How many more were born during the journey to the sea we know not. But they were eight years in the wilderness. (See 1 Ne. 17:20.) Those that entered the ship were, Lehi and Sariah, his wife; Laman and his wife; Lemuel and his wife; Sam and his wife; Nephi and his wife; Ishmael's wife (Ishmael having passed away at Nahom); two sons of Ishmael and their families (1 Ne. 7:6); Zoram and his wife (1 Ne. 16:7); Jacob and Joseph and others who may have been born in the wilderness. Elder George Reynolds ("Story of the Book of Mormon," p. 44) estimates the entire number that landed in the land of promise at from 60 to 80 souls.

VERSE 8. *Driven forth before the wind.* The ship was a sailing-vessel, and the start was made with a favorable wind.

9. And after we had been driven forth before the wind for the space of many days, behold, my brethren and the sons of Ishmael and also their wives began to make themselves merry, insomuch that they began to dance, and to sing, and to speak with much rudeness, yea, even that they did forget by what power they had been brought thither; yea, they were lifted up unto exceeding rudeness.

10. And I, Nephi, began to fear exceedingly lest the Lord should be angry with us, and smite us because of our iniquity, that we should be swallowed up in the depths of the sea; wherefore, I, Nephi, began to speak to them with much soberness; but behold they were angry with me, saying: We will not that our younger brother shall be a ruler over us.

11. And it came to pass that Laman and Lemuel did take me and bind me with cords, and they did treat me with much harshness; nevertheless, the Lord did suffer it that he might show forth

---

VERSE 9. *Merriment and rudeness.* After many days of sailing, a most extraordinary thing happened. The monotony of the daily routine was broken by merry-making. The brothers of Nephi and the sons of Ishmael and their wives "began to make themselves merry." From merriment they proceeded to dancing, singing and indecent language. The next step was utter disregard of their divine mission, and unseemly behavior. "They were lifted up unto exceeding rudeness."

"Rude" (from the Latin, "rudis") means "rough," and it is synonomous with "barbarous"; "vulgar," and "impudent." I can account for their behavior, only on the supposition that they were intoxicated. In their stock of provisions they undoubtedly had preserved grapes and grape juice, as well as honey and certain spices. They could easily make an alcoholic mixture, the wine ("mesech"), of which we read in Prov. 23:29-34: "At the last it biteth like a serpent, and stingeth like an adder. Thine eyes shall behold strange women and thine heart shall utter perverse things." That, it seems to me, is what happened.

VERSE 10. *Nephi began to speak to them with much soberness.* To Nephi, who was sober, their conduct was not merely offensive but alarming. He foresaw the possibility of failure and death in the deep. He, therefore, implored them to repent. But their reaction to his anxiety was drunken revelers' usual defence—anger. "We will not," they said, "have this youngster to rule over us."

Youth, of and by itself, is, of course, no virtue that can legitimately claim either adoration or submission. It is an advantage. And it is beautiful. But courageous, adventurous, strong youth full of faith in God, inspired by his Holy Spirit, is the best possible medium of leadership, when supported by the experience of age, ripened in the service of God. Israel needed both Samuel and David. Our colony in the ship needed both Lehi and Nephi.

VERSE 11. *The Lord did suffer it.* Laman and Lemuel, who seemed to be the leaders of the opposition, resorted to violence. They bound their brother with cords and treated him "harshly,"—with physical violence. But why did not the others interfere, meeting violence with violence? The answer to that question is given in the sentence beginning this paragraph. It was the conviction of Nephi and his friends, that, "The Lord did suffer it, that he might show forth his power." To have met violence with violence would have been to interfere with God's plan. Under the law of retaliation (lex talionis) they would have been justified in meeting

his power, unto the fulfilling of his word which he had spoken concerning the wicked.

12. And it came to pass that after they had bound me insomuch that I could not move, the compass, which had been prepared of the Lord, did cease to work.

13. Wherefore, they knew not whither they should steer the ship, insomuch that there arose a great storm, yea, a great and terrible tempest, and we were driven back upon the waters for the space of three days; and they began to be frightened exceedingly lest they should be drowned in the sea; nevertheless they did not loose me.

14. And on the fourth day, which we had been driven back, the tempest began to be exceeding sore.

15. And it came to pass that we were about to be swallowed up in the depths of the sea. And after we had been driven back upon the waters for the space of fours days, my brethren began to see that the judgments of God were upon them, and that they must perish save that they should repent of their iniquities; wherefore, they came unto me, and loosed the bands which were upon

my wrists, and behold they had swollen exceedingly; and also mine ankles were much swollen, and great was the soreness thereof.

16. Nevertheless, I did look unto my God, and I did praise him all the day long; and I did not murmur against the Lord because of mine afflictions.

17. Now my father, Lehi, had said many things unto them, and also unto the sons of Ishmael; but, behold, they did breathe out much threatenings against anyone that should speak for me; and my parents being stricken in years, and having suffered much grief because of their children, they were brought down, yea, even upon their sick-beds.

18. Because of their grief and much sorrow, and the iniquity of my brethren, they were brought near even to be carried out of this time to meet their God; yea, their grey hairs were about to be brought down to lie low in the dust; yea, even they were near to be cast with sorrow into a watery grave.

19. And Jacob and Joseph also, being young, having need of much nourishment, were grieved because of the afflictions of their mother; and also my wife with

force with force, as long as they did not exact any more than an eye for an eye and a tooth for a tooth; but the object the Lord had in view was their conversion and not vengeance; hence his patience and long-suffering. Nephi understood this by the Spirit within him. (See v. 16.) Non-resistance was his duty at this time.

VERSES 12-20. *The Lord showing his power.* First the "compass" ceased to work. They lost their course. (v. 12). Then a storm arose, which is characterized as a "great and terrible tempest." (v. 13.) For three days the ship was driven about, tossed hither and thither, up and down, shipping waves, pounding, rolling, the wind whistling in the rigging, howling, roaring, and the clouds hanging like a dark pall

her tears and prayers, and also my children, did not soften the hearts of my brethren that they would loose me.

20. And there was nothing save it were the power of God, which threatened them with destruction, could soften their hearts; wherefore, when they saw that they were about to be swal-

lowed up in the depths of the sea they repented of the thing which they had done, insomuch that they loosed me.

21. And it came to pass after they had loosed me, behold, I took the compass, and it did work whither I desired it. And it came to pass that I prayed unto the Lord; and after I had prayed

---

from the sky, ready for the funeral. The persecutors now were cowed, but not sufficiently to repent of their evil deeds. They hoped for an abatement of the tempest. But the fourth day came without any change for the better. The tempest increased in violence (v. 14). Then they began to relent. They acknowledged the hand of God in the storm, and set Nephi free (v. 15).

During the storm, Lehi and Sariah, now well advanced in years, unable to endure the anguish caused by the wickedness of their sons, and the physical discomforts of the uncontrolled vessel, became sick and were apparently brought near to death's door (vv. 17, 18). Jacob and Joseph, and, of course, the other children, were suffering a great deal during those four days, for in such weather on board a ship, little food is prepared: Little children are not attended to as usual. But the sickness of their parents and the tears of the children did not move the hearts of the rebels. It was the power of God to destroy that finally softened them (vv. 19, 20). As soon as Nephi had been set free, the storm abated, the compass worked, and the ship resumed its course (vv. 21, 22).

*The "compass"* (vv. 12 and 21) is the round ball of curious workmanship described in 1 Ne. 16:10. Some have assumed that the term was meant to convey the idea that Lehi, more than 500 years B. C. had the mariners' instrument which is supposed to have been unknown in the western world until the 12th century A. D., and that "compass" therefore, is an anachronism which furnishes evidence of the very human origin of the Book of Mormon. But that reasoning disregards two facts: First that the "compass" in question was not the magnetic instrument of the mariner, but a special contrivance which pointed the way they were to go, and that only in response to the faith of the sailor; secondly, that the word "compass" is a good English word, meaning not only the mariners' instrument but a circle or a globe in general, a round, a circuit. In Num. 34:5 and Joshua 15:13 it refers to the bend in the southern boundary line of the land of Israel, "from Azmon unto the river of Egypt" and from there to the sea. Luke, in Acts 28:13 uses the term for the course steered by the ship from Syracuse to Rhegium. In Ex. 27:5 and 38:4 it means the inside rim of the altar to which a metal net, or grate, was fastened, evidently in order to protect the wood work of the altar. In 2 Sam. 5:23 and 2 Kings 3:9, to "fetch a compass" means to surround a portion of the army of an enemy. In Prov. 8:23, "compass" refers to the circular horizon, and in Isaiah 44:13 to the compasses of a sculptor. It is clear from these references that the term as applied in the Book of Mormon to the little round ball of Lehi is correct. It is not an anachronism.[2]

---

[2]Some amusing anachronisms are on record. Shakespeare furnishes a few. For instance, he makes a "clock" in "Julius Caesar" strike three, long before anyone had heard of a striking clock. In Thackeray's "Esmond," in 1712 a book published in 1750 is mentioned. Schiller, in Piccolomini, has a lightning rod 150 years before it was invented.

the winds did cease, and the storm did cease, and there was a great calm.

22. And it came to pass that I, Nephi, did guide the ship, that we sailed again towards the promised land.

## 5. The journey continued.

24. And it came to pass that we did begin to till the earth, and we began to plant seeds; yea, we did put all our seeds into the earth, which we had brought from the land of Jerusalem. And it came to pass that they did grow exceedingly; wherefore, we were blessed in abundance.

25. And it came to pass that we did find upon the land of

23. And it came to pass that after we had sailed for the space of many days we did arrive at the promised land; and we went forth upon the land, and did pitch our tents; and we did call it the promised land.

promise, as we journeyed in the wilderness, that there were beasts in the forests of every kind, both the cow and the ox, and the ass and the horse, and the goat and the wild goat, and all manner of wild animals, which were for the use of men. And we did find all manner of ore, both of gold, and of silver, and of copper.

---

VERSE 23. *The Promised Land.* This was the first name given to America, on the landing of Lehi and his colony. It was one of the names by which Palestine was known in the Old Testament, because of God's promise to Abraham: "In the same day the Lord made a covenant with Abram, saying, Unto thy seed have I given this land, from the river of Egypt unto the great river, the river Euphrates." (Gen. 15:18) It was applied to America by the Lord himself, when he said to Nephi: "And insomuch as ye shall keep my commandments, ye shall prosper, and shall be led to a land of promise; yea, even a land which I have prepared for you." (1 Ne. 2:20) The very name was a constant reminder to the descendants of Lehi of their obligation to keep the commandments of God.

VERSE 24. *We did begin to till the earth.* As soon as the colony had landed, they prepared the soil for the seed they had brought with them. So did the pioneers that first came to Salt Lake valley for permanent settlement. Perhaps they found in this account of the Book of Mormon a needed inspiration. The soil was fertile, and they had an abundant harvest.

VERSE 25. *As we journeyed in the wilderness.* I understand this to mean that as soon as Lehi and his company had taken care of their first harvest they continued their journey "in the wilderness," which in this case would mean the bench land, or the mountain regions. If they landed in South America, this "wilderness" would be some part of the famous Cordillera of the Andes, or copper mountains which might well have been called "Gold mountains." Of these we read:

"Arranged sometimes in a single line, though more frequently in two or three lines running parallel or obliquely to each other, they seem to the voyager on the ocean but one continuous chain; while the huge volcanoes, which to the inhabitants of the tableland look like solitary and independent masses, appear to him only like so many peaks of the same vast and magnificent range. So immense is the scale on which nature works in these regions that it is only when viewed from a great distance that the spectator can in any degree comprehend the relation of the several parts to the stupendous whole. Few of the works of nature, indeed, are calculated to produce impressions of higher sublimity than the aspect of this coast, as it is gradually unfolded to the eye of the mariner sailing on the distant waters of the Pacific." ("Peru," by Wm. H. Prescott, Vol. 1, p. 28.)

*Beasts in the forest.* Nephi informs us: "There were beasts in the forests of every kind, both the cow and the ox, and the ass and the horse, and the goat and the wild goat, and all manner of wild animals."

This is one of the passages in the Book of Mormon, which has very generally been relied on by adverse critics to prove that the volume is but clumsy fiction. Even as painstaking an historian and keen reasoner as John Fiske pauses long enough in his masterly review of the story of the discovery of America,[3] to give vent to his sentiment in a cynical sneer at Nephi—"the veracious chronicler"; thereby justifying the doubtful compliment paid to himself, among others, by Dr. W. H. Holmes[4] in the following line: "The compilations of a Bancroft, a Winsor, or a Fiske, illumined as they are by exceptional genius, could not always rise above the vitiated records upon which they drew." But notwithstanding the cocksure criticism of the passage in the record of Nephi, I consider it one of the strong, irrefutable proofs of the authenticity of that book.

Let us remember that, when Lehi and those with him came to this side of the world, no matter where they landed, they saw here animals unlike any they had ever seen before, and yet bearing some resemblance to creatures familiar to them. If they landed in South America—and we may, for the time being, take that for granted for the sake of this argument—they saw, probably, the ancestor of the *llama*, an animal resembling the camel but smaller and without the hump. They saw the *alpaca*, an animal so closely related to the llama, that some have regarded the two as variations of the same species. Both bear a strong resemblance to sheep. The llama is about three feet high at the shoulder. It is not found wild any more.

They must have seen the *huanacu*, which some have classed as a variety of the llama, but which Dr. von Tschudi regards as an entirely different animal. The huanacus are about the same size as the llamas. They live in small herds and are very shy. They saw, probably, the *vicuña*, an animal somewhat smaller than the llama, being about two and a half feet high at the shoulder, and having a long, slender neck. Then they must have seen the *tapir*, an animal that has been compared to a pig, and also to a rhinoceros, although it has no horn.

It must also be remembered that none of the strange animals, peculiar to this continent, when first seen by the colonists of Lehi, had a name, known to them. How, then, was Nephi to mention them in his record? To be sure, he could have given them arbitrary names, but what useful purpose would that have served? He did exactly what any historian would have done in his place. He compared the strange animals he saw with animals he had known in his homeland, and gave to them familiar names, expressive of the peculiar qualities for which those names stood in his day. And that is the obvious reason why he called them "cows," "oxen," "asses," "horses," "goats," and "wild goats." The names were not meant to express "blood relationship" with the old-world animals known by these names, but resemblance in some characteristic or other.

The Spaniards, on their arrival here, encountered a difficulty similar to that which Nephi must have experienced. "The resemblance," says Prescott, "of the different species to those in the Old World, with which no one of them, however, was identical, led to a perpetual confusion in the nomenclature of the Spaniards, as it has since done in that of better instructed naturalists."[5] And yet, the Spaniards

---

[3] Discovery of Amercia, vol. 1, p. 3.
[4] Handbook of Aboriginal American Antiquities, Part 1, p. 11.
[5] Conquest of Mexico, vol. 1, p. 394.

had one advantage. When they arrived on the scene, all the animals had names, and they could learn these of the Indians, as they, of course, did, when they were able to make themselves understood.

Garcilasso Inca de la Vega, who wrote his delightful *Royal Commentaries* in the 16th or beginning of the 17th century, uses almost the same phraseology as Nephi, although he was a native of Peru and knew the Indian names for all the animals. He says:[*]

"There are other animals in the Antis, which are like *cows*. They are the size of a very small cow, and have no horns."

He refers to the tapir, which is so much like a cow that when European cattle were introduced into Brazil, the natives called them "tapyra." It is an animal about four feet from nose to tail, and the Spaniards used to call it *gran bestia*. But hear Garcilasso again:

"The male huanacu is always on the watch on some high hill, while the females browse in the low ground, and when he sees any man, he gives a neigh *like that of a horse*, to warn the others.

"The vicuna stands higher than the highest *goat*. They are swift, and a grey-hound cannot come near them."

In addition to the animals mentioned, the colonists must have seen deer and stags, the roe and the fallow deer, and such "wild animals" as foxes, lions, tigers, rabbits, etc. But the point to note is that the Inca, when describing the strange animals to his Spanish readers, compares them with "horses," "cows," "goats," just as the Prophet did twenty centuries before him, in his record. That I take to be a strong proof of its authenticity.

*Hebrew Classification of Animals.* Nephi was a Hebrew, and the expression of his thoughts, naturally, conformed to the idioms of his mother tongue. The Hebrews did not always classify objects as we do. For instance, observing that the animal we call "horse" had a peculiar way of "leaping" or galloping, they gave him a name expressive of that characteristic and called him *sus*, from a root, meaning "to leap." The horse was the "leaper." But presently they noticed the flight of a certain bird and fancied there was some resemblance between that mode of traveling and the leaping of a horse. Then they called the bird also *sus* or *sis*, and the swallow, as far as the name was concerned, was put in one class with the horse. For the same reason of classification a moth was called *sas* from the same root as the horse and the swallow. Again, they had at least six words for "ox." One of them was *aluph*, from a root meaning to be "tame," "gentle." It was used for both "ox" and "cow," because either could be "tame." For the same reason it might mean a "friend," and sometimes it meant the "head" of a family, or a tribe. Another word for "ox" was *teo*, translated "wild ox" on account of its swiftness, but the word also stands for a species of gazelle.

The enumeration by Nephi of "cow" and "ox," "ass," and "horse," "goat" and "wild goat," and all manner of "wild animals," meaning the strange specimens met with in the New World, conforms strictly to what might be expected of a Hebrew. The passage, therefore, as has already been said, is a strong proof of the truth of the record.

This method of naming strange objects was not confined to the Hebrews alone. It seems that all people entering a strange land adopted the same practice.

The English when they first came to America found the aborigines growing and cultivating a strange plant. They had never seen it before. It resembled, most closely, a plant familiar to them, which was corn. Now corn to them is what we, in

[*]*Royal Commentaries*, Translation by Sir Clements Markham, published by the Hakluyt Society, London, 1871; vol. 2, pp. 383 and 386.

America, call wheat. But it was not (wheat) corn, it was a plant indigenous to America. However, we would not think their historian false, let alone a liar, when he says that they found the Indians growing corn. This same procedure was characteristic of the Scandinavians and of other races.

*All manner of ore.* This would not have been found on the low, sandy coast strip, but in the mountains.

## GENERAL NOTES

1. *From Jerusalem to the Valley of Lemuel.* Lehi leaves Jerusalem and goes into the wilderness (1 Ne. 2:4).

2. He proceeds for three days in the wilderness near the Red Sea, and comes to the valley which he names, Lemuel (1 Ne. 2:6, 8, 14).

3. *From the Valley of Lemuel to Shazer.* Having crossed the river Laman in the valley of Lemuel, Lehi continues in a nearly south-southeasterly direction to a place which he gives the name of Shazer. Here the travellers replenish their supply of provisions (1 Ne. 16:13).

4. *From Shazer to an Unnamed Camp.* After a successful hunting expedition Lehi proceeds in the same direction as before, "for the space of many days," and then camps at some convenient resting place, not named. Here the steel bow of Nephi is broken by accident, and new bows and arrows are made of wood. The brothers of Nephi murmur and their father sides with them. (1 Ne. 16:14, 17, 20, 23)

5. *From the unnamed camp to Nahom.* From this station the journey is continued, still in nearly the same direction as before, and after "many days" they arrive at a place which they call Nahom. Here Ishmael passed away. They remained here for "many days." (1 Ne. 16:33, 34)

6. *From Nahom to Irreantum.* After having rested "many days" at Nahom, Lehi and his company change their course from nearly south southeast to nearly "eastward from that time forth." By following this new course, they finally arrive at a locality which they call Bountiful, situated at the sea shore. The sea they call "Irreantum." The entire time consumed in the wilderness is eight years. (1 Ne. 17:1, 4, 5) After many days Nephi is commanded to build a ship (c. 8). The ship is built (1 Ne. 18:4).

7. *Beginning of the Voyage.* Lehi began the voyage favored by the wind. (1 Ne. 18:8). "After many days" there is mutiny in the ship and a terrible storm is encountered (vv. 9-13). On the fourth day, the storm, instead of abating, increases in fury (v. 14). That is the end of the mutiny. The voyage is resumed (vv. 15-22).

8. *In the Land of Promise.* After "many days" the travelers disembark on the shores of the Promised land (v. 23).

*The Landing Place.* The question, Where did Lehi land? is discussed in, "An Introduction to the Study of the Book of Mormon," pp. 92-95 and 411-432. Several views are given.

If we accept the commonly held view, which has been stated by Elder George Reynolds, among others, that the landing place was on the coast of Chile, at about 30 degrees south latitude, we may suppose that Lehi and his colony embarked somewhere on the coast of the present sultanate of Oman in Arabia, and that their course was set nearly southeasterly. At first they might have encountered adverse trade winds and perhaps a turbulent sea, but as they reached the 30th parallel the trade wind would have been favorable for a course south of Australia, between that continent and Tasmania, and then north of New Zealand toward the coast of Chile. The nearest harbor in the northward path of the trade wind would be the place where Coquimbo now is located, not far from Valparaiso. (See a recent map of the World, published by the National Geographic Magazine.)

Coquimbo has one of the finest harbors in Chile. It is situated on the river that has the same name. And it is not very far from the Andes mountains. The population of the port was (in 1920) estimated at 160,256. Its latitude is 30 degrees south.

*Rowing or dancing.* In his Ancient Monuments of Mexico, Brasseur de Bourbourg gives a little bit of tradition that may be of interest to readers of this chapter. He quotes the native account of the settlement of Mexico thus:

"Here is the beginning of the accounts of the arrival of the Mexicans from the place named Aztlan. It was through the midst of the water that they made their way to this locality, being four tribes. And in coming they were rowing in their ships. In coming they placed their huts on piles in a place called The Cave of Quinevayan. It is from there that the eight tribes came to go out."

It appears very much as if we in this tradition had traces of both Jaredite and Lehite immigration. But the most interesting part of it is that the learned abbe and archaeologist informs us that the word which he has translated "rowing" does not mean "rowing" but "dancing"; the native story is, then, that the people, in coming over the sea, on some occasion were "dancing." The author says the word translated "rowing" is not so translated anywhere. But, he says, they did certainly not dance in the ship. This, he adds, is how I analyze the word, "macevaya": "Ma" means, the hand, the arm; "ceua" or "cehua" means, to unite or interlace, "ce," being the root. In the labor of rowing, the arms moved in unison and seemed to be interlaced, which is the sense in which I understand the verb, to "row."

This may be ingenious, but it is not worthy of an historian. The Book of Mormon statement that there was a dance on the ship, which came very near being disastrous to the entire company, receives confirmation in the tradition, fragmentary though the evidence may be.[7]

-----

[7]The argument of Brasseur de Bourbourg is remarkable enough to be recorded in his own language:

"Ils ramaent, *macevaya,* verbe a l'imparfait, de *maceva,* traduit, d'ordinaire, par dancer, faire penitence, etc., mais nulle part par le mot ramer que j'adopt ici. Ils ne dansaint certainment pas dans leurs bateaux, en voyageant. Voila pour qurquoi j'ai decompose le mot; *ma* signifie la main, le bras, et *ceua* ou *cehua,* unir ou entrelacer; *ce,* un, etant le radical. Dans le travail de rameurs, les bras vont a l'unison et semblent s'entrelacer, d'ou le sens du verbe ramer que j'ai pris."

## CHAPTER 19

*Two sets of plates, 1-6 — Zenos and other prophets, 7-21 — The brass plates, 22-24.*

### 1. *Two sets of plates.*

1. And it came to pass that the Lord commanded me, wherefore I did make plates of ore that I might engraven upon them the record of my people. And upon the plates which I made I did engraven the record of my father, and also our journeyings in the wilderness, and the prophecies of my father; and also many of mine own prophecies have I engraven upon them.

2. And I knew not at the time when I made them that I should be commanded of the Lord to make these plates; wherefore, the record of my father, and the genealogy of his fathers, and the more part of all our proceedings in the wilderness are engraven upon those plates of which I have spoken; wherefore, the things which transpired before I made these plates are, of a truth, more particularly made mention upon the first plates.

3. And after I had made these plates by way of commandment, I, Nephi, received a commandment that the ministry and the prophecies, the more plain and precious parts of them, should be written upon these plates; and that the things which were written should be kept for the instruction of my people, who should possess the land, and also for other wise purposes, which purposes are known unto the Lord.

4. Wherefore, I, Nephi, did make a record upon the other plates, which gives an account, or which gives a greater account of the wars and contentions and destructions of my people. And this have I done, and commanded

VERSE 1. *I did make plates of ore.* In accordance with divine instructions, Nephi made two sets of plates, (a) The Larger Plates which contained "the record of my father; also our journeyings in the wilderness," and prophecies of Lehi and Nephi; (b) The Smaller Plates.

VERSE 2. *The first plates.* When Nephi made the first plates, he knew not that he would be required to make another set, wherefore he gave on the first plates the genealogy of his father and ancestors and an account of the journey in the wilderness in great detail.

VERSE 3. *The second plates.* But he received instructions to make another set in addition to the first. On this second set he was to record their ministry, and the plain and precious parts of the prophecies; while the first plates were to be kept "for the instruction of my people, who should possess the land, and also for other wise purposes."

VERSE 4. *Upon the other plates.* That is, the first, a greater account is given "of the wars and contentions and destructions of my people."

my people what they should do after I was gone; and that these plates should be handed down from one generation to another, or from one prophet to another, until further commandments of the Lord.

5. And an account of my making these plates shall be given hereafter; and then, behold, I proceed according to that which I have spoken; and this I do that the more sacred things may be kept for the knowledge of my people.

6. Nevertheless, I do not write anything upon plates save it be that I think it be sacred. And now, if I do err, even did they err of old; not that I would excuse myslf because of other men, but because of the weakness which is in me, according to the flesh, I would excuse myself.

---

VERSE 5. *These plates.* Comp. 1 Ne. 9:4-6; 2 Ne. 5:30, D. and C. Sec. 10.

VERSE 6. *If I do err.* The aim of Nephi is to preserve in writing, for the benefit of posterity, only that which he considers "sacred." He acknowledges that he may err in the selection of subject matter; for all men err.

*Weakness . . . according to the flesh.* Nephi is aware of the fact that the "flesh," i. e. the mortal body, notwithstanding its marvelous construction, its endurance and recuperative, almost creative, powers, has its limitations and even imperfections. It is weak. It was owing to this characteristic of the "flesh" that Peter, James and John, during the hour of agony of our Lord in Gethsemane, were unable to keep awake with him, wherefore Jesus admonished them, "Watch and pray, that ye enter not into temptation: the spirit is willing, but the flesh is weak." (Matt. 26:41) Even the body of the Lord himself, the Holy One, the Sinless One, was subject to this condition. Otherwise he could not have died. This St. Paul states thus: "For though he was crucified through weakness, yet he liveth by the power of God." (2 Cor. 13:4)

This weakness, be it remembered, is not a moral but a physical condition. It is not sinful. But there is a weakness of the flesh, which is immoral and therefore sin.

St. Paul explains this at some length in his letter to the Romans (7:14-25). He there represents himself as he was before the Gospel of Jesus had made a new creature of him, and as many others are in their lives. He was, he says (v. 14), "sold" under sin. He was a slave of sin. "What I hate, that do I." (v. 15) But, he adds, it is not really I but the sin that dwelleth in me that is the active force: "For I know that in me (that is in my flesh) dwelleth no good thing: for to will is present with me; but how to perform that which is good I find not" (v. 18). That is to say, in other words—and this seems to be the doctrine of Paul—if a man or woman tampers with that which is wrong and becomes an habitual sinner, a slave of sin, then sin becomes a force within that man or woman, stronger than their understanding, their reason, and even their will. A human being may be endowed with intelligence by which he may become proficient in business, in the arts and sciences—even theology—but this is not enough to make him know, love and honor God by submission to his will. This is the work of the Holy Spirit in the human mind.

It may be interesting to recall that this doctrine of Paul is also the conclusion arrived at by philosophy. Ovid exclaims:

"My reason this, my passion that persuades; I see the right, and I approve it, too; Condemn the wrong and yet the wrong pursue."

## 2. *Zenos and other prophets.*

7. For the things which some men esteem to be of great worth, both to the body and soul, others set at naught and trample under their feet. Yea, even the very God of Israel do men trample un-der their feet; I say, trample under their feet but I would speak in other words—they set him at naught, and hearken not to the voice of his counsels.

---

Another philosopher: "—but I am overcome by sin, and I well understand the evil which I presume to commit. Passion, however, is more powerful than my reason, which is the cause of the greatest evils to mortal men." (Dr. Adam Clarke, in Commentary on Rom. 7:15)

Human will is, even by nature, inclined toward that which is right and good. It is, however, often too weak to overcome the evil influences. But if the will surrenders so completely to the evil powers, that it no longer urges man on in the right direction, that man is lost, indeed, as a ship without a propelling force and without a rudder.

### THE REJECTION OF THE MESSIAH

Nephi, in this section, mentions by name three prophets of the Old dispensation, not elsewhere recorded among the prophets, viz., Zenock, Neum and Zenos.

In contemplating the ever present possibility of man's falling into error, because of the weakness of the flesh, Nephi recalls the rejection of the Messiah, by the children of Israel, as an illustration of that fact, awful in its consequences, because, in setting him aside, they deliberately sinned against the light they had received. An angel, a messenger from heaven, had predicted his advent, and even stated the exact time when he would come (v. 8). Zenock and Neum had predicted his death by crucifixion, and Zenos had told them that his entrance into the realm of the dead would be signalized to the world, and especially to the House of Israel, by three days of darkness (vv. 10-12). And yet, notwithstanding these specific prophecies the people would refuse to accept him (v. 13). As a consequence they would be "scourged," rendered homeless, and be made a "hiss and a byword," the object of hatred among all nations. (v. 14) This is, indeed, an illustration of the truth everywhere apparent, that man, when not following the lead of the Holy Spirit, is liable to assume a wrong attitude, although well aware of the impropriety and also the dreadful consequences thereof.

VERSE 7. *The very God of Israel.* "Jehovah," or, as most scholars now believe, "Jahveh," is his name. (Ex. 6:2, 3)

Concerning the meaning of that sacred name, the opinions are divided. Some derive it from a form of the Hebrew verb "hajah," which would mean, "One who calls things into being," i. e., the Creator. The objection to this interpretation is chiefly that the form suggested does not appear anywhere but is merely assumed. Others point out that the verb "hajah," which is generally rendered "to be," "to exist," really means, "to become," "to come forth," and that the name therefore signifies, "One through whom God is coming forth," i. e. "revealing" himself. (See Gesenius, Hebr. und Aram. Handwörterbuch. This agrees with Ex. 33:19, 20; Matt. 11:27; John 1:18; Heb. 11:3; 1 Tim. 6:16.)

Some have understood Ex. 6:2, 3 to mean that the sacred name Jehovah was unknown before revealed to Moses, but that cannot be the true meaning of those verses. According to Ex. 3:13, 16, Moses said: "Behold, when I come unto the children of Israel, and shall say unto them, The God of your fathers hath sent me unto you; and they shall say to me, What is his name? what shall I say unto them?"

The Lord answered this question thus:

"*I am that I am: and he said,* Thus shalt thou say unto the children of Israel, I AM hath sent me."

Further:

"The Lord God [Jehovah Elohim] of your fathers, the God of Abraham, of Isaac and of Jacob, appeared unto me," etc.

This shows clearly that the Israelites in Egypt knew that Jehovah was the God of their fathers. For, otherwise the mention of his name would have had no effect.

In the Book of Abraham, Pearl of Great Price, the question is settled beyond a doubt. There we read:

"And his voice was unto me: Abraham, Abraham, behold, my name is Jehovah, and I have heard thee and have come down to deliver thee, and to take thee away from thy father's house, and from all thy kinsfolk . . . I will take thee, to put upon thee my name, even the Priesthood of thy father, and my power shall be over thee. As it was with Noah so shall it be with thee; but through thy ministry my name shall be known in the earth for ever, for I am thy God." (Pearl of Great Price, p. 30, vv. 16-19)

Note (1) that the sacred name was revealed to Abraham while he was in the city of Ur of the Chaldees; (2) that when the Lord puts his name upon a chosen servant, he confers upon him the Priesthood; (3) that the father of Abraham had the Priesthood, and therefore must have known the name of the divine Head; and (4) that as the knowledge of the name had come from Noah, so, through Abraham, it should be made known in all the world.

There is every reason to believe that the sacred name was well known to our first ancestors, Adam and Eve, from the early days of their existence on earth, first in the Garden of Eden, and then after the exodus from that paradise. This belief grows, as we read the second and third chapters of Genesis, and it becomes a certainty when, in the fourth chapter (v. 1) we hear the joyful exclamation of Eve at the birth of Cain, "I have gotten a man from Jehovah."

And then again, in Gen. 5:29, we learn that Lamech, the father of Noah, knew the sacred name. For, in naming his illustrious son, he said:

"This same shall comfort us concerning our work and toil of our hands, because of the ground which the Lord [Jehovah] has cursed."

The name was known all through the ages before the flood, and then to the patriarchs after the flood, but it had, undoubtedly, been dimmed in the consciousness of the Israelites in their wretched condition in Egypt, and therefore it was again revealed through Moses.

"It [Jehovah] is certainly not a new name that is introduced; on the contrary, the 'I am that I am' would be unintelligible, if the name itself were not presupposed as already known. The old name of antiquity, whose precious significance had been forgotten and neglected by the children of Israel, here, as it were, rises again to life, and is again brought home to the consciousness of the people." (Smith, Bible Dictionary)

In reading the Scriptures about the various manifestations of Jehovah, it is important to remember that a messenger authorized to represent Jehovah always speaks or acts as if he were the divine Person he represents. He stands, literally, in his stead. For instance:

We remember the account in Exodus of the rebellion of Israel, in consequence of which the Lord decreed to send an angel to go before the people in his stead.

The account is, briefly, this: The Lord instructed Moses to break camp and cause the people to proceed on their way to Canaan. But, he said, "I will not go up in the midst of thee; for thou art a stiffnecked people: lest I consume thee in the way" (Ex. 33:3). "And I will send an angel before thee" (v. 2). The Lord, however, would again be with the people when they should take possession of the land, for, he says, "I will drive out the Canaanite, the Amorite, etc." Now Moses was anxious to know more about the angel who was to be their guide. So he said to the Lord: "See, thou sayest unto me, Bring up this people; and thou hast not let me know whom thou wilt send with me." (v. 12) Then the Lord said, "My presence shall go with thee, and I will give thee rest" (v. 14). From Isaiah 63:9 we learn that "presence" here stands for, "The angel of his presence." Isaiah says: "In all their affliction he was afflicted, and the Angel of his Presence saved them." That, then, was the name of the messenger who was to represent Jehovah. Of this messenger we read in Ex. 23:20-23: "Behold I send an angel before thee . . . Beware of him, and obey his voice; provoke him not, for he will not pardon your transgressions: for my name is in him. But if thou shalt indeed obey his voice, and do all that I speak; then I will be an enemy unto thine enemies . . . For mine angel shall go before thee, and bring thee in unto the Amorites and the Hittites . . . and I will cut them off." Thus, the **Angel of the Presence of the** Lord occupied completely the position of the Lord himself during the entire journey through the wilderness.

Moses may have known who the Angel of the Presence was. Isaiah may have known. We do not. But we do know, according to the Scriptures, that Michael is the "first of the chief princes" (Dan. 10:13); and that he is specially the prince of the people of Daniel (v. 21), that is to say, the Hebrews. And we know, further, that it is Michael who, during the last days of unprecedented trouble, when the children of Israel are to be delivered a second time, shall "stand up" for them. (Dan. 12:1) May it not then have been Michael who was the Angel of the Presence in the wilderness? We also know that Adam is "Michael, the Prince, the Archangel" (D. and C. 107:54).

In the Doctrine and Covenants the important truth is revealed that Jesus Christ, our Redeemer, is Jehovah. We read, "Listen to the voice of Jesus Christ, your Redeemer, the Great I AM, whose arm of mercy hath atoned for your sins." (29:1) "I AM," as we have seen, is the same as "JEHOVAH."

Again:

"Thus saith the Lord, your God, even Jesus Christ, the great I AM, Alpha and Omega, the beginning and the end, the same which looked upon the wide expanse of eternity, and all the seraphic hosts of heaven, before the world was made; the same which knoweth all things, for all things are present before mine eyes; I am the same which spake, and the world was made, and all things came by me." (38:1-3; comp. 109:34, 68; 110:4)

This truth is definitely stated in "A Doctrinal Exposition," signed by the First Presidency and the Twelve Apostles of the Church, June 30, 1916. We read:

"A fourth reason for applying the title 'Father' to Jesus Christ is found in the fact that in all his dealings with the human family Jesus the Son has represented and yet represents Elohim, his Father, in power and authority. This is true of Christ in his pre-existent, antemortal, or unembodied state, in which he was known as Jehovah; also during his embodiment in the flesh; and during his labors as a disembodied spirit in the realm of the dead; and since that period in his resurrected state." ("Articles of Faith," James E. Talmage, p. 471)

### JEHOVAH

One description of the Deity is that found in the so-called Athanasian Creed. There we read:

"The Father is God, the Son is God, and the Holy Ghost is God. And yet, they are not three Gods but one God. So likewise the Father is Lord, the Son Lord, and the Holy Ghost Lord. And yet not three Lords but one Lord. . . . And in this Trinity none is afore or after another, none is greater or less than another, but the whole three Persons are eternal together and co-equal."

To those who find in this creed a sufficient and adequate presentation of their concept of the Deity, the question, "Who is Jehovah?" is not even likely to occur. But if they should meet it, they would probably answer something like this: "The Father is Jehovah, the Son is Jehovah, and the Holy Ghost is Jehovah. And yet, they are not three Jehovahs but One." In other words, Jehovah would to them stand sometimes for the Trinity, and sometimes for each of the three Divine persons.

But all Christians do not accept the Athanasian representation. Some of us understand that the Persons in the Godhead are three distinct Entities, or Beings, each possessing in the highest degree of perfection all the qualities that constitute what we call a "person," an individual, and that they are one in the same sense that the disciples of Christ are one, though separate beings, each living his own individual life. To those who so understand the Deity, the question stated is important as having a bearing on the divine nature of Jesus. Who is Jehovah?

If we endeavor to find the answer to that question, we must search the Scriptures. There is no other source of reliable information on that point. Philosophy cannot help us. Our own logic leads us nowhere. Our only concern in this inquiry is: "What is written in the law? How readest thou?" (Luke 10:26)

If we, then, first turn to the Doctrine and Covenants, this remarkable volume of revelations that largely pertain to our own dispensation, we learn that Jehovah is the Second Person in the Godhead, the Son, who, in his human manifestation became known as Jesus Christ, or Jesus, the Christ. There can be no controversy, or doubt, as to that.

Section 29 contains a revelation given in September 1830, consequently only a few months after the foundation of the Church. It is one of the outstanding revelations, given in the presence of six Elders; it reveals the doctrine of gathering, makes the important announcement that the coming of Christ is near, makes known the position of the first apostles in the Millennial kingdom, speaks of the first resurrection and the signs preceding the second advent, and of the general resurrection, and, finally, gives revelations concerning the creation, the fall, and the innocence of little children. And who is the divine personage that gives this important revelation? We read: "Listen to the voice of Jesus Christ, your Redeemer, the Great *I Am*, whose arm of mercy has atoned for your sins." (v. 1.) It is Jesus Christ, the Redeemer, who speaks, and it is he whose name is "The Great *I Am*."

That name is the English for Jehovah, as is clear from Exodus 3:14. Moses asks the divine personage who manifests himself to him for information as to his name: "When they (the children of Israel) shall say to me, "What is his name? what shall I say unto them?" And he said: "Thus shalt thou say unto the children of Israel, *I Am* hath sent me unto you." It was Jehovah who spoke to Moses, either in person or through his "angel" who represented him. (See verse 7, where the *Lord* is Jehovah)

The word Jehovah is derived from the Hebrew verb "to be" or "to cause to be," and means, therefore, the One who is, or who creates.

This truth is further confirmed in Section 110, which contains the account of the glorious appearance of Jehovah to the Prophet Joseph Smith and Elder Oliver Cowdery in the Kirtland temple on April 3, 1836. They saw our Lord standing upon the breastwork of the pulpit, as they rose from prayer, and they heard him speak. The Prophet says: "We saw the Lord . . . and his voice was as the sound of the rushing of great waters, even the voice of Jehovah, saying: 'I am the first and the last, I am he who liveth, I am he who was slain, I am your advocate with the Father.' " Here we learn that Jehovah is "the first and the last," "he who was slain" and "your advocate with the Father"; that is to say, the Son, Jesus Christ, the Lamb of God, our Mediator.

Note that Jehovah, according to his own word, is "our Advocate with the Father"; he is not our Father, the first Person in the Godhead, but one who represents us before the Father. In one sense, he is the father of the human race, because, as our representative, he stands at the head of the children of men, in the plan of redemption. He is the second Adam, and in that sense he is the Father, "Everlasting Father" (Is. 9:5) and he is also the Son (Mosiah 15:2-4), but that is figuratively speaking or rather, speaking with the law of adoption in view, as Abraham, figuratively speaking, is the "Father" of "all them that believe." (Rom. 4:11; Gal. 3:7)

Jehovah is, then, Jesus Christ, our Lord and Redeemer.

In the old Testament, Jehovah is one of the Elohim. This is very clear from numerous passages. Note that it was "the Lord God" who made the earth and the heavens. (Gen. 2:4) "The Lord God" is the English of "Jehovah Elohim," or, as I think we should understand it, "Jehovah, the Elohim." It was Jehovah Elohim who "planted a garden" (Gen. 2:8), who "took the man and put him into the garden" (Gen. 2:15), who commanded man concerning the tree (Gen. 2:16), and who appeared in the story of the fall and promise of redemption. It is Jehovah who has promised to create "new heavens and a new earth" (Is. 85:17).

It was Jehovah who spoke to Abraham, concerning Sodom and Gomorrah. (Gen. 18) Jehovah seems to have been one of the three men who stood before him, as he sat in the tent door. It may have been Jehovah in person, or it may have been one who was his representative, his "angel," having authority to speak in his name. Jehovah was the God of Abraham, Isaac, and Jacob. (Gen. 28:13 and many other passages.) He, probably, it was who wrestled with Jacob (Gen. 32:24-30). For, although he did not tell his name, he conferred upon Jacob, in blessing him, the authority of a "prince"—a title bestowed upon our Father, Adam, at Adam-ondi Ahman (Doc. and Cov. 107:54)—and Jacob felt impressed with the fact that he had seen Elohim "face to face."

It was "the angel," or messenger of Jehovah, who first appeared to Moses in the burning bush (Ex. 3:2), but later, as soon as the attention of Moses had been attracted to the miraculous manifestation and he drew near to investigate, then, it seems, Jehovah Elohim addressed him (v. 4-17).

At the exodus from Egypt, the Angel of Elohim[1] went before the camp of Israel, and when the Egyptians pursued, this divine Personage "removed and went behind them," so that he stood in the fiery cloud between Israel and the pursuers. (Ex. 14:19, 20) This Angel of Elohim was Jehovah, for so we read: "And Jehovah went before them by day in a pillar of a cloud, to lead them the way." (Ex. 13:21)

Jehovah, the great Angel, or Messenger, of Elohim,—the representative, in other words, of the great Council of Elohim, in which this plan of salvation was accepted, and on account of which he was afterwards known as the "Wonderful Counselor," (Is. 9:6), but when Israel, after the many manifestations of his power, turned to the golden calf, possibly with ceremonies of which obscene practices formed a part (Ex. 32:25), then he threatened to withdraw entirely. At this critical juncture of the history of Israel, Moses went up on the mountain and plead before Jehovah for Israel, whereupon Jehovah, in answer to the prayers of his faithful servant, gave him the promise that he would send his Angel with him. From this time Jehovah withdrew, and left one of his angels, or representatives, in charge.

Who this angel of Jehovah is, we are not expressly informed, but since Daniel

---

[1]The name here is not the same as "The angel of Jehovah," which occurs in so many places.

| 8. And behold he cometh, according to the words of the angel, | in six hundred years from the time my father left Jerusalem. |

says that "the great prince which standeth for the children of thy people" is Michael (Dan. 12:1; 10:13 and 21), there can be no harm in the suggestion that Michael, our venerable ancestor, possibly was the angel of Jehovah, who had already at this time performed the mission, of which Daniel speaks. But be this as it may, Jehovah withdrew, and as a sign of this, the tent in which religious ordinances were performed and which hitherto had stood in the center of the camp, was now removed a long distance from it. The cloudy pillar, in which the angel of Jehovah manifested his presence, rested there.

A remarkable interview between Moses and Jehovah took place at that tent, away from the camp. Moses reminded Jehovah, that although he had commanded him to be the visible leader of the people, he had not instructed him regarding the journey. "Show me now," he said, "thy way." Jehovah answered, "My presence shall go with thee." (Ex. 33:14) That is to say, Jehovah would not entirely abandon the people. He would be near, just as Jesus promised to be near his apostles, even after he had departed. In the same sense Jehovah would be present and manifest himself from time to time, as circumstances required. This promise was fulfilled throughout the entire journey in the wilderness.

After having obtained this promise, Moses said, "I beseech thee, show me thy glory." In answer to that prayer, Jehovah explained to him that he could not see his face, but that he (Jehovah) would show him all his goodness and proclaim, or explain, his name to him, and also permit him to see his back as he was passing by a certain place.

This last expression is in all probability a misunderstanding by the translators of the Hebrew word. The word may here mean "behind" in point of time, "afterwards," and in that case we may understand the meaning to be Moses was given the privilege of seeing Jehovah in the form in which he "afterwards" would appear in the flesh. This human form, we know was his "glory," for John says: "The Word was made flesh, and dwelt among us, and we beheld his glory (his body) as of the only begotten of the Father." If we understand the text in Exodus the same way, it is clear. Moses saw Jehovah, just as John saw the bodily form of the Word, all but his face. (Ex. 33:20-23)

This agrees perfectly with the beautiful narrative in the Book of Ether concerning the interview of the Brother of Jared with our Lord. The Lord showed himself unto him in "the body of his spirit," in the likeness of which he, Jesus Christ, had created man (Ether 3:14-16), and he says: "The time cometh that I shall glorify my name in the flesh." (v. 21) That was his "glory," and that was, we may feel sure, the glory which Moses, as well as the Brother of Jared, saw.

VERSE 8. *Six hundred years.* The messenger who brought the word of the Lord to Lehi concerning the destruction of Jerusalem, and the commandment to leave the city, (1 Ne. 10:4), told him that the Messiah would come six hundred years from the exodus of himself and family. This is one of the few divine predictions on record in which a definite time is set for the fulfilment of a divine decree.

Another prophecy of that class is the word of the Lord delivered by the angel Gabriel to the Prophet Daniel in Babylon (Dan. 9:24-27). This is one of the grandest predictions on record. The angel Gabriel declares that seventy "weeks"— 490 years—"are determined upon thy people and upon thy holy city, to finish"— or rather, to "restrain"—"the transgression," etc. That is, in 490 years the Mosaic dispensation would come to an end. The chronology from this time is at best uncertain, but the following is worthy of consideration:

9. And the world, because of their iniquity, shall judge him to be a thing of naught; wherefore they scourge him, and he suffereth it; and they smite him, and he suffereth it. Yea, they spit upon him, and he suffereth it, because of his loving kindness and his long-suffering towards the children of men.

10. And the God of our fathers, who were led out of Egypt, out of bondage, and also were preserved in the wilderness by him, yea, the God of Abraham, and of Isaac, and the God of Jacob, yieldeth himself, according to the words of the angel, as a man, into the hands of wicked men, to be lifted up, according to the words of Zenock and to be crucified, according to the words of Neum, and to be buried in a sepulchre, according to the words of Zenos, which he spake concerning the three days of darkness, which should be a sign given of his death unto those who should inhabit the isles of the sea, more especially given unto those who are of the house of Israel.

---

"That the seventy weeks mentioned by Daniel denote weeks of years is agreed by almost every commentator, but not the time when these seventy weeks, or 490 years, began. It is plain they began from an edict or warrant to build the city of Jerusalem, and not from an edict to rebuild the temple; they could not therefore begin at the edict of Cyrus, or Darius . . . but at the edict of Artaxerxes Longimanus, . . . either in the seventh year of his reign, when he gave Ezra his commission (Ezra 7 and 8), or in the twentieth year of it, when he gave Nehemiah his (Neh. 2). The edict in the seventh year . . . appears to have been just 490 years before our Savior's death, by which he finished transgression, and made an end of sin, by his complete atonement. Of these, seven weeks or forty-nine years, were spent in rebuilding the city and its walls and these ended about the [time of the] death of Nehemiah. Sixty-two more weeks, or 434 years, elapsed, before the ministry of John or Christ began. . . . Jesus, in the last half of the seventieth week, that is, at the end of it, made the sacrifice and oblation." (The Popular and Critical Bible Encyclopedia, Dr. Samuel Fallows, Editor, Vol. 2, p. 1558.)

It was Gabriel who communicated this message to Daniel. The matter, he said, had been "determined." (Dan. 9:24) Undoubtedly in a divine council meeting at which he had been present. There is no reason why we may not surmise that Gabriel perhaps was the angel who had visited Lehi, as he now visited Daniel. Lehi and Daniel were contemporary. But the latter, while still a young boy, was carried to Babylon. The vision in Chapter 9 is supposed to have been given in the year 538 B. C., in the first year of Darius the Mede.

A word of explanation may be called for here: Why read 490 "years" instead of seventy "weeks"? Why forty-nine "years" instead of seven "weeks"?

The answer is that the original text does not say seven "weeks," or seventy "weeks," but seven "sevenths," and, seventy "sevenths." The question, therefore, is, What does "sevenths," not "weeks," mean?

But the Jews had "sevens," (i.e. weeks) of years as well as "sevens" (or weeks) of days; for, every seventh year was a Sabbath year, and every period of years from Sabbath to Sabbath was a "seven" (or "week") of years. Now, inasmuch as the vision of Daniel was historical, necessarily referring to years and not to days, the "sevenths" mentioned must be "weeks" of years.

VERSE 10. *To be lifted up.* Refers to the death of our Lord on the cross. (See

11. For thus spake the prophet: The Lord God surely shall visit all the house of Israel at that day, some with his voice, because of their righteousness, unto their great joy and salvation, and others with the thunderings and the lightnings of his power, by tempest, by fire, and by smoke, and vapor of darkness, and by the opening of the earth, and by mountains which shall be carried up.

12. And all these things must surely come, saith the prophet Zenos. And the rocks of the earth must rend; and because of the groanings of the earth, many of the kings of the isles of the sea shall be wrought upon by the Spirit of God, to exclaim: The God of nature suffers.

13. And as for those who are at Jerusalem, saith the prophet, they shall be scourged by all people, because they crucify the God of Israel, and turn their hearts aside, rejecting signs and wonders, and the power and glory of the God of Israel.

14. And because they turn their hearts aside, saith the

---

v. 13)   Also the following: "And I, if I be lifted up from the earth, will draw all men unto me.   This he said, signifying what death he should die." (John 12:32, 33)

*Zenock.*  Possibly the Hebrew, *tsinok,* (Jer. 29:26), translated "stocks."  If so, the name may be an allusion to persecution which he may have suffered at the hands of his countrymen.  He was a Hebrew prophet. (See Alma 33:15; 34:7; Hel. 8:20; 3 Ne. 10:16)

*Neum.*  Among those who returned from Babylon with Zerubbabel was one Nehum (Heb., Nechum), one of the chiefs of the Jewish community.  It is probably the same name as Nahum.  Another, but longer, form of this name is, Nehemiah (Nehem-jah), which means, "Jehovah is full of consolation."  The name was not uncommon among the Hebrews.  The Neum referred to by Nephi prophesied of the crucifixion of our Lord.

*Zenos.*  A Hebrew prophet, who prophesied of the death of Christ and the darkness that would be a sign to the house of Israel of his descent into the realm of the dead. (See also Jac. 5:1; 6:1; Alma 33:3, 13, 15; 34:7)

VERSES 11-17.  *Thus spake the prophet.*  These verses contain a synopsis by Nephi of the predictions of Zenos on two important subjects: (1) the convulsions in nature by which all Israel might know that the great sacrifice of atonement had been made; (2) what the consequences would be to the House of Judah, of the rejection of this sacrifice of the Messiah.

VERSE 11.  *The thunderings and the lightnings of his power, by tempest, etc.*  The best commentary on these verses (11 and 12) is found in 3 Ne. 8:5-10:17.  The storm and the earthquake lasted about three hours, and the effects were felt both in the land southward and to the land northward.  The darkness lasted for three days. (See 3 Ne. 8:19 and 10:9)  And during all this time, nature was "groaning," while adjusting itself to the changes caused by the violent commotion.

VERSE 13.  *And so for those who are at Jerusalem.*  The prophet Zenos predicts that the Jews would be "scourged by all people," and that they would be dispersed among the nations, yet hated by all; they would become a "hiss and a by-word," because of their rejection of the "God of Israel," also called the "Holy One of Israel."

prophet, and have despised the Holy One of Israel, they shall wander in the flesh, and perish, and become a hiss and a by-word, and be hated among all nations.

15. Nevertheless, when that day cometh, saith the prophet, that they no more turn aside their hearts against the Holy One of Israel, then will he remember the covenants which he made to their fathers.

16. Yea, then will he remember the isles of the sea; yea, and all the people who are of the house of Israel, will I gather in, saith the Lord, according to the words of the prophet Zenos, from the four quarters of the earth.

17. Yea, and all the earth shall see the salvation of the Lord, saith the prophet; every nation, kindred, tongue and people shall be blessed.

Note the peculiarity of this prediction. The Jews would be dispersed among, but never assimilated with, other nations. Other peoples, or parts of other peoples, have been dispersed and made friends among the peoples of the world, while the Jews, in the dispersion (the "diaspora," as they call it) remain strangers, even when they acquire a new citizenship. History shows this to have been the rule, although there, of course, are many notable individual exceptions.

Dr. Keith, in his dissertations on the evidence for the truth of the Christian religion, calls attention to the fact that the Jews have always, since the crucifixion, been a suffering people. In the fifth century they were exiled from Alexandria, where they for centuries had had great influence. The emperor Justinian deprived them of their synagogues, and prohibited their use of any place whatever for religious purposes. He denied them the right to testify in court, and to dispose of any property they might have, by a will or testament. In Spain, at one time, they were given the choice between apostasy, imprisonment and exile. The same conditions were imposed on them in France. In Mohammedan countries they found equally bitter enemies. The head of the Roman Catholic world has, at sundry times, cursed all who befriended the Jews, as well as the Jews themselves. Christian holidays were sometimes made occasions of persecution. During the crusades, the hatred of the Jews increased. At Verdun, Trèves, Mainz, Speier and Worms thousands of Jews were robbed and murdered. At York, in England, it is said, on one occasion, 1500 Jews, including women and children, were captured, and when they were not permitted to ransom themselves, they murdered each other, in order to escape the fate prepared for them by the mob. In some countries the burning at the stake of a Jew was considered a great and noble "show." Even the women rejoiced when they witnessed the agony of the victim in the flames. For, was not the death of a Jew a victory of the faith? Neither high nor low, neither sex nor age, was spared when the flames of persecution were burning. Among the victims who perished in the flames was the great Portuguese dramatist, Antonio Joseph de Silvia, whose only crime was that he was a Jew.

The so-called "pogroms" of 1881, 1903 and 1905 are recent history. And the Jewish problem of the present day in some countries indicates that the prophetic word is still in force.

VERSE 15. *When . . . they no more turn aside their hearts against the Holy One of Israel.* This is the other side of the prophecy. It is a promise that, whenever the day comes that the Jews will accept Jesus as their Messiah, then the Lord will remember the covenants made with the fathers. Then He will gather them in, and all the earth will see the salvation of the Lord (v. 17).

18. And I, Nephi, have written these things unto my people, that perhaps I might persuade them that they would remember the Lord their Redeemer.

19. Wherefore, I speak unto all the house of Israel, if it so be that they should obtain these things.

20. For behold, I have workings in the spirit, which doth weary me even that all my joints are weak, for those who are at Jerusalem; for had not the Lord been merciful, to show unto me concerning them, even as he had prophets of old, I should have perished also.

21. And he surely did show unto the prophets of old all things concerning them; and also he did show unto man, concerning us; wherefore, it must needs be that we know concerning them for they are written upon the plates of brass.

## 3. *Brass plates.*

22. Now it came to pass that I, Nephi, did teach my brethren these things; and it came to pass that I did read many things to them, which were engraven upon the plates of brass, that they might know concerning the doings of the Lord in other lands, among people of old.

23. And I did read many things unto them which were written in the book of Moses; but that I might more fully persuade them to believe in the Lord their Re-

---

That the Jews still are a numerous people is one of the miracles of history. At present they are estimated at about fifteen and a half millions. Of these, there are 9,290,000 in Europe, 4,380,000 in North America, 200,000 in South America, 942,000 in Africa and 1,850,000 in Palestine.[1]

VERSE 22. *Engraven upon the plates of brass.* These were the records of which Laban was the custodian (1 Ne. 3:3; 3 Ne. 10:16, 17). Whether they were private property or records to which Lehi had as much legal right as he had, we are not informed. All we know is that he had them, and that the Lord commanded Lehi to claim them.

VERSE 23. *I did read many things to them.* Nephi read "in the book of Moses," and "that which was written by the prophet Isaiah."

*The Book of Moses.* Special attention is called to this phrase. Why does not Nephi say, "The books of Moses"? Or, even, "The five books of Moses"? For the simple reason that, to the Jews of his day, what we know as the five books of Moses were one volume which they called, "the Law," (Torah). The division into five parts took place centuries after the time of Nephi, probably in Alexandria, in Egypt. The title "Pentateuch"[2] means in Alexandrian Greek, "The five volumes." Origen is said to use it in that sense. It was introduced to the western world by Jerome (d. A. D. 418) and his contemporary, Rufinus. To the Jews it was, "Five Fifths of the Law." It was, "The Book of Moses." The term, "The book of Moses" in this

---

[1]1955.

[2]Teuchos, ordinarily, according to Liddel and Scott, means, a tool, implement, utensil, and in plural, implements of war, arms, armour.

deemer I did read unto them that which was written by the prophet Isaiah; for I did liken all scriptures unto us, that it might be for our profit and learning.

24. Wherefore I spake unto them, saying: Hear ye the words of the prophet, ye who are a remnant of the house of Israel, a branch who have been broken off; hear ye the words of the prophet, which were written unto all the house of Israel, and liken them unto yourselves, that ye may have hope as well as your brethren from whom ye have been broken off; for after this manner has the prophet written.

place, is therefore remarkable evidence of the genuineness of the record, which a well-informed student of the Book of Mormon will appreciate.

*I did read unto them.* Reading of the Scriptures is an indispensable part of spiritual training. Nephi was in daily communication with God and received wonderful revelations in dreams and visions and by means of the Liahona, but although he was thus favored, he found it necessary to read and study the Scriptures, and to understand them so he could explain and expound them to his brothers and fellow-travelers. He realized that it was necessary for him to know something "concerning the doings of the Lord in other lands, among people of old." (v. 22)

*I did liken all scriptures unto us.* This I take to mean that Nephi, in his sermons explained the Scriptures and applied their teachings to their own needs and circumstances. That is the correct way of reading the Scriptures.

In reading, for instance, the story of Abraham and Isaac on the mountain of Moriah, he would probably point out how the Lord rewards his faithful servants, who trust in him to the utmost and obey his commandments. He would, no doubt, draw a lesson from this solemn declaration of the Lord:

"And the Angel of the Lord called unto Abraham out of heaven a second time and said, By myself have I sworn, saith the Lord, for because thou hast done this thing, and hast not withheld thy son, thine only son: That in blessing I will bless thee, and in multiplying I will multiply thy seed as the stars of the heaven, and the sand which is upon the sea shore; and thy seed shall possess the gate of his enemies; and in thy seed shall all the nations of the earth be blessed; because thou hast obeyed my voice." (Gen. 22:15-18)

The reward of faith is a lesson offered in this Scripture, which is applicable to all times and all generations.

Or, in reading the story of the passage of Israel through the Red Sea, he might draw the lesson from it that God, who was mighty to take the Children of Israel across that sea, would also be able to take his father's company safely across the ocean to the land of promise.

That kind of reading is the most profitable literary exercise imaginable.

In reading any of the standard works of the Church it is well to ascertain the literal meaning of the passage read first, and the lesson it was intended to convey to those to whom it was first communicated. And then it might be well to ask, What lesson does it convey to my time and age? To my nation? My community? My family? Or to myself?

VERSE 24. *Hear ye the words of the prophet.*

A prophet of the Lord is one who speaks on behalf of the Lord, or in his name, whether he predicts future events, or unfolds the past, or gives commandments and rules for present conduct. To hear the words of the prophet is to consider them carefully and to do readily whatever the Lord, through his prophet, requests or commands.

The Lord said to his people concerning the Law, when all was prepared:

"For this commandment which I command thee this day, it is not hidden from thee, neither is it far off. It is not in heaven, that thou shouldst say, Who shall go up for us to heaven, and bring it unto us, that we may hear it and do it? Neither is it beyond the sea, that thou shouldst say, Who shall go over the sea for us, and bring it unto us, that we may hear it and do it? But the word is very nigh thee, in thy mouth, and in thy heart, that thou mayest do it." (Deut. 30:11-14)

Which is as much as to say that the Lord does not require anything strange and exceptional of his people. What he demands is that they do that which they know in their hearts to be true, and which perhaps they confess and proclaim with their lips as the word of the Lord.

## CHAPTER 20

*The words of the prophet, as recorded on the plates of brass—Compare Isaiah, 48.*

### 1. *Waters of Judah.*

1. Hearken and hear this, O house of Jacob, who are called by the name of Israel, and are come forth out of the waters of Judah, or out of the waters of baptism, who swear by the name of the Lord, and make mention of the God of Israel, yet they swear not in truth nor in righteousness.

---

The explanation of this chapter and the next, as given by Nephi in his discourse to his fellow travelers, is found in Chapter 22.

VERSE 1. *The waters of Judah.* This phrase in Isaiah has given commentators considerable trouble. "Hear ye . . . which are come forth out of the waters of Judah." What can the "waters of Judah" mean? Some read, "From the bowels of Judah"; others, "From the fountains of Jacob"; others, "From the days of Judah." From "the waters of baptism" is the true meaning. Whether this simple and obvious explanation came from the prophet Isaiah himself and had been engraved on the plates of Laban; or whether they are a gloss inserted by the prophet Nephi in his copy of the text, does not matter. In either case, it is an inspired explanation of an admittedly difficult passage.

Baptism was by no means unknown among the Jews at the time of Isaiah. When Jacob, returning from Haran, was about to re-enter the land of Canaan and build an altar to Jehovah at Bethel, he called his household together and said to them, "Put away the strange gods that are among you, and be clean, and change your garments." (Gen. 35:2) The word translated, "be clean," does not refer to the removal of dust and other impurities from the body, but to cleansing from sin, and in this case more particularly from the sin of worshiping "strange gods." It is the same word that is used in 2 Kings 5:14, where we read that Naaman, after having dipped himself in the Jordan, according to the word of the Lord, was cured of leprosy, "and he was clean." He was cleansed, not only of his sickness but of the contamination of paganism, for he exclaimed, "Behold, now I know that there is no God in all the earth, but in Israel." In other words, he was a new man, spiritually as well as physically.

From the Writings of Moses in the Pearl of Great Price we know that Adam was baptized. And when he had received the Holy Spirit, he heard a voice out of heaven, saying: Thou art baptized with fire, and with the Holy Ghost. This is the record of the Father, and of the Son, from henceforth and forever." (Chapter 6:64-66)

Baptism being a known ordinance among the Jews, the prophet could properly refer to it as the "waters of Judah."

*Swear by the name of the Lord.* Just how the custom of swearing by the divine Name originated is not known. It was common at the time of Moses, and became part of his law as a useful ceremony in the interest of peace and justice. In Ex. 22:11 an oath is ordered as an end of disputes concerning property rights. (Comp. Heb. 6:16) Instances of oaths in the Book of Mormon are found in 1 Ne. 4:33, 35 and 37, where Nephi and Zoram make a covenant with each other; also in Alma 52:39, where the son of Nephihah binds himself with an oath to judge in righteousness. Moroni regretted that he had sworn not to lead his people because

## 2. Thou hast seen . . . all this.

2. Nevertheless, they call themselves of the holy city, but they do not stay themselves upon the God of Israel, who is the Lord of Hosts; yea, the Lord of Hosts is his name.

3. Behold, I have declared the former things from the beginning; and they went forth out of my mouth, and I showed them. I did show them suddenly.

4. And I did it because I knew that thou art obstinate, and thy neck is an iron sinew, and thy brow brass;

5. And I have even from the beginning declared to thee; before it came to pass I showed them thee; and I showed them for fear lest thou shouldst say—Mine idol hath done them, and my graven image, and my molten image hath commanded them.

6. Thou hast seen and heard all this; and will ye not declare them? And that I have showed thee new things from this time, even hidden things, and thou didst not know them.

## 3. Behold I knew them.

7. They are created now, and not from the beginning, even before the day when thou heardest them not they were declared unto thee, lest thou shouldst say—Behold I knew them.

8. Yea, and thou heardest not; yea, thou knewest not; yea, from that time thine ear was not opened; for I knew that thou wouldst deal very treacherously, and wast called a transgressor from the womb.

---

of their wickedness, and he did not keep his oath. (Mormon 5:1) Evil and secret oaths are noted and condemned.

Our Lord, as is well known, condemns swearing in the daily intercourse between man and man. Whatever is beyond the mere affirmation, or negation, "cometh of evil." (Matt. 5:37) And the Apostle James reiterates this word of the Lord. (James 5:12). Yet, our Lord, when, during the legal proceedings against him, he was challenged under oath to say whether he was the Christ, the Son of God, he unhesitatingly replied in the affirmative; that is, as we should say, He testified under oath, not only that he was the Christ, the Son of God, but also that:

"Hereafter shall ye see the Son of man sitting on the right hand of power, and in the clouds of heaven." (Matt. 26:63, 64)

VERSE 6. *Thou hast seen and heard all this.* Our authorized version has, "Thou hast heard, see all this," which is anything but clear. "Thou hast seen and heard all this" is intelligible. The Lord had not only spoken, or "declared," "things from the beginning," but he had also "shown" them before they came to pass (vv. 3, 5). Consequently, they had both "seen" and "heard."[1]

---

[1]The Hebrew text is, "Shamaeta chatze kullah" ("thou hast heard, see all"). The text in the Book of Mormon suggests that the word translated "seen" has inadvertently dropped out of the Hebrew text, and that the copyist has erroneously written "chatze" for "hazze."

9. Nevertheless, for my name's sake will I defer mine anger, and for my praise will I refrain from thee, that I cut thee not off.

4. *I have refined thee.*

10. For, behold, I have refined thee, I have chosen thee in the furnace of affliction.

5. *For mine own sake.*

11. For mine own sake, yea, for mine own sake will I do this, for I will not suffer my name to be polluted, and I will not give my glory unto another.

6. *I am the first and the last.*

12. Hearken unto me, O Jacob, and Israel my called, for I am he; I am the first, and I am also the last.

13. Mine hand hath also laid the foundation of the earth, and my right hand hath spanned the heavens. I call unto them and they stand up together.

---

VERSE 9. *For my praise.* Means, "For the sake of my praise." The particle "for —sake" refers to both "my name" and "my praise." The longsuffering and mercy of God add to the honor and glory of his holy name.

VERSE 10. *I have refined thee.* The authorized version, in accordance with the Hebrew text, adds, "But not with silver." That sounds like an addition by a copyist. The plain meaning of the verse is that the Lord saw his people in the flames of affliction and chose them then, and undertook to refine them.

VERSE 11. *For mine own sake.* The repetition of this phrase gives emphasis to the fact that the selection of the children of Israel to be the people of God in a peculiar sense, was a divine act of sovereignty in no way merited by the people themselves. They have nothing to be proud of. Man is the clay. God is the artist. There is, perhaps, no truth more difficult to accept than that. And yet, there is no other way than perfect surrender to the Lord, that leads to eternal life and glory.

VERSE 12. *I am the first and the last.* Refers to Jehovah. Comp. Isa. 41:4; Rev. 1:8; 21:6; 22:13. The following comments from the Hebrew Daily Prayer Book, p. 3, are pertinent:

"He is the Lord of the universe, who reigned ere any creature yet was formed: At the time when all things were made by his desire, then was his name proclaimed king. And after all things shall have had an end, he alone, the dreaded one, shall reign Who was, who is, and who will be in glory."

Only, there will never be a time when all things shall have an end in the sense that they shall no longer exist. "Of the increase of his government and peace there shall be no end." (Is. 9:7)

VERSE 13. *They stand up together.* When the Creator calls to the inhabitants of the heavens or the earth, they stand up. It is a mark of respect. They stand at attention, to listen, and to comprehend his commands. This is not yet the case on

## 7. *Cyrus, prophecy concerning.*

14. All ye, assemble yourselves, and hear; who among them hath declared these things unto them? The Lord hath loved him; yea, and he will fulfil his word which he hath declared by them; and he will do his pleasure on Babylon, and his arm shall come upon the Chaldeans.

15. Also, saith the Lord; I the Lord, yea, I have spoken; yea, I have called him to declare, I have brought him, and he shall make his way prosperous.

16. Come ye near unto me; I have not spoken in secret; from the beginning, from the time that it was declared have I spoken; and the Lord God, and his Spirit, hath sent me.

17. And thus saith the Lord, thy Redeemer, the Holy One of Israel; I have sent him, the Lord thy God who teacheth thee to profit, who leadeth thee by the way thou shouldst go, hath done it.

18. O that thou hadst hearkened to my commandment—then had thy peace been as a river, and thy righteousness as the waves of the sea.

---

earth at all times. But the time will come when the majesty of the Lord will be thus recognized.

VERSE 14. *Who among them hath declared these things?* Which of the gods of the nations had declared beforehand what was about to happen? The Lord had previously announced, through his prophet, that he would raise up a "shepherd," "his anointed" i.e. his Messiah) to cause Jerusalem and the temple to be rebuilt, and Babylon to fall (Isa. 44:28; 45:1-4). He even gives his name, Cyrus (Heb. Koresh), and now he asks, Has any god thus lifted the veil of the future? True prophecy is strong evidence of the truth of the prophet and his religion.

*The Lord hath loved him.* Refers to Cyrus, and his conquest of Babylon.

VERSE 15. *He shall make his way prosperous.* The Lord would be on the side of Cyrus. The Chaldeans had had their opportunity. Through the prophet Daniel and other captives of Judah, the Lord had demonstrated his power so forcibly that Nebuchadnezzar proclaimed the God of Israel to be the only true God. He said: "Now I Nebuchadnezzar praise and extol and honor the King of heaven, all whose works are truth, and his ways judgment: and those that walk in pride he is able to abase." (Dan. 4:37) But the people fell back to the worship of idols and debauchery (Dan. 5:1-4). Thus their opportunity was lost. Now Cyrus was called to execute judgment.

VERSE 16. *Come ye near unto me.* The Lord now addresses the nations of the world.

*From the time that it was declared.* From the time the decree concerning Cyrus was determined on, the prophet had spoken of it, as the Lord God and his Spirit sent him to do. Note the three persons in the Godhead. In this verse we learn that the prophet was sent by "The Lord God" (Elohim) and his Spirit; in the next verse Jehovah, "the Holy One of Israel," speaks.

VERSE 18. *O that thou hadst hearkened!* A nation that will enjoy peace and righteousness, and not be torn by strife and crime waves, must, according to the word of God, hearken to his voice. That is applicable to all people in all ages.

*8. No peace . . . unto the wicked.*

19. Thy seed also had been as the sand; the offspring of thy bowels like the gravel thereof; his name should not have been cut off nor destroyed from before me.

20. Go ye forth of Babylon, flee ye from the Chaldeans, with a voice of singing declare ye, tell this, utter to the end of the earth; say ye: The Lord hath redeemed his servant Jacob.

21. And they thirsted not; he led them through the deserts; he caused the waters to flow out of the rock for them; he clave the rock also and the waters gushed out.

22. And notwithstanding he hath done all this, and greater also, there is no peace, saith the Lord, unto the wicked.

---

VERSE 19. *Like the gravel thereof.* Some commentators understand that "gravel" here refers to the fishes in the sea.

VERSE 20. *Go ye forth from Babylon.* The prophet predicts the return from Babylon, and that the people would come home with songs of joy.

VERSE 21. *They thirsted not.* The miracles here recounted—water from the rock, the cleaving of the rock—did take place when the Israelites came from Egypt, under Moses, and the captives on their way home from Babylon under Ezra and Nehemiah sang songs of this earlier deliverance, as the Latter-day Saints still are singing of the miraculous experiences of their fathers and mothers in the western deserts of their land of Zion.

VERSE 22. *No peace, saith the Lord, unto the wicked.* "Peace is the gift of God to those who repent of their sins and become reconciled to Him through the acceptance of the plan of salvation, whether they are far off or near—whether they be gentiles or Jews—but the wicked are like the troubled sea, whose waters cast up mire and dirt. Therefore they have no peace."

## CHAPTER 21

*The words of the prophet as recorded upon the plates of brass, continued
—Compare Isaiah, 49.*

### 1. A light to the Gentiles.

1. And again: Hearken, O ye house of Israel, all ye that are broken off and are driven out, because of the wickedness of the pastors of my people; yea, all ye that are broken off, that are scattered abroad, who are of my people, O house of Israel. Listen, O isles, unto me, and hearken ye people from far; the Lord hath called me from the womb; from the bowels of my mother hath he made mention of my name.

2. And he hath made my mouth like a sharp sword; in the shadow of his hand hath he hid me, and made me a polished shaft; in his quiver hath he hid me;

3. And said unto me: Thou art my servant, O Israel, in whom I will be glorified.

4. Then I said, I have labored in vain, I have spent my strength for naught and in vain; surely my judgment is with the Lord, and my work with my God.

5. And now, saith the Lord— that formed me from the womb that I should be his servant, to bring Jacob again to him— though Israel be not gathered, yet shall I be glorious in the eyes of the Lord, and my God shall be my strength.

6. And he said: It is a light thing that thou shouldst be my servant to raise up the tribes of Jacob, and to restore the preserved of Israel. I will also give thee for a light to the Gentiles, that thou mayest be my salvation unto the ends of the earth.

VERSE 3. *Thou art my servant, O Israel.* Some commentators recognize in the book of Isaiah four so-called "servant poems"; that is to say, four prophecies in poetic form, in which Israel, as a nation, is considered in the character and mission of a servant of the Lord. The first of these poems is Isa. 42:1-4; the second, 49:1-6; the third, 50:4-9; and the fourth, 52:13 to 53:12. Part of the last of these is quoted by Abinadi in his address to the priests of King Noah. (Mosiah 14)

This interpretation may be accepted as the first and literal meaning of these grand prophecies; in fact, the text itself seems to demand this. (See Isa. 42:18, 19; 49:6) But it is not the full meaning of them. Israel, as a servant of the Lord, is but a type, a shadow, of that perfect ideal of Man, the Messiah, the Holy One of Israel, the Son of God, and the complete and perfect fulfilment of these Scriptures is found only in the character and mission of our Lord Jesus Christ. The silence of Jesus before his persecutors and judges; the sufferings to which he voluntarily submitted; his death among the wicked and his burial with the rich; his vindication by the resurrection—all these are foretold, and the fulfilment is found only in the life and death of Him, who is, in the fullst meaning of the word, the Servant of the Lord.

VERSE 6. *A light to the Gentiles.* It is the mission of the children of Israel, as a nation, to be a light to the Gentiles. But that mission they cannot fill, until

## 2. O isles of the sea.

7. Thus saith the Lord, the Redeemer of Israel, his Holy One, to him whom man despiseth, to him whom the nations abhorreth, to servant of rulers: Kings shall see and arise, princes also shall worship, because of the Lord that is faithful.

8. Thus saith the Lord: In an acceptable time have I heard thee, O isles of the sea, and in a day of salvation have I helped thee; and I will preserve thee, and give thee my servant for a covenant of the people, to establish the desolate heritages;

9. That thou mayest say to the prisoners: Go forth; to them that sit in darkness: Show yourselves. They shall feed in the ways, and their pastures shall be in all high places.

10. They shall not hunger nor thirst, neither shall the heat nor the sun smite them; for he that hath mercy on them shall lead them, even by the springs of water shall he guide them.

11. And I will make all my mountains a way, and my highways shall be exalted.

12. And then, O house of Israel, behold, these shall come from far; and lo, these from the north and from the west; and these from the land of Sinim.

they themselves have, as it were, become transfigured by the glories of Bethlehem and Tabor and Golgotha and the Mount of Olives, and they can say with the Psalmist: "The Lord is my Light." (Ps. 27:1; comp. Luke 2:29-32; John 1:6-9; 12:35, 36; Rev. 21:23)

VERSE 7. *Kings shall see and arise.* The Lord addresses "him whom the nations abhorreth," the "servant of rulers," i.e. Israel, and gives the people the promise that they will not always be "despised' or "abhorred." He says the time will come when kings will "see and arise," they will stand up in reverence, in their presence.

VERSE 8. *O isles of the sea.* The Lord here addresses the nations of the earth. Sir Isaac Newton observes that to the Hebrews the continents of Asia and Africa were "the earth," because they had access to them by land, while the parts of the earth to which they sailed over the sea were "the isles of the sea." The Lord promises the nations of the earth that, through the help of Israel, the waste places will be redeemed (v. 8); liberty will be established (v. 9) prosperity will be general (v. 10); and means of communication will be multiplied (v. 11).

VERSE 12. *These shall come from afar.* Here the gathering of all Israel is predicted as part of the great work of the restoration of the earth. Some shall come from the north, and some from the west, and "these" from the land of Sinim.

That the gathering has already commenced from the North and the West is evident by the Latter-day work in America, and the movement toward Palestine from Great Britain and America. The land of Sinim is, according to some, Syene, in the south of Egypt, but Dr. Clark, in his Commentary, remarks that the word "sinim" means "bushes," and he suggests that the "land of sinim," therefore, probably refers to a land with great woods, to which Jews may have immigrated. He comments as follows:

13. Sing, O heavens; and be joyful, O earth; for the feet of those who are in the east shall be established; and break forth into singing, O mountains; for they shall be smitten no more; for the Lord hath comforted his people, and will have mercy upon his afflicted.

## 3. The Restoration of Jerusalem.

14. But, behold, Zion hath said: The Lord hath forsaken me, and my Lord hath forgotten me —but he will show that he hath not.

15. For can a woman forget

---

"The ten tribes are gone, no one knows whither.[1] On the slave coast in Africa, some Jewish rites appear among the people, and all the males are circumcized. The whole of this land, as it appears from the coast, may be emphatically the 'land of bushes' (eretz sinim), as it is all covered with woods as far as the eye can reach. Many of the Indians in North America, which also is a wood land, have a great profusion of rites, apparently in their basis Jewish. Is it not possible that the descendants of *the ten lost tribes* are among those in America, or among those in Africa whom European nations think they have a right to enslave? It is of these lost tribes that the 21st verse speaks: 'And these, where have they been?' "
Compare D. & C. 110:11; 133:23, 26.

VERSE 13. *Sing, O heavens; and be joyful O earth!* Describes the universal happiness that will be the result of the Latter-day work of restoration.

### THE RESTORATION OF JERUSALEM

VERSES 14-26. Here Zion is represented as a mother welcoming her children home. They are to gather in Zion in great numbers (v. 18); the land will appear too small for them (v. 19, 20); they will come from all parts of the world; gentiles will bring them in their "arms" and on their "shoulders" (v. 22); kings shall be their foster fathers, and queens their foster mothers (v. 23). The last three verses seem to indicate that the gathering will be completed amidst scenes of bloodshed and unspeakable atrocities (v. 24-26).

VERSE 14. *Zion.* This was originally the name of the upper part of Jerusalem. The city was built upon a high rock, with four hills, Zion, Acra, Moriah and Bezetha. The hill on the south-eastern side was called Zion. It was also known as the City of David, because he built his palace there. (2 Sam. 5:7-9) In the royal tomb of David on this hill, he and fourteen of his successors were buried. (I Kings 2:10; 11:43; 14:31) From the fact that David prepared a consecrated place for the sacred ark of Jehovah and erected over it a special tent on this Mount, (2 Sam. 6:12-17), Zion was called the "Holy Hill" (Ps. 2:6).

Immediately north of Zion was Acra. Between the two was a high wall. Moriah, supposed to be the hill on which Abraham was about to slay Isaac, is to the east of Acra. It was the site of the temple. Jewish rabbis hold that the altar of burnt offering of the temple stood on the very spot where the altar of Abraham was built. Zion and Moriah were connected by means of a bridge and a terrace. To the north was Bezetha which was joined to the city of Agrippa.

But Zion also stands for the entire City of Jerusalem (Isa. 10:24). The exiles in Babylon are "the captive daughters of Zion" (Isa. 52:2; Zech. 2:10, 11).

---

[1] This was published in 1853. Now, more is known of the ten tribes than was generally understood at that time.

her sucking child, that she should not have compassion on the son of her womb? Yea, they may forget, yet will I not forget thee, O house of Israel.

16. Behold, I have graven thee upon the palms of my hands; thy walls are continually before me.

17. Thy children shall make haste against thy destroyers; and they that made thee waste shall go forth of thee.

18. Lift up thine eyes round about and behold; all these gather themselves together, and they shall come to thee. And as I live, saith the Lord, thou shalt surely clothe thee with them all, as with an ornament, and bind them on even as a bride.

19. For thy waste and thy desolate places, and the land of thy destruction, shall even now be too narrow by reason of the inhabi-

In the Pearl of Great Price we learn more about Zion. "Zion" is the name which God gave his people, because they were of "one heart and one mind, and dwelt in righteousness; and there were no poor among them." (Book of Moses 7:18) Then Enoch built a city and called it Zion, adopting the name which God had given his people. It was the city of Holiness. (v. 19)

This city being built, Enoch seems to have had the hope that it would remain forever, the habitation of God. But the Lord enlightened him on that point. He said that he had blessed the inhabitants of Zion, but not the residue of the people. He, furthermore, showed Enoch all the inhabitants of the earth, and that he had taken Zion up into heaven, for they were the righteous inhabitants of the earth. (v. 21) The process of transferring the people of God from the earthly to the heavenly Zion did not belong exclusively to the time of Enoch. It was to be continued from generation to generation. For, Enoch beheld angels descending out of heaven bearing testimony of the Father and of the Son, and the Holy Ghost fell on many, and they were caught up by the powers of heaven into Zion. (v. 27) It is in this way that the Lord has taken Zion to his own bosom, "from all the creations, from all eternity to all eternity." (v. 31)

Enoch saw in his vision that he and the inhabitants of Zion were with the Father:

"And behold, Enoch saw the day of the coming of the Son of man in the flesh; and his soul rejoiced, saying: The Righteous is lifted up, and the Lamb is slain from the foundation of the world; and through faith I am in the bosom of the Father, and behold, Zion is with me." (v. 47)

But Zion will return to earth. The Lord assures Enoch that the time shall come, after a period of darkness and great distress, when righteousness shall be sent down from heaven, and truth come forth out of the earth. At that time the "elect" will be gathered out from the four quarters of the earth, to a place which the Lord will prepare, where his people may be looking forth for the coming of the Redeemer. For the tabernacle of God will be there, and it shall be called Zion, a New Jerusalem. There, the inhabitants of the heavenly Zion will meet the "elect," who are the inhabitants of Zion on earth:

"And the Lord said unto Enoch: Then shalt thou and all thy city meet them there, and we will receive them into our bosom, and they shall see us; and we will fall upon their necks, and they shall fall upon our necks, and we will kiss each other; and there shall be mine abode, and it shall be Zion, which shall come forth out of all the creations which I have made; and for the space of a thousand years the earth shall rest. . . . And Enoch and all his people walked with God, and he

tants; and they that swallowed thee up shall be far away.

20. The children whom thou shalt have, after thou hast lost the first, shall again in thine ears say: The place is too strait for me; give place to me that I may dwell.

21. Then shalt thou say in thine heart: Who hath begotten me these, seeing I have lost my children, and am desolate, a cap-

tive, and removing to and fro? And who hath brought up these? Behold, I was left alone; these, where have they been?

22. Thus saith the Lord God: Behold, I will lift up mine hand to the Gentiles, and set up my standard to the people; and they shall bring thy sons in their arms, and thy daughters shall be carried upon their shoulders.

23. And kings shall be thy

---

[God] dwelt in the midst of Zion; and it came to pass that Zion was not, for God received it up into his own bosom; and from thence went forth the saying, *Zion is fled.* (Moses 7:63, 64, 69)

In the Book of Mormon we have mainly three great truths concerning the Latter-day Zion: (1) That they who shall seek to bring forth Zion "at that day"—which evidently is the day in which we are living—are blessed (1 Ne. 13:37), (2) that opponents shall be destroyed (1 Ne. 22:14; 2 Ne. 6:13; 10:13; 27:3); (3) that it is dangerous to listen to the flattering voice of the adversary regarding Zion (2 Ne. 28:21).

A very large portion of the Doctrine and Covenants—the greatly inspired literary gem of our age—is devoted to the people and city of Zion. The student might read carefully the following passages, beginning with Section 21:7. This revelation was given the day the Church was organized. It tells us that the Prophet Joseph Smith was inspired to further the cause of Zion. That, then, is the mission of the Church.

Further: Zion, we read, shall rejoice upon the hills at the time of the salvation of Israel (36:24, 25). Zion shall be called the New Jerusalem, a land of peace, a city of refuge, a place of safety for the Saints, and the glory of the Lord shall be there (45:66, 67). Independence, Missouri, is the center place of Zion (57:4, 5; 58:13, 50, 57; 59:3). The Saints were to obtain an inheritance in Zion (64:30), but not the rebellious (64:35). Kirtland designated a city of the stake of Zion (94:1; 96:1-9; 97:10, 18, 19, 25). The *pure in heart are Zion* (97:21), and they shall return to Zion (101:18). A parable concerning the redemption of Zion (101:43-66). Revelation relating to the salvation and redemption of the Saints who are scattered on the land of Zion (103:1-18). Zion can be built up only by the principles of the law of the celestial kingdom (105:2-11, 13, 14, 32, 34). The bishops are judges in Zion (107:74). A prayer for Zion (109:59). The "strength" of Zion explained (113:7, 8). Meaning of, "Zion loosing herself from the bands of her neck" (113:9, 10). Far West, a holy city in the land of Zion (115:6-11). Baptism for the dead in Zion and in Jerusalem (124:36). Zion sanctified by the law of tithing (119:5, 6). The Saints among the gentiles to flee to Zion (133:9-12). The voice of the Lord in Zion (133:21-25). Zion to be redeemed (136:10, 18).

*The Lord hath forsaken me, my Lord hath forgotten me.* In the Hebrew text the first clause is, "Jehovah hath forsaken me; the second is, Adonai hath forgotten me. But both these names refer to the same divine Person. The Lord, in the following paragraphs shows how impossible it is that he should forget his people.

nursing fathers, and their queens thy nursing mothers; they shall bow down to thee with their face towards the earth, and lick up the dust of thy feet; and thou shalt know that I am the Lord; for they shall not be ashamed that wait for me.

24. For shall the prey be taken from the mighty, or the lawful captives delivered?

25. But thus saith the Lord, even the captives of the mighty shall be taken away, and the prey of the terrible shall be delivered; for I will contend with him that contendeth with thee, and I will save thy children.

26. And I will feed them that oppress thee with their own flesh; they shall be drunken with their own blood as with sweet wine; and all flesh shall know that I, the Lord, am thy Savior and thy Redeemer, the Mighty One of Jacob.

VERSE 16. *I have graven thee upon the palms of my hands.* I have delineated thee. An allusion to some practice of the ancients to mark the skin with some sort of symbol of a temple, or a city, to show respect for them. See Isa. 44:5:

"One shall say, I am the Lord's; and another shall call by the name of Jacob; and another shall write on his hand, To Jehovah."[1]

The early Christians used to mark their wrists or arms with the sign of the cross, or with the name of Christ. Comp. Rev. 20:4.

VERSE 17. *Shall go forth of thee.* Shall become thy offspring, spiritually speaking. Comp. Rom. 4:16, 17.

VERSE 21. *I have lost my children.* See v. 12.

VERSE 23. *Lick up the dust of thy feet.* The story is told of a prince who threw himself on the ground and kissed the prints that the horse of the victorious enemy had made with his hoofs in the dust, while he recited:

"While I shall have the happiness to kiss the dust of your feet, I shall think that fortune favors me with its tenderest caresses, and its sweetest kisses."

## GENERAL NOTES

"The past of Jerusalem is overflowing with thought. But the future is equally impressive. These ruins are not always to remain. The future temple, and the restored Israel, when Jerusalem shall be the throne of the Lord to all nations, claim the most earnest thought. The day when the feet of the Lord 'shall stand on the mount of Olives, which is over against Jerusalem on the east,' is full of importance; and whether we look backward or forward, we have to speak of Zion as 'the joy of the whole earth, for salvation is of the Jews' * * * Surely, there is no spot on Earth like Jerusalem." (Dr. Tyng)

*Origin of the Incas of Peru.* Speaking of the Nephites and other remnants of Israel, Elder J. Fred Evans calls attention to the fable of the origin of the Incas, as told by Pedro Sarmiento de Gamboa in his History of the Incas. According to this account:

Six leagues south southwest of Cuzco there is a place called Tampu-tocco (meaning, the Tavern of the Dawn). In the vicinity of this tavern there is a hill with three "windows." From one of these came a tribe of Indians, without parentage,

[1]Meaning, "I am Jehovah's."

called, Maras. From another window came a tribe called, Tampus, and from the chief window came four men and four women, who called themselves brothers and sisters. They knew no father nor mother. They came by order of Ticci Viracocha, who had created them to be lords. And for that reason, they took the name of Inca (lord).

The names of the four brethren are given thus: Manco Ccapac, Ayar Auca, Ayar Cachi, and Ayar Uchu. The names of the sisters: Mama Occlo, Mama Huaco, Mama Ipacura, and Mama Raua.

These settlers, however, were not the first inhabitants. There were others, with whom they entered into agreement to go out and look for fertile land and make war upon those who should oppose them.

These original settlers and the Incas elected Manco Ccapac and Mama Huaco to be their leaders, whereupon they set out from Tampu-tocco, in sufficient numbers to form a squadron. Manco Ccapac had a bird resembling a falcon, calling *Indi*, (the same as *Ynti*, the sun god). It must have been either a stuffed bird, or the image of a bird, for it was carefully carried in a hamper of straw, and it was left as an heirloom to succeeding Incas, to the time of Inca Yupanqui. It was through this Indi that Manco Ccapac became the leader. He also had a staff of gold, with which to test the soil in the countries they passed through.

They had many adventures on the road. At Huanacancha they remained for some time, sowing and looking for fertile land. At Tampo-quiro Mama Occlo gave birth to a son whom they called, Sinchi Rocca. At Hays-quiro they decided to get rid of their brother Ayar Cachi, wherefore they sent him back to Tampu-tocco, to fetch some golden vases which they had forgotten; and also some seed, called "napa." By reason of treachery, he perished. At Quiri-mauta Ayar Uchu remained as a "huaca," and Ayar Auca was from there to take possession of land set apart for him to people.

At a hill, two leagues from Cuzco, they saw a rainbow, which was regarded as good omen. Ayar Uchu went to a sacred statue and irreverently took a seat on it. His feet were immediately fastened to the image and he turned to stone.

At a place called Matahua, in the valley of Cuzco, the son of Manco Ccapac, Sinchi Rocca, was made a "knight." His ears were pierced, as a mark of nobility. A dance, called Ccapac Raymi, was performed. They remained here for two years. Then Mama Huaco hurled two wands of gold towards the north. One fell into a field, but did not drive in well, whereof they knew that the soil was not very fertile. The other went to a place near Cuzco. There they found deep fertile soil.

While still at Malahua, Manco Ccapac saw a heap of stones in the distance. He ordered his brother, Ayar Auca, to go thither and take possession of the land. He went "flying," for it seems that he had "wings" but, as so many aviators of our day, he perished. He was turned into stone. The heap was then called "cozco"; hence the name "Cuzco."

Manco Ccapac and Mama Occlo began to take possession of the land without the consent of the Huallas, the original inhabitants. Conflicts ensued and many cruelties were perpetrated.

Manco Ccapac, the story says, was 36 years old when he left Tampu-tocco. He was 8 years on the road to Cuzco, for he stayed one year in one place, and in another two years, and in other places more or less. He lived in Cuzco 100 years, and died at the age of 144 years.

The Inca rule is supposed to have lasted from 565 A.D. till 1533 A.D. But the history of Peru goes much further back than that.

## CHAPTER 22

*Prophecies, pertaining to things both temporal and spiritual, 1-6 — A marvelous work among the Gentiles, 7-12—Prophecies of war and bloodshed, 13-28—What is written is true, 29-31.*

### 1. *Prophecies pertaining to things temporal and spiritual.*

1. And now it came to pass that after I, Nephi, had read these things which were engraven upon the plates of brass, my brethren came unto me and said unto me: What meaneth these things which ye have read? Behold, are they to be understood according to things which are spiritual, which shall come to pass according to the spirit and not the flesh?

This chapter contains an explanation of the prophecies which Nephi had just read from the plates of brass. It begins with a question as to whether the Word of God is to be understood literally or spiritually, and the answer of Nephi. Then follows predictions concerning wars, the gathering of all Israel, and the final peaceful reign of the Holy One of Israel.

VERSE 1. *What meaneth these things?* When Nephi had finished reading, his brothers desired to know the true meaning of the words they had heard. Are they to be understood spiritually and not literally? This question may not appear to be important today, but it is one that has come down to us through many centuries. Is the Bible to be read literally, as any other book, or, has it a mystic sense, understood only by the initiated?

Philo, (20 B.C. to 40 A.D.) the Jewish Alexandrian philosopher, a contemporary of our Lord, was the great advocate in his day of the allegorical interpretation of the Scriptures, and he exerted an altogether remarkable influence upon the early church fathers and, through them, on the whole church. His philosophy was the Platonic, according to which all the things which our senses tell us exist are mere passing shadows, while the ideas in our minds are the realities. That is to say, an individual man, a horse, a book, etc. are only ephemeral phenomena, while the genus man or horse, or the class of objects we call book are the lasting things in the universe.

But Plato was also a Jew, and he believed in the literal inspiration of the Scriptures. How could this theory of the Bible be reconciled with his platonic philosophy? He found his solution in the "allegorical" interpretation of the Bible, which, by the way, is no interpretation at all but a re-writing of the text.

Clement of Alexandria (Cisca 150-215 A.D.), recognized four ways of interpreting the Scriptures, viz., The literal, the mystical, the moral and the prophetic. In his mystical system, the various details of the uniform of the high priest, for instance, had each a special meaning. The mitre signified the royal authority of our Lord. The breastplate of the ephod was a symbol of good works. The 360 bells on the priestly robe signified a year, viz., "the acceptable year of our Lord," and so on.

Origen, the most famous of the Alexandrian church fathers (185-253 A.D.), undertook the impossible task of harmonizing the Platonian philosophy of Philo with Christianity, as this great Jew had endeavored to do for said philosophy and Judaism. He, therefore, found in the words of the Scriptures a three-fold meaning, corresponding to the body, soul, and spirit of man. To him the letter was the "body." But, in addition to the literal sense, there was a moral and also a spiritual sense. In speaking of the Mosaic story of the creation, for instance, he asked if anyone

2. And I, Nephi, said unto them: Behold they were manifest unto the prophet by the voice of the Spirit; for by the Spirit are all things made known unto the prophets, which shall come upon the children of men according to the flesh.

3. Wherefore, the things of which I have read are things pertaining to things both temporal and spiritual; for it appears that the house of Israel, sooner or later, will be scattered upon all the face of the earth, and also among all nations.

---

can believe that the first three days were without sun, moon and stars, and the first day without a sky, even. These things, he suggests, are said figuratively by means of history, which is not to be understood literally, but as significant of certain "mysteries."

Some of these church fathers were so anxious to get a standing among the worldly wise of their day that they willingly reconstructed their theology in order to get room in it for pagan philosophy.[1]

VERSE 3. *Things both temporal and spiritual.* Nephi, realizing the importance of the question, perhaps even more than we do, explained to his brothers, that the prophecies were given by the Spirit, and that they pertained to both temporal and spiritual things, but that they were to be interpreted literally. Israel would be scattered (v. 3); some of the tribes would be lost to view to the rest of the world (v. 4); but they were to be "nursed by the gentiles" and again be remembered under the covenant with the fathers (v. 6). This is all to be understood literally.

Thus the question is completely and intelligently answered by Nephi. The words of the prophets, although referring to things both spiritual and temporal, are to be understood literally; unless, I think we may add, they are clearly shown to be used allegorically or figuratively, as for instance the "tree" and the "iron rod," etc., in the dream of Lehi. But let us note that the literal meaning of the word is that which it had at the time of the author, and as it was used by him and understood by his contemporaries, not as it is used and understood in our day, if the meaning has changed, as may be the case.

As an illustration: We read in Acts 21:15 that Paul and his companions took up their "carriages" and went up to Jerusalem. The literal meaning of the word

---

[1]Origen, for example, reading that Abraham, in his old age, married Keturah, and finding that "keturah" means "sweet odor" concluded that the true, mystical meaning of the statement is that Abraham, in his old age, became very holy.

The famous apocryphal author who writes under the name of Barnabas, possibly as early as the close of the first century, explained the Mosaic law concerning clean and unclean animals by saying that when Moses, for instance, prohibits the eating of swine flesh he does not mean what he says, but that we must not associate with people who, like swine, squander their time on pleasure and forget God, and then again call on him when they are in distress. For a sow, he says, does not know her owner when her belly is full, but when she is hungry, she makes a noise, and then keeps still again when she is fed. Then again, Moses says we must not eat the flesh of an hyena. That means, Be not an adulterer, or a seducer of others, and do not associate with such. But why? Because this animal changes sex every year, and is sometimes male and sometimes female. But why could they eat that which divideth the hoofs? That means that they must associate with the righteous, who live in the world but are expecting the world to come. That is the divided hoof! But let us quote:

"When Moses spoke about food, he gave the people three great commandments in a spiritual sense of the prescripts. But on account of the lusts of the flesh they understood him as if he had meant this of natural food." From this we may gather what the brothers of Nephi may have had in view when they asked for an explanation of the meaning of the text read.

4. And behold, there are many who are already lost from the knowledge of those who are at Jerusalem. Yea, the more part of all the tribes have been led away; and they are scattered to and fro upon the isles of the sea; and whither they are none of us knoweth, save that we know that they have been led away.

5. And since they have been led away, these things have been prophesied concerning them, and also concerning all those who shall hereafter be scattered and be confounded, because of the Holy One of Israel; for against him will they harden their hearts;

wherefore, they shall be scattered among all nations and shall be hated of all men.

6. Nevertheless, after they shall be nursed by the Gentiles, and the Lord has lifted up his hand upon the Gentiles and set them up for a standard, and their children have been carried in their arms, and their daughters have been carried upon their shoulders, behold these things of which are spoken are temporal; for thus are the covenants of the Lord with our fathers; and it meaneth us in the days to come, and also all our brethren who are of the house of Israel.

2. *A marvelous work among the Gentiles.*

7. And it meaneth that the time cometh that after all the house of Israel have been scattered and confounded, that the Lord God will raise up a mighty nation among the Gentiles, yea, even upon the face of this land; and by them shall our seed be scattered.

---

"carriages" at the time when the Bible translators wrote that, was, that which the traveler carried, that is to say, their baggage: In our day "carriages" does not mean baggage but a vehicle in which baggage is carried. The literal meaning of the word has changed. "Conversation" is another such word. When we read (Phil. 3:20), "Our conversation is in heaven," it is necessary to remember that when the translation was made, "conversation" meant, association, and not only an interchange of words.[2] To us, "conversation" does not convey any meaning in this connection. "Leasing" (Ps. 4:2) means, in modern English, "lying." To "let," (2 Thess. 2:7; Rom. 1:13) means "hinder." It is therefore clear that to understand even a translation not older than the authorized English version, it is necessary to be sure of the meaning of the words used at the time of the translation. This is just as important, and a great deal more difficult, when the question is of the original manuscripts.

VERSE 4. *Isles of the sea.* See 1 Ne. 21:8.

VERSES 7-12. This section refers to the dispersion and gathering of Israel, as predicted by the prophet in the previous chapter (vv. 8-23). The Lord addresses the "isles of the sea," (see 1 Ne. 21:8) and promises to give them "his servant," that is, Israel, "for a covenant." They are then in a position to liberate the captives and restore them to their lands (v. 12).

But how is this to be accomplished?

---

[2]The Revised Version has, "citizenship."

8. And after our seed is scattered the Lord God will proceed to do a marvelous work among the Gentiles, which shall be of great worth unto our seed; wherefore, it is likened unto their being nourished by the Gentiles and being carried in their arms and upon their shoulders.

9. And it shall also be of worth unto the Gentiles; and not only unto the Gentiles but unto all the house of Israel, unto the making known of the covenants of the Father of heaven unto Abraham, saying: In thy seed shall all the kindreds of the earth be blessed.

10. And I would, my brethren, that ye should know that all the kindreds of the earth cannot be blessed unless he shall make bare his arm in the eyes of the nations.

11. Wherefore, the Lord God will proceed to make bare his arm in the eyes of all the nations, in bringing about his covenants and his gospel unto those who are of the house of Israel.

12. Wherefore, he will bring them again out of captivity, and they shall be gathered together to the lands of their inheritance; and they shall be brought out of obscurity and out of darkness; and they shall know that the Lord is their Savior and their Redeemer, the Mighty One of Israel.

VERSE 7. *A mighty nation.* Nephi says God is to raise up a mighty nation among the Gentiles in "this land," referring, probably, to the United States. For Nephi delivered this discourse somewhere on this side of the Ocean. This mighty nation would disperse the descendants of Lehi.

VERSE 8. *A marvelous work.* After the dispersion of the remnant, a marvelous work would be done among the Gentiles, of special value to them and to the remnant.

VERSE 9. *Making the covenants with Abraham known.* The marvelous work would consist more especially in making the covenants with Abraham known to all the world.

VERSE 11. *The Gospel to be proclaimed.* The covenants will be known by their fulfilment "in the eyes of all the nations," and the preaching of the Gospel to the house of Israel.

VERSE 12. *He will bring them out of captivity.* The covenant people will again be brought out of captivity and be gathered in the lands of their inheritance. According to the law of God, the lands once allotted to his people can never be held, legally, by aliens. They are to revert, every fifth year, to the original heirs.

All this, according to Nephi, is predicted in the preceding chapters of the Prophet Isaiah.

America, and especially the United States of America, is God's great "melting pot." Here, the nations have met around the Constitution and under the aegis of the Starry Banner. Here the Lord, by his own processes of melting and alloying has demonstrated the possibility of producing a super-nation, as a pattern and a standard-bearer to all the world. Here, during the last one hundred years, more than thirty-seven millions of God's children have met. They have come as immigrants from all parts of the world. And now, the United States is the grandest possible monument in human history to the creative and regenerative power, to the honor and glory of the Redeemer of Man, the Mighty One of Israel.

## 3. *Prophecies of war and bloodshed.*

13. And the blood of that great and abominable church, which is the whore of all the earth, shall turn upon their own heads; for they shall war among themselves, and the sword of their own hands shall fall upon their own heads, and they shall be drunken with their own blood.

14. And every nation which shall war against thee, O house of Israel, shall be turned one against another, and they shall fall into the pit which they digged

---

The central thought of this part of the discourse of Nephi is the second coming of our Lord. He enumerates some of the events that are to precede his advent and the Millennium. (1) Certain nations connected with the "abominable church" are to be cursed with "war among themselves," until they are "drunken with their own blood." (v. 13) (2) Nations will war against the house of Israel, or against Zion, shall be turned one against another and be destroyed. (vv. 14, and 19) (3) Satan shall have no power over the hearts of men. (v. 15) (4) The fulness of wrath is to be poured out upon the wicked. (vv. 16 and 18) (5) Then, a prophet, like Moses, viz., the Holy One of Israel, will be raised up. (vv. 20-23) (6) The Lord will reign. (vv. 24-28) All this is to be understood "according to the flesh," that is to say, literally. (v. 27)

VERSE 13. *That great and abominable church.* The Book of Mormon, in several places, mentions an organization which it characterizes as an "abominable" church. It is also called the "church of the devil." (1 Ne. 14:17)

In the language of the Scriptures, any object or custom, that is detested or disliked for religious reasons, is called an abomination. That was the case in Egypt. (Gen. 43:32) Among the Hebrews, idols and idolatry were especially referred to as an "abomination" (Deut. 7:25, 26.) The "abominations" of which Daniel speaks (9:27) may refer to the altar (and probably the statue of the god Zeus) which Antiochus Epiphanes, in 168 B.C. set up in the temple as an insult to the Jews.[3] It was this blasphemy and the other outrages connected with it that drove the Maccabees out into the mountains, and prompted them to instigate the most heroic war of the entire history of the Jewish nation.

Our Lord, according to Matthew (24:15) and also Mark (13:14), quoted this prophecy of Daniel and predicted another profanation of the sanctuary, and left with the disciples the instruction that those who were in Judea at that time would better flee to the mountains, as the Maccabees had done in their day.[4]

VERSE 14. *Great shall be the fall.* They that fight against Zion shall be destroyed, and the abominable church shall fall. I understand this to mean that the

---

[3] Antiochus Epiphanes, also, with a sarcastic play on words, called "Epimanes" (the madman) is said to have caused his underlings to offer a sow as a sacrifice and to have had the sacred place sprinkled with the broth of swine flesh. (See 1 Macc. 1:41-49)

[4] The destruction of Jerusalem took place at the time of the passover (70 A.D.), when the city was full of pilgrims from all parts of the country. Before the arrival of the Roman legions, civil war was raging. There were three factions. The most fanatic of these were for a time victorious. They entered the sacred precincts with weapons concealed under their clothes. They murdered the priest at the altar, and continued the massacre, until the blood of their victims flowed like water. Thus the abomination of desolation (i. e., the abomination that is the cause of desolation) was a second time polluting the temple ground, as predicted by our Lord. The Romans surrounded the city. Famine soon was felt. It is said that hunger turned some into cannibals. A noble woman by the name of Mary, the daughter of one Eleazer, ate the flesh of her own baby. It is claimed that 1,100,000 people perished. The Romans reduced the city to a heap of stones, and Titus, is said to have declared that he was only an instrument of divine justice in destroying the city.

to ensnare the people of the Lord. And all that fight against Zion shall be destroyed, and that great whore, who hath perverted the right ways of the Lord, yea, that great and abominable church, shall tumble to the dust and great shall be the fall of it.

15. For behold, saith the prophet, the time cometh speedily that Satan shall have no more power over the hearts of the children of men; for the day soon cometh that all the proud and they who do wickedly shall be as stubble; and the day cometh that they must be burned.

16. For the time soon cometh that the fulness of the wrath of God shall be poured out upon all the children of men; for he will not suffer that the wicked shall destroy the righteous.

17. Wherefore, he will preserve the righteous by his power, even if it so be that the fulness of his wrath must come, and the righteous be preserved, even unto the destruction of their enemies by fire. Wherefore, the righteous need not fear; for thus saith the prophet, they shall be saved, even if it so be as by fire.

18. Behold, my brethren, I say unto you, that these things must shortly come; yea, even blood, and fire, and vapor of smoke must come; and it must needs be upon the face of this earth; and it cometh unto men according to the flesh if it so be that they will harden their hearts against the Holy One of Israel.

19. For behold, the righteous shall not perish; for the time surely must come that all they who fight against Zion shall be cut off.

20. And the Lord will surely prepare a way for his people, unto the fulfilling of the words of Moses, which he spake, saying: A prophet shall the Lord your God raise up unto you, like unto me; him shall ye hear in all things whatsoever he shall say unto you. And it shall come to pass that all those who will not hear that prophet shall be cut off from among the people.

21. And now I, Nephi, declare unto you, that this prophet of whom Moses spake was the Holy One of Israel; wherefore, he shall execute judgment in righteousness.

22. And the righteous need not fear, for they are those who shall

system of idolatry and falsehood on which antichristian governments and organizations are built will be destroyed, not the individuals who may have been deceived by the advocates of such a system, unless they harden their hearts against the influence of the Spirit of the Lord. (Comp. v. 18)

VERSE 15. *Satan shall have no more power.* The inference from this is that, as soon as the adversary is bound, error will have no attraction to the children of men.

VERSE 20. *A prophet . . . like unto me.* This prophet is the Holy One of Israel (v. 21). He will execute judgment in righteousness. Our Lord will, himself, have charge of the preparations for his second advent.

not be confounded. But it is the kingdom of the devil, which shall be built up among the children of men, which kingdom is established among them which are in the flesh—

23. For the time speedily shall come that all churches which are built up to get gain, and all those who are built up to get power over the flesh, and those who are built up to become popular in the eyes of the world, and those who seek the lusts of the flesh and the things of the world, and to do all manner of iniquity; yea, in fine, all those who belong to the kingdom of the devil are they who need fear, and tremble, and quake; they are those who must be brought low in the dust; they

are those who must be consumed as stubble; and this is according to the words of the prophet.

24. And the time cometh speedily that the righteous must be led up as calves of the stall, and the Holy One of Israel must reign in dominion, and might, and power, and great glory.

25. And he gathereth his children from the four quarters of the earth; and he numbereth his sheep, and they know him; and there shall be one fold and one shepherd; and he shall feed his sheep, and in him they shall find pasture.

26. And because of the righteousness of his people, Satan has no power; wherefore, he cannot be loosed for the space of many

VERSE 23. *Churches . . . to be consumed as stubble.* Five characteristics are here given, by which an honest inquirer may be guided if he has a desire to find the Church of God, and avoid the church of the adversary. He must avoid—

(1) All churches which are built up to get gain. A church operated for the purpose of "making money" is not God's church.

(2) All churches that are built up to get power over the flesh; that is, over fellowmen. Churches not governed in accordance with the recognition of the free agency of man and the law of common consent, are not of God.

(3) All churches which are built up to become popular in the eyes of the world are to be shunned. The "world" in this passage stands for such persons in the world whose interests are only worldly; who are seeking nothing but worldly pleasures, and who are dead to spiritual things. To become popular in such circles is to be outside the true church.

(4) All churches that seek the lusts of the flesh and the things of the world. The Apostle James had something like this in view, when he wrote:

"Ye ask, and receive not, because ye ask amiss, that ye may consume it upon your lusts. Ye adulterers and adulteresses, know ye not that the friendship of the world is enmity with God? Whosoever therefore, will be a friend of the world is the enemy of God. (James 4:3, 4)

(5) All churches that do all manner of iniquity. It is not only what is generally looked upon as immorality that disqualifies the church that tolerates and condones it; all manner of iniquities have the same effect.

"For I the Lord cannot look upon sin with the least degree of allowance." (D. and C. 1:31)

All such churches are to be consumed.

years; for he hath no power over the hearts of the people, for they dwell in righteousness, and the Holy One of Israel reigneth.

27. And now behold, I, Nephi, say unto you that all these things must come according to the flesh.

28. But, behold, all nations, kindreds, tongues, and people shall dwell safely in the Holy One of Israel if it so be that they will repent.

## 4. *What is written is true.*

29. And now I, Nephi, make an end; for I durst not speak further as yet concerning these things.

30. Wherefore, my brethren, I would that ye should consider that the things which have been written upon the plates of brass are true; and they testify that a man must be obedient to the commandments of God.

31. Wherefore, ye need not suppose that I and my father are the only ones that have testified, and also taught them. Wherefore, if ye shall be obedient to the commandments, and endure to the end, ye shall be saved at the last day. And thus it is. Amen.

VERSE 27. *All these things must come according to the flesh.* That is to say, they must be understood literally, and not as figurative expressions of something else.

VERSE 30. *Obedient to the commandments of God.* Obedience is the characteristic of the members of the true Church.

VERSE 31. *Salvation* at the last day is their reward.

### GENERAL NOTES

Note the 24th verse of this chapter. It gives us some idea of the character of the Millennial reign of the Holy One of Israel. During this time, the righteous must be led up as "calves of the stall."

The prophet Malachi makes use of this simile, as follows: "But unto you that fear my name shall the Sun of righteousness arise with healing in his wings; and ye shall go forth, and grow up as calves of the stall." (4:2) Which is as much as to say that, when the Millennial day dawns; when the Sun of righteousness arises, or, when the Son of God is revealed in glory his people will be taken care of spiritually. They will be fed and nourished in order that they may abound in grace and good works.

The prophet Hosea also uses the same expression: "Take with you words [words of repentance] and turn to the Lord: say unto him, Take away all iniquity, and receive us graciously: so will we render the calves of our lips." (14:2) And the apostle Paul (Heb. 14:15) interprets this verse thus: "By him therefore let us offer the sacrifice of praise to God continually, that is, the fruit of our lips giving thanks to his name."

Furthermore, during that blessed time to come, our Lord will actually reign. Not as a figure head, subject to the dicta of scheming statesmen, or the shifting winds and currents of misguided public opinion. No. He will reign—

(1) In dominion. That is, he will exercise sovereign prerogatives.

(2) In might. He will have ability to do that which his sovereign will dictates.

His resources will be unlimited, as they were in the days of the creation of our universe.

(3) In power. Might and power are about synonymous, but power may mean that he is empowered to exercise his might, or strength, as a sovereign, He has the authority. See the vision of Daniel (7:13, 14):

"Behold, one like a son of man * came to the Ancient of days, and they brought him near before him. And there was given him dominion, and glory, and a kingdom, that all people, nations, and languages, should serve him; his dominion is an everlasting dominion, which shall not pass away, and his kingdom that which shall not be destroyed."

This is his authority. The prophet saw in his vision that the Son of God, having become "like a son of man," received this commission of our common ancestor, the great patriarch and head of the human race, whose authority the Son of God, as a member of the human race, acknowledged and honored.

(4) In great glory. The reign of the Lord will be in splendor. He will bring with him the effulgence of the rising "Sun of righteousness," the glory of the presence of God, in the eternal mansions.

*What is a church?* The Hebrews of old had a representative assembly, or congregation, which is called "kahal," a word translated "ecclesia" (church) by the Seventy. This kahal, or Hebrew church, consisted of the elders and officers of the people, as is evident from Deut.: "Gather me all the elders of your tribes and your officers that I may speak these words in their ears . . . and Moses spake in the ears of all the congregation of Israel (all the "kahal" of Israel; that is, the entire assembly of elders and officers summoned to hear) the words of this song," etc. (Deut. 31:28-30)

Moses could, of course, not speak to the entire nation in one meeting. When he had a message to the people, he delivered it to a representative assembly, and they spoke to the people in their various subdivisions. That assembly was their "kahal," their "church." Comp. Num. 16:3, where it appears that the rebellion of Korah, Dathan and Abiram was a rising in the "congregation of the Lord" (literally, the "kahal of Jehovah"). See also Ex. 16:1-3. The entire congregation of the children of Israel (The Heb. here is "adath" for congregation) came to the wilderness of Sin. The whole congregation of the children of Israel (the Heb is again, "adath") murmured. But their complaint was undoubtedly voiced in the representative assembly; for they said to Moses and Aaron, Ye have brought us forth into this wilderness, to kill this whole assembly (Heb. "this kahal") with hunger.

There is a clear distinction between the entire people of Israel and the church of Israel.

The Greeks, and especially the Athenians, of old had their ecclesia. That was their legislative assembly, consisting of citizens, summoned to meet to transact public affairs. At Athens ordinary assemblies were held in each "prytaneia" (presidency"),* which would be about once a week. These assemblies were called "kyria ecclesia." Extraordinary assemblies were called whenever they were thought necessary. Note that "ecclesia" is the term by which the Church of our Lord is named in the famous passage, Matt. 16:18: "Upon this rock I will build my church" (ecclesia). Note also that the Greek term "kyria ecclesia," in a contracted form, has become the Scotch "kirk," the English "church," the German "Kirche," the Scandinavian "kyrka," and "Kirke"; the French have kept the same term in their "eglise."

---

*The prytaneia or presidency was a period of 35 or 36 days, about a tenth of a year, during which the princes (prytanes) of each tribe in turn presided in the council and the ecclesia. The first six periods contained 35, and the last four, 36 days each, or in the intercalary year of the cycle, 38 and 39 days resp. Thus the days of the prytaneia were counted as our days of the month

*The Church of the Firstborn.* "Let me explain what the Church of the Firstborn is. It is the first Church that ever was raised up upon this earth; that is, the firstborn Church. That is what I mean; and when God, our Father, organized that church, he organized it just as his Father organized the church on the earth where he dwelt; and that same order is organized here in the city of Great Salt Lake; and it is that order that Joseph Smith, the prophet of God, organized in the beginning in Kirtland, Ohio. Brother Brigham Young, myself, and others were present when that was done; and when those officers received their endowments, they were together in one place. They were organized and received their endowments and blessings, and those keys were placed upon them, and that kingdom will stand for ever." (Heber C. Kimball, J. of D., vol. 5, p. 129)

## LIAHONA

This interesting word is Hebrew with an Egyptian ending. It is the name which Lehi gave to the ball or director he found outside his tent the very day he began his journey through the "wilderness," after his little company had rested for some time in the Valley of Lemuel. (I Ne. 16:10; Alma 37:38)

*L* is a Hebrew preposition meaning "to," and sometimes used to express the possessive case. *Iah* is a Hebrew abbreviated form of "Jehovah," common in Hebrew names. *On* is the Hebrew name of the Egyptian "City of the Sun," also known as Memphis and Heliopolis. *L-iah-on* means, therefore, literally, "To God is Light"; or, "of God is Light." That is to say, God gives light, as does the Sun. The final *a* reminds us that the Egyptian form of the Hebrew name *On* is *Annu,* and that seems to be the form Lehi used.

Lehi had just received the divine command to begin his perilous journey. The question uppermost in his mind, after having received that call, must have been how to find the way. That must have been quite a problem. But he arose early in the morning, determined to carry out the command given. Undoubtedly he had prayed all night for light and guidance. And now, standing in the opening of the tent, perhaps as the first rays of the sun broke through the morning mists, his attention is attracted by a metal ball "of curious workmanship." He picks it up and examines it. And then, as he realizes that it is the guide for which he had been praying, he exclaims in ecstasy, *L-iah-on-a!* Which is as much to say, This is God's light; it has come from him! And that became the name of the curious instrument. This was not a compass. It was a miraculously formed instrument which served both as compass and octant.

Now, the fact is that this manner of giving names was an ancient Semitic custom. Hagar, when her son was perishing in the wilderness and she beheld the angel by the life-giving spring, exclaimed, *Beer-lachai-roi!* which means, literally, "Well, to live, to see." That is to say, "the well of him that liveth and seeth me," for that was the thought that came to her mind. (Gen. 16:13, 14) And that became the name of the well. In the same way, Abraham called the place where he had offered Isaac on the altar, *Jehovah-jireh,* "the Lord will provide"; because the Lord did provide for himself a ram instead of Isaac, as Abraham had assured his son the Lord would do. (Gen. 22:7-14) And that became the name of the Mount "to this day."

Lehi gave the metal ball a name commemorative of one of the great experiences of his life, just as these Old-Testament worthies had done. And, furthermore, he gave it a name that no one but a devout Hebrew influenced by Egyptian culture would have thought of. Is that not the strongest possible evidence of the truth of the historic part of the Book of Mormon?

# THE SECOND BOOK OF NEPHI

## AN INTRODUCTION

*Where written.* In the First Book of Nephi we have the account of the entire journey of Father Lehi and his company from Jerusalem to the Land of Bountiful, in Asia, and the voyage across the ocean to the Land of Promise. That is, America.

From the place of the first landing in America, after a bounteous harvest had been gathered in, the journey was continued in the wilderness. Judging from the fact that the company now traveled through a country where various specimens of animals were roaming, and where an abundance of ore, both precious and useful, was found (1 Ne. 18:25), they must have left the sea shore and continued their journey through the mountainous regions.

If we assume that the landing took place in South America, say, at thirty degrees south, where the city of Coquimbo, not far from Valparaiso, Chile, now is located, we may also assume that the colonists, in due time, may have come as far north as the Valley of Cusco, Peru, by way of the region around Lake Titicaca, Bolivia. As has been noted in a previous chapter, the Incas of Peru had a tradition according to which they had come into the valley after a journey that had lasted for eight years, and it is by no means impossible that future research will find the true connection between that tradition and the records of Nephi.

It was after the first more permanent settlement of Lehi in the Land of Promise, that Nephi was commanded to make the plates upon which the record was to be kept. (1 Ne. 19:1) Nephi did as commanded, and the beginning of the record was made in that first settlement. Later, after Nephi had founded the new settlement, which was called the Land of Nephi, he was instructed to make another set of plates on which to record a more condensed account of the history of the people (2 Ne. 5:29-33). It is a translation of the contents of this second set of plates that we now have in the Book of Mormon. The writing was done in the Land of Nephi.

---

*The Contents.* The main historical events noted in this book are:

1. Death of Lehi, 4:12.

2. Rebellion, 5:2-4.

3. Nephi, Sam, Jacob, Joseph, Zoram and their friends emigrate to a new location, 5:5-8.

4. They build a temple, 5:16.

5. Priests and teachers appointed, 5:26.

6. A second set of plates made, 5:30-33.

*Exhortations and prophecies:*

1. Lehi addresses the people on the Land of Promise—A land blessed to the righteous, but cursed to the wicked, 1:4, 7-12; exhortations, 1:28-32.

2. Lehi addresses his son, Jacob, on Redemption through the Messiah, 2:6-8; on opposition necessary in all things, 2:11-14; the forbidden fruit and the tree of life, 15; Adam fell that men might be, 25; the redemption of mankind, 2:28-30.

3. Lehi addresses his son Joseph on the prophecy of Joseph in Egypt, 3:5-16; on the mission of Moses, 17-22; the seed of Joseph not to be destroyed, 23-25.

4. Lehi blesses the sons and daughters of Laman and Lemuel, 4:3-9; the sons of Ishmael and all his household, 4:10; he blesses Sam, 4:11.

5. Jacob addresses the people of Nephi, 6:1-4; he quotes Isaiah, 5-7; he comments, 6:8-18.

6. Jacob quotes Isaiah, 50, 7:1-11.

7. Jacob quotes Isaiah, 51, 8:1-25.

8. Jacob on the resurrection, 9:3-6; on the infinite atonement, 9:7-11; on the judgment, 9:15-18; a nine-fold woe to sinners, 9:30-38; on prayer, 9:52; our seed not to be destroyed 9:53.

9. Jacob on the coming of Christ, 10:2-9; on a land of liberty with no kings, 10:10-17; gentiles numbered among Israel, 10:18-20.

10. Nephi's argument for the existence of God, 11:6-8.

11. Nephi quotes Isaiah, chapters 12-24.

12. Nephi's estimate of the value of the prophetic writings of Isaiah, 25:4-8; Nephi's comments and prophecies, 25:9-22; faith, the foundation of salvation, 25:23-30.

13. Nephi's prophecies continued on the coming of Christ to the Nephites, 26:1-9; on the destruction of the people, 26:10-11; on the last days, 26:14-33.

14. Nephi's prophecies continued on God's judgments on the wicked, 27:1-5; on the sealed book, 27:6-11; on the witnesses, 27:12-13; on "a marvelous work and a wonder," 27:26-35.

15. Nephi's prophecies continued on the churches of the world, 28:1-18; the kingdom of the devil, 28:19-23; a seven-fold wo and a curse, 28:24-32.

16. Nephi's prophecies continued, on the gentile attitude towards the Book of Mormon, "A Bible! A Bible!" 29:1-4.

17. Nephi's prophecies continued, on, repentant gentiles, the covenant people of the Lord, 30:1-2; on the Jews and the gentiles, 30:3-11; on the kingdom of peace, 30:12-18.

18. Nephi's prophecies continued, on baptism of the Lamb of God, 31:1-11; and, baptism and the Holy Ghost, 12-21.

19. Nephi's prophecies continued, on speaking with the tongue of angels, 32:1-6; and on prayer, 32:7-9.

20. Nephi's parting testimony, 33:1-12; an everlasting farewell, 33:13-15.

# THE SECOND BOOK OF NEPHI

*An account of the death of Lehi. Nephi's brethren rebel against him. The Lord warns Nephi to depart into the wilderness. His journeyings in the wilderness, &c.*

## CHAPTER 1

*Lehi addresses the people on, The Land of Promise, 1-12 — Exhortations, 13-32.*

### 1. *The death of Lehi.*

1. And now it came to pass that after I, Nephi, had made an end of teaching my brethren, our father, Lehi, also spake many things unto them — how great things the Lord had done for them in bringing them out of the land of Jerusalem.

2. And he spake unto them concerning their rebellions upon the waters, and the mercies of God in sparing their lives, that they were not swallowed up in the sea.

3. And he also spake unto them concerning the land of promise, which they had obtained — how merciful the Lord had been in warning us that we should flee out of the land of Jerusalem.

4. For, behold, said he, I have seen a vision, in which I know that Jerusalem is destroyed; and had we remained in Jerusalem we should also have perished.

5. But, said he, notwithstanding our afflictions, we have obtained a land of promise, a land which is choice above all other lands; a land which the Lord God hath covenanted with me should be a land for the inheritance of my seed. Yea, the Lord hath covenanted this land unto me,

---

VERSE 4. *I have seen a vision . . . Jerusalem is destroyed.* While Lehi and his company were still wanderers in the Arabian wilderness, the Lord gave him the promise that he would receive word of the destruction of Jerusalem. (1 Ne. 17:14) Now, after their arrival in America, the Lord gave them a vision in which the fate of that city was revealed.

The Prophet Ezekiel, who at that time was in Babylonia, among the exiles, also had a vision of the destruction of the holy city. He writes, "In the ninth year, in the tenth day of the month, the word of the Lord came unto me, saying, Son of man, write the name of the day, even of this selfsame day; the king of Babylon drew close unto Jerusalem this selfsame day." (Ezek. 24:1, 2) That is, Nebuchadnezzar, on that day began the siege which was to end in the capture of the city. The siege lasted a year and a half, and two years after the beginning of it, the news of the fall of the city reached Tel Abib in Babylon, where the prophet lived, and where many of the Jewish exiles were concentrated.

We note the fact that the Lord communicated the news of the calamity to his people, both in Asia and America, through his prophets. Did he also, by some means or other, reveal it to the so-called lost tribes? Who knows?

and to my children forever, and also all those who should be led out of other countries by the hand of the Lord.

6. Wherefore, I, Lehi, prophesy according to the workings of the Spirit which is in me, that there shall none come into this land save they shall be brought by the hand of the Lord.

---

VERSE 6. *There shall none come into this land save . . . by the hand of the Lord.* America has, by divine Providence, been set apart to be a "city of refuge" to men and women of every nation, kindred, tongue, and people, who should believe in the Gospel. (D. & C. 10:50-1) It was discovered and settled under the special direction of the Lord. In a special sense this may refer to the United States, but in a general way it is true of the entire country of Zion, North and South. (Alma 46:17)

When we read of the savagery that marked the first contact of some European conquerers of America with the natives, after the marvelous discovery of the country by Columbus, it may not be easy to recognize the hand of the Lord in the entire history of that time. But I think we may say that God directed the conquerors in the same way that he led the Assyrians under Sennacherib, or the Chaldeans under Nebuchadnezzar, or the Romans under Vespasian and Titus, and for very much the same reason, to overrun Palestine at various times.

The Aztec confederacy, which was broken up by Cortez, through his exploits in Mexico, was, in fact a "plunderbund" whose armed forces were maintained mainly for the purpose of robbing more or less defenseless communities, and carrying away corn and gold and other valuables, and especially human beings for slaves and cruel sacrifices; their worship was mostly revolting idolatry. Montezuma II, who was made a prisoner by Cortez, and who was killed while entitled to protection by the Spaniards, was really a despot, hated and feared even by some of his pretended allies. That is evident from the fact that thousands of the people of Tlascala joined Cortez in his march upon Tenochtitlan. That is perhaps also proved by the fact that a most efficient guide and pilot of the little army of Cortez was a young, brilliant woman, Marina, from Tabasco, who, by her loyalty to the invaders and her linguistic knowledge, saved the expedition from destruction at Cholula, and rendered valuable service at all times. Montezuma can not have been greatly beloved by the common people.

In Peru, the Incas, at the time of the arrival of Pizarro, who caused Atahualpa to accept "baptism" and then to be choked to death with a bow-string, and who burned the Chieftain Chalcuchima at the stake, were despots, who seemed to aim at the conquest of the world. Atahualpa himself had no legitimate claim to the position of ruler of Peru. Only a short time before the arrival of the Spaniards, he left Quito, where he was the governor, and marched upon Cuzco. His war was characterized by the utmost barbarity. He caused the family of the ruling Inca to be massacred, and the ruler himself, Inca Huascar, to be finally, murdered.

The culture of the Peruvians, although altogether remarkable and, in some respects superior to that of the Mayas and Nahuas, was nevertheless rigid, communistic despotism, made possible by the strangling of individual liberty and the establishment of superstitious class distinction. It rested on the falsehood that the Incas alone were the children of the Almighty, while the common people were their servants. The weakness of the system was seen clearly, when a handful of Spaniards could overthrow the structure, as easily as a child with the sweep of a hand destroys a house of cards.

If we remember that the Lord, according to the Book of Mormon, repeatedly

7. Wherefore, this land is consecrated unto him whom he shall bring. And if it so be that they shall serve him according to the commandments which he hath given, it shall be a land of liberty unto them; wherefore, they shall never be brought down into captivity; if so, it shall be because of iniquity; for if iniquity shall abound cursed shall be the land for their sakes, but unto the righteous it shall be blessed forever.

8. And behold, it is wisdom that this land should be kept as yet from the knowledge of other nations; for behold, many nations

cautioned the people here against despotism, which leads to destruction (see 2 Ne. 5:18; 10:11-14), we can see the hand of God even in the appearance of the executioners on the scene.[1]  See vv. 10-12)

However, it is only justice to say that not all the Spaniards were in the class referred to. There were men, such as Las Casas, for instance, and many others, who gladly gave themselves and all they had in the unselfish service of the natives, to the best of their ability and the understanding they had.

VERSE 7. *This land is consecrated.* The information is here given (1) that this land is a consecrated land, a holy land, to all those whom the Lord shall bring here, as the land of Canaan was to the Hebrews; (2) that if the people will serve God, they will enjoy the blessed gift of liberty, but that (3) if they become steeped in iniquity, the land itself will be cursed by that condition. It is only to the righteous —that is, the righteous people—that, "it shall be blessed forever."

And here it might be said that when Lehi speaks of a "righteous" people, he does not mean a nation consisting exclusively of righteous individuals. Such a people has not existed on earth since the days of Enoch. Sinners we have always with us. A righteous people is one which acknowledges the sovereignty of the Lord; a people whose legislators aim at making only just and equitable laws; whose judges judge in righteousness, and whose executives apply the laws in impartial warfare upon the unrighteous. That is a righteous people—a people that has the promises of divine blessings in the land of Zion.

VERSE 8. *This land should be kept as yet from the knowledge of other nations.* The reason given for this is that if not, many nations would overrun the land, and there would be no place for an inheritance.[2]

---

[1]"Intertribal warfare was perpetual, save now and then for truces of brief duration. Warfare was attended by wholesale massacre. As many prisoners as could be managed were taken home by their captors; in some cases they were adopted into the tribe of the latter as a means of increasing its fighting strength, otherwise they were put to death with lingering torments. There was nothing which afforded the red men such exquisite delight as the spectacle of live human flesh lacerated with stone knives or hissing under the touch of firebrands, and for ingenuity in devising tortures they have never been equalled. Cannibalism was quite commonly practiced.

"Women and children joined in these fiendish atrocities." (John Fiske, "The Discovery of America," vol. 1, p. 49.)

[2]In this connection the immigration statistics of the United States are interesting. On April 1, 1930, the total population of the country was 122,366,046. Of this number, 13,366,407 were classed as "foreign-born white" persons; 11,891,143 were negroes; 1,422,533 were Mexicans; 332,307 Indians. There were 74,954 Chinese, 138,834 Japanese, 45,208 Filipinos, 3,130 Hindus, 1,860 Koreans, and 780 other races. The possibilities of immigration were made known to Lehi, and also the wisdom of preventing a premature influx of immigrants. As for the United States, there was very little immigration prior to 1815. Between 1905 and 1914, the average annual total immigrants was over a million.

would overrun the land, that there would be no place for an inheritance.

9. Wherefore, I, Lehi, have obtained a promise, that inasmuch as those whom the Lord God shall bring out of the land of Jerusalem shall keep his commandments, they shall prosper upon the face of this land; and they shall be kept from all other nations, that they may possess this land unto themselves. And if it so be that they shall keep his commandments they shall be blessed upon the face of this land, and there shall be none to molest them, nor to take away

---

We recognize the hand of the Lord in the discovery of America by Columbus, and its subsequent settlement by so many people of all races. We also see the hand of Providence in the fact that detailed knowledge of this country was for centuries withheld from the rest of the world, notwithstanding the marvelous civilizations and millions of people who lived here. At sundry times it looked as if a discovery might have been made. Diodorus Siculus, a Greek historian, who lived during the time of Julius Cæsar (102-44 B.C.), relates that the Phoenicians discovered a large island in the Atlantic, several days' journey from the coast of Africa. Tyrians wanted to colonize the island, hearing of its wonderful clime and resources, but they were prevented by a decree of the senate at Carthage. Homer, Plutarch, and others are said to mention this "island." And yet, it remained, practically, an unknown land. Clement, supposedly a disciple of the Apostle Peter, wrote epistles to the Saints at Corinth, which have been preserved among the apocrypha of the New Testament. In the first of these letters (9:12-16) he says:

"The ocean, inaccessible to the human race, and the worlds beyond, are governed through the same laws of their grand master. Spring and summer, autumn and winter, peacefully succeed one another. The particular directions of the winds fulfil their work at all times without offending each other. The fountains, always flowing, made for pleasure and for health, always offer their bosoms, to sustain the life of man, and the smallest creatures are living together in peace and harmony."

"Worlds that are beyond" the ocean can refer only to countries on the American side of the globe, and the reference to its seasons, its directions of the wind, its fountains and its living creatures prove a rather astonishing information of this country, at that time. Without actual knowledge, how could Clement, or anybody, know that the natural laws operated here as in the Old World, and not in some other way?

Then, there is the myth about Votan, who is said to have conducted seven families from his country to America. According to Cabrera, quoted by Bancroft in Native Races (vol. 5, p. 69):

"Votan asserts that he is a descendant of Imox, of the race of Chan, and derives his origin from Chivim. He states that he conducted seven families from Valum Votan to this continent and assigned lands to them; that he is the third of the Votans; that, having determined to travel until he arrived at the root of heaven, in order to discover his relations to the Culebras (Serpents), and make himself known to them, he made four voyages to Chivim; that he arrived in Spain, and that he went to Rome; that he saw the great house of God building; that he went by the road which his brethren the Culebras had bored; that he marked it, and that he passed by houses of the thirteen Culebras. He relates that in returning from one of his voyages, he found seven other families of the Tzekil nation, who had joined

the land of their inheritance; and they shall dwell safely forever.

10. But behold, when the time cometh that they shall dwindle in unbelief, after they have received so great blessings from the hand of the Lord — having a knowledge of the creation of the earth, and all men, knowing the great and marvelous works of the Lord from the creation of the world; having power given them to do all things by faith; having all the commandments from the beginning, and having been brought by his infinite goodness into this precious land of promise —behold, I say, if the day shall come that they will reject the Holy One of Israel, the true Messiah, their Redeemer and their God, behold, the judgments of him that is just shall rest upon them.

11. Yea, he will bring other nations unto them, and he will give unto them power, and he will take away from them the lands of their possessions, and he will cause them to be scattered and smitten.

12. Yea, as one generation passeth to another there shall be bloodsheds, and great visitations among them, wherefore, my sons, I would that ye would remember; yea, I would that ye would hearken unto my words.

the first inhabitants, and recognized in them the same origin as his own, that is, of the Culebras."

This is, of course, myth; but even a myth must have an historical basis, be it ever so weak; otherwise it would be mere Munchausenian balderdash. This historical basis of the Votan-myth is, no doubt, actual intercourse between the Old World and the New in the dim past of the history of mankind. Some students of American history believe that Tyrians, after their city had been destroyed by Alexander the Great, went to the Fortunate Island and from there to the coast of Florida; further, to the Gulf of Mexico around Yucatan and into the bay of Honduras, where they ascended a river, and, finally, founded the city of Copan. Garcia, Kingsborough, and many others, favor the theory that the Indians are of Jewish origin, a theory that we know, from the Book of Mormon, to be true as far as some of them are concerned.

When we come down to historical times, we find Greenland, geographically considered, a part of America, settled toward the end of the 10th century, and afterwards the North American coasts explored by Leif Ericson and other Icelanders, some of whom penetrated to the interior, how far is not yet fully known. But the route to America was again closed, as if by a Supernatural power, and history lost all knowledge of this part of the world.

Just how the intercourse was broken off, may not be fully known. But we know that during the 14th century, "black death" carried off twenty-five million people in Europe, and almost as many in China and other parts of Asia, and that, during the fifteenth century, Greenland was devastated, presumably by Indians from the mainland, who left only the ruins on the sites of numerous settlements. No wonder if, after such devastations, the children of men for a long time lost all ambition to explore and colonize unknown lands.

VERSE 11. *He will bring other nations unto them.* See notes on v. 6.

## 2. *Exhortations.*

13. O that ye would awake; awake from a deep sleep, yea, even from the sleep of hell, and shake off the awful chains by which ye are bound, which are the chains which bind the children of men, that they are carried away captive down to the eternal gulf of misery and woe.

14. Awake! and arise from the dust, and hear the words of a trembling parent, whose limbs ye must soon lay down in the cold and silent grave, from whence no traveler can return; a few more days and I go the way of all the earth.

---

VERSES 13-32. In these verses Lehi addresses specially Laman, Lemuel, Sam, the sons of Ishmael, and Zoram.

VERSE 13. *O that ye would awake!* Lehi considers the opponents of Nephi as spiritually "asleep," and bound with chains, and that they had been reduced to that condition by influences from hell. Their opposition was a kind of hypnotic influence from the infernal regions, but their condition was voluntary on their part. He, therefore, exhorts them to awake and shake off the chains. No one needs to be held in bondage by the adversary against his own will.

VERSE 14. *Grave from whence no traveler can return.* Critics of the Book of Mormon have without reason asserted that this is plagiarism from Shakespeare. There is not the slightest ground for that assumption. To compare the grave (the Hebrew Sheol) with a country from which a traveler could not return, was but natural to one who as Lehi, had spent so many years traveling and now was nearing the grave. The simile is at once striking and simple and original.

The lines from Shakespeare which have been mentioned as plagiarized are the following, which the immortal bard credits to Hamlet in Act I, scene 3:

> . . . "Who would fardels bear,
> To grunt and sweat under a weary life;
> But that the dread of something after death,
> The undiscovered country, from whose bourn
> No traveler returns—puzzles the will;
> And makes us rather bear those ills we have,
> Than fly others that we know not of,"

Shakespeare, it will be observed, considers that our ignorance of the world beyond, on account of absence of communication between the two worlds, keeps some of us from committing suicide, because we prefer battling with the evils with which we are familiar to venturing out against unknown evils. That thought is as far from the expression of Lehi as the east is from the west.

The probability is that Shakespeare borrowed his line from Job and misunderstood it, and therefore gave it a meaning which Job never intended it to have.

Job, speaking of the days of man as few and full of trouble says, in part,

"Seeing his days are determined, the number of his months are with thee, thou hast appointed his bounds that he cannot pass." (Job 14:5; 16:22)

The idea that Job expresses is this that the days and months of man on earth are determined by the Lord, and that no living man can pass those boundaries set for his life. Like the grass and the flowers, man flourishes in the time deter-

15. But behold, the Lord hath redeemed my soul from hell; I have beheld his glory, and I am encircled about eternally in the arms of his love.

16. And I desire that ye should remember to observe the statutes and the judgments of the Lord; behold, this hath been the anxiety of my soul from the beginning.

17. My heart hath been weighed down with sorrow from time to time, for I have feared, lest for the hardness of your hearts the Lord your God should come out in the fulness of his wrath upon you, that ye be cut off and destroyed forever;

18. Or, that a cursing should come upon you for the space of many generations; and ye are visited by sword, and by famine, and are hated, and are led according to the will and captivity of the devil.

19. O my sons, that these things might not come upon you, but that ye might be a choice and a favored people of the Lord. But behold, his will be done; for his ways are righteous forever.

20. And he hath said that: Inasmuch as ye shall keep my commandments ye shall prosper in the land; but inasmuch as ye will not keep my commandments ye shall be cut off from my presence.

21. And now that my soul might have joy in you, and that my heart might leave this world with gladness because of you, that I might not be brought down with grief and sorrow to the grave, arise from the dust, my sons, and be men, and be determined in one mind and in one heart, united in all things, that ye may not come down into captivity;

22. That ye may not be cursed

---

mined, and then the harvester comes and cuts him down. Job is not speaking of the boundaries between this life and the life hereafter; he is speaking of the days and months which the Almighty, as he understood it, had determined for him on earth. He considered himself as a hireling, who had a certain task to perform before he was entitled to a rest. (See v. 6) The question of the status of the dead in Sheol is not involved in this passage of the Book of Job, although he had wonderfully clear ideas on this subject, as on the subject of the resurrection. (See Job 16:22; 19:23-27)

VERSE 15. *The Lord hath redeemed my soul.* As the Lord had redeemed his soul, so he would redeem the soul of his rebellious children, if they would turn to him, repentant and prayerful.

VERSE 16. *Observe the statutes and judgments of the Lord.* Rebellion is slavery. Obedience is the price for liberty.

*Statutes and judgments.* A statute is a legislative enactment; any authoritatively declared rule, ordinance, decree or law.

A judgment may be a sentence pronounced by God as the Supreme Judge. Or, it may be a ruling, when a statute needs an explanation. Such rulings may come through the inspired word of the Lord, either written or spoken by his authorized servants.

with a sore cursing; and also, that ye may not incur the displeasure of a just God upon you, unto the destruction, yea, the eternal destruction of both soul and body.

23. Awake, my sons; put on the armor of righteousness. Shake off the chains with which ye are bound, and come forth out of obscurity, and arise from the dust.

24. Rebel no more against your brother, whose views have been glorious, and who hath kept the commandments from the time that we left Jerusalem; and who hath been an instrument in the hands of God, in bringing us forth into the land of promise; for were it not for him, we must have perished with hunger in the wilderness; nevertheless, ye sought to take away his life; yea, and he hath suffered much sorrow because of you.

25. And I exceedingly fear and tremble because of you, lest he shall suffer again; for behold, ye have accused him that he sought power and authority over you; but I know that he hath not sought for power nor authority over you, but he hath sought the glory of God, and your own eternal welfare.

26. And ye have murmured because he hath been plain unto you. Ye say that he hath used sharpness; ye say that he hath been angry with you; but behold, his sharpness was the sharpness of the power of the word of God, which was in him; and that which ye call anger was the truth, according to that which is in God, which he could not restrain, manifesting boldly concerning your iniquities.

27. And it must needs be that the power of God must be with him, even unto his commanding you that ye must obey. But behold, it was not he, but it was the Spirit of the Lord which was in him, which opened his mouth to utterance that he could not shut it.

---

VERSE 24. *Rebel no more.* The great weakness of Laman was his pride. He was a man with a strong personality, capable of impressing others as a leader. He, no doubt, had as much education as his younger brothers. He was skilled in oratory, and he had the legal advantage of being the firstborn. But with all these qualifications he was weak, because he lacked humility.

Laman had his chance. But he did not stand the test. We have seen how he failed. When the question of obtaining the brass plates from Laban came up, the Lord gave Laman the opportunity to lead. Boldly he went to Laban with his request, but at the first sign of danger he fled. Not so Nephi. He relied on the Lord and succeeded.

Then Laman again showed his weakness in anger and acts of violence. Read the account again in 1 Ne. 3:10-14, 28-31. At length he became a rebel and a leader of rebellion against the Lord, (vv. 25, 26).

VERSE 27. *Ye must obey.* Lehi here defines the principles of divine authority. It is the voice of God through his inspired servant. "It was not he . . . it was the Spirit of the Lord . . . which opened his mouth to utterance, that he could

28. And now my son, Laman, and also Lemuel and Sam, and also my sons who are the sons of Ishmael, behold, if ye will hearken unto the voice of Nephi ye shall not perish. And if ye will hearken unto him I leave unto you a blessing, yea, even my first blessing.

29. But if ye will not hearken unto him I take away my first blessing, yea, even my blessing, and it shall rest upon him.

30. And now, Zoram, I speak unto you: Behold, thou art the servant of Laban; nevertheless, thou hast been brought out of the land of Jerusalem, and I know that thou art a true friend unto my son, Nephi, forever.

31. Wherefore, because thou hast been faithful thy seed shall be blessed with his seed, that they dwell in prosperity long upon the face of this land; and nothing, save it shall be iniquity among them, shall harm or disturb their prosperity upon the face of this land forever.

32. Wherefore, if ye shall keep the commandments of the Lord, the Lord hath consecrated this land for the security of thy seed with the seed of my son.

---

not shut it." Divine authority must not be assumed, no matter how great faith we may have. It cannot be acquired by study—not even of theology. It is given by God and received—by faith, yes! But faith is only the hand that receives. It is God that puts the gift into the hand. Until that is done, the hand is empty.

VERSE 28. *My first blessing.* This promise is given especially to Laman, Lemuel, Sam, and the sons of Ishmael. If they would hearken to Nephi, the blessing of his father would be theirs. See vv. 7, 20, 22.

VERSE 29. *Zoram.* His special blessing was, no doubt, deserved. He was very much attached to Nephi, from their first acquaintance. And when Nephi sought a place of gathering away from Laman, Zoram went with him. (2 Ne. 5:6) How he came to join the company of Lehi is related in 1 Ne. 4:20-38. He was at that time a trusted servant of Laban. Later he took the eldest daughter of Ishmael for wife. (1 Ne. 16:7) One of his descendants was Ammoron, who called himself a bold Lamanite (Alma 54:23), and engaged in a war of revenge on account of supposed wrongs committed centuries before he was born. It is not impossible that the name "Ammoron" still survives in the Aymara linguistic stock in South America, which some students consider a member of the Kechua stock, while Dr. Brinton treats it as a distinct linguistic stock. ("The American Race," p. 216)

The name Zoram is, probably from the Hebrew, "Zur," a rock,[3] signifying a trustworthy, reliable character. It is perpetuated throughout Book of Mormon history. There was a righteous, God-fearing Nephite general by that name in the days of the judges (Alma 16:5-7). Also an apostate by the same name (Alma 30:59; 31:1). There was also, at one time, an apostate sect, Zoramites, in the country of Antionum.

---

[3]"*Lo khezuranu Zuram,*" ("Not as our rock is their rock," Deut. 32:31.)

## CHAPTER 2

*Lehi addresses his son Jacob, 1-13—Lehi addresses all his sons, 14-30.*

### 1. *Lehi's address to Jacob.*

1. And now, Jacob, I speak unto you: Thou art my firstborn in the days of my tribulation in the wilderness. And behold, in thy childhood thou hast suffered afflictions and much sorrow, because of the rudeness of thy brethren.

2. Nevertheless, Jacob, my firstborn in the wilderness, thou knowest the greatness of God; and he shall consecrate thine afflictions for thy gain.

3. Wherefore, thy soul shall be blessed, and thou shalt dwell safely with thy brother, Nephi; and thy days shall be spent in the service of thy God. Wherefore, I know that thou art redeemed, because of the righteousness of thy Redeemer; for thou hast beheld that in the fulness of time he cometh to bring salvation unto men.

4. And thou hast beheld in thy youth his glory; wherefore, thou

---

VERSE 1. *Jacob.* The first of two sons born to Lehi in the wilderness before the travelers arrived in the Land of Bountiful, about 595 B.C. The name is derived from a verb which means, "to overreach," "to circumvent." The name of the second son was Joseph. In due time these two brethren were made priests and teachers in the Land of Nephi. (2 Ne. 5:26)

*In the day of my tribulation.* This refers to the journey from Nahom to Bountiful in Arabia, during which time children were born and miraculously sustained. (1 Ne. 17:1-6)

VERSE 2. *He shall consecrate thy afflictions for thy gain.* Lehi reminds his son of the great truth that trials and afflictions are necessary in the preparation for the reception of special blessings. That is a difficult lesson to learn. Especially in days of pleasure hunting, who wants to hear that afflictions are necessary for purification and glorification; that, to the followers of the Captain of our salvation, the road to victory goes over Calvary? Who can truthfully say, with the poet:

> "We take with solemn thankfulness
> Our burden up, nor ask it less,
> And count it joy that even we
> May suffer, serve, or wait for thee,
> Whose will be done?"
> —John G. Whittier.

VERSE 3. *Thy days shall be spent in the service of thy God.* The greatest blessing a human being can receive: To belong to the entourage of the King of kings!

*Thou art redeemed.* Not because of the afflictions suffered, but, "because of the righteousness of thy Redeemer." It is the righteousness of the Redeemer that is the foundation of the redemption of man, and Lehi repeats this again and again. (See vv. 6, 8, 26, 28) A slave, who is bought and set free, is redeemed.

art blessed even as they unto whom he shall minister in the flesh; for the Spirit is the same, yesterday, today, and forever. And the way is prepared from the fall of man, and salvation is free.

5. And men are instructed sufficiently that they know good from evil. And the law is given unto men. And by the law no flesh is justified; or, by the law men are cut off. Yea, by the temporal law they were cut off; and also, by the spiritual law they perish from that which is good, and become miserable forever.

6. Wherefore, redemption cometh in and through the Holy Messiah; for he is full of grace and truth.

7. Behold he offereth himself

---

VERSE 4. *And thou hast beheld in thy youth.* Most of the great men of God have been called in their childhood. The age of youth is the age of vision.

> Youth sees, age tests,
> Youth soars, age rests.
> While Youth is out for detection,
> Old age is in for perfection.
> And both are one, as flower and pod,
> Both serving well the kingdom of God.

*His glory.* Jacob had beheld his coming in the flesh, his ministry, his atoning sacrifice, his resurrection, and his glorious return to the Father. All this constituted his glory. Jacob, therefore, knew the plan of salvation by revelation, just as we know it by the inspired proclamation of the Gospel. He could look forward toward Calvary, as we are looking backward in history to that central place of interest both in heaven and on earth. (See Pearl of Great Price, Mos. 5:4-9)

*Salvation is free.* "For God so loved the world, that he gave his only begotten Son, that whosoever believeth in him should not perish, but have everlasting life." (John 3:16) And that reminds me of a twice-told tale.

A young missionary had preached a powerful sermon on "free salvation." He felt sure that the audience had been impressed with his explanations and exhortations. Consequently, at the close of his effort, he turned to a woman who seemed especially moved upon by the good spirit and asked her if she had enjoyed his talk. "Well," she said, "to be frank, I remember only the text. What a wonderful text! The Spirit of God was filling my heart so full of the love of God, while you were speaking, that I felt as if I were in the divine Presence all the time." That was a good missionary. A good missionary always brings the Spirit of God with him to his meetings and gives Him a chance to speak.

VERSE 5. *Instructed sufficiently.* Not only is salvation free, but sufficient knowledge has been imparted to all men in all ages, to enable them to do that which brings salvation and to shun the opposite. "For unto whomsoever much is given, of him shall much be required: and to whom men have committed much, of him they will ask the more." (Luke 12:48) It follows, that to him whom little is given, little will be required. See notes under verse 14.

VERSES 6-10. *Redemption through Christ.* He answers the ends of the law for the benefit of all who have a broken heart and a contrite spirit. That is to say, when the law, as the accuser, urges the penalty of separation of the transgressor from God and all that is good, the Holy Messiah, as the Defender, replies that the

a sacrifice for sin, to answer the ends of the law, unto all those who have a broken heart and a contrite spirit; and unto none else can the ends of the law be answered.

8. Wherefore, how great the importance to make these things known unto the inhabitants of the earth, that they may know that there is no flesh that can dwell in the presence of God, save it be through the merits, and mercy, and grace of the Holy Messiah, who layeth down his life according to the flesh, and taketh it again by the power of the Spirit, that he may bring to pass the resurrection of the dead, being the first that should rise.

9. Wherefore, he is the first-fruits unto God, inasmuch as he shall make intercession for all the children of men; and they that believe in him shall be saved.

10. And because of the intercession for all, all men come unto God; wherefore, they stand in the presence of him, to be judged of him according to the truth and holiness which is in him. Wherefore, the ends of the law which the Holy One hath given, unto the inflicting of the punishment which is affixed, which punishment that is affixed is in opposition to that of the happiness which is affixed, to answer the ends of the atonement—

11. For it must needs be, that there is an opposition in all things. If not so, my first-born in the wilderness, righteousness could not be brought to pass, neither wickedness, neither holiness nor misery, neither good nor bad. Wherefore, all things must needs be a compound in one; wherefore, if it should be one body it must needs remain as dead, having no life neither death, nor corruption nor incorruption, happiness nor misery, neither sense nor insensibility.

accused is his, by virtue of his sacrifice for sin. The law has no further claim on him. Christ rose from the dead by the power of the Spirit, for the purpose of bringing a general resurrection to pass; and he rose first in order to make intercession for all men, and save those who believe in him. Through his intercession all will be resurrected; the believers will be saved.

Furthermore, through his intercession for all men, they will be judged in accordance with divine principles of truth and holiness. There can be no mistake. Even those who are under condemnation will acknowledge the justice of the decrees of God.

"Even so, Lord God Almighty, true and righteous are thy judgments."

On the subject of the law, see Rom. 2:19-25; 3:20-26.

VERSE 10. Holy One. This is the Messiah, and we are here told that the resurrected dead, as a consequence of his intercession, will be judged by the law which he has given. Paul, in his letter to the Romans, expresses the same thought: "In the day when God shall judge the secrets of men by Jesus Christ according to my gospel." (Rom. 2:12-16. Compare Words of Mormon, v. 11) The title, "the Holy One," and particularly, "the Holy One of Israel," is frequently applied by Isaiah to our Savior. It occurs 25 times in the book that bears his name, and only

12. Wherefore, it must needs have been created for a thing of naught; wherefore there would have been no purpose in the end of its creation. Wherefore, this thing must needs destroy the wisdom of God and his eternal purposes, and also the power, and the mercy, and the justice of God.

13. And if ye shall say there is no law, ye shall also say there is no sin. If ye shall say there is no sin, ye shall also say there is no righteousness. And if there be no righteousness there be no happiness. And if there be no righteousness nor happiness there

be no punishment nor misery. And if these things are not there is no God. And if there is no God we are not, neither the earth; for there could have been no creation of things, neither to act nor to be acted upon; wherefore, all things must have vanished away.

14. And now, my sons, I speak unto you these things for your profit and learning; for there is a God, and he hath created all things, both the heavens and the earth, and all things that in them are, both things to act and things to be acted upon.

---

six times elsewhere in the Old Testament. In Is. 29:23 the title is, "the Holy One of Jacob," followed by this explanation, "the God of Israel." Jacob and Israel were two names of the same patriarchal ancestor.

There is a reason why the Prophet Isaiah prefers this title. When he was called to the prophetic office, he saw, in a vision, the Lord sitting upon a throne, high and lifted up, and he heard the attendant seraphim crying, one to another, "Holy, holy, holy is the Lord of Hosts; the whole earth is full of his glory." (Is. 6:1-4) To Isaiah our Lord after that was "The Holy One," or, "The Holy One of Israel," or "Jacob." The use of this title by Lehi in an address to his son Jacob, who was named after the patriarch, is appropriate and full of meaning. In Luke 4:34 an evil spirit refers to our Lord as "The Holy One of God." Holiness is a divine quality without which no one can please God (Rom. 8:1-8); nor abide in his presence. It should be noted that this title is found in the latter part of Isaiah, from chapter 40 to chapter 60, and not only in the first part; which should go far to prove the unity of the book, both in design and authorship.

*Opposition in all Things.* Here the prophet seems to refute the theory of monists who maintain that all existences may be considered as ultimately belonging to only one category. They find in this view an escape from what appears to be contradictions, conflict, war and confusion between the natural forces of the universe; for, they argue, if there is but one fundamental essence, one principle, there can be no fundamental conflict. But Lehi teaches that there is an opposition in all things. If not, he says, there would be neither righteousness nor wickedness; neither good nor bad; and, consequently, no responsibility, and neither rewards nor punishment.

Were there no law, there would be no sin, no virtue, no happiness and even no God. But, if there were no God, we ourselves would not exist, for there would have been none that could have given us existence.

That is an inevitable conclusion from the premises of an absurd philosophy.

VERSE 14. *My Sons.* Lehi calls special attention to what he now is about to say.

He is speaking of the existence of God, the creation, the fall of man, free agency and the atonement.

*There is a God.* Only a "fool"—that is, one who is deficient in moral qualities (see Rom. 1:22)—contradicts this self-evident truth, and his negation is determined by the heart rather than the intellect; that is to say, he wishes that there were no God, and he talks accordingly. "The fool has said in his heart, There is no God." (Psalm 14:1) That is his wish, his desire.

Such an individual may, perhaps, find comfort in the conclusion of Kant, that the existence of God, a First Cause, cannot be proved by any argument known to logic, since every cause seems to require a previous cause to account for it, wherefore a First Cause can never be located. But St. Paul does not agree with this conclusion. His assertion is that all that which can be known by mortal man concerning God has been made manifest by our Lord himself, for "God has showed it unto them." Paul is also of the opinion that his eternal power and Godhead "are clearly seen in the creation." (Rom. 1:19, 20) The Hebrew poet expresses the same thought:

> "The heavens declare the Glory of God,
> And the firmament showeth his handiwork.
> Day unto day poureth forth speech,
> And night unto night showeth knowledge.
> There is no speech nor language;
> Their voice cannot be heard.
> Their sound is gone out through all the earth,
> And their words to the end of the World."
> —Psalm 19:1-3.

There is absolutely no excuse for the assertion that there is no God, even in the form of a wish.

*He hath created all things.* Not only is there a God, but he has created all things. All that human senses can contact and human understanding can comprehend; all that divine revelation can unveil to a soul quickened by the Holy Spirit —all is created, and God is the Creator.

As is well known, after the publication of the Darwinian hypothesis of natural selection and "Origin of Species" during the years 1858 and 1859, the theory of evolution became fashionable as a substitute for the doctrine of creation. It was hailed by many as a new discovery and as the very key of the universe.

But this attitude toward it has begun to undergo a notable change.

It is being recalled that surmises regarding evolution are not new; that, in fact, some ancient Greek philosophers in the dim past dreamed of evolution, and that Descartes, the famous French mathematician (1596-1650), and after him Leibnitz, considered it possible that higher forms of existences had originated in lower. Stripped of its assumed character of an ultra-modern scientific discovery, the theory has lost some of its prestige.

The soundness of it is also being doubted, notwithstanding the seemingly strong support of intellectual giants, such as Kant (1724-1804), La Place (1749-1829), Lyell (1830) and many others. Dr. Henry Fairfield Osborn has been quoted in a magazine, May 15, 1932, as having made the sweeping statement, that man lived on the earth not 50,000 years ago, as Darwinists assume, but at least 50 million years ago, and that he was never anything but a man.

Shortly afterwards Dr. Austin H. Clark, of the U. S. National Museum, Washington, is said to have declared, by the same publication:

"Applying our knowledge of embryology, we may assume without possibility of contradiction that all major groups of animals were formed at the same time.

15. And to bring about his eternal purposes in the end of man, after he had created our first parents, and the beasts of the field and the fowls of the air, and in fine, all things which are created, it must needs be that there was an opposition; even the forbidden fruit in opposition to the tree of life; the one being sweet and the other bitter.

16. Wherefore, the Lord God gave unto man that he should act for himself. Wherefore, man could not act for himself save it should be that he was enticed by the one or the other.

There is no evidence which leads us to suppose that any major group was derived from another."

The argument for evolution which compares that process with the growth of a plant from the seed may be ornamental, but it is not logical. The development of plants from the seed, one generation after another of the same kind, is a wonderful illustration of the resurrection (1 Cor. 15:35-49), but not of evolution. When our Lord (Mark 4:28) compares the kingdom of God with a plant that bears fruit, "first the blade, then the ear, then the full corn in the ear," he is not speaking of evolution, for no plant evolves from the blade, it grows, blade and all, from the seed (vv. 26, 27). The plant thus illustrates the gradual growth of the kingdom from a small beginning, but not evolution.

The arguments for evolution which at one time seemed justified by the Mendelian law have been shattered by the discovery that hybrids return to their original characteristics after two or three generations, if not subject to special care. Here, again, nature presents to our view the wonderful picture of a circular movement, from seed to seed, but not evolution.

The gravest indictment against the Darwinian theory is its tendency to develop agnosticism, or even infidelity. Darwin himself became an agnostic. He rejected the Bible's conception of God and of Christ, and said, as quoted by his son: "I for one must be content to remain an Agnostic." (Quoted by Wm. Jennings Bryan in his great speech before the judge in the Scopes' trial, July 21, 1925.) That the theory of evolution leads to infidelity is admitted by the best informed evolutionists. Arthur Cushman McGiffert, in his, "The Rise of Modern Religious Thought," declares that it has had this effect upon "many," but he finds comfort in the fact that it has given us the idea of the immanence of God in everything as a substitute—a poor compensation, I must say, for the loss of the personal God of the Revelations, the Father and Governor of us all!

If we are justified in judging of the attributes of a tree from the quality of the fruit, we must conclude that a theory that produces infidelity cannot be true, not from God.

VERSES 15-16. *Forbidden fruit.* We are here taught that something forbidden was necessary in man's experience on earth. Man had been endowed with free agency, but unless there had been something not lawful to do, there could not have been freedom of choice. Man could have willed only that which was lawful, there being nothing unlawful. Kant puts this thought fairly well when he says that to act in response to duty is to give a law to oneself, and that is to be autonomous, or free. Hence I say, the very prohibition made man free, as long as he was at liberty to choose between obedience and disobedience, with a clear understanding of the consequences.

17. And I, Lehi, according to the things which I have read, must needs suppose that an angel of God, according to that which is written, had fallen from heaven; wherefore, he became a devil, having sought that which was evil before God.

18. And because he had fallen from heaven, and had become miserable forever, he sought also the misery of all mankind. Wherefore, he said unto Eve, yea, even that old serpent, who is the devil, who is the father of all lies, wherefore he said: Partake of the forbidden fruit, and ye shall not die, but ye shall be as God, knowing good and evil.

19. And after Adam and Eve

---

VERSE 17. *Fallen from Heaven.* The record of the story of the fall of man on earth begins properly with an account of the rebellion of Lucifer in heaven.

According to the Book of Abraham (3:22-28), when the proposition to arrange a dwelling place in which the noble intelligences embodied, might have an opportunity of proving themselves worthy of advancement, and the question of leadership came up, one like unto the Son of Man said,

"Here am I, send me."

And another said, "Here am I, send me."

God said, "I will send the first."

Then the second became angry and rebelled, and many followed after him.

In the Book of Moses we read (4:1-4) that the fallen angel, later, repeated his proposition. He offered to redeem all mankind, provided God would make him his Son and give him his glory. Not a soul would be lost.

When this amended proposition came before the Son, he replied humbly, "Father, thy will be done and the glory be thine for ever."

God, then, confirmed the first decision, and gave the Son authority to cast the rebels out of heaven. There was war in heaven. (Rev. 12:7, 8) Michael, our Father Adam, fought against the "dragon" and his angels, until these were cast out. It was then that our Lord (Luke 10:18) "beheld satan fall from heaven as lightning."

*He Became a Devil.* This word is from the Greek "diabolos," which means "calumniator," or "accuser." Here it stands for the Hebrew "satan," which means an enemy, an adversary. Cast out of heaven, the enemy became an accuser, he became satan, yea, even the devil, the father of lies, to deceive and to blind men. (Mos. 4:4)

In the New Testament "devil" often signifies a "demon," a spirit, whether good or evil. See, for ex., 2 Tim 4:1, where "doctrines of devils," might better be rendered, "doctrines concerning spirits,"—referring, perhaps, to the practices of certain so-called spiritists.

VERSE 18. *Partake of the Forbidden Fruit.* Adam came to this earth as innocent and devoid of worldly knowledge and experience as a babe. The Garden had been prepared for him by his heavenly Father, to be his first home. There, under divine care and tuition, he became capable of performing his mission on earth.

When he was sent out of the Garden, he knew how to take care of trees and cultivate the soil. He knew the different animals, for he had named them according to their characteristics. He could observe some of the heavenly constellation, which, like a celestial timepiece, indicated not only day and night, but also seasons, particular days and years, and, we may add, cycles. (Gen. 1:4)

had partaken of the forbidden fruit they were driven out of the garden of Eden, to till the earth.

20. And they have brought forth children; yea, even the family of all the earth.

21. And the days of the children of men were prolonged, according to the will of God, that they might repent while in the flesh; wherefore, their state became a state of probation, and their time was lengthened, according to the commandments which the Lord God gave unto the children of men. For he gave commandment that all men must repent; for he showed unto all men that they were lost, because of the transgression of their parents.

22. And now, behold, if Adam had not transgressed he would not have fallen, but he would have remained in the garden of Eden. And all things which were created must have remained in the same state in which they were after they were created; and they must have remained forever, and had no end.

23. And they would have had no children; wherefore they would have remained in a state of innocence, having no joy, for they knew no misery; doing no good, for they knew no sin.

---

Our first parents began their career outside the Garden of Eden with a high degree of culture. That is the picture presented by sacred history; also by profane history. It is corroborated by archeology, for, no matter how deep scientists dig in the earth, wherever they find human remains, they unearth evidence of culture.

Adam and Eve lived as happy as children in the Garden until they came in contact with a temptor, who prevailed upon them to eat the forbidden fruit. In the Pearl of Great Price (Mos. 4:5-7) two agents appear in this plot against man, Satan and the Serpent. We read: "And Satan put it into the heart of the Serpent . . . to beguile Eve, for he knew not the mind of God." In the D. & C. 29:40 we read that "it came to pass that the devil tempted Adam, and he partook of the forbidden fruit and transgressed the commandment, wherein he became subject to the will of the devil, because he yielded unto temptation." St. Paul (1 Tim. 2:14) says, "Adam was not deceived," which is understood to mean that he voluntarily and deliberately ate of the fruit, in order not to be separated from Eve.

There is not necessarily any discrepancy between these three accounts. Satan inspired the Serpent to tempt Eve. The chief of the fallen angels then turned to Adam, who, probably, had already made up his mind what to do.

But who was the serpent? It may have been a reptile in the Garden. Dr. Adam Clark, in his great work on the Bible, maintains that the "serpent" was a baboon, supposed by some to have been the monkey to which honors were paid in Egypt under the name of Anubis. But his arguments are not convincing. It is more probable that it was one of the fallen angels who were expelled from heaven together with Satan, and who was known as the "serpent."

"The devil had truth in his mouth as well as lies when he came to Mother Eve . . . She did eat, her eyes were opened, and she saw good and evil. She gave of the fruit to her husband, and he ate, too. What would have been the consequence if he had not done so? They would have been separated, and where would we have been? I am glad he did eat." (Brigham Young, Jour. of Dis., Vol. 12, p. 70)

24. But behold, all things have been done in the wisdom of him who knoweth all things.

25. Adam fell that men might be; and men are, that they might have joy.

26. And the Messiah cometh in the fulness of time, that he may redeem the children of men from the fall. And because that they are redeemed from the fall they have become free forever, knowing good from evil; to act for themselves and not to be acted upon, save it be by the punishment of the law at the great and last day, according to the commandments which God hath given.

27. Wherefore, men are free according to the flesh; and all things are given them which are expedient unto man. And they are free to choose liberty and eternal life, through the great mediation of all men, or to choose captivity and death, according to the captivity and power of the devil; for he seeketh that all men might be miserable like unto himself.

---

VERSE 25. *Men are that they might have joy.* Brigham Young: "When I look at the economy of heaven, my heart leaps for joy, and if I had the tongue of an angel, or the tongues of the whole human family combined, I would praise God in the Highest for his great wisdom and condescension in suffering the children of men to fall into the very sin into which they have fallen, for he did it that they, like Jesus, might descend below all things and then press forward and rise above all." (Jour. of Dis., Vol. 13, p. 145)

### REDEMPTION

VERSE 26. *The Messiah Cometh.* The great purpose of the advent of the Messiah in the fulness of time was to redeem the children of men from certain consequences of the fall. For, although that experience was necessary in the development of man, and was, as has been said, a "fall upwards," it had certain consequences that called for redemption. One of these was death, from which there would have been no resurrection but for the redemption. See v. 27.

To redeem property, or a person, was, under the Mosaic law, to pay a legal ransom, and thereby to procure freedom for the land attached, or the servant in bondage. Any near relative could act as the redeemer. (See Lev. 25:25-28; 47-52) The Messiah is our Redeemer. (Gal. 3:13.)

Man by setting aside the commandment of God and doing the will of Satan, in the matter of the forbidden tree, became, as it were, his property, his bondservant. That appears from the word of our Lord, "No man can serve two masters . . . ye cannot serve God and mammon" (Matt. 6:24). Note that it cannot be done. We belong either to one or the other. And St. Paul says expressly, "Know ye not, that to whom ye yield yourselves servants to obey, his servants ye are to whom ye obey; whether of sin unto death, or of obedience unto righteousness?" (Rom. 6:16.) If mankind had not had a Redeemer, it would have been in thraldom; because of the redemption, "they have become free for ever."

*In the Fulness of Time.* This meant, anciently, the time when the child became of age. St. Paul gives that explanation. The heir, he says, as long as he is a child, is under tutors and governors until the time appointed by the father; even so we, "but when the fulness of time was come, God sent forth his Son . . .

28. And now, my sons, I would that ye should look to the great Mediator, and hearken unto his great commandments; and be faithful unto his words, and choose eternal life, according to the will of his Holy Spirit;

29. And not choose eternal death, according to the will of the flesh and the evil which is therein, which giveth the spirit of the devil power to captivate, to bring you down to hell, that he may reign over you in his own kingdom.

30. I have spoken these few words unto you all, my sons, in the last days of my probation; and I have chosen the good part, according to the words of the prophet. And I have none other object save it be the everlasting welfare of your souls. Amen.

---

to redeem those that were under the law, that we might receive the adoption of sons, . . . and the Spirit of his Son into your hearts, crying Abba, Father." (Gal. 4:4-6.) "Abba" is the Aramaic for "father," the word used by Jesus in his prayers in Gethsemane. It has been compared to our, "daddy," which, when used as a term of endearment is rather pretty and indicates intimate comradeship in the family.

VERSE 28. *Look to the Great Mediator.* Study the character and work of the Messiah, who by his atonement became the Mediator and Redeemer.

During the Mosaic dispensation, one day of the year was devoted to that great theme. It was part of the Temple service. The day was called, "the day of atonement." It was a general fast day, a day of repentance and prayer.

On this day Aaron attired in priestly vestments offered a sin offering for himself and his house. Blood of this offering was sprinkled on the covering of the ark in the Holy of Holies.

Then two goats were presented before the Lord on behalf of the people. The high priest selected by lot one of these for Jehovah as a sin offering. The other was to belong to Azazel, who by some has been supposed to be one of the fallen angels, who led the "sons of God" in the wickedness that brought the flood upon the race. (Gen. 6:1-4.) The high priest laid his hands upon this goat, confessed the sins of the people, thereby conferring them symbolically on the animal, which then was set free in the wilderness for the fallen angel. The burnt offering for the High priest and the people ended the solemn ceremonies. It was thus that the Lord, during the Old dispensation; impressed the people with the seriousness of transgression and the necessity of atonement and a Mediator.

It has been stated that on this day, perhaps at sunset, when the day ended, the young maidens used to meet in the vineyards and dance and sing, and give the young men an opportunity to form an idea of their future wives, whom the mothers, I believe, generally selected for them.

NOTES

The atonement of Christ is not limited to his death on the cross. His entire life was a sacrifice.

It is efficacious as regards man, in so far as man, in accepting his teachings and obeying his commandments becomes able and worthy, morally, intellectually and physically, to be associated with God. Faith, repentance and baptism are the first steps back to the house of the Father.

The humiliation and sufferings of Christ should be an object lesson to all of the nature and consequences of sin. If we contemplate the infinite love of Jesus for humanity, the purity of his life, and his holiness, and then gaze on the picture of his sufferings—then, we should be able to form some faint idea of what a loathsome thing sin is; also of the need of a Mediator.

The heavens hid their face in darkness, and the earth shook and trembled with fear, when the Holy One of Israel ended his mortal career on the cross; but his cry of victory penetrated the veil and went ringing through all creation:

### "IT IS FINISHED"

## CHAPTER 3

*Lehi Addresses his Son Joseph—He Quotes Joseph, the Son of Jacob—Speaks of a Choice Seer.*

### 1. *Introduction.*

1. And now I speak unto you, Joseph, my last-born. Thou wast born in the wilderness of mine afflictions; yea, in the days of my greatest sorrow did thy mother bear thee.

2. And may the Lord consecrate also unto thee this land, which is a most precious land, for thine inheritance and the inheritance of thy seed with thy brethren, for thy security forever, if it so be that ye shall keep the commandments of the Holy One of Israel.

3. And now, Joseph, my last-born, whom I have brought out of the wilderness of mine afflictions, may the Lord bless thee forever, for thy seed shall not utterly be destroyed.

4. For behold, thou art the fruit of my loins; and I am a descendant of Joseph who was carried captive into Egypt. And great were the covenants of the Lord which he made unto Joseph.

5. Wherefore, Joseph truly saw our day. And he obtained a promise of the Lord, that out of the fruit of his loins the Lord God would raise up a righteous branch unto the house of Israel; not the Messiah, but a branch which was to be broken off, nevertheless, to be remembered in the covenants of the Lord that the Messiah should be made manifest unto them in the latter days, in the spirit of power, unto the bringing of them out of darkness unto light — yea, out of hidden darkness and out of captivity unto freedom.

---

VERSE 1. *Joseph.* Born in the wilderness. See 1 Ne. 18:7, 19. The name means "He will increase." It was the name given also to the firstborn of the Patriarch Jacob and his beloved Rachel; one of the noblest and most perfect characters of history.

VERSE 2. *Holy One of Israel.* See 1 Ne. 19:14, 15; 2 Ne. 2:10.

VERSE 3. *Not Utterly Destroyed.* 1 Ne 13:30. There must be numerous descendants of Joseph, the son of Lehi, among the millions of aborigines now living in the American countries.

VERSE 4. *Lehi's Ancestors.* Lehi was a descendant of Joseph, the son of Jacob, through the lineage of Manasseh. (Alma 10:3.) The family of Ishmael, however, were descendants of Ephraim. In this land of inheritance, the children of Manasseh have precedence over those of Ephraim, according to the natural order of the birthright. This is consistent with the list of 144,000 "sealed" servants of the Lord, as recorded in Rev. 7:5-8, where the name of Ephraim is left out, and Manasseh is inserted between Naphtali and Simeon.

VERSE 5. The Patriarch Jacob, in blessing his son Joseph in Egypt, referred to him as a fruitful bough by a well, the branches of which "run over the wall." In

6. For Joseph truly testified, saying: A seer shall the Lord my God raise up, who shall be a choice seer unto the fruit of my loins.

7. Yea, Joseph truly said: Thus saith the Lord unto me: A choice seer will I raise up out of the fruit of thy loins; and he shall be esteemed highly among the fruit of thy loins. And unto him will I give commandment that he shall do a work for the fruit of thy loins, his brethren, which shall be of great worth unto them, even to the bringing of them to the knowledge of the covenants which I have made with thy fathers.

8. And I will give unto him a commandment that he shall do none other work, save the work which I shall command him. And I will make him great in mine eyes; for he shall do my work.

9. And he shall be great like unto Moses, whom I have said I would raise up unto you, to deliver my people, O house of Israel.

10. And Moses will I raise up, to deliver thy people out of the land of Egypt.

---

the Scriptures a "branch" often refers to the Messiah, as for ex. in Isaiah 11:1-5. Our Lord himself says he is the true vine, and the disciples are the branches. (John 15:1-8.) But here, Lehi explains that Joseph did not refer to the Messiah, but to some one who was to be broken off from his genealogical tree and yet to be remembered in the latter days. In the Old Testament, Joshua and Zerubbabel (Zechariah 4:9-14) are said to be two olive trees, representing, as we in modern terms should say, one the church and the other the state. Joseph in Egypt uses a common term when he speaks of Lehi as a branch that was to be broken off the main tree, but to be restored in the latter days by the Messiah.

A CHOICE SEER

In the next verse we are informed that Joseph in Egypt prophesied of his descendants in future generations. In this chapter, vv. 6-21, we have a record of one of these prophecies.

VERSE 6. *A Seer.* Before the days of Samuel, a prophet was known as a seer. A seer is one who communicates with God in visions, or dreams. He sees. A prophet is one who speaks for God about that which belongs to either the future, past or present. This paragraph refers to Joseph Smith, the latter-day prophet.

VERSE 7. *His Work.* His especial work is here said to be to bring to the descendants of Joseph, the son of Jacob, knowledge of the covenants of the Lord with their ancestors. The publication of the Book of Mormon is, therefore, of special importance to the Indians of Hebrew origin. The covenants of the Lord were made with their ancestors.

VERSE 9. *Great Like unto Moses.* The Prophet Joseph Smith is here compared to Moses. The comparison is striking. (1) Both saw and spoke with Jehovah. (2) Both were liberators who led multitudes in exodus for the sake of liberty from oppression. (3) Both were law-givers by divine inspiration. (4) Both were prophets and seers. (5) Both performed mighty miracles. (6) Both encountered opposition, from "friends" and enemies. (7) Both depended largely on a brother for success: Moses on Aaron; Joseph on Hyrum.

11. But a seer will I raise up out of the fruit of thy loins; and unto him will I give power to bring forth my word unto the seed of thy loins—and not to the bringing forth my word only, saith the Lord, but to the convincing them of my word, which shall have already gone forth among them.

12. Wherefore, the fruit of thy loins shall write; and the fruit of the loins of Judah shall write; and that which shall be written by the fruit of thy loins, and also that which shall be written by the fruit of the loins of Judah, shall grow together, unto the confounding of false doctrines and laying down of contentions, and establishing peace among the fruit of thy loins, and bringing them to the knowledge of their fathers in the latter days, and also to the knowledge of my covenants, saith the Lord.

13. And out of weakness he shall be made strong, in that day

---

VERSE 12. *The two Books.* The writings "by the fruit of thy loins" are the Book of Mormon; those by the "fruit of the loins of Judah" are the Bible. The results of the union of these two volumes will be marvelous. False doctrines will be "confounded"; Peace will be established in the world, and the descendants of Joseph will receive knowledge of the covenants made with their fathers.

The Book of Mormon is essentially a book of doctrines, and its teachings are gradually leavening the religious thought of the world. As for establishing peace, it can be said that the great peace movement among the nations, as far as it has had any success, is distinctly American, and I venture the assertion that it has been made a reality, very largely through the proclamation of the Gospel by the Elders of the Mormon Church.

The descendants of Joseph will yet receive the Gospel. The Indians are quick to understand, when given a chance. In August, 1841, a number of Sac and Fox Indians visited the Prophet Joseph in Nauvoo. He explained the Gospel to them and exhorted them not to make war and kill each other. The spokesman for the Indians said that he had a Book of Mormon in his wick-i-up, and he added: "I believe that you are a great and good man. I look rough, but I also am a son of the Great Spirit. I have heard your advice. We intend to quit fighting and follow the good talk you have given us." (From "Joseph Smith, the Prophet," by Andrew Jenson.)

It may be mentioned here that at the peace conference at Buenos Aires, Argentina, which was attended Dec. 1, 1936, by the U. S. President, representatives of 21 American republics unanimously endorsed a plan designed to banish war for ever from the American continents. Previous to that, a special session of the conference, presided over by a lady delegate from Salt Lake City, Utah, Mrs. Burton Musser, had received a petition for some such action, signed by over a million men and women from all parts of the world. U. S. Secretary of State Cordell Hull described the action of the conference as "epochal." And it was. But it is the preaching of the Gospel — the Bible and the Book of Mormon — that has prepared the way for it.

VERSE 13. *Out of Weakness . . . Strong.* The important truth is taught here that spiritual strength is derived from missionary work. Elders who have filled missions with honor, will endorse this proposition. Many of them have received their strongest testimony when testifying to others.

when my work shall commence among all my people, unto the restoring thee, O house of Israel, saith the Lord.

14. And thus prophesied Joseph, saying: Behold, that seer will the Lord bless; and they that seek to destroy him shall be confounded; for this promise, which I have obtained of the Lord, of the fruit of my loins, shall be fulfilled. Behold, I am sure of the fulfilling of this promise;

15. And his name shall be called after me; and it shall be after the name of his father. And he shall be like unto me; for the thing, which the Lord shall bring forth by his hand, by the power of the Lord shall bring my people unto salvation.

16. Yea, thus prophesied Joseph: I am sure of this thing, even as I am sure of the promise of Moses; for the Lord hath said unto me, I will preserve thy seed forever.

17. And the Lord hath said: I will raise up a Moses; and I will give power unto him in a rod; and I will give judgment unto him in writing. Yet I will not loose his tongue, that he shall speak much, for I will not make him mighty in speaking. But I will write unto him my law, by the finger of mine own hand; and I will make a spokesman for him.

---

At a time when leaders in the Church, friends and brothers, apparently, were conspiring to overthrow the Prophet, Heber C. Kimball, Orson Hyde, Willard Richards, and Joseph Fielding were called on a mission to England. This was in 1837. The Prophet and the Church, in their condition of seeming weakness, were made strong. The Church has increased in vigor and activity with the development of missionary work for the restoration of Israel.

*All my People.* That includes the so-called "lost tribes." See 3 Ne. 16:1, 3; 17:4.

VERSE 14. *Shall be Confounded.* This promise the Lord has kept, even although the Prophet Joseph suffered martyrdom. "Confounded" means "confused," "put to shame," "defeated." That has always been the fate of the enemies of the servants of the Lord.

VERSE 15. *The Name of the Seer.* "It shall be called after me"—Joseph—and "after the name of his father"—Joseph Smith, Senior. He was, furthermore, to resemble Joseph, in this respect that "the thing that the Lord shall bring forth by his hand"—the Book of Mormon—will bring "my people" salvation.

VERSE 16. *I will Preserve thy Seed Forever.* The descendants of Joseph, the son of Jacob. See v. 3.

VERSE 17. *The spokesman of Moses.* Aaron. See Exodus 4:10-17. The Lord appointed Aaron to that office in these words: "He shall be thy [Moses] spokesman unto the people, even he shall be to thee instead of mouth, and thou shalt be to him instead of God." (Ex. 4:16.) That is to say, Moses was to deliver to him, and through him to the people, the word of God, as revealed from time to time.

18. And the Lord said unto me also: I will raise up unto the fruit of thy loins; and I will make for him a spokesman. And I, behold, I will give unto him that he shall write the writing of the fruit of thy loins, unto the fruit of thy loins; and the spokesman of thy loins shall declare it.

19. And the words which he shall write shall be the words which are expedient in my wisdom should go forth unto the fruit of thy loins. And it shall be as if the fruit of thy loins had cried unto them from the dust; for I know their faith.

20. And they shall cry from the dust; yea, even repentance unto their brethren, even after many generations have gone by them. And it shall come to pass that their cry shall go, even according to the simpleness of their words.

21. Because of their faith their words shall proceed forth out of my mouth unto their brethren who are the fruit of thy loins; and the weakness of their words will I make strong in their faith, unto the remembering of my covenant which I made unto thy fathers.

## 2. Conclusion.

22. And now, behold, my son Joseph, after this manner did my father of old prophesy.

23. Wherefore, because of this covenant thou art blessed; for thy seed shall not be destroyed, for they shall hearken unto the words of the book.

---

VERSE 18. *Another Spokesman.* Refers to Sidney Rigdon, whom the Lord, in a revelation given October 12, 1833, promised to ordain "to be a spokesman to my servant Joseph." (D. and C. 100:9.) Joseph was to be mighty in testimony, and Sidney in expounding all scriptures. Joseph was to be the revelator, Sidney the spokesman.

Immediately after the martyrdom, Sidney Rigdon asked for the guardianship of the Church on the ground of this appointment ("Essentials of Church History," Joseph Fielding Smith, p. 387), forgetting that his office of spokesman to Joseph Smith necessarily ended with the death of the Prophet.

VERSES 19-21. *Cry from the Dust.* Refers to the Book of Mormon. It is a divine promise that, by means of this volume, although its words are simple (v. 20) and weak (v. 21) the descendants of Joseph will be converted to the covenants God made with their fathers. Among the millions of Indians now inhabiting the Americas there are many children of Manasseh and Ephraim. The promise concerns them first. As for all others, they become the seed of Abraham, when they embrace the Gospel.

"If a pure gentile firmly believes the gospel of Jesus Christ, and yields obedience to it, in such a case I will give you the words of the Prophet Joseph: 'The effect of the Holy Ghost upon a gentile is to purge out the old blood, and make him actually of the seed of Abraham.'" (Discourses of Brigham Young, Selected by Dr. John A. Widtsoe, p. 669.)

VERSE 23. *Thou art Blessed.* Lehi now speaks to his son Joseph. He repeats the promise that his descendants will not be destroyed. (Comp. v. 3, 1 Ne. 13:30, 31.)

24. And there shall rise up one mighty among them, who shall do much good, both in word and in deed, being an instrument in the hands of God, with exceeding faith, to work mighty wonders, and do that thing which is great in the sight of God, unto the bringing to pass much restoration unto the house of Israel, and unto the seed of thy brethren.

25. And now, blessed art thou, Joseph. Behold, thou art little; wherefore hearken unto the words of thy brother, Nephi, and it shall be done unto thee even according to the words which I have spoken. Remember the words of thy dying father. Amen.

---

VERSE 24. Lehi restates, briefly, the prophecy of Joseph, the son of Jacob, concerning the "choice seer." He is not only a great prophet, but a mighty restorer of the house of Israel.

VERSE 25. *Amen.* This familiar word is an adjective, meaning, "true," or "faithful." In Rev. 3:14 Christ is called, "the Amen, the true and faithful witness." . . .

The word was well known to the Hebrews. In the trial by ordeal, common among the ancients, the accused person was made to drink a potion cursed by the officiating priest before the altar of Jehovah. An oath was then read, and the suspect responded, "Amen, Amen!" (So be it!). (Numb. 5:22.) According to Deut. 27:14-26, the Levites were commanded to put a motion before the assembly of Israel, that twelve offenses, specified, be declared grave crimes, some of them calling for the penalty of death, and that the motion was to be accepted by the people answering, "Amen."

In Isaiah 65:16 the Lord is called the "God of Truth," which is a translation of the original, "God of Amen."

Our Lord often repeated the word for the sake of emphasis: "Amen, amen, I say unto you." (John 13:16, 20, 21; 14:12, etc.) The translators have, "Verily, verily, I say unto you."

Some of the Psalms, for example 41 and 72, end with, "Amen and Amen!" and the Christian churches very early adopted this form, as we infer from 1 Cor. 14:16, where St. Paul asks: "If thou shalt bless with the spirit"—and not with the understanding—"how shall the unlearned say Amen at thy giving thanks, seeing he understandeth not what thou sayest?" Justin Martyr (100-165) informs us that, at the Sacrament meetings, the entire congregation responded to the benediction by saying, Amen!

But Amen was also the Egyptian god of whom Dr. Wallis Budge (Osiris and the Resurrection, Vol. 1, p. 360) says that he was a god unlike any of the other gods of Egypt, for he symbolized the hidden Power, the source of the world and all life, the highest conception of the Deity which the Egyptians ever imagined.

The famous Egyptian pharaoh, Rameses II, generally supposed to have been the pharaoh of the oppression of the Israelites, is said to have offered up this prayer to Ammon, after having been defeated in a battle:

"I call upon thee, my Father Ammon! My many soldiers have abandoned me; none of my horsemen hath looked towards me; and when I called them, none hath listened to my voice. But I believe that Ammon is worth more to me than a million of soldiers, than a hundred thousand horsemen." (Hibbert Lectures, 1879, p. 228.)

## CHAPTER 4

*Last Hours of Lehi—Rebellion of Laman, Lemuel and the Sons of Ishmael
—Two Sets of Plates—A Song Composed by Nephi.*

### 1. *Introduction.*

1. And now, I, Nephi, speak concerning the prophecies of which my father hath spoken, concerning Joseph, who was carried into Egypt.

2. For behold, he truly prophesied concerning all his seed. And the prophecies which he wrote, there are not many greater. And he prophesied concerning us, and our future generations; and they are written upon the plates of brass.

### 2. *The last hours of Lehi.*

3. Wherefore, after my father had made an end of speaking concerning the prophecies of Joseph, he called the children of Laman, his sons, and his daughters, and said unto them: Behold, my sons,

---

VERSE 1. *Joseph in Egypt a Prophet.* The information is here given that Joseph, the son of Jacob, prophesied concerning the descendants of Lehi, and that these prophecies were recorded on the plates of brass which once were in the custody of Laban. (1 Ne. 3:3.) Joseph may, therefore, properly be called a great prophet.

This is also evident from the accounts of his dreams (Gen. 37:5-11); his interpretation of the dreams of the butler and the baker (Gen. 40:5-19); and the pharaoh (Gen. 41:25-36) and also from his address to his brothers (Gen. 45:3-14).

To the ordinary reader of the Bible it would perhaps not occur to regard Joseph in Egypt as a prophet, but to the Hebrews anciently one who spoke for God, whether about things present, past or future, was a prophet. Abraham was a prophet (Gen. 20:7). Aaron was called the prophet of Moses, because he spoke for his brother (Ex. 7:1). Many prophets are mentioned in the Old Testament. Among these are Samuel, Nathan, Gad (1 Chron. 29:29), and Ahijah and Iddo (2 Chron. 9:29). The Hebrew Bible includes the authors of the books Joshua, Judges, Samuel and Kings among the prophets. The Hebrews had also prophetesses. Among these were Deborah, (Judges 4:4.), Huldah (2 Kings 22:14) and Miriam (Ex. 15:20). Among the New Testament prophetesses can be mentioned, Anna, (Luke 2:36) and the four daughters of Philip, the evangelist. (Acts 21:9)

No details are given concerning the visit of Paul and Luke in the home in Caesarea, but as Philip was one of the first seven bishops in Jerusalem (Acts 6:5), it is evident that Luke, the historian, could get much valuable information from him concerning the earliest days of the church, for the book of the Acts he was writing at that time.

The last of the prophets of the Old Dispensation was John the Baptist, the greatest of them all (Matt. 11:9-11; Luke 16:16), because with him the dispensation covered by the Law and the Prophets (Acts 13:15) was completed. But the prophetic gift remained one of the great characteristics of the New dispensation. (1 Cor. 14:1, 3, 5, 22, 31, 32.)

Only a Jew, I believe, educated as Nephi was, would have regarded Joseph, the son of Jacob, as a prophet, as Nephi does. Another evidence of the authenticity of the Book of Mormon!

and my daughters, who are the sons and the daughters of my first-born, I would that ye should give ear unto my words.

4. For the Lord God hath said that: Inasmuch as ye shall keep my commandments ye shall prosper in the land; and inasmuch as ye will not keep my commandments ye shall be cut off from my presence.

---

VERSE 4. *Ye shall prosper in the land.* On one condition: Inasmuch as ye shall keep my commandments. Special favors from God produce a special obligation to keep his laws.

Recent researches furnish evidence of the prosperity that once was enjoyed at least by some of the former inhabitants of America.

Excavations in burial grounds in Panama under the direction of H. B. Roberts and S. K. Lathrop, Peabody archeologists, during the years 1930, 1931 and 1933, have revealed that, in the province of Cocle, there once lived a people which in wealth rivaled the Incas of Peru. Numerous objects of gold in the form of rich adornments were found. Also pottery and implements of copper, stone and bone.

The wealth of the Incas was fabulous. Atahualpa, when a prisoner of the Spaniards, piled up gold to the value of more than fifteen million dollars as ransom, although to no avail. According to Prescott, after Sarmiento, the interior of the temple at Cuzco was, literally, a mine of gold. On the western wall was a representation of the Deity, consisting of a human countenance looking forth from amidst innumerable rays of light, in the same manner as the sun is often personified. The figure was engraved on a massive plate of gold of enormous dimensions, thickly powdered with emeralds and precious stones. It was so situated that the rays of the morning sun fell upon it, lighting up the apartment with an effulgence that seemed more than natural, and which was reflected back from the golden ornaments on the walls and ceiling. The cornices which surrounded the walls were of gold, and a broad frieze of the same costly material, let into the stone work, encompassed the whole exterior of the edifice. (Prescott, Peru, Vol. I, p. 89)

In Yucatan, where the Maya civilization at one time rivaled the culture of Egypt in the days of King Tut, priceless relics of jade and gold have been recovered in recent years.

In Panama, Mr. John Q. Critchlow, of Salt Lake City, for many years a resident of the South American republic, ascended the mountain El Volcan, a short distance from the settlement Divala in the province of Chiriqui. The mountain rises to an elevation of about 11,000 feet above the sea level, and from the top an observer can see the Pacific on one hand and the Atlantic on the other. It was in May, 1922, that Mr. Critchlow made the ascent. According to the published reports, it was his good fortune to discover, on this excursion, in the ruins of an ancient pueblo, "wonders of ancient art, enormous workings in solid gold, examples of excellence attained in pottery, and the strange carvings of hieroglyphics." The report accepts this as evidence that a nation of Maya people lived and flourished in Panama long before Caesar made his journey to the British Isles, and that their civilization was topped only by that of ancient Rome.

Julius Caesar invaded Britain in the year 54 B.C.

The tombs at Monte Alban, in the state of Oaxaca, Mexico, where rich archeological finds have been made, have also furnished evidence that the ancient Zapotecs were experts in relief painting. In November, 1932, Dr. Alfonso Caso, government archaeologist, announced that remarkable works of ancient art had been found on the floor and door jamb of a tomb. The paintings were done in brilliant greens, reds, and yellows, and the colors were well preserved. Among objects unearthed

5. But behold, my sons and my daughters, I cannot go down to my grave save I should leave a blessing upon you; for behold, I know that if ye are brought up in the way ye should go ye will not depart from it.

6. Wherefore, if ye are cursed, behold, I leave my blessing upon you, that the cursing may be taken from you and be answered upon the heads of your parents.

7. Wherefore, because of my blessing the Lord God will not suffer that ye shall perish; wherefore, he will be merciful unto you and unto your seed forever.

8. And it came to pass that after my father had made an end of speaking to the sons and daughters of Laman, he caused the sons and daughters of Lemuel to be brought before him.

9. And he spake unto them, saying: Behold, my sons and my daughters, who are the sons and the daughters of my second son; behold I leave unto you the same blessing which I left unto the sons and daughters of Laman; wherefore, thou shalt not utterly be destroyed; but in the end thy seed shall be blessed.

10. And it came to pass that when my father had made an end of speaking unto them, behold, he spake unto the sons of Ishmael, yea, and even all his household.

---

were incense burners, two translucent green axes, ear ornaments, bits of jade and hollow engraved bones.

VERSE 5. *If ye are brought up in the way ye should go ye will not depart from it.* Here Lehi teaches his household the principle taught long before his time, "Train up a child in the way he should go: and when he is old, he will not depart from it." (Prov. 22:6) To bring up a child does not mean only to teach him the right way, but to train him in walking in it. Training, says Layman Abbott, is the production of habit. Actions oft repeated become a habit; habit long continued becomes a second nature. When a child is trained in telling the truth and doing what is right, he will do so, even at the cost of his life, because it has become his nature.

VERSE 6. *Your Parents.* On the duty of parents toward their children, see D. and C. 68:28, 29; and D. and C. Commentary pp. 515, 518, 737, and 738. Children are gifts of God; parents are responsible for their proper care. "Ye fathers, provoke not your children to wrath: but bring them up in the nurture and admonition of the Lord. (Eph. 6:4)

VERSE 8. *Lemuel, the second son of Lehi.* (1 Ne. 2:5) The name means, "devoted," or, "dedicated," to God. It is found in Proverbs 31:1, where it may refer to King Solomon.

VERSE 9. *Not Utterly Destroyed.* Lehi gave Lemuel the same blessing that the firstborn received (vv. 4-7), including the promise that his descendants would not be exterminated.

VERSE 10. *The Sons of Ishmael.* Lehi blessed the household of Ishmael, who died and was buried in the Old Country, at a place which they called Nahom (1 Ne. 16:34). The name Ishmael means, "[Whom] God Hears." The blessing bestowed upon the house of Ishmael is not recorded.

"Ishmael was of the lineage of Ephraim, and his sons married into Lehi's family, and Lehi's sons married Ishmael's daughters, thus fulfilling the words of Jacob upon

11. And after he had made an end of speaking unto them, he spake unto Sam, saying: Blessed art thou, and thy seed; for thou shall inherit the land like unto thy brother Nephi. And thy seed shall be numbered with his seed; and thou shalt be even like unto thy brother, and thy seed like unto his seed; and thou shalt be blessed in all thy days.

12. And it came to pass after my father, Lehi, had spoken unto all his household, according to the feelings of his heart and the

Ephraim and Manasseh in the 48th chapter of Genesis which says: 'And let my name be named on them, and the name of my fathers, Abraham and Isaac; and let them grow into a multitude in the midst of the Earth.' Thus these descendants of Manasseh and Ephraim grew together upon this American continent, with a sprinkling from the house of Judah, from Mulek descended . . . thus making an intermixture of Ephraim and Manasseh with the remnants of Judah, and for aught we know, the remnants of some other tribes that may have accompanied Mulek." (Apostle Erastus Snow, Jour. of Dis., Vol. 23, pp. 184-5)

Apostle Snow says that the Prophet Joseph informed the Saints that the genealogical record of Lehi was contained on the 116 pages first translated and subsequently lost, and that Ishmael was, as stated, of the lineage of Ephraim.

In the history of Israel in America, Lehi, a descendant of Manasseh, the firstborn of Joseph, took the lead over the descendants of Ephraim, although Jacob, in his blessing gave him the first place. It was different in the historic development in Palestine. There Ephraim was in the front ranks. Joshua, the successor of Moses, was an Ephraimite. To this day, when a Hebrew blesses his son, he repeats the very words of the dying Patriarch and says, "God make thee as Ephraim and Manasseh," —Ephraim first. But Jacob predicted also that a people would come from Manasseh, and that he, too, would be great. (Gen. 48:19) The Nephites are the literal fulfilment of this prophecy. And, if, as I surmise, the Nahuas of American ethnology are the Nephites of the Book of Mormon, the fulfilment is a matter of history. (See Introduction to the Study of the Book of Mormon, Sjodahl, pp. 146 and 367)

The Nahuas, according to Dr. Daniel Brinton, "occupied the Pacific coast from about the Rio del Fuerte in Sinaloa, N. lat. 26 degrees, to the frontiers of Guatemala, except a portion at the isthmus of Tehuantepec . . . On the borders of the lakes in the valley of Mexico were the three important states, Tezcuco, Tlacopan and Tenochtitlan, who at the time of the conquest were formed into a confederacy of wide sway. The last mentioned, Tenochtitlan, had its chief town where the city of Mexico now stands, and its inhabitants were the Aztecs." (The American Race, p. 128)

If my theory is sound, the history of the Nahuas should be studied in the light of the blessings given Joseph by his father, Jacob, in Egypt.

VERSE 11. *Sam.* Lehi blesses his third son. His name is Egyptian. It was the name of the chief priest of the priesthood of *Ptah*, at Memphis, the primordial god who, according to Egyptian ideas, furnished *Ra* the elements out of which the world was organized. (Paul Pierret, Dictionaire d'Archeologie Egyptienne, Paris, 1875, p. 490) Lehi, in his blessing, links him and his descendants to Nephi and the offspring of this younger brother.

VERSE 12. *He Waxed Old.* This is perfectly good English, although now archaic. It means, "he became exhausted," "tired out." (See Deut. 29:5; Heb. 8:13)

*He Died and was Buried.* Lehi's last act in mortality was to bless his posterity. And, let no one regard this as a mere formality. A father's blessing by the power

Spirit of the Lord which was in | to pass that he died, and was
him, he waxed old. And it came | buried.

## 3. *After the death of Lehi.*

13. And it came to pass that | of Ishmael were angry with me
not many days after his death, | because of the admonitions of the
Laman and Lemuel and the sons | Lord.

---

of the Priesthood, is a draft on the unlimited resources of heaven, which our Eternal Father has obligated himself to honor, according to the words of our Savior: "Verily I say unto you, Whatsoever ye shall bind on earth shall be bound in heaven: and whatsoever ye shall loose on earth, shall be loosed in heaven." (Matt. 18:18) That is the value of a father's, or a patriarchal, blessing.

Lehi died. Tenderly the angel of death pressed a kiss on the dimming eyes, and he fell asleep, surrounded by his devoted children and household.

> Reader, pause a while at Lehi's grave,
> Honor here a hero, faithful, brave.
>
> O'er Arabia's shifting, burning sand,
>     Irreantum's turbulent expanse,
>     Where the windstorms howled and whirled in dance,
> Led by faith and Liahona's hand,
> Lehi came to Joseph's hallowed land.
>
> 'Midst sorrows and turmoil and strife
>     He gather'd no wealth, no renown;
> He gave to his God all his life,
>     God gave him a heavenly crown

Death is sometimes spoken of as the separation of soul and body. It would be more correct to say, that the separation of the soul—or, rather, the spirit—and the body is one of the effects of death. Death itself, like life, is a mystery. The spirit clings, as long as possible, to the body, even when this is sick, or tortured, but when they are separated, the body must be disposed of. In the words of Abraham, at the death of Sarah: "Give me a possession of a buryingplace with you, that I may bury my dead out of my sight." (Gen. 23:4)

"What of friends that have gone beyond the veil—are they dead? No, they live, and they move in a more exalted sphere. Did they fight for the kingdom of God when here? Yes, they did. Are they battling for it now? Yes; and the time is approaching when the wicked nations have to be destroyed; and the time is near when every creature is to be heard saying, 'Honor and power and might and majesty and dominion be ascribed to him that sitteth upon the throne, and to the Lamb, for ever and ever.' We have got to bring this about, whether we do it in this world, or that which is to come." (John Taylor, J. of D., vol. 5, p. 191)

VERSE 13. *Angry with me.* Nephi, after the death of Lehi, naturally, felt it his duty to admonish his brethren and associates, as his father had done. Undoubtedly, they held services at regular times, similar to our fast meetings, where all had an opportunity to bear testimony, or to admonish and teach. It must have been on such occasions that Laman, Lemuel and the sons of Ishmael became angry. The brothers were jealous of the greater gifts and influence of Nephi, the youngest of the four. The sons of Ishmael thought, perhaps, that they, as belonging to the lineage

14. For I, Nephi, was constrained to speak unto them, according to his word; for I had spoken many things unto them, and also my father, before his death; many of which sayings are written upon mine other plates; for a more history part are written upon mine other plates.

15. And upon these I write the things of my soul, and many of the scriptures which are engraven upon the plates of brass. For my soul delighteth in the scriptures, and my heart pondereth them, and writeth them for the learning and the profit of my children.

---

of Ephraim should not be subordinate to a son of Manasseh. But whatever the cause, the old hatred broke out again.

Lest this experience of Nephi should be regarded as a refutation of the truth of the principle stated in the 5th verse of this chapter, let it be said that a very important part of training is the will of the person to be trained. There must be co-operation on his, or her, part; otherwise the object in view will not be attained. No one can be trained to become a great musician, a painter, a runner, an orator, a linguist, or what not and certainly not a good Latter-day Saint against his, or her will. The principle is true, but it does not destroy the free agency of man. Our heavenly Father himself exclaims, through the Prophet Isaiah (1:2): "I have nourished and brought up children, and they have rebelled against me."

VERSE 14. *Mine Own Plates.* As is well known, Nephi was the author of two volumes of plates—the larger and the smaller. In the first of these he preserved the history of the kings and the wars and contentions of his people. (1 Ne. 9:2-6) It was a political history. The second, or smaller, volume was chiefly a history of the ministry. (1 Ne. 19:1-7; Jac. 1:1-4; Words of Morm. 3-8) It was a brief ecclesiastical history.

VERSE 15. *My Soul Delighteth in the Scriptures.* Who can truthfully say, with Nephi, that he finds real pleasure in reading and studying the sacred scriptures? Or, with the Psalmist: "O how love I thy law! it is my meditation all the day." (Psalm 119:97) Many, I am afraid, forget the Author of the Scriptures and lay them aside as antiquated and not up to date.

Let me tell a little story. A young man in the American forces in France during the World war, had the misfortune of becoming a prisoner of war. He was reported as dead, and connection with his home was interrupted for years, because he was sick and unable to keep up the correspondence. When, finally, after years of isolation, he received a letter from his father, his joy was boundless. It was a precious piece of paper. But much of it was unintelligible to him. Children had grown up. Old persons had become older, and most of them had passed away. Automobiles had become common. New roads had been built. There were new business houses. As far as the letter referred to such changes, it was strange to him. But it was from his father, and he read it over and over again.

One day this young man met another fellow who argued against the Bible on the flimsy ground that nobody can understand it. But he got the correct reply this time.

Our friend took up his letter and said, "This is from my father. On account of my imprisonment and sickness and long absence I do not understand all of it, but, try to get it away from me! When I get home, it will all be clear to me. If you do not like the Word of God, I am afraid that you do not care for your Eternal Father or your eternal home."

## 4. *Introduction to Nephi's Song.*

16. Behold, my soul delighteth in the things of the Lord; and my heart pondereth continually upon the things which I have seen and heard.

## 5. *A confession of sin.*

17. Nevertheless, notwithstanding the great goodness of the Lord, in showing me his great and marvelous works, my heart exclaimeth: O wretched man that I am! Yea, my heart sorroweth because of my flesh; my soul grieveth because of mine iniquities.

---

### A SONG OF NEPHI

The remainder of this chapter, from verse 16, is a remarkable piece of poetry composed by Nephi. It was, clearly, written at a time when he was depressed because of the death of his father and the enmity manifested towards him by his older brothers.

Hebrew ancient poetry was essentially different from modern compositions in the poetical style. It lacked rhymes and meter. It was the rhythm of thought, rather than of words, as for instance:

"Why art thou cast down, O my soul?
And why art thou disquieted within me?"—Ps. 43:5.

Two lines expressing the same thought?

The Hebrews were fond of poetry. Parts of the Bible were written in that form, although this is not apparent in the translations. Not only the Psalms, but also the book of Job and a portion of the Prophets are poetry. For instance:

"His grave was appointed with the wicked
And with the rich man was his sepulcher."—Is. 53:9.

The book of Job and the Song of Songs are dramatic poetry. In the New Testament, parts of the Revelation by John are poetry.

The song of Nephi can be divided as follows: (1) Introduction, v. 16; (2) A Confession of Sin, vv. 17-19; (3) Contemplation of God's Fatherly Love, vv. 20-25; (4) Folly of Giving Way to Despair, vv. 26-30; (5) A Prayer, vv. 31-35.

VERSE 16. Blessed he is who can say this truthfully. See notes to v. 15.

VERSE 17. *O Wretched Man that I Am!* To one who has read the marvelous story of Nephi, as related so far, this exclamation may come as an unexpected surprise. To what iniquities does he refer? To what sins? (v. 18) We know not. But whatever they were, Nephi had no intention to minimize, or excuse them. He had not any desire to say, with the Pharisee: "I thank thee, O God, that I am not as other men are"; nor with a young man whom I happen to remember, who, in a public prayer meeting, asked God to forgive him his "little" faults, for, he said, "If I have done anything wrong, I did not mean to." Nephi seems to have felt the solemn truth of the Scriptural doctrine that the imagination of man's heart is evil from his youth. (Gen. 8:21) But the nobility of the character of Nephi is clearly shown in his confession. There is no word of criticism of his brothers, no prayer

18. I am encompassed about, because of the temptations and the sins which do so easily beset me.

19. And when I desire to rejoice, my heart groaneth because of my sins; nevertheless, I know in whom I have trusted.

## 6. God's fatherly love.

20. My God hath been my support; he hath led me through mine afflictions in the wilderness; and he hath preserved me upon the waters of the great deep.

21. He hath filled me with his love, even unto the consuming of my flesh.

22. He hath confounded mine enemies, unto the causing of them to quake before me.

23. Behold, he hath heard my cry by day, and he hath given me knowledge by visions in the night-time.

24. And by day have I waxed bold in mighty prayer before him; yea, my voice have I sent up on high; and angels came down and ministered unto me.

25. And upon the wings of his Spirit hath my body been carried away upon exceeding high mountains. And mine eyes have beheld great things, yea, even too great for man; therefore I was bidden that I should not write them.

---

for retaliation, although they were plotting against him. Nephi did not assume the responsibility of an accuser, nor a judge. (See Matt. 7:1, 2)

VERSE 18. *Beset.* Nephi uses this word in the same sense the Old Testament writers which he had read used it, viz., "encompassed about," or, "surrounded by." See Judges 19:22; Ps. 22:12, and Hos. 11:12. St. Paul, in his letter to the Hebrews, (12:1) compares sin to the weights and clinging garments which the contestants in a race must get rid of, if they want to win the prize, while the spectators are a "cloud" of witnesses,—for to the runners in the arena, in their swift progress toward the goal, they must have appeared just like one indistinct mass. Sin always is an obstacle to the contestants for the heavenly crown.

From the depressing contemplation of weaknesses and shortcomings, Nephi now directs his thoughts toward God. Then the depression vanishes. He counts the many blessings God has bestowed upon him from the day he accompanied his father out of Jerusalem. This section (vv. 20-25) is in the nature of an epic.

VERSE 20. *God hath been my support.* 1 Ne. 30-32; 17:1, 2; *He hath preserved me upon the great deep.* 1 Ne. 18:9-23.

VERSE 21. *He hath filled me with his love.* 1 Ne. 11:22-26.

VERSE 22. *He hath confounded mine enemies.* 1 Ne. 17:52. *Causing them to quake before me.* 1 Ne. 16:27.

VERSES 23-24. 1 Ne. 3:29-31; 11:14.

VERSE 25. *Visions on a high mountain.* 1 Ne. 11:1; *Visions not to be written.* 1 Ne. 1:14. This may be read together with 2 Cor. 12:4-9, where St. Paul relates that he, before his missionary journeys, was caught up into the third heaven, also known as Paradise, where he heard unspeak-

*7. Folly of giving way to despair.*

26. O then, if I have seen so great things, if the Lord in his condescension unto the children of men hath visited men in so much mercy, why should my heart weep and my soul linger in the valley of sorrow, and my flesh waste away, and my strength slacken, because of mine afflictions?

27. And why should I yield to sin, because of my flesh? Yea, why should I give way to tempta- tions, that the evil one have place in my heart to destroy my peace and afflict my soul? Why am I angry because of mine enemy?

28. Awake, my soul! No longer droop in sin. Rejoice, O my heart, and give place no more for the enemy of my soul.

29. Do not anger again because of mine enemies. Do not slacken my strength because of mine afflictions.

able words, "which it is not lawful for man to utter." But, lest he should feel proud on account of such visions or revelations, he was given a "thorn in the flesh"—some sickness causing excruciating pain—which he compared to a messenger of Satan, sent to buffet him.

VERSE 26. *Why . . . sorrow?* Nephi is calm and composed now. He recognizes the folly of doubting God's Fatherly care, after he had been the recipient of so great mercy.

VERSE 27. *Why am I Angry?* In this paragraph Nephi further opens his heart, and makes it clear that it was anger that had "beset" him, as we have read in vv. 17-19. That was the "iniquity," the "sin," that caused his flesh to "waste away," and opened his heart to the adversary, to destroy his peace.

Nephi is absolutely correct in his estimate of the effects of paroxysms of anger on the body and mind of those who yield to it. I may state that I remember from the early years of my life an estimable lady, a good, faithful wife and the mother of beautiful children. At intervals she suffered outbursts of wrath to such a degree, that doctors told her that, unless she conquered those attacks, they would be her death. That is just what happened. She passed away after such an unreasonable outburst of passion.

I do not believe that Nephi suffered in a similar manner in any degree. I am rather inclined to the belief that he composed this song for the benefit of his brothers. They were angry with him. He may also have felt anger. They refused to listen to his sermons. Hence he may have hoped to reach them with a piece of poetry, as the Prophet Nathan had reached King David with a rebuke. Nathan had a little composition which he humbly submitted to the criticism of the king, the greatest writer of fiction at the time, in Israel. And it was not until the royal poet had given his opinion of the conduct of the hero of Nathan's story that the Prophet let the thunderbolt fall: "Thou art the man!" (2 Sam. 12:1-14) In the case of David it had the desired effect.

Anger, like fire, may be good, if kept under proper control. And some commentators tell us that that is what the Apostle had in mind when he wrote to the Ephesians (4:26), "Be ye angry and sin not." Perhaps it is. I am not prepared to say it is not. But I have a suspicion that the negation belongs to both clauses of the sentence, and that the true meaning is, "Be [not] angry, and sin not."

30. Rejoice, O my heart, and cry unto the Lord, and say: O Lord, I will praise thee forever: yea, my soul will rejoice in thee, my God, and the rock of my salvation.

## 8. A Prayer.

31. O Lord, wilt thou redeem my soul? Wilt thou deliver me out of the hands of mine enemies? Wilt thou make me that I may shake at the appearance of sin? 32. May the gates of hell be shut continually before me, because that my heart is broken and my spirit is contrite! O Lord, wilt thou not shut the gates of thy righteousness before me, that I may walk in the path of the low valley, that I may be strict in the plain road! 33. O Lord, wilt thou encircle me around in the robe of thy righteouness! O Lord, wilt thou make a way for mine escape before mine enemies! Wilt thou make my path straight before me! Wilt thou not place a stumbling block in my way—but that thou

---

For, in the same chapter he says: "Let all bitterness, and wrath, and anger, and clamour, and evil speaking, be put away from you, with all bitterness." (v. 31)

VERSE 30. *Rejoice, O my Heart.* This section closes with a shout of joy, which may be rendered thus, in the form of modern blank verse:

Rejoice, my heart, cry out to God, and say,
O Lord, I praise thee now and ever.
My soul, my heart, rejoice in thee, my God,
Who art the Rock of my salvation.

VERSE 31. *Redeem my Soul.* Nephi prays for deliverance from the hands of his enemies who were plotting against him, and from the bondage of sin. His desire was that he might be made to fear even the appearance of sin. He, evidently, realized the importance of the principle which the Apostle expressed thus: "Work out your own salvation with fear and trembling" (Phil. 2:12); and which Soeren Kierkegaard, the eccentric Danish philosopher, (1813-1855) gave the form of a striking paradox: "If you fear, then fear not; but if you do not fear, then fear."

VERSE 32. *Gates of Hell.* Nephi prays that these may be closed to him continually. To the Hebrews, "hell" was either merely the grave; or a region of gloom and misery where the spirits of evil-doers were awaiting the resurrection and final judgment. The gates of hell were the entrance to this region. The spirits of the righteous were in Paradise. But "gates" was also a figurative expression for a town (Gen. 22:17; Ps. 87:2, 3). In Ps. 24:7, 9, "Lift up your heads, O ye gates and be ye lifted up, ye everlasting doors." "Gates" also means kingdoms or empires, and I believe that Nephi uses the word in that sense. There are on earth two great kingdoms: One is the kingdom of hell, or evil; the other is the kingdom of righteousness. And now he prays that the entrance to the first of these may be closed to him for ever, while he may always have free entrance to the other.

The special lesson of this prayer is that it is safer to keep out of the way of temptation than to rely on one's will power to resist it. "Blessed the man who walketh not in the counsel of the ungodly, nor standeth in the way of sinners, nor sitteth in the seat of the scornful." (Ps. 1:1, 2)

wouldst clear my way before me, and hedge not up my way, but the ways of mine enemy.

34. O Lord, I have trusted in thee, and I will trust in thee forever. I will not put my trust in the arm of flesh; for I know that cursed is he that putteth his trust in the arm of flesh. Yea, cursed is he that putteth his trust in man or maketh flesh his arm.

35. Yea, I know that God will give liberally to him that asketh. Yea, my God will give me, if I ask not amiss; therefore I will lift up my voice unto thee; yea, I will cry unto thee, my God, the rock of my righteousness. Behold, my voice shall forever ascend up unto thee, my rock and mine everlasting God. Amen.

VERSE 35. *Amiss.* This means "wrong," or "improper." (2 Chron. 6:37) To ask "not amiss" is, therefore, to ask for that which is right and proper. "Ye ask, and receive not, because ye ask amiss, that ye may consume it upon your lusts," (James 4:3).

The prayer ends with an expression of perfect confidence in God:—

> I will lift up unto thee, O God, my cry,
> Thou wilt my humble petitions not deny.
> Therefore my voice shall forevermore ascend
> God, Everlasting, to thee, worlds without end.

### GENERAL NOTES

In his prayer, Nephi asks God fervently for deliverance from the hands of his enemies (v. 31). "Wilt thou," he prays, "make a way for mine escape before mine enemies" (v. 34), and, he adds, "I will trust in thee for ever."

The Lord heard this prayer; for, shortly after it had been uttered, he directed Nephi to form a company of faithful friends and lead them to another part of the country. (2 Ne. 5:5-8) Nephi did so, and they became exceedingly prosperous. (vv. 13-17)

The Nephites, as the colonists were called (v. 9), in all probability, became the founders of the great Nahua civilization which flourished in Mexico and Central America, while the Peruvian civilization in South America developed out of seeds planted by Laman and his followers; the older civilizations of which monuments have been left in Yucatan (so named, perhaps from Joktan, the brother of Peleg, in whose days the earth was divided); and in Bolivia, at Lake Titicaca, were, perhaps the work of the Jaredites, of whom the Lord said that they would become a great nation: "And there shall be none greater than the nation which I will raise up unto me of thy seed, upon all the face of the earth." (Ether 1:43)

When I say that I regard this passage (vv. 16-35) as poetry, I do not have the modern form, with rhymes and meters, in mind, but ancient Hebrew poetry, such as we find in Job, the Psalms, the Proverbs and some of the Prophets.

I am aware that some have affirmed, on the authority of Josephus, and others, that the Psalms were originally composed in meter, but I believe that is an open question which we need not discuss here.

The chief characteristic of the ancient Hebrew poetry has been called "parallelism," because of a certain correspondence as to thought and language or both, between two or more lines which form a period, or stanza.

For example:—

"Keep not thou silence, O God;
Hold not thy peace, and be not still, O God." (Ps. 83:1)

"My soul longeth, yea even fainteth for the courts of the Lord;
My heart and my flesh crieth out for the living God." (Ps. 84:2)

"For the Lord hath chosen Zion;
He hath desired it for his habitation." (Ps. 132:13)

Sometimes the form is antithetical, rather than parallel, strictly speaking:—

"The memory of the just is blessed,
But the name of the wicked shall rot." (Prov. 10:7)

Sometimes it is a double antithetical form:

"The bricks are fallen down
But we will build them with hewn stones;
The sycamores are cut down,
But we will change them into cedars." (Isa. 9:10)

Sometimes there is a gradual extension of the thought, thus:—

"Blessed is the man
That walketh not in the counsel of the ungodly,
Nor standeth in the way of sinners,
Nor sitteth in the seat of the scornful." (Ps. 1:1)

The Lamentations of Jeremiah, a book which in our Bibles has been placed between Jeremiah and Ezekiel, but in the Hebrew canon between Ruth and Ecclesiastes, furnishes an illustration of another form of ancient poetry. It consists of five songs, each of 22 periods, or stanzas, corresponding to the number of letters in the Hebrew alphabet. In four of the songs, each line, or stanza, begins with a letter of that alphabet, all placed in alphabetical order, from the first (Aleph) to the last (Tau). Other acrobatics of this kind are Psalms 111, 112, 119 and 145; but it is evident that we cannot look for similar arrangements in the Book of Mormon, because we know nothing of the alphabet in which it was engraved.

Students of this subject will find that the parallelism is less strict in the Psalms than in the Book of Job. In this composition there is, besides, a very effective musical cadence.

The song of Nephi arranged in parallel lines, might look somewhat like this:

### A Song of Lamentation by Nephi, the Son of Lehi

Behold, my soul delighteth in the things of the Lord;
And my heart pondereth continually upon the things
    which I have seen and heard.

Nevertheless, notwithstanding the great goodness of the
Lord, in showing me his great and marvelous works, my
    heart exclaimeth:

O, wretched man that I am!
Yea, my heart sorroweth because of my flesh;
My soul grieveth because of mine iniquities.

I am encompassed about,
Because of the temptations and the sins
Which do so easily beset me.
And when I desire to rejoice, my heart groaneth because
    of my sins

Nevertheless, I know in whom I have trusted.
My God hath been my support.

He hath led me through mine afflictions in the wilderness;
And he hath preserved me upon the waters of the great deep.

He hath filled me with his love,
Even unto the consuming of my flesh,

He hath confounded mine enemies,
Unto the causing of them to quake before me.

Behold, he hath heard my cry by day,
And he hath given me knowledge by visions in the night-time.

And by day have I waxed bold in mighty prayer before him;
Yea, my voice have I sent up on high,
And angels came down and ministered unto me.

And upon the wings of his spirit hath my body been carried
        away upon exceeding high mountains.
And mine eyes have beheld great things, yea, even too
        great for man; therefore I was bidden that I
        should not write them.

O then, if I have seen so great things,
If the Lord in his condescension unto the children of men
        hath visited men in so much mercy,
Why should my heart weep and my soul linger in the Valley
        of Sorrow,
And my flesh waste away, and my strength slacken, because
        of mine afflictions?

And why should I yield to sin because of my flesh?
Yea, why should I give way to temptations that the evil
        one have place in my heart to destroy my
        peace and afflict my soul?
Why am I angry because of mine enemy?

Awake my soul! No longer droop in sin.
Rejoice O my heart, and give place no more for the enemy
        of my soul,

Do not anger again because of mine enemies.
Do not slacken my strength because of mine afflictions.

Rejoice, O my heart, and cry unto the Lord and say:
O Lord, I will praise thee forever;
Yea, my soul will rejoice in thee, my God, and the Rock
        of my salvation.

O Lord, wilt thou redeem my soul?
Wilt thou deliver me out of the hands of mine enemies?
Wilt thou make me that I may shake at the appearance of sin?

May the gates of hell be shut continually before me,
Because that my heart is broken and my spirit is contrite!

O Lord, wilt thou not shut the gates of righteousness
        before me, that I may walk in the path of
        the low valley,
That I may be strict in the plain road!

O Lord, wilt thou encircle me around in the robe of thy
        righteousness!

O Lord, wilt thou make a way, for mine escape before
    mine enemies!

Wilt thou make my path straight before me!
Wilt thou not place a stumbling block in my way.

But that thou wouldst clear my way before me,
And hedge not up my way, but the ways of mine enemy.

O Lord, I have trusted in thee,
And will trust in thee for ever.
I will not put my trust in the arm of flesh;
For I know that, Cursed is he that putteth his trust in
    the arm of flesh.

Yea, cursed is he that putteth his trust in man
Or maketh flesh his arm.

Yea, I know that God will give liberally to him that
    asketh
Yea, my God will give me, if I ask not amiss.

Therefore I will lift up my voice unto thee;
Yea, I will cry unto thee, my God, the rock of my
    righteousness.

Behold, my voice shall forever ascend up unto thee,
My rock and mine everlasting God.   Amen.

                                        **(2 Nephi 4:16-35)**

## CHAPTER 5

*The Great Schism, 1-8, — Nephites, 9-19 — Lamanites, 20-25 — Jacob and Joseph Ordained, 26-28 — The Two Volumes of Plates, 29-34.*

### 1. *The Great Schism.*

1. Behold, it came to pass that I, Nephi, did cry much unto the Lord my God, because of the anger of my brethren.

2. But behold, their anger did increase against me, insomuch that they did seek to take away my life.

3. Yea, they did murmur against me, saying: Our younger brother thinks to rule over us; and we have had much trial because of him; wherefore, now let us slay him, that we may not be afflicted more because of his words. For behold, we will not have him to be our ruler; for it belongs unto us, who are the elder brethren, to rule over this people.

4. Now I do not write upon these plates all the words which they murmured against me. But it sufficeth me to say, that they did seek to take away my life.

5. And it came to pass that the Lord did warn me, that I, Nephi, should depart from them and flee

---

VERSES 1-8. *I, Nephi, . . . did cry unto the Lord.* The account of the great schism in the family of the departed prophet begins with the statement that the anger of the oldest brother against the younger had increased to the degree that Laman had begun to consider plans for the destruction of Nephi. The refuge and defense of Nephi, then, was prayer. Such was his education and training. But to all appearances prayer did not avail. The enmity increased. Laman forgot that he had had his chance of leadership and failed. (See 1 Ne. 3:11, 14)

God hears and answers prayer. That is an eternal truth, solid as the everlasting hills. The Apostle John assured the members of the church in his day that, "Whatever we ask, we receive of him, because we keep his commandments and do those things that are pleasing in his sight." (1 John 3:22) But he also said in the same epistle (5:16) that there is a sin "unto death"; and, "I do not say that ye shall pray for it."

From the tenor of this epistle it appears that the "sin unto death" which the Apostle had in mind, was apostasy; see, for instance, 2:22, 24; 4:15, 20. For when a sinner rejects the Savior which God has provided, and his atonement, there is no other savior, no other means of salvation. But Laman was about to add fratricide to apostasy. Hence the Lord commanded Nephi to depart. Evidently this was the only means of preventing Laman from plunging himself headlong into the whirlpool of everlasting destruction. For, by following the divine promptings and leaving the settlement, Nephi prevented the heinous crime of fratricide. And by departing voluntarily, he, seemingly, assumed part of the responsibility for the deplorable separation.

Nephi left. (v. 5) He was accompanied by Zoram, Sam, Jacob, Joseph and their families, his sisters and all those who would go with him. (6) Nephi explains that "all those who would go with him" were those who believed in the warnings and revelations of God. But were they only the children and grandchildren of Lehi and his company, who less than thirty years previously had left Jerusalem?

into the wilderness, and all those who would go with me.

6. Wherefore, it came to pass that I, Nephi, did take my family, and also Zoram and his family, and Sam, mine elder brother and his family, and Jacob and Joseph, my younger brethren, and also my sisters, and all those who would go with me. And all those who would go with me were those who believed in the warnings and the revelations of God; where-fore, they did hearken unto my words.

7. And we did take our tents and whatsoever things were possible for us, and did journey in the wilderness for the space of many days. And after we had journeyed for the space of many days we did pitch our tents.

8. And my people would that we should call the name of the place Nephi; wherefore, we did call it Nephi.

## 2. The Nephites.

9. And all those who were with me did take upon them to call themselves the people of Nephi.

10. And we did observe to keep the judgments, and the statutes, and the commandments of the Lord in all things, according to the law of Moses.

---

(v. 28) Were these as numerous already at this time as the expression, "all those who would go with me," seems to imply? Or, is it possible that Lehi and his family had established their first settlement in a locality where they found aborigines—Jaredites, for instance—who had identified themselves with the newcomers, as the Mulekites did with the immigrants led by Mosiah (Omni vv. 12-19)?

There may be no definite information on this point in the record of Nephi, but see also v. 14. It is a peculiar fact, which may, or may not, be significant, that, in the numerous traditions of the Indians concerning the appearance of civilizers and reformers in various places, widely separated, these always found aborigines to teach and elevate. This is true of Quetzalcoatl in Cholula, Votan in Chiapas, Wixepecocha in Oajaca, Zamna and Cukulcan in Yucatan, Gucumatz in Guatemala, Viracocha in Peru, Sume and Paye-Tome in Brazil and Bochica in Colombia.

The journey lasted for the "space of many days," (v. 7), which means that it was a long journey, and it went through the wilderness. In the Book of Mormon, the term "wilderness" means a country inhabited by wild beasts, or only sparsely settled. In Brazil, according to George Church in "Aborigines of South America," p. 19, this meaning of the word "desert" has been retained to this day. It means a "wild, upland pasture country."

Having traveled for many days, they found a place suitable for settlement, and they called it Nephi. It became the "Land of Nephi." (v. 8)

VERSE 10. *Judgments.* Judicial decisions.

*Statutes.* May refer to rules and regulations for the guidance of social intercourse.

*Commandments.* The authoritative edicts of God, the ruler of the universe.

The Nephites endeavored to carry out these obligations, as recorded in the books of Moses—the Law.

11. And the Lord was with us; and we did prosper exceedingly; for we did sow seed, and we did reap again in abundance. And we began to raise flocks, and herds, and animals of every kind.

12. And I, Nephi, had also brought the records which were engraven upon the plates of brass; and also the ball, or compass, which was prepared for my father by the hand of the Lord, according to that which is written.

13. And it came to pass that we began to prosper exceedingly, and to multiply in the land.

14. And I, Nephi, did take the sword of Laban, and after the manner of it did make many swords, lest by any means the people who were now called Lamanites should come upon us and destroy us; for I knew their hatred towards me and my children and those who were called my people.

---

VERSE 11. *Prosper Exceedingly.* The Nephites were agriculturists and stock raisers. It may be recalled here that the Indians, their descendants, are credited with having developed twenty-five kinds of crops, among which are corn or maize, peanuts, beans, squashes, pumpkins, sunflowers, gourds and the exceedingly important cotton plant. They understood seed selection, irrigation and cultivation. Prescott says of the Peruvians:

"Terraces were raised upon the steep sides of the Cordillera; and, as the different elevations had the effect of difference of latitude, they exhibited in regular gradation every variety of vegetable form, from the stimulated growth of the tropics to the temperate products of a northern clime; while flocks of llamas—the Peruvian sheep—wandered with their shepherds over the broad, snow-covered wastes on the crests of the sierra, which rose beyond the limits of cultivation. An industrious population settled along the lofty regions of the plateaus, and towns and hamlets, clustering amidst orchards and wide-spreading gardens, seemed suspended in the air far above the ordinary elevation of the clouds."

VERSE 12. *Nephi had Records . . . Brass.* The plates that had been in the custody of Laban. These enabled them to study history and genealogy.

*The Ball, or Compass.* Critics of the Book of Mormon, at one time, used to quote this as an evidence against the authenticity of the Book, the compass, they said, not being known before the 12th century A.D. But they had the mariners' compass in mind. This compass in the Book of Mormon was a special instrument prepared by the Lord to guide Lehi on the road, and it was operated by faith. (1 Ne. 16:10; 26-29) The word "compass" occurs in several places of the Bible. In Ex. 27:5 and 38:4, it means a brim or moulding in the altar, on which a metal net was suspended to catch the embers after the firebrands on which the sacrificial offerings were consumed. That contrivance encompassed the altar and was, therefore, a "compass." (See also Acts 28:13 for another meaning of that word)

VERSE 14. *Sword of Laban.* See notes under 1 Ne. 4:9 and 22-27. Nephi certainly believed in preparation for self-defense, but that is not an argument in favor of war. The Lamanites he feared were those who might come in order to murder and plunder and who, therefore, were mere criminals. The Book of Mormon is a great and important "pacifist" document. It represents war as a "fountain of filthy water," originating in hell (1 Ne. 12:15, 16), and it shows in

15. And I did teach my people to build buildings, and to work in all manner of wood, and of iron, and of copper, and of brass, and of steel, and of gold, and of silver, and of precious ores, which were in great abundance.

16. And I, Nephi, did build a temple; and I did construct it after the manner of the temple of Solomon save it were not built of so many precious things; for they were not to be found upon the land, wherefore, it could not be built like unto Solomon's temple. But the manner of the construction was like unto the temple of Solomon; and the workmanship was exceeding fine.

17. And it came to pass that I, Nephi, did cause my people to be industrious, and to labor with their hands.

---

the Fourth Book of Nephi that where Christianity prevails Millennium is the rule. (See Fourth Ne., vv. 15-18)

*Those who were Called my People.* See notes under v. 5.

VERSES 15-17. *Buildings.* See in connection with these paragraphs the excellent treatise on the "Seven Claims of the Book of Mormon" by Dr. John A. Widtsoe and Dr. Franklin S. Harris, Jr., pp. 67-85. The meaning of "steel" and "brass" is discussed briefly in "An Introduction to the Study of the Book of Mormon," pp. 74-76. It is safe to accept the statements of the Book of Mormon on debatable questions, and then wait for the final verdict of scientific investigation.

In the meantime it is a source of satisfaction, and faith promoting to contemplate the fact that the descendants of Lehi, both Nephites and Lamanites, for a long time contributed largely to the activities that lifted the ancient Americans to a very high level in culture and civilization. The record of their past is a promise of a glorious future.

*Nephi Did Build a Temple.* It was patterned after the Temple of Solomon. So did Onias, the Jew, in Egypt. (Antiq. of the Jews, by Josephus, p. 461, Boston, 1849) Only, these temples were, of necessity, smaller and less costly.

Temple building in accordance with the divine pattern is the greatest of all civilizing agencies. It is the art of arts. Not only architecture, but all other arts —sculpture, painting, music, poetry, etc., are its humble servants. Wherever the Lord has a temple, he has a palace, a dwelling, of his own. And where he dwells, there is a portion of heaven, where glorious hosts are in attendance, carrying out his least bidding and praising him continually with songs of everlasting joy.

VERSE 17. *Nephi caused his people . . . to labor with their hands.* This may, perhaps, be thought strange in our machine age. But, after all, the human hand is still the most efficient tool in existence, if beauty and durability of workmanship are desired. For speed and mass-production, machinery has the advantage, but in other respects the old masterpieces, mostly "handmade," are unsurpassed. It is a moot point, too, whether people would not be better off with fewer machines and more employment for willing laborers, trained to do the world's work. Every honest working man is a genuine nobleman. Remember the word of our Lord: "My Father worketh hitherto, and I work." (John 5:17) Somebody has well said: "As it is the property of fire to burn, of snow to chill, so of God to work." And we are his children.

18. And it came to pass that they would that I should be their king. But I, Nephi, was desirous that they should have no king; nevertheless, I did for them according to that which was in my power.

19. And behold, the words of the Lord had been fulfilled unto my brethren, which he spake concerning them, that I should be their ruler and their teacher. Wherefore, I had been their ruler and their teacher, according to the commandments of the Lord, until the time they sought to take away my life.

---

VERSE 18. *No King.* The Nephites must have been quite numerous at this time, since they felt the need of a "king." They proposed to confer that title upon Nephi, but he declined the honor. Undoubtedly, Nephi was well informed on the history of the Orient, the cradle of his forefathers (1 Ne. 1:1), and he knew the fate of nations under autocratic kings and tyrants. He had read that the Prophet Samuel had counseled Israel against the election of a king, on the ground that such an official would make the people his slaves. Probably he had the solemn warning of that great prophet in mind, who said: "And ye shall cry out in that day because of your king which ye shall have chosen you: and the Lord will not hear you in that day." (1 Sam. 8:10-18)

At first the king was merely the chief, the father and counselor, of his tribe or community. In Assyria he held the priesthood. He was anointed in the temple, and the officiating priest said, in part: "May thy foot in the temple and thy hands at the altar of Ashur, thy god, be pleasing. May thy priestship and the priestship of thy sons be pleasing before Ashur, thy god." Later the rulers of Assyria became commanders of armies and great conquerors. But that was the beginning of the end, which came about 25 years before Lehi left Jerusalem, when the government was overthrown by a Scythian invasion and the revolt of Media and Babylonia. The Assyrian monarch perished in the flames of his palace, and the invaders divided the country between them.

In Babylonia the king, from being the first of his tribe, the head and leader, because of physical strength, mental superiority, or wealth, in time became the owner of his subjects and disposed of them as he saw fit. Nebuchadnezzar was such a despot.

The famous Hammurabi called himself "the god of kings."

In Egypt, the ruler, from being the father and counselor of the people, became the absolute master. As his title, pharaoh, indicates, he was regarded as the scion, or son, of one of their many gods, and therefore divine. He was supposed to be the son of the god Horus.[1]

In Peru, where government and social institutions, judging from the accounts, may have taken form under Lamanite influence, the kings, or ruling Incas, finally became autocrats, exalted in pride, who, even if in some instances benevolent, by forging chains of serfdom around the necks of their humble subjects, rendered them practically helpless, because deprived of self-reliance and initiative, when these qualities were highly needed, in the face of aggressive, arrogant enemies. In the fate of all these empires we see the results of kingly despotism, under various names.

---

[1] This subject is discussed at length by Dr. H. F. Lutz, University of California, in the "American Anthropologist," Oct.-Dec. 1924, pp. 435-453.

## 3. *The Lamanites.*

20. Wherefore, the word of the Lord was fulfilled which he spake unto me, saying that: Inasmuch as they will not hearken unto thy words they shall be cut off from the presence of the Lord. And behold, they were cut off from his presence.

---

VERSE 20. *The Presence of the Lord.* Through his Spirit, God is everywhere.

> "Whither shall I go from thy Spirit?
> Or whither shall I flee from thy presence?
> If I ascend up into heaven, thou art there:
> If I make my bed in hell, behold thou art there.
> If I take the wings of the morning,
> And dwell in the uttermost parts of the sea:
> Even there shall thy hand lead me,
> And thy right hand shall hold me."          —Psalm 139:7-10.

But on special occasions, the presence of God, or his messengers, have had special manifestations.

When the law was given on Sinai, the presence of God was manifested in a dark electric cloud. The lightnings flashed, the thunders rolled, the voice of the Lord came like trumpet blasts. The entire mountain shook. (Ex. 19:16-19)

Then, when the tabernacle was all completed and dedicated, a cloud descended on it and the glory of the Lord filled it. All Israel could see this cloud by day, and the fire by night, and follow its indications. (Ex. 40:34-38)

When the temple of Solomon was dedicated, "the cloud filled the house of the Lord, so that the priests could not stand to minister because of the cloud: for the glory of the Lord had filled the house of the Lord." (1 Kings 8:10-11)

This manifestation of the presence of God among his children has been called the "Shekina," a word that means "to dwell in a tent," to "tabernacle." John, in his Gospel (1:14) says, of our Lord: "And the Word became flesh and dwelt among us." That is, he "tabernacled" among us.[2]

There was a rabbinical saying to the effect that, "Where two or three are together to study the Torah"—the Law of Moses—"the Shekina is in their midst." Our Lord, it will be recalled, said to his disciples, "Where two or three are gathered together in my name, there am I in the midst of them"; (Matt. 18:20) thereby comparing himself to the Shekina of the Old Testament—The Glory of God. His parting promise was: "And, lo, I am with you always even unto the end of the world." (Matt. 28:20)

The "presence of the Lord" means, first, his omnipresence. The Lamanites were not outside this all-embracing sphere. But it means, secondly, the special manifestations which God gives his children, "that through the power and manifestation of the Spirit, while in the flesh, they may be able to bear his presence in the world of glory" (D. and C. 76:118). From such special manifestations the Lamanites had cut themselves off. They no longer had revelations, and were, therefore, on the road to moral degeneration and final destruction. For,

> "Where there is no vision, the people perish;
> But he that keepeth the law, happy is he."          —Prov. 29:18.

These two lines must be read together. They mean that when revelation is withdrawn, lawlessness takes its place. But the end of lawlessness is destruction.

---

[2]The original is, "eskænosen en hæmin."

21. And he had caused the cursing to come upon them, yea, even a sore cursing, because of their iniquity. For behold, they had hardened their hearts against him, that they had become like unto a flint; wherefore, as they were white, and exceeding fair and delightsome, that they might not be enticing unto my people the Lord God did cause a skin of blackness to come upon them.

22. And thus saith the Lord God: I will cause that they shall be loathsome unto thy people, save they shall repent of their iniquities.

23. And cursed shall be the seed of him that mixeth with their seed; for they shall be cursed even with the same cursing. And the Lord spake it, and it was done.

24. And because of their curs-

VERSE 21. *White, Fair and Delightsome.* There can be no doubt that the Indians originally were "white." Dr. Ales Hrdlicka, the famous Smithsonian anthropologist, is quoted to the effect that the American Indian is a closer cousin to the white man, physically, than popularly supposed. He founded this conclusion on thousands of measurements and observations on individuals of both races, beginning with his original work on the Pueblo Indians in 1898.

In this verse the darkening of the skin is said to be one result of transgression, and for a special purpose. Microscopists are said to have ascertained that,

"Complexions are not permanent physical characteristics, but are subject to change. Climate is a cause of physical differences, and frequently in a single tribe may be found shades of color extending through the various transitions from black to white." (Bancroft, Native Races, Vol. 1, p. 14)

*Skin of Blackness.* While the family of Lehi was camping in the Valley of Lemuel (1 Ne. 2:23), the Lord manifested to Nephi, then a young boy, that he would be made a ruler among his brethren, and that if they rebelled, a great curse would be the consequence. Later, he saw in a vision (1 Ne. 12:23) that the descendants of his brethren had become dark and loathsome. See also Alma 3:6-11, and Mormon 5:15. That was the curse, due to rebellion.

To those who still divide the human race according to color and consider each class a race, separated from all the others by an impassable gulf, this explanation of the mystery of color may not appear satisfactory. But the classification on color lines —in view of the statement of the Apostle Paul on Marshill, at Athens, that God has made of one blood all nations of men, (Acts 17:26)—cannot be accepted as scientific, although it is convenient for common purposes. We must after all agree with a contributor to the "American Anthropologist" for Oct.-Dec., 1924, p. 489, who says:

"It must be observed that the colors assigned to these five types are purely imaginary. We are all of us, 'black' and 'white,' really brown. The Negro is not black but chocolate colored (a fact which some artists have not discovered yet). The Chinese is not yellow, the Indian is not red, and the white are by no means white, as anyone may see for himself by viewing his hand on a sheet of note paper. The actual pigment is a sepia colored material known as melanin, which is the same in all, the Negroes having a plentiful supply of it, while others have a scanty suffused charge."

If we believe in the unity of the human race, we can also believe that the complexion of individuals and groups can be affected by food, climate, habits and even emotions.

VERSES 22-24. In these paragraphs further consequences of the great schism are enumerated.

ing which was upon them they did become an idle people, full of mischief and subtlety, and did seek in the wilderness for beasts of prey.

25. And the Lord God said unto me: They shall be a scourge unto thy seed, to stir them up in remembrance of me; and inasmuch as they will not remember me, and hearken unto my words, they shall scourge them even unto destruction.

### 4. Jacob and Joseph Ordained.

26. And it came to pass that I, Nephi, did consecrate Jacob and Joseph, that they should be priests and teachers over the land of my people.

27. And it came to pass that we lived after the manner of happiness.

28. And thirty years had passed away from the time we left Jerusalem.

### 5. The two volumes of plates.

29. And I, Nephi, had kept the records upon my plates, which I had made, of my people thus far.

30. And it came to pass that the Lord God said unto me: Make other plates; and thou shalt engraven many things upon them which are good in my sight, for the profit of thy people.

31. Wherefore, I, Nephi, to be obedient to the commandments of the Lord, went and made these plates upon which I have engraven these things.

32. And I engraved that which is pleasing unto God. And if my people are pleased with the things of God they will be pleased with mine engravings which are upon these plates.

33. And if my people desire to know the more particular part of the history of my people they must search mine other plates.

34. And it sufficeth me to say that forty years had passed away, and we had already had wars and contentions with our brethren.

---

VERSE 25.   Here is a warning to the descendants of Nephi: Lamanites would be a scourge to them, and unless they (that is, the descendants of Nephi) would remember the Lord and hearken to his words, they would be scourged to destruction.

VERSES 26-28.   *Jacob and Joseph were ordained Priests and Teachers.* Nephi had built a temple (v. 16). In it the Mosaic law was observed. Under that law, the priests were appointed to offer up sacrifices for the people as well as for themselves. (Lev. 4:5, 6) Under that law, priests were also the teachers of the people, as appears from the following:

"Do not drink wine or strong drink, thou, nor thy sons with thee, when ye go into the tabernacle of the congregation, lest ye die: it shall be a statute for ever throughout your generations: and that ye may put difference between holy and unholy, and between clean and unclean; and that ye may teach the children of Israel all the statutes which the Lord hath spoken to them by the hand of Moses. (Lev. 10:9-11)

VERSES 29-34.   On the two volumes of plates, see 1 Ne. 9, and notes.

## CHAPTER 6

*A Discourse by Jacob—The Introduction, 1-5—Isaiah* (49:22, 23) *Quoted* 6, 7—*Comments by Jacob, 8-15—Isaiah* (49:24-26) *Quoted, 16-18.*

### 1. *The Introduction.*

1. The words of Jacob, the brother of Nephi, which he spake unto the people of Nephi:

2. Behold, my beloved brethren, I, Jacob, having been called of God, and ordained after the manner of his holy order, and having been consecrated by my brother Nephi, unto whom ye look as a king or a protector, and on whom ye depend for safety, behold ye know that I have spoken unto you exceeding many things.

3. Nevertheless, I speak unto you again; for I am desirous for the welfare of your souls. Yea, mine anxiety is great for you; and ye yourselves know that it ever has been. For I have exhorted you with all diligence; and I have taught you the words of my father; and I have spoken unto you concerning all things which are written, from the creation of the world.

4. And now, behold, I would speak unto you concerning things which are, and which are to come; wherefore, I will read you the words of Isaiah. And they are the words which my brother has

VERSE 1. *The Words of Jacob.* Jacob, the brother of Nephi, begins a discourse, in which he, at the request of his brother, quotes at length from the prophet Isaiah. It is, perhaps, his first public discourse after he had been appointed a priest and teacher. (2 Ne. 5:26)

For various reasons it is an important sermon. It proves that the latter part of Isaiah, which some modern critics like to consider as the work of a "second" Isaiah, was accepted as genuine at the time of Nephi, as it was in the days of our Lord. It shows us that the Nephites held meetings for worship and instruction, as is done in our days, and that they based their addresses on the holy Scriptures, as we do.

VERSE 2. *His Authority.* Jacob was "called" of God. He was "ordained" after the manner of his holy order, and he was "consecrated" by his brother.

*King.* Nephi was regarded as a king, but not as a despot. As a "protector." As a king he was the servant of the people. But he was also a prophet, and as such, he spoke and acted for the Lord.

VERSE 3. *The Words of my Father.* Jacob had spoken to the people before. He had given them the same instructions that his father had given him. And he had spoken concerning "all things which are written, from the creation of the world." He had evidently told the people the story of the world, as we have it in Genesis, and of the dealings of God with his people, as recorded in other Scriptures. Those are the proper subjects of discourses at all times, in religious meetings. The Bible contains the word of God to man, as do the other sacred Scriptures.

VERSE 4. *The Words of Isaiah.* Jacob is about to deliver an address on the present and the future, and begins by quoting a section of the Prophet Isaiah, commencing with chapt. 49:22. The Prophet Mormon (8:23) exhorts the people to,

desired that I should speak unto you. And I speak unto you for your sakes, that ye may learn and glorify the name of your God.

5. And now, the words which I shall read are they which Isaiah spake concerning all the house of Israel; wherefore, they may be likened unto you, for ye are of the house of Israel. And there are many things which have been spoken by Isaiah which may be likened unto you, because ye are of the house of Israel.

## 2. Isaiah 49:22, 23 Quoted.

6. And now, these are the words: Thus saith the Lord God: Behold, I will lift up mine hand to the Gentiles, and set up my standard to the people; and they shall bring thy sons in their arms, and thy daughters shall be carried upon their shoulders.

7. And kings shall be thy nursing fathers, and their queens thy nursing mothers; they shall bow down to thee with their faces towards the earth, and lick up the dust of thy feet; and thou shalt know that I am the Lord; for they shall not be ashamed that wait for me.

---

"Search the prophecies of Isaiah." His name signifies, "The Salvation of God," and he has been called the evangelical prophet, because his chief theme is the advent of the Savior, the first and second, his character and work, and the extension of his kingdom. He is, moreover, worth studying for the real excellency of his style, which is simple, clear, elegant and dignified.

VERSE 6. *Lift up mine hand to the Gentiles.* Signifies to "beckon them" to come.

*Set up my Standard.* During the journey of Israel from Egypt, each tribe was marching under some standard. On the east side of the Tabernacle were Judah, Issachar and Sebulon under the standard of Judah. On the south side were Reuben, Simeon and Gad under the standard of Reuben. On the west side were Ephraim, Manasseh and Benjamin under the standard of Ephraim. On the north side were Dan, Asher and Naphtali under the standard of Dan. (Numb, chap. 2) Now the Lord has another standard, under which both Jews and Gentiles may unite on their way to the Land of Promise. That standard is the Everlasting Gospel. Comp. Is. 13:2:

> "Lift ye up a banner upon the high mountains,
> Exalt the voice unto them;
> Shake the hand that they may go
> Into the gates of the nobles."

*On their Shoulders.* The palanquins in which the wealthy Orientals traveled were carried on the shoulders of men.

VERSE 7. *Kings . . . Nursing Fathers.* This prediction was literally fulfilled when, in November, 1917, Lord Balfour declared that the British government would look with favor upon the restoration of Palestine as the Jewish homeland, a declaration that was ratified later by a conference of statesmen at San Remo, and, on July 22, 1922, by the League of Nations, when that world organization assigned to Great Britain the mandate for the country.

*Lick up the dust.* A figure of speech which signifies humble submission.

## 3. Comments by Jacob.

8. And now I, Jacob, would speak somewhat concerning these words. For behold, the Lord has shown me that those who were at Jerusalem, from whence we came, have been slain and carried away captive.

9. Nevertheless, the Lord has shown unto me that they should return again. And he also has

---

The interpretation of Jacob may be stated briefly.

Jerusalem had fallen. Some of the inhabitants had been slain; others had been carried away into captivity. Jacob had seen this, probably in a vision, (v. 8) as had Nephi. (2 Ne. 1:4) But he had also seen that "they shall return." (v. 9) He had seen that the Messiah would come at the appointed time, and that he would be rejected and slain on a cross. (v. 9) Then the people would be ripe for the judgments of God. They would be "driven to and fro," and many would be "smitten and afflicted." (v. 10) They would be scattered and hated, but on account of the prayers of those who are faithful, they would be gathered when they accept the Crucified One as their Redeemer. (v. 11)

Now the Gentiles that have befriended Zion and not fought against the covenant people, nor joined the abominable church "shall be saved" (vv. 12, 13); for the Messiah will come a second time and recover his people. He will manifest himself in "fire, tempests, earthquakes, bloodshed, pestilence and famine," and thus demonstrate that the Lord—that is, Jesus Christ—"is God, the Holy One of Israel." (vv. 14, 15)

VERSE 8. *Carried Away.* Bible scholars recognize two great deportations. The first took place in the year 596 B.C., four years after the departure of Lehi from Jerusalem. Lehi was then about half way through the desert journey, which lasted eight years in all, and Jacob must have been a baby, since he was born in the desert. Lehi may have had a vision of this deportation. If so, he would certainly have related that vision to his family many times.

On this occasion Nebuchadnezzar carried away King Jehoiachin and family, the Prophet Ezekiel and thousands of nobles and craftsmen. He destroyed the sacred vessels in the temple and looted the treasuries. And, finally, he appointed an uncle of Jehoiachin, Zedekiah, king in Jerusalem. (2 Kings 24:10-14)

The second deportation took place in the year 586 B.C., ten years after the first. On that occasion all monumental and otherwise valuable buildings in Jerusalem were destroyed by fire. Everything of value was carried to Babylon. Some of the children of Zedekiah were cruelly butchered before his eyes, and that was the last thing he saw, before his eyes were put out. Gedaliah was made ruler in Jerusalem.

As near as can be judged from Book of Mormon chronology, Lehi had passed away at that time. The Nephites had established themselves as an independent colony, and Jacob and Joseph had been appointed priests and teachers. (See 2 Ne. 5:28) It is more than probable that the Lord gave Jacob a vision of this second deportation shortly after it had taken place in the year 586 B.C., as he gave Lehi a vision of the first deportation. The Prophet Ezekiel and the captives in Babylon were notified by a special messenger of the epochal event. (Ex. 33:21)

VERSE 9. *They Should Return.* They did return under Zerubbabel in 537 B.C. The rebuilding of the temple was begun in 520 B.C., and in 444 B.C., Ezra read the law in Jerusalem.

shown unto me that the Lord God, the Holy One of Israel, should manifest himself unto them in the flesh; and after he should manifest himself they should scourge him and crucify him, according to the words of the angel who spake it unto me.

10. And after they have hardened their hearts and stiffened their necks against the Holy One of Israel, behold, the judgments of the Holy One of Israel shall come upon them. And the day cometh that they shall be smitten and afflicted.

11. Wherefore, after they are driven to and fro, for thus saith the angel, many shall be afflicted in the flesh, and shall not be suffered to perish, because of the prayers of the faithful; they shall be scattered, and smitten, and hated; nevertheless, the Lord will be merciful unto them, that when they shall come to the knowledge of their Redeemer, they shall be gathered together again to the lands of their inheritance.

12. And blessed are the Gentiles, they of whom the prophet has written; for behold, if it so be that they shall repent and fight not against Zion, and do not unite themselves to that great and abominable church, they shall be saved; for the Lord God will fulfill his covenants which he has made unto his children; and for this cause the prophet has written these things.

13. Wherefore, they that fight against Zion and the covenant people of the Lord shall lick up the dust of their feet; and the people of the Lord shall not be ashamed. For the people of the Lord are they who wait for him; for they still wait for the coming of the Messiah.

14. And behold, according to the words of the prophet, the Messiah will set himself again the second time to recover them; wherefore, he will manifest himself unto them in power and great glory, unto the destruction of their enemies, when that day cometh when they shall believe in him; and none will he destroy that believe in him.

15. And they that believe not in him shall be destroyed, both by fire, and by tempest, and by earthquakes, and by bloodsheds, and by pestilence, and by famine. And they shall know that the Lord is God, the Holy One of Israel.

---

VERSE 11. *Gathered Again.* Jacob had seen that, after they had rejected the Messiah, they would be scattered and subjected to many sufferings, but also gathered for a second time. In the year 70 A.D. Titus destroyed Jerusalem. Our Lord had said (Luke 21:24) that Jerusalem should be trodden down by the Gentiles "until the times of the Gentiles be fulfilled." Emperor Julian (331-63 A.D.), in order to discredit the prophecies and please the Jews, encouraged these to rebuild the city and the temple. But the work was interrupted by earthquakes and flames of fire—remarkable phenomena for which even the famous Gibbon has found it difficult to account. Furthermore, during the so-called Crusades a series of "holy" wars, started by Pope Urban II, begun in 1096 and lasting, off and on, until

## 4. *Isaiah 49:24-26 Quoted.*

16. For shall the prey be taken from the mighty, or the lawful captive delivered?

17. But thus saith the Lord: Even the captives of the mighty shall be taken away, and the prey of the terrible shall be delivered; for the Mighty God shall deliver his covenant people. For thus saith the Lord: I will contend with them that contendeth with thee—

18. And I will feed them that oppress thee, with their own flesh; and they shall be drunken with their own blood as with sweet wine; and all flesh shall know that I the Lord am thy Savior and thy Redeemer, the Mighty One of Jacob.

---

1272 A.D., all western Europe was united in efforts at rescuing the Holy Land from the domination of the Gentiles. But it was all in vain. Romans, Greeks, Persians, Turks and Arabs continued to trample Jerusalem under foot.

VERSE 16. *The Mighty.* Refers to Nebuchadnezzar and others who held Judah captive. The skeptic would ask whether anyone would be able to rescue the Jews from the power of the mighty world conquerors. God answers in vv. 17 and 18.

VERSE 18. *Their own Flesh . . . their own Blood.* Signifies internal wars. And they will go on, until all shall know that Jesus Christ is their Savior and Redeemer.

### GENERAL NOTES

Alma, the valiant defender of the martyr Abinadi, and the preacher of repentance at the Waters of Mormon, ordained priests—one to each fifty members, "to preach unto them, and to teach them concerning the things pertaining to the kingdom of God." (Mosiah 18:18-22) They were instructed to preach and teach what he, Alma, had taught them, and especially repentance and faith on the Lord. He was a High Priest. (Mos. 23:16; 26:7; 29:42)

Alma, the son of Alma the First, also consecrated "teachers and priests and elders over the church." (Alma 4:7)

Priests and Elders were ordained by Alma, in Zarahemla, "by laying on his hands according to the order of God, to preside and watch over the church." (Alma 6:1) In Moroni, Chap. 3, we have the words spoken by the elders when they ordained priests and teachers. They were undoubtedly given to them by our Lord himself.

Jacob was called of God. "No man"—not even the Son of God—"taketh this honor unto himself," but he must be called by God, as was Aaron. (Heb. 5:4-10)

Concerning the consecration of Aaron we read in Exodus 28th and 29th chapters. Special garments were made for him, "for glory and for beauty," consisting of a breastplate, an ephod, a robe, an embroidered coat, a mitre and a girdle. The breastplate was a pocket worn on the chest, made of fine linen and embroidered with gold, blue, purple and scarlet yarn. Some of the other pieces were made of the same kind of material and similarly ornamented. In the breastplate, Aaron carried the urim and thummim, wherefore it became known as the "breastplate of judgment." On his shoulders Aaron had two onyx stones, on which the names of the twelve tribes of Israel were engraved, six names on each stone, "for a memorial before the Lord," and on the mitre there was a gold plate, on which the words, "Holiness to the Lord" were engraved.

## CHAPTER 7

*The Cause of Separation from God, 1-3 — A "Servant Poem," 4-9 — An Important Question, 10, 11.*

### 1. *The Cause of Separation.*

1. Yea, for thus saith the Lord: Have I put thee away, or have I cast thee off forever? For thus saith the Lord: Where is the bill of your mother's divorcement? To whom have I put thee away, or to which of my creditors have I sold you? Yea, to whom have I sold you? Behold, for your iniquities have ye sold yourselves, and for your transgressions is your mother put away.

2. Wherefore, when I came, there was no man; when I called, yea, there was none to answer. O house of Israel, is my hand shortened at all that it cannot redeem, or have I no power to deliver? Behold, at my rebuke I dry up the sea, I make their rivers a wilderness and their fish to stink because the waters are dried up, and they die because of thirst.

3. I clothe the heavens with blackness, and I make sackcloth their covering.

### 2. *A "Servant" Poem.*

4. The Lord God hath given me the tongue of the learned, that I should know how to speak a word in season unto thee, O house of Israel. When ye are weary he waketh morning by morning. He waketh mine ear to hear as the learned.

---

VERSE 1. *To Whom Have I Put Thee Away?* Our Lord is still discussing the question in the preceding chapter, paragraph 16: "Shall the prey be taken from the mighty?" In this passage he sees Israel, the nation, as a mother of many children, the individual Israelites, all absent from their home, but not through any act of his. He had not given her a bill of divorcement. He had not sold the children to satisfy any creditor. In either case he might not have a legal right to reclaim them. But, they had given themselves away by their iniquities and transgressions. They had "sold" themselves.

VERSES 2 and 3. *An Empty House.* And so, the Lord says, when I came home, there was no man to take care of my carriage and animals; when I called, there was no one to answer.

The Lord now reminds Israel of his omnipotence, as a warning of what they may expect as a consequence of their desertion to a strange master.

#### "SERVANT POEMS"

Some commentators recognize in the Prophet Isaiah four pieces of poetry to which they have given the name of "Servant Poems," because they refer to Israel, the nation, as the servant of the Lord, and its mission in the world.

In the first of these, Is. 42:1-4, God says he has sent his Spirit to his "servant," enabling him to bring justice to the world, and that the isles are waiting for the

5. The Lord God hath opened mine ear, and I was not rebellious, neither turned away back.
6. I gave my back to the smiter, and my cheeks to them that plucked off the hair. I hid not my face from shame and spitting.

---

revelation of the law of God. In the second, Is. 49:1-6, Israel, the servant, says he was called to his mission, even before he was born. In the third, Is. 50:4-10, the servant relates his sufferings and expresses implicit faith in God. In the fourth, Isaiah 52:13-53:12, the author predicts future glory of the servant, after a period of sufferings and humiliation.

Note the last verse:

> "Therefore will I divide him a portion with the great,
> And he shall divide the spoil with the strong;
> Because he has poured out his soul unto death,
> And he was numbered with the transgressors,
> And he bare the sins of many,
> And made intercession for the transgressors."

If we understand this to refer to Israel, the nation, it was fulfilled, partly, when Palestine, after World War I, was recognized as the homeland of the Jews. They certainly, at that time, received a portion of the spoil with the great and strong nations of the world. If we understand it to refer more particularly to the Messiah, as it certainly does, it has also been fulfilled in part, by the preponderance of the Christian civilization in the world. Our Lord has, if only nominally a large portion in the distribution of the earth among the strong and mighty. But the greatest glory is yet to come. (See Is. 54)

VERSE 4. *The Tongue of the Learned.* It is the "Servant" who is speaking. God, he says, had inspired him to speak with the tongue of a scholar, to encourage the weary. The prophets of old did not speak except by divine guidance. Com. Ezekiel 33:22, where the prophet says that the Lord opened his mouth, so that he was no longer silent as to prophesying concerning Israel, as he had been for about three years. (Ez. 24:1, 27)

VERSE 5. *Opened mine Ear.* Part of the ceremony of consecration of Aaron, in the Mosaic dispensation, was the application of a drop of sacrificial blood to the right ear, to signify his willingness to hear and obey the laws of God (Ex. 29:20). A similar ceremony, with the same import, was part of the healing of a leper. (Lev. 14:14) The "servant" in this paragraph, therefore, says that the Lord had healed him, giving him the Priesthood, and made him willing to obey. This is particularly true in our day when the restored Gospel is received chiefly by those in whose veins the blood of Israel is flowing.

VERSE 6. *The Smiter.* The persecutor. The history of the Jews in the dispersion is a most marvelous section of human annals. With the ascendency of the religion of the professedly Christian world, the persecution of the Jews assumed, at times, cruel and decidedly unchristian forms. In some countries they were taxed exorbitantly, and yet prohibited from making a decent living. They were driven from pillar to post, and at times exiled, although there was no place of refuge for them. The 11th-15th centuries were a dark period. In 1290 they were driven from England. In 1395, from France. In Germany they were at times, regarded as the property of the sovereigns, who considered themselves at liberty to buy them and sell them at will. And yet, the Jews, notwithstanding all persecution and suffering, have multiplied until today they number over fifteen

7. For the Lord God will help me, therefore shall I not be confounded. Therefore have I set my face like a flint, and I know that I shall not be ashamed.

8. And the Lord is near, and he justifieth me. Who will contend with me? Let us stand together. Who is mine adversary? Let him come near me, and I will smite him with the strength of my mouth.

9. For the Lord God will help me. And all they who shall condemn me, behold, all they shall wax old as a garment, and the moth shall eat them up.

## 3. An Important Question

10. Who is among you that feareth the Lord, that obeyeth the voice of his servant, that walketh in darkness and hath no light?

11. Behold all ye that kindle fire, that compass yourselves about with sparks, walk in the light of your fire and in the sparks which ye have kindled. This shall ye have of mine hand—ye shall lie down in sorrow.

---

million souls in all parts of the world. They have given to the world statesmen, musicians, philosophers, writers and, of course, financiers of great eminence. It has been said with truth that there is not now one country which does not count Jews among the foremost and most brilliant representatives of its progress. In World War I Great Britain had five battalions of the Royal fusiliers, exclusively Jews, many of whom lived in the United States. They were known as "Judeans," and they served with distinction in Allenby's campaign in Palestine in 1918. The Jews, as a nation, have their peculiarities, but as a whole they have, as stated in this poem of the servant, suffered patiently, and generally returned good for evil.

Verses 7-9. This is the language of perfect confidence in the protection of God. "God will help me." "The Lord is near." "He justifieth me." And the enemies will wear themselves out, until they look like old, discarded garments, destroyed by moths.

Verses 10-11. *Who hath no Light?* In these paragraphs the prophet challenges the world to point out anyone who fears the Lord and listens to the voice of his servant and yet walks in the dark, without light. Is there any such, whether an individual or a nation?

On the other hand, he claims that those who enter into an alliance with Egypt, or, in a modern theological term, "the world," are only encircling themselves with sparks, that splutter a moment and then leave them in the dark, where they are liable to stumble and fall.

"And this shall ye have of my hand—Ye shall lie down in sorrow." Behold and lo, there are none to deliver you; for ye obeyed not my voice when I called to you out of the heavens; ye believed not my servants, and when they were sent unto you ye received them not. Wherefore, they sealed up the testimony and bound up the law, and ye were delivered over unto darkness." (D. and C. 133:70-72)

### GENERAL NOTES

I have taken the view that the so-called "servant poems," in the first place, refer to Israel, as a nation, its world-wide mission, its sufferings because of the wickedness of its opponents, its final deliverance and restoration to glory and of happiness in the presence of the Lord. It should be added that, in the second place, it refers to the spiritual Israel, which is the church and kingdom of Christ, entrusted with the mission of bringing the message of salvation to the world, by the proclamation of the Gospel, obedience to God's laws and patient suffering. In the third place, it refers to the Messiah, the Lamb of God, who came to the children of men as their Savior and Redeemer. He was, and is, the Servant in whose life, death, and resurrection to glory these prophecies were, and will be, literally fulfilled in everything, except that he was sinless, so that his sufferings were wholly as a substitute for his brethren. They refer, in fact to every servant of the Lord, who has engaged in the work of the Master, and especially to every martyr for his cause. As the Apostle Paul says: "Now I rejoice in my sufferings for your sake and fill up on my part that which is lacking of the afflictions of Christ in my flesh for his body's sake, which is the church." (Col. 1:24)

Every faithful martyr for Christ is a "lamb of God" slain for the benefit of the world; not in the sense of atonement for sin; but in this sense: Faithfulness that endures sufferings, and even death, for a cause, is the strongest possible evidence of truth and the value of that cause. The testimony of martyrdom brings, therefore, more converts than a mere verbal testimony. The blood of the martyrs has always been the "seed of the church." Millions have been converted to Christ by that testimony. (Comp. 2 Cor. 4:8-12)

The financial power of the Jews may be inferred from the fact that Palestine during the years 1934-36 absorbed 150,000 of that race, and that American Jews alone, during 1936, contributed $2,076,327 for colonization, immigration and improvement of the country.

## CHAPTER 8

*God Speaks to His People, 1-8 — The People of God Responds, 9-11 — God Speaks, 12-25.*

### 1. *God speaks to his people.*

1. Hearken unto me, ye that follow after righteousness. Look unto the rock from whence ye are hewn, and to the hole of the pit from whence ye are digged.

2. Look unto Abraham, your father, and unto Sarah, she that bare you; for I called him alone, and blessed him.

3. For the Lord shall comfort Zion, he will comfort all her waste places; and he will make her wilderness like Eden, and her desert like the garden of the Lord.

Joy and gladness shall be found therein, thanksgiving and the voice of melody.

4. Hearken unto me, my people; and give ear unto me, O my nation; for a law shall proceed from me, and I will make my judgment to rest for a light for the people.

5. My righteousness is near; my salvation is gone forth, and mine arm shall judge the people. The isles shall wait upon me, and on mine arm shall they trust.

---

This chapter is a dialogue between God and his people. In the first eight verses God speaks. In the next three, the people respond. Then God speaks again, to the end of the chapter.

VERSE 1. *The Rock.* Means ancestors. See next verse. Wise are the children who remember their parents and lineage, and profit by their experiences.

VERSE 2. *Look unto Abraham and Sarah.* The Lord reminds his people that he had called Abraham while he was alone—that is, without children, and blessed him.

VERSE 3. *The Lord shall comfort Zion.* He who kept his promises to Abraham and Sarah, will also keep his promises to their descendants. This concerns specially Palestine. Her wilderness will be turned into a "garden of the Lord." Joy and gladness will be found there. But it is true also of every place where Zion is established. There will be no deserts, only gardens, with thanksgiving and the voice of melody.

VERSE 4. *Law shall Proceed from Me.* The Lord here promises to give his people a new law. That means a new dispensation. See Heb. 7:11-19, where the Apostle tells us that if perfection had been obtained by means of the Levitical legislation and Priesthood, there would have been no need of another Priesthood—the Melchizedek—or other legislative enactments. But, he says, when the Priesthood is changed, there is also a change of the law. But it must come from God. "Wherefore I, the Lord, knowing the calamity which should come upon the inhabitants of the earth, called upon my servant Joseph Smith, Jun., and spake unto him from heaven, and gave him commandments . . . that mine everlasting covenant might be established." (D. and C. 1:17-22; see also D. and C. 22:1; 45:9; 54:4, 5)

VERSE 5. *Mine Arm shall Judge the People.* This means that the Lord will exercise the judiciary functions as well as the legislative. The isles, which refers specially to the smaller kingdoms, will rely on him.

6. Lift up your eyes to the heavens, and look upon the earth beneath; for the heavens shall vanish away like smoke, and the earth shall wax old like a garment; and they that dwell therein shall die in like manner. But my salvation shall be forever, and my righteousness shall not be abolished.

7. Hearken unto me, ye that know righteousness, the people in whose heart I have written my law, fear ye not the reproach of men, neither be ye afraid of their revilings.

8. For the moth shall eat them up like a garment, and the worm shall eat them like wool. But my righteousness shall be forever, and my salvation from generation to generation.

## 2. *The people of God respond*: 9-11.

9. Awake, awake! Put on strength, O arm of the Lord; awake as in the ancient days. Art thou not he that hath cut Rahab, and wounded the dragon?

10. Art thou not he who hath dried the sea, the waters of the great deep; that hath made the depths of the sea a way for the ransomed to pass over?

---

VERSE 6. *My Salvation for Ever.* Abraham was directed to look up to heaven and count, if he could, the sparkling stars. He could not. He was then informed that his descendants would also be innumerable. (Gen. 15:5) The stars were now an evidence to him of the unlimited powers of God. His descendants are here told to behold the heavens and to remember that, although the entire universe is subject to change, and apparent destruction, as a smoke that vanishes, yet the salvation of God remains the same for ever, and his righteousness will never be abolished. Here is something permanent, not depending on changing fashions not left behind because of the progress of civilization or the increase of knowledge. What was right and good and pleasing to our heavenly Father at the beginning, is good and right and pleasing today and will remain so for ever and ever. It is interesting to note, what the sacred Scriptures say of the stars,

"Instead of supposing a thousand, as ancient astronomers did (Hipparchus says 1022, Ptolemy 1026), they declare that they are innumerable; a declaration which modern telescopes discover to be not even a figure of speech. 'God,' says Sir John Hershel, after surveying the groups of stars and nebulae in the heavens, 'has scattered them like dust through the immensity of space.' And when the Scriptures speak of their hosts, it is as dependent, material, obedient things." (Dr. Joseph Angus)

VERSES 7-8. *In whose Heart . . . my Law.* Those in whose hearts the law of God is written, so that it has become part of their nature to live accordingly, have no occasion to fear their enemies. God will destroy these like old rags eaten by moths. But the principles of salvation remain for ever.

VERSE 9. *Rahab.* Means "defiance," "pride," and refers here to Egypt, as in Psalm 87:4: "I will make mention of Rahab and Babylon to them that know me: behold Philistia, and Tyre, with Ethiopia; this was born there."

This is a remarkable plea of the people of God before his throne. The very mention of Rahab in this place recalls the day of judgment when all nations shall be gathered before the Son of Man, and he shall separate them (the nations) as a shepherd divideth his sheep. (Matt. 25:31-3) The same thought is expressed in

11. Therefore, the redeemed of the Lord shall return, and come with singing unto Zion; and everlasting joy and holiness shall be upon their heads; and they shall obtain gladness and joy; sorrow and mourning shall flee away.

## 3. God speaks again.

12. I am he; yea, I am he that comforteth you. Behold, who art thou, that thou shouldst be afraid of man, who shall die, and of the son of man, who shall be made like unto grass?

13. And forgetest the Lord thy maker, that hath stretched forth the heavens, and laid the foundations of the earth, and hast feared continually every day, because of the fury of the oppressor, as if he were ready to destroy? And where is the fury of the oppressor?

14. The captive exile hasteneth, that he may be loosed, and that he should not die in the pit, nor that his bread should fail.

15. But I am the Lord thy

---

the Psalm, (87) where the text, however obscure, seems to teach that on the day of reckoning, some countries, among others, Egypt, Babylonia, Philistia, Tyre and Ethiopia, will be registered as natives, or friends, of Zion, when the Almighty (see verse 6) shall establish her. Consequently, the people of God will return to Zion, as to a country inhabited by friends.

At present (1955 A.D.) there seem to be troubles between natives and immigrating Jews in Palestine, but we may expect that these will be settled to the satisfaction of all, in due time.

VERSE 11. *Gladness and Joy.* Not frivolity. "My soul shall be joyful in the Lord: it shall rejoice in his salvation." (Psalm 35:9)

*The Word of the Lord.* In this section the Lord rebukes his people for fearing man, whose glory is but that of the grass, which, as our Lord says, "today is and tomorrow is cast into the oven." (Matt. 6:30), while forgetting the Almighty. "Awake, awake, O Jerusalem!" he says,—a call that is being heard throughout the world today. Jerusalem is awakening.

The Lord, further, reminds Jerusalem that she has none to guide her—no inspired prophets as of old, with divine authority to speak for him. Her sons, he says, have "fainted," while desolation and destruction have clung to her as a "wild bull in a net." (verse 20) Therefore, hear now, he says, the Lord. The Lord pleads her cause. The cup of trembling will be put into the hands of the oppressor (v. 23), while Zion will clothe herself in festive garments and rejoice in her new-born liberty. (vv. 24, 25)

The great lesson here is that the people of God must have that implicit faith in him, which is the fruit of obedience.

VERSE 12. *The son of man.* This sometimes refers to the Messiah. Christ used the title himself (Matt. 26:64), but here it means human beings generally.

VERSE 13. *Forgetting the Lord, thy Maker.* God expresses, as it were, astonishment at the possibility of this forgetfulness, since it was he that made the heavens and the earth. How can anybody, who lives in this glorious palace, forget the builder thereof?

God, whose waves roared; the Lord of Hosts is my name.

16. And I have put my words in thy mouth, and have covered thee in the shadow of mine hand, that I may plant the heavens and lay the foundations of the earth, and say unto Zion: Behold, thou art my people.

17. Awake, awake, stand up, O Jerusalem, which hast drunk at the hand of the Lord the cup of his fury—thou hast drunken the dregs of the cup of trembling wrung out—

18. And none to guide her among all the sons she hath brought forth; neither that taketh her by the hand, of all the sons she hath brought up.

19. These two sons are come unto thee, who shall be sorry for thee—thy desolation and destruction, and the famine and the sword—and by whom shall I comfort thee?

20. Thy sons have fainted, save these two; they lie at the head of all the streets; as a wild bull in a net, they are full of the fury of the Lord, the rebuke of thy God.

21. Therefore hear now this, thou afflicted, and drunken, and not with wine:

22. Thus saith thy Lord, the Lord and thy God pleadeth the cause of his people; behold, I have taken out of thine hand the cup of trembling, the dregs of the cup of my fury; thou shalt no more drink it again.

23. But I will put it into the hand of them that afflict thee; who have said to thy soul: Bow down, that we may go over—and thou hast laid thy body as the ground and as the street to them that went over.

24. Awake, awake, put on thy strength, O Zion; put on thy beautiful garments, O Jerusalem, the holy city; for henceforth there shall no more come into thee the uncircumcised and the unclean.

25. Shake thyself from the dust; arise, sit down, O Jerusalem; loose thyself from the bands of thy neck, O captive daughter of Zion.

VERSE 15. *The Lord of Hosts.* The sun is not the ruler of the planets and other stars. God is the Maker and the Lord of the sun and all the heavenly "hosts."

VERSE 16. *Plant the Heavens.* The heavens and the earth have been set up as a tent, like the tabernacle in the desert, God's dwelling, in order that he might say to Zion, Behold thou art my people. The Temple service is one connecting link between God and his people.

VERSES 24-25. *Awake, awake!* The section closes with the assurance that Jerusalem will be restored to more than her former independence, importance and glory. Note that the city is addressed as the "captive daughter of Zion." And the Lord says: "Shake thyself from the dust!" Arise from thy lowly position! Take the seat of honor! Throw off the yoke, O captive daughter of Zion!

## GENERAL NOTES

Old Testament prophecies concerning countries, and particularly those referred to in the notes under verse 9, are highly instructive.

*Egypt.* This was at one time one of the mighty kingdoms of the world. It is stated on the authority of Herodotus, the Greek historian, that it had no less than 20,000 cities and that the number of inhabitants was incredibly large. It was the cradle of art, industry, religion and learning. Some of its monuments in stone are still so many riddles of the ages.

But prophets of the Lord declared that it would become "the basest of kingdoms" —that is to say, a kingdom with little political influence—"neither shall it exalt itself any more above the nations; for I will diminish them, that they shall no more rule over the nations." (Ezek. 29:15) Egypt, in fulfilment of this prophecy, and others, has seen its extraordinarily productive fields occupied in succession by Persians, Macedonians, Romans, Greeks, Arabs and the Ottomans. Strangers have ruled the richest of God's strip of earth, and the native inhabitants have been serfs. Isaiah (19:4-10) and Ezekiel (chaps. 30-31) predicted the complete downfall and desolation of Egypt.

But the prophets also predicted the restoration of Egypt. Isaiah (19:22-25) has this remarkable forecast:

"And they"—the Egyptians—"shall return to the Lord, and he shall be intreated of them, and shall heal them. In that day shall there be a highway out of Egypt to Assyria, and the Assyrian shall come into Egypt, and the Egyptian into Assyria, and the Egyptians shall serve with the Assyrians. In that day shall Israel be the third with Egypt and with Assyria, even a blessing in the midst of the land: whom the Lord of hosts shall bless, saying, Blessed be Egypt my people, and Assyria the work of my hands, and Israel mine inheritance."

The Lord also says through the Prophet Isaiah, to Israel:

"I am the Lord thy God, the Holy One of Israel, thy Savior: I gave Egypt for thy ransom, Ethiopia and Seba for thee." (Is. 43:3. Read the entire chapter)

It has been our privilege to see these prophecies, at least partly, fulfilled. Egypt now has a population of 14,213,000. Cairo, the capital, has 1,064,400, and Alexandria, 573,000 inhabitants. Her constitution, promulgated in 1930, declares Egypt an independent, sovereign state, with Islam as the state religion and Arabic the official language. A treaty of friendship with the United States was ratified by Parliament on May 26, 1930.

*Babylon.* If, says Dr. Keith, there ever was a city that could defy predictions of destruction, it was Babylon. For a long time it was the most famous city of the world. With its temples and palaces, its walls and hanging gardens, its dams for the control of the flood waters, its gigantic gates of copper, its artificial lake, it was the wonder of the world. The soil of the surrounding country was so rich that agriculture, according to Herodotus and others, yielded 200-fold, sometimes 300-fold. It was the center of a venerable civilization, of military power, of commerce, of arts and literature[1] and of worldly glory. But while the city was yet on the summit of power, prophets of the Lord predicted its downfall. (See 2 Ne. 23; or Is. 13) Isaiah says:

"Come down and sit in the dust, O virgin daughter of Babylon, sit on the ground: there is no throne, O daughter of the Chaldeans: for thou shalt no more be called tender and delicate . . . desolation shall come upon thee suddenly, which thou shalt not know." (Is. 47:1-11)

[1]It may interest the reader to know that, while many of the Babylonian records were preserved on cylinders of clay, baked in ovens or in the sun, some were engraved on metal plates, and that the characters on some are so small that they cannot be read except by the aid of a magnifying glass. It is said that there are specimens of this kind of records in the British Museum.

Jeremiah 50:1-3:

"Declare ye among the nations, and publish, and set up a standard; publish and conceal not; say, Babylon is taken, Bel is confounded, Merodach is broken in pieces; her idols are confounded, her images are broken in pieces. For out of the north there cometh up a nation against her, which shall make her land desolate, and none shall dwell therein: they shall remove, they shall depart, both man and beast."

These and other prophecies have all come true. During the 16th century ghostly remnants of the walls, built to last, seemingly for ever, were still marking the place whence Babylon once radiated its glory to the world; after that even these melancholy monuments of the past were buried so deeply that no trace of them could be found for centuries.

Babylonia, now resurrected in the kingdom of Irak, also spelled Iraq, is teeming with a population of Assyrians, Babylonians or Chaldeans, Arabs and Ottomans. It has a population of about three million souls. In 1932 it became an independent state under British protection. It is a limited monarchy with a parliament consisting of two chambers.

*Tyre.* This famous city, about 50 miles south of Beiruth, was once a mercantile world center, comparable in importance to New York, or London, of today. It was the capital of Phoenicia, the mother country of Carthage, the great rival of Rome, in the Mediterranean. Her sailors and merchants roamed all over the then known world.

But the prophets of the Lord predicted her downfall and destruction. Isaiah foretold that Tyre would fall and be utterly forgotten. (Is. 23:5, 8, 15) Ezekiel has this prediction:

"Thus saith the Lord God; Behold I am against thee, O Tyrus, and will cause many nations to come up against thee, as the sea causeth his waves to come up. And they shall destroy the walls of Tyrus, and break down her towers: I will also scrape her dust from her, and make her like the top of a rock. It shall be a place for the spreading of nets in the midst of the sea: for I have spoken it, saith the Lord God." (Ez. 26:1-6)

This has been fulfilled. Nebuchadnezzar laid siege to the city. It lasted for thirteen years, until, as Ezekiel says, "every head"—of his vast army—"was made bald and every shoulder was peeled"—from carrying burdens—"yet had he no wages, nor his army." (Ez. 29:18) The time had not yet come. About 270 years later, Alexander the Great accomplished its downfall.

Tyre was built on rocks in the sea, about a mile and a half from the shore. Alexander caused a road to be constructed through the water. This gigantic task completed, he threw the city with its 150 feet high walls into the deep, and swept the rocks on which it had stood. Fishermen did actually spread their nets on these rocks, to dry in the sun.

Isaiah has a remarkable prediction that may be noted here. He says: "Howl, ye ships of Tarshish; for it (Tyre) is laid waste, so that there is no house, no entering in; from the land of Chittim it is revealed to them. . . . Howl, ye ships of Tarshish: for your strength is laid waste." (Is. 23:1-14) "Ships of Tarshish" were sometimes absent on their voyages for two or three years. Imagine the consternation of the crews, when such ships came back and found no harbor in which to enter, no houses where the city had stood, only naked rocks, connected with the shore by means of a mole!

At the beginning of our era, a new Tyre was visited by the disciples of Christ. It had a temple and some churches. During the 7th century it came into the hands of the Saracenes, and then, in the 12th century, the crusaders. It was then a place of some importance. For 300 years it was ruled by the Turks. In 1834 it was visited by a destructive earthquake. Ten years later a traveler relates that when he and others came to the place and looked for a shop in which to buy some souvenirs, they found none. Fishermen were still spreading their nets on the rocks.

For a correct understanding of the movement known as Zionism, it is essential to study the prophecies concerning these and other near Oriental countries—their devastation, but also their restoration. For the convenant made with Abraham included all his descendants, and not only the Jews and the comparatively small country of Palestine. (See Gen. 15:18-21) It is a great problem, which, perhaps, only our Lord himself can solve.

*The Resurrection.* The doctrine of the resurrection of Jesus is the very keystone of Christianity. Peter, the Apostle, begins his First letter to the Saints thus:

"Blessed be the God and Father of our Lord Jesus Christ, which according to his abundant mercy hath begotten us again unto a lively hope by the resurrection of Jesus Christ from the dead" (1 Pet. 1:3); for, it was his resurrection that brought new life to his dismayed followers, and made them willing to die for their Master. St. Paul (1 Cor. 15:17-18) argues, that if Christ be not raised, then our faith is in vain; the dead have perished, and "we are of all men most miserable." Jacob, the son of Lehi, gives us a definite understanding of this, in this sermon (2 Ne. 9:8, 9), by explaining that, if "the flesh should rise no more," our spirits would become like the fallen angel and remain with him in misery, as his slaves forever.

In view of the importance of this doctrine, we may well ask, Is there sufficient evidence of its actuality?

Paul, the Apostle, who wrote a letter to the Corinthians as early as about 22 years after the crucifixion, gives, in that epistle a list of eye-witnesses to the appearance of Jesus after his death, thus: (1) Peter, (2) the Twelve, (3) more than 500 brethren, (4) James, (5) all the Apostles, and (6) himself. This list is confined to what we should call the Church authorities, who were well known, and to a conference, presumably in Galilee. The women, whose names are given by the evangelists, and the two men on their way to Emmaus, are not referred to by Paul, as they would be less known to the Corinthians.

But, it might be said, all these were friends of the Master, and not impartial witnesses.

Not quite all. Paul was a persecutor, when Jesus appeared to him, and he became a disciple as a result of that appearance—a miracle almost as great as the resurrection itself.

But there are other witnesses.

It appears that the governors of the Roman provinces always reported important events to the emperor in Rome. Pilate, therefore, kept memoirs of Jewish affairs during his procuratorship, called *Acta Pilati.* Referring to this usage, Eusebius, who has been called "the Father of Church History," and who lived at the close of the third and beginning of the fourth century, says, "Our Savior's resurrection being much talked of throughout Palestine, Pilate informed the emperor of it, as likewise of his miracles, of which he had heard; and that, being raised up after he had been put to death, he was already believed by many to be a God."

Such accounts were deposited in the archives of Rome and served as a source of information to historians. Hence, Justin Martyr, about the year 140 A.D., in his first "Apology," having mentioned the crucifixion of Jesus, adds, "And that these things were so done, you may know from the Acts made in the time of Pontius Pilate."

Tertullian, a prominent church father, about 200 A.D., in his "Apology," after speaking of the crucifixion, the resurrection and ascension, proceeds thus, "Of all these things relating to Christ, Pilate, himself in his conscience already a Christian, sent an account to Tiberius, then emperor. Tertullian also relates the following: "There was an ancient decree that no one should be received for a deity, unless he was first approved by the senate. Tiberius, in whose time the Christian name had its rise, having received from Palestine an account" of Christ, proposed to the senate that he should be enrolled among the Roman gods. But the senate rejected his proposition, because the emperor had declined a similar honor for himself.

I have quoted these paragraphs from Dr. Horne's monumental work, "An Introduction to the Critical Study of the Holy Scriptures." He mentions many other Hebrew and pagan witnesses for the historic accuracy of the New Testament narratives.

The only objection worth mentioning is the one that is recorded by Matthew. He says that the soldiers, detailed to guard the tomb, were bribed to report that the disciples had "stolen" the body while they slept.

Just a line of comment on that.

According to the Mosaic law (Num. 21:22, 23), the body of a malefactor that had been hung on a tree, should not remain in that position over night, "that thy land be not defiled." Accordingly, the conspirators went to Pilate, as soon as they learned that their innocent victim had passed away, to get the body. But when they came to Pilate, probably in order to get permission to dispose of the remains in the Valley of Hinnom, also called Tophet and Gehenna, where bodies of malefactors were sometimes cremated, and where "their worm dieth not, and the fire is not quenched" (Mark 9:44, 46, 48), they learned that Joseph of Arimathæa, who was a member of the Sanhedrin and in secret a disciple, had, by consent of Pilate, taken Jesus from the cross and laid him in his own tomb. When, immediately after the Sabbath, it was reported that Jesus had arisen and it became necessary, from their point of view, to account for the absence of the body, they naturally said, thinking of Joseph of Arimathæa, that the disciples had taken it away. They had; the disciples had taken it; but only from the cross, not from the grave. God had thwarted the plan of the wicked to have the body of his beloved Son cremated in the ever burning flames in the filthy valley of Gehenna.

Resurrection is a demonstrated fact. Because he lives, we shall live. And every Sunday, our Lord's day, should be, to us, an Easter Sunday.

## CHAPTER 9

*Jacob, on the Resurrection, 1-6—On the Atonement, 7-13—On the Judg-*
*ment, 14-22—On Salvation Through Repentance, Baptism, Faith, 23-26—A*
*Tenfold Wo, 27-38—On the Awfulness of Sin, 39-49—Exhortations, 50-54.*

## 1. On the Resurrection.

1. And now, my beloved brethren, I have read these things that ye might know concerning the covenants of the Lord that he has covenanted with all the house of Israel—

2. That he has spoken unto the Jews, by the mouth of his holy prophets, even from the beginning down, from generation to generation, until the time comes that they shall be restored to the true church and fold of God; when they shall be gathered home to the lands of their inheritance, and shall be established in all their lands of promise.

---

Having read Isaiah 49:22-26 and chapters 50 and 51, Jacob delivers a series of discourses, recorded in 2 Ne. chapters 9-10. The Nephites, evidently, spent considerable time in their religious meetings, reading and expounding the holy Scriptures. In other words, they kept the Sabbath, and other days of worship, as prescribed by the laws of God. (Ex. 20:8-11; 23:14-16; see D. and C. 59:12-16; 68:29)

VERSE 1. *I have read . . . that ye may know.* The object of reading the Scriptures is, and should always be, to obtain knowledge of the plan of salvation; and more especially as this plan concerns our children and descendants, since it is the sacred duty of parents, as the representatives of God in the family, to transmit the knowledge they need for development and progress in all that is good and therefore promotive of temporal and eternal happiness.

VERSE 2. *They Shall be Restored.* This is a promise of the restoration of the Jews to the true Church and fold of God "when they shall be gathered home."

*The Lands of their Inheritance.* When Israel entered Canaan under Joshua, the country was divided by lot "for an inheritance" among the families of the various tribes. In the division the larger tribes received a larger territory than those with a smaller number of families. The country east of the Jordan was allotted to Reuben, Gad and half the tribe of Manasseh. The rest of the people were settled between the Jordan and the Mediterranean. To the descendants of Levi, who were devoted to the temple service and literary pursuits, a certain number of cities with surrounding land for grazing purposes were to be allotted. (See Numb. 33:54-34:1-15) The total number of Levitical cities was to be 48, six of which were to be cities of refuge, where one guilty of manslaughter, but accused of murder, might find protection against the "avenger," which was the next of kin to the victim. (Numb. 35:1-8) This was the land of their inheritance. The southern boundary was the "River of Egypt" (Numb. 34:5), which is a brook running through the Sinai peninsula to the Mediterranean south of Gaza. The northern boundary was a line drawn through Hazar-enan, which some have identified as the modern Kuryetein, sixty miles northeast of Damascus.

*Their Lands of Promise.* This, probably, refers to the entire territory which the Lord promised the descendants of Abraham. (Gen. 15:18-21)

3. Behold, my beloved brethren, I speak unto you these things that ye may rejoice, and lift up your heads forever, because of the blessings which the Lord God shall bestow upon your children.

4. For I know that ye have searched much, many of you, to know of things to come; wherefore I know that ye know that our flesh must waste away and die; nevertheless, in our bodies we shall see God.

5. Yea, I know that ye know that in the body he shall show himself unto those at Jerusalem, from whence we came; for it is expedient that it should be among them; for it behooveth the great Creator that he suffereth himself to become subject unto man in the flesh, and die for all men, that all men might become subject unto him.

6. For as death hath passed upon all men, to fulfil the merciful plan of the great Creator, there must needs be a power of resurrection, and the resurrection must needs come unto man by reason of the fall; and the fall came by reason of transgression; and because man became fallen they were cut off from the presence of the Lord.

## 2. On the Atonement.

7. Wherefore, it must needs be an infinite atonement—save it should be an infinite atonement this corruption could not put on incorruption. Wherefore, the first judgment which came upon man must needs have remained to an endless duration. And if so, this flesh must have laid down to rot and to crumble to its mother earth, to rise no more.

---

VERSES 3-4. *Blessings upon Your Children.* Among these Jacob mentions first the resurrection of their bodies. "In our bodies we shall see God." The Nephites were familiar with the Book of Job. (Compare Job 19:26)

VERSES 5-6. *Death and Resurrection.* Jacob, consistently, refers to the prophetic word concerning the first advent of Christ, his death and resurrection, as irrefutable evidence of our own resurrection and eternal existence.

VERSE 7. *An Infinite Atonement.* The literal meaning of the word in the Old Testament translated "atone" is, to "cover," and "atonement" means "covering." The idea conveyed is that, by the atonement, two parties, separated by a serious offense committed, are again united, because satisfaction has been rendered. The offense is not "covered" in the sense of being hidden. It is covered by righting the wrong done and the pardon of the offended party.

There is, I believe, general agreement on the literal meaning of the word, but concerning the significance, the nature, of the act of covering, opinions differ.

One view is that Christ atoned for the transgression of many by paying, vicariously, the penalty which Divine justice had affixed to the breaking of the law; thus appeasing Divine justice, procuring pardon and opening the way for the pardoned sinner back to the presence of the reconciled Father. Anselm, archbishop of Canterbury (A. D. 1093), is generally regarded as the chief exponent of this view.

8. O the wisdom of God, his mercy and grace! For behold, if the flesh should rise no more our spirits must become subject to that angel who fell from before the presence of the Eternal God, and became the devil, to rise no more.

9. And our spirits must have become like unto him, and we become devils, angels to a devil, to be shut out from the presence of our God, and to remain with the father of lies, in misery, like unto himself; yea, to that being who beguiled our first parents, who transformeth himself nigh unto an angel of light, and stirreth up the children of men unto secret combinations of murder and all manner of secret works of darkness.

10. O how great the goodness of our God, who prepareth a way for our escape from the grasp of this awful monster; yea, that

Another view is that the coming of Christ and his sufferings were entirely a manifestation of the love of God, not a plan for appeasing his wrath. Abelard, the storm-tossed French philosopher (A. D. 1141), maintained this aspect of the doctrine. Man, he held, had become estranged from God by transgression; he was brought back by love, not wrath.

Grotius (A. D. 1617), in his controversy with the Socinians, maintained that the atonement was an act of satisfaction demanded by the the moral government of God, rather than by his justice.

The entire doctrine is stated by Paul thus:

"God hath reconciled us to himself by Jesus Christ, and hath given to us the ministry of reconciliation; to wit, that God was in Christ, reconciling the world unto himself, not imputing their trespasses unto them; and hath committed unto us the word of reconciliation. Now, then, we are ambassadors for Christ,"—that is the authority of the holy Priesthood—"as though God did beseech you by us: we pray you in Christ's stead, be ye reconciled to God. For he hath made him to be sin for us, who knew no sin; that we might be made the righteousness of God in him." (2 Cor. 5:18-21)

*Infinite Atonement.* "God was in Christ, reconciling the world unto himself." This is the Christian doctrine. The atonement of Christ is infinite because of the value of the sacrifice. It was not by the shedding of the blood of goats or calves but his own precious blood, that the reconciliation was effected. (Heb. 9:12-14) It is infinite because of its infinite efficacy. "For by one offering he hath perfected for ever them that are sanctified." (Heb. 10:14) It is infinite because of its universal application: "In whom we have redemption through his blood, the forgiveness of sins . . . that in the dispensation of the fulness of times he might gather together in one all things in Christ, both which are in heaven, and which are on earth; even in him." (Eph. 1:7-10)

Jacob here adds an important thought: But for the infinite atonement, corruption could not have put on incorruption; that is, the body would not have been resurrected; and there would have been no appeal from the first sentence of the Divine court.

VERSES 8-13. *If the Flesh should rise no More.* There are those who rebel at the thought of a resurrection and the prospect of a life after this. Jacob tells us here what the consequences would be but for the redemption of the body from the grave. Our spirits would have become the subjects of the fallen angel. They would

monster, death and hell, which I call the death of the body, and also the death of the spirit.

11. And because of the way of deliverance of our God, the Holy One of Israel, this death, of which I have spoken, which is the temporal, shall deliver up its dead; which death is the grave.

12. And this death of which I have spoken, which is the spiritual death, shall deliver up its dead; which spiritual death is hell; wherefore, death and hell must deliver up their dead, and hell must deliver up its captive spirits, and the grave must deliver up its captive bodies, and

the bodies and the spirits of men will be restored one to the other; and it is by the power of the resurrection of the Holy One of Israel.

13. O how great the plan of our God! For on the other hand, the paradise of God must deliver up the spirits of the righteous, and the grave deliver up the body of the righteous; and the spirit and the body is restored to itself again, and all men become incorruptible, and immortal, and they are living souls, having a perfect knowledge like unto us in the flesh, save it be that our knowledge shall be perfect.

## 3. The Judgment.

14. Wherefore, we shall have a perfect knowledge of all our guilt, and our uncleanness, and our nakedness; and the righteous shall have a perfect knowledge of their enjoyment, and their righteousness, being clothed with purity, yea, even with the robe of righteousness.

15. And it shall come to pass that when all men shall have passed from this first death unto life, insomuch as they have become immortal, they must appear before the judgment-seat of the Holy One of Israel; and then cometh the judgment and then must they be judged according

---

have been like unto him. They would have become devils, and messengers of Lucifer, shut out from the presence of our heavenly Father for ever. (v. 9) But because of the atonement, death and hell shall deliver up the dead. (v. 10) On the other hand, Paradise must deliver up the spirits of the righteous, and the grave their bodies, and these will be reunited in a state of immortality, with a perfect knowledge. (vv. 12, 13)

"Temporal Death" (v. 11) means the grave; "spiritual death" is the existence in hell. (v. 12)

VERSE 14. *Knowledge.* Perfect consciousness of our deeds of unrighteousness, or righteousness; of our guilt or innocence; of our condition, whether it is one of purity or impurity. In this respect our resurrected existence will be different from our present state in mortality. Here a veil is drawn over our prenatal life, and we begin writing our biography, as it were, on a clean sheet of paper. In our next existence all our previous experience on earth, and perhaps even before our life on earth, will be before us as in a book.

VERSE 15. *Then Cometh the Judgment.* Immediately after the resurrection.

to the holy judgments of God.

16. And assuredly, as the Lord liveth, for the Lord God hath spoken it, and it is his eternal word, which cannot pass away, that they who are righteous shall be righteous still, and they who are filthy shall be filthy still; wherefore, they who are filthy are the devil and his angels; and they shall go away into everlasting fire, prepared for them; and their torment is as a lake of fire and brimstone, whose flame ascendeth up forever and ever and has no end.

17. O the greatness and the justice of our God! For he executeth all his words, and they have gone forth out of his mouth, and his law must be fulfilled.

18. But, behold, the righteous, the saints of the Holy One of Israel, they who have believed in the Holy One of Israel, they who have endured the crosses of the world, and despised the shame of it, they shall inherit the kingdom of God, which was prepared for them from the foundation of the world, and their joy shall be full forever.

19. O the greatness of the mercy of our God, the Holy One of Israel! For he delivereth his saints from that awful monster the devil, and death, and hell, and that lake of fire and brimstone, which is endless torment.

20. O how great the holiness of our God! For he knoweth all things, and there is not anything save he knows it.

21. And he cometh into the world that he may save all men if they will hearken unto his voice; for behold, he suffereth the pains of all men, yea, the pains of every living creature,

---

VERSE 16. *The Righteous will Remain Righteous,* and they who are filthy shall be filthy still. Lucifer and his followers will be sent to a place where their torment will be as the pain caused by burning brimstone.

VERSE 18. *The Verdict in the Case of the Saints.* They shall inherit the kingdom of God. Note that they will be awarded the kingdom as their inheritance; not as their servants' wages. As St. Paul puts it:

"The Spirit itself beareth witness with our spirit, that we are the children of God: and if children, then heirs; heirs of God, and joint-heirs with Christ; if so be that we suffer with him, that we may also be glorified together. (Rom. 8:16, 17)

VERSE 20. *He Knoweth All Things.* There is infinite comfort in the thought that the Judge knoweth all things. He knows our frailties better than we know them ourselves. He knows our temptations, our efforts to combat them and the reasons for failures, if we have failed. He knows precisely what our surroundings have been and their influence upon our character; also how much of our shortcomings is due to inherited tendencies. He knows perfectly how much responsibility we must justly bear. "For we have not an High Priest which cannot be touched with the feeling of our infirmities; but was in all points tempted like as we are, yet without sin. Let us therefore come boldly unto the throne of grace, that we may obtain mercy, and find grace to help in the time of need." (Heb. 4:15, 16) In the case of the Saints of God, the judgment seat is also the throne of grace, the mercy seat, of our heavenly Father.

both men, women, and children, who belong to the family of Adam.

22. And he suffereth this that the resurrection might pass upon all men, that all might stand before him at the great and judgment day.

## 4. Conditions of Salvation.

23. And he commandeth all men that they must repent, and be baptized in his name, having perfect faith in the Holy One of Israel, or they cannot be saved in the kingdom of God.

---

VERSE 23. *He commandeth.* Note that repentance, baptism, and faith are the conditions on which salvation in the kingdom of God is obtained. God commands all men to repent, to be baptized and to have perfect faith in Christ. It is not optional in any case. He who will not repent, believe and be baptized "must be damned." (v. 4)

The doctrine of repentance is an essential part of the Gospel. It occupies the second place in the Articles of Faith of the Church: (1) Faith; (2) Repentance; (3) Baptism: (4) Laying on of hands for the reception of the Holy Ghost.

But repentance is not only a doctrine. It is the main manifestation of the new life of those who have been "born again" and thereby became citizens of the kingdom of God. All are commanded to repent, and genuine repentance brings forgiveness. (Mos. 26:31; Alma 5:49, 51, 54, 56; 9:30. Also D. and C. 64:10-14)

*Baptism.* This is another condition of salvation. Together with repentance it is the "gate" to the kingdom. (v. 41: 2 Ne. 31:17, 18; Moroni 6:8) It is also a witness before God that the one who has been baptized has thereby entered into a covenant with him to keep his commandments. (Mos. 18:10) According to the Apostle Paul (1 Cor. 10:1, 2) the Hebrews anciently had a remarkably clear conception of baptism, both as to its form and significance. Referring to the passage of the children of Israel through the Red Sea (Ex. 13:21 and 14:22) he says: "Our fathers were all under the cloud, and all passed through the sea; and were all baptized unto"—literally, "into," Moses, that is, into the Mosaic dispensation—"in the cloud and in the sea."

This was a baptism of the entire Hebrew nation, symbolically cleansing them from all impurities clinging to them after the captivity in Egypt, and obligating them to follow Moses as their leader, appointed by God, to the land of Promise. It was a complete immersion in the waters of the sea and the cloud. And we note that the very means by which Israel was saved became the means of destruction of their God-defying pursuers.

*Perfect Faith.* This is another condition of salvation. The Apostle Paul (Heb. 11:1-3), after having quoted Habakkuk 2:4: "The just shall live by his faith," explains what faith is: "The substance of things hoped for, the evidence of things not seen." The word "substance" means that which "stands under," or, the underlying reality of things. It is that which sustains the qualities by which matter becomes perceptible to us. For instance. Here is an object. We examine it. We find that it has a certain weight, and a peculiar color; that it is impervious to the action of most acids; that it amalgamates readily with mercury, and that, for practical purposes, it forms valuable alloys with silver, or copper, etc., etc. We call it gold. Another object, with a different combination of qualities, we call silver; another, copper, etc., etc. That which sustains these qualities is the "substance."

24. And if they will not repent and believe in his name, and be baptized in his name, and endure to the end, they must be damned; for the Lord God, the Holy One of Israel, has spoken it.

25. Wherefore, he has given a law; and where there is no law given there is no punishment; and where there is no punishment there is no condemnation; and where there is no condemnation the mercies of the Holy One of Israel have claim upon them, because of the atonement; for they are delivered by the power of him.

26. For the atonement satisfieth the demands of his justice upon all those who have not the law given to them, that they are delivered from that awful monster, death and hell, and the devil, and the lake of fire and brimstone, which is endless torment; and they are restored to that God who gave them breath, which is the Holy One of Israel.

---

What substance is in the material world, faith is in the spiritual world. It is the very foundation of the qualities—love, humility, peace, joy, benevolence, etc., etc.—which are the essential characteristics of the Christian character.

St. Paul, further, explains that "through faith we understand that the worlds were framed by the word of God, so that things that are seen were not made of things which do appear;" for, no matter what scientists may assert, the beginning of things, origins, being outside our sphere of experience or observation, can be known only through faith. Only through faith do we comprehend that the universe of which we are a part is the Divine ideas which received form in the material creation. Abel, Enoch, Noah, Abraham, Sarah, Isaac, Jacob, Joseph, Moses, Joshua, Samuel, and many others are mentioned as examples of what mortals can accomplish, if they have the power that comes from faith in God.

It is important to remember that "faith" means not only the conviction in the mind, but also that which is believed, the Gospel, the creed, which, in the mind of the Apostle, is a long step in advance of the Mosaic law. See Acts 6:7; 13:8; 14:22-27; Rom. 1:5; 3:27; 10:8; Gal. 1:23; 2:16; 3:2, 5; Eph. 2:8; 1 Tim. 1:2; 4:1. When this is kept in mind, it is evident that there is no conflict between the views of Paul and James. For when it is argued that salvation is by faith and not by works, as for instance in Gal. 3, it is not maintained that a Christian is without works of righteousness, but that it is the Gospel and not the law of Moses that has "saved" him, and made him capable of living a righteous life.

A Scientific View. Dr. Arthur H. Compton of the University of Chicago, a Noble prize winner in physics in 1927, was quoted in a dispatch dated Dec. 26, 1933, as having said in a Christmas interview, that faith in God may be a thoroughly scientific attitude, even if we are unable to establish the correctness of our belief. Science, he said, further, as reported, can have no quarrel with a religion which postulates a God to whom men are as children, "not that science shows such a relationship . . . but the evidence for an intelligent Power working in the world which science offers does make such postulate plausible."

VERSE 25. No Law . . . no Condemnation. This is a complete and satisfactory reply to the question, what will become of those who have never heard the Gospel message? God is just. He is also merciful. And the Atonement is infinite. There is a "justice" which is injustice; sometimes infinite mercy is perfect justice.

## 5. A Tenfold Wo!

27. But wo unto him that has the law given, yea, that has all the commandments of God, like unto us, and that transgresseth them, and that wasteth the days of his probation, for awful is his state!

28. O that cunning plan of the evil one! O the vainness, and the frailties, and the foolishness of men! When they are learned they think they are wise, and they hearken not unto the counsel of God, for they set it aside, supposing they know of themselves, wherefore, their wisdom is foolishness and it profiteth them not. And they shall perish.

29. But to be learned is good if they hearken unto the counsels of God.

30. But wo unto the rich, who are rich as to the things of the world. For because they are rich they despise the poor, and they persecute the meek, and their hearts are upon their treasures; wherefore, their treasure is their God. And behold, their treasure shall perish with them also.

31. And wo unto the deaf that will not hear; for they shall perish.

32. Wo unto the blind that will not see; for they shall perish also.

33. Wo unto the uncircumcised of heart, for a knowledge of their iniquities shall smite them at the last day.

34. Wo unto the liar, for he shall be thrust down to hell.

35. Wo unto the murderer who deliberately killeth, for he shall die.

36. Wo unto them who commit whoredoms, for they shall be thrust down to hell.

37. Yea, wo unto those that worship idols, for the devil of all devils delighteth in them.

38. And, in fine, wo unto all those who die in their sins; for they shall return to God, and behold his face, and remain in their sins.

---

VERSES 27-38. The sins here condemned should be carefully noted. (1) Wo unto those who have received the law of God, and do not keep it; they show contempt for the Lawgiver. (2) Wo unto those who are rich and despise the poor. (v. 42; James 1:9-11) (3) Wo unto those who will not hear; (4) and not see; (5) and those who harden their hearts in iniquity. (6) Wo unto the liars. (7) Wo unto the murderers. Murder is rightly considered the greatest of crimes. By it a sacrilege is committed upon the image of God, and a time of probation is ruthlessly cut short in the death of the victim. But, according to the word of our Lord himself, a liar is also a great criminal. He says to his persecutors, John 8:44:

"Ye are of your father the devil, and the lusts of your father it is your will to do. He was a murderer from the beginning, and stood not in the truth, because there is no truth in him. When he speaketh a lie, he speaketh of his own; for he is a liar and the father thereof."

If the devil is the father of lies, the liar must be, in a special sense, related to, or associated with him. (8) Wo unto the violators of the laws of chastity, "for they shall be thrust down to hell." Wo unto the worshipers of idols (9), and (10)

## 6. On the Awfulness of Sin.

39. O, my beloved brethren, remember the awfulness in transgressing against that Holy God, and also the awfulness of yielding to the enticings of that cunning one. Remember, to be carnally-minded is death, and to be spiritually-minded is life eternal.

40. O, my beloved brethren, give ear to my words. Remember the greatness of the Holy One of Israel. Do not say that I have spoken hard things against you; for if ye do, ye will revile against the truth; for I have spoken the words of your Maker. I know that the words of truth are hard against all uncleanness; but the righteous fear them not, for they love the truth and are not shaken.

41. O then, my beloved brethren, come unto the Lord, the Holy One. Remember that his paths are righteous. Behold, the way for man is narrow, but it lieth in a straight course before him, and the keeper of the gate is the Holy One of Israel; and he employeth no servant there; and there is none other way save it be by the gate; for he cannot be deceived, for the Lord God is his name.

42. And whoso knocketh, to him will he open; and the wise, and the learned, and they that are rich, who are puffed up because of their learning, and their wisdom, and their riches — yea, they are they whom he despiseth; and save they shall cast these things away, and consider themselves fools before God, and come down in the depths of humility, he will not open unto them.

43. But the things of the wise

---

those who die in their sins; they shall return to God, and even see his face, but they shall, nevertheless, remain in their sins.

VERSE 39. *Carnally-minded . . . Spiritually-minded.* The struggle of Lucifer for supremacy on earth is sometimes manifested in the prevalence of agnosticism, atheism, or other philosophies of doubt or infidelity; but frequently it appears in the substitution of empty ceremonies for the active spiritual life; materialistic performances for the actual communion of the soul with heaven. Then religion is likely to become an instrument for the furtherance of ambition, power, social recognition, wealth, or even gross indulgence. It becomes a "carnal" religion and an asset of the "carnally-minded." Hence we are told that to be spiritually-minded is to have life eternal, while the opposite is death.

VERSES 41-43. *Come unto the Lord.* Jacob here speaks of the conversion of a sinner and his surrender to the Lord as "coming" to him. The road is narrow. Each one must walk it for himself. There is no room for an easy conveyance of any kind. But it is straight. It is not unnecessarily long with curves and turnings. At the end of it there is a gate (see notes under v. 23): Repentance and baptism. There is no other entrance. Our Lord is the keeper; not St. Peter. And "whoso knocketh, to him will he open," provided he is not proud on account of learning, wisdom or wealth, but that he, in all humility considers himself a "fool" before God. Comp. 1 Cor. 1:21, 23, 25: "But we preach Christ crucified, unto the Jews a stumblingblock and unto the Greeks foolishness."

and the prudent shall be hid from them forever—yea, that happiness which is prepared for the saints.

44. O, my beloved brethren, remember my words. Behold, I take off my garments, and I shake them before you; I pray the God of my salvation that he view me with his all-searching eye; wherefore, ye shall know at the last day, when all men shall be judged of their works, that the God of Israel did witness that I shook your iniquities from my soul, and that I stand with brightness before him, and am rid of your blood.

45. O, my beloved brethren, turn away from your sins; shake off the chains of him that would bind you fast; come unto that God who is the rock of your salvation.

46. Prepare your souls for that glorious day when justice shall be administered unto the righteous, even the day of judgment, that ye may not shrink with awful fear; that ye may not remember your awful guilt in perfectness, and be constrained to exclaim: Holy, holy are thy judgments, O Lord God Almighty—but I know my guilt; I transgressed thy law, and my transgressions are mine; and the devil hath obtained me, that I am a prey to his awful misery.

47. But behold, my brethren, is it expedient that I should awake you to an awful reality of

VERSE 44. *I Take off my Garments, and I Shake them before You.* At this stage of the address, when Jacob was about to explain the serious nature of the sin of rejecting the message of salvation, the Spirit prompted him to employ an impressive gesture. Wherefore he took off his outer garments and shook them before the people. At the same time he prayed God to be his witness on the day of judgment that he had freed himself for responsibility for their iniquities, by delivering the message faithfully. I am, he said, rid of your blood.

We are reminded by this of the instruction our Lord gave his Apostles when he first sent them on a mission. They were not to go as beggars asking for alms, but as ambassadors of a King with favors to bestow. Into whatsoever city or town ye shall enter, he said, ask if there is anybody there who is worthy, and stay there. If they are worthy, your peace will rest on them; if not, it will return to you. And in that case, "when ye depart out of that house or city, shake off the dust of your feet." (Matt. 10:14; Mark 6:11; Luke 1:12)

"Dust" has several figurative and symbolic meanings in the Scriptures. To sit in the dust and to sprinkle dust on the head was a sign of deep mourning. (Job 1:12, 13; Isa. 47:1) To lick the dust of one's feet, as it is said was customary at some Oriental courts, when subjects were admitted to the presence of sovereigns (Isa. 49:23) was, of course, a degrading humiliation. When the Serpent (Gen. 3:14; Isa. 65:25) was condemned to "eat dust" all the days of his life, he was, in modern language, doomed to an existence of the most degrading nature imaginable. He who, in the Garden of Eden, was the spokesman of Satan, became, as it were, a slave of slaves of the fallen angel. (Pearl of Great Price, Mos. 4:6-7)

VERSES 45-48. We infer from the concluding paragraphs that the demonstration made a deep impression on his hearers, who understood the meaning of it. He allays the commotion, and concludes with this stanza:

these things? Would I harrow up your souls if your minds were pure? Would I be plain unto you according to the plainness of the truth if ye were freed from sin?

48. Behold, if ye were holy I would speak unto you of holiness; but as ye are not holy, and ye look upon me as a teacher, it must needs be expedient that I teach you the consequences of sin.

49. Behold, my soul abhorreth sin, and my heart delighteth in righteousness; and I will praise the holy name of my God.

## 7. Exhortations.

50. Come, my brethren, every one that thirsteth, come ye to the waters; and he that hath no money, come buy and eat; yea, come buy wine and milk without money and without price.

51. Wherefore, do not spend money for that which is of no worth, nor your labor for that which cannot satisfy. Hearken diligently unto me, and remember the words which I have spoken; and come unto the Holy One of Israel, and feast upon that which perisheth not, neither can be corrupted, and let your soul delight in fatness.

52. Behold, my beloved brethren, remember the words of your God; pray unto him continually

---

VERSE 49:   Behold, my soul abhorreth sin,
And my heart delighteth in righteousness;
And I will praise the holy name of my God.

VERSES 50, 51. *Come . . . everyone that thirsteth.* These two verses are evidently a quotation from Isaiah 55:1, 2. But they are not a literal repetition of the words of the prophet. When *we* quote the inspired word of God, we must repeat it literally; otherwise we cannot be certain that we are saying what the Spirit intended to say. But the Divine Author, or Inspirer, of the Scriptures does not come under that rule. His word is always the truth.

Some commentators hold that the Prophet Isaiah, in these verses, on behalf of the Lord, invites the gentile nations to come and join Israel in the establishment of the Millennial Kingdom of God, (see vv. 6-8) where water, wine, milk, bread, etc.; that is, abundant prosperity, will be had without money and without price. Probably, there is some truth in that; for, undoubtedly, social and economic conditions will, during the Millennium, be different from what they now are. For one thing, there will probably be no interest-bearing debt, and to that extent the prosperity promised will not cost anything. It will be had "without money and without price." But that does not say that there will be no money as a medium of exchange. When Jacob reads this passage of Isaiah, he means not only temporal prosperity, but above all, spiritual abundance; for he explains: "Feast upon that which perisheth not, neither can be corrupted, and let your soul delight in fatness." (v. 51)

Jesus had this passage in mind, possibly, when he stood on the Temple ground one day and said with a loud voice: "If any man thirst, let him come unto me and drink." (John 7:37. Comp. 4:13, 14) John comments thus: "But this he spake of the Spirit which they that believe on him should receive." (John 7:39)

VERSE 52. *Pray Continually.* Note that prayer and a joyful heart go together.

by day, and give thanks unto his holy name by night. Let your hearts rejoice.

53. And behold how great the covenants of the Lord, and how great his condescensions unto the children of men; and because of his greatness, and his grace and mercy, he has promised unto us that our seed shall not utterly be destroyed, according to the flesh, but that he would preserve them; and in future generations they shall become a righteous branch unto the house of Israel.

54. And now, my brethren, I would speak unto you more; but on the morrow I will declare unto you the remainder of my words. Amen.

VERSE 53. *Not Utterly Destroyed.* The Book of Mormon does not teach that the Nephites were at any time utterly exterminated, with the exception of a very few individuals. It tells us that the people on this continent, shortly after the ministration of Jesus among them were united. Even the racial distinction between Nephites and Lamanites was obliterated. There were no "Lamanites or any manner of -ites." They were all one in Christ. (4 Ne. vv. 17, 18) This Millennial condition lasted until the spirit of antichrist made its appearance in the form of pride and love of the world. Then different churches were organized. (v. 27) Some became persecutors. (v. 29) In the 131st year after the advent of Christ a religious organization was formed, which became known as Nephites, because they believed in Christ, as Nephi had done. Their opponents became known as Lamanites, because they followed Laman in their religious tendencies. The distinction between Nephites, Jacobites, Josephites and Zoramites on one side, and Lamanites, Lemuelites and Ishmaelites on the other, from now on was on religious lines, not because of descent, just as the distinction between Lutherans, Calvinists, etc., is one of confession of faith, not of parental lineage. (4 Ne. vv. 36-39) The great battle at Cumorah was fought, as I understand it, between these two religious organizations. (Mormon 1:8, 9) The Nephite religious organization was broken up at Cumorah. The Nephite government came to an end. But among the victorious so-called Lamanites, there were descendants of Nephi, Jacob, Joseph and Zoram, as well as of Laman and his friends, as there are among the Indians to this day.

On May 1, 1950, reports issued from the office of the commissioner of Indian affairs in Washington indicated that the Indians in the United States were gaining in numbers. In 1910 the census showed 301 tribes north of Mexico with a total of 291,014 individuals. In 1950 the total had increased to 343,000. The birth rate exceeded deaths by 1300 annually. Some tribes, the report said, are independent, operate sawmills, herd sheep and cattle, raise hay and grain, build irrigation systems and contribute to education and the care of their indigents. Many are riding in automobiles. All of which may indicate that the descendants of Lehi, both through Nephi and Laman, will be preserved and become a righteous branch, in due time, "unto the house of Israel."

VERSE 54. *On the Morrow.* Jacob closes his remarks with the announcement that he would continue his discourse the following day. This suggests that it may have been delivered at a time, when more than one holiday was observed in succession, as for instance on the 15th day of the first month of the year, the month of Abib, which corresponds almost to our April. According to the ancient regulations, the 14th of Abib was the day of the passover. The 15th was the weekly Sabbath and the beginning of the feast of unleavened bread. The 16th was the day, when the priest, on behalf of the people, presented a sheaf of the first fruit of the harvest before the Lord together with certain offerings of meat and drink and a burnt offering. (Comp. Lev. 23:2-12) These three days were very much like holidays, as our general conferences, which also include a Sabbath. On those days public "convocations," or assemblies, were held, when, no doubt, addresses were made by the prophets of the Lord.

Or, the remarks may have been delivered later, in the third month of the year, Tisri, at the time of the Pentecost, also called the Feast of Weeks. Concerning this, the instructions were, to count, from the 16th of Abib, seven complete weeks, or Sabbaths, 49 days, and then add one day, making a total period of fifty days. This was the annual day of Jubilee. On this day the people were to bring to the Sanctuary liberal offerings of meat. They were to come with bread, now baked with leaven, with a young bullock, rams, goats and lambs. At this time, too, a holy convocation was proclaimed. (See Lev. 23:15-21)

If we count, beginning with Abib 16th, the 4th of Tisri is the 49th day. That is also one of the seven weekly Sabbaths. The next day, the 5th of Tisri, is the 50th day, the yearly Jubilee Sabbath. This season corresponds somewhat to our month of June. These two annual Jubilee Sabbaths can well, if we so choose, be considered one sabbath, one cessation of work, one rest, with forty-eight hours' duration instead of the usual twenty-four hours'. On this Jubilee Sabbath, as we may call it, a sermon could be preached on the first part of it and conveniently continued on the second, and that would be "on the morrow."

A similar arrangement obtained in the calendar of years. The recorders counted 49 years. Every seventh was a Sabbath year. Nothing was planted, nothing was harvested that year. When they had counted seven complete weeks of years, or 49 years, they added one, making a complete cycle of 50. This was the year of Jubilee. (See Lev. 25:3-17) The fifty-first year began a new cycle. It was a complete repetition of the weekly Sabbaths. Two Sabbath years came together in uninterrupted succession every fifty years, as two weekly Sabbaths did every year.

## A SYNOPSIS OF THE DISCOURSE

This chapter is a discourse, or at least a homily, by Jacob, the son of Lehi. It ought to have an interest to missionaries and other public speakers of the Church, as giving us material for judging of the nature of the sermons of those remote days, both as to subject-matter and form of delivery.

Having read a portion of the Prophet Isaiah (49:22; 52:2) as a text, he states the subject of his remarks: "The Covenants of the Lord which he has Covenanted with all the House of Israel." (v. 1)

A covenant may be defined as a solemn contract between two parties who bind themselves to certain requirements. When God is one of the parties, he prescribes the requirements and states the conditions on which the rewards for obedience, or fearful consequences of disobedience, invariably follow. The other party humbly accepts. In this case, the covenant may be regarded as, "the Plan of Salvation," which is a briefer statement of the theme of the discourse. (Comp. vv. 6 and 13)

A suggested synopsis of the homily follows:

### INTRODUCTION

In his introduction Jacob states the object of his remarks: "That ye may rejoice . . . because of the blessings which the Lord God shall bestow upon your children." (v. 3)

### PART ONE

I. Death, Resurrection, the Coming and Sufferings of Christ, and also the Fall, necessary parts of "The Merciful Plan of the Great Creator" (vv. 4-6)—the Plan of Salvation.

II. An Infinite Atonement.

    A. No Resurrection but for an Infinite Atonement (v. 7)
    B. The Wisdom, Mercy and Grace of God shown in the Atonement and the Resurrection. (vv. 8, 9)
    C. The Goodness of God as shown in his preparation of a way of escape from death and hell. (vv. 10-12)
    D. The Greatness of the Plan of Salvation, as shown in the deliverance of the spirits of the righteous from Paradise and their bodies from the grave, and the union of the two in immortality. (vv. 13, 14)

III. The Judgment.

    A. All must appear before the Judgment-seat of the Holy One of Israel. (v. 15)
    B. The righteous shall remain righteous, and the filthy shall continue in that condition, the "filthy" being the devil and his angels; their fate, everlasting fire. (v. 16)
    C. The greatness and justice of God as shown in his judgment. (vv. 17, 18)
    D. The greatness of the mercy of God, as shown in the deliverance of his Saints from the devil, death, hell and the lake of fire. (v. 19)
    E. The greatness of the holiness of God, a consequence of his perfect knowledge of all things. (v. 20)
    F. The object of his coming into the world, to save all the children of men, on condition of repentance, baptism, faith and obedience. (vv. 21-26)

PART TWO

Having emphasized the magnitude of the work of the Atonement, Resurrection and Redemption from all evil, Jacob, in a tenfold exclamation of Woe! expresses his abhorrence of the transgression of the laws of the Redeemer. (vv. 27-38)

I. Transgression is a waste of the days of probation. (v. 27)

II. The Tenfold Woe.

    A. Woe unto him that has the laws given and that transgresseth them; who think they are wise, but whose wisdom is foolishness. (vv. 27-29)
    B. Woe unto the money-worshipers, who despise the poor and persecute those who are humble; for their treasure shall perish with them. (v. 30)
    C. Woe unto the deaf that will not hear. (v. 31)
    D. Woe unto the blind that will not see. (v. 32)
    E. Woe unto the uncircumcised of heart, for the consciousness of their guilt will remain with them to the last. (v. 33)
    F. Woe unto the liar, for he shall be thrust down to hell. (v. 34)
    G. Woe unto the murderer who deliberately killeth, for he shall die. (v. 35)
    H. Woe unto them who commit whoredoms, for they shall be thrust down to hell. (v. 36)
    I. Woe unto those that worship idols, for the devil delighteth in them. (v. 37)
    J. Woe unto all who die in their sins; for . . . they shall remain in their sins. (v. 38)

PART THREE

The magnitude of the work of redemption and the terrible consequences of transgression suggests these earnest admonitions:

A. Remember that "to be carnally minded is death; to be spiritually-minded is life eternal." (v. 39)
B. Remember the greatness of the Holy One of Israel. (v. 40)
C. Come to the Holy One. (v. 41)
D. But he receives only those who come through the depths of humility. (v. 42)
E. The happiness that only the wise and the prudent can enjoy is prepared for the Saints. (v. 43)

Having said this, a highly dramatic scene followed. Jacob took off his outer garments and shook them in full view of the audience. At the same time he prayed the Lord to look upon him with his all-searching eye, and to bear witness for him at the last day, that he was clean of their iniquities and had no responsibility for their blood. (v. 44) Then he resumed his exhortations:

F. Turn away from sin. (v. 45)
G. Prepare for the glorious day of judgment. (v. 46)
H. The reason why he spoke so much about sin and not of holiness. (vv. 47-48) Verse 49 is possibly a quotation, to give emphasis to this part of the discourse. It can be read thus:

"Behold, my soul abhorreth sin,
And my heart delighteth in righteousness;
And I will praise the holy name of God."

I. Free Salvation. (vv. 50, 51) These verses are a free quotation from Isa. 55:1 and 2.
J. A final reminder of the duty of prayer. (v. 52)

## CONCLUSION

In conclusion Jacob reminds the people of the magnitude of the covenants of God, and of his condescension, his grace and mercy, as a consequence of which he has promised the Nephites that their descendants "shall not utterly be destroyed, according to the flesh, but that he would preserve them"; and that they shall become a righteous branch unto the house of Israel. (v. 53)

## CHAPTER 10

*Consequences of the Rejection of the Messiah, 1-6—National Restoration Promised, 7-14 — The Secret Works of Darkness to be Destroyed, 15-19 — Closing Admonitions, 20-25.*

### 1. *Consequences of Rejecting the Messiah.*

1. And now I, Jacob, speak unto you again, my beloved brethren, concerning this righteous branch of which I have spoken.

2. For behold, the promises which we have obtained are promises unto us according to the flesh; wherefore, as it has been shown unto me that many of our children shall perish in the flesh because of unbelief, nevertheless, God will be merciful unto many; and our children shall be restored, that they may come to that which will give them the true knowledge of their Redeemer.

3. Wherefore, as I said unto you, it must needs be expedient that Christ—for in the last night the angel spake unto me that this should be his name—should come among the Jews, among those who are the more wicked part of the world; and they shall crucify him—for thus it behooveth our God, and there is none other

VERSES 1-2. *This Righteous Branch.* Jacob closed his discourse in the previous chapter by reminding the people of the promise of God that the descendants of Lehi, in the future, would become a "righteous branch" to the house of Israel. In his address in this chapter, he again refers to this promise.

"Branch" has different meanings in the Scriptures, besides the literal one. The disciples of Jesus are called branches, in their relationship to the Master as the "vine." (John 15:5) Kings are called "branches" (Ezek. 17:3), of their ancestral houses, because they spring from them, as twigs from a stem, or root. In this chapter the descendants of Lehi are referred to. They are "many of our children"; and, "our children," in verse 2. Many of them will perish, because of unbelief, but not all. There will be a restoration.

VERSES 3-6. *Christ Shall Come* among the Jews (v. 3).

VERSE 3. Jacob, the brother of Nephi, informs us here that the sacred Name had been revealed to him, by an angel, and that it would be "Christ," and Nephi, in the same book (25:19) records that, according to the prophets, "his name shall be Jesus Christ, the Son of God." Mosiah, also, says his name shall be Jesus Christ. (Mos. 3:8)

Such passages indicate that the early inhabitants of America long before the arrival of the Spaniards, had definite knowledge of the plan of salvation as set forth in the Hebrew Scriptures. They furnish an explanation of the origin of some traditions current among Indians at the time of the conquest and recorded by Cieza de Leon, Sarmiento, and others, according to which a white man, coming from the south, had visited their fore-fathers and taught them from a book, referred to as a "stick"—an expression which reminds us of the Biblical "stick of Ephraim," or "stick of Judah." (See The Ayar Incas, by Dr. Miles Poindexter, Vol. 2, pp. 86, 87)

Two objections have been advanced against these and similar passages in the Book of Mormon.

nation on earth that would crucify their God.

4. For should the mighty miracles be wrought among other
nations they would repent, and

know that he be their God.

5. But because of priestcrafts
and iniquities, they at Jerusalem
will stiffen their necks against
him, that he be crucified.

---

It has been said that "Christ" is not a name but a title; that we ought to say "the Christ," as we say, "John the Baptist," or "Paul the Apostle." It has also been urged that, as "Jesus Christ" is the English equivalent of two Greek words in the New Testament, their appearance in the Book of Mormon proves that volume to be the work of a plagiarist.

To the first of these objections we need only say that the English word "Christ," from the Greek "Christos," certainly is a title, an adjective, but it has also in common usage become a proper noun, a name. A great many words descriptive of the status, occupation, or quality of a person have become names, as for instance King, Taylor, Armstrong, etc. In the same way, "Christ," the adjective, which means, "anointed" has become one of the names of our Redeemer, as the angel told Jacob would happen. Even among his contemporaries he was known as "Christ, the King of Israel." (Mark 15:32)

The reply to the second objection is equally obvious. If the plates of the Book of Mormon were accessible and it could be shown that the Greek form of the sacred name was part of the text, the objection referred to might appear well founded, although even in that case, it might be truthfully said that a divinely inspired prophet might have had a vision of a future event and also of the name, or title, of the central hero of it, as Isaiah had of the Babylonian captivity and the name, or title (Cyrus or Kores) of the Persian ruler who was to end it and authorize the re-building of the temple. (Is. 45:1)

But the Prophet Joseph, in a letter published in *The Times and Seasons,* May 15, 1843, informs us that, "There was no Greek or Latin upon the plates from which I, through the grace of the Lord, translated the Book of Mormon." That disposes of the objection under consideration. The Greek form of the names did not appear on the plates.

The probability is that the Hebrew form was the one that the Prophet Joseph found in those records. The Hebrew equivalent of the two sacred names is, "Jehoshuah Hammashiach." The Prophet, in his translation, naturally rendered these words by their English equivalents, "Jesus Christ," which names, in their various forms, are known all over the world.

These names, however, have a much greater meaning than at first may be apparent. They mean that our Redeemer has been anointed by his Father, to a position of Ruler in the universe. As Paul, the Apostle says: "Wherefore God also hath highly exalted him, and given him a name which is above every name. That at the name of Jesus every knee should bow, of things in heaven, and things in earth, and things under the earth; and that every tongue should confess that Jesus Christ is the Lord, to the glory of God the Father." (Phil. 2:9-11)

VERSE 5. *Priestcrafts.* The rejection of the Messiah and the consequent dispersion of the people are traced to the existence of priestcrafts and iniquities. The meaning of the first of these words is not merely such subtlety as is ascribed to the serpent in the Garden (Gen. 3:1), or such wickedness as generally originates in the realm of Lucifer. It has a special meaning which should be carefully noted. It means, according to 2 Ne. 26:29, the practice of religion for worldly gain and the praise of men. The Lord says: "Priestcrafts are that men preach and set

6. Wherefore, because of their iniquities, destructions, famines, pestilences, and bloodshed shall come upon them; and they who shall not be destroyed shall be scattered among all nations.

---

themselves up for a light unto the world, that they may get gain and praise of the world."

> To preach for pay,
> For gold to pray

is to turn religion into an industrial craft, and that is "priestcraft."

VERSE 6. *Scattered among All Nations.* The dispersion and restoration of the descendants of Abraham, Isaac and Jacob was a subject in which all well informed Israelites were interested and with which they were familiar. It was a subject which was impressed upon the people by Moses, before they entered Canaan. (See Deut. 28:16-68) This was partly fulfilled at the time of the destruction of the city and the temple of Nebuchadnezzar. According to Josephus, the most revolting features foretold in this prophecy actually took place during the siege. Other prophets dwelt on the same subject.

Some of the last discourses of our Lord in Jerusalem concerned the signs that would precede the end of the Mosaic dispensation and the subsequent dispersion of the Jews. These signs are definitely and clearly stated (See Matt. 24, Mark 13, and Luke 21:6-33.)

Dr. Alexander Keith points out the following, in his Testimony to the Truth of the Christian Religion:

1. *Many shall come in my name and say, I am Christ.* Simon Magus claimed authority. The Samaritan, Dositheus, claimed authority. Theudas deceived many (Acts 5:36). The country was full of deceivers who tried to induce people to follow them.

2. *They were to hear of wars and rumors of war.* The Jews refused to give the Romans permission to unveil a statue of Emperor Caligula in the Temple, and as a consequence they were seized by fear of their masters to such a degree that they neglected their fields and vineyards. In Caesarea Jews and Syrians fought for possession of the city. Twenty thousand Jews were massacred, the others were scattered. In Alexandria 50,000 Jews were slain, and in Damascus, 10,000. Italy was shaken to its foundations, by internal wars about the throne. Four emperors, Nero, Galba, Otho and Vitellius perished in two years.

3. *Famines, pestilences and earthquakes.* (Matt. 4:7) During the reign of Emperor Claudius (41-54 A.D.) famine was frequent. The distress lasted for years in Palestine. Then came pestilence. Earthquakes visited Rome, Crete and other places. During the reign of Nero there were destructive seismic disturbances in Campania, Laodicea, Hierapolis and Colosse. All nature was in commotion and, as Josephus remarks, it was generally felt that the disaster foreshadowed was not a common occurrence.

4. *Fearful sights and great signs shall there be from heaven.* (Luke 21:11) Josephus and Tacitus both mention such signs. Tacitus is quoted to the effect that hosts in shining armour appeared battling in the sky, and that a fiery cloud enveloped the temple; also, that, suddenly the gates to the sanctuary were opened, and that a loud voice was heard, causing exceeding commotion.

5. *The disciples were to be persecuted.* (Mark 13:9; Luke 21:12) Peter, Paul, Matthew, Thomas, Mark, Luke, and many other prominent disciples suffered mar-

tyrdom in different places and by different means of torture. The very name "Christian" became the object of hatred in the pagan world.

6. *The disciples were to be betrayed by parents, brethren, kinsfolk and friends.* (Luke 21:16) That happened. St. Paul had that experience. (See 2 Cor. 11:13-15, 26, 27; Gal. 2:4; 2 Tim. 3:1-5.) Tacitus avers that many martyrs suffered death, having been betrayed by so-called fellow-Christians, which themselves had been delivered to the authorities by alleged brethren. And Paul expressly states that at the beginning of his trial in Rome, "no man stood with me, but all forsook me." (2 Tim. 4:16)

7. *The Gospel shall be preached in all the world.* (Matt. 24:14) We know that Christianity had been made known in almost every part of the vast Roman empire before the destruction of Jerusalem, through the missionary efforts of the chief Apostles, the Apostle Paul and others. We know that it had been brought to Ethiopia, in Africa, by the Ethiopian secretary of state under Queen Candace. (Acts 8:27-39) We know not in how many directions the first Christian missionaries traveled, but we may safely assume that Christianity, from the first, followed the main trade routes to the principal parts of the world. Mr. Bancroft ("The Native Races," Vol. 5, p. 25) says that St. Thomas has been identified with Topiltzin Quetzalcoatl, the two names having the same meaning in Greek (Didymos), and Nahua respectively. But that is, of course, mere speculation.[1]

8. *The end of the dispensation and the dispersion of the people were attended by great tribulation,* "such as was not since the beginning of the world to this time, no, nor ever shall be." (Matt. 24:21) Jacob was familiar with the terrible scenes to be expected at the end of the Mosaic dispensation, for Moses as stated in a previous paragraph had described them with soul stirring realism, before his departure. (Deut. 28:49-68) He said the country would be invaded by foreign barbarians who would spare neither women nor men, neither young nor old. There would be famine, until, "Thou shalt eat the fruit of thine own body." "The tender and delicate woman . . . her eye shall be evil toward the husband of her bosom . . . and toward the children which she shall bear; for she shall eat them for want of all things, secretly, in the siege and straitness, wherewith thine enemy shall distress thee in thy gates." All this was fulfilled literally. The altar, the temple, the walls and the entire city were destroyed by greedy soldiers who plowed up the very ground, digging for buried treasures. Josephus is authority for the statement that one million three hundred thousand Jews perished in this war and that ninety-seven thousand fell into captivity. Of these 2,500 were sacrificed in the arena in honor of the birthday of the Emperor Domitian.[2] Others perished in different ways. No wonder that the prophets of the Nephites spoke about this time so earnestly. No wonder that our Savior wept (Luke 19:41), when contemplating the winding-up scenes.

Such were the signs of the approach of the end of the Mosaic dispensation. Similar signs precede every change broad enough to be called the end of an epoch, or the coming of the Lord to judgment. They infallibly warn us of what is to come, as the falling leaves and the first frost tell us that winter is near.

---

[1]Others, among whom Lord Kingsbury is prominent, identify Quetzalcoatl with the Messiah himself. This might be supposed to agree with the remarkable story in the Book of Mormon concerning the appearance of Jesus in the Land of Bountiful after his crucifixion. (3 Ne. 11:26)
[2]Historians relate that the Christians, through the providence of the Lord, escaped the final calamities, in accordance with the words of Jesus: "When ye shall see Jerusalem encompassed * * * then let them which are in Judea flee to the mountains." (Luke 21:20) It appears that after General Cestius Gallus had enclosed the city, he suddenly, for some reason not now known, relaxed his vigilance, although leading men had offered to open the gates and surrender. When, later, Vespasian advanced, many fled to the mountains around Jericho, and especially to the little city of Pella, where they were comparatively safe.

## 2. *National Restoration Promised.*

7. But behold, thus saith the Lord God: When the day cometh that they shall believe in me, that I am Christ, then have I covenanted with their fathers that they shall be restored in the flesh, upon the earth, unto the lands of their inheritance.

8. And it shall come to pass that they shall be gathered in from their long dispersion, from the isles of the sea, and from the

---

VERSE 7. *They Shall Be Restored.* On this Condition: when "they shall believe in me, that I am Christ." The Hebrews have certainly not yet, as a whole, accepted Jesus of Nazareth as the Messiah, although many individuals have done so; but the ancient prejudices and inherited hatred have been greatly allayed among the educated classes. The Lord, apparently anxious to fulfil his promises to Abraham, Isaac and Jacob, has, therefore, already begun the gathering of their descendants in the Land of Promise. In 1896, Dr. Theodore Herzl was prompted to issue his famous pamphlet, "The Jewish State," which became the foundation stone of modern Zionism. In November 1917 Lord Balfour declared that "the British government would look with favor upon the restoration of Palestine as the Jewish homeland." This declaration may at first have been intended as a statement of the British policy only, and it may have been chiefly a bid for the support of the fifteen million Jews in the world for the cause of the allies in the world war. A Hebrew battalion was also organized against the Turks in Palestine, and Zionism obtained a recognized status in the world. After the great war, in 1922, the Balfour declaration was ratified by the League of Nations, and since then the gathering has proceeded rapidly. According to Mr. Gedaliah Bublick, a noted newspaper editor in Tel Aviv, Palestine, there were in 1920 only 55,000 Jews in the country. Sixteen years later there were 400,000, of whom ten thousand were immigrants from America. Owing to the anti-Semitic pressure in many countries, Zionism is one of the most important movements, at present.

During the month of August, 1929, sporadic attacks were made by Arabs on Jewish settlements, which were vigorously repulsed by the Jews. A royal British commission found, after inquiry, that the Arabs had very little reason for complaint, the Palestinian government having favored them in the matter of employment, taxation and budgetary allotments. But the discontent continued.

During the summer of 1936 an American commission, unofficial, consisting of U. S. Senators Copeland, Austin and Hastings, went to Palestine to investigate the cause of Arab outbreaks. During the month of December, that year, they reported the existence in the country of a political conflict between Jewish and Arab aspirations. Certain agitators, they found, were seeking to establish an Arabian state, and they feared that the Jews nourished similar plans. But the Balfour declaration did not contemplate anything but a Palestinian state, in which Jews and Arabs would have equal rights. The commission found no ground for prohibition of Jewish immigration. There is room for hundreds of thousands more settlers in Palestine, and if the Trans-Jordan is opened to the Jews, millions can find refuge in the land promised to Abraham and his descendants. (Gen. 15:18-21)

Zionism is a question of more than academic interest to the United States. For, on December 3, 1924, Great Britain and the United States, represented by the late Lord Balfour and the then Secretary of State, Charles Evans Hughes, resp., entered into a treaty by which the United States consented to the mandate of Great Britain

four parts of the earth; and the nations of the Gentiles shall be great in the eyes of me, saith God, in carrying them forth to the lands of their inheritance.

9. Yea, the kings of the Gentiles shall be nursing fathers unto them, and their queens shall become nursing mothers; wherefore, the promises of the Lord are great unto the Gentiles, for he hath spoken it, and who can dispute?

10. But behold, this land, said God, shall be a land of thine inheritance, and the Gentiles shall be blessed upon the land.

11. And this land shall be a land of liberty unto the Gentiles, and there shall be no kings upon the land, who shall raise up unto the Gentiles.

12. And I will fortify this land against all other nations.

13. And he that fighteth against Zion shall perish, saith God.

14. For he that raiseth up a king against me shall perish, for I, the Lord, the king of heaven, will be their king, and I will be a light unto them forever, that hear my words.

## 3. Secret Works of Darkness to be Destroyed.

15. Wherefore, for this cause, that my covenants may be fulfilled which I have made unto the children of men, that I will do unto them while they are in the flesh, I must needs destroy the secret works of darkness, and of murders, and of abominations.

over the Holy Land, as given by the League of Nations, and stipulated that the consent of the United States would be required to any change in that mandate.

VERSE 9. *Kings Shall Be Nursing Fathers.* See notes under verse 7.

VERSE 10. *This Land Shall Be . . . Thine Inheritance.* The important truth here stated would not be known but for the Book of Mormon. True, Jacob, the patriarch, foretold in his dying blessing that Joseph, as a fruitful bough, would send his branches over the wall, and that his blessings would include the "utmost bound of the everlasting hills." In the Book of Mormon it is shown how this was fulfilled.

VERSES 11-14. *No Kings Upon This Land.* See Mosiah 29:25-40; Deut. 17:14-17; 1 Sam. 9:17. Mosiah (29:13) explains that if it were possible to have kings always who would establish the laws of God and judge the people according to his commandments, there would be no objection to the title, as such, but (v. 16), "because all men are not just it is not expedient that ye should have a king or kings to rule over you." It is better to have officials that can be dismissed without revolutions.

VERSE 15. *Secret Works of Darkness.* Transgressions and plots planned in secret, and carried out under the cover of darkness. They are in the same class as murder and abominations. They are to be destroyed. But there is also another class of secret works. Our Lord says: "Take heed that ye do not your alms before men. . . . But when thou doest alms, let not thy left hand know what thy right hand doeth." Again: "And when thou prayest, thou shalt not be as the hypocrites . . . but pray to thy Father in secret; and the Father which seeth in secret, shall reward thee openly." (Matt. 6:1-18)

16. Wherefore, he that fighteth against Zion, both Jew and Gentile, both bond and free, both male and female, shall perish; for they are they who are the whore of all the earth; for they who are not for me are against me, saith our God.

17. For I will fulfil my promises which I have made unto the children of men, that I will do unto them while they are in the flesh—

18. Wherefore, my beloved brethren, thus saith our God: I will afflict thy seed by the hand of the Gentiles; nevertheless, I will soften the hearts of the Gentiles, that they shall be like unto a father to them; wherefore, the Gentiles shall be blessed and numbered among the house of Israel.

19. Wherefore, I will consecrate this land unto thy seed, and them who shall be numbered among thy seed, forever, for the land of their inheritance; for it is a choice land, saith God unto me, above all other lands, wherefore I will have all men that dwell thereon that they shall worship me, saith God.

### 4. Closing Admonitions.

20. And now, my beloved brethren, seeing that our merciful God has given us so great knowledge concerning these things, let

---

VERSE 16. *He That Fighteth Against Zion.* Fighting against Zion is one of the deeds that bring destruction upon the guilty individuals, be they Jews or Gentiles, bond or free, male or female.

*They Are They Who Are the Whore of All the Earth.* This is an exceedingly important revelation. In some Protestant circles it has been customary to regard a certain religious body as alone deserving that opprobrious epithet; but here we learn that it does not refer to any religious body in particular, but that everyone who engages in hostility against the people of God is a member of the abominable multitude, no matter what the religion, race or sex may be. Compare Rev. 17:14, where we read that the woman, arrayed in purple and scarlet and sitting on a scarlet colored beast "shall make war with the Lamb, and the Lamb shall overcome them;" both the woman and the beast; "for he is Lord of lords, and King of kings: and they that are with him are called, and chosen, and faithful."

VERSE 17. *I Will Fulfil My Promises.* The promises given to Noah, to Abraham and his descendants; to David, and many others, concerning his kingdom on earth. (See Pearl of Great Price, Moses 7:43-65; Gen. 17:16, 19; Ps. 46:9, 10; 76:2, 10) Secret works of darkness must be destroyed, if the promises are to be fulfilled.

VERSE 18. *Gentiles to be Blessed.* The prediction is here made that the descendants of Lehi would first be afflicted by Gentiles, but later treated kindly by the same class of people; wherefore these would be "numbered" among the children of Israel and become partakers of their blessings. (Comp. Rom. 9:4-8)

VERSE 19. *I Will Consecrate This Land.* For an inheritance of the descendants of Lehi and also the children of those who are numbered among them. A solemn warning is added. God will that all who live here shall worship him, this being a "choice" land, above all others; a consecrated land. Where the laws of God are enforced, none but those who really love and worship God will care to live.

us remember him, and lay aside our sins, and not hang down our heads, for we are not cast off; nevertheless, we have been driven out of the land of our inheritance; but we have been led to a better land, for the Lord has made the sea our path, and we are upon an isle of the sea.

21. But great are the promises of the Lord unto them who are upon the isles of the sea; wherefore as it says isles, there must needs be more than this, and they are inhabited also by our brethren.

22. For behold, the Lord God has led away from time to time from the house of Israel, according to his will and pleasure. And

now behold, the Lord remembereth all them who have been broken off, wherefore he remembereth us also.

23. Therefore, cheer up your hearts, and remember that ye are free to act for yourselves— to choose the way of everlasting death or the way of eternal life.

24. Wherefore, my beloved brethren, reconcile yourselves to the will of God, and not to the will of the devil and the flesh; and remember, after ye are reconciled unto God, that it is only in and through the grace of God that ye are saved.

25. Wherefore, may God raise you from death by the power of

---

VERSE 20. *We Are Upon An Isle of the Sea.* Comp. v. 8. For the comments of George Reynolds on this, see "Story of the Book of Mormon," p. 253, fifth edition; quoted in, "An Introduction to the Study of the Book of Mormon," p. 223. Dr. Brinton, "Library of Aboriginal American Literature," vol. 5, p. 134, says:

"The Indians almost universally believed the dry land they knew, to be part of a great island, everywhere surrounded by wide waters whose limits were unknown. Many tribes had vague myths of a journey from beyond this sea; many placed beyond it the home of the sun and of light, and the happy hunting grounds of the departed souls."

The Prophet Isaiah, speaking of the restoration of Israel, mentions "the Islands of the Sea" among the countries from which the people are to be gathered. (2 Ne. 21:11) Assyria, Elam, Pathros, Egypt, Cush, Shinar and Hamath are known. But where is the country he calls, "The Islands of the Sea?" Here is the answer. Read also verses 21 and 22.

VERSE 22. *God has Led Away from Time to Time from the House of Israel, According to His Will and Pleasure.* Modern research inclines to the view that immigration from Asia across the Pacific ocean and Islands in the south, and the Bering Strait in the north, furnished America with a mixed population thousands of years ago, and that a lively commerce was carried on between North and South America many centuries before the discovery by Columbus and subsequent adventurers. (See the Preface to "The Ayar Incas" by Dr. Miles Poindexter.) The evidence in favor of this opinion is also a testimony to the authenticity of the record in the Book of Mormon of the voyage of Lehi, and the information that "The Lord did bring Mulek into the land North" (Hel. 6:10), and this further revelation that the Lord has, from time to time, led colonies of Israelites from their main home to distant parts of the world.

the resurrection, and also from everlasting death by the power of the atonement, that ye may be received into the eternal kingdom of God, that ye may praise him through grace divine. Amen.

---

VERSE 25. *By the Power of the Atonement.* Note that Jacob, closes his sermon with a final testimony that it is through the Atonement of Christ alone that man can gain an entrance into the eternal kingdom of God, there to praise him for his grace divine. That is the sum and substance of the sermon. And it is stated in sentences which, through their beauty of literary style bear the marks of divine inspiration in every word.

> Christ died: His love and his atoning death we preach.
> Christ rose, and thus broke down the awful gates of hell.
> Christ went to heav'nly glory, as the Scriptures teach;
> The universal choir soon sings that, "All is Well."

## NOTES

"We are upon an isle of the sea." The statement refers to the American continents. Could the Prophet Isaiah possibly have had any knowledge of America? I am inclined to believe that he had.

King Solomon, about two hundred years before the time of the prophet, when the kingdom of Israel had attained its greatest height of glory in power, wealth, influence and fame, had two mercantile navies. One was stationed at Ezion-geber, on the Red Sea, in the land of Edom. (I Kings 9:26) The other was anchored at Tyre, the Liverpool of antiquity, where King Hiram harbored his own vessels between voyages. By means of these two fleets, one in the Mediterranean, and one in the Red Sea, Palestine was undoubtedly connected with the rest of the world along the usual sea routes to a much greater extent than now generally believed. That the ships of Solomon went on very long voyages is clear from 1 Kings 1:22, where it is stated that they made one voyage in three years. They would hardly need three years for a trip to the British Isles and return. It is more probable that they sometimes went out as far as Iceland, and from there to America.

## CHAPTER 11

*Nephi's Introduction to His Excerpts from the Book of the Prophet Isaiah.*

### 1. Introduction.

1. And now, Jacob spake many more things to my people at that time; nevertheless only these things have I caused to be written, for the things which I have written sufficeth me.

2. And now I, Nephi, write more of the words of Isaiah, for my soul delighteth in his words. For I will liken his words unto my people, and I will send them forth unto all my children, for he verily saw my Redeemer, even as I have seen him.

3. And my brother, Jacob, also has seen him as I have seen him; wherefore, I will send their words forth unto my children to prove unto them that my words are true. Wherefore, by the words of three, God hath said, I will establish my word. Nevertheless, God sendeth more witnesses, and he proveth all his words.

4. Behold, my soul delighteth in proving unto my people the truth of the coming of Christ; for, for this end hath the law of Moses been given; and all things which have been given of God from the beginning of the world, unto man, are the typifying of him.

VERSE 2. *My Soul Delighteth in his Words.* This chapter may be considered an introduction by Nephi to the excerpts he is about to make from the records of the Prophet Isaiah. There are twelve chapters from this book, from 2 to 13, inclusive, besides the paragraphs quoted by Jacob. (2 Ne. 7 and 8) Nephi states the reason why he reads and quotes that portion of the Old Testament. His soul delighteth in it. The Prophet had seen the Redeemer and his testimony of that fact was a strong corroboration of the testimony of Nephi, who also said he had seen our divine Savior. In addition, Isaiah spoke of the gathering of Israel and Judah, and that must have been a gospel of infinite consolation to the exiles on the Islands of the Sea.

VERSE 3. *Jacob,* too, had seen the Savior. Three witnesses were fully competent to establish the fact itself of the existence of Jesus, even before his birth in the flesh.

VERSE 4. *The Coming of Christ.* Isaiah has been called "The Evangelical Prophet," because of his abundant predictions concerning the Messiah, his birth, his character, ministry, passion, death, his final victory and the majesty and glory of his kingdom. Nephi, who lived long before the Advent, delighted in the study of these themes. And it was necessary to study them in order to prove their truth to others.

*The Law of Moses* was given for the same purpose. To explain the Gospel of Christ. Refers especially to the ceremonial law. The dedication of the firstborn (Ex. 12:2); The distinction between clean and unclean food; the rules for purification; lawful and unlawful marriages; the laws regarding priestly orders, holy places, times of holding services; the Sabbath, the sabbatical year (every 7th); the year of

5. And also my soul delighteth in the covenants of the Lord which he hath made to our fathers; yea, my soul delighteth in his grace, and in his justice, and power, and mercy in the great and eternal plan of deliverance from death.

6. And my soul delighteth in proving unto my people that save Christ should come all men must perish.

7. For if there be no Christ there be no God; and if there be no God we are not, for there could have been no creation. But there is a God, and he is Christ, and he cometh in the fulness of his own time.

8. And now I write some of the words of Isaiah, that whoso of my people shall see these words may lift up their hearts and rejoice for all men. Now these are the words, and ye may liken them unto you and unto all men.

---

jubilee; passover; the feast of weeks; of tabernacles of trumpets, and the day of atonement. All such precepts were given for the purpose of teaching the children of Israel the first principles of the Gospel.

VERSE 5. *The Covenants of the Lord.* See notes 2 Ne. 10:17.

*In his Grace, Justice, Power, and Mercy,* in the plan of deliverance from death. *Grace* means the love of God, which is the source of all the benefits we receive from him. But it means also, in a secondary sense, the benefits themselves which we receive, among all of which the Gospel of Jesus Christ is the greatest. When John, in his Gospel, says: "The Law was given by Moses, but grace and truth came by Jesus Christ (John 1:17); he means to say that, as the Old Mosaic dispensation came through Moses, so the New Gospel dispensation has come through Jesus Christ. Paul uses the word, grace, in the same sense: "As sin has reigned unto death, even so, might grace"—the Gospel—"reign through righteousness unto eternal life by Jesus Christ, our Lord." (Rom. 5:21.)

*Mercy.* Justice does not exclude mercy. Sometimes what we call "justice" may be rank injustice, because we do never know for certain what mitigating circumstances, due to heredity or environment, are responsible in a case of transgression. Sometimes mercy is justice. In the Old dispensation the tables of law were covered by the "Mercy Seat," a most wonderful type of the government of God, who has said: "I, the Lord, will forgive whom I will forgive, but of you it is required to forgive all men." (D. and C. 64:10.)

VERSE 6. *Save Christ Should Come All Men Must Perish.* Nephi says he delights in proving this truth. His argument here takes the form of a compound syllogism, known as "sorites," of which we have had several examples in this book.

## CHAPTER 12

*The Millennial Government, 1-4—Apostasy of the House of Jacob, 5-9—*
*Punishment of Pride, 10-21—Conclusion, 22. Comp. Is. 2.*

### 1. *The Millennial Government.*

1. The word that Isaiah, the son of Amoz, saw concerning Judah and Jerusalem:

2. And it shall come to pass in the last days, when the mountain of the Lord's house shall be established in the top of the mountains, and shall be exalted above the hills, and all nations shall flow unto it.

3. And many people shall go and say, Come ye, and let us go up to the mountain of the Lord, to the house of the God of Jacob; and he will teach us of his ways, and we will walk in his paths; for out of Zion shall go forth the law, and the word of the Lord from Jerusalem.

---

VERSE 1. *The Word that Isaiah, the Son of Amoz, Saw.* That is all we know about the authorship of this prophetic word. It is almost identical with Micah 4:1-3. Either of these prophets may be the author, or, they may be quoting from a common source. It is one of the sure words of prophecy, of which the Apostle Peter says: "Whereunto ye do well that ye take heed, as unto a light that shineth in a dark place." It is a "word" of more than common importance; otherwise it would not have been incorporated in the texts of two great Old Testament Prophets, and then in the record of Nephi.

*Concerning Judah and Jerusalem.* Judah and Jerusalem are concerned, as being the immediate objects of the prophecy, but, as the context shows, it concerns the entire world. God has so ordained it, that the blessings of light and life are to come to mankind through one chosen family, the descendants of Abraham. They are the wires by means of which the power from the central, Divine Source has been, and will continue to be, diffused to all the world. So, the Apostle Paul: "If the casting away of them"—their dispersion—"be the reconciling of the world, what shall the receiving of them"—their gathering—"be, but life from the dead?" (Rom. 11:15)

VERSE 2. *In the Last Days.* Refers clearly to the Millennium. See D. and C. 29:11, 22, 23; 43:30, 31.

*Mountain of the Lord's House.* The word "mountain" is used in the Scriptures in different allegorical, or figurative, meanings, besides the literal sense. Here it stands for the Church of God, which, as the fifth kingdom, is destined to grow from the size of a stone to that of a mountain and fill the world. (Dan. 2:35, 45) The meaning is, therefore, that when the Church of God shall be established in the top of the mountains and be exalted above the hills, then all nations shall flow unto it.

VERSE 3. *Many People.* When the Church shall be thus established and exalted, then "many people"—not everybody, for even during the Millennium there will be different creeds and modes of worship (Micah 4:5)—but many people shall come and join the Church, enter the house of the Lord, to learn his will, accept his instructions and walk in his paths.

4. And he shall judge among the nations, and shall rebuke many people: and they shall beat their swords into plow-shares, and their spears into pruning-hooks—nation shall not lift up sword against nation, neither shall they learn war any more.

## 2. The Apostasy of the House of Jacob.

5. O house of Jacob, come ye and let us walk in the light of the Lord; yea, come, for ye have all gone astray, every one to his wicked ways.

6. Therefore, O Lord, thou hast forsaken thy people, the house of Jacob, because they be replenished from the east, and hearken unto soothsayers like the Philistines, and they please themselves in the children of strangers.

7. Their land also is full of silver and gold, neither is there any end of their treasures; their land is also full of horses, neither is there any end of their chariots.

8. Their land is also full of idols; they worship the work of their own hands, that which their own fingers have made.

9. And the mean man boweth not down, and the great man humbleth himself not, therefore, forgive him not.

---

VERSE 4. *Then the Earth will have Peace.* The result will be as stated in this verse. National affairs will be regulated by divine law, and international differences will be adjusted by divinely inspired arbitration. Peace will reign, and temple work will go on undisturbed.

"He shall judge among the Nations." That is the explanation of the expression in the previous verse: "The word of the Lord from Jerusalem."

VERSE 5. *The Light of the Lord.* The light of revelation. They had gone astray from that light.

VERSE 6. *Replenished from the East.* As the darkness around became more and more intense in the progress away from the light, and the minds became more and more empty as regards divine impressions, they tried to "replenish"—refill—them with Oriental superstitions, "soothsaying" — fortunetelling, which is the poorest possible substitute for the divine word of prophecy.
*One Consequence.* This led to intimate association with strangers, the adoption of their social habits and forms of devotion.

VERSE 7. *Other Consequences.* They accumulated enormous wealth, gold and silver. But also an enormous military organization, horses and chariots.

VERSE 8. *Idolatry.* Great prosperity and militarism are a combination incompatible with the worship of God. Devotion to the Maker of the heavens and the earth, revealed in the Prince of Peace, naturally makes a worshiper abhor an institution of which the archenemy of God and man is the originator and the perpetuator.
*Their Own Hands—Made.* To worship the conceptions of one's own mind —the creations of one's own hands—indicates ignorance and simplicity.

VERSE 9. *Forgive him not.* The meaning of this verse is: Although the people are simple-minded and ignorant, yet, both the common and the outstanding individuals are too proud to be humble; therefore God cannot forgive them.

### 3. *Punishment of Pride.*

10. O ye wicked ones, enter into the rock, and hide thee in the dust, for the fear of the Lord and the glory of his majesty shall smite thee.

11. And it shall come to pass that the lofty looks of man shall be humbled, and the haughtiness of men shall be bowed down, and the Lord alone shall be exalted in that day.

12. For the day of the Lord of Hosts soon cometh upon all nations, yea, upon every one; yea, upon the proud and lofty, and upon every one who is lifted up, and he shall be brought low.

13. Yea, and the day of the Lord shall come upon all the cedars of Lebanon, for they are high and lifted up; and upon all the oaks of Bashan;

14. And upon all the high mountains, and upon all the hills, and upon all the nations which are lifted up, and upon every people;

15. And upon every high tower, and upon every fenced wall;

16. And upon all the ships of the sea, and upon all the ships of Tarshish, and upon all pleasant pictures.

17. And the loftiness of man shall be bowed down, and the haughtiness of men shall be made low; and the Lord alone shall be exalted in that day.

---

The previous section closes (v. 9) with the observation that, since neither the common people nor the outstanding individuals humble themselves before the Lord, there can not be any forgiveness. In this section the consequences of pride are enumerated.

VERSE 12. *The Day of the Lord of Hosts Soon Cometh.* The day of the Lord, also called the day of judgment and the coming of the Lord, sometimes stands for any period of time during which nations, or countries, are visited with great calamities. (Is. 63:4; 2 Pet. 3:12:13; Ps. 36:13-15)

"Jesus has been upon the earth a great many more times than you are aware of. When Jesus makes his next appearance upon the earth, but few of this Church will be prepared to receive him and see him face to face and converse with him; but he will come to his temple. Will he remain and dwell upon the earth a thousand years, without returning? He will come here and return to his mansions where he dwells with his Father, and come again to the earth, and again return to his Father, according to my understanding. Then angels will come and begin to resurrect the dead, and the Savior will also raise the dead, and they will receive the keys of the resurrection, and will begin to assist in that work. Will the wicked know of it? They will know just as much about that as they now know about 'Mormonism' and no more." (Brigham Young, Discourses, Selected and Arranged by Dr. John A. Widtsoe, p. 176.)

VERSE 16. *Upon All Pleasant Pictures.* "Pleasant Pictures" refers to the standards or figure heads of the ships. The prophet has, in the previous verses of this section, emphasized the fact that humiliation would be the consequence of pride. All that was high and exalted in its own estimation would be debased and humiliated. (vv. 12. Comp. v. 17.) He enumerates: The cedars of Lebanon, the oaks of Bashan, the mountains and hills, the nations and people, the towers and walls and, finally, the ships of the sea, even the largest, the Tarshish ships, with

18. And the idols he shall utterly abolish.

19. And they shall go into the holes of the rocks, and into the caves of the earth, for the fear of the Lord shall come upon them and the glory of his majesty shall smite them, when he ariseth to shake terribly the earth.

20. In that day a man shall cast his idols of silver, and his idols of gold, which he hath made for himself to worship, to the moles and to the bats;

21. To go into the clefts of the rocks, and into the tops of the ragged rocks, for the fear of the Lord shall come upon them and the majesty of his glory shall smite them, when he ariseth to shake terribly the earth.

## 4. Conclusion.

22. Cease ye from man, whose breath is in his nostrils; for wherein is he to be accounted of?

their proud standards or figure heads. All shall be made low, and the Lord alone shall be exalted. (v. 17)

VERSES 18-20. *Idols.* In verse 8 the prophet notes that the land is full of idols. Here he predicts the destruction of all images that are being worshiped, be they ever so costly. Idols of gold and silver shall be thrown into the dark and dusty corners infested by "moles and bats."

VERSE 22. *Cease Ye from Man.* The meaning seems to be: Do not rely on man whose mortal existence is but as a breath of air. Rely on God.

### GENERAL NOTES

In Acts 28:11 the student will find an illustration of the meaning of the expression, "pleasant pictures." There we are informed that the ship in which Paul traveled from Malta to Rome had Castor and Pollux for a "sign." Those mythical twin sons of Zeus were the supposed protectors of the ship, and their images were painted, or sculptured in a prominent place on the ship. Others had different protectors and therefore different images and standards. But idols, whether on land or sea will be utterly destroyed in the wrath of the day of the Lord.

## CHAPTER 13

*Oppression and Anarchy, 1-15 — Fashionable Luxury Doomed, 16-26. Comp. Isaiah 3.*

### 1. *Oppression and Anarchy.*

1. For behold, the Lord, the Lord of Hosts, doth take away from Jerusalem, and from Judah, the stay and the staff, the whole staff of bread, and the whole stay of water—

2. The mighty man, and the man of war, the judge, and the prophet, and the prudent, and the ancient;

3. The captain of fifty, and the honorable man, and the counselor, and the cunning artificer, and the eloquent orator.

4. And I will give children unto them to be their princes, and babes shall rule over them.

5. And the people shall be oppressed, every one by another, and every one by his neighbor; the child shall behave himself proudly against the ancient, and the base against the honorable.

6. When a man shall take hold of his brother of the house of his father, and shall say: Thou hast clothing, be thou our ruler, and let not this ruin come under thy hand—

7. In that day shall he swear, saying: I will not be a healer; for in my house there is neither bread nor clothing; make me not a ruler of the people.

8. For Jerusalem is ruined, and Judah is fallen, because their tongues and their doings have been against the Lord, to provoke the eyes of his glory.

9. The show of their countenance doth witness against them, and doth declare their sin to be even as Sodom, and they cannot hide it. Wo unto their souls, for they have rewarded evil unto themselves!

---

VERSE 1. *Stay and Staff.* Refer to articles of food, but also to the leaders of the people enumerated in verses 2 and 3.

VERSE 4. *Children shall Rule.* Consequently, children would be the rulers. This was particularly unfortunate when the country had been swept by destructive tornadoes and devastated, needed the wise and steady counsel of experienced men.

VERSE 5. *The People Shall be Oppressed.* Anarchy prevailed. Everybody took advantage of his neighbor. Children defied and humiliated their elders; the unworthy crowded those who were entitled to honor and respect to the wall.

VERSES 6-9. *Thou hast Clothing, etc.* Thou hast, at least, a respectable-looking raiment. Take the government of the ruined state into thy hands. But the individual approached shall refuse emphatically to accept the offer. His answer is: It is a physician the people need, and I am not a healer (v. 7). I have no food and no clothes in my house to distribute. It would do you no good to put me at the head of the government, if it is maintenance you are expecting. Look at their faces. (v. 9) Their appearance testifies against them. They cannot hide their sin.

10. Say unto the righteous that it is well with them; for they shall eat the fruit of their doings.

11. Wo unto the wicked, for they shall perish; for the reward of their hands shall be upon them!

12. And my people, children are their oppressors, and women rule over them. O my people, they who lead thee cause thee to err and destroy the way of thy paths.

13. The Lord standeth up to plead, and standeth to judge the people.

14. The Lord will enter into judgment with the ancients of his people and the princes thereof; for ye have eaten up the vineyard and the spoil of the poor in your houses.

15. What mean ye? Ye beat my people to pieces, and grind the faces of the poor, saith the Lord God of Hosts.

## 2. Fashionable Luxury Doomed.

16. Moreover, the Lord saith: Because the daughters of Zion are haughty, and walk with stretched-forth necks and wanton eyes, walking and mincing as they go, and making a tinkling with their feet—

17. Therefore the Lord will smite with a scab the crown of the head of the daughters of Zion, and the Lord will discover their secret parts.

18. In that day the Lord will take away the bravery of their

---

VERSES 10-11. *The Righteous — the Wicked.* The righteous need really not fear. They have the fruit of their works to draw on. The wicked perish as a result of the unnatural use to which they have put their own hands. God is just.

VERSES 12-15. *Children are Oppressors, etc.* Inexperienced rulers are likely to become tyrants and to bring about all kinds of misgovernment. This happened (v. 12), but the Lord would stand up to plead and to judge (13). "The Lord will enter into judgment with the ancients." I understand this to mean, probably, that he would inspire the elders of the people, and strengthen them to state their grievance and pronounce the consequences.

*Lord God of Hosts.* The same as "Lord of Sabaoth" (Rom. 9:29; James 5:4), or, Zebaoth, The hosts of the Lord are his angels, the ministers of the Lord and his people, or, the innumerable heavenly bodies in the firmament, all of which are the subjects of his will.

VERSES 16-17. *Because the Daughters of Zion are Haughty.* The wealthy, fashionable women were, undoubtedly as guilty as the men in the oppression of the poor, wherefore the poor, wherefore the vengeance of the Almighty fell upon them, too, in the form of loathsome diseases, or captivity, with scanty clothing (v. 17).

VERSES 18-24. *Feminine Ornaments.* In this section a very complete list of feminine jewelry and ornaments is furnished by the prophet. We notice, "tinkling ornaments," probably rings worn on the feet; "cauls," nets, or perhaps

tinkling ornaments, and cauls, and round tires like the moon;

19. The chains and the bracelets, and the mufflers;

20. The bonnets, and the ornaments of the legs, and the headbands, and the tablets, and the ear-rings;

21. The rings, and nose jewels;

22. The changeable suits of apparel, and the mantles, and the wimples, and the crisping-pins;

23. The glasses, and the fine linen, and hoods, and the veils.

24. And it shall come to pass, instead of sweet smell there shall be stink; and instead of a girdle, a rent; and instead of well set hair, baldness; and instead of a stomacher, a girding of sackcloth; burning instead of beauty.

25. Thy men shall fall by the sword and thy mighty in the war.

26. And her gates shall lament and mourn; and she shall be desolate, and shall sit upon the ground.

diadems; "round tires," necklaces (v. 18); "chains, bracelets and mufflers;" probably, earrings, bracelets and veils (v. 19); "ornaments of the legs," chains connecting the legs, to prevent the wearer from taking too long steps when walking; "headbands, tablets and ear-rings," (v. 20), also translated, "girdles, perfume bottles and amulets, or charms;" "glasses," (v. 20) means "mirrors." The Lord would cause all these to be removed. Instead of finery there would be the misery of women in slavery, even "burning instead of beauty" (v. 24), which evidently refers to the mark of the cruel brand-iron on slaves. To these sufferings would be added the agony of seeing the men in every grade of society swept away by war. In the gates (v. 26) where, under normal conditions, business was transacted and affairs of state and communities discussed, lamentations and mourning were heard. Zion, desolate, was sitting in the dust on the ground.

## CHAPTER 14

*Millennial Conditions Promised—Compare Isaiah 4.*

### 1. *Take away our reproach.*

1. And in that day, seven women shall take hold of one man, saying: We will eat our own bread, and wear our own apparel; only let us be called by thy name to take away our reproach.

2. In that day shall the branch of the Lord be beautiful and glorious; the fruit of the earth excellent and comely to them that are escaped of Israel.

3. And it shall come to pass, they that are left in Zion and remain in Jerusalem shall be called holy, every one that is written among the living in Jerusalem—

---

VERSE 1. *In that Day.* That is, when a large part of the male population shall have been exterminated by war and its concomitants, seven women shall offer themselves to one man, as here stated.

*To Take Away our Reproach.* In the old times a woman, as a rule, considered it unfortunate not to have the privilege of motherhood. See the story of Rachel in the Old Testament, Gen. 30:33; or, in the New Testament, Elizabeth, the mother of John the Baptist, Luke, 1:25. The misfortune must have been felt more keenly at a time when the population had been practically decimated. A plurality of wives in one household, under the protection of one man may, according to this prophetic utterance, be a more desirable arrangement than one by which six women of every seven are excluded from the joys and responsibilities of a mother. It is no defense of lawlessness to say that under similar circumstances the same remedy might be applied again. But only by divine revelation through the Prophet authorized to speak for the Lord. (See Jacob 2:27-30; D. and C. 43:2-6.)

VERSE 2. *The Branch.* This is generally understood to refer to the Messiah. But see 2 Ne. 3:5; 10:1; Is. 60:21; 61:3.

VERSE 3. Holiness has been defined as "conformity to the nature and the will of God, whereby a Saint is distinguished from the unrenewed world; and is not actuated by their principles and precepts, nor governed by their maxims and customs." (Cruden's Concordance under "Holiness.") Israel was commanded to be a "holy nation, a sanctified nation, a nation of saints. (Ex. 19:6) The followers of our Savior are in the New Testament often referred to as "saints," which indicates that they were regarded as sanctified, separated from the "world" by their purer faith and more perfect practices. In this remarkable prophecy the prediction is made that, in the latter days, when Israel and Judah (v. 4) are being gathered in from the dispersion, those who remain after having passed through the fiery trials, whether in Zion or Jerusalem, will be known as "holy,"—that is, as "Saints."

*Written Among the Living.* Mme. Lydia M. von Finkelstein Mountford, in her little gem of a book, "Jesus Christ in His Homeland," explains that the book of the living in the Roman empire, at the time our Savior was born, was a volume in which property owners were registered as living, when they had fulfilled their duties, as required of them. The book was Caesar's "Book of Life." Mme. Mountford tells an incident to which she was an eyewitness during the late reign of the Turks in

4. When the Lord shall have washed away the filth of the daughters of Zion, and shall have purged the blood of Jerusalem from the midst thereof by the spirit of judgment and by the spirit of burning.

5. And the Lord will create upon every dwelling-place of mount Zion, and upon her assemblies, a cloud and smoke by day and the shining of a flaming fire by night; for upon all the glory of Zion shall be a defence.

6. And there shall be a tabernacle for a shadow in the daytime from the heat, and for a place of refuge, and a covert from storm and from rain.

---

her homeland, Palestine. The occasion was one of registration of tax payers. A man brought up, she says, weak and feeble. In fact, he was carried on a stretcher. The tax gatherer asked the secretary to ascertain his name and to write it down, if he was worthy. Then he asked:

"Hast thou written it?"

The Secretary: "Yes, my lord, for it is worthy to be written in the Book of Life."

"Then," the narrator says, that man raised himself up on his elbow, and he looked at us with wondrous eyes and said: "Praise and thanks unto God, my name is written in the Book of Life." Whereupon he again reclined upon the stretcher and passed away, peacefully and happy. This may help us to understand, better, this expression, "written among the living," and also, "The Book of Life," and, "The Lamb's Book of Life," in Rev. 20:12 and 21:27.

VERSE 4. *Spirit of Burning.* The divine punishment is like a fire which separates the good from the evil, and then consumes the bad element while it purifies that which is good.

VERSE 5. *A Defense.* A protecting cover. But even so, the expression needs explanation. Perhaps a question might help. Suppose the prophet, seven hundred years before our era, had been carried away, in the spirit, to Ensign Peak and been permitted to see Salt Lake valley, as it is today, first at noon, then at sunset with its indescribable beauty of colors; then, let us suppose that he had seen the shadows of night fall, and, all of a sudden, the entire valley, as by a miracle, lit up by thousands of lights, the Temple radiant among all the glittering little stars; how would he have described this vision to a public not aware of electricity, and he, himself, just as ignorant in that particular as his hearers, except by saying just what he did say, that the Lord had created upon every dwelling place on Mount Zion, and upon her assemblies, a cloud and smoke by day, and the shining of a flaming fire by night; and that this marvelous beauty, this evidence of progress and prosperity, would be the protection of the glory of Zion? Or, suppose that the prophet had been standing on the Mount of Olives in Palestine, at a future day, viewing the New Jerusalem and the new temple across the Valley of Kedron, and the thousands of homes that will be there, even more wonderfully illuminated, as scientific marvels are multiplied; what could he have said in a description? That the modern glory of Zion reminded him of the cloud and the fire by which God anciently manifested his glory to Israel is certain. (See Ex. 13:21; 33:18; Numb. 9:15; 2 Chron. 5:13, 14. See also Ezek. 11:22, 23; 43:1-5)

VERSE 6. *Shadow.* An explanation of the "cloud" in the preceding verse.

*Covert.* Means "shelter," the same as "defense."

## GENERAL NOTES

Some scholars regard the first verse of this chapter as belonging to the preceding chapter. It might be well, therefore, to remember that the division of the Bible into chapters and verses is not part of the original arrangement of the sacred volume.

"The present division of the Scriptures into chapters and verses . . . are not of divine origin, nor are they of great antiquity. The Vulgate was the first version divided into chapters: a work undertaken by Cardinal Hugo, in the 13th century, or, as Jahn thinks, by Langton, archbishop of Canterbury, 1227. He introduced the division into chapters only. The Hebrew Scriptures were similarly divided by Mordecai Nathan, in 1445, and in 1661 Athias added in his printed text, the division into verses. The New Testament was divided in the same way by Robert Stephens, who is said to have completed it in the year 1551, during a journey (inter equitandum), from Paris to Lyons.

"As might be expected, these divisions are very imperfect, and even when not inaccurate, they tend to break the sense and to obscure the meaning." (Bible Handbook, by Dr. Joseph Angus, p. 60)

Modern Jews use the present division of the Old Testament, but anciently, when referring to their sacred scriptures, they mentioned the subject of the paragraph, as, for instance "in Elias" (Rom. 11:2), which is 1 Kings 17:19. "The Bow" in 2 Sam. 1:18 refers to a poem so called, in the Book of Jasher, and, in "The Bush" (Mark 12:26, and other places), may refer to Exodus 3.

## CHAPTER 15

*The Vineyard of the Lord, 1-7—A Sixfold Wo, 8-24—When the Anger of the Lord is Kindled, 25-30. Compare Isaiah 5.*

### 1. *The Vineyard of the Lord.*

1. And then will I sing to my well-beloved a song of my be-loved, touching his vineyard. My well-beloved hath a vineyard in a very fruitful hill.

2. And he fenced it, and gathered out the stones thereof, and planted it with the choicest vine, and built a tower in the midst of it, and also made a wine-press therein; and he looked that it should bring forth grapes, and it brought forth wild grapes.

3. And now, O inhabitants of Jerusalem, and men of Judah, judge, I pray you, betwixt me and my vineyard.

4. What could have been done more to my vineyard that I have not done in it? Wherefore, when I looked that it should bring forth grapes it brought forth wild grapes.

5. And now go to; I will tell you what I will do to my vine-yard—I will take away the hedge thereof, and it shall be eaten up; and I will break down the wall thereof, and it shall be trodden down;

6. And I will lay it waste; it shall not be pruned nor digged; but there shall come up briers and thorns; I will also command the clouds that they rain no rain upon it.

The Israelites had a yearly festival, at the end of their year, called the feast of ingathering (Ex. 23:16; 34:22), because on that occasion the people were required to give thanks especially for the harvest of fields and vineyards. It has been suggested that this song, or poem, was composed and recited on such an occasion. It contains a parable in which Israel is represented as a vineyard (as in Is. 3:14), and the consequences of the neglect of unfaithful keepers. (Matt. 21:33-41) As a literary composition, no less than as a prophetic utterance, it is regarded as an outstanding piece of sacred reading.

VERSE 1. *The Vineyard.* This is Israel, (See v. 7)

*My Well-beloved is the Lord.* The Prophet says that in this composition he is singing God's own song—a song inspired by the divine Spirit—concerning his people—his vineyard.

VERSE 2. *A Tower.* From which the vineyard and surrounding territory could be watched, and the approach of enemies, or animals, could be seen in time to prevent depredations.

*Wild Grapes.* The small, sour variety that has but little commercial value, if any.

VERSE 5. *What Will I Do?* In the preceding verse the Lord asks what more he could do to the vineyard to make it a success. In this and the following verses he explains, in words of burning wrath, what he is about to do.

*Eaten Up.* The hedge and the wall would be broken down and the vineyard overrun with grazing animals.

7. For the vineyard of the Lord of Hosts is the house of Israel, and the men of Judah his pleasant plant; and he looked for judgment, and behold, oppression; for righteousness, but behold, a cry.

## 2. A Sixfold Wo.

8. Wo unto them that join house to house, till there can be no place, that they may be placed alone in the midst of the earth!

9. In mine ears, said the Lord of Hosts, of a truth many houses shall be desolate, and great and fair cities without inhabitant.

10. Yea, ten acres of vineyard shall yield one bath, and the seed of a homer shall yield an ephah.

11. Wo unto them that rise up early in the morning, that they may follow strong drink, that continue until night, and wine inflame them!

12. And the harp, and the viol, the tabret, and pipe, and wine are in their feasts; but they regard not the work of the Lord, neither consider the operation of his hands.

13. Therefore, my people are

---

VERSE 7. *Oppression.* Means here more particularly the shedding of blood. The closing sentences present an instance of rhyme rarely found in Hebrew poetry. It might be rendered somewhat like this, approximately:

> He looked for legal intercession,
> But, lo, oppression!
> For righteousness (none would deny),
> But heard a cry.
> —"A Cry." Comp. James 5:4.

VERSES 8-24. In this section the Prophet enumerates some of the principal causes of the downfall of Israel and Judah. It is a mirror in which modern nations may look with profit. They are:

VERSES 8-10. Wo unto them that join house to house. Property acquired for selfish purposes is not a blessing. Greed is never satisfied. Ownership of property is not condemned. The only question is, how did the owner get it, and to what use does he put it?

*Ten Acres.* With the curse of God upon the land, ten acres would yield only one bath of wine (about 8 gallons); an ephah (v. 10) was a tenth part of a homer, so that the yield was only a tenth part of the sowing.

VERSE 11. *Intoxication.* Slaves of strong drinks have no time, nor inclination, for useful endeavor. Early and late, their craving, like a burning flame, consumes what is good in them.

*Drink and Music.* The art of music is of divine origin, and its proper purpose is to enable man to praise the Creator and to consider the marvelous operations of his hands. (v. 12) But the music of the drunkard drowns the nobler thoughts and sinks the victim to the level of the lower brutes. The music of satan in bar rooms and places of revelry, where intoxicants flow, is poison to all spiritual and intellectual life, and a source of destruction of nations. (vv. 14-17)

gone into captivity, because they have no knowledge; and their honorable men are famished, and their multitude dried up with thirst.

14. Therefore, hell hath enlarged herself, and opened her mouth without measure; and their glory, and their multitude, and their pomp, and he that rejoiceth, shall descend into it.

15. And the mean man shall be brought down, and the mighty man shall be humbled, and the eyes of the lofty shall be humbled.

16. But the Lord of Hosts shall be exalted in judgment, and God that is holy shall be sanctified in righteousness.

17. Then shall the lambs feed after their manner, and the waste places of the fat ones shall strangers eat.

18. Wo unto them that draw iniquity with cords of vanity, and sin as it were with a cart rope;

19. That say: Let him make speed, hasten his work, that we may see it; and let the counsel of the Holy One of Israel draw nigh and come, that we may know it.

20. Wo unto them that call evil good, and good evil, that put darkness for light, and light for darkness, that put bitter for sweet, and sweet for bitter!

---

VERSES 18-19. *Iniquity and Sin.* Generally refer to all kinds of wickedness and transgression of the law, but in the languages of the Scriptures "iniquity" also means, the punishment by which sin is atoned for. As for instance, when it is said that Aaron "may bear the iniquity of the holy things" (Ex. 28:38), it means that he was to atone for the impurity which may have adhered to them. In the same way, "sin" means not only an overt act, but also the atonement for sin. The sense here seems to be:

> Wo unto them who, in their vanity, are clamoring
> for the punishment of others,
> And pulling for retribution
> As with cart ropes,
> Saying, Let him make speed and hasten his work
> That we may see it;
> And let the counsel of the Holy One of
> Israel draw nigh and come
> That we may know it.

Comp. 2 Peter 3:3-14: "There shall come, in the last days, scoffers, walking after their own lusts and saying, Where is the promise of his coming? For since the fathers fell asleep, all things continue as they were from the beginning of the creation. . . . The Lord is not slack concerning his promise as some men count slackness; but is long suffering to usward, not willing that any should perish but that all should come to repentance. But the day of the Lord will come as a thief in the night."

VERSE 20. *Falsehood.* The Prophet denounces falsehood as one of the causes of the downfall of the nation. And justly so. To say that darkness is light and light darkness, that sweet is bitter and bitter sweet, etc., is to take a stand of opposition to our Lord, who in his life, in his very existence, was, and is, the embodiment of Truth. The great mystery of Pilate, which, some say, has come down through

21. Wo unto the wise in their own eyes and prudent in their own sight!

22. Wo unto the mighty to drink wine, and men of strength to mingle strong drink;

23. Who justify the wicked for reward, and take away the righteousness of the righteous from him!

24. Therefore, as the fire devoureth the stubble, and the flame consumeth the chaff, their root shall be rottenness, and their blossoms shall go up as dust; because they have cast away the law of the Lord of Hosts, and despised the word of the Holy One of Israel.

### 3. *When the Anger of the Lord is Kindled.*

25. Therefore, is the anger of the Lord kindled against his people, and he hath stretched forth his hand against them, and hath smitten them; and the hills did tremble, and their carcasses were

---

the centuries as an unanswered question, was anticipated by our Lord, when he declared, "I am the way, the truth and the life," and when he added, "No man cometh unto the Father, but by me," (John 14:6), he virtually said that the road of Truth is the only way there is to progress, back to the Father. He was that road. From one point of view considered, truth is the correct knowledge of the present, the past and the future (D. and C. 93:24). But the source of such knowledge is Christ (D. and C. 88:7-15, 50). It is he that is in the sun, the moon, the stars, the earth, and human intelligence, the immensity of space, and in all things. The perversion of truth, be it in religion, in politics, in business, or in family and social circles, in the pulpit or the press or radio, on the rostrum or the soap box, is really warfare against Him, to whom has been given all power in heaven and on earth.

VERSE 21. *Pride.* The prophet here pronounces wo unto those who are putting a too high estimate upon their own wisdom and prudence. Lacking humility, they are unfit for leadership. Not knowing obedience, they cannot command. Their wisdom is apt to be folly; their prudence ignorance. If a man is truly great, he need not blow his own trumpet; his friends know it before he himself does.

VERSES 22-24. *Intemperance in Officers.* In vv. 11-17 drunken revelry in general has been condemned as a cause of the downfall of the nation. Here a special wo is pronounced because of the indulgence of the administrators of the law in strong drink. Wo the drunkards who justify the wicked for reward, and condemn the righteous! Verse 24 may be paraphrased thus:

> "As fire devoureth stubble
> And the flame consumeth chaff,
> So shall their roots rot
> And their foliage blow away as dust,
> Because they have despised the law of the
> Lord of Hosts,
> And set aside the word of the Holy One of Israel."

VERSE 25. *Anger of the Lord.* Can God be angry? The Scriptures say he can. For instance, Num. 25:4; 32:14; Deut. 21:20, and many other passages. The question is similar to another: "Can God hear?" Or "see?" The Psalmist answers that query

torn in the midst of the streets. For all this his anger is not turned away, but his hand is stretched out still.

26. And he will lift up an ensign to the nations from far, and will hiss unto them from the end of the earth; and behold, they shall come with speed swiftly; none shall be weary nor stumble among them.

27. None shall slumber nor sleep; neither shall the girdle of their loins be loosed, nor the latchet of their shoes be broken;

28. Whose arrows shall be sharp, and all their bows bent, and their horses' hoofs shall be counted like flint, and their wheels like a whirlwind, their roaring like a lion.

29. They shall roar like young lions; yea, they shall roar, and lay hold of the prey, and shall carry away safe, and none shall deliver.

30. And in that day they shall roar against them like the roaring of the sea; and if they look unto the land, behold, darkness and sorrow, and the light is darkened in the heavens thereof.

---

by propounding another: "He that planted the ear, shall he not hear? He that formed the eye, shall he not see? He that chastiseth the heathen, shall he not correct?" (Psalm 94:9, 10) May we not continue and ask: He that made his children sensitive to the injustice and sufferings of fellow beings, shall he be immovable, himself as a cold marble statue?" That is unthinkable. The Scriptures speak not only of his wrath, but of his "fierce wrath." However, they also give us to understand that,

"His anger endureth but a moment,
But his favor all our life:
There may be weeping in the evening,
But in the morning there is joy."
—Psalm 30:6.

*The Hills Did Tremble.* Refers to an earthquake, as a result of which corpses littered the streets as refuse.

*His Hand is Stretched Out Still.* His anger is not yet appeased. He is ready to strike again. Which is but another way of saying that the object of the correction had not yet been attained. More punishment is coming.

VERSES 26-30. *Further Calamities.* These consisted in the invasion of the country by the eastern nations. God would summon them. The Prophet refers to the Assyrians (10:5, 6) as "The Rod of God's Anger." Here their invasion is graphically depicted as the roaring sea and the covering of the land with darkness.

CHAPTER 16

*Isaiah Called to the Prophetic Office, 1-8—His Message to the People, 9-13. Compare Isaiah 6.*

1. *Isaiah Called to the Prophetic Office.*

1. In the year that king Uzziah died, I saw also the Lord sitting upon a throne, high and lifted up, and his train filled the temple.

2. Above it stood the seraphim; each one had six wings; with twain he covered his face, and with twain he covered his feet, and with twain he did fly.

3. And one cried unto another, and said: Holy, holy, holy, is the Lord of Hosts; the whole earth is full of his glory.

4. And the posts of the door moved at the voice of him that cried, and the house was filled with smoke.

5. Then said I: Wo is unto me! for I am undone; because I am a man of unclean lips; and I dwell

---

VERSE 1. *In the Year That King Uzziah Died.* Uzziah, also called Azariah (2 Kings 15:1), was the son of Amaziah. He was the ninth king of Judah and ascended the throne in Jerusalem at the age of sixteen years. He reigned between the years 810 and 759 B.C. It is said of him that he did that which was right in the sight of the Lord in the early part of his government, as long as he followed the counsel of Zechariah, the prophet. (2 Chron. 26) But later in life, pride inspired him to attempt to usurp the prerogatives of the priesthood. He went into the temple and insisted on burning incense on the altar. When he defied the High Priest Azariah and his assistants, he was stricken with leprosy, and remained a sufferer of that loathsome affliction until his death. Jotham, his son, succeeded him on the throne. Isaiah was called to the prophetic office during the last year of the life of Uzziah in his exclusion from family, friends and society.

*The Vision of the Prophet.* Isaiah saw the Lord sitting on his throne, in the Holy of Holies, which represented the invisible abode of the Deity. He was enrobed in a robe of light (Psalm 104:2), the train of which filled the front part of the temple, as the light from the Presence of God fills the visible creation and the immensity of space. (D. and C. 88:12)

VERSE 2. *Seraphim.* Above the throne were seen Seraphim. This word is said to mean "fire spirits." But whatever the etymology of the name may be, these beings of the vision of the prophet were glorious beings, engaged in the service of the Almighty. They were intelligent beings, glorifying their Maker. As seen by the Prophet, they had wings. With two they covered the upper part, and with two the lower part of their bodies, out of respect for Him who occupied the throne. With the other two they were flying; they kept themselves floating in the air, as it were, ever ready for service without delay, and while they were waiting for the divine command, they were praising the Lord.

VERSE 3. *One Cried to Another.* "Holy, Holy, Holy is the Lord of Hosts, etc."

VERSE 4. *Smoke.* A cloud which surrounded the radiant glory, thereby making it possible for mortal eye to endure it. (See Ex. 33:18-22; 1 Kings 8:10, 11; Ezek. 10:4)

VERSE 5. *Wo Unto Me.* The Prophet, in the presence of the glory of God, realized that his lips were unclean, and that he lived among a people with unclean

in the midst of a people of unclean lips; for mine eyes have
seen the King, the Lord of Hosts.

6. Then flew one of the seraphim unto me, having a live coal
in his hand, which he had taken
with the tongs from off the altar;

7. And he laid it upon my

mouth, and said: Lo, this has
touched thy lips; and thine iniquity is taken away, and thy sin
purged.

8. Also I heard the voice of
the Lord, saying: Whom shall I
send, and who will go for us?
Then I said: Here am I; send me.

## 2. His Message to the People.

9. And he said: Go and tell
this people—Hear ye indeed, but
they understood not; and see ye
indeed, but they perceived not.

10. Make the heart of this people fat, and make their ears
heavy, and shut their eyes—lest
they see with their eyes, and hear
with their ears, and understand
with their heart, and be converted
and be healed.

11. Then said I: Lord, how
long? And he said: Until the
cities be wasted without inhabi-

tant, and the houses without
man, and the land be utterly
desolate;

12. And the Lord have re-
moved men far away, for there
shall be a great forsaking in the
midst of the land.

13. But yet there shall be a
tenth, and they shall return, and
shall be eaten, as a teil-tree, and
as an oak whose substance is in
them when they cast their leaves;
so the holy seed shall be the substance thereof.

---

lips; that is, that his and their conversation had not always been pure. He felt
as if he were about to perish, because he had seen the Lord, before he was perfectly clean.

VERSE 6. *Live Coal.* Probably one of the hot rocks lying on the altar and
used for cooking purposes. One of the seraphs picked up one of these.

VERSE 7. *His Message.* Applying it to the mouth of the Prophet, he said:
"Thine iniquity is taken away, and thy sin is purged." Sin and Iniquity. (See
2 Ne. 15:18)

VERSE 8. *Whom Shall I Send?* Now the Prophet was equipped for his
mission. He could hear the voice of the Lord. He was ready and willing to go
wherever the Lord would send him. Comp. Pearl of Great Price, Mos. 4:1, 2;
and Ab. 3:27, 28.

VERSES 9-10. *Hear Ye Indeed; See Ye Indeed.* The tenth verse explains the
ninth. It may be expressed thus: "Ye may hear and see all ye want, but hearing
the word of God and seeing his wonders does not bring salvation. On the contrary. The result of the preaching, the hearing and seeing would be "fat," that
is, insensible hearts, blind eyes, deaf ears, and dull understanding, instead of conversion and healing.

VERSE 11. *Lord, How Long?* The Prophet, naturally, wondered how long
this condition was to last, and the Lord answered his humble question in these
closing verses of the chapter: Until the cities and homes be depopulated, the land

utterly desolate, and the people driven into exile. But, (v. 13), a remnant, a tenth part, would be left, and return. This remnant is a "holy seed."

"For I would not, brethren, that ye should be ignorant of this mystery, lest ye should be wise in your own conceits; that blindness in part is happened to Israel, until the fulness of the Gentiles be come in, and so all Israel shall be saved: as it is written. These shall come out of Zion the Deliverer, and shall turn away ungodliness from Jacob." (Paul, Rom. 11:25, 26)

## CHAPTER 17

*Syria and Israel Combine Against Judah, 1-2 — The Message of Isaiah to Ahaz, 3-9 — Ahaz Offered a Sign, 10-16 — Desolation Predicated, 17-25. Compare Isaiah 7.*

### 1. *Syria and Israel Combine Against Judah.*

1. And it came to pass in the days of Ahaz the son of Jotham, the son of Uzziah, king of Judah, that Rezin, king of Syria, and Pekah the son of Remaliah, king of Israel, went up toward Jerusalem to war against it, but could not prevail against it.

2. And it was told the house of David, saying: Syria is confederate with Ephraim. And his heart was moved, and the heart of his people, as the trees of the wood are moved with the wind.

### 2. *The Message of Isaiah to Ahaz.*

3. Then said the Lord unto Isaiah: Go forth now to meet Ahaz, thou and Shearjashub thy son, at the end of the conduit of the upper pool in the highway of the fuller's field;

4. And say unto him: Take heed, and be quiet; fear not, neither be faint-hearted for the two tails of these smoking firebrands, for the fierce anger of Rezin with Syria, and of the son of Remaliah.

5. Because Syria, Ephraim, and the son of Remaliah, have taken evil counsel against thee, saying:

6. Let us go up against Judah and vex it, and let us make a breach therein for us, and set a king in the midst of it, yea, the son of Tabeal.

7. Thus saith the Lord God: It shall not stand, neither shall it come to pass.

8. For the head of Syria is Damascus, and the head of Damascus, Rezin; and within three score and five years shall Ephraim be broken that it be not a people.

---

VERSE 1. *Jerusalem Threatened.* Isaiah was an historian as well as a prophet. Here he records the fact that two kings, Rezin, king of Syria, and Pekah, king of Israel, formed an alliance against Ahaz, king of Judah, for the purpose of invading Jerusalem.

VERSE 2. *His Heart was Moved.* The rumor of their movements caused a panic in Jerusalem. In the graphic language of the prophet, the hearts of the king and the people were "moved," swaying back and forth, as trees in the wind.

VERSE 6. *A Breach Therein for Us.* Isaiah reveals to Ahaz that the plot of the two kings was nothing to be afraid of, for more than one reason. The first was this, that it was merely a personal scheme, by which they hoped to benefit themselves. It was "for us."

VERSE 8. *The Head of Syria.* Is Resin.

9. And the head of Ephraim is Samaria, and the head of Samaria is Remaliah's son. If ye will not believe surely ye shall not be established.

### 3. *Ahaz was Offered a Sign.*

10. Moreover, the Lord spake again unto Ahaz, saying:

11. Ask thee a sign of the Lord thy God; ask it either in the depths, or in the heights above.

12. But Ahaz said: I will not ask, neither will I tempt the Lord.

13. And he said: Hear ye now, O house of David; is it a small thing for you to weary men, but will ye weary my God also?

14. Therefore, the Lord himself shall give you a sign—Behold, a virgin shall conceive, and shall bear a son, and shall call his name Immanuel.

15. Butter and honey shall he eat, that he may know to refuse the evil and to choose the good.

16. For before the child shall know to refuse the evil and choose the good, the land that thou abhorrest shall be forsaken of both her kings.

VERSE 9. *The Head of Ephraim.* Is Pekah, the son of Remaliah. Neither had the nation they governed with them in this selfish enterprise. In fact, there was no Syria, no Ephraim; only two smoking firebrands (v. 4), who assumed an authority to speak for those nations which they did not have. The Prophet was commissioned to tell Ahaz that the Lord had decided that their plot would not succeed. (v. 7) That was another reason why he need not fear.

VERSE 11. *Ask Thee a Sign.* The Prophet was commissioned to offer Ahaz some miraculous evidence of the truth of this message.

VERSE 12. *I Will Not Ask.* Ahaz refused to accept this gracious offer, on the alleged ground that he was afraid of offending the Lord. Perhaps he had already made some arrangement with the Assyrians.

VERSE 14. *The Sign.* Isaiah, then, declared that the Lord would, nevertheless, give him a sign: Behold, a virgin—a young wife, possibly the wife of the Prophet—would become the mother of a son, whom she would call Immanuel, meaning, "God is with us."

VERSE 16. *The Land That Thou Abhorrest.* Syria and the land of Ephraim. Both would be overrun by the Assyrians before the child would be old enough to discern between evil and good.

This prophecy was literally fulfilled in the days of Ahaz, but it had another fulfilment in the person of our Lord. According to Matthew (1:20-24), Joseph, when thinking of leaving Mary secretly, without causing a public scandal, had a dream, in which an angel appeared to him and explained that he had no cause against Mary. The evangelist adds that, all this was done, that it might be fulfilled which was spoken of the Lord by the Prophet, saying: "Behold, a virgin shall be with child, and shall bring forth a son, and they shall call his name Emmanuel." A most notable instance of the double application of a prophetic utterance!

## 4. *Desolation Predicted.*

17. The Lord shall bring upon thee, and upon thy people, and upon thy father's house, days that have not come from the day that Ephraim departed from Judah, the king of Assyria.

18. And it shall come to pass in that day that the Lord shall hiss for the fly that is in the uttermost part of Egypt, and for the bee that is in the land of Assyria.

19. And they shall come, and shall rest all of them in the desolate valleys, and in the holes of the rocks, and upon all thorns, and upon all bushes.

20. In the same day shall the Lord shave with a razor that is hired, by them beyond the river, by the king of Assyria, the head, and the hair of the feet; and it shall also consume the beard.

21. And it shall come to pass in that day, a man shall nourish a young cow and two sheep;

22. And it shall come to pass, for the abundance of milk they shall give he shall eat butter; for butter and honey shall every one eat that is left in the land.

23. And it shall come to pass in that day, every place shall be, where there were a thousand vines at a thousand silverlings, which shall be for briers and thorns.

24. With arrows and with bows shall men come thither, because all the land shall become briers and thorns.

25. And all hills that shall be digged with the mattock, there shall not come thither the fear of briers and thorns; but it shall be for the sending forth of oxen, and the treading of lesser cattle.

---

VERSE 17. *The King of Assyria.* The Prophet, in this and the following verses, predicts trouble over Judah. Ahaz felt it when Tiglath-Pileser, the Assyrian king exacted a heavy tribute without rendering any service. (2 Chron. 28:19-21)

VERSES 18-20. *Egypt and Assyria.* The attack of Syria and Ephraim on Judah gave Tiglath-Pileser a welcome opportunity to plan the conquest of Egypt, which was also attempted by Shalmaneser, Sargon and Sennacherib. During the reign of Sennacherib the Assyrians came as bees over Judah, the ally of Egypt, and (in 614 B.C.) the Egyptians attacked Judah.

VERSES 21-22. *A Young Cow and Two Sheep.* The country would be reduced to almost a desert, in which the remaining inhabitants would depend on a few animals for a living. Comp. v. 15.

VERSE 23. *Silverlings.* Pieces of silver, used as a medium of exchange.

VERSES 24-25. *With Arrows and Bows.* The land would be so desolate that even where there once were well tended vineyards, there were "briers and thorns," and it would be necessary to go armed on account of the wild animals. In once expensive vineyards oxen and cattle would graze.

## CHAPTER 18

*The Great Roll Concerning Maher-Shalal-Hash-Baz, 1-4—The Invasion of the Assyrians, 5-8—The Enemy Nations Finally to be Crushed, 9-15—The Roll to be Sealed and Hidden, 16-17—Isaiah to Remain, with His Children, as a Sign, 18-22—Compare Isaiah 8.*

### 1. *The Great Roll Concerning Maher-Shalal-Hash-Baz.*

1. Moreover, the word of the Lord said unto me: Take thee a great roll, and write in it with a man's pen, concerning Maher-shalal-hash-baz.

2. And I took unto me faithful witnesses to record, Uriah the priest, and Zechariah the son of Jeberechiah.

3. And I went unto the prophetess; and she conceived and bare a son. Then said the Lord to me: Call his name, Maher-shalal-hash-baz.

4. For behold, the child shall not have knowledge to cry, My father, and my mother, before the riches of Damascus and the spoil of Samaria shall be taken away before the king of Assyria.

### 2. *The Invasion of the Assyrians.*

5. The Lord spake also unto me again, saying:

6. Forasmuch as this people refuseth the waters of Shiloah that go softly, and rejoice in Rezin and Remaliah's son;

7. Now therefore, behold, the Lord bringeth up upon them the

---

VERSE 1. *About the Great Roll.* Two years—as it has been supposed—after the preceding prophecy, Isaiah received the instructions in this chapter. He is directed to take a great roll, a prepared skin, and write "with a man's pen;" that is, with common, readable letters, the story concerning Maher-Shalal-Hash-Baz. This has been translated, "Speedy to rob; swift to plunder." The name was given, to indicate to the people the character of the enemy nations.

VERSE 2. *Uriah and Zechariah.* The Prophet, according to instructions summoned two reliable witnesses (for Uriah, see 2 Kings 16:11).

VERSE 3. *The Prophetess.* His wife.

VERSE 4. *Before the King of Assyria.* The son born was given a name to remind the people of the prophecy of Isaiah, that before long the riches of Damascus and Samaria, the capital of Ephraim, would be carried in a triumphal procession before the king of Assyria, whom Ahaz had bribed. (2 Kings 16:7-9)

VERSE 6. *This People.* The people of Judah.

*Shiloah* was a spring, the clear, pure and clear water of which came slowly running from the mountain on which the temple of God had been erected. It was, therefore a striking symbol of the word of God and his government. Because the people of Judah were dissatisfied with this gentle rule, and preferred the domination of Rezin and Remaliah's son—Syria and Ephraim.

VERSE 7. *The Waters of the River.* The Euphrates with its canals and confluents. Stands here for the king of Assyria with his hosts. Since the people

waters of the river, strong and many, even the king of Assyria and all his glory; and he shall come up over all his channels, and go over all his banks.

8. And he shall pass through Judah; he shall overflow and go over, he shall reach even to the neck; and the stretching out of his wings shall fill the breadth of thy land, O Immanuel.

## 3. Enemy Nations Finally to be Crushed.

9. Associate yourselves, O ye people, and ye shall be broken in pieces; and give ear all ye of far countries; gird yourselves, and ye shall be broken in pieces; gird yourselves, and ye shall be broken in pieces.

10. Take counsel together, and it shall come to naught; speak the word, and it shall not stand; for God is with us.

11. For the Lord spake thus to me with a strong hand, and instructed me that I should not walk in the way of this people, saying:

12. Say ye not, A confederacy, to all to whom this people shall say, A confederacy; neither fear ye their fear, nor be afraid.

13. Sanctify the Lord of Hosts himself, and let him be your fear, and let him be your dread.

14. And he shall be for a sanctuary; but for a stone of stumbling, and for a rock of offense to both the houses of Israel, for a gin and a snare to the inhabitants of Jerusalem.

15. And many among them shall stumble and fall, and be broken, and be snared, and be taken.

---

despised the waters of Shiloah, they would be given a devastating inundation from Assyria.

VERSE 8. *His Wings.* The divisions of his armies.

*Thy Land, O, Immanuel!* Immanuel was, as I understand it, the name of the second son of Isaiah (2 Ne. 17:14). Judea was, therefore, the country of his birth. But Immanuel was also a type of our Redeemer, and the country was his in a much more real sense.

VERSE 9. *O Ye People!* The Prophet now addresses the enemies of Judah. He says, in substance, You may combine — associate yourselves — all you want, nevertheless, ye shall be broken in pieces. Arm yourselves, counsel together, all in vain. Immanuel! God is with us.

VERSE 11. *With a Strong Hand.* The Prophet was sure of this, for the Lord had, as it were, gripped him in his firm hand while he instructed him what to say and what to do. Do not, the Lord said, shout confederacy with the crowd. (v. 12)

VERSES 13-15. *Sanctify the Lord.* He will be a city of refuge to those who are true, but a "rock of offense" to those who are unfaithful to him.

## 4. *The Roll to be Sealed and Hidden.*

16. Bind up the testimony, seal the law among my disciples.

17. And I will wait upon the Lord, that hideth his face from the house of Jacob, and I will look for him.

## 5. *Isaiah and his Children to Remain as a Sign.*
### *Comp. Is. 8.*

18. Behold, I and the children whom the Lord hath given me are for signs and for wonders in Israel from the Lord of Hosts, which dwelleth in Mount Zion.

19. And when they shall say unto you: Seek unto them that have familiar spirits, and unto wizards that peep and mutter—should not a people seek unto their God for the living to hear from the dead?

20. To the law and to the testimony; and if they speak not according to this word, it is because there is no light in them.

---

VERSE 16. *Bind Up the Testimony.* The contents of the roll ended with verse 15. It now remained for the Prophet to have the parchment rolled up and sealed, and put away for future reference.

VERSE 17. *As for the Prophet,* he would wait for the Lord to fulfil his word.

VERSE 18. *Behold I and the Children.* The Prophet reminds the people of the fact that both he and his children were signs and wonders given them by the Lord as testimonies of his predictions. The names of two of his sons are recorded: Shear-Jashub (Is. 7:3) and Maher-Shalal-Hash-Baz. (Is. 8:3) Whether Immanuel, mentioned in Is. 7:14 and 8:8, was the second son of Isaiah is a debated question. Among early Hebrew commentators Kimschi held that view. Grotius, Faber, Fritche, Gesenius, Hitzig and others have also advocated that opinion. Others have regarded the prophecy concerning Immanuel applicable only to our Lord and his virgin Mother. But, notwithstanding the preponderance of this interpretation, it seems to me that the context of Is. 7:14 compels us to regard the virgin, the "alma" of that text as a young woman living at the time of King Ahaz and the prophet; for, how could her motherhood otherwise have been a sign to the skeptic king, for whom it was intended? But, if the virgin was the contemporary of the king and the prophet, she was, in all probability the wife of the latter. We notice that Isaiah, before the birth of Maher-Shalal-Hash-Baz, undoubtedly following divine instructions, summoned two competent witnesses to accompany him to the mother of the expected child, to ascertain to their own satisfaction and to disarm public criticism, that she, the "prophetess," was the legal wife of the Prophet. And, is it not probable that she was given that title, because she was the mother of the prophetic child Immanuel,—the type of the Messiah?

VERSE 19. *Familiar Spirits.* The Prophet warns the people against spiritism. When the people from the East shall try to induce you to establish communication with family spirits, then say, Should not a people ask God, if the living want to hear from the dead?

VERSE 20. *The Law and the Testimony.* That is the revealed word of God. If they do not speak in accordance with that word, there will—literally

21. And they shall pass through it hardly bestead and hungry; and it shall come to pass that when they shall be hungry, they shall fret themselves, and curse their king and their God, and look upward.

22. And they shall look unto the earth and behold trouble, and darkness, dimness of anguish, and shall be driven to darkness.

---

translated—"be no dawn," and, consequently, no daylight, for them. Comp. 2 Pet. 1:19.

VERSES 21-22. *Bestead.* Harassed, beset. Apostasy from the word of God causes all kinds of sufferings, because of the spiritual darkness that takes the place of the light of truth.

## CHAPTER 19

*The Prince of Peace and His Reign, 1-7 — A Prophecy Against Israel, 8-21. Compare Isaiah 9.*

### 1. *The Prince of Peace and his Reign.*

1. Nevertheless, the dimness shall not be such as was in her vexation, when at first he lightly afflicted the land of Zebulun, and the land of Naphtali, and afterwards did more grievously afflict by the way of the Red Sea beyond Jordan in Galilee of the nations.

2. The people that walked in darkness have seen a great light; they that dwell in the land of the shadow of death, upon them hath the light shined.

3. Thou hast multiplied the nation, and increased the joy— the joy before thee according to the joy in harvest, and as men rejoice when they divide the spoil.

4. For thou hast broken the yoke of his burden, and the staff of his shoulder, the rod of his oppressor.

5. For every battle of the warrior is with confused noise, and garments rolled in blood; but this shall be with burning and fuel of fire.

---

VERSE 1. *Galilee of the Nations.* The northern part of Palestine, allotted to Zebulon and Naphtali and bordering on Phoenicia and Syria, was known as the "Galilee of the Nations," or, Gentiles, because of its mixed population. The manners and customs of the people, and even the dialect spoken became affected by foreign settlers. From time to time the region was invaded by hostile hordes. Concerning the invasion of Benhadad, the Syrian, see Kings 15:20. Of the havoc wrought by Tiglath Pileser, the Assyrian, see 2 Kings 15:29-32.

VERSE 2. *A Great Light.* Isaiah was shown, in this vision, that God had selected this darkened portion of the land of promise for the appearance there of a great Light, even the Messiah, Jesus, of Nazareth. See Matt. 4:15, 16.

VERSE 3. *The Joy of the Nation.* The Prophet sees in the coming of the Messiah the beginning of an era of liberty and prosperity. There will be general rejoicing, as in the time of harvest, or after a notable victory over an enemy. The same thought is continued in the next verse.

This verse reads somewhat different from the text in the authorized version: "Thou hast multiplied the nation, *and not* increased the joy." In connection with what follows, this makes poor sense. Nephi had the copy of the prophecy that had been in the possession of Laban, and we may conclude that its text was purer than that of some later manuscripts. The word translated "not" can be a word meaning, "to him;" that is, to the nation, and that makes quite a difference.

VERSE 4. *Oppressor.* In this verse, after the last word, the translators of King James' Bible have added, "as in the day of Midian," evidently referring to the story of Gideon in Judges 6-8. The words may be a marginal note which, somehow, has crept into the text in later copies.

VERSE 5. *Burning and Fuel.* The meaning seems to be this: The era of peace and prosperity will not come through war, for wars bring only confusion,

6. For unto us a child is born, unto us a son is given; and the government shall be upon his shoulder; and his name shall be called, Wonderful, Counselor, The Mighty God, The Everlasting Father, The Prince of Peace.

7. Of the increase of government and peace there is no end, upon the throne of David, and upon his kingdom to order it, and to establish it with judgment and with justice from henceforth, even forever. The zeal of the Lord of Hosts will perform this.

---

noise and bloodshed. It will come when the nations are sensible enough to consign all their blood-stained war equipments to the flames—make a bonfire of them. And that time is near, for,—

VERSE 6. *A Child Is Born.* The Messiah. To the vision of the Prophet this event, marking a new epoch in the existence of the world, was a present reality: "Unto us a child is born, unto us a son is given." It was already done in the great Council in heaven. Even the names of the Messiah, indicating his mission on earth, had been selected. These names, if we drop the comma after Wonderful, as I believe we may do safely, since punctuation marks are very arbitrary, are four:

Wonderful Counselor,
Mighty God,
Everlasting Father,
Prince of Peace.

*Wonderful Counselor.* See Pearl of Great Price, Mos. 4:1-3; Abraham 3:27, 28. The full meaning of this name is better understood when read in the light of the revelations in the Pearl of Great Price concerning the plan of salvation. The translators who made the Greek translation known as the Septuagint, must have had a Hebrew text different to that now commonly accepted. Their rendition of the passage, transformed into English, is:

"For unto us a child is born, and to us a son is given, whose government is on his own shoulder; and his name shall be called, Messenger of a Great Counsel. Great is his government and to his peace there is no boundary," etc.

The important and remarkable fact is here made clear that the early translators of the Hebrew text of Isaiah, understood the "Wonderful," "Counselor" of the English version to mean, "The Messenger of a Great Counsel," as revealed in the Pearl of Great Price.

*Mighty God.* Some modern scholars would like to understand this to mean that our Redeemer is here referred to as mighty "warrior." He was that in the conflict that ended with the expulsion of the fallen angel from the presence of God. See Luke 10:18; Rev. 12:9; 2 Ne. 2:17, 18; D. and C. 29:36, 37; Pearl of Great Price, Mos. 4:3, 4. But he was also "God." The name indicates his divinity.

*Everlasting Father.* Literally: "Father of Eternity." Meaning the originator and ruler of ages, or eras. Comp. Isaiah 57:15; Jer. 10:10; Micah 5:2.

*Prince of Peace.* If we divide mankind into two great divisions, one governed by law and the peaceful administration of the law, and the other by tyrannic violence, then we will find the Prince of peace at the head of the first of these divisions. That is his kingdom, as the Prince of Peace.

VERSE 7. *The Throne of David.* Refers, evidently, to Jerusalem. Palestine has yet an important role in the making of world history. The mission of the Prince

## 2. A Prophecy against Israel.

8. The Lord sent his word unto Jacob and it hath lighted upon Israel.

9. And all the people shall know, even Ephraim and the inhabitants of Samaria, that say in the pride and stoutness of heart:

10. The bricks are fallen down, but we will build with hewn stones; the sycamores are cut down, but we will change them into cedars.

11. Therefore the Lord shall set up the adversaries of Rezin against him, and join his enemies together;

12. The Syrians before and the Philistines behind; and they shall devour Israel with open mouth. For all this his anger is not turned away, but his hand is stretched out still.

13. For the people turneth not unto him that smiteth them, neither do they seek the Lord of Hosts.

14. Therefore will the Lord cut off from Israel head and tail, branch and rush in one day.

15. The ancient, he is the head; and the prophet that teacheth lies, he is the tail.

16. For the leaders of this people cause them to err; and they that are led of them are destroyed.

17. Therefore the Lord shall have no joy in their young men, neither shall have mercy on their fatherless and widows; for every one of them is a hypocrite and an evildoer, and every mouth speaketh folly. For all this his anger is not turned away, but his hand is stretched out still.

18. For wickedness burneth as the fire; it shall devour the briers and thorns, and shall kindle in the thickets of the forests, and they shall mount up like the lifting up of smoke.

---

of Peace will be carried out, not with murderous war implements, but with the burning love—zeal—of the Lord of Hosts for his people.

VERSE 8. *A Word Unto Jacob.* This is a prophecy against Israel. It begins with verse 9 of this chapter and ends with verse 4 of the next. Jacob and Israel here stand for Israel, also called Ephraim.

VERSE 11. *The Adversaries of Rezin.* The Assyrians, who had conquered Rezin, the head of Damascus. The Lord would now send the Assyrians against Israel.

VERSE 12. *Other Enemies.* Also the Syrians and Philistines, who, as conquered peoples, were compelled to fight in the ranks of the conquerors.

VERSE 14. *Head and Tail.* See verse 15.

VERSE 17. *Young Men.* A timely warning to youth of all Times. The Lord loves young people who dedicate themselves to his service, but he has no joy in evil doers, whether young or old.

VERSE 18. *Wickedness.* Is here compared to a flame that begins in the briers and thorns in the field, spreads little by little and ends in a raging forest fire, darkening the sky with masses of thick smoke.

19. Through the wrath of the Lord of Hosts is the land darkened, and the people shall be as the fuel of the fire; no man shall spare his brother.

20. And he shall snatch on the right hand and be hungry; and he shall eat on the left hand and they shall not be satisfied; they shall eat every man the flesh of his own arm—

21. Manasseh, Ephraim; and Ephraim, Manasseh; they together shall be against Judah. For all this his anger is not turned away, but his hand is stretched out still.

---

VERSE 20. *The Flesh of His Own Arm.* Internal strife, brother against brother, is just like tearing one's own flesh to pieces and eating the shreds. It is raving madness.

VERSE 21. *Ephraim and Manasseh.* But that was the condition. The two brothers were fighting each other. But they were uniting in attacks on Judah.

## CHAPTER 20

*The Last of the Prophecy Against Israel, 1-4 — A Prophecy Against Assyria, 5-16 — A Remnant of Israel Shall Return, 17-27 — The Assyrians Halted, 28-34. Compare Isaiah 10.*

### 1. *The Last of the Prophecy against Israel.*

1. Wo unto them that decree unrighteous decrees, and that write grievousness which they have prescribed;

2. To turn away the needy from judgment, and to take away the right from the poor of my people, that widows may be their prey, and that they may rob the fatherless!

3. And what will ye do in the day of visitation, and in the desolation which shall come from far? to whom will ye flee for help? and where will ye leave your glory?

4. Without me they shall bow down under the prisoners, and they shall fall under the slain. For all this his anger is not turned away, but his hand is stretched out still.

### 2. *A Prophecy against Assyria.*

5. O Assyrian, the rod of mine anger, and the staff in their hand is their indignation.

6. I will send him against a hypocritical nation, and against the people of my wrath will I give him a charge to take the spoil, and to take the prey, and to tread them down like the mire of the streets.

---

VERSE 1. *Unrighteous Decrees.* Those who make unrighteous laws and render partial judgments are denounced.

VERSE 2. *To Turn Away the Needy.* The victims of bad legislation and wrong judgments are generally the poor and needy; the widows and the fatherless.

VERSE 3. *The Day of Visitation.* A day of visitation is approaching. A day when enemies from afar will invade the country of Israel. The Lord now asks: What will ye do then?

*Your Glory.* Meaning, your wealth and armed soldiers. What is going to become of them?

VERSE 4. *Without Me.* Without God, the defenders of the people would be humiliated by carrying burdens among the prisoners, or fall among the slain.

VERSE 5. *O Assyrian.* The prophecy begins with this verse and ends with chapter 22. (Is. 12)

*The Rod.* The Assyrian king would be only a rod to be used for the correction of an erring people; a staff indicating indignation.

VERSE 6. *A Hypocritical Nation.* I will send him against a hypocritical nation, the Lord says, and charge him to take spoil and prey upon the people, and trample them down as mire in the streets.

7. Howbeit he meaneth not so, neither doth his heart think so; but in his heart it is to destroy and cut off nations not a few.

8. For he saith: Are not my princes altogether kings?

9. Is not Calno as Carchemish? Is not Hamath as Arpad? Is not Samaria as Damascus?

10. As my hand hath founded the kingdoms of the idols, and whose graven images did excel them of Jerusalem and of Samaria;

11. Shall I not, as I have done unto Samaria and her idols, so do to Jerusalem and to her idols?

12. Wherefore it shall come to pass that when the Lord hath performed his whole work upon Mount Zion and upon Jerusalem, I will punish the fruit of the stout heart of the king of Assyria, and the glory of his high looks.

13. For he saith: By the strength of my hand and by my wisdom I have done these things; for I am prudent; and I have moved the borders of the people, and have robbed their treasures, and I have put down the inhabitants like a valiant man;

14. And my hand hath found as a nest the riches of the people; and as one gathereth eggs that are left have I gathered all the earth; and there was none that moved the wing, or opened the mouth, or peeped.

15. Shall the ax boast itself against him that heweth therewith? Shall the saw magnify itself against him that shaketh it? As if the rod should shake itself against them that lift it up, or as if the staff should lift up itself as if it were no wood!

16. Therefore shall the Lord, the Lord of Hosts, send among his fat ones, leanness; and under his glory he shall kindle a burning like the burning of a fire.

---

VERSE 7. *He Meaneth Not So.* However, the Assyrians did not understand his mission. He rejoiced in destruction, gloried in violence as if it were an evidence of greatness.

VERSE 8. *Princes . . . Kings.* Are not, he asks, my princes kings? Eastern potentates often called his governors and satraps kings, and themselves king of kings.

VERSES 9-11. *Calno as Carchemish, etc.* In his pride, the Assyrian looks over his conquests. Carchemish (Fort of Chemosh) was the chief city of the Hittites from 1100 to 850 B.C. It was there that Pharaoh Necho was defeated in 605 B.C., five years before Lehi left Jerusalem. See Jer. 46:2; 2 Chron. 25:20.

The Assyrian king is represented as saying, Since I have made myself the master of kingdoms, the images of which were more powerful than those of Jerusalem and Samaria, why should I not gain possession of Jerusalem and her idols?

VERSES 12-16. *I Will Punish . . . the King of Assyria.* The Lord replies to that proud question. He says, in substance, that when he has chastised his people on Mount Zion and in Jerusalem, the king of Assyria will be made to eat the fruit of his boasting.

*Leanness.* (v. 16) Literally, a "pining sickness in his fat body." May refer to the miraculous destruction of the Assyrian army under Sennacherib. (Is. 37:30-38)

### 3. *Remnant of Israel shall Return.*

17. And the light of Israel shall be for a fire, and his Holy One for a flame, and shall burn and shall devour his thorns and his briers in one day;

18. And shall consume the glory of his forest, and of his fruitful field, both soul and body; and they shall be as when a standard-bearer fainteth.

19. And the rest of the trees of his forest shall be few, that a child may write them.

20. And it shall come to pass in that day, that the remnant of Israel, and such as are escaped of the house of Jacob, shall no more again stay upon him that smote them, but shall stay upon the Lord, the Holy One of Israel, in truth.

21. The remnant shall return, yea, even the remnant of Jacob, unto the mighty God.

22. For though thy people Israel be as the sand of the sea, yet a remnant of them shall return; the consumption decreed shall overflow with righteousness.

23. For the Lord God of Hosts shall make a consumption, even determined in all the land.

24. Therefore, thus saith the Lord God of Hosts: O my people that dwellest in Zion, be not afraid of the Assyrian; he shall smite thee with a rod, and shall lift up his staff against thee, after the manner of Egypt.

25. For yet a very little while, and the indignation shall cease, and mine anger in their destruction.

---

In a manuscript found at Nineveh Sennacherib has left this account of his exploits: "This Hasakijahu Jahudu, fear of the greatness of my majesty swept him away and the guards and soldiers he had scraped up to defend the city Ursalimmo (Jerusalem), his powerful city; their ships he sent away with thirty talents of silver * * * and his daughters, the women in the palace, his slaves, male and female, to Ninua, the city of my dominion, and he sent his equerry to pay the tribute and to acknowledge his submission."

This shows to perfection the accuracy of the character drawn of the Assyrian ruler by the Prophet Isaiah.

VERSE 17. *The Light of Israel.* God is a light to his people, but a burning flame to his enemies.

*Thorns and Briers.* The Assyrian armies.

VERSE 18. *Forest and Fruitful Field.* Another reference to his armed forces— an army without standard-bearers: a disorganized mob.

VERSE 19. *The Rest of the Trees Few.* The rest of the soldiers will be so few that a child may count them.

VERSE 20. *Him That Smote Them.* The Assyrians. Israel will no longer trust their enemies, but in the Lord.

VERSES 21-23. *Return* here means repentance, a "return" to God. The remnant will return to him, because what he has decreed will certainly be carried out.

26. And the Lord of Hosts shall stir up a scourge for him according to the slaughter of Midian at the rock of Oreb; and as his rod was upon the sea so shall he lift it up after the manner of Egypt.

27. And it shall come to pass in that day that his burden shall be taken away from off thy shoulder, and his yoke from off thy neck, and the yoke shall be destroyed because of the anointing.

## 4. The Assyrians Halted.

28. He is come to Aiath, he is passed to Migron; at Michmash he hath laid up his carriages.

29. They are gone over the passage; they have taken up their lodging at Geba; Ramath is afraid; Gibeah of Saul is fled.

30. Lift up the voice, O daughter of Gallim; cause it to be heard unto Laish, O poor Anathoth.

31. Madmenah is removed; the inhabitants of Gebim gather themselves to flee.

32. As yet shall he remain at Nob that day; he shall shake his hand against the mount of the daughter of Zion, the hill of Jerusalem.

33. Behold, the Lord, the Lord of Hosts shall lop the bough with terror; and the high ones of stature shall be hewn down; and the haughty shall be humbled.

34. And he shall cut down the thickets of the forests with iron, and Lebanon shall fall by a mighty one.

---

VERSE 26. *The Slaughter of Midian.* Refers to the victory of Gideon over the Midianites. (Judges 7)

*After the Manner of Egypt.* See Ex. 14.

VERSE 27. *Because of the Anointing.* Refers to the power of the Priesthood. The Prophet employs the figure of speech of a slave carrying a burden, whose yoke will be destroyed, because of his Priesthood. One who honors his Priesthood cannot but be a free man. See the letter of Paul to Philemon concerning Onesimus. (vv. 8-16)

VERSE 28. *He is Come.* The Prophet, in a vision, sees the Assyrian army enter the territory of Judah at Aiath, leave their carriages at Michmash; then march through the narrow pass between Michmash and Geba and camp at the latter place. The inhabitants of Rama and Gibea of Saul are panic-stricken and flee. (v. 29) The people of other cities prepare to follow their example. (vv. 30-31) When the Assyrians are at Nob (v. 32), the fate of Jerusalem seems to be sealed, but the Lord intervenes for the salvation of his people. (vv. 33-34)

### GENERAL NOTES

Sennacherib reigned in Assyria between 705-681 B.C. At the beginning of his reign he faced a revolt of his western dependencies, led, it seems, by Hezekiah, and supported by Egypt. In 701 he invaded Palestine and destroyed a number of cities, but at Jerusalem his army was decimated by a terrible sickness. (2 Kings 18:13; 19:37) Shortly afterwards he was assassinated and succeeded by Esarhaddon. Historians divide Assyrian history into three periods. Sennacherib belongs to the third. This period is regarded as the golden age of Assyria. The sculptured marbles, they tell us, which have been brought from the palaces of Sargon, Sennacherib and Asshurbanipal, show a skill reminding of the Greeks. During the same period, the sciences of geography and astronomy were cultivated with great diligence; studies of languages and history occupied many learned men. Modern scholars are filled with admiration, as they discover and decipher the evidences of the mental activity of the ancient Assyrians.

## CHAPTER 21

*The Rod of Jesse, 1-10—A Second Gathering, 11-16. Compare Isaiah 11.*

### 1. *The Rod of Jesse.*

1. And there shall come forth a rod out of the stem of Jesse, and a branch shall grow out of his roots.

2. And the Spirit of the Lord shall rest upon him, the spirit of wisdom and understanding, the spirit of counsel and might, the spirit of knowledge and of the fear of the Lord;

3. And shall make him of quick understanding in the fear of the Lord; and he shall not judge after the sight of his eyes, neither reprove after the hearing of his ears.

4. But with righteousness shall he judge the poor, and reprove with equity for the meek of the earth; and he shall smite the earth with the rod of his mouth, and with the breath of his lips shall he slay the wicked.

5. And righteousness shall be the girdle of his loins, and faithfulness the girdle of his reins.

---

VERSE 1. *The Rod of the Stem of Jesse.* The Messiah. Literally, the "stem" means the "stump" of the tree left in the ground, after the branches had been cut down and the luxuriant foliage removed. The meaning is that the Messiah would come when the family of Jesse had been reduced to the social status it occupied at the time of its ancestor, before the golden age of David and Solomon. The Messiah would come as a shoot from the stump of the family tree, but the tender twig would grow and become a flourishing, fruitful Tree.

VERSES 2-5. *His Characteristics.* In Isaiah 9:6 four names of the Messiah are given:

Wonderful Counselor,
Mighty God,
Everlasting Father,
Prince of Peace.

In the Pearl of Great Price, Moses 7:35, these names appear:

ı am [Jehovah?] God,
Man of Holiness,
Man of Counsel,
Endless and Eternal.

Here (Is. 11:2) are four characteristics of the Messiah. He was endowed with—

The Spirit of the Lord,
The Spirit of Wisdom and Understanding,
The Spirit of Counsel and Might,
The Spirit of Knowledge and
the Fear of the Lord.

The Spirit of the Lord came upon Jesus at his baptism (Matt. 3:16, 17; Mark 1:10, 11; Luke 3:21, 22; John 1:32-34). Through the influence and guidance of the Divine Spirit he had wisdom to recognize the difference between right and wrong, truth and error, and understanding to do what is right and avoid what is wrong.

6. The wolf also shall dwell with the lamb, and the leopard shall lie down with the kid, and the calf and the young lion and fatling together; and a little child shall lead them.

7. And the cow and the bear shall feed; their young ones shall lie down together; and the lion shall eat straw like the ox.

8. And the sucking child shall play on the hole of the asp, and the weaned child shall put his hand on the cockatrice's den.

9. They shall not hurt nor destroy in all my holy mountain, for the earth shall be full of the knowledge of the Lord, as the waters cover the sea.

10. And in that day there shall be a root of Jesse, which shall stand for an ensign of the people; to it shall the Gentiles seek; and his rest shall be glorious.

## 2. A Second Gathering.

11. And it shall come to pass in that day that the Lord shall set his hand again the second time to recover the remnant of his people which shall be left, from Assyria, and from Egypt, and from Pathros, and from Cush, and from Elam, and from Shinar, and from Hamath, and from the islands of the sea.

---

He had the Spirit of "counsel and might;" he was resourceful and strong in difficulties, and he had the loving fear of the Father, which is founded on a knowledge of his Fatherhood. (v. 2) The Messiah, by the guidance of the Spirit, is also "quick" of understanding: sensitive and exact in judgment. He is not deceived by those who falsely profess to fear the Lord. (v. 3) He sees the heart and judges accordingly. The poor and those who are humble are the special objects of his care. (vv. 4 and 5) For their benefit he will "smite the earth with the 'rod' of his mouth," or,—which is the same—"the breath of his lips," as did Moses when he sent plagues on Egypt, waving the rod of Aaron, as the symbol of the power of the Almighty. (Ex. 7 et seq.) Note that the "sword" of the Messiah is the "rod of his mouth," his word, his gospel, and that his "armour" is righteousness and faithfulness. There are no other sure roads to peace in the world.

VERSES 6-9. *The Millennium* is here described. That Millennial conditions are possible on earth is proved by the story in Fourth Nephi 15-36.

VERSE 10. *Root of Jesse.* Commentators generally take it for granted that the "root of Jesse" in this verse is the same as the "rod out of the Stem of Jesse" in verse 1. They apply both the "rod out of the stem" and the "root" to the Messiah. But in verses 4-9 the Millennium is clearly introduced, and in this verse we read that the root of Jesse stands for an "ensign;" that is, a banner around which even the Gentiles will gather. We read that the "rest" of the Messiah, that is, his resting place, the temple (1 Chron. 28:2), will be "glorious," and in the next verse we are told that the gathering of the remnant of Israel and Judah has begun for a second time. All of which seems to me to point to the time in which we are now living, and the preparations now being made for the Millennium, through the Church of Jesus Christ of Latter-day Saints.

VERSE 11. *A Second Time.* This gathering is, evidently, the one now going on. *The Islands of the Sea.* See 2 Ne. 10:8, 20, 21.

12. And he shall set up an ensign for the nations, and shall assemble the outcasts of Israel, and gather together the dispersed of Judah from the four corners of the earth.

13. The envy of Ephraim also shall depart, and the adversaries of Judah shall be cut off; Ephraim shall not envy Judah, and Judah shall not vex Ephraim.

14. But they shall fly upon the shoulders of the Philistines towards the west; they shall spoil them of the east together; they shall lay their hand upon Edom and Moab; and the children of Ammon shall obey them.

15. And the Lord shall utterly destroy the tongue of the Egyptian sea; and with his mighty wind he shall shake his hand over the river, and shall smite it in the seven streams, and make men go over dry shod.

16. And there shall be a highway for the remnant of his people which shall be left, from Assyria, like as it was to Israel in the day that he came up out of the land of Egypt.

---

VERSES 12-13. *An Ensign.* Is a banner, or flag, to guide a traveler, or mark a gathering place; in this case, the central camp of both Ephraim and Judah, when the two great divisions of Israel are united.

VERSE 14. *They Shall Fly Upon.* The context shows the meaning to be that the people united will dominate people to the west, where the Philistines lived at one time; as well as the people to the east.

VERSE 15. *The Tongue of the Egyptian Sea.* May refer to the construction of the Suez Canal.
*The River.* The Euphrates.

VERSE 16. *A Highway.* The meaning of the verse is that there will be a highway for the remnant of his people left after the fall of what was once Assyria, as there was for the people that came out of Egypt.

## CHAPTER 22

*God No Longer Angry, 1-2 — Israel Rejoices, 3 — The People Commissioned to Declare the Gospel, 4-6. Compare Isaiah 12.*

### 1. *God No longer Angry.*

1. And in that day thou shalt say: O Lord, I will praise thee; though thou wast angry with me, thine anger is turned away, and thou comfortedst me.

2. Behold, God is my salvation; I will trust, and not be afraid; for the Lord JEHOVAH is my strength and my song; he also has become my salvation.

### 2. *Israel Rejoices.*

3. Therefore, with joy shall ye draw water out of the wells of salvation.

### 3. *The People to Declare the Gospel.*

4. And in that day shall ye say: Praise the Lord, call upon his name, declare his doings among the people, make mention that his name is exalted.

5. Sing unto the Lord; for he hath done excellent things; this is known in all the earth.

6. Cry out and shout, thou inhabitant of Zion; for great is the Holy One of Israel in the midst of thee.

VERSE 1. *Thine Anger is Turned Away.* In this song we learn the important truth that the anger of God is not an ever burning flame, but that he is ready to comfort his children when they flee him.

VERSE 3. *Wells of Salvation.* Has reference to the feast of tabernacles, or tents, celebrated by the Jews at the close of the year in grateful remembrance of the goodness of God to their fathers in the wilderness, and to themselves, as evidenced by abundant harvests and other blessings in the land of Rest. (Lev. 23:34) The observance lasted for seven days. A libation was an important part of the services every day. It was at the close of such a festival that our Lord stood on the temple ground and invited the people to come unto him. It was the last day. The water was perhaps flowing gently in the trench. But the crowd was about to disperse. Each one had to go to his own home and leave the life-giving stream for, perhaps, less pleasant water containers. Then Jesus cried with a loud voice: "If any man thirst, let him come unto me, and drink. He that believeth on me, as the scripture hath said, out of his innermost parts shall flow rivers of living water." You need not thirst, because you cannot always stay by this stream. (John 7:37, 38. Comp. John 4:14) Jesus spoke of the spirit which they that believe on him should receive. (John 7:39)

VERSES 4-6. *Declare His Doings.* The people are called upon to praise the Lord by proclaiming the greatness of his Name (4), which means his character; his works (5), in creation, and salvation, and his leadership in Zion (6).

### GENERAL NOTES

This is called The Song of Moses and the Lamb. It was sung by Moses and the Children of Israel on the shore of the Red Sea, when the people had passed safely through the deep in which Pharaoh's armies had found a watery grave. (Ex. 15:1-18)

Compare Rev. 15:1-18. In the vision here recorded, John sees the transfigured throng at the shore of a sea of molten, fiery glass. They have overcome the "beast," his "image," his "mark," and "the number of his name," To the sweet accompaniment of harps, their harmonies are rolling out over the illimitable expanse:

> "Great and marvelous are thy works, Lord God Almighty,
> Just and true are thy ways, thou King of Saints.
> Who shall not fear Thee, Lord, and glorify thy Name,
> And worship before thee?
> For thy judgments are made manifest."

## CHAPTER 23

*A Graphic Description of the Destruction of Babylon. Compare Isaiah* 13.

1. The burden of Babylon, which Isaiah the son of Amos did see.

2. Lift ye up a banner upon the high mountain, exalt the voice unto them, shake the hand, that they may go into the gates of the nobles.

3. I have commanded my sanctified ones, I have also called my mighty ones, for mine anger is not upon them that rejoice in my highness.

4. The noise of the multitude in the mountains like as of a great people, a tumultuous noise of the kingdoms of nations gathered together, the Lord of Hosts mustereth the hosts of the battle.

5. They come from a far country, from the end of heaven, yea, the Lord, and the weapons of his indignation, to destroy the whole land.

6. Howl ye, for the day of the Lord is at hand; it shall come as a destruction from the Almighty.

7. Therefore shall all hands be faint, every man's heart shall melt;

8. And they shall be afraid; pangs and sorrows shall take hold of them; they shall be amazed one at another; their faces shall be as flames.

9. Behold, the day of the Lord cometh, cruel both with wrath and fierce anger, to lay the land desolate; and he shall destroy the sinners thereof out of it.

10. For the stars of heaven and the constellations thereof shall not give their light; the sun shall be darkened in her going forth, and the moon shall not cause her light to shine.

11. And I will punish the world for evil, and the wicked for their iniquity; I will cause the arrogancy of the proud to cease, and will lay down the haughtiness of the terrible.

12. I will make a man more precious than fine gold; even a man than the golden wedge of Ophir.

---

VERSE 1. *Burden.* The word translated "burden" means that which is borne, and, therefore, figuratively speaking, a prediction of a calamity which falls on you like a weight, a "burden." Comp. Jer. 23:33.

VERSE 2. *Exalt the Voice Unto Them.* The people of Babylon are here told, ironically, I think, to call on the Medes and Persians and hurry them up to come and enter the gates of the city. Through abandoning themselves to wickedness, people are always inviting destruction.

VERSE 3. *My Sanctified Ones.* The Lord had commanded the armies of the Medes and the Persians to begin a holy war. They were, for the time being, in his service; sanctified, that is, set apart, to execute his judgments.

VERSES 4-5. *The Noise of the Multitude.* There is an unusual noise in the mountains. What is it? The Lord is mobilizing nations from far-off countries, intending to use them for the destruction of the entire land.

13. Therefore, I will shake the heavens, and the earth shall remove out of her place, in the wrath of the Lord of Hosts, and in the day of his fierce anger.

14. And it shall be as the chased roe, and as a sheep that no man taketh up; and they shall every man turn to his own people, and flee every one into his own land.

15. Every one that is proud shall be thrust through; yea, and every one that is joined to the wicked shall fall by the sword.

16. Their children also shall be dashed to pieces before their eyes; their houses shall be spoiled and their wives ravished.

17. Behold, I will stir up the Medes against them, which shall not regard silver and gold, nor shall they delight in it.

18. Their bows shall also dash the young men to pieces; and they shall have no pity on the fruit of the womb; their eyes shall not spare children.

19. And Babylon, the glory of kingdoms, the beauty of the Chaldees' excellency, shall be as when God overthrew Sodom and Gomorrah.

---

VERSES 6-16. *The Day of the Lord is at Hand.* To the Babylonians the invasion of the Medes and Persians, the destruction of their homes and cities, was "the day of the Lord." It was the day of his vengeance and judgment upon them. The prophetic imagery, which here refers to the destruction of Babylon, is applicable to all such catastrophes of historic import. It is, therefore, also descriptive of the last judgment before the Millennium, which is, the fullest meaning of the word, "the day of the Lord."

The destruction comes from the Almighty (v. 6); it is not a peaceful, painless operation. On the contrary, under it, people will faint with pain and anguish. (v. 7-9); stars and constellations ("Orions"), meaning, individuals and organizations renowned throughout the world for their brilliancy, will fail to give their light; even the sun and the moon—even kings and queens, and governments in general (Gen. 37:8-10)—will be darkened, or fail to function (v. 10); for the Lord will punish the world for evil and wickedness, and humiliate the proud and haughty. (v. 11) In this process the population will be decimated (v. 12); the heavens will be shaken—government systems will be dissolved—the earth removed out of her place—boundaries of kingdoms will be obliterated in the wrath of the Lord (v. 13); armies will be scattered like sheep (v. 14), and those who are found among the wicked will be slain by the sword (v. 15); in the savagery of the war, even women and children will be destroyed. (v. 16) Such is the prophetic sketch of the day of the Lord which was to end the Babylonian empire. And that catastrophe was a type of the termination of our own era, too.

VERSE 17. *Not Regard Silver and Gold.* It is here said that the Medes would not accept bribes. They could not be bought off.

VERSE 18. *Dash the Young Men to Pieces.* The cruelty of the soldiers in former days was almost unbelievable. To some little extent the human race has undeniably advanced from the moral level of the ancient Babylonians, Medes and Persians, but military ethics are yet very low. Aeronautics has not yet had the elevating influence on warfare it might have had in our time, but it is coming gradually, slowly.

20. It shall never be inhabited, neither shall it be dwelt in from generation to generation: neither shall the Arabian pitch tent there; neither shall the shepherds make their fold there.

21. But wild beasts of the desert shall lie there; and their houses shall be full of doleful creatures; and owls shall dwell there, and satyrs shall dance there.

22. And the wild beasts of the islands shall cry in their desolate houses, and dragons in their pleasant palaces; and her time is near to come, and her day shall not be prolonged. For I will destroy her speedily; yea, for I will be merciful unto my people, but the wicked shall perish.

---

VERSES 19-22. *Babylon Utterly Destroyed.* Babylon was one of the great cities of the ancient world, perhaps the greatest. Its walls were, for height and width, one of the wonders of the world. The temple of Bel, the terraced ("hanging") gardens, the immense copper gates, and the artificial lake were, up to that time, the greatest achievements of human skill and ingenuity. The fields and farms and flocks yielded almost incredible returns, and the wealth, luxury and power of the ruling classes were correspondingly great. If any city, or country, could be regarded as invincible, Babylonia and Babylon might be so considered. But centuries before their fall Isaiah predicted, with supernatural knowledge of the details, the destruction of the city and the overthrow of the government.

It was done by means of strategy. After a long siege, apparently without effect, Cyrus, who led the besieging Medes and Persians, decided to turn the Euphrates out of its course and enter on the dry river bed. That was a gigantic undertaking. The river was 1500 feet wide and 12 feet deep. However, the undertaking was successful. The invaders entered from two sides, the former inflow and outflow of the river, and so quietly did they take possession that most of the people did not know what was happening till it was too late to make resistance. Aristotle had been informed that some of the inhabitants did not know until three days afterwards that the city had fallen. When the king of Babylon learned that Cyrus was at the gate of the palace, he commanded that he be admitted. He was. The king and all the revelers surrounding him perished. Many Babylonian princes, at that time, ended their useless earthly lives, in a drunken debauch. The kingdom was divided and given to the Medes and the Persians. Comp. Dan. 5.

## CHAPTER 24

*Israel to be Gathered, 1-3 — A Song on Babylon, 4-23 — About Assyria, 24-27—Against Philistia, 28-32. Comp. Is. 14.*

## 1. *Israel to be Gathered.*

1. For the Lord will have mercy on Jacob, and will yet choose Israel, and set them in their own land; and the strangers shall be joined with them, and they shall cleave to the house of Jacob.

2. And the people shall take them and bring them to their place; yea, from far unto the ends of the earth; and they shall return to their lands of promise. And the house of Israel shall possess them, and the land of the Lord shall be for servants and handmaids; and they shall take them captives unto whom they were captives; and they shall rule over their oppressors.

3. And it shall come to pass in that day that the Lord shall give thee rest, from thy sorrow, and from thy fear, and from the hard bondage wherein thou wast made to serve.

## 2. *A Song on Babylon.*

4. And it shall come to pass in that day, that thou shalt take up this proverb against the king of Babylon, and say: How hath the oppressor ceased, the golden city ceased!

5. The Lord hath broken the staff of the wicked, the scepters of the rulers.

6. He who smote the people in wrath with a continual stroke, he that ruled the nations in anger, is persecuted, and none hindereth.

7. The whole earth is at rest, and is quiet; they break forth into singing.

8. Yea, the fir-trees rejoice at

VERSE 1. *Yet.* Means, once more, for a second time. They will again be established in their own land, as when they came out of Egypt; but with this difference, that this time they will not be required to exterminate the strangers. The strangers will be joined with them and cleave to the house of Jacob.

VERSE 2. *People shall Take them and Bring them to their Place.* In this paragraph and the following the promise is made that the nations of the earth will help the Children of Israel to return home and settle down. Strangers will gladly serve them, not, indeed as slaves that are bought and sold, but as "servants and handmaids" (v. 2)—members of the household. There was no slavery among the Hebrews, as practiced among the Egyptians and Romans, for instance. The servants were protected by law, equally with the masters.

VERSES 4-23. This song of Babylon is considered an excellent specimen of Hebrew poetry. It may be divided thus:

VERSES 4-8. *The Earth at Rest.* The oppressor being removed, there is no longer any disturber of the peace. The nations are singing for joy; even nature partakes of the rest.

thee, and also the cedars of Lebanon, saying: Since thou art laid down no feller is come up against us.

9. Hell from beneath is moved for thee to meet thee at thy coming; it stirreth up the dead for thee, even all the chief ones of the earth; it hath raised up from their thrones all the kings of the nations.

10. All they shall speak and say unto thee: Art thou also become weak as we? Art thou become like unto us?

11. Thy pomp is brought down to the grave; the noise of thy viols is not heard; the worm is spread under thee, and the worms cover thee.

12. How art thou fallen from heaven, O Lucifer, son of the morning! Art thou cut down to the ground, which did weaken the nations!

13. For thou hast said in thy heart: I will ascend into heaven, I will exalt my throne above the stars of God; I will sit also upon the mount of the congregation, in the sides of the north;

14. I will ascend above the heights of the clouds; I will be like the Most High.

15. Yet thou shalt be brought down to hell, to the sides of the pit.

16. They that see thee shall narrowly look upon thee, and shall consider thee, and shall say: Is this the man that made the earth to tremble, that did shake kingdoms?

17. And made the world as a wilderness, and destroyed the cities thereof, and opened not the house of his prisoners?

18. All the kings of the nations, yea, all of them, lie in glory, every one of them in his own house.

19. But thou art cast out of thy grave like an abominable branch, and the remnant of those that are slain, thrust through with a sword, that go down to the stones of the pit; as a carcass trodden under feet.

20. Thou shalt not be joined with them in burial, because thou hast destroyed thy land and slain thy people; the seed of evil-doers shall never be renowned.

21. Prepare slaughter for his

---

VERSES 9-15. *Commotion in Hell.* The reception of the tyrant among the dead in Sheol is described with vivid imagination. There is excitement and commotion, as there would be in any great center of population in the Orient, waiting for the arrival of a great potentate; only, this time they are expecting one whom they hated in life. Kings rise from their thrones and taunt him with questions, sneeringly: "Art thou become weak as we?" (v. 10) Where is thy music? Look at the worms all over you! (v. 10) The king of Babylon is next compared to Lucifer, the son of the morning, who fell because of pride. "For thou hast said in thy heart I will ascend into heaven . . . I will be like the Most High. Yet thou shalt be brought down to hell." (v. 15)

VERSES 16-21. *The Corpse of the King Unburied on the Battlefield.* Other

children for the iniquities of their fathers, that they do not rise, nor possess the land, nor fill the face of the world with cities.

22. For I will rise up against them, saith the Lord of Hosts, and cut off from Babylon the name, and remnant, and son, and nephew, saith the Lord.

23. I will also make it a possession for the bittern, and pools of water; and I will sweep it with the besom of destruction, saith the Lord of Hosts.

---

kings lie in their tombs "in glory," but the king of Babylon is cast out of his grave as a rotten limb of a tree, and, as a carcass trodden under feet. (v. 19)

*Thrust through with a Sword.* This became literally true. Nabonadius, the last king of Babylonia, fled to Borsippa, after having been defeated in battle by Cyrus, and left his son, Belshazzar, in Babylon to look after the affairs of state. The young prince was surprised by the invaders, in the midst of revelry, and slain in the confusion, at the gate of his magnificent palace, "thrust through with a sword;" whereupon Nabonadius, his father, crushed in body and spirit by his losses, surrendered to the conquerer.

*Thou hast Destroyed thy Land and Slain thy People.* Through the incessant war expeditions. Even "successful" wars are a curse to a country.

VERSES 22-23. *Pools of Water.* At the beginning of our era, Babylon was still partly inhabited and the surrounding country was cultivated. In the second century, the walls were still standing. During the fourth century they served as an enclosure for wild animals, and Persian monarchs went there to amuse themselves hunting. By and by the location was lost sight of and forgotten. More modern writers—Dr. Alexander Keith, among others—note the utter desolation of the once famous city. From the place where once the temple of Bel and the royal palaces rose in majestic heights, to the streets, everything has been reduced to gravel hills. Some are large; others are smaller. One who sees the innumerable parallel hills and the depressions between them does not know whether they are remnants of streets or canals. Babylon is fallen. Its foundations could not have been brought lower. Its "pomp has been brought down to the grave." It has literally become "pools of water." For laborers have made innumerable excavations to get gravel, or clay, for industrial purposes, and when the Euphrates overflows its banks, its water fills these hollows forming pools, or swamps. Such was the glory of Babylon less than a century ago. (Comp. Jer. 51:42)

*Bittern.* The Hebrew is "kippod," a word that occurs only in three places in the Bible: here, Is. 34:11, and Zeph. 2:14. Opinions differ concerning the meaning of it. Gensenius derives it from "kappad," to "shorten," or "contract" oneself, and translates it, "leech" (Grm. "Igel"). Our accepted translation, "bittern" is a species of heron, a bird with long feathers on the breast and neck, and a strong, pointed bill, which is known to frequent the marshes and rivers of western Asia and eastern Europe.

Concerning the desolation of the place that once was Babylon, Dr. Keith says there was no trace of vegetation. The ground looked as if it had been washed again and again by the rising and falling river, until every vestige of good soil had been swept away. Yet, the higher located sections had not been reached by the overflow and were therefore dry and parched as a desert, while the lower land was a swamp.

### 3. *About Assyria.*

24. The Lord of Hosts hath sworn, saying: Surely as I have thought, so shall it come to pass; and as I have purposed, so shall it stand—

25. That I will bring the Assyrian in my land, and upon my mountains tread him under foot; then shall his yoke depart from off them, and his burden depart from off their shoulders.

26. This is the purpose that is purposed upon the whole earth; and this is the hand that is stretched out upon all nations.

27. For the Lord of Hosts hath purposed, and who shall disannul? And his hand is stretched out, and who shall turn it back?

### 4. *Against Philistia.*

28. In the year that king Ahaz died was this burden.

29. Rejoice not thou, whole Palestina, because the rod of him that smote thee is broken; for out of the serpent's root shall

VERSE 24. *As I have Thought.* Note that God's thoughts are realities. "As I have thought, so shall it come to pass." Also, his purposes "stand." They are perfect, as God is perfect. Any change in his thoughts or purposes would be from perfection to imperfection, and that is unthinkable.

VERSE 25. *I Will Bring the Assyrian.* These paragraphs can be read to advantage as part of 2 Ne. 20, where the destruction of the army of Sennacherib is foretold. God brought the Assyrian to the mountains of Judah, for his defeat and destruction, and the liberation of his people.

But the prophetic word does not finish the history of Assyria, nor of Egypt, with descriptions of destruction. The Prophet Isaiah unveils this view of the future:

"And the Lord shall smite Egypt; he shall smite and heal it, and they shall return even to the Lord, and he shall be intreated of them, and shall heal them. In that day shall there be a highway out of Egypt to Assyria, and the Assyrian shall come into Egypt, and the Egyptian into Assyria, and the Egyptians shall serve with the Assyrians. In that day shall Israel be the third with Egypt and with Assyria, even a blessing in the midst of the land: Whom the Lord of Hosts shall bless, saying, Blessed be Egypt my people, and Assyria, the work of my hands, and Israel mine inheritance." (Is. 19:22-25)

If we read "Mesopotamia," or, "Irak," instead of "Assyria," and remember that Palestine was recognized as the homeland of the Jews; that Egypt obtained a liberal measure of political freedom, and that a considerable portion of ancient Assyria, under the name of Irak, or, Mesopotamia, was created an independent state, by the treaty of Versailles June 28, 1919, all under the mandate of Great Britain, we may be justified in looking forward to further developments along the lines here indicated. God recognizes, in this prophecy, the Egyptians as his people, in its resurrected existence, as his creation, and Israel as his inheritance.

VERSE 28. *In the Year that King Ahaz Died.* 728 B. C. The Philistines revolted and took several cities in Judah. The Prophet warned them not to exult too soon.

come forth a cockatrice, and his fruit shall be a fiery flying serpent.

30. And the first-born of the poor shall feed, and the needy shall lie down in safety; and I will kill thy root with famine, and he shall slay thy remnant.

31. Howl, O gate; cry, O city; thou, whole Palestina, art dissolved; for there shall come from the north a smoke, and none shall be alone in his appointed times.

32. What shall then answer the messengers of the nations? That the Lord hath founded Zion, and the poor of his people shall trust in it.

---

VERSE 29. *"Because the Rod of him that Smote thee is Broken,"* For the Lord had a fiery, flying serpent ready to sink his fangs into them, instead; referring to the Assyrian invader, Sargon. (Is. 20:1)

*Palestina.* Here and in verse 31 means Philistia, the country of the Philistines (Heb. Peleshet), the southern part of the coast plain of Canaan. This country was once one of the most flourishing, and, consequently, one of the most important and wealthy in Syria. Its cities, particularly Gaza, Askelon and Ashdod, were famous in the Old World, when the prophets predicted their destruction. Even long after their doom was proclaimed, they continued to prosper. Alexander the Great, the conqueror of the Persian army, was halted outside Gaza and delayed for two months. Askelon was famous for its flourishing vineyards, which made it an important commercial center. Ashdod was a strongly fortified city, strong enough to hold the Egyptian conquerors at bay for twenty years. It was demolished by the Turks in 1270 A. D., and Ibrahim Pasha carried away a considerable part of the ruins, to use for building material elsewhere. The surrounding country was fertile enough for many years. Wheat, peas, beans, fig trees, almonds and pomegranates were produced in abundance, but gradually the curse seemed to settle upon the soil. It became barren, and the few inhabitants who survived eked out a precarious existence by taking care of a few sheep and goats. Gaza was destroyed by Alexander the Great, 333 B. C. Strabo, at the beginning of our era, refers to it as a "desert." That is the very expression the angel of the Lord used when he sent Philip to go and meet the Ethiopian. He said "rise and go . . . unto the way that goeth down from Jerusalem unto Gaza, which is desert." (Acts 8:26) True, Constantine rebuilt Gaza, and established an ecclesiastic see there, but not on the old site but some distance from it. It was the new Gaza, known as "Ghuzze," which figured in the world war and fell into the hands of General Sir Henry Allenby, Nov. 6, 1917.

VERSE 30. *The Firstborn of the Poor.* The Jews shall prosper, while the Philistines were destroyed by famine and war.

VERSE 31. *There shall Come from the North a Smoke.* Referring to the Assyrians.

VERSE 32. *What to Answer the Messengers of the Nations.* This is a remarkable verse. The implication is that when the descendants of Abraham are being gathered for the last time, the nations of the world will be in commotion on account of war and war rumors. They will then send ambassadors to Palestine, or to the leading Jews, wherever they dwell, and ask them how they are getting along. The Prophet here, at least (see date in verse 28) 2265 years ago, formulated the correct answer to that question: "The Lord hath founded Zion, and the poor of his people shall trust in it." In other words, "All is well with Zion. God has founded it."

## CHAPTER 25

*Nephi's Introduction to His Comments, 1-11—Prediction Concerning the Death of Christ, 12-14—Dispersion and Gathering of the Jews a Second Time, 15-16—The Last Gather, 17-23—The Law and the Gospel, 24-30.*

## 1. Nephi's Introduction to his Comments.

1. Now I, Nephi, do speak somewhat concerning the words, which I have written, which have been spoken by the mouth of Isaiah. For behold, Isaiah spake many things which were hard for many of my people to understand; for they know not concerning the manner of prophesying among the Jews.

---

*Comments by Nephi.* Chapter 24 concludes the extracts of Nephi from the book of the Prophet Isaiah. In this chapter (25) he begins his exegesis of the section quoted. This extends to the end of chapter 31. It is one of the very important sections of the Book of Mormon.

VERSE 1. *My People.* Nephi realizes that the Prophet Isaiah, as, indeed, all the prophets, are difficult to understand, without special instruction. His people, he says, had not had the information needed because their works were works of darkness and abomination. (v. 2) We note that righteous living is necessary to a correct understanding of the Word of God, and especially the prophetic word.

*The Prophetic Language.* We may here note some peculiarities of the prophetic language, "the manner of prophesying among the Jews."

The prophets sometimes speak of future events as present, because they are present to them in their visions. For instance, "Unto us a Child is born." (Isa. 9:6)

Similarly, they sometimes speak of the future as already past. For instance: "He hath borne our grief and carried our sorrows; yet we did esteem him stricken, smitten of God, and afflicted." (Is. 53:4)

Another peculiarity is that the prophets sometimes group together future events very much as one combines stars into constellations in the wide expanse, according to their apparent position to an observer on earth, rather than their actual distance from each other. We have seen an example of this in the prophecies (see Is. 10 and 11), where the prophet speaks of the deliverance from Assyrian captivity and the deliverance by the Messiah, still future, as closely following, one upon the other. This peculiarity is very striking in the prophecies of our Lord concerning the destruction of Jerusalem and the "end of the world."

Nephi claimed to understand the prophecies, not only because he, himself, had the Spirit of prophecy (v. 4), but because he had lived in Jerusalem and was familiar with the religious observances of the Jews, their national customs, habits and history (v. 5), and the topographical surroundings of Jerusalem (v. 6). Without this knowledge the prophetic word is to a large extent unintelligible.

Prophecies are often uttered in figurative, or symbolic, terms. Some examples are here offered:

Arm means strength, or power, and arms made bare, power manifested. (Is. 52:40)

Babylon stands for an idolatrous, persecuting enemy of the people of God. (Is. 47-12; Rev. 17, 18)

Beast means a worldly power, especially a tyrannical, usurping government. (Dan. 7:3; Ezek. 34:28)

2. For I, Nephi, have not taught them many things concerning the manner of the Jews; for their works were works of darkness, and their doings were doings of abominations.

3. Wherefore, I write unto my people, unto all those that shall receive hereafter these things which I write, that they may know the judgments of God, that they come upon all nations, ac-

---

Dragon (Job 7:12 "Whale," should probably be crocodile) is often a symbol of Egypt (Is. 27-1, 51:9, Ezek. 19:3) and therefore in Rev. 12:3 and 13:1 refers to some oppressive worldly power.

Book, received, is the symbol of inauguration (2 Kings 11:12, "testimony,"); a book written within and without is a list of a long series of events; sealed is said of what is not yet revealed; to eat a book is to study it closely (Jer. 15:16; Rev. 10:9) The Book of Life, see Ezra 2:62; Rev. 3:5.

Breastplate is a symbol of something that is a protection for a vital part of the body, and which, at the same time, strikes terror into the breast of an adversary, (Is. 59:17; 1 Thess. 5:8; Rev. 9:9).

Crowns, symbol of delegated authority (Rev. 19:12, here, literally, "diadems.").

Earthquakes, violent agitations (Joel 2:10; Hag. 21:22; Rev. 6:12).

Forehead, written on, was the mark of a priest (Lev. 19:28); or a servant or a soldier (Rev. 22:4). Priests of idols wore a mark, a name or a number (Rev. 13:16-18).

Harp, a symbol of praise and joy (Ps. 33:2; Rev. 14:3).

Heaven and Earth, has a threefold sense. It means the material world, perceptible to our senses; sometimes it refers to the moral invisible world, and sometimes to the political organizations of the world. When used in this sense, heaven is the symbol of rulers and earth of subjects (Matt. 24:29).

Horn, stands for Power and regal dignity. (Dan. 8:9; Rev. 13:1)

Virgins (Rev. 14:4) stands for faithful worshipers, not corrupted by false doctrines and empty ceremonies. As the "woman" in Rev. 12, clothed with the Sun, having the moon under her feet and on her head a crown of twelve stars, undoubtedly refers to the Church of Christ, which is represented as adorned with the righteousness of which our Redeemer is the Author; standing on the Mosaic dispensation with its reflected light, and sustaining, as a crown of stars, the rule of the twelve Apostles; so "women" here (Rev. 14:4) is the symbol of anti-christian churches, and they who are not polluted by the doctrines and practices of such organizations, are "virgins."

These few examples, chiefly from Dr. Angus' Bible Handbook, illustrate the nature of the symbolic terms used by the Prophets. They are, as it were, hieroglyphs made audible by means of the spoken word. The student should be cautioned, however, against the not uncommon mistake of regarding as hieroglyphic, or figurative, terms which are used in their literal sense. He needs the constant guidance of the Spirit of the Lord not to err in this respect.

In this introduction Nephi explains that he has not been prompted to teach his people many things concerning the manners of the Jews, including, of course, the prophetic terms ,(v. 2), because their works were the works of darkness. That he refers to his people in the Land of Nephi, and not to the Jews in Palestine, must be inferred from the fact that he, in verse 5, makes this statement, "I know that the Jews do understand the things of the prophets." He, therefore speaks of another class of people, gathered around him in his new American settlement.

VERSE 3. *My People.* This surmise is strengthened by this verse, in which he regards all "that shall receive hereafter these things which I write," as his people.

cording to the word which he hath spoken.

4. Wherefore, hearken, O my people, which are of the house of Israel, and give ear unto my words; for because the words of Isaiah are not plain unto you, nevertheless they are plain unto all those that are filled with the spirit of prophecy. But I give unto you a prophecy, according to the spirit which is in me; wherefore I shall prophesy according to the plainness which hath been with me from the time that I came out from Jerusalem with my father; for behold, my soul delighteth in plainness unto my people, that they may learn.

5. Yea, and my soul delighteth in the words of Isaiah, for I came out from Jerusalem, and mine eyes hath beheld the things of the Jews, and I know that the Jews do understand the things of the prophets, and there is none other people that understand the things which were spoken unto the Jews like unto them, save it be that they are taught after the manner of the things of the Jews.

6. But behold I, Nephi, have not taught my children after the manner of the Jews; but behold, I, of myself, have dwelt at Jerusalem, wherefore I know concerning the regions round about; and I have made mention unto my children concerning the judgments of God, which hath come to pass among the Jews, unto my children, according to all that which Isaiah hath spoken, and I do not write them.

VERSE 4. *My People, which are of the House of Israel.* Here again a distinction seems to be made between his people, which were the descendants of Jacob, the Patriarch, whose other name was Israel (Gen. 32:28), and those of some other origin. But who could they be?

It would not be wise to speak categorically on a subject of which Revelation is silent and the sciences still are groping in the dark. But it is not to anticipate revelation, nor to assume scientific superiority, to call attention to the promise of the Lord to the Brother of Jared, when he instructed him to cross over to the western world: "There,"—in what to us is America—"I will raise up unto me of thy seed, and the seed of thy brother, and they who shall go with thee, a great nation. And there shall be no greater nation than the nation which I will raise up unto me of thy seed, upon all the face of the earth." (Ether 1:43) Nor would it be unreasonable to suppose, in view of this marvelous divine promise, that the Jaredites, although a vast number of them were destroyed at Ramah, were scattered, at that time, 19 hundred years after their arrival here, all over the American continents, as were the Indians at the time of the discovery, in the 15th century. If this assumption is correct—and there can be little doubt about that—we may also assume that some of them joined the Nephites in their settlements and the Lamanites in theirs, as well as the Mulekites, as these joined the people of Mosiah (Omni 19). Others may have rejected the message of Nephi and remained idolaters. Conditions in the first settlements of both the Nephites and the Lamanites may have developed during the first fifty years very much as they did during the first few decades in Utah after the colonization by President Brigham Young and the Pioneers. That would explain some difficult passages in the Book of Mormon.

But, whoever they were, neither they nor the descendants of Nephi and his

7. But behold, I proceed with mine own prophecy, according to my plainness; in the which I know that no man can err; nevertheless, in the days that the prophecies of Isaiah shall be fulfilled men shall know of a surety, at the times when they shall come to pass.

8. Wherefore, they are of worth unto the children of men, and he that supposeth that they are not, unto them will I speak particularly, and confine the words unto mine own people; for I know that they shall be of great worth unto them in the last days; for in that day shall they understand them; wherefore, for their good have I written them.

9. And as one generation hath been destroyed among the Jews because of iniquity, even so have they been destroyed from gener-ation to generation according to their iniquities; and never hath any of them been destroyed save it were foretold them by the prophets of the Lord.

10. Wherefore, it hath been told them concerning the destruction which should come upon them, immediately after my father left Jerusalem; nevertheless, they hardened their hearts; and according to my prophecy they have been destroyed, save it be those which are carried away captive into Babylon.

11. And now this I speak because of the spirit which is in me. And notwithstanding they have been carried away they shall return again, and possess the land of Jerusalem; wherefore, they shall be restored again to the land of their inheritance.

followers, had been instructed sufficiently to understand the prophets (vv. 4 and 6). For that reason Nephi wrote this discourse, this "prophecy," (v. 7), for the benefit of future generations. (v. 8)

VERSE 7. *Men Shall Know of a Surety.* At the time when a prophecy is fulfilled, it is understood perfectly, and the time is made known by the fulfilment. Nephi here enunciates a principle recognized by Bible students, viz., that it is the fulfilment of a prophecy that is the evidence of its divine inspiration and origin. Were this not so, every reader of future generations would, undoubtedly, be deprived of the strongest possible evidence of the divine inspiration of the Word of God. (Comp. Is. 42-26; 43:9)

VERSE 9. *Destroyed.* We note, "destroyed from generation to generation." "Destroyed" is sometimes read, as if it could only mean "exterminated." But it is evident that a race cannot be exterminated more than once, and not from generation unto generation. "Destroyed," however, also means "brought to ruin," "overthrown," or even very much "damaged," as a dress torn or hopelessly soiled. In this sense we may say that a race can be "destroyed" from generation to generation, although it does not cease to exist. We note especially "destroyed" in verse 10.

VERSE 10. *"The Land of Jerusalem."* Palestine. Note again, that although they were to be "destroyed," they "shall be restored again to the land of their inheritance." They were never to be exterminated.

## 2. Prediction Concerning the Death of Christ.

12. But, behold, they shall have wars, and rumors of wars; and when the day cometh that the Only Begotten of the Father, yea, even the Father of heaven and of earth, shall manifest himself unto them in the flesh, behold, they will reject him, because of their iniquities, and the hardness of their hearts, and the stiffness of their necks.

---

VERSE 12. *Heaven and Earth.* If this expression is to be understood in its figurative, prophetic meaning, it stands for all mankind, both rulers and subjects. (Notes under v. 1)

*They will Reject Him.* Nephi ascribes the rejection of Jesus by the leaders of the people to their iniquities, their hardness of heart, and their pride (stiff necks).

(1) *Their Iniquities.* Caiaphas was the high priest at the time of the crucifixion, and presided over the sanhedrin, the Jewish tribunal that condemned Jesus to death. This Caiaphas was the son-in-law of Annas, who had been the high priest but had been deposed by the Roman authorities for conduct unbecoming his exalted office. But the Jews generally did not recognize the authority of the Romans to depose the high priest. He was, therefore, considered the actual head of the council, and influenced its decisions. These men were Sadducees. As such they virtually denied a life after this and the obligation to conform to moral standards. They were tolerant enough in questions of doctrine, and indifferent to the opposition encountered by the Pharisees from time to time; but they were financially interested in the cattle market and the tables of the money changers by which the temple grounds were desecrated. When Jesus, possibly for the second time (comp. Matt. 21:12, 13, Mark 11:15-18, Luke 19:45, 46, with John 2:13-17), drove the cattle and cattle vendors from the temple grounds and spilled their money all over the place, they gladly paid Judas a pittance for delivering him into their hands secretly, so as not to risk a popular demonstration in his favor such as that which had stirred up the people of Jerusalem at his triumphant entrance into the city a few days previously. (2) *Hardness of Heart.* This was as conspicuous as their iniquity. For although they had no convicting proof of their accusations, and were told so repeatedly, they insisted on the death of Jesus as a blasphemer. When Pilate suggested that he be set free on the strength of a humane holiday custom, they seemed panic-stricken and clamored for the liberation of a real criminal. Their hearts were hard as flint against the Holy One of Israel. And not only did they demand his death. They wanted to make sure that his end would be the most degrading and painful imaginable. We can hear Pilate, trying to calm the raving mob, crying that Jesus was innocent, and telling their leaders that if they wanted an innocent man crucified, they would have to do it themselves. (John 19:6.) They might have put our Lord to death by stoning, as, later Stephen suffered martyrdom. But stoning was, comparatively speaking, a humane mode of capital punishment. It was crucifixion they wanted, and they finally obtained their object by intimating to Pilate that he might be accused in Rome of disloyalty to Caesar, if he should set Jesus free. (John 19:8-16.) (3) *Pride.* The officials, both Sadducees and Pharisees, were deeply wounded in their pride by the appearance of Jesus on the temple grounds, in the power and spirit of Elijah of old; previously he had broken off all connection with the Pharisees as a sect, by denouncing them publicly as usurpers of the "seat of Moses," by their additions to his law. He had accused them of love of adulation and flattery, of hypocrisy, folly and blindness, of the teaching of false doctrines, and of being the

13. Behold, they will crucify him; and after he is laid in a sepulchre for the space of three days he shall rise from the dead, with healing in his wings; and all those who shall believe on his name shall be saved in the kingdom of God. Wherefore, my soul delighteth to prophesy concerning him, for I have seen his day, and my heart doth magnify his holy name.

cause of the destruction of Jerusalem and the temple, now near at hand, by their persecution of the messengers of God. (Matt. 23) Their besetting sin was vanity and pride, as noted by Nephi. Wherefore Jesus says, in part: "Be not ye called Rabbi, for one is your Master, even Christ, and all ye are brethren. And call no man your father upon the earth; for one is your Father, which is in heaven. Neither be ye called masters; for One is your Master, even Christ. But he that is greatest among you shall be your servant. And whosoever shall exalt himself shall be abased, and he that shall humble himself shall be exalted. (Matt. 23:8-12)

VERSE 13. *For the Space of Three Days.* The commonly accepted understanding is that Jesus died on the cross on Friday, the 14th of Abib, shortly after 3 p.m., and that, as soon as the necessary permission had been obtained, he was hurriedly wrapped in a shroud and laid in the tomb of Joseph of Arimathaea. Saturday, Abib the 15th which began Friday at sunset and ended at sunset Saturday, was the Sabbath. All were then resting. But when the Sabbath ended, some of the women bought the necessary ingredients for the preparation of the body. (Luke 24:1-8) Sunday, Abib the 16th, began at sunset Saturday. Early Sunday morning about sunrise, Mary of Magdala came to the tomb and found it empty. Shortly afterwards the other women came with the ointment and also found that the Master was not there. (John 20:1-16; Luke 24:1-10) According to this account, the body of Jesus was in the tomb part of Friday, all Saturday and about half of the Sunday. This would, it is argued, in Hebrew colloquialism, be three days-and-nights.

There may be a difference of opinion as to the day of the crucifixion and burial, but that our Lord rose on the first day of the week, our Sunday, is the universal opinion, founded both on tradition and history. Sunday was the day on which the first Christians came together for Christian worship. (Acts 20:7; 1 Cor. 16:2) The resurrection of Christ was their only known reason for so doing. The day was, therefore, called the "Lord's Day." (Rev. 1:10) Pliny, in the first or beginning of the second century, reported to the emperor, Trajan, that the Christians had a certain day on which they sang a hymn to Christ as a God. That could not have been on the Mosaic Sabbath. Justin Martyr (140 A.D.) states positively that the Christians had the custom of assembling the first day of the week, because on that day our Lord rose from the dead, and Tertullian (200 A. D.) speaks of Sunday as the day of the resurrection of our Lord (die Domini resurrexionis.—Critical and popular Bible Encyclopaedia, Lord's Day).

The change from the seventhday to the firstday Sabbath at the end of the old dispensation was as natural as it was inevitable. As good Jews, the first Christians kept the established day of rest. But that day ended at sunset, at six p.m., say, and the first day began at the same hour. They, therefore, had ample time, on the first day, before retiring, to gather in the homes, for Christian worship, for love feasts, for testimonies concerning the crucified and resurrected Savior. And that is just what happened. Thus, the day after the Sabbath became, naturally, the Lord's day, and the Christian Sabbath, from the very first day of the resurrection.

The Mosaic Sabbath was instituted in commemoration of the work of God in creation (Ex. 31:15-17); the Lord's day, similarly, is a reminder to us that the res-

14. And behold it shall come to pass that after the Messiah hath risen from the dead, and hath manifested himself unto his people, unto as many as will believe on his name, behold, Jerusalem shall be destroyed again; for wo unto them that fight against God and the people of his church.

### 3. A Second Dispersion and Gathering.

15. Wherefore, the Jews shall be scattered among all nations; yea, and also Babylon shall be destroyed; wherefore, the Jews shall be scattered by other nations.

16. And after they have been scattered, and the Lord God hath scourged them by other nations for the space of many generations, yea, even down from generation to generation until they shall be persuaded to believe in Christ, the Son of God, and the atonement, which is infinite for all mankind—and when that day shall come that they shall believe in Christ, and worship the Father in his name, with pure hearts and clean hands, and look not forward any more for another Messiah, then, at that time, the day will come that it must needs be expedient that they should believe these things.

---

urrection of Jesus was the beginning of a new creation, affecting the entire universe, (Rom. 8:19-23)—the beginning of new heavens and a new earth (Is. 65:17-25; 2 Pet. 3:13, 14; Rev. 21:1-5).

VERSE 14. *Jerusalem Shall be Destroyed.* This was done by the Romans under Titus, 70 A.D. Jesus, who foresaw what the consequences of Hebrew politics would be, wept when he took a last look at the city, before his passion. And well might he weep. The city at the time of the destruction, was overfilled with visitors who had come to celebrate a yearly festival. Suddenly the gates were closed and the multitudes were trapped. Food supplies were consumed. A difference of opinion between the dominant parties, concerning the defense, developed into a civil war. Pharisees, Sadducees and Zealots fought each other, with sword and fire. The Zealots took charge of the temple grounds and massacred the priests at the altars. When the food supplies were finished, famine added horrors to the situation. Cases of cannibalism were observed under heart-rending circumstances, as when mothers were slaying their own children. When, finally, the Roman soldiers gained an entrance into the city, they strewed the streets with corpses. It is estimated that 1,100,000 perished in this insane conflict. When Titus was lauded for his victory, he disclaimed all honor for it. He was, he said, only an instrument of divine retribution.

VERSE 15. *The Jews Shall be Scattered.* Although the city and the temple had been destroyed and thousands of the inhabitants were driven into foreign lands, some of the exiles returned sixty years later, led by a pretender to Messianic authority. These tried again to defy Rome. A war began which lasted two years. It is claimed that 580,000 of the people fell in this conflict, besides those who perished by famine, pestilence and fire. At that time, it is said, fifty cities were totally destroyed, and Judaea was left a desert. From that time Jews have been a foreign element in nearly every country on earth, in Asia, in Europe, in Africa and America.

## 4. *The Last Gathering.*

17. And the Lord will set his hand again the second time to restore his people from their lost and fallen state. Wherefore, he will proceed to do a marvelous work and a wonder among the children of men.

18. Wherefore, he shall bring forth his words unto them, which words shall judge them at the last day, for they shall be given them for the purpose of convincing them of the true Messiah, who was rejected by them; and unto the convincing of them that they need not look forward any more for a Messiah to come, for there should not any come, save it should be a false Messiah which should deceive the people; for there is save one Messiah spoken of by the prophets, and that Messiah is he who should be rejected of the Jews.

19. For according to the words of the prophets, the Messiah cometh in six hundred years from the time that my father left Jerusalem; and according to the words of the prophets, and also the word of the angel of God, his name shall be Jesus Christ, the Son of God.

---

According to a decree of Emperor Hadrian, Jews were prohibited, on the pain of death, to enter Jerusalem.

VERSE 17. *The Second Time.* The restoration from the servitude in Egypt was the first.

*Marvelous Work and Wonder.* (Isa. 29:13, 14) Refers to the restoration of the Church previous to the restoration of Israel in the latter days.

VERSE 18. *He Shall Bring Forth His Words.* The Book of Mormon and the Latter-day revelations. One of the great objects of the Book of Mormon is to convince the Children of Israel that Jesus, whom their ancestors rejected, is the promised Messiah. It should not be difficult for well-informed, intelligent descendants of Abraham to accept Jesus as their Messiah, their deliverer; for, wherever his principles have been accepted and his divine authority acknowledged, liberty, religious and civil, has prevailed. In 1654 A. D. the first Jews in the United States, 23 in number, arrived in what was then New Netherlands. They came from Brazil, to escape persecution there, and found a warm welcome and perfect freedom here. And since then, wherever American democracy has prevailed over autocracy, the Jews have been on an equal level with other citizens. War on the American democracy is, therefore, in many places, also an attack on the Jews and the Messiah, the divine Author of human freedom.

VERSE 19. *In Six Hundred Years.* We are here informed that prophets had stated that the Messiah would come 600 years from the exodus of Lehi (comp. 1 Ne. 10:4; 19:8). This, however, does not furnish a clue to the actual year of the birth of Jesus, counting, for instance from the year of the foundation of Rome, which is generally given as 753 B. C. The popular view is that the Nativity occurred 4 years, but some scholars place it as much as from 5 to 7 years, before Christ.

*His Name Shall Be Jesus Christ.* See Article on "The Sacred Name," 2 Ne. 10.

20. And now, my brethren, I have spoken plainly that ye cannot err. And as the Lord God liveth that brought Israel up out of the land of Egypt, and gave unto Moses power that he should heal the nations after they had been bitten by the poisonous serpents, if they would cast their eyes unto the serpent which he did raise up before them, and also gave him power that he should smite the rock and the water should come forth; yea, behold I say unto you, that as these things are true, and as the Lord God liveth, there is none other name given under heaven save it be this Jesus Christ, of which I have spoken, whereby man can be saved.

21. Wherefore, for this cause hath the Lord God promised unto me that these things which I write shall be kept and preserved, and handed down unto my seed, from generation to generation, that the promise may be fulfilled unto Joseph, that his seed should never perish as long as the earth should stand.

22. Wherefore, these things shall go from generation to generation as long as the earth shall stand; and they shall go according to the will and pleasure of God; and the nations who shall possess them shall be judged of

VERSE 20. *Heal the Nations.* Refers to the incident related in Numbers 21:4-9, where we read that Moses, under divine instruction, had a serpent made of "brass," also translated "copper," on which repentant Israelites, bitten by poisonous serpents as a punishment for rebellion against Moses, might "look and live." The serpent was a type of Jesus (John 3:14, 15). It was kept for at least seven hundred years, as a national relic, and was destroyed by Hezekiah, king of Judah, because it had become an object of idoltry. (2 Kings 18:4) And when he had it broken up, he called it, in derision, "nehushtan," a "thing made of brass."

Nephi, commenting on this incident in the wilderness, refers to the twelve tribes as "nations." To his prophetic eye the tribes represented the nations of the world, and the serpent was the picture of their crucified Savior. (See notes on "the prophetic language" under verse 1) But the expression is also literally correct. For the tribes of Israel were, in fact, so many little republics, each independent of the rest, except as common interests dictated cooperation. The book of Judges gives ample evidence for this proposition. (See 8:1-3; 12:1-3; 18:1-12 and chapter 20)

*None Other Name.* Comp. Phil. 2:9-12. There is only one Savior, one Mediator between man and God. That is Jesus Christ. And the testimony of St. Paul is that the day will come when every tongue shall "confess that Jesus Christ is the Lord, to the glory of God the Father." And this, he says, applies to everything, in heaven, on earth and under the earth. (Phil 2:10)

VERSES 21-22. *These Things.* Refers to the Book of Mormon. Nephi discloses important information in these paragraphs.

First, he says God has promised him that his writings would be preserved and handed down to his seed, from generation to generation, in fulfilment of a promise given to Joseph, that "his seed should never perish as long as the earth should stand." Just when Joseph received that promise is not stated, but see the blessings of Ephraim and Manasseh (Gen. 48:15, 16) and of Joseph (Gen. 49:22-26). Jacob said to Joseph, in part:

them according to the words which are written.

23. For we labor diligently to write, to persuade our children, and also our brethren, to believe in Christ, and to be reconciled to God; for we know that it is by grace that we are saved, after all we can do.

---

"The blessings of thy father have prevailed
Above the blessings of my progenitors,
Unto the utmost bounds of the everlasting hills,
They shall be on the head of Joseph."

It is evident that Nephi did not expect that his descendants would ever be exterminated, and they never were. He believed that the promise to Joseph would be fulfilled in his descendants, to the end of days.

Secondly, Nephi tells us that his writings would be distributed from generation to generation, as long as the earth shall stand, and that the distribution would be under the special direction of God. This is a natural deduction, since He alone knows for certain where the descendants of Joseph would be from generation to generation.

Third, Nephi tells us that the nations, to whom these writings become known, will be judged according to the moral and ethical standards they reveal. This is one reason why the statesmen of the world would do well to study the Book of Mormon. For a day will come, when the Lord shall return in glory, at the beginning of the Millennium. Then he will summon the nations before him. Their records will be scrutinized, and a place will be assigned to each in accordance with the treatment accorded "one of the least" of these. For there is a national, as well as an individual, day of Judgment. (Matt. 25:31-46)

VERSE 23. *By Grace We are Saved.* The doctrine here stated is, salvation is freely given and cannot be "earned." We find the same thought in the Doctrine and Covenants (6:13): "There is no gift greater than the gift of salvation." And the Apostle Paul recognizes the difference between earnings and favors, when he says that the "wages of sin" is death, but the "gift" of God is eternal life through Jesus Christ our Lord. (Rom. 6:23) We can earn death, but we must receive life as a gift, or not at all.

The Prophet Joseph explains that to be saved is to be placed beyond the reach of all enemies, even death, and that this can be done only through the Priesthood. (Hist. of the Church, Vol. 5, p. 403)

A seemingly hopeless discussion has been carried on by philosophers, as well as theologians, on the question of the ability of man to earn salvation, and his responsibility in case of failure to do so. Great thinkers, such as Kant, Schleiermacher, Hegel, Ritschi, and many others, have contributed their conclusions on the all-important problems presented. The old notion that human history is but a marionette show in which the strings are being pulled by some one behind a screen to make the dolls move, has been abandoned long ago, for the only rational concept presented by the revelations of God, that the human family is his children, being fostered under his care and gradually educated for their eternal testing. God, because of his love, has provided this course for us, and, as the Apostle says (1 John, 4:19): "We love God, because he first loved us"; but where there is genuine mutual love, the question of "wages" is far in the background. Love engenders love, but if our love of God is real, it finds expression in unselfish service of our fellowmen. (1 John 3:17; 4:20, 21) In recent years the gospel doctrine of the Fatherhood of God, with the infinite love and the immeasurable responsibility of a Divine Father, possess-

## 5. *The Law and the Gospel.*

24. And, notwithstanding we believe in Christ, we keep the law of Moses, and look forward with steadfastness unto Christ, until the law shall be fulfilled.

25. For, for this end was the law given; wherefore the law hath become dead unto us, and we are made alive in Christ because of our faith; yet we keep the law because of the commandments.

26. And we talk of Christ, we rejoice in Christ, we preach of Christ, we prophesy of Christ, and we write according to our prophecies, that our children may know to what source they may look for a remission of their sins.

---

ing unlimited power and wisdom, has replaced the contradictory notions of God of former ages.

VERSES 24-27. *The Law of Moses.* Nephi here explains that he and his people are keeping the Law of Moses, while, at the same time, they are looking forward to the coming of Christ, with faith, as the true Source of the remission of sins and life eternal. He argues that the very purpose of the Law is to prepare the people for the coming of Christ to fulfil its requirements, in his life and death.

VERSE 26. *We Talk of Christ.* The central truth in the Mosaic dispensation was the doctrine of the Messiah, the Christ, as it is in the new dispensation, the Gospel. Hence Nephi: We talk of, we rejoice in, we preach and prophesy of Christ, and we write according to our prophecies for the instruction of our children concerning to what Source "they may look for a remission of their sins."

From this point of view we may regard the Old and New covenants as grades of the same school, the second being the more advanced of the two. Or, we may say that the Law is the Gospel foreshadowed, promised, and that the Gospel is the Law substantiated, realized, fulfilled.

The tabernacle (and, later, the temple) with its dividing veil, furniture and Glory of the Lord, represented the entire universe, visible and invisible, and was the palace of the King, the center of the divine government.

The sacrifices were the visible representations of the first and chief principle of true religion and worship, the doctrine of the atonement. They were impressive lessons on the holiness, Fatherly love, justice, and responsibility of God in the government of his children; and of the obligations of man to him, as members of his household.

The festivals, weekly, monthly, yearly and cyclic, were further reminders of the duty to serve God by taking care of his children. They were sermons on true worship, as expressed in human fellowship and brotherly love. (See 1 John 3:14-28)

The education furnished by these two grades, is necessary for the advancement of man to the next dispensation—the Millennial reign of the Son of God on earth.

But although the Law and the Gospel are parts of the same divine educational system, and therefore one, they present marked differences. It is the differences between Moses and Jesus, Sinai and Calvary; or, the destructive forces of nature that passed before Elijah at Mt. Horeb, and the still small voice in which the prophet immediately recognized the presence of God. (I Kings 19:9-18)

A more detailed review of the Mosaic dispensation may be offered here.

*The Tabernacle.* This was the temple of Israel in the wilderness, the sanctuary of Jehovah, as their God, and his palace as their King. Here he dwelt, here he manifested himself. It was a rectangular structure, representing heaven in the "holy of holies," and earth in the "holy place." (Heb. 19-18) In the holy of holies were the ark of the covenant, surmounted by cherubim with outstretched wings, and on this throne, the Shekina, the Glory of God, rested. Near the ark were the tables of stone with the ten commandments, a pot of manna, and the rod of Aaron. In the holy place were the golden altar of incense, the golden candlestick, and a table on which bread was placed daily. (Ex. 25)

*The Temple.* Later, the temple of Solomon was built according to the same pattern. It was similarly furnished, and, in addition, it had a great baptismal font resting on twelve oxen of copper. This was placed in the court of the priests "on the right side of the east end, over against the south," near the altar of burnt offering.

*The Priests.* All the priests were the descendants of Levi, and they were all devoted to the public service. (Num. 4:1-20) During the reign of David they were divided into three divisions, of which one assisted the priests, another furnished the singing and music, and the third acted as porters and guards of the temple.

*Sacrifices* formed one of the chief parts of the divine service under the Mosaic Law. From the vegetable kingdom were offered flour, cakes, parched corn, frankincense, and wine for drink offering. The animals offered were oxen, sheep, goats, and, in some cases, doves, but never fishes. Human sacrifices were expressly forbidden. (Lev. 18:21; 20-25)

Sacrifices were either an expression of gratitude for blessings received, or an expiation for sin. There were, therefore, thank-offerings, sin- or trespass offerings and burnt-offerings. The latter were offered in atonement for sin in general. They were consumed by fire and were presented daily. Sin-offerings were atoning for sins of commission, and trespass-offerings for sins of omission. (Lev. 7:1-10) In all these the principle of vicarious suffering is illustrated. The life of the victim was substituted for the life of the offender. In the thank-offering a bull, a sheep, or a goat was slain. The blood was sprinkled around the altar. The breast and shoulder belonged to the officiating priest. The rest appeared on the festive table in the circle of the family and their friends. (Lev. 6:1-17; 1 Cor. 10:18) Sacrifices for special favors were called "sacrifices of praise."

By all this shedding of blood, God impressed upon the minds of the people his abhorrence of sin and his demand for holiness in his worshipers.

*The Festivals* of the Mosaic dispensation were equally significant. The weekly Sabbath—one day of every seven—was devoted to rest, worship and instruction. (Lev. 24:8; Num. 28:9) The day of the new moon was also a festival. (Num. 28:9) Three annual festivals were observed, when all the men were required to appear at the sanctuary. (Ex. 23:14-17) These were: (1) The Passover, in remembrance of the exodus from Egypt. This began on the 14th of Abib in the evening and lasted till the 21st of the month. It was during the beginning of this festival, the 14th of Abib, that our Lord instituted the Sacrament of the Supper. (Matt. 26:20-28; Mark 14:12-25; Luke 22:14-38; John 13:1-30; 1 Cor. 10:16-18, 11:23-29) (2) The fiftieth day after the second day of the passover week was Pentecost, the festival of weeks. (Ex. 23:16; Lev. 23:9-21) During this festival Jews came to Jerusalem from many countries. (Acts 2:2-11) (3) In the autumn, from the 15th to 23rd of the seventh month (Tisri, October) the feast of Tabernacles was celebrated. This was a festival of great joy. (Lev. 23:33-37)

*The Day of Atonement.* The tenth day of this month was the day of Atonement, which was a day of fasting and confession of sins. It was on this day that the high priest entered the Holy of Holies and sprinkled the atoning blood before the Lord. (Lev. 23:26-32)

*The Sabbath Year and Year of Jubilee.* Every seventh year was a sabbath year, a year of rest, as every seventh day of the week was a day of rest. (Ex. 23:10-11; Lev.

27. Wherefore, we speak concerning the law that our children may know the deadness of the law; and they, by knowing the deadness of the law, may look forward unto that life which is in Christ, and know for what end the law was given. And after the law is fulfilled in Christ, that they need not harden their hearts against him when the law ought to be done away.

28. And now behold, my people, ye are a stiffnecked people; wherefore, I have spoken plainly unto you, that ye cannot misunderstand. And the words which I have spoken shall stand as a testimony against you; for they are sufficient to teach any man the right way; for the right way is to believe in Christ and deny him not; for by denying him ye also deny the prophets and the law.

29. And now behold, I say unto you that the right way is to believe in Christ, and deny him not; and Christ is the Holy One of Israel; wherefore ye must bow down before him, and worship him with all your might, mind, and strength, and your whole soul; and if ye do this ye shall in nowise be cast out.

30. And, inasmuch as it shall be expedient, ye must keep the performances and ordinances of God until the law shall be fulfilled which was given unto Moses.

---

23:5-7; Deut. 31:10-13) and the year after every seven Sabbatic years, that is to say, every fiftieth year in the cycle of years was the year of jubilee. (Lev. 25:8-17) Then two Sabbath years, the 49th and the 50th, came together. (Lev. 25:8-17)

*Double Sabbaths.* The weekly Sabbaths were similarly arranged. Once a year two Sabbaths came together, the 49th and the 50th day after the first offering of the first fruit of the harvest as a wave offering. The harvest was then completed, and bread made of the new flour, as well as new grain, were offered as a second first fruit. Many burnt offerings were also presented at this time. This festival was the "feast of weeks," also called Pentecost. (Lev. 23:15-21)

VERSE 27. *Deadness of the Law.* St. Paul uses this term in Rom. 4:19, 20, where he refers to the natural lack of physical vigor of Abraham and Sarah, at the time when they were promised a son and heir in their advanced age. The Apostle says the patriarch "staggered" not through unbelief, but was strong in faith, giving glory to God. Further, "For what the Law could not do, in that it was weak through the flesh"—that is, on account of the weakness of human nature—"God, sending his own Son in the likeness of sinful flesh, and for sin, condemned sin in the flesh." (Rom. 8:3) And again: "For I through the Law am dead to the Law, that I might live unto God." (Gal. 2:19)

VERSE 28. *The Prophets and the Law.* To Nephi, as to the Apostle Paul, Christ is all in all. (Eph. 1:23; Col. 3:11) Whosoever denies Christ, denies also the Prophets and the Law. That is, the entire Scriptures. For anciently the Hebrews classed Joshua, Judges and Ruth, Samuel 1 and 2, Kings 1 and 2, Chronicles 1 and 2, Daniel, Ezra and Nehemiah, Esther and Job among the Prophets. Nephi was acquainted with some of these books, the socalled Nebiim Reshonim, as well as with the Law, the Torah. He, therefore, refers to the Scriptures as "The Prophets and the Law."

## CHAPTER 26

*Christ to Appear in America, 1-11 — Gentiles, as Well as Jews, Must Believe, 12-18—Gentiles in the Last Days, 19-29—Latter-day Commandments of God, 30-33.*

### 1. *Christ to Appear in America.*

1. And after Christ shall have risen from the dead he shall show himself unto you, my children, and my beloved brethren; and the words which he shall speak unto you shall be the law which ye shall do.

2. For behold, I say unto you that I have beheld that many generations shall pass away, and there shall be great wars and contentions among my people.

3. And after the Messiah shall come there shall be signs given unto my people of his birth, and also of his death and resurrection; and great and terrible shall that day be unto the wicked, for they shall perish; and they perish because they cast out the prophets, and the saints, and stone them, and slay them; wherefore the cry of the blood of the saints shall ascend up to God from the ground against them.

4. Wherefore, all those who are proud, and that do wickedly, the day that cometh shall burn them up, saith the Lord of Hosts, for they shall be as stubble.

5. And they that kill the prophets, and the saints, the depths of the earth shall swallow them up, saith the Lord of Hosts; and mountains shall cover them, and whirlwinds shall carry them away, and buildings shall fall upon them and crush them to pieces and grind them to powder.

6. And they shall be visited with thunderings, and lightnings, and earthquakes, and all manner of destructions, for the fire of the anger of the Lord shall be kindled against them, and they shall be as stubble, and the day that cometh shall consume them, saith the Lord of Hosts.

7. O the pain, and the anguish of my soul for the loss of the slain of my people! For I, Nephi, have seen it, and it well nigh consumeth me before the presence of the Lord; but I must cry unto my God: Thy ways are just.

---

VERSE 1. *He Shall Show Himself Unto You.* This promise was fulfilled. See 3 Nephi 4:8-11.

*The Law which ye Shall Do.* The story of the appearance of Jesus in the land of Bountiful, his ministrations and sermons, is recorded in 3 Ne. 11:1-27:12. This is the Law of the Gospel. It is the "fulness of the Gospel." It is a story that should be studied diligently and intelligently.

VERSES 3-7. *A Sign of the Birth of Jesus.* The descendants of Nephi are here promised to receive notice of the birth of the Messiah, by unmistakable signs in the heavens. Comp. Alma 6:20; Hel. 14:3-13.

*Also of his Death and Resurrection.* Hel. 14:14, 20-29. These signs were given in order that believers might have a strong foundation for their faith, and that doubters would have no excuse for their rejection of the Messiah. (Hel. 14:29)

8. But behold, the righteous that hearken unto the words of the prophets, and destroy them not, but look forward unto Christ with steadfastness for the signs which are given, notwithstanding all persecution—behold, they are they which shall not perish.

9. But the Son of righteousness shall appear unto them; and he shall heal them, and they shall have peace with him, until three generations shall have passed away, and many of the fourth generation shall have passed away in righteousness.

10. And when these things have passed away a speedy destruction cometh unto my people; for, notwithstanding the pains of my soul, I have seen it; wherefore, I know that it shall come to pass; and they sell themselves for naught; for, for the reward of their pride and their foolishness they shall reap destruction; for because they yield unto the devil and choose works of darkness rather than light, therefore they must go down to hell.

11. For the Spirit of the Lord will not always strive with man. And when the Spirit ceaseth to strive with man then cometh speedy destruction, and this grieveth my soul.

## 2. Gentiles, as well as Jews, Must Believe.

12. And as I spake concerning the convincing of the Jews, that Jesus is the very Christ, it must needs be that the Gentiles be convinced also that Jesus is the Christ, the Eternal God;

13. And that he manifesteth himself unto all those who believe in him, by the power of the Holy Ghost; yea, unto every nation, kindred, tongue, and people working mighty miracles, signs,

*The Wicked Shall Perish.* Persecutors are here referred to. To reject the prophets who came with a divine message, and to slay the Saints because they live righteous lives, is wickedness in the last degree. The sinners are being warned even by the voice of nature, as heard in earthquakes, rolling thunders, lightnings, storm-winds and destruction. (v. 5-7)

On the other hand, the righteous shall not perish with the wicked. Those who believe on Christ will be preserved. (v. 8) And not only that, but, for their sake, the destruction will be postponed for three generations and part of the fourth (v. 9), during which time the Son of Righteousness will heal them and cause them to live in peace. But, after that, when pride and foolishness and crime again abound, the destruction will no longer be postponed, but will come suddenly (v. 10). For, when the Spirit of the Lord ceases to "strive;" that is, to struggle, to argue with men, their fate is sealed. (v. 11)

VERSES 12-13. *What All Must Believe.* That Jesus is the Christ. To regard him as a great Teacher, an incomparable Reformer, a perfect Man, is not to have faith in salvation. Both Jews and Gentiles must be convinced (1) that Jesus is the Christ, the Eternal God (v. 12); (2) that he manifest himself by the Power of the Holy Ghost (v. 13); that, in other words, he still is in the midst of those who worship him, an ever present Savior and Redeemer, according to his promise: "Lo, I am with you always even unto the end of the world." (Matt. 28:20)

and wonders, among the children of men according to their faith.

14. But behold, I prophesy unto you concerning the last days; concerning the days when the Lord God shall bring these things forth unto the children of men.

15. After my seed and the seed of my brethren shall have dwindled in unbelief, and shall have been smitten by the Gentiles; yea, after the Lord God shall have camped against them round about, and shall have laid siege against them with a mount, and raised forts against them; and after they shall have been brought down low in the dust, even that they are not, yet the words of the righteous shall be written, and the prayers of the faithful shall be heard, and all those who have dwindled in unbelief shall not be forgotten.

16. For those who shall be destroyed shall speak unto them out of the ground, and their speech shall be low out of the dust, and their voice shall be as one that hath a familiar spirit; for the Lord God will give unto him power, that he may whisper concerning them, even as it were out of the ground; and their speech shall whisper out of the dust.

17. For thus saith the Lord God: They shall write the things which shall be done among them, and they shall be written and sealed up in a book, and those who have dwindled in unbelief shall not have them, for they seek to destroy the things of God.

18. Wherefore, as those who have been destroyed have been destroyed speedily; and the multitude of their terrible ones shall be as chaff that passeth away— yea, thus saith the Lord God: It shall be at an instant, suddenly—

VERSE 14. *The Last Days.* The "latter days" is an expression which, in the parlance of the Old Testament prophets, refers to the reign of the Messiah. Here Nephi says he is speaking of the "last days," meaning the time after the bringing forth of "these things,"—the Book of Mormon—"unto the children of men." This makes the date of the appearance of the Book of Mormon an epochal date in history. The plates were delivered to the Prophet Joseph on September 22, 1827. In June, 1829, the translation was finished, and in the spring of 1830, the first printed edition was ready for distribution. Nephi, if I understand him correctly, regards this as the beginning of the last days of the Old, and the dawn of a new dispensation.

VERSES 15-18. *The Sermon Out of the Ground.* Nephi, in these paragraphs, as in the following chapter, applies the prophecy of Isaiah 29 to the coming forth of the Book of Mormon, giving us, probably, another illustration of the double application of a prophecy. (See notes on the prophetic language in the previous chapter.) Also a hasty sketch of the history of his descendants in America—their dwindling in unbelief and their sufferings at the hands of gentiles, until they are brought down low into the dust (v. 15); yet, he says, their testimony will not be silenced; for the words of the righteous and the prayers of the faithful, on endurable records, will speak out of the ground. And although the voice will be weak, like a whisper from the grave, yet the Lord will give unto "him"—that is, unto the "righteous" (v. 15)— power to bring about a sudden change in the affairs of the children of men, by his testimony. (v. 16) The "book sealed up," refers clearly to the Book of Mormon.

## 3. Gentiles in the Last Days.

19. And it shall come to pass, that those who have dwindled in unbelief shall be smitten by the hand of the Gentiles.

20. And the Gentiles are lifted up in the pride of their eyes, and have stumbled, because of the greatness of their stumbling block, that they have built up many churches; nevertheless, they put down the power and miracles of God, and preach up unto themselves their own wisdom and their own learning, that they may get gain and grind upon the face of the poor.

21. And there are many churches built up which cause envyings, and strifes, and malice.

22. And there are also secret combinations, even as in times of old, according to the combinations of the devil, for he is the foundation of all these things; yea, the foundation of murder, and works of darkness; yea, and he leadeth them by the neck with a flaxen cord, until he bindeth them with his strong cords forever.

23. For behold, my beloved brethren, I say unto you that the Lord God worketh not in darkness.

---

VERSE 19. *Smitten by the hand of the Gentiles.* The story of the invasion of America by Europeans in the 16th century, is a tragic illustration of the truth of this prophecy. Witness the appearance in Mexico of Cortes with his 450 Spaniards and 1000 Tlascalan allies. From the very first of his contact with the natives, strife and slaughter ensued. Cortes, having occasion to leave Tenoctlican—the ancient name of the city of Mexico—left Pedro de Alvarado in charge. The Aztecs celebrated their May festival with the sacrifice of a handsome youth, as was their custom. This was, we may say, their pentecost. But the sacrifice was too horrible to Alvarado. Under the impression that the Aztecs were cowards, he fell upon the crowds of worshipers and massacred 600 of them, among whom were prominent chiefs. When Cortes returned, he found the people excited. Montezuma, practically a prisoner among the Spaniards, had been deposed, and his brother, Cuitlahuatzin, had been elected ruler in his stead. They now attacked the Spaniards. Spanish cannon swept the streets with terrible effects. Some idea of the losses of the Aztecs can be formed from the fact that the battle and the retreat cost Cortes 750 of his 1250 white soldiers and 4000 of his 6000 Tlascalan allies.

But Cortes came back. On April 28, 1521, he began a siege of the city, which Dr. John Fiske compares to the siege of Jerusalem by Titus, on a smaller scale, of course. On August 18, Cortes was master of the situation. But then the city was a ruin. A new era had been inaugurated, in which the natives lost their culture, their literature, and arts, and were, practically, buried in the "dust."

The first contact of the natives of Peru with the Spaniards under Pizarro and Almargro—both of whom were finally murdered in a feud between themselves—was a duplicate of the so-called conquest of Cortes. We shall not here repeat the almost incredible stories of cruelties perpetrated on the Indians by some of the early invaders. Suffice it to say that this prophecy was literally fulfilled. The Indians were everywhere sorely "smitten by the hands of the Gentiles."

VERSES 20-23. *Churches and Secret Combinations.* Gentiles, Nephi says, are "lifted up in their pride." They are, as it were, not looking where they are

24. He doeth not anything save it be for the benefit of the world; for he loveth the world, even that he layeth down his own life that he may draw all men unto him. Wherefore, he commandeth none that they shall not partake of his salvation.

25. Behold, doth he cry unto any, saying: Depart from me? Behold, I say unto you, Nay; but he saith: Come unto me all ye ends of the earth, buy milk and honey, without money and without price.

26. Behold, hath he commanded any that they should depart out of the synagogues, or out of the houses of worship? Behold, I say unto you, Nay.

27. Hath he commanded any that they should not partake of his salvation? Behold I say unto you, Nay; but he hath given it free for all men; and he hath commanded his people that they should persuade all men to repentance.

28. Behold, hath the Lord commanded any that they should not partake of his goodness? Behold I say unto you, Nay; but all men are privileged the one like unto the other, and none are forbidden.

29. He commandeth that there shall be no priestcrafts; for, behold, priestcrafts are that men preach and set themselves up for a light unto the world, that they may get gain and praise of the world; but they seek not the welfare of Zion.

## 4. *Latter-day Commandments of God.*

30. Behold, the Lord hath forbidden this thing; wherefore, the Lord God hath given a commandment that all men should have charity, which charity is love. And except they should have charity they were nothing. Wherefore, if they should have charity they would not suffer the laborer in Zion to perish.

---

going; they lack humility, and as a consequence, they are stumbling. They are building up "churches," and combinations, in which they are preaching human wisdom for gain, and even committing works of darkness (vv. 21, 22). But, says Nephi, the "Lord God," is not working in the dark (v. 23). The result of the multiplication of churches and secret societies is envy, strife, and malice. (v. 21) Never progress.

VERSES 24-29. *God Loveth the World.* The substance of these paragraphs is this: Our Lord God never does anything but that which will benefit his children (v. 24). He loveth the world. He invites all to come unto him and get "milk and honey" freely. (v. 25; comp. Isa. 55:1, 2.) In other words, salvation is offered freely to all (vv. 27, 28); there shall be no "priestcrafts"—no preaching for money and fame, but only for the welfare of Zion. (v. 29; comp. 2 Ne. 10:5; 3 Ne. 16:10-20)

VERSE 30. *All Men Should have Charity.* See Moroni 7:47, 48. In Moroni 8:26 the word "love" is, probably, the same as "charity" here.

Special attention is called to the brief but important explanatory note: "Charity is Love." That is the exact meaning of the Hebrew "ahabah." The word translated "charity" in I Cor. 13 is "agape," which also means "love" It is so rendered in Luke

31. But the laborer in Zion shall labor for Zion; for if they labor for money they shall perish.

32. And again, the Lord God hath commanded that men should not murder; that they should not lie; that they should not steal; that they should not take the name of the Lord their God in vain; that they should not envy; that they should not have malice; that they should not contend one with another; that they should not commit whoredoms; and that they should do none of these things; for whoso doeth them shall perish.

33. For none of these iniquities come of the Lord; for he doeth that which is good among the children of men; and he doeth nothing save it be plain unto the children of men; and he inviteth them all to come unto him and partake of his goodness; and he denieth none that come unto him, black and white, bond and free, male and female; and he remembereth the heathen; and all are alike unto God, both Jew and Gentile.

---

11:42 and Rom. 5:5, 8. Why the authorized version has "charity" instead of "love" is not clear, unless the translators were anxious to avoid a word which, in their judgment, might be misunderstood by some readers. The version revised by the Anglo-American Bible Commission translates "love," as required by the original. Nephi, probably, uses the Hebrew word "ahabah."

VERSE 31. *If They Labor for Money They shall Perish.* That seems to be a difficult assertion, since our Lord himself (Luke 10:7) teaches that "the laborer is worthy of his hire," and James, the Apostle and (probably) brother of our Lord, in his epistle (5:4, 5) severely rebukes the wealthy property owners for withholding the wages due the laborers, contrary to the Mosaic law (Deut. 24:14 15), which prescribes that servants be paid promptly.

"Thou shalt not oppress an hired servant that is poor and needy, whether he be of thy brethren or of thy strangers that are in the land within thy gates; at his day thou shalt give him his hire, neither shall the sun go down upon it; for he is poor and setteth his heart upon it; lest he cry against thee unto the Lord, and it be sin unto thee."

Our Lord does certainly not condemn the wage system, either in Zion or elsewhere, if it is practised in righteousness, for the benefit of his people. But he puts the mark of disapproval upon the sordid materialism that has no higher aim than the making and hoarding of money for selfish purposes. We can, I believe, safely read: "If they labor for money"—only—"they shall perish."

VERSE 32. *Men Should Not Murder.* In the light of Christian ethics, as expounded by our Lord himself in his Sermon on the Mount (Matt. 5:21, 22; 3 Ne. 12:21, 23), this commandment prohibits not only the slaying of a fellow-being but the anger and hatred in which manslaughter originates. Our Lord says: "Whosoever is angry with his brother without cause shall be in danger of the judgment . . . but whosoever shall say, Thou fool, shall be in danger of hell fire." And John, the Apostle, in his First Epistle (3:15) explains this further: "Whosoever hateth his brother is a murderer: and ye know that no murderer hath eternal life abiding in him."

*They Should Not Lie.* There is, perhaps, no crime more common among men.

In this paragraph, prevarication, as it is sometimes called, politely, is placed where it rightly belongs, between murder and stealing. Good old Wm. Paley, in his Philosophy, justly condemns even so-called "white lies," thus: "They always introduce others of a darker complexion." I have, he says further, "seldom known anyone who deserted truth in trifles, that could be trusted in matters of importance!" The habit of lying, he adds, "is easily extended to serve the designs of malice or interest; like all habits, it spreads indeed of itself."

In other words, there may be harmless "white lies," as there are guns "not loaded;" but neither white lies nor guns are safe toys to play with.

*They Should Not Steal.* All acts of dishonesty in the dealings of a person with God, with society in its entirety or in smaller lawful organizations, or with individuals, are theft. They are prohibited because they are an injury to our neighbor, or neighbors, or (in the case of stealing from God) to ourselves. Opinions may differ as to how far it may be permissible to go in the furtherance of personal interests, but our Lord has given us the well known, perfect, "golden" rule: "All things whatsoever ye would that men should do to you, do ye even so to them: for this is the Law and the Prophets." (Matt. 7:12; Luke 6:31, 3 Ne. 14:12)

The following sentiments in the apocryphal book of Tobit may be interesting as showing the influence of the Mosaic law on the popular consciousness of the Israelites even before the Christian era:

"Let not the wages of any man, which hath wrought for thee, tarry with thee, but give it him out of hand: for if thou serve God, he will also repay thee." "Do that to no man which thou hatest." "Give of thy bread to the hungry, and of thy garments to them that are naked. And according to thine abundance give him; and let not thine eye be envious, when thou givest alms." (Tob. 4:14, 16)

The divine prohibition of theft is an endorsement of private property rights, and, under present conditions, no other arrangement seems desirable. Whatever may happen when the world is more advanced in civilization, moral and spiritual, is another question. Under present conditions, if there were no private property rights, enabling a person to lay by for future use such articles as he does not need immediately, everyone would have to be his own farmer, hunter, carpenter, tailor, shoemaker, etc., etc. Progress in any one line would be out of the question. But when everyone can devote himself to at least one line of pursuit and save, as his property, the results of his endeavors, and exchange them for the results of the labors of his neighbors, then a way is opened up out of barbarious primitivity to desirable civilization, with all its complex problems and responsibilities.

*They Should Not Take the Name of the Lord Their God in Vain.* The Jews anciently interpreted this commandment in the Decalogue so literally that they ceased to pronounce the sacred Name entirely. Where it occurred in the inspired writings, they read "Adonai" (Lord), or "Elohim" (God) instead. But, as they, originally, did not have vowel points to indicate the correct pronunciation, this, in course of time, was entirely forgotten. Vowel points came into use in the early part of the sixteenth century, but at that time no one could tell for certain what points to put under the letters YHVH, which represented the sacred Name. This is still a debated question, but it is quite generally supposed that "YAVETH" best represents the original pronunciation. The meaning of the name is given by the Divine representative who spoke to Moses in the flaming bush, as "I AM"; i. e. "The Existent One" (Ex. 3:14). This conception of God, I understand, was expressed in an inscription in an Isis temple at Sais, Egypt, thus: "I am all that has been, that is, and that will be." (Smith's Bible Dictionary, under "Jah.") When, therefore, Moses came to the Pharaoh of the oppression in the Name of "I AM," that potentate had no excuse for pretending ignorance of the authority of the messenger (Ex. 5:1, 2).

*They Should Not Envy.* "Envy" has been described as a disposition to grieve and fret at the supposed success of others. Asaph, the Hebrew poet, confesses: But as for me, my feet were almost gone; my steps had well nigh slipped. For I was envious at the foolish, when I saw the prosperity of the wicked." (Ps. 73:3, 4) The seriousness of this sin may be realized when we reflect on some of its consequences. It was envy that caused Lucifer to fall. Because of envy Joseph was sold into Egypt. Envy caused almost perpetual strife between Ephraim and Judah. St. Paul (Rom. 1:29) says that when God gives rebellious trangressors over to a "reprobate mind," they become "full of envy, murder, debate, deceit, malignity." Envy prepares the human heart as a dwelling place for evil impulses.

*They Should Not Have Malice.* "Malice" is defined as a disposition to injure another. In law it is a wilfully formed plan to do damage to another. The Apostle Paul (1 Cor. 5:8) compares "malice" and "wickedness" to a leaven, and mentions as their opposites, "sincerity" and "truth." Malice, then, is a hideous sin. As all sin it is contagious. It has an influence for evil on all who come in close contact with the sinner.

*They Should Not Contend One With Another.* In the language of the Scriptures to "contend" signifies to strive to reclaim a person from his evil ways, as in Prov. 29:9; or, to manifest an ardent zeal for the truth, as in Jude 3. It is the duty of a true Christian to "contend" for the faith, in this sense of the word. But it also signifies to "dispute," as in Acts 11:2, where we read that some church members "contended" with Peter, accusing him of having broken the Mosaic ceremonial law. It means even to "fight" in battle, as in Deut. 2:9. In this sense of the word it stands for an evil to be avoided. For "Contention" see Acts 13:39; Phil. 1:16, 1 Cor. 1:11; Tit. 3:9.

*They Should Not Commit Whoredoms.* The marriage is of divine origin. The home is, of necessity, prior to any other organization on earth. As a matter of fact, all other social structures, including church and state, exist, or should exist, for the benefit of the home, and home life.

There is no greater physical comfort to a man, or a woman, or to children who are growing up, than a well regulated home; no stronger stimulant to intellectual endeavors or spiritual achievements than the atmosphere of pure love, in which husband and wife, parents and children, live, in a home dedicated to the lord. Such a home is a true "Bethel," in which God's children communicate with their heavenly home, even in their pure dreams, as Jacob on his way to Pandan-Aram. No matter, if the pillow is but a stone, the presence of heavenly messengers make it the "gate," the entrance to heaven. (Gen. 28:17)

The object of this commandment is to safeguard the home by the preservation of chastity, the foundation of it. Irregular indulgence against the commandment of God is destructive of the home. It depraves and corrupts the mind more readily and thoroughly than any other vice, and prepares the mind of the morally weakened individual for the commission of other crimes, even against the protests of conscience. Let us not forget the solemn warning of our Lord: "For out of the heart proceed evil thoughts, murders, adulteries, fornications, thefts, false witness, blasphemies." (Matt. 15:19) Our Lord places sins of lust among the greatest crimes known to man. He also places under this prohibition all acts that are calculated to inflame the mind, when he says: "Whosoever looketh on a woman to lust after her hath committed adultery with her already in his heart." (Matt. 5:28, 3 Ne. 12:28) This is, by inference, a condemnation of filthy literature, pictures, conversation, indecent dances or gestures. Hear St. Paul on this subject: "Let no corrupt conversation proceed out of your mouth." (Eph. 4:29) Again: "Marriage is honorable in all, and let the bed be undefiled: for fornicators and adulterers God will judge. (Heb. 13:4)

## GENERAL NOTES.

The commandments in this chapter (vv. 30-32) we may call the Decalogue as taught to the Nephites. The student of the Book of Mormon may wish to compare this summary with versions presented in the Exodus and the Deuteronomy. A comparison will bring out the important truth that the fundamental principles of morality are essentially the same in all ages.

### THE DECALOGUE OF THE NEPHITES.

1. All men should have charity (love).
2. Laborers in Zion shall labor for Zion (not for fame or money.)
3. Men should not murder.
4. They should not lie.
5. They should not steal.
6. They should not take the Name of God their Lord in vain.
7. They should not envy.
8. They should not have malice.
9. They should not contend one with another.
10. They should not commit whoredoms.

*Conclusion.* They should do none of these things; for whoso doeth them shall perish.

### THE DECALOGUE OF THE EXODUS.

Commentators have displayed a vast amount of learning and ingenuity in attempting to prove that the narrative in Exodus concerning the giving of the Law is a mixture of but poorly connected fragments of various texts, and that parts of it, therefore, are now almost unintelligible. We need not feel alarmed at this proposition. The information offered in Exodus may have originated in different documents. That is neither improbable nor destructive of the historical value. But that the editing was careless, or that there appears to be impassable breaks in the text is not admitted.

Let us read the account in Exodus:

*The First Interview of Moses with the Lord.* In the Third month, the same day (the third), Israel arrived at Mount Sinai and camped there. Moses proceeded up on the mount, and was commissioned to take the message to the representatives of the people, that if they would obey God and keep his covenant he would make them his people before all others. Moses delivered this message.

*Second Interview.* The people agreed. Moses reported this fact, whereupon the Lord instructed him to "sanctify" them—that is, prepare them for a solemn meeting —and let them draw near to the mountain, but not too near. The assembly convened, all attired in their holiday raiments. The Lord descended. The mountain seemed to be afire. Lightnings struck, thunders rolled. Smoke rose as from a furnace. A trumpet sounded louder and louder, and the entire mountain shook, as if trembling in awe and fear. Moses and Aaron, who had been instructed to come up closer to the divine Presence, did so. Then the Lord spoke the "Words" in Ex. 20:1-17, and the two brothers, after some further instructions, went to the camp.

## Two Texts

| No. 1 | No. 2 |
|---|---|

*God's Spoken Decalogue* — *God's Written Decalogue*

**Introduction:**

I am the Lord thy God, which have brought thee out of the land of Egypt, out of the house of bondage.

1. Thou shalt have no other gods before me.

2. Thou shalt not make unto thee any graven image, or any likeness of anything that is in heaven above, or that is in the earth beneath, or that is in the water under the earth:
Thou shalt not bow down thyself to them, nor serve them: for I the Lord thy God am a jealous God, visiting the iniquity of the fathers upon the children unto the third and fourth generation of them that hate me;
And shewing mercy unto thousands of them that love me, and keep my commandments.

3. Thou shalt not take the name of the Lord thy God in vain; for the Lord will not hold him guiltless that taketh his name in vain.

4. Remember the sabbath day, to keep it holy.
Six days shalt thou labour, and do all thy work:
But the seventh day is the sabbath of the Lord thy God: in it thou shalt not do any work, thou, nor thy son, nor thy daughter, thy manservant, nor thy maidservant, nor thy cattle, nor the stranger that is within thy gates:
For in six days the Lord made heaven and earth, the sea, and all that in them is, and rested the seventh day: wherefore the Lord blessed the sabbath day, and hallowed it.

5. Honor thy father and thy mother: that thy days may be long upon the land which the Lord thy God giveth thee.

---

**Introduction:**

I am the Lord thy God, which brought thee out of the land of Egypt, from the house of bondage.

1. Thou shalt have none other Gods before me.

2. Thou shalt not make thee any graven image, or any likeness of any thing that is in heaven above, or that is in the earth beneath, or that is in the waters beneath the earth:
Thou shalt not bow down thyself unto them, nor serve them: for I the Lord thy God am a jealous God, visiting the iniquity of the fathers upon the children unto the third and fourth generation of them that hate me,
And shewing mercy unto thousands of them that love me and keep my commandments.

3. Thou shalt not take the name of the Lord thy God in vain: for the Lord will not hold him guiltless that taketh his name in vain.

4. Keep the sabbath day to sanctify it, as the Lord thy God hath commanded thee.
Six days shalt thou labour, and do all thy work:
But the seventh day is the sabbath of the Lord thy God: in it thou shalt not do any work, thou, nor thy son, nor thy daughter, nor thy manservant, nor thy maidservant, nor thine ox, nor thine ass, nor any of thy cattle, nor thy stranger that is within thy gates; that thy manservant and thy maidservant may rest as well as thou.
And remember that thou wast a servant in the land of Egypt, and that the Lord thy God brought thee out thence through a mighty hand and by a stretched out arm: therefore the Lord thy God commanded thee to keep the sabbath day.

5. Honor thy father and thy mother, as the Lord thy God hath commanded thee; that thy days may be prolonged, and that it may go well with thee, in the land which the Lord thy God giveth thee.

## Two Texts (Continued)

|  |  |
|---|---|
| No. 1 | God's Written Decalogue |
| God's Spoken Decalogue | No. 2 |

| | |
|---|---|
| 6. Thou shalt not kill. | 6. Thou shalt not kill. |
| 7. Thou shalt not commit adultery. | 7. Neither shalt thou commit adultery. |
| 8. Thou shalt not steal. | 8. Neither shalt thou steal. |
| 9. Thou shalt not bear false witness against thy neighbour. | 9. Neither shalt thou bear false witness against thy neighbour. |
| 10. Thou shalt not covet thy neighbour's house, thou shalt not covet thy neighbour's wife, nor his manservant, nor his maidservant, nor his ox, nor his ass, nor any thing that is thy neighbor's. —Ex. 20:2-17 | 10. Neither shalt thou desire thy neighbour's wife, neither shalt thou covet thy neighbour's house, his field, or his manservant, or his maidservant, his ox, or his ass, or any thing that is thy neighbour's. —Deut. 5:6-21 |

*A Third Interview.* Some time afterwards Moses was commanded to come to the mountain, accompanied by Aaron, Nadab, Abihu and seventy Elders. Moses recorded the Words of the Lord—the Ten commandments given orally during the second interview—built an altar, offered a peace offering and read the record to the people. Then he and the companions selected went to the mountain, where they were favored with a glorious vision of God. (Ex. 24:1-11)

After this manifestation Moses was called to come nearer, but alone. He was then privileged to remain in the divine Presence forty days and forty nights. It was during this time that he received the two tables of stone, a law, and commandments, which, the Lord says, I have written that thou mayest teach them. (v. 12) However, Moses destroyed these tables, when, on his way to the camp, he found that the people had returned to the indecent idolatry of the Egyptians. (Ex. 32:19, 25)

*The Fourth Interview.* After a humble and most patriotic intercession, Moses was directed to make another set of tables, on which, the Lord said, I will write the same Words which were upon the first set. Again the Lord descended and met his servant. Again Moses remained forty days and forty nights in the divine Presence. Again he received the Ten Commandments, this time on the stone tables he had brought with him. And this time, when he descended, his countenance shone, reflecting the glory of the divine Presence. (Ex. 34.)

These tablets were carefully guarded. They were deposited in the ark (Deut. 10:2-6; Heb. 9:4), where no profane hands could touch them.

Shortly before his death, Moses incorporated a copy of these commandments in the book known as the Deuteronomy. (Deut. 5:1-21; see also "God's Written Decalogue" above)

*Two Texts or One?* It is generally believed that the version of the Decalogue, proclaimed in the hearing of Israel during the 2nd interview with Moses is identically the same as that which was handed to him on the stone tables during the third and fourth interviews. Opinions are divided on that point. But it appears that there is a fundamental discrepancy in the two versions in the reasons given for the observance of the Sabbath. In the first text (see above) the motive emphasized for keeping the weekly Sabbath is of general application to mankind, wherever men live. God, we read, after 6 days of creation work, "rested" on the 7th day, wherefore he blessed that day and sanctified it, to be a day of godly rest. (Gen. 2:2, 3) The explanation in the second text is entirely different. It is chiefly of national application. The people are there enjoined to keep the seventh day holy, remembering that they had been in bondage in Egypt, undoubtedly overworked by hard taskmasters, and that they had been delivered by the mighty power of Jehovah, their God. The Decalogue, and more particularly the Sabbath commandment, was to be a reminder of the covenant between God and Israel. The tables of stone were therefore the "tables of testimony." (Ex. 34:29) In this view the version in Ex. 20 is identical with the law given to our first parents in the garden of Eden, when "God blessed the seventh day and sanctified it." (Gen. 2:3) It was the version that was proclaimed orally to Israel on the mountain. The other version, it is supposed, is the one that was engraved on the stone tables by the finger of God. It is of this version that Moses says: "These words God spoke unto all your assembly in the mount out of the midst of the fire . . . and he added no more. And he wrote them on two tables of stone, and delivered to me." ( Deut. 4:13; 5: 22. Comp. Neh. 9:13, 14)

If we understand that there are two decalogues in the Pentateuch, one for the guidance of the human race under the Patriarchal era, and one for the special guidance of Israel under the Mosaic era, we can also understand the attitude of St. Paul to the Mosaic Sabbath law. (See Rom. 14:5, 6; Gal. 4:9, 10) Although the Mosaic law came to an end, the Patriarchal law remained.

*The Nephite Decalogue.* The Ten Commandments as recorded in a condensed form in this chapter, are the substance of the Patriarchal version of the Law. They are arranged differently, and some are epitomized, but they are all there.

"All men should have charity." This is the first and second commandments in one brief sentence. "Charity" means "love," and he who loves God will have no other gods before him; nor will he make and revere images instead of God.

It will be remembered that our Lord on one occasion was asked by a lawyer: "Which is the great commandment in the Law? Jesus answered: "Thou shalt love the Lord, thy God, with all thy heart, and with all thy soul, and with all thy mind. This is the first and great commandment." (Matt. 22:35-38) It is also the first and foremost in the Nephite version of the Law. Comp.: "Thou shalt love the Lord thy God." (Deut. 5:6)

The Sabbath commandment comes next in the synopsis of Nephi. But it is condensed in one brief sentence: "Laborers in Zion shall labor for Zion." That means that laborers, whether engaged in physical and mental activities, or spiritual endeavors, will gladly give one day of every seven days to the Lord. That is, they will keep the Sabbath, if they work for Zion. If they labor for selfish ends, for money and fame, they will not have time to give God his day.

The fourth commandment is not specially mentioned in this brief synopsis of the Law by Nephi. But it is included in the Law of love. Our Lord, in his conversation with the lawyer, says, after having recited a second commandment from Lev. 19:18: "Thou shalt love thy neighbor as thyself," that "On these two commandments hang all the Law and the Prophets. (Matt. 22:39, 40) And St. Paul (Rom. 13:10) says "Love is the fulfilling of the Law." We may well consider that the fourth commandment is included in the first: that love of God also means love and reverence of parents, who are the representatives of God in the family on earth.

## CHAPTER 27

*Characteristics of the Last Days, 1-5—The Book of Mormon, 6-11—Witnesses, 12-23—A Marvelous Work, 24-28—Jacob not to be Ashamed, 29-35.*

### 1. *Characteristics of the Last Days.*

1. But, behold, in the last days, or in the days of the Gentiles—yea, behold all the nations of the Gentiles and also the Jews, both those who shall come upon this land and those who shall be upon other lands, yea, even upon all the lands of the earth, behold, they will be drunken with iniquity and all manner of abominations—

2. And when that day shall come they shall be visited of the Lord of Hosts, with thunder and with earthquake, and with a great noise, and with storm, and with tempest, and with the flame of devouring fire.

3. And all the nations that fight against Zion, and that distress her, shall be as a dream of a night vision; yea, it shall be unto them, even as unto a hungry man which dreameth, and behold he eateth but he awaketh and his soul is empty; or like unto a thirsty man which dreameth, and behold he drinketh but he awaketh and behold he is faint, and his soul hath appetite; yea, even so shall the multitude of all the nations be that fight against Mount Zion.

4. For behold, all ye that doeth iniquity, stay yourselves and wonder, for ye shall cry out, and cry; yea, ye shall be drunken but not with wine, ye shall stagger but not with strong drink.

5. For behold, the Lord hath poured out upon you the spirit of deep sleep. For behold, ye have closed your eyes, and ye have rejected the prophets; and your rulers, and the seers hath he covered because of your iniquity.

VERSE 1. *The Last Days.* See 2 Ne. 26:14.

*Drunken with Iniquity.* That is one of the signs of the last days. Comp. 2 Thess. 2:7-12, where the Apostle reminds the Saints that the "mystery of iniquity" was already then at work, and that when "he that letteth," which at that time was the imperial Roman power, "that Wicked" would be revealed, "whom the Lord shall consume with the spirit of his mouth, and shall destroy with the brightness of his coming." St. Paul adds that God would send the followers of the wicked one, strong delusion, "that they should believe a lie," and thus perish.

VERSE 2. *They Shall be Visited of the Lord of Hosts.* Another sign is here given. There will be disturbances in nature, in the form of thunder, earthquakes, "noise," tempests, fire.

VERSE 3. *Nations That Fight Against Zion.* This seems to indicate that one of the signs of the end is war on Zion and persecution of her people, not only by hostile armies invading the countries known as Zion, but also by the stirring up of strife and rebellion against the heaven-inspired principles of government given for the protection of human liberty. All nations, we are told here, that fight against

## 2. *The Book of Mormon.*

6. And it shall come to pass that the Lord God shall bring forth unto you the words of a book, and they shall be the words of them which have slumbered.

7. And behold the book shall be sealed; and in the book shall be a revelation from God, from the beginning of the world to the ending thereof.

8. Wherefore, because of the things which are sealed up, the things which are sealed shall not be delivered in the day of the wickedness and abominations of the people. Wherefore the book shall be kept from them.

9. But the book shall be delivered unto a man, and he shall deliver the words of the book, which are the words of those who have slumbered in the dust, and he shall deliver these words unto another;

10. But the words which are sealed he shall not deliver, neither shall he deliver the book. For the book shall be sealed by the power of God, and the revelation which was sealed shall be kept in the book until the own due time of the Lord, that they may come forth; for behold, they reveal all things from the foundation of the world unto the end thereof.

11. And the day cometh that the words of the book which were sealed shall be read upon the house tops; and they shall be read by the power of Christ; and all things shall be revealed unto the children of men which ever have been among the children of men, and which ever will be even unto the end of the earth.

---

Zion, whether by open warfare or "undeclared war," will be as sleepers who feast in their dreams. They will awake as hungry and thirsty as ever. See 2 Ne. 26:15, 16 and notes.

VERSE 6. *The Words of a Book.* Nephi, in these paragraphs, describes the Book of Mormon and its coming forth in the latter days in the language of the Prophet Isaiah 29:9-12. It is the words of those that slumbered (v. 6). It is sealed. (v. 7 Comp. 2 Ne. 18:16) It is a revelation from God on the history of the world, from the beginning to the end thereof (v. 7). But the sealed part is not to be published in the "day of wickedness."

VERSES 9 and 10. In these paragraphs Nephi describes his vision of the interview of Martin Harris with learned men concerning the Book of Mormon. The Prophet Joseph was living on his little farm near Harmony, Pa. Here he studied the characters on the plates, and between December 1827 and February 1828 he had copied and translated some of them by the aid of the urim and thummim. Martin Harris visited the Prophet at this time and obtained a transcript of the glyphs with the translation. These he submitted first to Professor Anthon, New York, and then to Professor Samuel Mitchell. When he returned, he was more than ever convinced of the inspiration of Joseph Smith and his divine calling. (See Essentials in Church History, Joseph Fielding Smith, pp 62-64; also Introduction to the Study of the Book of Mormon, pp. 10-14.)

VERSE 11. *The Sealed Part of the Book.* Nephi has told us (v. 10) that the sealed part of the Book will come forth in the due time of the Lord, and that then

### 3. Witnesses.

12. Wherefore, at that day when the book shall be delivered unto the man of whom I have spoken, the book shall be hid from the eyes of the world, that the eyes of none shall behold it save it be that three witnesses shall behold it, by the power of God, besides him to whom the book shall be delivered; and they shall testify to the truth of the book and the things therein.

13. And there is none other which shall view it, save it be a few according to the will of God, to bear testimony of his word unto the children of men; for the Lord God hath said that the words of the faithful should speak as if it were from the dead.

the entire story of the world will be revealed. Here he adds some notable particulars. (1) The words of the book "which were sealed shall be read upon the housetops." An evident allusion to the radio, by means of which, in our day, the last days, the Gospel in word and song is proclaimed all around the world. (2) "They shall be read by the power of Christ. Compare the D. and C. 88:5-13, where we are told that the light of Christ is the light of the sun, and the power thereof, by which it was made; that this light also is in the moon and the stars, and the earth: "which light proceedeth forth from the immensity of space. The light which is in all things, which giveth life to all things: which is the law by which all things are governed; even the power of God who sitteth upon his throne, who is in the bosom of eternity, who is in the midst of all things."

It is a question whether this ubiquitous force, this omnipresent power of Christ, this cosmic light, manifested in the flashing lightnings and rolling thunders of Sinai, in the remarkable phenomenon that was a cloud at day and a flame at night, and which rested on the mercy seat in the Tabernacle and, later, in the Temple, was not the same mysterious forces which we now know as electricity, or atomic.

VERSE 12. *Three Witnesses.* The best commentary on this section is early Church history. In June, 1929, the translation of the Book of Mormon had been finished. Martin Harris had been promised, on condition of obedient faith, the privilege of being one of the three witnesses mentioned in this paragraph, as in 2 Ne. 11:3 and Ether 5:1-4 (D. and C. see 5). Oliver Cowdery and David Whitmer, naturally, hoped to be the other two.

The translation finished, Joseph invited his parents to come to him for a visit. They gladly came. Martin Harris accompanied them. The evening of the day on which they arrived at the home of the Whitmers, was spent in reading portions of the translation. Shortly before the manifestation the Prophet and his three friends, in answer to fervent prayers, received the revelation in the D. and C. sec. 17, in which the Lord instructed them to have faith, and, after they had seen the plates, to testify thereof to the world, "that my servant Joseph Smith, Jr., may not be destroyed, that I may bring about my righteous purposes unto the children of men in this work." When the day came, Joseph Smith, Oliver Cowdery, David Whitmer and Martin Harris went out into the woods to engage in prayer. While they were so engaged, a heavenly messenger appeared, to Joseph Smith, Oliver Cowdery and David Whitmer and showed them the plates, and gave them this assurance: "These plates have been revealed by the power of God, and they have been translated by the power of God. The translation of them which you have seen is correct, and I command you to bear record of what you now see here."

Martin Harris, who had left his companions for private prayer, now was joined

14. Wherefore, the Lord God will proceed to bring forth the words of the book; and in the mouth of as many witnesses as seemeth him good will he establish his word; and wo be unto him that rejecteth the word of God!

15. But behold, it shall come to pass that the Lord God shall say unto him to whom he shall deliver the book: Take these words which are not sealed and deliver them to another that he may show them unto the learned, saying: Read this, I pray thee. And the learned shall say: Bring hither the book, and I will read them.

16. And now, because of the glory of the world and to get gain will they say this, and not for the glory of God.

17. And the man shall say: I cannot bring the book, for it is sealed.

18. Then shall the learned say: I cannot read it.

19. Wherefore it shall come to pass, that the Lord God will deliver again the book and the words thereof to him that is not learned; and the man that is not learned shall say: I am not learned.

20. Then shall the Lord God say unto him: The learned shall not read them, for they have rejected them, and I am able to do mine own work; wherefore thou shalt read the words which I shall give unto thee.

21. Touch not the things which are sealed, for I will bring them forth in mine own due time; for I will show unto the children of men that I am able to do mine own work.

---

by the Prophet, and while the two were praying, the heavenly messenger again appeared with the volume and turned the leaves, whereupon Martin Harris arose and full of joy exclaimed: " 'Tis enough! 'Tis enough! Hosannah!"

On some other occasion, before the plates had been finally delivered to the heavenly messenger, the Prophet Joseph had shown them to Christian, Jacob, Peter, Jr. and John Whitmer, Hiram Page, Joseph Smith, Sr., Hyrum and Samuel Smith, and they had handled as many plates as he had translated, and examined the engravings. They so testify.

There are those who tell us that all this is deceit. What is their supposition? They pretend to believe—and they expect the rest of us to believe—that the Prophet Joseph, knowing that he had fabricated a story of three witnesses, succeeded in persuading his friends, in their full senses, that they were, actually and really, those three fictitious characters, and that they retained that conviction until death silenced their lips. Can any sane person believe that? Can anyone believe that it would have been possible for Cervantes to persuade one of his associates that he was actually Don Quixote, and another that he was Sancho Panza? If not, why should we suppose that the Prophet Joseph might have convinced Oliver Cowdery, David Whitmer, and Martin Harris that they were three persons existing nowhere except in the imagination of the prophet? (For a detailed account of the witnesses, see Essent. of Church Hist., Joseph Fielding Smith, pp. 72-81.)

VERSE 21. *Touch not the Things which are Sealed* may indicate that the volume was divided into two parts, of which the Prophet, during the translation, needed to handle only the smaller.

22. Wherefore, when thou hast read the words which I have commanded thee, and obtained the witnesses which I have promised unto thee, then shalt thou seal up the book again, and hide it up unto me, that I may preserve the words which thou hast not read, until I shall see fit in mine own wisdom to reveal all things unto the children of men.

23. For behold, I am God; and I am a God of miracles; and I will show unto the world that I am the same yesterday, today, and forever; and I work not among the children of men save it be according to their faith.

## 4. A Marvelous Work.

24. And again it shall come to pass that the Lord shall say unto him that shall read the words that shall be delivered him:

25. Forasmuch as this people draw near unto me with their mouth, and with their lips do honor me, but have removed their hearts far from me, and their fear towards me is taught by the precepts of men—

26. Therefore, I will proceed to do a marvelous work among this people, yea, a marvelous work and a wonder, for the wisdom of their wise and learned shall perish, and the understanding of their prudent shall be hid.

27. And wo unto them that seek deep to hide their counsel from the Lord! And their works are in the dark; and they say: Who seeth us, and who knoweth us? And they also say: Surely, your turning of things upside down shall be esteemed as the potter's clay. But behold, I will show unto them, saith the Lord of Hosts, that I know all their

---

VERSE 24. *Him That Shall Read the Words.* Refers to the Prophet Joseph Smith. Comp. vv. 12 and 15.

VERSE 25. *Their Fear Towards Me.* Their worship, which is but a repetition of precepts of mere human origin.

VERSE 26. *A Marvelous Work and Wonder.* Isaiah says that the Lord, because of the emptiness of the worship, would perform a "marvelous work and wonder," by means of which the wisdom of their wise and the understanding of their prudent would perish and be hid; and Nephi applies this language to the coming forth of the Book of Mormon, as the beginning of a marvelous work and wonder, the effects of which would be the humiliation of the wisdom and learning of the world.

VERSE 27. *Wo unto Them That Seek Deep to Hide Their Counsel from the Lord.* Some of the Jews, at the time covered by the prophecy of Isaiah, were planning an alliance with Egypt, hoping to hide their conspiracy from the prophet, and even from the Lord. "Who seeth us? Who knoweth us?" they asked. The Prophet answered that God does see and know their secret work, although done in the dark. Nephi applies this prophecy on the conditions prevalent during the last days, when men would have similar ideas about the indifference of the Almighty to human affairs. Nephi says he is not indifferent. He knows "all their works."

works. For shall the work say of him that made it, he made me not? Or shall the thing framed say of him that framed it, he had no understanding?

28. But behold, saith the Lord of Hosts: I will show unto the children of men that it is yet a very little while and Lebanon shall be turned into a fruitful field; and the fruitful field shall be esteemed as a forest.

## 5. Jacob Not to be Ashamed.

29. And in that day shall the deaf hear the words of the book, and the eyes of the blind shall see out of obscurity and out of darkness.

30. And the meek also shall increase, and their joy shall be in the Lord, and the poor among men shall rejoice in the Holy One of Israel.

31. For assuredly as the Lord liveth they shall see that the terrible one is brought to naught, and the scorner is consumed, and all that watch for iniquity are cut off;

32. And they that make a man an offender for a word, and lay a snare for him that reproveth in the gate, and turn aside the just for a thing of naught.

33. Therefore, thus saith the Lord, who redeemed Abraham,

---

VERSE 28. *Lebanon Shall Be Turned into a Fruitful Field.* As a proof of the Divine power and interest in human affairs, Lebanon shall be turned into a fruitful field; and the fruitful field shall be esteemed as a forest. That is to say, the fertility and productiveness of the country will be so great, with the blessings of God, that there will seem to be no difference between a natural forest and an artificial park. All will have the appearance of a well cultivated garden.

This has been corroborated in our own day. In less than 25 years, the actual development of Palestine, agriculturally, commercially and intellectually, is the marvel of history. The Jews in Palestine, as the Latter-day Saints in America, have, literally, turned a desert into a garden. They have brought money, knowledge, idealism, and the type of people settled there is the best human material available for the building up of a country. Of the 400,000 Jews in Palestine about 10,000 are said to be immigrants from America. They have contributed much, particularly through investments, toward development of the orange groves, shipping and commercial companies and industries.

VERSE 29. *The Deaf Shall Hear the Words of the Book.* The blind shall see out of darkness. Those who pretended not to hear and not to see the inspiration of the Book of Mormon, will awake to the effects of it on the world. They will realize that outside the revelation of God there is spiritual darkness.

VERSE 30. *The Meek Shall Increase.* The humble, the lowly among men, shall feel strong under the conditions established by the Holy One of Israel.

VERSES 31-32. *The Terrible One is Brought to Naught.* The tyrant who has accused and persecuted men "for a word." An allusion to unjust and harassing lawsuits, if "word" (Heb. "debar") is understood to mean a legal statute.

VERSE 33. *The Lord Who Redeemed Abraham.* Commentators note that there is no reference in the Old Testament to any incident in the life of the Patriarch

concerning the house of Jacob: Jacob shall not now be ashamed, neither shall his face now wax pale.

34. But when he seeth his children, the work of my hands, in the midst of him, they shall sanctify my name, and sanctify the Holy One of Jacob, and shall fear the God of Israel.

35. They also that erred in spirit shall come to understanding, and they that murmured shall learn doctrine.

to which this redemption can refer specially, but that there is a tradition that he, at some time, was threatened with the fire of a burning furnace. In the Book of Abraham, Pearl of Great Price, I think, we find the story of the redemption of Abraham to which Isaiah (29:22) and Nephi here refer.

Abraham was a native of Ur of the Chaldees. (Gen. 11:28)

According to the Book of Abraham, the Egyptians had an altar and a religious establishment there, just as, for instance, Americans in our day have churches and congregations in some of the principal cities of the world, such as London, Paris, etc. The paternal relatives of Abraham, it seems, had turned away from the religion of their ancestors and were worshiping pagan idols, and especially the divinities of Egypt. They even delighted in the sacrifice of children.

Then a time came, when the priests of Pharaoh seized Abraham, intending to take his life on the altar. But when he lifted up his voice to God, the "Angel of his (God's) Presence" appeared, unloosened the bands of the intended victim, promised him the Priesthood, and declared that: "Through thy ministry my name shall be known in the earth forever, for I am thy God." Then, "the Lord broke down the altar of Elkenah and of the gods of the land, and utterly destroyed them, and smote the priest that he died." The country must have been visited by some unusual calamity, for the record says: "There was great mourning in Chaldea, and also at the court of Pharaoh." (Book of Abraham 1:5-20)

It was thus that God redeemed Abraham by almighty power and taught him one of the lessons that enabled him to become the "father of all that believe." (Rom. 4:11)

### GENERAL NOTES

In recent years the site of Ur has been explored by the eminent British archaeologist Dr. C. Leonard Woolley. He reports that he found unmistakable evidence of trade connections between Ur and Egypt as early as about the first dynasty. He also claims to have discovered common features in the religions of the two countries—the valley of the Nile and the valley of the Tigris and the Euphrates. (The Sumerians, by C. Leonard Woolley, Oxford, 1928, pp. 46 and 186-190.)

The story of Abraham is, or might be, the common ground on which Christians, Jews and Mohammedans might meet for a final great reunion. To all these he is "the father of the faithful," and, "the friend of God."

*Read from the House Tops.* On Sunday, March 31, 1935, President Heber J. Grant, at 12:30 a.m. read a message from the Latter-day Saints to the people of the entire world which may well be regarded as the beginning of the literal fulfilment of this prophecy in 2 Ne. 27:11, in as much as it was broadcast by radio and consisted of a masterly resume of the essence of "Mormonism." President Grant said, in part:

"What the world needs today more than anything else is an implicit faith in God, our Father, and in Jesus Christ, his Son, as the Redeemer of the world. The message of The Church of Jesus Christ of Latter-day Saints to the world is that

God lives, that Jesus Christ is his Son, and that they appeared to the boy Joseph Smith, and promised him that he should be an instrument in the hands of the Lord in restoring the true Gospel to the world. I quote from a Vision given to Joseph Smith and Sidney Rigdon:

"And this is the Gospel, the glad tidings, which the voice of the heavens bore record unto us—

"That he came into the world, even Jesus, to be crucified for the world, and to bear the sins of the world, and to sanctify the world, and to cleanse it from all unrighteousness;

"That through him all might be saved whom the Father had put into his power and made by him.

"Who glorifies the Father, and saves all the works of his hands, except those sons of perdition who deny the Son after the Father has revealed him.

"And again from the same Vision:

"And we beheld the glory of the Son, on the right hand of the Father, and received of his fulness;

"And saw the holy angels, and them who are sanctified before his throne worshiping God, and the Lamb, who worship him forever and ever.

"And now, after the many testimonies which have been given of him, this is the testimony, last of all, which we give of him: That he lives!

"For we saw him, even on the right hand of God; and we heard the voice bearing record that he is the Only Begotten of the Father—

"That by him, and through him, and of him, the worlds are and were created, and the inhabitants thereof are begotten sons and daughters unto God.

"It has been my great privilege to bear this testimony in England, Ireland, Scotland, Wales, Germany, France, Holland, Belgium, Switzerland, Italy, Norway, Sweden, Denmark, Canada, Mexico, in the Hawaiian Islands and in far-off Japan, and to lift up my voice declaring that our Heavenly Father and his beloved Son have again spoken from the heavens, that the Gospel of our Redeemer has been restored to the earth, and to bear witness that I know that God lives, that I know that Jesus is the Christ, the Son of the living God and the Redeemer of mankind, and that I know that Joseph Smith was the instrument in the hands of the Lord in restoring the everlasting Gospel.

"My appeal to all members of the Church who possess this same testimony is so to live that other men seeing their good deeds shall be inspired to investigate the Gospel of our Redeemer.

"Words fail me in expressing my heartfelt gratitude to God for the radio, which gives me this opportunity of bearing my testimony to all the people of the world of the restoration of the Gospel of Jesus Christ. I pray the Lord to bless all mankind in these troublous times, that wisdom may be given to men in every land so to live that peace may come to the peoples of the world." President Heber J. Grant, Annual Conference Report, April, 1935, pp. 9, 10.

## CHAPTER 28

*Concerning the Churches, 1-18—The Kingdom of the Devil to be Shaken,
19-23—The Precepts of Men and the Power of God, 24-32.*

### 1. *Concerning the Churches.*

1. And now, behold, my brethren, I have spoken unto you, according as the Spirit hath constrained me; wherefore, I know that they must surely come to pass.

2. The things which shall be written out of the book shall be of great worth unto the children of men, and especially unto our seed, which is a remnant of the house of Israel.

3. For it shall come to pass in that day that the churches which are built up, and not unto the Lord, when the one shall say unto the other: Behold, I, I am the Lord's; and the others shall say: I, I am the Lord's; and thus shall every one say that hath built up

---

VERSES 1-18. In this section Nephi relates what had been revealed to him concerning the churches in the latter days.

In 1 Ne. 13:6 and 14:10-17 we read that there are but two churches, one being founded by the devil and the other by the Son of God. The Prophet Nephi explains the meaning of this (2 Ne. 10:16) in the following words: "Wherefore, he that fighteth against Zion, both Jew and Gentile, both bond and free, both male and female, shall perish; for they are they who are the whore of all the earth." (1 Ne. 14:10; 22:22, 23.) In this sense there are but two churches. Those who are not for our Lord are against him. (Matt. 12:30; Mark 9:10) And membership in this "church" of the devil is by no means limited to one organization, or one denomination.

But the word "church" is also used in a more limited sense. It stands for an organized body of worshipers.

*No Invisible Church.* In the opinion of some scholars the church of Christ is an entirely invisible body, consisting of all true believers in our Lord, no matter what denomination they belong to, or do not belong to; no matter what their forms of worship may be. This church, they say, has no need of forms, ceremonies, chapels, creeds or ministry. Only Christ knows who the members are. And this church they explain, is the only one in which salvation can be obtained.

But this invisible, to men unknown, multitude is not a "church."

The word in the Old Testament, as Nephi knew it, is "kahal" which means an assembly, a gathering, called or invited to meet for certain purposes. (Psalm 22:22) In the Septuagint the Hebrew word "kahal" was rendered "ekklesia," which word, according to Liddel and Scott, means, "an assembly of the citizens summoned by the crier, the legislative assembly." At Athens the regular assembly with the "kyriai ekklesia," meaning the ruling body. From the Septuagint the word found its way to Greek-speaking Christians and was by them applied to Christian assemblies, and especially to the Church of Christ. Nephi, probably, did not know the Greek word "ekklesia," but he knew the Hebrew "kahal," which means the same; and the Prophet Joseph, properly, translates it "church."

VERSE 3. *I Am the Lord's.* Nephi hears the various churches boasting of being the Lord's church. Some people may sincerely believe that if they make an or-

churches, and not unto the Lord—

4. And they shall contend one with another; and their priests shall contend one with another, and they shall teach with their learning, and deny the Holy Ghost, which giveth utterance.

5. And they deny the power of God, the Holy One of Israel; and they say unto the people: Hearken unto us, and hear ye our precept; for behold there is no God today, for the Lord and the Redeemer hath done his work, and he hath given his power unto men;

6. Behold, hearken ye unto my precept; if they shall say there is a miracle wrought by the hand of the Lord, believe it not; for this day he is not a God of miracles; he hath done his work.

7. Yea, and there shall be many which shall say: Eat, drink, and be merry, for tomorrow we die; and it shall be well with us.

8. And there shall also be many which shall say: Eat, drink, and be merry; nevertheless, fear God—he will justify in committing a little sin; yea, lie a little, take the advantage of one because of his words, dig a pit for thy neighbor; there is no harm in this; and do all these things, for tomorrow we die; and if it so be that we are guilty, God will beat us with a few stripes, and at last we shall be saved in the kingdom of God.

9. Yea, and there shall be many which shall teach after this manner, false and vain and foolish doctrines, and shall be puffed up in their hearts and shall seek deep to hide their counsels from the Lord; and their works shall be in the dark.

10. And the blood of the saints shall cry from the ground against them.

11. Yea, they have all gone out of the way; they have become corrupted.

12. Because of pride, and be-

---

ganization of believers with a creed in imitation of Biblical doctrines and a corps of officers with Biblical names, or titles, they have a church of Christ. But that is a mistake. A church of Christ must be founded by Divine authority. A number of American citizens could not go abroad and organize an embassy, that would be recognized as such, without authority from the government in Washington, no matter how honest and able they might be. Nor can any man, or any number of men, without authority from the Lord, build a church which he will recognize as his. What the psalmist says of the material creation is applicable to the spiritual existences also: "The earth is the Lord's and the fulness thereof; the world and they that dwell therein. For he hath founded it," (Ps. 24:1-2). The Church, we may say, is his, only if he is the founder of it. No painter, no matter how much of an artist he is, can make a genuine Rembrandt.

VERSES 5-6. *Behold There is no God Today.* The meaning is, as stated in verse 6: Do not believe in miracles, for now there are no miracles; God has done his work. This is exactly what rationalists during the "age of enlightenment" in the 19th century maintained. They made human, scientific knowledge the highest standard of truth. Unable to explain the miraculous scientifically, they treated it as myth, or denied it. Rationalism became the nurse of infidelity.

# THE SECOND BOOK OF NEPHI

---

cause of false teachers, and false doctrine, their churches have become corrupted, and their churches are lifted up; because of pride they are puffed up.

13. They rob the poor because of their fine sanctuaries; they rob the poor because of their fine clothing; and they persecute the meek and the poor in heart, because in their pride they are puffed up.

14. They wear stiff necks and high heads; yea, and because of pride, and wickedness, and abominations, and whoredoms, they have all gone astray save it be a few, who are the humble followers of Christ; nevertheless, they are led, that in many instances they do err because they are taught by the precepts of men.

15. O the wise, and the learned, and the rich, that are puffed up in the pride of their hearts, and all those who preach false doctrines, and all those who commit whoredoms, and pervert the right way of the Lord, wo, wo, wo be unto them, saith the Lord God Almighty, for they shall be thrust down to hell!

16. Wo unto them that turn aside the just for a thing of naught and revile against that which is good, and say that is of no worth! For the day shall come that the Lord God will speedily visit the inhabitants of the earth; and in that day that they are fully ripe in iniquity they shall perish.

17. But behold, if the inhabitants of the earth shall repent of their wickedness and abominations they shall not be destroyed, saith the Lord of Hosts.

18. But behold, that great and abominable church, the whore of all the earth, must tumble to the earth, and great must be the fall thereof.

## 2. The Kingdom of the Devil.

19. For the kingdom of the devil must shake, and they which belong to it must needs be stirred up unto repentance, or the devil will grasp them with his everlasting chains, and they be stirred up to anger, and perish;

20. For behold, at that day shall he rage in the hearts of the children of men, and stir them up to anger against that which is good.

21. And others will he pacify, and lull them away into carnal

VERSE 18. *The Abominable Church.* This organization is described in verses 8-18. She teaches false doctrines and is full of pride (v. 9); she persecutes and robs the poor in order to have fine sanctuaries (vv. 10-13); she is corrupt and unjust (vv. 15-16), but she will end in perdition. (vv. 15 and 18)

VERSE 19. *The Kingdom of the Devil.* The sacred Scriptures do not favor the view that there is no personal devil, no kingdom of the devil.

In this section he is said to be stirring men up to hostility against that which is good, and that, if they do not repent, they will perish, because of his "rage" in their hearts (v. 20). He will drive them to destruction, as prisoners in security, that they will say: All is well in Zion; yea, Zion prospereth, all is well—and thus the devil cheateth their souls, and leadeth them away carefully down to hell.

22. And behold, others he flattereth away, and telleth them there is no hell; and he saith unto them: I am no devil, for there is none—and thus he whispereth in their ears, until he grasps them with his awful chains, from whence there is no deliverance.

23. Yea, they are grasped with death, and hell; and death, and hell, and the devil, and all that have been seized therewith must stand before the throne of God, and be judged according to their works, from whence they must go into the place prepared for them, even a lake of fire and brimstone, which is endless torment.

---

chains.   Some he will lead to hell with infatuating siren songs about all being well, although death lurks on either side (v. 21), be it Scylla or Charybdis.   Others he convinces that there is no devil and no hell, while he leads them to the place from which "there is no deliverance." (vv. 22-23).

Our Lord, during his earthly mission, recognized the existence of the devil. He referred to him as "the prince of this world" (John 12:31; 14:30; 16:11). Which means, not only that he exists, but that he has great power in the world. It means, in fact, that his power is so great that St. Paul could consistently call him the "god of this world" (2 Cor. 4:4). That this is not exclusively a figure of speech appears from the fact that he is also described as the "prince of the power of the air" (Eph. 2:22), which seems to mean that, if permitted by the Ruler of the universe, he has intelligence and power enough to use the forces of nature to the injury and undoing of men.   The story of Job confirms this thought.   In that magnificent drama, he causes not only the Sabaens to slay the servants of the patriarch (Job 1:15), but also the lightning to fall from heaven and destroy his flocks together with the shepherds (v. 16). He caused Chaldeans to kill the camels and their keepers, and he directed a cyclone to crush the house in which the children of Job were feasting, burying them in the ruins (vv. 17-19). And, finally, satan, after divine permission, attacked Job himself, with "boils" that covered his entire body (2:1-8).

In his encounter with our Lord immediately after the baptism of the Christ, satan claimed dominion over the entire world and offered it to the Son of God as reward for joining his worshipers—a proposition which our Savior had rejected long before, when the great apostasy in heaven took place.   (Pearl of G. P., Mos. 4:1-2; Ab. 3:27) But when he said to Jesus: "To thee will I give all this authority and the glory of them; for it hath been delivered unto me, and to whomsoever I will give it" (Luke 4:6), he did not speak the truth; for no part of the world belongs legally to him; much less the entire world.   And yet, our Lord recognized his great power when he said: "If satan is divided against himself, how shall his kingdom stand?" (Luke 11:18.) Judging from certain Scripture passages, it appears that satan has always endeavored to obtain control of goverments by means of religious and political, as well as social organizations and personal influences.   And so we read of his "throne" (Rev. 2:13); his "synagogue" (Rev. 3:9); and "world-rulers of darkness." (Eph. 6:12) In Daniel 10:13, 20 it appears that rulers of kingdoms sometimes are on the side of satan and that Michael, the archangel, is still actively engaged against him.

Satan has great power.   But he can never obtain possession of anyone that does not surrender voluntarily.   "Resist the devil, and he will flee from you."

## 3. *The Precepts of Men.*

24. Therefore, wo be unto him that is at ease in Zion!

25. Wo be unto him that crieth: All is well!

26. Yea, wo be unto him that hearkeneth unto the precepts of men, and denieth the power of God, and the gift of the Holy Ghost!

27. Yea wo be unto him that saith: We have received, and we need no more!

28. And in fine, wo unto all those who tremble, and are angry because of the truth of God! For behold, he that is built upon the rock receiveth it with gladness; and he that is built upon a sandy foundation trembleth lest he shall fall.

---

(James 4:7) Comp. the remarkable story in the Pearl of G. P., Moses 1:18-22, where we read that satan fled from Moses, weeping and wailing, because he could not persuade the great prophet to join him and his rebellion.

VERSES 24-32. In this section Nephi reviews the religious condition of the world during the latter days, and pronounces an eight-fold wo unto those who are responsible for the evils existing.

VERSE 24. (1) *Wo Unto Him That is at Ease in Zion.* The people of God are expected to be active, laboring for their own salvation and that of others. The world is, as it were, afire. Millions are in jeopardy. There is no time for idleness; nor for folly.

VERSE 25. (2) *"All is Well."* Wo unto him who excuses his indifference with the assumption that all is well, when it is not.

VERSE 26. (3) *The Precepts of Men.* Empty forms without spirituality. (Is. 29:13) Wo unto him who hearkeneth to such precepts, for he, naturally, is in danger of becoming an infidel, denying the power of God, and the gift of the Holy Ghost. False doctrines are likely to take the form of futile ceremonies: vain worship may prepare the way for soul-destroying doctrines.

VERSE 27. (4) *We Need No More.* Progress is necessary to the welfare of man. Wo to him who saith: We need no more. When a person needs no more prayer, no more instruction, no more work for the Lord, no more fellowship, his condition is one of stagnation, which will, unless cured in time, end in spiritual death.

> Do strive, and you'll survive,
> Have done, and you are gone.

VERSE 28. (5) *Angry Because of the Truth.* Wo to all such. For their anger is a proof that they have built their spiritual house upon loose sand. They are trembling for fear of falling. If they had built upon the Rock, they would have faith and stand firm. They would rejoice in the truth. They would recognize it when they heard it, as the sheep recognizes the voice of the shepherd. "My sheep hear my voice, and I know them, and they follow me. And I give unto them eternal life." (John 10:27, 28)

29. Wo be unto him that shall say: We have received the word of God, and we need no more of the word of God, for we have enough!

30. For behold, thus saith the Lord God: I will give unto the children of men line upon line, precept upon precept, here a little and there a little; and blessed are those who hearken unto my precepts, and lend an ear unto my counsel, for they shall learn wisdom; for unto him that receiveth I will give more; and from them that shall say, We have enough, from them shall be taken away even that which they have.

31. Cursed is he that putteth his trust in man or maketh flesh his arm, or shall hearken unto the precepts of men, save their precepts shall be given by the power of the Holy Ghost.

32. Wo be unto the Gentiles, saith the Lord of Hosts! For notwithstanding I shall lengthen out mine arm unto them from day to day, they will deny me; nevertheless, I will be merciful unto them, saith the Lord God, if they will repent and come unto me; for mine arm is lengthened out all the day long, saith the Lord God of Hosts.

VERSES 29-30. (6) *Line Upon Line.* The parallel passage in Isaiah: "For precept must be upon precept, precept upon precept, line upon line; here a little, there a little." A popular commentator suggests that these words may not be intended to convey any sense, but the fact that they are part of the text in the possession of Nephi ought to be proof of their genuineness, and, therefore, of their authenticity. The thoughtful reader might also observe that the text in Nephi is notably condensed, supporting the claim of the Book of Mormon on the title page, to be an abridgment of more lengthy records.

Isaiah, in the chapter under consideration (28) saw the fall of the kingdom of Ephraim and its sudden destruction, as a fig ripe before the season (1-6). He saw the people in captivity among foreigners, where they would be taught as small children, a little at a time, and that in a foreign tongue, with "stammering lips," as it were. But, the Prophet says, Judah would have to pass through a similar experience, because of the drunkenness of her spiritual leaders (7-9) and the folly of her political rulers (14-15).

But Nephi applies these words in a different sense. He understands them to convey the great truth that the revelations of God are progressive, given "line upon line" as men are capable of understanding them, and willing to carry them out in practice.

The revelations of God begin, we may say, with "paradise lost," and show the road to "paradise regained."

"The truths and purposes of God are in themselves incapable of progress; but not the revelation of those truths. In nature, the rising sun scatters the mists of the morning, and brings out into light first one prominence, and then another, till every hill and valley is clothed in splendour. The landscape was there before, but it was not seen. So in revelation, the progress is not in the truth, but in the clearness and impressiveness with which Scripture reveals it."—Dr. Joseph Angus.

VERSE 31. (7) *Cursed is he, etc.* A strong condemnation of those who rely on weak man and human wisdom, instead of God, for salvation.

VERSE 32. (8) *Infidelity Condemned*. The greatest calamity that can befall the nations is denial of God. Infidelity is rebellion against "the Lord God of Hosts." And yet, The lord opens his arms all day to those who return to him, repentant.

> The Lord is merciful and gracious,
> Slow to anger and plenteous in mercy.
> He will not always chide:
> Neither will he keep his anger for ever.
> He hath not dealt with us after our sins,
> Nor rewarded us according to our iniquities.
> For as the heaven is high above the earth,
> So great is his mercy toward them that fear him.
> As far as the east is from the west,
> So far hath he removed our transgressions from us.
> Like as a father pitieth his children,
> So the Lord pitieth them that fear him.
> For he knoweth our frame;
> He remembereth that we are dust.
> —Psalm 103:14.

CHAPTER 29

*The Book of Mormon and the Bible, 1-7—Two Witnesses, 8-10—Several Records, 11-14.*

## 1. *The Book of Mormon and the Bible.*

1. But behold, there shall be many—at that day when I shall proceed to do a marvelous work among them, that I may remember my covenants which I have made unto the children of men, that I may set my hand again the second time to recover my people, which are of the house of Israel;

2. And also, that I may remember the promises which I have made unto thee, Nephi, and also unto thy father, that I would remember your seed; and that the words of your seed should proceed forth out of my mouth unto your seed; and my words shall hiss forth unto the ends of the earth, for a standard unto my people, which are of the house of Israel;

3. And because my words shall hiss forth—many of the Gentiles shall say: A Bible! A Bible! We have got a Bible, and there cannot be any more Bible.

4. But thus saith the Lord God: O fools, they shall have a Bible; and it shall proceed forth from the Jews, mine ancient covenant people. And what thank

In this section Nephi states that many Gentiles, at the time when the "marvelous work of the Lord," foretold by Isaiah, was about to begin, by the coming forth of the Book of Mormon, would reject it on the ground that they had a Bible and would not need another. The Lord, therefore, he says, reminds them they had not received the Bible with gratitude to the Jews, through whom it had come to them. But, he would, nevertheless, bring forth the Book of Mormon, as another witness to prove the fact that he is the same today, yesterday, and for ever.

VERSE 1. *A Marvelous Work.* See 2 Ne. 25:17.
*The Second Time.* 2 Ne. 6:14.

VERSE 2. *Promises Which I have Made.* 2 Ne. 3:21-25.
*Hiss Forth.* 2 Ne. 15:26.
*Standard.* Or ensign, 2 Ne. 15:26.

VERSE 3. *A Bible! A Bible!* If "Bible" (biblion, or, biblon) means "book," and the plural (biblia), "books," and more particularly inspired, and, therefore, sacred books, the Book of Mormon is a Bible. It is not a substitute for the Old and New Testaments, commonly so known; it is a corroborative witness for the same divine cause.

Quite a few years ago, a prominent clergyman in Salt Lake City criticized the Church for, as he thought, trying to impose a Fifth Gospel on the public, referring more especially to the Third Book of Nephi. I remember that President B. H. Roberts, in replying, expressed regret that the recognition of that book as a fifth Gospel had come first from an outsider. Little did that clergyman realize that he was fulfilling prophecy by raising an objection against the Book of Mormon, on the assumed ground that it is too much like the Bible.

they the Jews for the Bible which they receive from them? Yea, what do the Gentiles mean? Do they remember the travels, and the labors, and the pains of the Jews, and their diligence unto me, in bringing forth salvation unto the Gentiles?

5. O ye Gentiles have ye remembered the Jews, mine ancient covenant people? Nay; but ye have cursed them, and have hated them, and have not sought to recover them. But behold, I will return all these things upon your own heads; for I the Lord have not forgotten my people.

6. Thou fool, that shall say: A Bible, we have got a Bible, and we need no more Bible. Have ye obtained a Bible save it were by the Jews?

---

VERSE 5. *Have Ye Remembered the Jews?* It is the Lord who asks. How have the Jews, through whom the Bible came, been received? History answers by turning its blood-stained pages to the light, one by one, seemingly for endless ages.

We, who have reached an advanced age, remember a time when the brilliant rays of civilization seemed about to break through the mists and give hope of the early dawn of a better day. Already Napoleon I, in 1806, summoned a Sanhedrin of Jews, to learn the qualifications of their people for citizenship. And during the so-called Victorian era, the freedom of the Hebrews grew with the ever increasing influence of democracy.

The World War made a great change. During those dark years, the world was easily pushed back a century, or more, in some parts of the world, and with this recession of civilization, barbarism has gained ground, and with it, persecution of the Jews.

According to newspaper clippings:

At the beginning of 1938, the unfortunate Jews in Germany appealed to the ruler of that nation for the mercy of salvation from destitution and extermination, they being forcibly scattered and then persecuted for not having visible means of support, or passports.

In Bucharest, about the same time, a Rumanian government official is said to have announced that plans were being laid for a world-wide anti-Semitic congress, which would, of course, mean world-wide persecution.

In Italy, the ruler is said to have informed the Jews (Feb. 16, 1938) that they would not be permitted to play a more important part in the national life than their individual abilities merit.

In Austria, in Jan. 1938, the state council considered measures for the closing of the country to refugees from Poland and Rumania, somewhat after the pattern of the old slave legislation in the United States before the Civil War.

*Austrian Jews.* On March, 1938, the situation of the Jewish population in Austria had become so critical that Jewish World congress in Geneva petitioned the League of Nations to consider the problem of the "Martyrdom of Austrian Jews." The congress showed that the Jewish death rate in Austria had risen from an average of 4 a day to 140. If the Jews ever were in need of a Messiah, they are now. Meanwhile agitation in Palestine has been rife between Jews and Arabs, until the strongholds seem to have been in the hands of the opponent of the Prince of Peace.

*I Have Not Forgotten My People.* That is the promise of the Lord. The settlement of 200,000 Jews in recent years (this was written in 1955) is regarded as one of the miracles of history. Rabbi Samuel H. Gordon, Salt Lake City, is quoted as having said in a recent address that the spectacle of Palestine of today, is one of "a

7. Know ye not that there are more nations than one? Know ye not that I, the Lord your God, have created all men, and that I remember those who are upon the isles of the sea; and that I rule in the heavens above and in the earth beneath; and I bring forth my word unto the children of men, yea, even upon all the nations of the earth?

## 2. Two Witnesses.

8. Wherefore murmur ye, because that ye shall receive more of my word? Know ye not that the testimony of two nations is a witness unto you that I am God, that I remember one nation like unto another? Wherefore, I speak the same words unto one nation like unto another. And when the two nations shall run together the testimony of the two nations shall run together also.

9. And I do this that I may prove unto many that I am the same yesterday, today, and forever; and that I speak forth my words according to mine own pleasure. And because that I have spoken one word ye need not suppose that I cannot speak another; for my work is not yet finished; neither shall it be until the end of man, neither from that time henceforth and forever.

10. Wherefore, because that ye have a Bible ye need not suppose that it contains all my words; neither need ye suppose that I have not caused more to be written.

## 3. Several Records.

11. For I command all men, both in the east and in the west, and in the north, and in the south, and in the islands of the sea, that they shall write the words which I speak unto them; for out of the

race of agriculturally astute people becoming wedded to the soil after centuries of being confined to commercial activities." The land which 20 years ago could feed only 700,000 people now supports a population of about 1,500,000, and has an orange export business of $18,000,000 a year, two-thirds of it produced by Jews, he said. Industrial development in Palestine also is being stimulated by the Jewish migration, he said. (Salt Lake Trib., Feb. 5, 1938.)

God has not forgotten his people.

VERSE 7. *The Isles of the Sea.* See 2 Ne. 10:22-24.

VERSE 9. *Yesterday, Today and Forever.* One of the attributes of God is indicated here. He is not subject to changes as we are. He works in accordance with eternal laws, or rules. If he has caused inspired writings to be given to men at any time, he will do so again, when necessary for their guidance. We may expect "bibles" in different ages and localities. Comp. Heb. 13:4: "Jesus Christ the same yesterday, and today and forever."

VERSES 11-12. *I Command All Men . . . That They Shall Write.* In view of this statement and the following in verse 12: "And I shall also speak to all the nations of the earth, and they shall write it," the utter indifference to all sacred literature,

books which shall be written I will judge the world, every man according to their works according to that which is written.

12. For behold, I shall speak unto the Jews and they shall write it; and I shall also speak unto the Nephites and they shall write it; and I shall also speak unto the other tribes of the house of Israel, which I have led away, and they shall write it; and I shall also speak unto all nations of the earth and they shall write it.

13. And it shall come to pass that the Jews shall have the words of the Nephites and the Nephites shall have the words of the Jews; and the Nephites and the Jews shall have the words of the lost tribes of Israel; and the lost tribes of Israel shall have the words of the Nephites and the Jews.

14. And it shall come to pass that my people, which are of the house of Israel, shall be gathered home unto the lands of their possessions; and my word also shall be gathered in one. And I will show unto them that fight against my word and against my people, who are of the house of Israel, that I am God and that I covenanted with Abraham that I would remember his seed forever.

except the Bible, is rather unfortunate. As Latter-day Saints we have accepted the Bible, the Book of Mormon, the Doctrine and Covenants, and the Pearl of Great Price as inspired guides to eternal life. But we also acknowledge our obligation to accept truth from whatever source it comes. All the sacred writings will some day be gathered together. (v. 13)

VERSE 14. *The Lands of Their Possessions.* The promise is here repeated that the descendants of Abraham, and especially the house of Israel, will be gathered. Note the plural. I take "lands of their possessions" to mean all the countries in which their possessions once were allotted to them—the entire region between the River of Egypt and the Euphrates, once inhabited by Kenites, Kenizzites, Kadmonites, Hittites, Perizzites Rephaims, Canaanites, Girganites and Jebusites. (Gen. 15:18-21) According to the Mosaic law, land possessions returned automatically every fiftieth year to the original owner: "In the year of the jubilee the field shall return to him of whom it was bought, even to him to whom the possession did belong." (Numb. 27:24) The original covenant was made with the descendants of Abraham, and this fact may have to be considered in the solution of what now seems to be a difficult problem, involving perfect justice between Hebrews and Arabs.

### GENERAL NOTES

*Tel Aviv.* This is the name of a city on the Mediterranean near the city of Jaffa. It was founded in 1909. In 1913 it had only 908 inhabitants. In 1930 there were 40,000. In Tel Aviv, the ancient Hebrew language, for centuries regarded as dead, has been revived. Newspapers are printed in pure Hebrew. Theaters and even signboards use that tongue. The streets are thronged with well-dressed people, with shiny motor cars, mostly of American manufacture, and motor buses. The traffic policemen are dressed much like the American policemen in summer uniform. The shops are bright and modern. The homes are either of the California bungalow type or flat buildings. There are Jews from South Africa, from Argentina and Brazil, from the United States, from Yemen in central Arabia, from Russia in large numbers, from Poland, Austria, England and many other countries. There they are adapting and building up a new civilization in a purely Jewish atmosphere.

The Jews of the United States have furnished a large part of the means for experiment. Statistics show that the Keren Hayesod, an organization engaged in assisting immigration received more than 2,000,000 pounds sterling from the United States of a total of 3,774,000 pounds. And in 1923 there was floated in the United States a Tel Aviv municipal loan of 75,000 pounds sterling.

Tel Aviv is only one of the manifestations of the establishment of the Jewish home. More than 100 villages and agricultural colonies have been established in various parts of Palestine, with a population of more than 100,000.

*Concerning the Book of Mormon.* Only recently in Los Angeles I called upon a gentleman, now in his seventy-first year, an eminent geologist who devotes a great deal of time to the study of American archaeology. He said to me: "Dr. Merrill, *Joseph Smith knew more about the ancient inhabitants of America than all the scholars that have lived.*" He had read the Book of Mormon because it came into his possession, because he was reading everything that had come to his notice concerning ancient America, and he had been examining the results of every archaeological investigation, and that was his testimony to me. He said: "I would like, if I had the strength, to devote my time to writing a book that would prove to my associate scientists the validity of that book."

Anyhow, our testimony is that the Book of Mormon is genuine. As I said, *the divinity of the establishment of this Church stands or falls with the validity of that book. I say this, of course, in perfect confidence* that no matter what discoveries may be made, the validity of that book will never be impeached—Extract from a sermon in the Tabernacle, Salt Lake City, by Dr. Joseph L. Merrill, Jan. 13, 1929. Deseret News, Jan. 19, that year.

*Northern Myths.* As a sample of pre-Christian literature, the following rendition of a few paragraphs of the Icelandic poem "Voeluspa" (the Oracles of the Wolf) is offered. They are from the Danish edition of the Older Edda, by Frederik W. Horn, Copenhagen, 1869. According to this poem, Oden visited Neji, a Northern seeress, in search of knowledge. He paid her costly rings, an ancient medium of exchange, indicating the high age of the composition. She took her runic wand. Then:

> Far and wide around her,
> Through the worlds existing,
> Went the searching eyes.

She said she remembered nine worlds—a plausible allusion to the generations between Adam and Noah. Then:

> That was time's beginning.
> Yme was the builder.
> Cooling waves there were not,
> Neither sand nor sea.
> Land existed nowhere,
> Nor the vaulted heaven,
> Or the fragrant flowers,
> Nothing but expanse.

The sons of Bure, somehow, made land. The sun shone. The rocks became warm. Vegetation sprouted. The moon appeared. But:

> Little knew the Sun-king
> Where to find his palace;

Little knew the new moon
All the power it wielded;
Stars had not been given
    Their allotted place.

Then the Mighty Powers
Took their seats in council
And the gods, the holy,
    Asked for good advice.
Night and light they named,
And to reckon seasons,
They gave Morning, Mid-day,
    Forenoon, Ev'ning, names.

On the field of Ida
All the Aesir gathered.
There they timbered temples,
    Rising t'ward the sky.
There they strength exerted,
There they allthing started.
There they made their smithies,
Forged their tongs of iron,
And their tools for labor,
    Worked the noble ore.

They did not lack gold. They were happy, until giant damsels appeared among
them. These brought misfortune.

Again the mighty Powers gathered in council.

Prophecies describing the latter-day conditions of the world are quite remarkable:

Brothers will, in battle,
Slaughter one another.
Kindred will be tearing
    Friendship's dearest ties.
Earth is full of evil,
Unclean lusts are ruling,
Swords and battle-axes,
    Useless are the shields.

Wolves and whirling stormwinds
Shall appear together,
Ere the world shall perish,
    Ere the Ragnaroek.
Crash! go rolling thunders
Giants shall be flying,
No one cares for any
    Other than himself.

Then the sun is darkened,
Waves the earth engulfing.
Brilliant stars of heaven
    Pale, give no more light.
Flames 'gainst flames are raging
Crashing, thundering, sparkling;
Towards heaven's arches
    Reach the greedy fires.

That is Ragnaroek.   But it is not the end.   The seeress continues:

Now I see a landscape
O'er the sea arising,
On the lofty hill sides
    Eagles catching fish.
Wild, in frothy freshets,
Water rushes downward,
Green is earth, and glorious,
    Fair, as ne'er before.

On the field of Ida
Aesir meet together,
Tell again the saga
    Of the Midgard Snake.
Great things they remembered,
All they had experienced,
Runes they had been given
    By the Highest God.

Now the Strong is coming,
He who is the Ruler
Over things existing,
    Judgment to dispense.
Everything he judges,
Every feud he settles,
Tells what things are sacred
    Here upon the earth.

Fairer than the sunshine
Now I see a castle,
Walls with gold all covered,
    Gimle is its name.
There shall all the righteous
Live in joy and happy,
    All eternity.

*Other Sacred Books.*  The bibles of the Brahmnists and Buddhists, the Vedas, are thought to have originated as early as 2000 B. C. Those books recognize one God, Brahmah, "almighty, eternal, omnipresent, the great Soul, of whom all other gods are parts. They are concerned with prayers and ceremonies. Brahmahnism is said to hold that there is no essential difference between gods and men; that the gods are only farther advanced, and that men, by means of transmigration of souls, are coming after as fast as possible.

*Buddhism.*  This is claimed to be "reformed" Brahmahnism.  Protestantism in the world of paganism! It is named after Gautama Buddha, whose birth year is given as 568 B.C. Buddhism now claims 150 million followers in Burma, Nepal, Ceylon, Siam, Tibet, China and Japan, and about 180,000 in America, besides some in European countries. According to Buddhism, salvation from the evils of existence can be attained by right faith, right judgment, right language, right purpose, right practice, right effort, right thinking, and meditation.

It is not improbable that these and other Asiatic religions have a common origin, viz., the Patriarchal faith of Noah, which, in the course of time, degenerated, just as various systems of Christianity have done, although they have the same historical origin.

*Zoroastrianism.*  The bible of this religion is the Zend Avesta.  The founder or rather, reformer was Zoroaster, whose birth is placed about 600 B.C., or, as others hold, 1000 B.C.  According to Zoroaster, the realm of good is ruled by Ormazd and six attendant spirits.  They represent good thoughts, righteousness, wished-for kingdom, harmony on earth, salvation, immortality.  Next to these stand the angels who guide the forces of nature, chief of whom is Mithra.  Atar, the fire, Apo, the waters, and others repesenting the sun, the moon, stars, etc., are carrying out the divine decrees regarding the universe.  On the other hand, Ahriman is the leader of a rabble of archfiends, demons and evil spirits, who are at war with the good spirits and seeking to destroy the soul of man.  Cyrus, who played such an important part in the history of Israel, and to whom God, through the Prophet Isaiah, referred as "my servant" (Is. 44:28), may have been an adherent of the creed of the great Oriental reformer.  The Magi, who came to Bethlehem and worshiped at the manger, leaving there their costly gifts of gold, frankincense and myrrh (Matt. 2:11), may have been Zoroastrian priests, possibly with royal blood in their veins.

During the 7th century, the worshipers of Zoroaster were driven to India by the Mohammedan invasion of Persia.  There they became known as Parsees (Persians).  There is still a remnant of them, with headquarters at Bombay.  They are noted for generosity, have a priesthood, and revere fire as an emblem of purity.

*Islam.*  Founded by Mohammed about 600 A. D.  Its "bible" is the Koran, a word meaning, "reading."  It contains readings concerning religious, social, civil, legal 'and many other subjects, all of which, it is claimed, was revealed to the prophet by the angel Gabriel.  The book professes to be "a guide for those who believe in the mysteries of faith, who pray, give alms, and believe in revelations given to the prophets."  Its main doctrines are that God is one; that there is but one true religion, and that there is a day of judgment.  Mohammedans recognize Moses and Jesus as great prophets, but to them Mohammed is *the* prophet.

*Some Figures.*  According to a recent census, there are 331 million Roman Catholics in the world; 206 million Protestants and 144 million Orthodox Catholics.  On the other hand there are said to be 230 million Hindus, 209 million Mohammedans and 150 million Buddhists.  The entire number of non-Christians is given as 1,167,100,000 to 689,000,000 Christians.

CHAPTER 30

*Jews and Gentiles, 1-2 — The Book of Mormon, 3-6 — The Jews, 7 — All Nations, 8-11—The Millennium, 12-18.*

## 1. *Jews and Gentiles.*

1. And now behold, my beloved brethren, I would speak unto you; for I, Nephi, would not suffer that ye should suppose that ye are more righteous than the Gentiles shall be. For behold, except ye shall keep the commandments of God ye shall all likewise perish; and because of the words which have been spoken ye need not suppose that the Gentiles are utterly destroyed.

2. For behold, I say unto you that as many of the Gentiles as will repent are the covenant people of the Lord; and as many of the Jews as will not repent shall be cast off; for the Lord covenanteth with none save it be with them that repent and believe in his Son, who is the Holy One of Israel.

## 2. *The Book of Mormon.*

3. And now, I would prophesy somewhat more concerning the Jews and the Gentiles. For after the book of which I have spoken shall come forth, and be written unto the Gentiles, and sealed up again unto the Lord, there shall be many which shall believe the words which are written; and they shall carry them forth unto the remnant of our seed.

VERSES 1-2. *The Covenant People.* Jews and Gentiles are on a level of equality before God, for Gentiles who repent, thereby join the covenant people and share its privileges and prerogatives, as well as its duties and responsibilities. On the other hand, Jews, who will not repent, are cast off. St. Paul teaches the same doctrine: "or the promise that he"—Abraham—"should be the heir of the world, was not to Abraham, or to his seed through the law, but through the righteousness of faith"—the gospel. (Rom. 4:13) Again: "There is no difference between the Jew and the Greek"—Gentile—"for the same Lord over all is rich unto all that call upon him." (Rom. 10:12.) And: "As many as are led by the Spirit of God, they are the sons of God." (Rom. 8:14)

VERSE 3. *Many Shall Believe.* "There are 756,000 living members of the Church, besides those who have died in the faith, or who once accepted it in their faith and afterwards by transgression lost the spirit of the work and departed from the Church, but, who, singularly enough in the majority of cases, still continue to assert their faith in the truth of the Book of Mormon; and those who have been brought to a belief in the Book of Mormon, but who have not had the courage to make the sacrifices involved in a public profession of their faith. A further evidence is the many tongues and languages into which the Book of Mormon has been translated."—B. H. Roberts, quoted in, "Seven Claims of the Book of Mormon," by Dr. John A. Widtsoe and Dr. Franklin S. Harris, Jr., p. 176.

4. And then shall the remnant of our seed know concerning us, how that we came out from Jerusalem, and that they are descendants of the Jews.

5. And the gospel of Jesus Christ shall be declared among them; wherefore, they shall be restored unto the knowledge of their fathers, and also to the knowledge of Jesus Christ, which was had among their fathers.

6. And then shall they rejoice; for they shall know that it is a blessing unto them from the hand of God; and their scales of darkness shall begin to fall from their eyes; and many generations shall not pass away among them save they shall be a white and delightsome people.

### 3. *The Jews.*

7. And it shall come to pass that the Jews which are scattered also shall begin to believe in Christ; and they shall begin to

---

VERSES 4-6. *The Book of Mormon Is Written for the Gentiles.* Many will believe it. These will carry it to the Nephites and Lamanites, "the remnant of our seed." (v. 3) By this means these will obtain knowledge of their origin and kinship with the Jews. (v. 4) This may not seem important to some just now, before the plan of salvation is completed. But we must not judge of the importance of any single part of an educational system devised by Infinite Skill, before we know it in its entirety. The real necessity for genealogical connections may not be fully known until the kingdom of God is established during the Millennium.

Alexander Campbell, who came in contact with the first missionaries of our Church, urged as an objection against the Book of Mormon that it deals with a number of modern theological controversies. And so it does. But that is not a valid ground for rejection. Truth is eternal. It has neither beginning nor end. Truths that we know were known to the first ancestors of our race, and to Noah and his children, through whom they were handed down to the various branches of the human family. Religious controversies must have been, to a large extent, the same anciently as they are today. Were this not so, the Bible, too, would have to be rejected, for there is not a modern heresy, hardly a modern, general theological question, that has not been anticipated by the authors of that sacred volume. God's books never become antiquated.

"Mr. Campbell lists the controversial points on which the Book of Mormon passes decision. An unlearned boy would hardly know these subjects, much less be able to deal with them intelligently. Here is the list of Campbell's subjects: "a. Infant baptism. b. Ordination. c. The Trinity. d. Regeneration. e. Repentance. f. Justification. g. The fall of man. h. The Atonement. i. Transubstantiation. j. Fasting. k. Penance. l. Church government. m. Religious experience. n. The call to the ministry. o. General resurrection. p. Eternal punishment. q. Who may baptize. r. Free masonry. s. Republican government. t. The rights of man.

"Many of the solutions of these controversies offered by the Book of Mormon have been adopted during the last century by most of controversialists, without of course, mentioning the Book of Mormon. This may be verified by an examination of the present creeds of the churches as compared with the creeds one hundred years ago." (Dr. John A. Widtsoe and Dr. Franklin S. Harris, Jr. in *Seven Claims of the Book of Mormon*, p. 146.)

gather in upon the face of the land; and as many as shall be-

lieve in Christ shall also become a delightsome people.

## 4. All Nations.

8. And it shall come to pass that the Lord God shall commence his work among all nations, kindreds, tongues and people to bring about the restoration of his people upon the earth.

9. And with righteousness shall the Lord God judge the poor,

and reprove with equity for the meek of the earth. And he shall smite the earth with the rod of his mouth; and with the breath of his lips shall he slay the wicked.

10. For the time speedily cometh that the Lord God shall cause a great division among the people, and the wicked will he de-

VERSE 7. *Jews.* We have read in 2 Ne. 25:16, 17 and other passages that when the Jews accept Jesus as their Messiah and worship the Father in his name, the Lord will set his hand again the second time to restore his people. In this paragraph we are told that when they "begin" to believe in Christ, they will also "begin" to gather in upon the face of the land—Palestine. This is being fulfilled in our day.

Judging from the little volume by Rabbi Joseph Klausner of Jerusalem on "Jesus of Nazareth," we may expect the coming of a radical change in the attitude of educated Jews toward the mission and work of that greatest of Jews of all ages. The rabbi describes the political, economic, religious, and intellectual conditions of the time in which Jesus lived. He repudiates some of the common legends and traditions concerning him, and thus prepares the way for his acceptance as the Messiah. See also 2 Ne. 29:5.

*A Delightsome People.* A living faith in our Lord will break down prejudices between Jews and Gentiles. Each branch of the human family will be "delightsome" to the other. "If Jews had been allowed to preserve the ideals of the prophets in matters of tolerance and equality, the race would have taken its place in the world today."—Dr. Levi Edgar Young, quoted in the Deseret News, March 11, 1938, p. 17.

VERSES 8-11. *In Literary Construction,* as in contents, this section is one of the gems of the Book of Mormon. For one thing, it has unity of plan. It begins with the proposition that Jews and Gentiles are on a level of equality before God. (vv. 1-2) Then it states the mission of the Book of Mormon to be to reveal the origin of the descendants of Lehi and their kinship with the Jews. (vv. 3-6) It continues by asserting that the Jews, including the descendants of the Nephites and Lamanites, shall be gathered (v. 7). Next we are given to understand that the work of restoration of the people of God is extended to "all nations, kindreds, tongues and people" (v. 8). Thus it shows the progression of the work of the Lord from a comparatively speaking, limited beginning to its completion in the Millennium (vv. 9-18).

*Another Characteristic.* The importance of the section may be judged from the fact that a portion of its appears twice in this Book of Nephi. Paragraphs 9, 11-15 are all but perfectly identical with paragraphs 4-9 of chapter 21, which is a copy of Is. 11. The 10th verse is new here. In the early part of his book, Nephi

stroy; and he will spare his peo- | 11. And righteousness shall be
ple, yea, even if it so be that he | the bridle of his loins and faith-
must destroy the wicked by fire. | fulness the girdle of his reins.

---

copies Is. 2-14. After having reproduced these chapters, he comments on them. When, in the course of his explanations, he comes to Is. 11:4, he reads that verse a second time, and it becomes verse 9 in this chapter. Verse 10 is his comment. Verses 5-9 in Is. become 11-15 here. An evidence, I would think, of the importance attached to the passage by Nephi. And no wonder. For it deals with latter-day visitations by the Lord, the judgment on nations, and the Millennium.

VERSE 8. *Among All Nations.* I suppose that this work of restoration among all nations, kindreds, tongues, and people, of which the coming forth of the Book of Mormon was the beginning, embraces activity on both sides of the veil, for the salvation of the race. St. Paul, certainly, had such an application in view, when he wrote to the Saints in Ephesus "That in the dispensation of the fulness of times" —and that is the times of which Nephi speaks—"he might gather together in one all things in Christ, both which are in heaven and which are on earth; even in him." (Eph. 1:10)

*Work for the Dead.* But, is there any evidence that the descendants of Lehi at this time knew of work for those on the other side of the veil?
Perhaps not!
And yet, they were temple builders. And they must have had some temple service.
Alma, speaking of the resurrection of the dead to Zeezrom, said, in part:

"It is given unto many to know the mysteries of God; nevertheless they are laid under a strict command that they shall not impart only according to the portion of his word which he doth grant unto the children of men, according to the heed and diligence which they give unto him. And therefore, he that will harden his heart, the same receiveth the lesser portion of the word; and he that will not harden his heart, to him is given the greater portion of the word, until it is given him to know the mysteries of God, until he know them in full." (Alma 12:9-11)

VERSE 9. *The Wicked.* Here and in the next verse, is antichrist. (Comp. 2 Thess. 2:3-10; 1 John 4:1-3)

VERSE 10. *A Great Division.* Refers, possibly, to the judgment of nations, as described by our Lord, Matt. 25-31-46.

VERSE 11. *Girdle.* The Orientals, when walking fast, or working, found it convenient to gather up their long, flowing robes by means of a girdle. During the Millennium, it seems, the Lord will take part in the activities of his people. But righteousness and faithfulness, not militarism and hypocrisy, will be his strength, the force of his reign, his girdle.

*Loins.* Were supposed to be the seat of strength. To gird up the loins was, in prophetic parlance, to make ready for work, or for traveling untrammeled.

*Reins.* The same as kidneys. Supposed to be the symbols of desire; also of knowledge, joy, pleasure. Sometimes coupled with the heart. (Psalm 7:9; Jer. 17:10; Rev. 2:23)

## 5. *The Millennium.*

12. And then shall the wolf dwell with the lamb; and the leopard shall lie down with the kid, and the calf, and the young lion, and the fatling, together; and a little child shall lead them.

13. And the cow and the bear shall feed; their young ones shall lie down together; and the lion shall eat straw like the ox.

14. And the sucking child shall play on the hole of the asp, and the weaned child shall put his hand on the cockatrice's den.

15. They shall not hurt nor destroy in all my holy mountain; for the earth shall be full of the knowledge of the Lord as the waters cover the sea.

16. Wherefore, the things of all nations shall be made known; yea, all things shall be made known unto the children of men.

17. There is nothing which is secret save it shall be revealed; there is no work of darkness save it shall be made manifest in the light; and there is nothing which is sealed upon the earth save it shall be loosed.

18. Wherefore, all things which have been revealed unto the children of men shall at that day be revealed; and Satan shall have power over the hearts of the children of men no more, for a long time. And now, my beloved brethren, I must make an end of my sayings.

---

VERSES 12-18. *The Wolf and the Lamb, etc.* Millennial conditions under the scepter of the Prince of Peace are described in these paragraphs. Revealed knowledge will be so abundant among men that satan will have no power over their hearts. Their enlightenment and consequent refinement will be so dominant that even the brute creation, and especially the higher animals, will feel the influence thereof. (Comp. Rom. 8:19-25)

Opinions among Bible students differ concerning the Millenium. Is it a literal kingdom on earth, governed by our Lord in person? Or, is it all spiritual? The answer depends largely on how the Revelation by John, and especially chapters 20 and 21, are understood. The Book of Revelations is—in passing—a connecting sacred literary link between the Old Testament prophetic era, especially Ezekiel and Daniel, and the prophetic office of the Church of Jesus Christ of Latter-day Saints, in as much as a "key" to it is incorporated in the Doctrine and Covenants, Sec. 77. The Lord, evidently, expects the Saints to study it. What then does the Book of Revelation itself say?

*The Revelation by John.* This book is divided into two parts, "The things which are," and "The things which shall be hereafter" (1:19).

The first part refers mainly to the churches in Asia Minor at the time of John. It is a message sent to them by our Lord himself, through the Apostle. (1:10, 11) It is recorded in Rev. 1 to 3.

The second part was shown to him (a) in a sequence of visions beyond the veil, in heaven, (Rev. 4:1), depicting, as generally understood, the history of the world and the church in the world; or, as stated better in D. and C. 77:6: "The revealed will, mysteries and works of God; the hidden things of his economy concerning this earth during the seven thousand years of its continuance, or its temporal existence." This first division of the second part ends with chapter 11.

That chapter also ends the "key" given to the Church through the Prophet Joseph, showing that his information on the subject of the construction of the book was more correct than that possessed by most scholars of our day. What follows chapter 11 is visions added by inspiration and so carefully selected that the Apostle assures us that if any undertake to add anything, or to take anything therefrom, he would be excluded from access to the tree of life and the holy city. (Rev. 22:18, 19) These additions (b) are: The vision of a woman pursued by the dragon and fleeing into the wilderness (Rev. 12); a beast rising up out of the sea, and another out of the earth (13); the Lamb and 144,000 on Mt. Sion; three angels, one of whom has the everlasting gospel to proclaim, followed by a harvest and a vintage (14), and then the pouring out of seven vials of plagues (15, 16). Then comes the vision of the woman on the beast (17); the destruction of "Babylon" (18); songs of praise (19:1-10), when Christ, followed by heavenly hosts, establishes his reign as "King of kings and Lord of lords" (19:11-21); new heavens and a new earth (20-22:5); and the conclusion (22:6-21).

These added visions appear to be explanations in greater detail, nearer views or "close-ups," as it were, of visions in the first portion of the second, or prophetic, part of the book. Thus, the vision of the angel with the everlasting gospel (14:6, 7) adds details to the vision of the angel with the little book (Chapt. 10), and the vision of the millennium (chapt. 20) is a nearer view of the briefer revelation in 11:15-19:

"And there followed great voices in heaven, and they said, The Kingdom of the world is become the kingdom of our Lord, and his Christ; and he shall reign for ever and ever * * * We give thee thanks, O Lord God, the Almighty, which art and which wast; because thou hast taken thy great power, and didst reign." (Rev. 11:17, 18)[1]

We note that, according to the Revelation, "the kingdom of the world" has become "the Kingdom of our Lord," because he has, by his great power, taken possession as its King. That is the Millennium. That is the Kingdom of God.

*The Kingdom.* We now turn to other parts of the New Testament for further information of the nature of the kingdom of God.

John the Baptist, the last and greatest of the prophets of the Mosaic dispensation (Matt. 11:11) began his ministry by urging repentance on the ground that "the kingdom of heaven is at hand." (Matt. 3:2) Our Lord opened his career with the same message. (Matt. 4:17) He commissioned his disciples when he first sent them out on a mission, to preach the same glad tidings and to prove it by performing miracles in his name. (Matt. 10:7-15) Later, when Pharisees demanded to know where the kingdom, the near advent of which he and his disciples had preached, was, he stated plainly that it had already come. It does not, he said, come with outward manifestations, as a worldly kingdom. It has no armies, no navies, no diplomatic service, no police force, no gorgeous palaces. You cannot point to its capital and say, "lo here! Lo there!" It has not come to that yet. Nevertheless, "the kingdom of God is within you;" that is, among you, in the midst of you. For, where Jesus and his Apostles are, there is the Kingdom of God with all the power and authority of that kingdom. (Luke 17:20, 21) This kingdom our Lord "appointed," that is, bequeathed, to the Twelve. (Luke 12:32; 22:29) Its spiritual nature is evident from the Sermon on the Mount (its fundamental law), from the life of Jesus as portrayed in the Gospels, and from his own declaration before Pilate:

---

[1] "Didst reign" in the original is, "ebasileausas" which means, literally, "hast become a King."

"Thou sayest that I am a king. To this end have I been born, and to this end am I come into the world, that I should bear witness unto the truth. Every one that is of the truth heareth my voice." (John 18:37)

Which is as much as to say, that the kingdom of Christ is the kingdom of truth, reality, not pretense; that its subjects are those only who are true, genuine, honest; and that the world will be redeemed from its condition of hypocrisy and falsehood by the testimony of the citizens of the kingdom of Christ bearing witness of the truth, not by violence. Thus the kingdoms of the world, under whatever form of government they may exist, will become the kingdom of Christ, for him to mould and govern, in accordance with the demands of the eternal principles of truth.

*Christ to Return.* When our Lord was preparing for his departure, his disciples asked him whether he now was about "to restore the kingdom of Israel." He was not, But, he said, "ye shall receive power, when the Holy Ghost is come upon you: and ye shall be my witnesses." (Acts 1:6-8)

The day for the departure of Jesus had come. While the disciples were looking intently into heaven, on the cloud behind which he had disappeared from their view, two men "in white apparel" stood by them, who said: "Ye men of Galilee . . . this Jesus, which was received up from you into heaven, shall so come in like manner as ye beheld him going into heaven." (Acts 1:11) Literally, personally; not figuratively speaking. And this coming will be before the Millennium. (2 Thess. 2:8)

This is the testimony of the Scriptures.

They bear witness of a long time of apostasy. But that is not the end. The wicked one will be destroyed. Babylon, the woman on the beast, will be judged. Christ will return. There will be joy and thanksgiving in heaven. "Again and again, and again, the cry is heard there, 'Allelujah;' and the servants of God on earth are summoned to join in the song." (Dr. Joseph Angus.)

Students of this important subject are, further, referred to the D. & C. 23:11-22; 43:18-26; 45:45-55; 49:22-25, 88:86-110; Pearl of Great Pr., Mos. 7:47-67.

VERSE 12. *A Little Child.* Isaiah refers to the Messiah (9:6) as a "Child," a "Son," whose insignia of government are on his shoulders; who shall occupy the throne of David.

## GENERAL NOTES

The subjoined extracts from a sermon by President Rudger Clawson, the Apostle, delivered in the Tabernacle, Salt Lake City, April 7, 1933, may properly complete my notes on this chapter. President Clawson said, in part:

### WORK FOR THE DEAD

"The following piece of information, I am sure, will be very interesting to you, and will also be instructive. Something over six millions of endowments have been administered in The Church of Jesus Christ of Latter-day Saints up to December, 1932. Something over eight millions of baptisms for the dead have been solemnized in The Church of Jesus Christ of Latter-day Saints up to December 31st, 1932. Many thousands of sealings of wives to husbands, and of children to parents, have taken place.

"I think we may reasonably expect that the great majority of these who have had the work done for them will accept it, and if that be the case, brethren and sisters, you will see at a glance that the Church of the First-born in heaven is much greater and stronger, and the membership there is much more numerous than it is in the Church of Jesus Christ, or the First-born, here upon the earth.

"When I saw these figures I was very much impressed with them."

*The Last Sermon of President Woodruff.* President Clawson continued, "Perhaps I will just have time, possibly, to allude to the last sermon of President Wilford Woodruff. It was delivered in this Tabernacle, April 10, 1898. He bore a very powerful and impressive testimony. He said:

"At the close of this conference I have a desire to bear my testimony before you upon a few principles. I have rejoiced very much during this conference in listening to the testimonies of the apostles and elders who have spoken. It has brought to my remembrance a little of my history.

"In April of 1838, while in the town of Kirtland, in walking across the street, I met two men who held the apostleship. They said to me: 'Brother Woodruff, we have something that we want you to join us in.' Said I, 'What is it?' 'We want another prophet to lead us.' 'Whom do you want?' 'We want Oliver Cowdery. Joseph Smith has apostatized.' After listening to them, I said: 'Unless you repent of your sins, you will be damned and go to hell, and you will go through the fulness of eternal damnation, and all your hopes in this life will pass before you like the frost before the rising sun. You are false. Joseph Smith holds the keys of the kingdom of God on earth, and will hold them until the coming of the Son of Man, whether in this world or in the world to come.' I am happy to say that these men did repent pretty soon, turned to the Church, and died in it.

"I feel thankful today that Joseph F. Smith is with us as a son of Hyrum Smith. He bears a true and faithful testimony of his father. I would to God that Joseph Smith had a son in the flesh who would do as Joseph F. Smith does here— bear testimony to the truth of his father. The Prophet Joseph Smith has no son that stands in the midst of the Church of God and bears record of his father. He never has had, possibly never will have.

"I will give you a testimony here that will show you where I stand with regard to this matter. Joseph Smith never ordained his son Joseph, never blessed him, never set him apart to lead this Church and kingdom on the face of the earth. When he or any other man says he did, they state that which is false before high heaven.

"The last speech that Joseph Smith ever made to the quorum of the apostles was in a building in Nauvoo, and it was such a speech as I never heard from mortal man before or since. He was clothed upon with the spirit and power of God. His face was clear as amber; the room was filled as with consuming fire. He stood three hours upon his feet. Said he:

*The Prophet Joseph:* "You Apostles of the Lamb of God have been chosen to carry out the purposes of the Lord on earth. Now, I have received, as the Prophet, Seer and Revelator, standing at the head of this dispensation, every key, every ordinance, every principle and every priesthood that belongs to the last dispensation and fulness of times. And I have sealed all these things upon your heads. Now, you Apostles, if you do not rise up and bear off this kingdom, as I have given it to you, you will be damned.

*President Woodruff:* "I am the only witness left on earth that can bear record of this, and I am thankful that I have lived to see the day in which I stand. I am thankful to see the sons of these prophets and apostles holding the Holy Priesthood in our day and generation. I do not believe the day will ever come— it is too late in the day, in my opinion—when any elder in this Church will be called to stand before any two of the apostles with us today and give unto them the declaration that I gave unto the two apostles I have referred to. I do not think any of the apostles will occupy that position. I have faith to believe that these men will bear the apostleship, will hold it, and live their religion. They have been called and ordained of God for this purpose. I do not think that one of them will apostatize. I believe that they will be with you and with this Church while they stand in the flesh, true and faithful to God."

There is another clause here which I wish to read. It has some bearing on what I have said.

*President Woodruff:* "Brother Cannon"—meaning George Q. Cannon—"has been laying before you something with regard to the nation in which we live, and what has been said concerning it. I am going to bear my testimony to this assembly, if I never do it again in my life, that the men who laid the foundation of this American government, and signed the Declaration of Independence, were the best spirits the God of Heaven could find on the face of the earth. They were choice spirits, not wicked men. General Washington and all the men that labored for that purpose were inspired of the Lord. Another thing I am going to say here, because I have a right to say it, every one of those men that signed the Declaration of Independence, with General Washington, called upon me, as an apostle of the Lord Jesus Christ, in the temple at St. George, two consecutive nights, and demanded at my hands that I should go forth and attend to the ordinances of the House of God for them. Men are here, I believe, that know of this, Brother J. D. T. McAllister, David H. Cannon and James S. Black. Brother McAllister baptized me for all those men, and then I told these brethren that it was their duty to go into the temple and labor until they had got endowments for all of them. They did it. Would those spirits have called upon me as an elder of Israel, to perform that work, if they had not been noble spirits before God? They would not. I bear this testimony because it is true. The Spirit of God bore record to myself and the brethren while we were laboring in that way.

"What has been said with regard to this nation and to our position is coming to pass, and all the powers of earth and hell will not stay the hand of Almighty God in the fulfilment of the great prophecies that have come to pass to prepare the way for the coming of the Son of Man.

"You who have gathered here are my witnesses of this. I feel as though the day has come when every elder and every Latter-day Saint ought to stop and consider the position he is in, and the covenants he has entered into. Is there anything on the face of the earth that will pay you to depart from the oracles of God and from the Gospel of Christ? Is there anything that will pay you to lose the principles of salvation, to lose a part in the first resurrection, with the privilege of standing in the morning of the resurrection clothed with glory, immortality and eternal life, at the head of your father's house? No, there is nothing. I feel sorry many times when I see men who have the priesthood almost forget that they have any interest in the work of God.

"I feel thankful to God that I have lived as long as I have, and to see as much as I have in fulfilment of the words of the Prophet of God. His days were few.

"We live in the last dispensation, and in the midst of the great work that all the patriarchs and prophets since God made the world have spoken of. Afflictions and tribulations await the world. The destroying angels have got their sharp sickles in their hands, and are going to reap down the earth. Everything that has been spoken by the prophets under the inspiration of the Holy Ghost will come to pass in the generation in which we live. Do not forget it!"

## CHAPTER 31

*Baptism, the Doctrine of Christ, 1-4 — His Need of Baptism, 5-8 — A Pattern, 9-13—Endurance Necessary, 15-18—Steadfastness in Christ, 19-21.*

### 1. *Baptism, the Doctrine of Christ.*

1. And now I, Nephi, make an end of my prophesying unto you, my beloved brethren. And I cannot write but a few things, which I know must surely come to pass; neither can I write but a few of the words of my brother Jacob.

2. Wherefore, the things which I have written sufficeth me, save it be a few words which I must speak concerning the doctrine of Christ; wherefore, I shall speak unto you plainly, according to the plainness of my prophesying.

3. For my soul delighteth in plainness; for after this manner doth the Lord God work among the children of men. For the Lord God giveth light unto the understanding; for he speaketh unto men according to their language, unto their understanding.

4. Wherefore, I would that ye should remember that I have spoken unto you concerning that prophet which the Lord showed unto me, that should baptize the Lamb of God, which should take away the sins of the world.

### 2. *His Need of Baptism.*

5. And now, if the Lamb of God, he being holy, should have need to be baptized by water, to fulfil all righteousness, O then, how much more need have we, being unholy, to be baptized, yea, even by water!

---

VERSE 2. *Doctrine of Christ.* Nephi refers to baptism. He proposes to discuss that ordinance as taught by our Lord himself.

VERSE 4. *That prophet which the Lord showed unto me.* John the Baptist. See 1 Ne. 10:7-10.

*The Lamb of God.* The Lamb that (1), as a sacrifice, bears our iniquity (Is. 53:6, 7), or, (2) furnishes the material for protecting and ornamental covering. (v. 7), or, as in the Revelation by John, (5:6; 6:1; 14:1; 22:1), where the Lamb is the head of the entire creation, visible and invisible, who leads all that exists to victory and glory.

*The sins of the world.* Attention might be called to the plural form of the first noun referring, evidently, to individual transgressors, which the Lamb taketh away on condition of repentance and obedience. The singular form, the "sin of the World," which is the term used by John the Baptist (John 1:29), is the transgression of our first parents, the evil consequences of which would have been the inheritance of all their descendants, had they not been removed. But the guilt was taken away, when Adam repented, was baptized and forgiven, through faith in the Lamb of God, who was slain "from the foundations of the world." (Rev. 13:8)

6. And now, I would ask of you, my beloved brethren, wherein the Lamb of God did fulfil all righteousness in being baptized by water?

7. Know ye not that he was holy? But notwithstanding he being holy, he showeth unto the children of men that, according to the flesh he humbleth himself before the Father, and witnesseth unto the Father that he would be obedient unto him in keeping his commandments.

8. Wherefore, after he was baptized with water the Holy Ghost descended upon him in the form of a dove.

### 3. A Pattern.

9. And again, it showeth unto the children of men the straightness of the path, and the narrowness of the gate, by which they should enter, he having set the example before them.

10. And he said unto the children of men: Follow thou me. Wherefore, my beloved brethren, can we follow Jesus save we shall be willing to keep the commandments of the Father?

VERSE 6. *To Fulfil all Righteousness.* John, the forerunner of the Messiah, the herald of the kingdom of God, was commanded to baptize in water, (John 1:33) in fulfilment of such prophecies as Ezek. 36:25, or Zech. 13:1, 2. His baptism was, therefore, the entrance to the kingdom to be established by Jesus.

In his divine nature, Jesus would not have had need of baptism; in fact, the ordinance would have been an empty ceremony; but Jesus, in his human existence had divested himself of every vestige of specially divine attributes, and become like his brethren in everything but sin. (Phil. 2:5-8) In his human nature he was the second Adam, (Rom. 5:17-21). As such, he passed through the entrance to the kingdom which John proclaimed. The reformation, or regeneration, he was to effect, would have to come from within and not from without. Again, as a baptism of repentance, the ceremony was a public confession of sin and regret, and an outward sign of a decision by the penitent sinner to begin a new life, as a little child. In his human nature, Jesus, as the representative of the race, carrying the sin of the world, had the same need of baptism, as other human beings had, and have. St. Luke, in his account, notes that our Lord was praying, when the heavens were opened and he heard the voice: "Thou art my beloved Son!" (Luke 3:21, 22). Luke also says the ordinance administered by John was "baptism for the remission of sins." (3:3)

VERSE 9-13. As an example to follow, the baptism of Jesus showed the "straightness of the path and the narrowness of the gate." When he says, "follow me," or, "come after me," (Matt. 4:19, 16:24; Luke 9:59; John 10:2, he means, "keep the commandments of the Father." But one of these is, "repent and be baptized in the name of my beloved Son." Compliance with this commandment brings the Holy Ghost.

VERSE 9. *The Straightness of the Path.* "Straightness," as applied to the road, is its quality of leading directly to the goal, as a straight line, without turnings or deviations. "Behold, the way for man is narrow, but it lieth in a straight course before him." (2 Ne. 9:41; comp. Is. 40:3, 4; 42:16)

11. And the Father said: Repent ye, repent ye, and be baptized in the name of my Beloved Son.

12. And also, the voice of the Son came unto me, saying: He that is baptized in my name, to him will the Father give the Holy Ghost, like unto me; wherefore, follow me, and do the things which ye have seen me do.

13. Wherefore, my beloved brethren, I know that if ye shall follow the Son, with full purpose of heart, acting no hypocrisy and no deception before God, but with real intent, repenting of your sins, witnessing unto the Father that ye are willing to take upon you the name of Christ, by baptism — yea, by following your Lord and your Savior down into the water, according to his word, behold, then shall ye receive the Holy Ghost; yea, then cometh the baptism of fire and of the Holy Ghost; and then can ye speak with the tongue of angels, and shout praises unto the Holy One of Israel.

## 4. *Endurance Necessary.*

14. But, behold, my beloved brethren, thus came the voice of the Son unto me, saying: After ye have repented of your sins, and witnessed unto the Father that ye are willing to keep my command-

---

VERSE 11. *In the Name of my Beloved Son.* Critics have found some difficulty in reconciling this shorter baptism formula, "In the Name of the Son," with the formula given by Matthew (28:19), "In the Name of the Father and of the Son and of the Holy Ghost."

In defense it has been replied that baptism in the first church was administered "in the name of Christ," meaning, by his authority, "for" him; but "into the name of the Trinity," or, into the communion with the Tri-une Godhead. It has been said that the use by the authors of the New Testament of two different particles[1] to denote the authority by which it is performed and its object, warrants this conclusion. But I am afraid the argument can not be substantiated. For the two particles are used indiscriminately. Thus, St. Luke, in his record of the re-baptism of the Johannine disciples at Ephesus, says when they had heard St. Paul speak, "they were baptized, 'into' "—not in—"the name of the Lord Jesus" (Acts 19:4). Luke here uses the formula of Matthew, as far as the particle "into" is concerned. The inference is fair that the briefer formula, "in the name of Jesus" is the same as the longer formula, only abbreviated, but meaning the same. That, in other words, baptism in the name, or into the name, of Jesus, means in the New Testament, as here, baptism both "in" and "into" the name of the Godhead. (See vv. 12 and 13; also 21)

VERSES 14-16. *He that Endureth to the End.* The solemn truth is taught here, that repentance, baptism, and the reception of the Holy Ghost, although necessary for perfect salvation, do not save anyone, unless he continues faithful to the end. One who denies Jesus cannot be saved by ordinances. St. Paul expresses the same thought, when he writes that one who falls away, crucifying Christ anew, after having been enlightened and tasted the heavenly gift, cannot be renewed to

---

[1] "In" and "Into" (Greek, "en" or "epi," and "eis,") prove their contention.

ments, by the baptism of water, and have received the baptism of fire and of the Holy Ghost and can speak with a new tongue, yea, even with the tongue of angels, and after this should deny me, it would have been better for you that ye had not known me.

15. And I heard a voice from the Father, saying: Yea, the words of my Beloved are true and faithful. He that endureth to the end, the same shall be saved.

16. And now, my beloved brethren, I know by this that unless a man shall endure to the end, in following the example of the Son of the living God, he cannot be saved.

17. Wherefore, do the things which I have told you I have seen that your Lord and your Redeemer should do; for, for this cause have they been shown unto me, that ye might know the gate by which ye should enter. For the gate by which ye should enter is repentance and baptism by water; and then cometh a remission of your sins by fire and by the Holy Ghost.

18. And then are ye in this straight and narrow path which leads to eternal life; yea, ye have entered in by the gate; ye have done according to the commandments of the Father and the Son; and ye have received the Holy Ghost, which witnesses of the Father and the Son, unto the fulfilling of the promise which he hath made, that if ye entered in by the way ye should receive.

### 5. Steadfastness in Christ.

19. And now, my beloved brethren, after ye have gotten into this straight and narrow path, I would ask if all is done? Behold, I say unto you, Nay; for ye have not come thus far save it were by the word of Christ with unshaken faith in him, relying

---

repentance (Heb. 6:4-6). And the Apostlt John (1 John 5:16, 17) says he does not even ask the Saints to pray for a deserter from the Lord. His inspired instruction is that if any man see his brother commit a sin "not to death,"—not apostasy from the Lord—he may pray for him, and God will renew his life. But, he says, "there is sin unto death: not concerning this do I say that he should make a request."

Naturally. For there is but one Savior. Only One Name, in which to accept salvation. If a sinner reject him and his atoning sacrifice, there is no other, whether in heaven or on earth, by whom he can be saved. Salvation depends entirely on the acceptance of Jesus as the Savior, by keeping his commandments, and keeping on keeping them, to the end.

VERSES 17-18. *This Straight and Narrow Path.* Nephi is still speaking of endurance as a struggle forward on a straight and narrow path. He seems reluctant to leave the subject. He is delivering his farewell address, and he lays the emphasis on the necessity of being faithful to the end.

VERSES 19-21. Nephi, having exhorted the Saints to endurance, now calls their attention to the importance of "steadfastness in Christ," which means, firm-

wholly upon the merits of him who is mighty to save.

20. Wherefore, ye must press forward with a steadfastness in Christ, having a perfect brightness of hope, and a love of God and of all men. Wherefore, if ye shall press forward, feasting upon the word of Christ, and endure to the end, behold, thus saith the Father: Ye shall have eternal life.

21. And now, behold, my beloved brethren, this is the way; and there is none other way nor name given under heaven whereby man can be saved in the kingdom of God. And now, behold, this is the doctrine of Christ, and the only and true doctrine of the Father, and of the Son, and of the Holy Ghost, which is one God, without end. Amen.

---

ness or solidity of faith in him, as explained in paragraph 19: having "unshaken faith in him, relying wholly upon the merits of him who is mighty to save." He whose faith is not shaken by every wind that blows, every adversity that arises, is steadfast. Note that steadfastness is accompanied by "perfect brightness of hope, and a love of God and all men." That is the characteristic of enduring faith. (20)

VERSE 21. *This Is the Way.* Under par. 11 it was suggested that, "in the name of the Son" means, "in the name of the entire Godhead." This is certainly the meaning here:

"This is the doctrine of Christ,"

which statement is thus amplified:

"And the only true doctrine of the Father, and of the Son, and of The Holy Ghost."

*Which Is One God.* Doctrine and Covenants has the same testimony: "Which Father, Son, and Holy Ghost are One God, infinite and eternal without end." (20:28)

"They are one in essence, in purpose, in spirit, in attributes, in power and glory, but they are, nevertheless, three personages.

" 'The Scriptural facts are (a) The Father says I; The Son says I; The Spirit says I. (b) The Father says Thou to the Son, and the Son says Thou to the Father; and in like manner the Father and the Son use the pronouns He and Him in reference to the Spirit. (c) The Father loves the Son, the Son Loves the Father; the Spirit testifies of the Son. The Father, Son, and Spirit are severally subject and object. They act and are acted upon, or are the objects of action * * * The Son is of the Father, and the Spirit is of the Father and the Son. The Father sends the Son, and the Father and the Son send the Spirit.' " (Charles Hodge, D.D., Systematic Theology, Vol. 1, pp. 444-5; quoted in D. and C. Commentary, p. 144.)

## THE MODE OF BAPTISM DISCUSSED

It is customary to speak of immersion, sprinkling, and affusion as so many different modes of baptism, but, as a matter of fact, there is only one mode of that ordinance, and there can be no more. Sprinkling is sprinkling and affusion is affusion, but neither is baptism, for baptism is a complete burial, or submersion, in water, such as is easily and most naturally accomplished by immersion. No application of water which fails to entirely surround, or cover, the person who is being baptized, is baptism.

In revelations contained in the Doctrine and Covenants this is plainly taught. He who baptizes is there instructed to "immerse him or her in the water, and come forth again out of the water" (Sec. 20:74). Baptism is a "burial": "They are they who received the testimony of Jesus, and believed on his name and were baptized after the manner of his burial, being buried in the water in his name, and this according to the commandment which he has given" (Doc. and Cov. 76:51). Further: "The baptismal font was instituted as a simile of the grave, and was commanded to be in a place underneath where the living are wont to assemble, to show forth the living and the dead" (Doc. and Cov. 128:13). In the Book of Mormon we are shown how baptism was performed by Alma: "After Alma had said these words, both Alma and Helam were buried in the water; and they arose and came forth out of the water rejoicing" (Mosiah 18:14). In 3 Nephi 11:26 we read: "And then shall ye immerse them in the water, and come forth again out of the water." This is the instruction of our Lord to the Nephites, and He also declares: "And according as I have commanded you thus shall ye baptize. And there shall be no disputations among you" (3 Nephi 11:28).

The Prophet Joseph Smith: "The gospel requires baptism by immersion for the remission of sins, which is the meaning of the word in the original language; namely, to bury, or immerse" (History of the Church, Vol. 5, page 499).

Heber C. Kimball: "If you have a little water sprinkled in your face, poured upon your head, or you kneel in the water, is that baptism? No! you must go and be buried with Christ—be immersed—overwhelmed in the water. This requirement is binding upon all, both high and low . . . And I will say to you, gentlemen and ladies, who have not complied with this, you will have to do so in a day to come, before you can receive an exaltation in the kingdom of God" (Journal of Discourses, Vol. 8, page 210).

B. H. Roberts: "The terms 'buried' and 'planted' are in plain allusion to the manner in which the saints had received the ordinance of baptism, which could not have been by sprinkling or pouring, as there is no burial, or planting, in the likeness of Christ's death, or being raised in the likeness of his resurrection, in that; but in immersion there is (The Gospel, page 185).

Dr. James E. Talmage: "Scriptural authority warrants none other form than immersion" (Articles of Faith, page 141).

This is the doctrine of the Church.

Those who hold that sprinkling and pouring are valid modes of baptism assert that "baptism is washing with water." "By washing," they say, "is meant any such application of water to the body as effects its purification. This may be done by immersion, affusion, or sprinkling." And, in proof of this proposition they argue, in the first place, that the word "baptizo" means, as inferred from its use in classical Greek, the Septuagint, and the New Testament, not only to "immerse," but to "ye," to "gild," to "wet," to "moisten," to "wash," to "pour upon"; secondly, that there is no passage in the New Testament in which "baptism" necessarily implies "immersion," while there are several in which "immersion" is necessarily excluded.

The first of these arguments is mere sophistry. Competent scholarship declares that "baptizo," and "bapto" from which "baptizo" is derived, mean to "dip, to immerse, to plunge in water." Luther: "The term baptism is a Greek word; it may be rendered by 'dipping,' as when we dip anything in water that it may be entirely covered with water." Beza: "Christ commanded us to be baptized; by which word it is certain immersion is signified." John Wesley: "'Buried with Him,' alluding to the ancient manner of baptizing by immersion." Mosheim: "The sacrament of baptism was administered in this [the first] century without the public assemblies, in places appointed and prepared for that purpose, and was performed by immersion of the whole body in the baptismal font." Calvin: "The word 'baptize' signifies to 'immerse,' and the rite of immersion was observed by the ancient church." Vitringa: "The act of baptizing is the immersion of believers in water." Such is the testimony of scholarship, founded upon the use of the words "bapto" and "baptizo," by both secular and sacred authors.    In the classics those words are employed to describe the sinking of ships in the sea; of immersion by crossing rivers, or sinking in swamps; dipping vessels or other objects in a liquid, etc. (The reader who cares to examine this subject further is referred to a paper by Elder Henry Whittal, published in volumes XXI, and XXII, of the *Millennial Star*.)

This, then, is the meaning of the words in question.

But human language is imperfect.    No tongue has a word for every thought, or every shade of thought a man may wish to express, and, therefore, it happens that most words are employed to denote acts, or objects, akin or analogous to, or resembling in some respects those for which they stand originally.    But that does not affect their original meaning.    For instance, to "bathe" means to "wash by immersion," but the poet, nevertheless, speaks of bathing "in the dimples of her cheek." That, however, does not justify the conclusion that "bathing" means "looking at" an object.    If a friend tells us that he "bathed" in the Dead Sea, we do not understand him to say that perhaps he merely had a look at that beautiful sheet of water, for to "bathe" does not mean that, although a poet may with propriety use the word in that sense to express his rapture.    In the same way, "bapto" and "baptizo" may be used to express a number of ideas, such as to "stain," to "gild," to "glaze," to "moisten," to "temper" steel in oil, and even to "imbue," but the original meaning of the words remain, to "dip," to "immerse," to "plunge," and their use to denote the other ideas is justified only because of the resemblance, or fancied resemblance, between the original and secondary meaning.    Thus, when an author says a lake, or a garment, was "baptized" in blood, meaning "stained," he conveys the idea that the stains covered a large area, as if the lake, or garment, had been dipped in blood.    And when the word is used to denote "gilding," "glazing," "tempering," it is needless to say that it refers to the fact that the objects gilded, glazed, or tempered had been entirely covered, as if plunged into the liquid used in each case.    For this is the meaning of the words, no matter what poetical or metaphorical purposes they are made to serve.

The second argument, or the assertion that there are passages in the New Testament in which the idea of immersion is excluded from baptism, is baseless.

For instance, we are told that the three thousand persons who were converted on the day of Pentecost at Jerusalem (Acts 2:41) could not have been baptized by immersion because there were no private baths available for that purpose, and no water close by, in which the multitude could have been baptized in that manner. The same remark is made to apply to the five thousand (Acts 4:4).

But the author of the Acts does not say that the three thousand were baptized all on one day; nor at Jerusalem.   Luke says: "They that gladly received his word were baptized: and the same day there were *added* unto them about three thousand souls" (Acts 2:41). They may have been "added" to the disciples that day, by applying for baptism and placing their names on the records of the church. As to the time when the baptism took place, that is not stated. They were undoubtedly baptized as soon as the opportunity would permit, and if there was not a sufficient quantity of water for the purpose in Jerusalem, or the immediate vicinity, the river Jordan was less than twenty miles to the east, and that to the Jews, who were used to journeys over much longer distances, was not an obstacle. They could walk down to the Jordan in, say, five or six hours. Many of them were visitors at the capital at this time, and would return home by way of Jericho and the Jordan valley. And as for the five thousand (Acts 4:4), they were not baptized in one day. Luke says that was the total number of disciples at the time of the story of the fourth chapter of Acts. They had, of course, been baptized at various times.

There is, therefore, no argument in either of these passages against immersion, and in favor of sprinkling, or affusion.

The assertion is also made that the Ethiopian who was baptized by Philip (Acts 8:38) could not have been immersed, for "he was traveling through a desert part of the country towards Gaza, when Philip joined him," and there is no stream, it is said, in that region of sufficient depth to allow the immersion of a man. But this objection ignores the obvious fact that Philip must have traveled with the Ethiopian a considerable distance before the baptism took place. Philip joined him somewhere near Gaza, but they did not separate there. Thy continued the journey together, for we read: "As they went on their way they came to a certain water" (Acts 8:36). This may have been a place where the road from Gaza southward came close to the shore of the Mediterranean; or Philip may have traveled in company with the Ethiopian as far as the so-called "River of Egypt," at the southern boundary of Palestine, a distance of perhaps fifty miles. It would take that long time to explain the gospel to the Ethiopian. To say that there was no water anywhere between Gaza and Egypt in which to immerse this distinguished convert is an evidence of desperation.

It is generally alleged that the jailer at Philippi and his household were baptized in the jail (Acts 16:33), and that they could not have been immersed. But the narrative shows plainly that the baptism took place outside the building in which the jailer lived, and in one part of which the place of imprisonment perhaps was located; for he took Paul and Silas to some place where he could wash their wounds, after which he and his family were baptized, and then, as is stated, he "brought them into his house" for refreshments. Neither the washing nor the baptism took place in the house, for the simple reason that immersion was necessary for the sacred rite, if not for the washing of the wounds.

We are told that the presumption against immersion is still stronger in Mark 7:4, where it is said that the Pharisees do not eat except they "wash" (baptize) themselves, and that they "wash" cups, pots, and tables. Are we, it is asked, to believe that the Pharisees immersed themselves before each meal, when they came from the market; or that they washed their tables as well as their cups and pots by immersion?

The fact is that the Jews, who, like all Orientals, used their fingers as we use knives and forks, washed their hands before meals, and between courses, for obvious reasons; that was "washing themselves," just as we say that we wash ourselves, when we lave our hands and faces. But besides this washing they had a ceremonial cleansing. In the former, water was poured on their hands; in the latter their hands were immersed in the water. The disciples did not observe "the traditions of the elders" (Mark 7:3.) That is, they neglected the ceremonial purifications, but certainly not common cleanliness. Concerning the "washing" mentioned in the fourth verse, the following comment appears in the Cambridge Bible: " 'Wash' here implies complete immersion as contrasted with the mere washing of the hands in verse 3." It should be said, further, in this connection, that the word which in the New Testament signifies Christian baptism (baptisma) is not used for the ceremonial washings of the Jews. This word is "baptismos," and there is about the same difference between them as between "petra" (a rock) and "petros" (a piece of rock). "The very use of the two similar words seems intended to mark off the Christian rite of baptism as separate and unique" (*Helps to the Study of the Bible,* page 362). At all events, it is not safe to apply conclusions drawn from the ceremonial washings of the Pharisees to the baptism instituted by our Lord.

It is, finally, alleged that when New Testament writers speak about baptism of the Spirit, immersion is excluded, since the Holy Spirit is a person. But the same argument would exclude both sprinkling and pouring, since a person can neither be sprinkled nor poured out. Matthew, Mark, Luke, John, Paul, all speak of baptism "in" Holy Spirit (Matt. 3:11; Mark 1:8, John 1:33; Acts 1:5, I Cor. 12:13; in all of which passages the Greek preposition is "in," not "with," or "by"). And they mean just what they say. On the day of Pentecost the Holy Spirit "filled all the house" where the disciples were assembled, and they were, consequently, immersed in it and filled with it, as completely as we are immersed in the air we breathe. It was a true baptism in Spirit. The same miracle was repeated in the house of Cornelius, and it is repeated whenever two or three come together in the name of the Lord, when the divine Presence is manifested.

The Scriptures tell us that John baptized at a place where there was "much water" (John 3:23); that those who were baptized went into the water and came up "out of the water" (Matt. 3.16; Acts 8:38, 39); that Israel passing through the Red Sea, with water on both sides and the cloud hiding the people completely, from the Egyptians, were "baptized in the cloud and the sea" (I. Cor. 10:1, 2). No clearer illustration of baptism could be given.

We have seen now that the Scriptures employ a word meaning "immersion" for "baptism," and "immerse" for "baptize"; that this is the only mode of performing that ordinance which corresponds to that which it signifies, viz., a burial and resurrection, and that the main objections to that understanding of the sacred ordinance are without basis in fact. We therefore reiterate: There is only one mode of baptism, and there can be no other, and that is complete submersion.

## CHAPTER 32

*The Doctrine of Christ Concerning the Holy Ghost, 1-6—An Exhortation to Prayer, 7-9.*

### 1. *The Doctrine of Christ Concerning the Holy Ghost.*

1. And now, behold, my beloved brethren, I suppose that ye ponder somewhat in your hearts concerning that which ye should do after ye have entered in by the way. But, behold, why do ye ponder these things in your hearts?

2. Do ye not remember that I said unto you that after ye had received the Holy Ghost ye could speak with the tongue of angels? And now, how could ye speak with the tongue of angels save it were by the Holy Ghost?

3. Angels speak by the power of the Holy Ghost; wherefore, they speak the words of Christ. Wherefore, I said unto you, feast upon the words of Christ; for behold, the words of Christ will tell you all things what ye should do.

4. Wherefore, now after I have spoken these words, if ye cannot understand them it will be because ye ask not, neither do ye knock; wherefore, ye are not brought into the light, but must perish in the dark.

5. For behold, again I say unto you that if ye will enter in by the way, and receive the Holy Ghost, it will show unto you all things what ye should do.

6. Behold, this is the doctrine of Christ, and there will be no more doctrine given until after he shall manifest himself unto you in the flesh. And when he shall manifest himself unto you in the flesh, the things which he shall say unto you shall ye observe to do.

---

In the preceding chapter, Nephi has stated the doctrine of Christ concerning baptism. In this he sets forth, briefly, the doctrine of the Master concerning the Holy Ghost.

VERSE 2. *The Tongue of Angels.* One who has received the Holy Ghost can speak "with the tongue of angels." For, after all, angels, too, speak the words of Christ, as dictated to them by the Holy Ghost. In 2 Ne. 31:14 the "tongue of angels" is called a "new" tongue, and so it is, because it is different from the speech of one who is not guided by the holy Spirit. Men and women of the world are known by their conversation, and so are the Saints. In 1 Cor. 13:1 "tongues of angels seems to mean superhuman eloquence, but "tongues" the Apostle says, are but "sounding brass or a tinkling cymbal," if they are without love.

VERSES 4-5. *The Holy Ghost Will Show You All Things.* This is the special mission of the Holy Spirit. (John 16:13-15; 1 Ne. 10:17-19.)

VERSE 6. *The Doctrine of Christ.* This, Nephi says, is the doctrine of Christ. Further revelations on this subject may be looked for when the Lord himself appears. (See 1 Ne. 12:6-8; 3 Ne. 11:3-17)

## 2. *An Exhortation to Prayer.*

7. And now I, Nephi, cannot say more; the Spirit stoppeth mine utterance, and I am left to mourn because of the unbelief, and the wickedness, and the ignorance, and the stiffneckedness of men; for they will not search knowledge, nor understand great knowledge, when it is given unto them in plainness, even as plain as word can be.

8. And now, my beloved brethren, I perceive that ye ponder still in your hearts; and it grieveth me that I must speak concerning this thing. For if ye would heark-en unto the Spirit which teacheth a man to pray ye would know that ye must pray; for the evil spirit teacheth not a man to pray, but teacheth him that he must not pray.

9. But behold, I say unto you that ye must pray always, and not faint; that ye must not perform any thing unto the Lord save in the first place ye shall pray unto the Father in the name of Christ, that he will consecrate thy performance unto thee, that thy performance may be for the welfare of thy soul.

VERSE 7. *The Spirit Stoppeth Mine Utterance.* Here Nephi feels prompted to cease speaking. One who is guided by the Spirit is always conscious of the proper time to quit as well as to begin. And so Nephi brings his comments to a close by an exhortation to pray always.

VERSE 9. *Ye Must Pray Always.* Prayer has been defined as the direct approach of man to God, to make requests or to commune. Prayers, says Dr. John A. Widtsoe, the Apostle, are always heard and always answered, even if not as we expect. To arise from prayer, refreshed in spirit, is of itself an answer. Dr. Widtsoe recommends regular times of prayer in the household, if possible. It might be well, he says, to pray with the family just before the family meal, when most members of the family are present. (Program of The Church of Jesus Christ of Latter-day Saints, p. 119.)

*Family Prayer.* If there were more family prayers, there would be an increased disposition in the home to overlook and forgive such little failings as are common to weak mortals; there would be greater unity in the home and fewer divorces to curse the community; children would have more respect for the parents; the ties of love would be stronger, and there would be few prodigal sons and daughters and less crime; there would be better health, increased contentment and prosperity, because of more general observance of the Word of Wisdom and the law of tithing and fast offerings.

*Personal Prayers.* But family prayers do not, and are not intended to, take the place of private devotion. As is well known, our Lord says on that subject: "But thou, when thou prayest, enter into thine inner chamber, and having shut thy door, pray to thy Father, which is in secret and thy Father which seeth in secret, shall recompense thee." Every human being is exposed to temptations and has weaknesses which should prompt to private prayer; perhaps to confession, and humble petitions for pardon, and for increased power of resistance—which can be of no possible interest to anybody else. Frequent private prayer is the telephone message to our heavenly home. It is best sent in a booth secluded from the noise and confusion of a busy world.

*Public Prayers.* And then there are the meetings for public devotion. To attend them is a duty we owe to the community in which they are held. The Apostle Paul warns against the habit of "forsaking the assembling ourselves together, as the custom of some is." If that example were followed generally, public assemblies for devotion would dwindle away, and the community would lose their influence for morality and spiritual activity.

The common excuse for lack of interest in religious meetings is that there is nothing to learn by attending them. "You hear the same thing over and over again."

That criticism is, of course, a not infrequent estimate of the average sermon. Whether it is justified or not depends largely on the frame of mind of the critic. But the sermon is not the only part of the service. Perhaps not even the most essential. The presence of our Savior, in his Holy Spirit, as on the day of Pentecost, wherever two or three are gathered in his name; the sacrament, in which our covenants with the Lord are renewed; the inspiring songs of joy and praise, the prayers and thanksgivings and devotion, are the essential features of Christian divine services. They are as necessary to a healthy spiritual life as a pure atmosphere is to the vigor of the body. Men and women must have companionship. Frequently those who forsake the congregations of the Church join secular organizations with questionable objects and activities.

Still, the sermon is an important part of the divine service. The speaker who accepts the call to occupy the pulpit has a great responsibility. As a messenger from God he must have a message to deliver to the congregation. He must not regard the rostrum as a place from which to exhibit real or supposed talents; still less as a platform on which to practice public speaking, which can be done more properly in the family circle, at the time of the family devotion. Enlightened by the Holy Spirit, he will regard the pulpit as a banqueting table from which to distribute the bread of life abundantly, not in the form of stale crusts nor as half-baked dough, but in delicious loaves, fresh from the glowing embers on the altar of private meditation and fervent prayers.

## GENERAL NOTES

An anecdote is told about Martin Luther. It is said that he on one occasion was asked to examine a young candidate for the pulpit, to ascertain his qualifications for the ministry, and that the first question the venerable leader of Protestantism asked was: "What do you know about the devil?"

Many a shaft of sarcasm has been aimed at the immortal Wittenberg professor, ex-friar and author of, "On the Babylonish Captivity of the Church," on account of this seeming overestimation of the importance of the role of Satan in the world. But Luther was right. No one can successfully combat the evil influences at work who knows nothing about them; or who underestimates their power.

\* \* \*

The sacred Scriptures everywhere teach the personality of the adversary of the Son of God. Here, in the Book of Nephi, he is said to be stirring up the children of men to hostility against that which is good. It is said that, unless they escape by repentance, he will drive them, as prisoner in chains, to destruction. Some he will lead enchanted with siren songs about all being well, although death lurks on either side, Scylla and Charybdis. Others he convinces that there is no personal evil angel, no place where he reigns, while he is taking them to the region from which there is no deliverance. (2 Ne. 28:22, 23)

\* \* \*

Our Lord, during his earthly mission, recognized the existence of the adversary. He recognized his power, when he spoke of him as "the prince of this world" (John 12:31; 14:30, 16:11). Which means not only that he exists, but that he wields immense influence in the world. It means, in fact, that his power is so great that St. Paul can consistently call him, "the god of this world" (2 Cor. 4:4). That this is not merely a figure of speech appears from the fact that he is also described as the "prince of the power of the air" (Eph. 2:22), which can only mean that, if God permitted him, he could, by his intelligence and resources, engage the forces of nature to the injury of men.

The story of Job confirms this thought. In that magnificent drama, he causes not only the Sabacans to slay the servants of the patriarch (Job 1:15), but also the lightning to strike his flocks, together with the shepherds (v. 16). He makes the Chaldeans kill the camels and their keepers, and he directs a cyclone to destroy the house in which the children of Job are feasting, burying them in the debris (17-19). And, finally, Satan, having obtained divine permission, attacked Job himself with "boils" that covered the entire body (2:1-8).

In his encounter with our Lord immediately after the baptism of the Holy One, Satan claimed ownership of the world and offered it to him as a reward for joining his worshipers—a proposition which the Son of God has had rejected long before, when the great apostasy in heaven took place (Pearl of Great P., Mor. 4:1-2; or Ab. 3:27) But when he said to Jesus: "To thee will I give all this authority and the glory of them; for it hath been delivered unto me, and to whomsoever I will give it." (Luke 4:1), he did not speak the truth; for no part of the earth belongs legally to him; much less the entire world. And yet, our Lord recognized his immense importance, when he said: "If Satan is divided against himself, how shall his kingdom stand?" (Luke 11:18.) Judging from Scripture passages, Satan has always endeavored to obtain control over men by means of their own organizations, religious, political and social. And so we read of his "throne" (Rev. 2:13); his "synagogue" (Rev. 3:9); and "world-rulers of darkness" (Eph. 6:12), etc. In Daniel 10:13, 20, it appears that rulers of kingdoms sometimes are on the side of Satan, and that Michael, the archangel, still is actively engaged against him.

Yes, he has great power in the world. But he can never obtain possession of anyone that does not surrender voluntarily. "Resist the devil, and he will flee from you." (James 4:7) Read the remarkable story in the Pearl of Great Price, Moses 1:18-22, where Satan is said to have fled from Moses, weeping and wailing, because he could not persuade the great prophet to join him in rebellion.

Hurl your inkstand in his face, as Luther is said to have done at Wartburg, if you have no other weapon handy. He fears and hates the written as well as spoken word of God. And so do his servants.

## THE OFFICE OF THE HOLY GHOST

According to the Word of God, those who have repented and received baptism have the assurance that the gift of the Holy Ghost will be bestowed upon them. Peter, speaking on behalf of the Divine Master, said to the converts on the day of Pentecost: "Repent, and be baptized . . . and ye shall receive the gift of the Holy Ghost" (Acts 2:38). Ananias was sent to Saul with the message of salvation, in order that he might be "filled with the Holy Ghost," as well as receive his sight (Acts 9:6). The apostles, though instructed and given authority to preach and baptize in the name of the Lord, were not fully equipped for the ministry until they had received the power of the Holy Spirit for themselves and to impart to those who should believe through their word. For that reason the Master commanded them to wait in Jerusalem, for the fulfilment of "the promise of the Father, which, saith he, ye have heard of me" (Acts 1:4). Then He ascended. It was, as He had previously explained to them (John 16:7), necessary that He should "go away," for, "if I go not away, the Comforter will not come unto you." Just why the gift of the Spirit could not be bestowed until our Lord had departed, we may not comprehend; but it was so, in accordance with the pre-arranged plan of salvation. Our Lord completed His mission by ascending to His Father, and then He sent the Comforter with power from on high.

This outpouring of the Holy Spirit was foretold by the prophets of old, for it was as necessary as the atonement for the establishment of the kingdom of God. God says through Joel: "And it shall come to pass afterward that I will pour out my Spirit upon all flesh (Joel 2:28); and Zechariah undoubtedly refers to the same glorious manifestation of the divine Presence in these words: "And I will pour upon the house of David, and upon the inhabitants of Jerusalem, the spirit of grace and of supplications" (Zech. 12:10).

The same promises for the gift of the Spirit have been given in our day (Doc. and Cov. 33:15, 39:23, and many other places).

The pouring out of the gift of the Holy Ghost is frequently spoken of as "baptism." John the Baptist told the multitudes on the banks of the Jordan: "He that cometh after me . . . shall baptize you with the Holy Ghost and with fire" (Matt. 3:11; John 1:33). In the Book of Mormon the same expression occurs. For "Behold, then shall ye receive the Holy Ghost; yea, then cometh the baptism of fire and the Holy Ghost (2 Ne. 31:13). "Whoso cometh unto me with a broken heart and a contrite spirit, him will I baptize with fire and with the Holy Ghost" (3 Ne. 9.20).

The question has been asked. How can the Holy Spirit be "poured out"? Or, how can baptism be performed in Holy Spirit? Who, or what, is the Holy Spirit?

The Holy Spirit, or the Holy Ghost, is, in the first place, a person, or personage, though not dwelling in a tabernacle as tangible as that of the Father, or the Son (Doc. and Cov. 130:22). As a person he is one with the Father and the Son, and the three "constitute the great, matchless, governing and supreme power over all things; by whom all things were created and made that were created and made, and these three constitute the Godhead, and are one" (Lectures on Faith 5:2). It would be inconsistent and meaningless to speak of the "outpouring" of the *person* of the Holy Spirit, or baptism *in* a person.

But the Holy Spirit is also something which we, for lack of better terms, may characterize as energy, a force, a power, an influence, which proceedeth from the Godhead and fills the universe, both the visible and invisible, as David says: "Whither shall I go from thy Spirit? or whither shall I flee from thy presence? If I ascend up into heaven, thou art there: if I make my bed in hell, behold, thou art there. If I take the wings of the morning, and dwell in the uttermost parts of the sea; even there shall thy hand lead me, and thy right hand shall hold me. If I say, Surely the darkness shall cover me; even the night shall be light about me. Yea, the darkness hideth not from thee; but the night shineth as the day: the darkness and the light are both alike to thee" (Psalm 139:7-12). This energy, this influence, can be poured out; the inner man can be immersed in it as the body in the waters of baptism.

It is necessary to make this distinction between the Holy Ghost as a person, and the omnipresent, divine Influence. Careful writers and speakers of the Church observe this difference.

The Prophet Joseph Smith says "There is a difference between the Holy Ghost and the gift of the Holy Ghost. Cornelius received the Holy Ghost before he was baptized, which was the convincing power of God unto him of the truth of the gospel, but he could not receive the gift of the Holy Ghost until after he was baptized. Had he not taken this sign, or ordinance, upon him, the Holy Ghost, which convinced him of the truth of God, would have left him" (*History of the Church*, Vol. 4, page 555).

The Holy Ghost personally, as it were, opened the door through which the gospel message should be delivered to the Gentile world, by pouring out upon those in the house of Cornelius a portion of the power and influence which enabled them to accept the truth, speak with tongues, and magnify God. But the full measure of this divine gift came after baptism and the laying on of hands; otherwise, baptism in water would have been superfluous. The Prophet Joseph Smith again observes: "Until he [Cornelius] obeyed these ordinances and received the gift of the Holy Ghost, by the laying on of hands, according to the order of God, he could not have healed the sick or commanded an evil spirit to come out of a man."

Doctor James E. Talmage makes the distinction between the Holy Ghost as a person and an influence, as follows: "The term Holy Ghost and its common synonyms, Spirit of God, Spirit of the Lord, or simply, Spirit, Comforter, and Spirit of Truth, occur in the scriptures with plainly different meanings, referring in some cases to the person of God, the Holy Ghost, and in other instances to the power or authority of this great Being. The context of such passages will show which of these significations applies . . . Much of the confusion existing in our human conceptions concerning the nature of the Holy Ghost, arises from the common failure to segregate our ideas of His person and powers" (*Articles of Faith,* pages 164, 165).

President Joseph F. Smith, in a discourse delivered in the Tabernacle, Salt Lake City, on March 16, 1902, said in regard to this subject: "The question is often asked, Is there any difference between the Spirit of the Lord and the Holy Ghost? The terms are frequently used synonymously. We often say the Spirit of God when we mean the Holy Ghost; we likewise say the Holy Ghost when we mean the Spirit of God. The Holy Ghost is a personage in the Godhead, and is not that which lighteth every man that comes into the world. It is the Spirit of God which proceeds through Christ to the world, that enlightens every man that comes into the world, and that strives with the children of men, and will continue to strive with them, until it brings them to a knowledge of the truth and the possession of the greater light and testimony of the Holy Ghost" (Quoted by B. H. Roberts, *The Mormon Doctrine of the Deity,* page 288).

Orson Pratt, speaking of the Holy Spirit, as distinct from the person of the Holy Ghost, says: "When I speak of the Holy Spirit, I speak of it as being a substance that is precisely the same in its attributes as those of the Father and Son; I speak of it as being a substance that is diffused throughout space, the same as oxygen is in pure water or air. . . . This light, then, recollect, is so universally diffused, that it giveth light to all things. This is the same light that governs all things, and it is called 'the power of God.' . . . It is this same spirit that acts in connection with the Father and Son in governing all things in the heavens and upon the earth, and through all the boundless extent of space. Cause this oneness, this union, among the particles of the Spirit, to cease, and you would soon see all things go into confusion. Take away this Spirit, and you would immediately see some things going up, others down; some moving horizontally; one portion of the earth would divide from the other; one part would be flying here and another there. . . . Portions of this Spirit, we say, exist throughout every part of space, and they perform all the work of governing and keeping that perfect harmony which we behold in all nature. All nature is by these means made to submit to the great law of oneness" (*Journal of Discourses,* Vol. 2, pp. 337, 339, 340, 341).

This thought is expressed in the Doctrine and Covenants as follows: "And the light which now shineth, which giveth you light, is through him who enlightened your eyes, which is the same light that quickeneth your understandings, which light proceedeth forth from the presence of God to fill the immensity of space. The light which is in all things; which giveth life to all things: which is the law by which all things are governed: even the power of God who sitteth upon his throne, who is in the bosom of eternity, who is in the midst of all things" (Doc. and Cov. 88:11-13). And again: "He comprehendeth all things, and all things are before him, and all things are round about him: and he is above all things, and in all things, and is through all things, and is round about all things; and all things are by him, and of him, even God, for ever and ever" (Doc. and Cov. 88:41).[1]

When the reception of the Holy Spirit, or the gift of the Spirit, is compared to baptism, it is, as already observed, this power, this influence, this light which is meant by the term "Spirit."

Human language is but imperfect, and it is doubtful whether there is another word expressive of the true nature of this divine element. Orson Pratt calls it a "substance." We may, with Dr. Talmage, refer to it as a "power," or an influence, or as some authors do, call it "light," or couple it with the term "fire." And it is all this. But it is also much more. It is "Holy Spirit"—a substance, an influence, a power, a light, a "fire," that proceeds from the Godhead, and permeates everything; an element in which "we live, and move, and have our being" (Acts 17:28). It is the glory of God, the manifestation of the divine presence; the "fire and smoke" which made Sinai tremble and which consumed those who came near without bearing the priesthood; the glory which rested on the Mercy seat in the Tabernacle; the "wind" which filled the house on the day of Pentecost, and the flames over the heads of the disciples. It is divine intelligence, since "the glory of God is intelligence" (Doc. and Cov. 93:36). It is the force before which mountains flee and worlds perish; for, "the presence of the Lord shall be as the melting fire that burneth, and as the fire which causeth the waters to boil" (Doc. and Cov. 133:41). There is no better word for this omnipresent, divine power than "Holy Spirit."

When a person has received baptism in Holy Spirit, the presence of this divine intelligence, this energy, is manifested in various ways.

Through it the believer is enabled to *know* that Jesus is the Christ, the Messiah, the promised Redeemer of the world, and the Son of God, just as surely as he knows, through the testimony of his senses, that the world exists and that he is part of it. This no man can know except by the "Holy Ghost" (I Cor. 12:3); that is, except he has the baptism in "Holy Spirit," for so the verse may be rendered: "No one speaking *in* God's Spirit says that Jesus is accursed; and no one can say Jesus is Lord except in Holy Spirit." Truth and knowledge depend upon

[1]Philosophers should, perhaps, be cautioned against going too far beyond the revealed word. One of the early speakers of the Church came to the conclusion that every particle of the Spirit is in itself all powerful and all wise, full of intelligence and possessing all the attributes of God—a mere philosophical speculation, which Brigham Young, in a public discourse, characterized as incorrect. To quote: "Brother ............ was upon this same theory once, and in conversation with Brother Joseph Smith advanced the idea that eternity or boundless space was filled with the Spirit of God, or the Holy Ghost. After portraying his views upon that theory very carefully and minutely, he asked Brother Joseph what he thought of it. He replied that it appeared very beautiful, and that he did not know of but one serious objection to it. Says the brother, 'What is that?' Joseph replied, 'It is not true' " (*Journal of Discourses,* vol. 4, p. 266.) The omnipresence of God's Spirit is a truth clearly revealed, but if we go beyond that revelation we are apt to become lost in speculation.

this divine outpouring in the soul. In the same chapter (verse 13) we read, translated literally, "For *in* one Spirit are we all baptized into one body . . . and have been all given to drink, into one Spirit." The Spirit, therefore, becomes part of every believer, as a member of the body of the Church of Christ, just as the spirit of man is indwelling in every part of the natural body. It is a possession guaranteed by the covenant into which he has entered, and which remains with him as long as he is faithful to that covenant, for enlightenment and knowledge concerning the things of God.

Some of the effects of the Spirit may be enumerated. "The fruit of the Spirit," Paul says, "is love, joy, peace, longsuffering, gentleness, goodness, faith, meekness, temperance" (Gal. 5:22, 23). Another effort of the gift of the Spirit is liberty; for, "Where the Spirit of the Lord is, there is liberty" (II Cor. 3:17). There is freedom from the bondage of the Mosaic laws and statutes which were enacted for the temporary guidance of the people of God during the period of minority. There is also free access to the Mercy Seat, which ancient Israel could approach only through a representative.

Through the Spirit we enter into an actual experience of divine sonship. We learn to say with full confidence, "Abba Father!" and have the testimony of the Spirit, that, " if [we are] children, then heirs; heirs of God, and joint heirs with Christ" (Rom. 8:16, 17)—not servants in the house of the Father, but heirs.

This confidence is sometimes spoken of as the "assurance" of faith, as different from the timid confession: "Lord, I believe; help thou mine unbelief." Because of this assurance Paul says: "We . . . rejoice in hope of the glory of God. . . . because the love of God is shed abroad in our hearts by the Holy Ghost which is given unto us" (Rom. 5:2-5). And John says: "He that believeth on the Son of God hath the witness in himself" (I John 5:10), which accords with Rom. 8:16: "The Spirit itself beareth witness with our spirit, that we are the children of God."

The Spirit enables us to pray. It "helpeth our infirmities: for we know not what we should pray for as we ought: but the Spirit itself maketh intercession for us with groanings which cannot be uttered. And he that searcheth the hearts knoweth what is the mind of the Spirit, because he maketh intercession for the saints according to the will of God" (Rom. 8:26, 27). "And it shall come to pass that he that asketh in Spirit shall receive in Spirit" (Doc. and Cov. 46:28).

Through the Spirit we become one with Christ and one with each other, "for intelligence cleaveth unto intelligence." (Doc. and Cov. 88:40), and our Lord prays: "That they may be one, even as we are one: I in them, and thou in me, that they may be made perfect in one" (John 17:22, 23).

These are fruits of the Spirit, common to all who have been endowed with "power from on high." But there are also special gifts "For to one is given by the Spirit the word of wisdom; to another the word of knowledge by the same Spirit; to another faith by the same Spirit; to another the gifts of healing by the same Spirit; to another the working of miracles; to another prophecy; to another discerning of spirits; to another divers kinds of tongues; to another the interpretation of tongues; but all these worketh that one and the selfsame Spirit" (I Cor. 12:4-11). Of Bezaleel the Lord said: "I have filled him with the Spirit of God to work in gold, and in silver, and in brass" (Exodus 31:3, 4). In the like manner Moses, and after him the Judges, were qualified by special gifts of the Spirit for their work, and so were the prophets, from Samuel to Malachi. The Brother of Jared, had, in the highest degree, the gift of performing miracles. Moroni tells us that he spoke to Mount Zerin, and it was removed (Ether 12:30). Nephi, Alma, Moroni, and, in our own day and generation, the Prophet Joseph Smith, and his successors, and associates have been qualified for their work by the same Spirit.

By that Spirit man became a "living soul"—a class different from the animals. Job says, the inspiration of the Almighty giveth men understanding; that is, reason and intelligence, for we read: He "teaches us more than the beasts of the earth" (Job 35:11). But it is especially the source of all spiritual life.

Finally, as this Spirit is the source of knowledge and truth, and spiritual power, so it is also the medium through which the resurrection and the quickening of our mortal bodies will be effected. Paul tells us (Rom. 8:11): "If the Spirit of him that raised up Jesus from the dead dwell in you, he that raised up Christ from the dead shall also quicken your mortal bodies by his Spirit that dwelleth in you." This verse is rather obscure, but the meaning seems to be that, if we have within us the Spirit of God, who brought our Savior's body out of the grave, then He who raised up Christ, as the head and representative of His people, shall quicken our mortal bodies by His Spirit that dwelleth in us. And thus not only the saints who are dead at the coming of Christ, but also those who live at that time, shall be quickened by the Spirit (I Thess. 4:14-17), and meet the Lord in His coming.

As has been stated, laying on of hands is the ordinance by which the gift of the Holy Spirit is imparted. But it must be performed by one having authority to do so.

## CHAPTER 33

*A Last Word of the Prophet Nephi — His Anxiety for the Salvation of the World.*

### 1. *Not Mighty in Writing like unto Speaking.*

1. And now I, Nephi, cannot write all the things which were taught among my people; neither am I mighty in writing, like unto speaking; for when a man speaketh by the power of the Holy Ghost the power of the Holy Ghost carrieth it unto the hearts of the children of men.

2. But behold, there are many that harden their hearts against the Holy Spirit, that it hath no place in them; wherefore, they cast many things away which are written and esteem them as things of naught.

3. But I, Nephi, have written what I have written, and I esteem it as of great worth, and especially unto my people. For I pray continually for them by day, and mine eyes water my pillow by night, because of them; and I cry unto my God in faith, and I know that he will hear my cry.

4. And I know that the Lord God will consecrate my prayers for the gain of my people. And the words which I have written in weakness will be made strong unto them; for it persuadeth them to do good; it maketh known unto them of their fathers; and it speaketh of Jesus, and persuadeth them to believe in him, and to endure to the end, which is life eternal.

5. And it speaketh harshly against sin, according to the plainness of the truth; wherefore, no man will be angry at the words which I have written save he shall be of the spirit of the devil.

6. I glory in plainness; I glory in truth; I glory in my Jesus, for he hath redeemed my soul from hell.

7. I have charity for my people, and great faith in Christ that I shall meet many souls spotless at his judgment-seat.

8. I have charity for the Jew— I say Jew, because I mean them from whence I came.

9. I also have charity for the Gentiles. But behold, for none of these can I hope except they shall be reconciled unto Christ, and enter into the narrow gate, and walk in the straight path which leads to life, and continue

Nephi, standing at the border line of the great Hereafter, opens his heart to his people, as, perhaps, never before.

*Imperfection Confessed.* First, his own laboriously executed work passes before him, and he finds it imperfect in high degree. In all humility he confesses its defects (v. 1). At the same time he finds consolation in the fact that he has written under the inspiration of the Holy Spirit (vv. 2, 3), and that he has consecrated his work by constant prayers and supplications (v. 4), and warning against sin (v. 5). This makes him feel to sing for joy (v. 6).

in the path until the end of the day of probation.

10. And now, my beloved brethren, and also Jew, and all ye ends of the earth hearken unto these words and believe in Christ; and if ye believe not in these words believe in Christ. And if ye shall believe in Christ ye will believe in these words, for they are the words of Christ, and he hath given them unto me; and they teach all men that they should do good.

11. And if they are not the words of Christ, judge ye—for Christ will show unto you, with power and great glory, that they are his words, at the last day; and you and I shall stand face to face before his bar; and ye shall know that I have been commanded of him to write these things, notwithstanding my weakness.

12. And I pray the Father in the name of Christ that many of us, if not all, may be saved in his kingdom at that great and last day.

13. And now, my beloved brethren, all those who are of the house of Israel, and all ye ends of the earth, I speak unto you as the voice of one crying from the dust: Farewell until that great day shall come.

14. And you that will not partake of the goodness of God, and respect the words of the Jews, and also my words, and the words which shall proceed forth out of the mouth of the Lamb of God, behold, I bid you an everlasting farewell, for these words shall condemn you at the last day.

15. For what I seal on earth, shall be brought against you at the judgment bar; for thus hath the Lord commanded me, and I must obey. Amen.

---

*This Clears the Atmosphere,* and the outlook becomes brighter. He loves his people and knows that many of them will stand spotless before the judgment seat (v. 7). He loves the Jews, the people whence he came (v. 8). He loves the Gentiles who have accepted Christ as their Redeemer (v. 9). He assures all, Jews and Gentiles, that if they believe in Christ, they will also believe the words which he (Nephi) has written; for, he says, they are the words of Christ; and his prayer for all is that we may be saved in the kingdom of Christ at the last day. (vv. 10-12).

To believers in Christ he says: "Farewell until that great day shall come." (v. 13)

To unbelievers: "I bid you an everlasting Farewell, for these words shall condemn you at the last day. (v. 14) For what I seal on earth"—meaning, what he had written—"shall be brought against you at the judgment bar." (v. 15)

I do not know that we can do better than close this study with verse 6, as the last word of Nephi. They express his lovely character to perfection:

> "I glory in plainness;
> I glory in truth;
> I glory in Jesus,
> For he hath redeemed my soul from Sheol."

## THE PROPHET ISAIAH

*Isaiah in the Book of Mormon.* As is well known, there are no less than 18 chapters of the Book of Isaiah in the Book of Mormon. That is a considerable part of the prophetic record.

In the First Book of Nephi we have chapters 48 and 49. Part of the 49th chapter is also quoted in the Second Book of Nephi, in the account of the Teachings of Jacob (2 Nephi 6:6, 7, 16-18). Is. 50 and 51 are also quoted by Jacob (2 Ne. 7 and 8).

Is. 2 to 14 are quoted by Nephi (2 Ne. 12 to 24).

Is. 53 is quoted by Abinadi as part of his address to the priests of Noah. (Mos. 14)

Whether this order of the chapters is an indication of the order in which they appeared on the plates of Laban, which Nephi had, we have no means of knowing. It might pay scholarship to look into that question from a Book-of-Mormon point of view. That the original chronological order has been upset in the Hebrew manuscripts, is not impossible.

*Who was Isaiah?* He was the son of one Amoz and he is said to have prophesied during the reigns of Uzziah, Jotham, Ahaz and Hezekiah, kings of Judah. (Isa. 1:1) One tradition has it that he was put to death during the reign of Manasseh, son of Hezekiah. It is supposed that his prophetic activities fell during the period of 758-690 B.C. That would make him a contemporary of Hosea, Micah, and Nahum. It would bring him quite close to the time of Lehi, who left Jerusalem in the year 600 B.C.

*The Policy of Isaiah.* The Jews, at the time of this prophet, came in contact with questions relating to world politics, through the movements of the Assyrians toward the Mediterranean, and the countermovements of the Medes and other nations. Uzziah, following the demand of militarists, built fortresses and heaped up war implements, as a matter of safety against invaders. King Ahaz, not confident of the military strength of the kingdom, thought it better to pay tribute and trust in the generosity of the Assyrians. Others sought political expedients, as unworthy of the people of Jehovah. He assured them that the only guaranty of safety was implicit trust in God and obedience to his commandments. Hezekiah followed this sound advice, and the Lord took charge of the defense of the city of Jerusalem against the Assyrians. (Is. 37:35-38)

*Fate of Isaiah.* The tradition that regards the beginning of the reign of Manasseh as the time in which the prophetic activities of Isaiah came to an end, avers that the prophet was condemned to death because he rebuked the apostate king and predicted the destruction of Jerusalem and the temple by the Babylonians.

*Further Particulars About Isaiah.* The prophet was married to a "prophetess" and he had at least two sons, Shear-Jashub (meaning, "the remnant shall return") Is. 7:3, and Maher-shalal-hash-baz (meaning, "making speed to the spoil he hasteneth the prey") Is. 8:1. During the reign of Hezekiah, he was highly respected. That he wielded considerable influence in the state is evident from the fact that he caused Sheba, who plotted with the Egyptians, to be removed from the office he held.

As a prophet, Isaiah foresaw the apostasy of the nation and the destruction of the city and temple by the Babylonians. But to him this was not the end; it was not the *ragnorok.* It was rather a change of seasons. The land would not remain desolate for ever, parched by the burning sun and swept by torrid blasts. The dry season would have an end and be followed by the early rains and a complete resurrection of the apparently dead kingdom of Judah; and not only that, but he saw a new-born world, glorified under the rule of Jehovah. It is only when we understand the outlook of Isaiah upon the development of the world, that we can understand his wonderful prophecies.

*The Book of Isaiah.* The Prophet Isaiah, as already stated, delivered his prophecies during a period of many years. The same is true of other prophets. Each discourse was no doubt recorded in substance at the time it was delivered, by whoever performed the duties of the secretary of the prophet at the time. By and by there was a number of discourses, and when it became desirable to gather them into one volume, or roll, for the benefit of the friends of the prophet at home, or for the people abroad, as for instance those in the Assyrian captivity, or for the benefit of coming generations, or for any other purpose, the first selection, collation, arrangement and editing were, naturally, done under the direction of the prophet himself.

This is not mere assumption. The events recorded in the 36th chapter of Jeremiah, the great prophet who lived about seventy years after Isaiah, illustrate this plausible explanation of the origin of the prophetic books.

It was during the reign of King Jehoiakim, whom the Egyptian Pharaoh Necho had placed on the throne of the kingdom of Judah. The defeat of the Egyptians in Syria and the consequent fall of Judah were drawing near. Then, the Lord commanded Jeremiah to take a "roll of a book" and "write therein all the words that I have spoken unto thee against Judah, and against all the nations, from the day I spake unto thee, from the days of Josiah, even unto this day." The prophet immediately called Baruch to be his secretary, and this able scribe wrote down the words of the Lord as dictated by Jeremiah. This, then, was the procedure.

The roll as completed was presented to the king. It was meant to be a warning to him and to all the Jews. But Jehoiakim, after having heard a few pages, became enraged and threw the entire manuscript into the fire, where it was completely destroyed. Later, Jeremiah was commanded by the Lord to take another roll and "write in it all the former words that were in the first roll." He did so, "and there were added besides unto them many like words." (Jer. 36:1-4, 20-23, 27, 32)

It is evident that the prophet had the written material on hand from which he could have copies made whenever needed, and that copies were made when required. In such copies the chronological arrangement would not be observed, if some other principle of classification were considered more effective for the purpose in view. Prophecies of other prophets may have been incorporated in the text as proofs or confirmation of the truths conveyed. Diversities of style may have crept in, owing to the difference in education and natural gifts and endowments of various scribes employed.

*The Unity of the Book.* This is a much discussed subject. The argument started when, toward the end of the 18th century, someone expressed doubts regarding the authorship of the 50th chapter of the book. Soon learned men suggested that the entire latter section, chapters 40-66, must have been written by an unknown author whom they proposed to call the Second Isaiah, (Deutero-Isaiah). Rosenmueller, Eichhorn, Gesenius, Ewald, Delitzsch and many others were among the defenders of this view.

But the process of critical disintegration did not stop with this proposition. Presently the critics asserted that they had discovered contributions of several unknown authors, some of whom lived after the exile in Babylonia. The idea of a plurality of Isaiahs grew. Moderate skeptics, represented by such men as Drs. Driver, Davidson and others, were willing to admit that Isaiah was responsible for about 800 verses of the book, but that the remaining 492 verses must have been written by others. A more radical group would not give Isaiah credit for more than 262 verses of the 1292 comprising the book. The remaining 1030 verses, they say, are from the pens of other writers. All seem to agree in regarding the last chapters, 40-66, as belonging to the time after the Babylonian exile.

The question has an actual interest to the student of the Book of Mormon, because portions of Isaiah, which the critics say, were first composed after the exile, are quoted by Nephi as part of the plates of Laban, which record was carried out of Palestine long before the captivity. How could those plates contain predictions that were first made three or four hundred years after their removal by Lehi to America? I remember my late friend, the Right Rev. Bishop Spaulding, used to put that question as an argument, to him irrefutable, against the authenticity and genuineness of the Book of Mormon. (Episcopalian Bishop residing in Salt Lake City.)

The question sounds formidable in view of the profound learning of the advocates of a plurality of Isaiahs and the disintegration of his book.

But the truth is that every learned objection to the view that Isaiah is one author and one book, has been met and refuted by equally weighty scholarship.

Consider, for instance, the assumption that the Chaldean words in the book prove that it was written after the exile, when the Jews had learned the language of the Chaldeans. It has been shown that Chaldean words are found in Hebrew writings, just as Latin, Greek, and other foreign words are found in English literature. But what does that prove as to authorship? It has, furthermore, been shown that there are only four indisputably Chaldean words in Isaiah, and that they occur in the part that even the critics admit belongs to him.

Thus every objection has been answered. And in addition it has been shown that for a period of 2,500 years after Isaiah no one had any doubt of the genuineness of his book, but that it was accepted even by the authors of the New Testament and by our Lord Himself as the work of Isaiah, the son of Amoz. It has been shown that 47 chapters of the 66 in the book, are quoted, directly or indirectly, by our Lord and his apostles. Among the passages quoted as the words of Isaiah are parts of chapters 1, 6, 9, 10, 11, 29, 40, 42, 53, 61 and 65. And thus the Book of Mormon is amply justified in giving the writings of Isaiah as part of the contents of the plates of Laban.

*A Rational View.* Some modern scholars regard chapters 36-39 as the central section. The preceding discourses, they hold, relate chiefly to the Assyrian period, while the latter portion is, as it were, a preview of the Babylonian era.

This should be supplemented by the statement that through the entire book references are made to the final redemption and gathering of Israel and Judah, and the salvation of all the world in the kingdom of the Messiah. On this understanding of the origin and construction of the book, it is easily seen that it is one composition and not a patchwork of scrolls. Also, that it has one author, not many authors and still more editors. Klostermann, speaking of the two parts of Isaiah, in which it is naturally divided, observes: "Since in both, the general view of the Holy Land and Jerusalem is that of a desolate and depopulated region to be re-peopled by the return of the exiled, doubtless the editor meant to convey the idea that, of both parts, the Isaiah of 36-39 is the prophetic author. It is therefore unscientific arbitrariness, instead of setting apart chapters 28-66, and employing chapters 28-39 as the key to 60-66, to break off after 35-39, and to imagine oneself in a new region. He who holds 35:3-4 does not stumble at 49:1; and only he who reads 28-29 can understand 48:3-11, and can regard the same prophet as basing a second prediction upon the fulfillment of the first." (*The New Shaff-Herzog Encyclopedia.*)

## THE FIVE BOOKS OF MOSES

### 1 Nephi 5:11

*The Pentateuch.* As regards the first books of the Old Testament, we must suppose that Moses, or his secretaries under his supervision, recorded the chief events of the day. The notes, properly collated and edited, became the law. They were, in all probability, kept near the sacred chest, or ark, in which the stone tables, the pot of manna, and the rod of Aaron, were deposited. See Deut. 31:26, where we read, "Take this book of the law, and put it in the side of the ark of the covenant of the Lord your God, that it may be there for a witness against thee." There must also have been copies of this law in the possession of the leaders of the people, whose duty it was to expound it and to administer the ordinances.

At some time Moses wrote, or caused to be written, under his direction, the introduction to the law which we have in Genesis—the account of the creation, the flood, the building of the tower, the history of the Patriarch Abraham and his immediate descendants down to the exodus. And towards the end of his life he added the fifth book, which is called Deuteronomy, because it is a recapitulation of many things previously recorded. It contains chiefly the moral law, as promulgated by Moses just before his departure. Jesus and his first Apostles loved this book. It is quoted at least 32 times in the New Testament, and scholars have recognized about 80 references to it in the latter part of the Bible.

The Mosaic authorship of the Pentateuch cannot be successfully denied. By that I do not mean that Moses wrote everything in that volume with his own hand. But no matter who did the mechanical work, or when, the books are Mosaic. They came from him. Genesis is no doubt based upon documents and literature to which Moses had access, and which he had studied in Egypt, and in the land of Midian. The story of the expedition of Amraphel for instance, is probably based on records then existing. But besides such sources of information, revelations were given to Moses concerning the heavens and the earth, and the children of men to the last generations. (See the Pearl of Great Price, Book of Moses.) He had first-hand information from the Source of all truth.

# THE BOOK OF JACOB

## THE BROTHER OF NEPHI

*The words of his preaching unto his brethren. He confoundeth a man who seeketh to overthrow the doctrine of Christ. A few words concerning the history of the people of Nephi.*

## CHAPTER 1

*Nephi's commandment to Jacob regarding the small plates, 1-8—Death of Nephi, 9-12—No more dividing into tribes, 13-14—Under reign of second king, Nephites began to embark upon evil ways, 15-17—Jacob and Joseph minister in their priestly calling, 18-19.*

### 1. *Nephi's commandment to Jacob regarding the small plates.*

1. For behold, it came to pass that fifty and five years had passed away from the time that Lehi left Jerusalem; wherefore, Nephi gave me, Jacob, a commandment concerning the small plates, upon which these things are engraven.

2. And he gave me, Jacob, a commandment that I should write upon these plates a few of the things which I considered to be most precious; that I should not touch, save it were lightly, concerning the history of this people which are called the people of Nephi.

3. For he said that the history of his people should be engraven upon his other plates, and that I should preserve these plates and hand them down unto my seed, from generation to generation.

4. And if there were preaching which was sacred, or revelation which was great, or prophesying, that I should engraven the heads of them upon these plates, and touch upon them as much as it were possible, for Christ's sake, and for the sake of our people.

5. For because of faith and great anxiety, it truly had been made manifest unto us concerning our people, what things should happen unto them.

6. And we also had many revelations, and the spirit of much prophecy; wherefore, we knew of Christ and his kingdom, which should come.

7. Wherefore we labored dili-

---

VERSES 1-8. *What "I should write upon these plates."* Here the thread of narrative is again broken, to be resumed by Jacob. Fifteen years passed and then Jacob was instructed to take charge of the second set of plates and to hand them down to his descendants, properly completed with the history of his times.

Readers of the Book of Mormon know that Nephi had been instructed to make a set of smaller plates for the record of sacred history, and that he did so, while the

gently among our people, that we might persuade them to come unto Christ, and partake of the goodness of God, that they might enter into his rest, lest by any means he should swear in his wrath they should not enter in, as in the provocation in the days of temptation while the children of Israel were in the wilderness.

8. Wherefore, we would to God that we could persuade all men not to rebel against God, to provoke him to anger, but that all men would believe in Christ, and view his death, and suffer his cross and bear the shame of the world; wherefore, I, Jacob, take it upon me to fulfil the commandment of my brother Nephi.

## 2. Death of Nephi.

9. Now Nephi began to be old, and he saw that he must soon die; wherefore, he anointed a man to be a king and a ruler over his people now, according to the reigns of the kings.

10. The people having loved Nephi exceedingly, he having been a great protector for them, having wielded the sword of Laban in their defence, and having labored in all his days for their welfare—

11. Wherefore, the people were desirous to retain in remembrance his name. And whoso should reign in his stead were called by the people, second Nephi, third Nephi, and so forth, according to the reigns of the kings; and thus they were called by the people, let them be of whatever name they would.

12. And it came to pass that Nephi died.

---

larger plates, which had been kept by Lehi were devoted to secular events, chiefly. (See 1 Ne. 6:16) This arrangement was not new, or original, in the days of Nephi. Dr. Leonard Wooley, an English archaeologist who has spent years of successful research in the land of the Near East, tells us in his little but immensely interesting book on the Sumerians, that about 2000 years B.C. scribes of that race undertook to record the glories of the past. They, he says, had at their disposal, a mass of documentary evidence and from this they compiled, on the one hand the political history of the people and on the other, their religious traditions. The original records were lost long ago but this set of duplicate tables undoubtedly facilitated the making of such excerpts and lists of kings as do exist and which enabled Berosus, the Greek historian (about 260 B.C.) to write his Babylonian-Chaldean history. Jacob was instructed by Nephi to write upon the small plates mainly that which he considered "most precious," such as "sacred preaching" or "revelations" or "prophecies."

VERSES 9-12. Nephi was now advanced in years. He appointed a king over the people. The people, however, decided to make *nephi* a title as well as a name and let their *kings* be known as *nephis*, Nephi I and Nephi II, etc. Thus the king-title was virtually set aside for the title of *Nephi*, which means *prophet*.

Having set his house in order, Nephi passed away.

The late President George Q. Cannon in his *Story of the Life of Nephi* offers this beautiful tribute to this mighty servant of God:

"Fifty-five years from the time that Lehi left Jerusalem, Nephi gave a commandment to his brother Jacob concerning the small plates upon which he had engraved so many revelations and so much doctrine. He desired his brother to keep them and to hand them down to his children after him; and to be sure and pursue the same course with them that he had—engrave upon them sacred things which were preached and any great revelations or prophecies that might be given. Jacob did this; and they remained in the hands of his lineage until Amaleki, who was a descendant of his, placed them in the custody of King Benjamin. Jacob does not inform us, in his book that we have received, how long this was before the death of Nephi; but, as he says in the same connection, that Nephi began to be old, and saw that he must die, it is probable that it was only a short time.

"It was then that Nephi anointed a man to be ruler and a king over his people. He was so greatly beloved by them, through his self-sacrificing and continuous labors for them and his courage in defending them; (for he had been compelled to have recourse to the sword of Laban, and to wield it in their defense against the attacks of the Lamanites); that they were desirous to retain in remembrance, his name. They, therefore, called his successors Second Nephi, Third Nephi, etc., 'let them be of whatever name they would.'

"The government was, without doubt, more patriarchal than monarchial in its character. Upon one occasion, Nephi's brother, Jacob, in addressing the people, uses this language: 'Having been called of God, and ordained after the manner of his holy order, and having been consecrated by my brother, Nephi, *unto whom ye look as a king or a protector, and on whom ye depend for safety'* Yet Nephi himself informs us that his people desired that he should be their king; 'but,' he adds, 'I, Nephi, was desirous that they should have no kings; nevertheless, I did for them according to that which was in my power.' This explains the relationship which he bore to them. He taught them the will of God, administered ordinances unto them, was their leader in all civil and religious matters in repelling the attacks of their enemies and was able to teach them mechanism and the arts of manufacturing. To such a man his people would naturally look, as Jacob says, as a king or protector. Before his death, it appears that he chose his brother, Jacob—who was a man of great faith and a prophet, and who with Joseph, another brother, had been ordained a priest and teacher by him over the land of the Nephites—to take the lead in all matters and to have charge of the records upon which the more sacred things were to be kept, and anointed another to be ruler in civil affairs. Whether it was one of his own sons or not, we are not informed, neither is it stated that this office was made hereditary. From what is said subsequently in the record respecting the kings, however, it seems clear that this office did descend from father to son; but the people also had a voice in choosing the king. The brief allusion that is made to these kings by Jarom nearly two centuries after Nephi's death, shows that for that period they had been mighty and faithful men of God. Upwards of four hundred years after Nephi's departure, a glimpse is given us of the mode of life which the king led. Speaking of Mosiah, son of Benjamin, it is said, 'And King Mosiah did cause his people that they should till the earth. And he also, himself, did till the earth, that thereby he might do according to that which his father had done in all things.'

"Such a monarchy as is here described, would be an inexpensive form of government, and it is probable that it was chiefly of this character from the beginning. We know that the two kings who preceded Mosiah II were like himself—prophets of God. He, himself, was a seer, also, as was his grandfather of the same name, and most likely his father, Benjamin; and he had in his possession the Urim and Thummim. Such men ruled the people in righteousness and as kind fathers, and kept the expense of government down to the lowest point. Whether or not there was a change of dynasty when the first Mosiah was chosen king, is not certain from what is written by Amaleki in the Book of Omni, though it does not appear improbable. Neither does it appear why the kings, Mosiah, Benjamin, and Mosiah were not called by the dynastic name of *Nephi*, according to the custom which prevailed through the long life-time of Jacob and probably afterwards. If a change of dynasty did occur, this custom may have been changed, though scarcely for that cause alone, as Nephi was still the revered founder of the nation; it may be that the dynastic name was omitted and their own names mentioned, for the purpose of better distinguishing them. When the record which was kept by the kings upon the other plates of Nephi shall be brought forth, we shall have the knowledge respecting the history of the Nephites covering this period of upwards of four centuries that will be of inestimable value. One thing, however, is plain from that which has come to us, that when the first Mosiah became king, in him was again united the kingly and priestly authority.

"'And it came to pass that Nephi died.' In this simple language does Jacob record the event. He leaves Nephi's works to speak for him. And their consideration cannot fail to be of profit to all who will give them attention. The example of such a life is of immense benefit to mankind; it strengthens, elevates and inspires with noble purpose all who become acquainted with it. No Latter-day Saint can read the life of Nephi, as he has given it to us in his record, without being incited to exercise greater faith, to live nearer to God and to cherish loftier aims.

"It can be said about the writings of Nephi (and this is also true of the entire Book of Mormon and in fact of all saving truth) that they bring the conviction of their divinity to the heart of every one who reads them in the spirit in which they were written. Read in that spirit, they fill the soul with a sweet and heavenly joy which only the spirit of God can produce.

"The career of Nephi was a most eventful one. He passed through many trials and afflictions; he was often in positions of peril: but he never yielded, never faltered, nor never shrunk from any ordeal to which he was exposed. In every relation of life he admirably performed his part. As a son, he was all a father could desire and of this Lehi bore ample testimony before he died. As a brother he did all in his power to benefit and save his kindred. What his course was with those who followed him and cast their lots with him, we can understand by reading his teachings, his labors and the love in which they held him while living and his memory when dead. He was patient, persevering, energetic and skillful; a man who was evidently born to lead. He exhibited these qualities when required to return to Jerusalem. Afterwards in the wilderness it seemed as though the company would all have perished had it not been for his good sense and capacity as a hunter. In building the ship, in its management upon the ocean, in teaching his people to work in wood and in metals of all kinds—iron, copper, brass, steel, silver and gold—he exhibited his skill as a mechanic, a miner, a seaman, chemist and metallurgist. He manufactured swords and other weapons of defense, he built houses, he cultivated the ground, he raised flocks and herds, he built a temple, which though not so costly as Solomon's, was constructed after its pattern, and the workmanship upon it was exceedingly fine; he taught his people to be skillful, industrious and how to apply their labor to the best advantage; as a statesman he organized society upon a firm and permanent basis, laid the foundation of civil and religious liberty; gave shape to the government and polity and implanted in the breasts of his people such a love for and a determination to maintain equal rights that the effects were felt, it may be said in truth, through all the generations of his race. Understanding as he did the government of the Lord, before whom there are no privileged classes, he respected the rights of the people; and while he knew there must be officers to bear responsibility and a properly organized government, he knew also that it should be based upon the consent of the people. He brought with him to this 'promised land' the broadest conceptions respecting the principle of human equality and the rights of men. Some of his views we gather from his teachings. Speaking of the Lord, he says, 'And he inviteth them all to come unto him and partake of his goodness; and he denieth none that come unto him, black and white, bond and free, male and female; and he remembereth the heathen and all are alike unto God, both Jew and Gentile.' The nobility in which he evidently believed, was the nobility of good deeds. The perfect performance of duty would enoble the poorest and the lowliest and make him the peer of the richest and the best born. While his people were true to his teachings, this sentiment always prevailed. They enjoyed the largest liberty consistent with the preservation of good order. Every man had the greatest freedom of belief. Theft, robbery, violence, adultery and murder were all punished under the law; but there was no law against a man's belief; persecution of religion, however

## 3. *No more dividing into tribes.*

13. Now the people which were not Lamanites were Nephites; nevertheless, they were called Nephites, Jacobites, Josephites, Zoramites, Lamanites, Lemuelites, and Ishmaelites.

14. But I, Jacob, shall not hereafter distinguish them by these names, but I shall call them Lamanites that seek to destroy the people of Nephi, and those who are friendly to Nephi I shall call Nephites, or the people of Nephi, according to the reigns of the kings.

## 4. *Under reign of second king, Nephites began to embark upon evil ways.*

15. And now it came to pass that the people of Nephi, under the reign of the second king, began to grow hard in their hearts,

erroneous or false the religion might be, was expressly forbidden and was made punishable. In this way the quality and free agency of the people was preserved, and they were left at liberty to choose for themselves their faith and form of worship. So far as his influence and teachings went among the people, they were free and the country was a land of liberty unto them.

"We here close the life of Nephi. He has shown us how much a mortal man, who devotes himself to God and his work, can accomplish for himself and his fellow-mortals, and how near, by the exercise of faith, man can draw to God."

VERSES 13-14. *Nephites and Lamanites.* An important change in the division of the people is noted in this connection. Hitherto, the tribal arrangement into Nephites, Jacobites, Josephites, Zoramites, Ishmaelites, Lamanites and Lemuelites had been maintained for civic and genealogical purposes. Now, Jacob says, "I, Jacob, shall not hereafter distinguish them by these names, but I shall call them Lamanites that seek to destroy the people of Nephi, and those who are friendly to Nephi I shall call Nephites, or the people of Nephi."

The term *Nephites* or *Lamanites* is generally supposed to refer only to the literal descendants of Lehi, through Nephi and Laman, respectively. This is not strictly correct.

A few years after this change in giving names after tribal ancestors, as indicated, was made, we read,

"And it came to pass that whosoever would not believe in the tradition of the Lamanites, but believed those records which were brought out of the land of Jerusalem, and also in the tradition of their fathers, which were correct, who believe in the commandments of God and kept them, were called the Nephites, or the people of Nephi, from that time forth. . . ." (Alma 3:11)

May not the reason for this deviation from the original and obvious rule of naming the people in accordance with their lineage been necessitated by the accession to the pioneer colonies of people, those whose genealogies were not known? Descendants of the Jaredites, for instance? Or from other arrivals here, of whom the Book of Mormon has no record? It is easier to understand what follows concerning the wickedness of the people at that early day of their history and their having a temple with temple ordinances and service, if we suppose that they had been joined by other elements.

VERSES 15-16. *Began to grow hard in their hearts.* The death of Nephi was a great spiritual loss to the people. This became evident already during the reign of his

and indulge themselves somewhat in wicked practices, such
as like unto David of old desiring
many wives and concubines, and
also Solomon, his son.

16. Yea, and they also began
to search much gold and silver,
and began to be lifted up somewhat in pride.

### 5. Jacob and Joseph minister in their priestly calling.

17. Wherefore I, Jacob, gave
unto them these words as I
taught them in the temple,
having first obtained mine errand
from the Lord.

18. For I, Jacob, and my brother Joseph had been consecrated
priests and teachers of this people, by the hand of Nephi.

19. And we did magnify our
office unto the Lord, taking upon

us the responsibility, answering
the sins of the people upon our
own heads if we did not teach
them the word of God with all
diligence; wherefore, by laboring
with our might their blood
might not come upon our garments; otherwise their blood
would come upon our garments,
and we would not be found spotless at the last day.

successor. The people began to adopt the practices of David and Solomon regarding
marriage and concubinage. They also began to prospect for gold and silver and as
a consequence of worldly success, their hearts were filled with pride. Jacob reproved
them severely, having obtained the Lord's will concerning these things.

VERSES 17-19. *Jacob and Joseph ordained priests and teachers.* Sometime before
Nephi died, he appointed Jacob and Joseph, his brothers, to the office of priest in
the Holy Order of God. At the death of Nephi, Jacob succeeded him as the leader
and head of the spiritual concerns of the people. Another was appointed to rule
over their civil affairs.

## CHAPTER 2

*Jacob's denunciation of unchastity and other sins, 1-22—Plurality of wives forbidden because of wickedness, 23-35.*

### 1. *Jacob's denunciation of unchastity, etc.*

1. The words which Jacob, the brother of Nephi, spake unto the people of Nephi, after the death of Nephi:

2. Now, my beloved brethren, I, Jacob, according to the responsibility which I am under to God, to magnify mine office with soberness, and that I might rid my garments of your sins, I come up into the temple this day that I might declare unto you the word of God.

3. And ye yourselves know that I have hitherto been diligent in the office of my calling; but I this day am weighed down with much more desire and anxiety for the welfare of your souls than I have hitherto been.

---

VERSES 1-11. *Commanded of the Lord to reprove the People.* In this chapter and the two which follow, a continued sermon or a series of sermons, preached by Jacob, is recorded by him. They can easily be understood by all who desire to know and understand the truth. They bear the mark so plainly seen in Jacob's addresses, that of being devoid of any attempt to minimize or to apologize for what he has to say. He realized that a truth, spoken in plainness, is more quickly recognized than one decked in apologies, pretexts, and excuses. Besides this, he knew that such a one carried with it a conviction of right which would endure, while all else, no matter how pleasant, would "sooner or later perish" and as a dream, pass from the mind. Therefore, the plainness of the Gospel of Christ.

There are times, when as a reproof, a truth is spoken in love and kindness. It is often more painful to him who imparts it than to those who should receive it. This seems to have been so in the case of Jacob. He expresses a deep concern for those who have been made to suffer because of the wrongdoings of others. To add grief and misery to the sufferings of those who had come to the temple to be comforted by God's holy word caused him to shrink with shame before the Lord, in whose presence he must testify to them of their guilt. He says, "And also it grieveth me that I must use so much boldness of speech concerning you, before your wives and your children, many of whose feelings are exceedingly tender and chaste and delicate before God, which thing is pleasing unto God." (Verse 7)

Jacob first tells those who have gathered there of his purpose in coming up to the temple that day. He points out the obligation he has under God "to magnify mine office with soberness" that in no way could their sins be accounted against him, "I came up to the temple this day that I might declare unto you the word of God." (Verse 2)

VERSE 3. *And ye yourselves know, etc.* To the end expressed in verse 2, he, as they all knew, had been most diligent. But he says, "I this day am weighed down with much more desire and anxiety for the welfare of your souls than I have hitherto been." No doubt the growing iniquities among the people had been a source of great sorrow to Jacob. The increasing pride of their hearts had come as a wedge between their duties and their pleasures. He consoles himself with the fact that they, as yet, had been obedient to the "Word of the Lord" that beforetime he had given unto them.

4. For behold, as yet, ye have been obedient unto the word of the Lord, which I have given unto you.

5. But behold, hearken ye unto me, and know that by the help of the all-powerful Creator of heaven and earth I can tell you concerning your thoughts, how that ye are beginning to labor in sin, which sin appeareth very abominable unto me, yea, and abominable unto God.

6. Yea, it grieveth my soul and causeth me to shrink with shame before the presence of my Maker, that I might testify unto you concerning the wickedness of your hearts.

7. And also it grieveth me that I must use so much boldness of speech concerning you, before your wives and your children, many of whose feelings are exceedingly tender and chaste and delicate before God, which thing is pleasing unto God;

8. And it supposeth me that they have come up hither to hear the pleasing word of God, yea, the word which healeth the wounded soul.

9. Wherefore, it burdeneth my soul that I should be constrained, because of the strict commandment which I have received from God, to admonish you according to your crimes, to enlarge the wounds of those who are already wounded, instead of consoling and healing their wounds; and those who have not been wounded, instead of feasting upon the pleasing word of God have daggers placed to pierce their souls and wound their delicate minds.

10. But, notwithstanding the greatness of the task, I must do according to the strict commands of God, and tell you concerning your wickedness and abominations, in the presence of the pure in heart, and the broken heart, and under the glance of the piercing eye of the Almighty God.

11. Wherefore, I must tell you the truth according to the plainness of the word of God. For behold, as I inquired of the Lord, thus came the word unto me, saying: Jacob, get thou up into the temple on the morrow, and declare the word which I shall give thee unto this people.

12. And now behold, my brethren, this is the word which I declare unto you, that many of you have begun to search for gold, and for silver, and for all manner of precious ores, in the which this land, which is a land of promise

VERSES 12-19. *Lifted up in pride.* Many of the Saints residing in the Land of Nephi had grown exceeding rich in search for gold and silver, which, in the land where they lived, did "abound most plentifully."[1] Some of them, more than others,

[1] The land in which Jacob wrote this was a rich mineral country. This does not agree with conditions in Guatemala, whose "silver, gold, copper, iron and lead are mined only in small quantities." Still less does it fit Yucatan. It reminds us rather of Colombia or Equador. According to the Minister of Industry, Colombia in 1929, had the world's largest production of emeralds and platinum and the largest production of gold in South America. Silver, copper, and salt are other mineral products. British Honduras, too, is an agricultural country.

unto you and to your seed, doth abound most plentifully.

13. And the hand of providence hath smiled upon you most pleasingly, that you have obtained many riches; and because some of you have obtained more abundantly than that of your brethren ye are lifted up in the pride of your hearts, and wear stiff necks and high heads because of the costliness of your apparel, and persecute your brethren because ye suppose that ye are better than they.

14. And now, my brethren, do ye suppose that God justifieth you in this thing? Behold, I say unto you, Nay. But he condemneth you, and if ye persist in these things his judgments must speedily come unto you.

15. O that he would show you that he can pierce you, and with one glance of his eye he can smite you to the dust!

16. O that he would rid you from this iniquity and abomination. And, O that ye would listen unto the word of his commands, and let not this pride of your hearts destroy your souls!

17. Think of your brethren like unto yourselves, and be familiar with all and free with your substance, that they may be rich like unto you.

18. But before ye seek for riches, seek ye for the kingdom of God.

19. And after ye have obtained a hope in Christ ye shall obtain riches, if ye seek them; and ye will seek them for the intent to do good—to clothe the naked, and to feed the hungry, and to liberate the captive, and administer relief to the sick and the afflicted.

20. And now, my brethren, I have spoken unto you concerning pride; and those of you which have afflicted your neighbor, and persecuted him because ye were

---

obtained many riches and in the pride engendered thereby, wore costly apparel and went about with "stiff necks and high heads." They persecuted the poor and in vainglory imagined they were better than they. Jacob reproved and admonished them, saying that God did not justify them in so doing, "Let not the pride of your hearts destroy your souls." Be free with your substance and think of those who may be less fortunate than you, because, he warned them, God can destroy all your wealth and even you with one glance of his piercing eye. You will recall a previous sermon in which Jacob said, "But wo unto the rich, who are rich as to the things of the world. For because they are rich they despise the poor, and they persecute the meek, and their hearts are upon their treasures; wherefore, their treasure is their God." (2 Ne. 9:30) In any event, "But before ye seek for riches, seek ye for the kingdom of God." He assures them that after they receive a "hope in Christ" that then, if they still want riches, they will obtain them. However, he tells them that then their wants will be for a different purpose; they will seek for riches only to do good.

VERSES 20-22. *Ye were proud in your hearts.* Why be proud in your hearts and afflict your neighbor because of the things God hath given you? Jacob asks for a reason. "What say ye of it?" He wants them to ponder it in their hearts. "Do ye not suppose such things are abominable unto him who created all flesh?" One man he says, is as precious in the sight of God as is another and that, for the same reason

proud in your hearts, of the things which God hath given you, what say ye of it?

21. Do ye not suppose that such things are abominable unto him who created all flesh? And the one being is as precious in his sight as the other. And all flesh is of the dust; and for the selfsame end hath he created

them, that they should keep his commandments and glorify him forever.

22. And now I make an end of speaking unto you concerning this pride. And were it not that I must speak unto you concerning a grosser crime, my heart would rejoice exceedingly because of you.

## 2. *Plurality of wives forbidden because of iniquity.*

23. But the word of God burthens me because of your grosser crimes. For behold, thus saith the Lord: This people begin to wax in iniquity; they understand not the scriptures, for they seek to excuse themselves in committing whoredoms, because of the things which were written concerning David, and Solomon his son.

24. Behold, David and Solomon truly had many wives and

concubines, which thing was abominable before me, saith the Lord.

25. Wherefore, thus saith the Lord, I have led this people forth out of the land of Jerusalem, by the power of mine arm, that I might raise up unto me a righteous branch from the fruit of the loins of Joseph.

26. Wherefore, I the Lord God will not suffer that this people shall do like unto them of old.

---

all are created to keep His commandments and, thereby, glorify Him. There is a lesson we all may learn here. Pride, too often, leads our footsteps astray. It crowds all thoughts of God from our hearts. We are so engrossed in the world and the things thereof that we have no time or thought for other than, "What shall I eat? or what shall I drink? or wherewithal shall I be clothed?" We forget his wisdom and guidance. It is then we should remember, "Man shall not live by bread alone, but by every word that proceedeth from the mouth of God." When we recognize that great truth, all pride, envyings, hardheartedness, and deceit will be banished and in their place, love of God and our fellowmen will fill our hearts and in humility, we will recognize all men as brethren, they having one Father, and we will profit by the lessons they shall teach us.

VERSES 23-35. *This people . . . understand not the scriptures.* We know but little of what occurred among the Nephites in Jacob's time. The people, however, appear in some respects to have fallen into sin. They had grown in worldly pride and devoted much time and energy to the search of wealth. By reason of their isolated position and because the Jews had abused the principle of plural marriage, the people of Lehi had been commanded that each man should have but one wife. Some of them did not heed this special law and took other wives, not only without God's sanction but entirely contrary to his express command. Indeed, they committed other grievous sins, excusing themselves therefor by quoting the actions of Kings

27. Wherefore, my brethren, hear me, and hearken to the word of the Lord: For there shall not any man among you have save it be one wife; and concubines he shall have none;

28. For I, the Lord God, delight in the chastity of women. And whoredoms are an abomination before me; thus saith the Lord of Hosts.

29. Wherefore, this people shall keep my commandments, saith the Lord of Hosts, or cursed be the land for their sakes.

30. For if I will, saith the Lord of Hosts, raise up seed unto me, I will command my people; otherwise they shall hearken unto these things.

31. For behold, I, the Lord, have seen the sorrow, and heard the mourning of the daughters of my people in the land of Jerusalem, yea, and in all the lands of my people, because of the wickedness and abominations of their husbands.

32. And I will not suffer, saith the Lord of Hosts, that the cries of the fair daughters of this people, which I have led out of the land of Jerusalem, shall come up unto me against the men of my people, saith the Lord of Hosts.

33. For they shall not lead away captive the daughters of my people because of their tenderness, save I shall visit them with a sore curse, even unto destruction; for they shall not commit whoredoms, like unto them of old, saith the Lord of Hosts.

34. And now behold, my brethren, ye know that these commandments were given to our father, Lehi; wherefore, ye have known them before; and ye have come unto great condemnation; for ye have done these things which ye ought not to have done.

35. Behold, ye have done greater iniquities than the Lamanites, our brethren. Ye have broken the hearts of your tender wives, and lost the confidence of your children, because of your bad examples before them; and the sobbings of their hearts ascend up to God against you. And because of the strictness of the word of God, which cometh down against you, many hearts died, pierced with deep wounds.

David and Solomon, his son. At this the Lord was greatly displeased and he instructed Jacob to reprove them sharply. This, he did in the temple. He re-affirmed the law that the Nephites of that age should have only one wife, but he added, in the name of "the Lord of Hosts," that if he wanted to raise up a holy seed unto himself, he would command his people. This, we have reason to believe he did, though we find no direct statement on the matter.

Plural marriage is wrong where the Lord does not permit it. And the Lord, who commands his people to be loyal and law-abiding, is not going to give his consent to law-breaking. Matrimony, whether single or plural, is sanctified by the commandment of God, but he will not command his people to break the laws of the land. "Let no man break the laws of the land, for he that keepeth the laws of God hath no need to break the laws of the land." (D. and C. 58:21)

## GENERAL NOTES

*David and Solomon.* Different opinions concerning the true meaning of this text have been expressed by readers of the Book of Mormon. The reference to David and Solomon shows clearly *what* the Lord censored and *why.*

In the case of David, the Lord said through the Prophet Nathan:

"Thus saith the Lord God of Israel, I anointed thee king over Israel, and I delivered thee out of the hand of Saul; and I gave thee thy master's house, and thy master's wives into thy bosom, and gave thee the house of Israel and Judah; and if that had been too little, I would moreover have given unto thee such and such things. Wherefore hast thou despised the commandment of the Lord, to do evil in his sight? Thou hast killed Uriah the Hittite with the sword, and hast taken his wife to be thy wife, and hast slain him with the sword of the children of Ammon. (II Sam. 12:7-9)

That was David's awful sin. He had not only taken a wife without divine sanction—another man's wife at that—but he had committed foul murder, in order to get possession of her. I fancy his sin would be no greater, had he committed murder to come in possession of houses or land, or even, as Nathan expressed it, "one little ewe lamb." Ahab and Jezebel were both sentenced to death, through the mouth of the Prophet Elijah, for the murder of Naboth for the sake of his vineyard. (I Kings 21:17-24)

In the case of Solomon we read:

"But King Solomon loved many strange women, together with the daughter of Pharaoh, women of the Moabites, Ammonites, Edomites, Zidonians, and Hittites; of the nations concerning which the Lord said to the children of Israel, Ye shall not go in to them, neither shall they come in to you: for surely they will turn away your heart after other gods: Solomon clave unto these in love. . . . For it came to pass, when Solomon was old, that his wives turned away his heart after other gods: and his heart was not perfect with the Lord his God, as was the heart of David his father." (I Kings 11:1-4)

Solomon, as is here shown, sinned in making social alliances with idolaters, contrary to the commandment of God, and in adopting features of their worship. It was this that kindled the anger of the Lord against him. (*Ibid.,* vv. 5-11)

Now it appears that the Nephites, shortly after the death of Nephi, began to yield to the desires of depraved hearts, and sought to justify their carnal practices by what is recorded of David and Solomon. The Prophet Jacob, who had succeeded Nephi, was, therefore, directed by the Lord to explain to them the awful consequences of sexual indulgences outside the sacred precincts of divine sanction, as exemplified in the experiences of those two kings of the Jews, and to command them to have only one wife and no concubines, unless the Lord for some special purpose, should give them a different law.

## CHAPTER 3

*Jacob's denunciation continued—Lamanites more righteous than Nephites —The former commended for fidelity in marriage—The latter again warned.*

## 1. Jacob's denunciation continued. Nephites again warned.

1. But behold, I, Jacob, would speak unto you that are pure in heart. Look unto God with firmness of mind, and pray unto him with exceeding faith, and he will console you in your afflictions, and he will plead your cause, and send down justice upon those who seek your destruction.

2. O all ye that are pure in heart, lift up your heads and receive the pleasing word of God, and feast upon his love; for ye may, if your minds are firm, forever.

3. But, wo, wo, unto you that are not pure in heart, that are filthy this day before God; for except ye repent the land is cursed for your sakes; and the Lamanites, which are not filthy like unto you, nevertheless they are cursed with a sore cursing, shall scourge you even unto destruction.

4. And the time speedily cometh, that except ye repent they shall possess the land of your inheritance, and the Lord God will lead away the righteous out from among you.

5. Behold, the Lamanites your brethren, whom ye hate because of their filthiness and the cursing which hath come upon their skins, are more righteous than you; for they have not forgotten the commandment of the Lord, which was given unto our fathers —that they should have save it were one wife, and concubines they should have none, and there should not be whoredoms committed among them.

6. And now, this commandment they observe to keep; wherefore, because of this observance, in keeping this commandment, the Lord God will not destroy them, but will be merciful unto

VERSES 1-14. Whilst the early Nephites were polygamists and unfortunately for them, unrighteous ones, the Lamanites were monogamists, which form of marriage they appear to have ever after retained.

One phase of Lamanite character, originating, doubtless, in their Israelitish ancestry is worthy of our praise. It was the great strength of their domestic affections, their love for their wives and their children and their kindness to their families. As we shall have to refer so often to their vices, we must, in justice to them, insert here the description of their virtues given by Jacob. He says, "Behold, their husbands love their wives, and their wives love their husbands; and their husbands and wives love their children; and their unbelief and their hatred towards you is because of the iniquity of their fathers." Nor is there anything in this incompatible with the ferocity of their character or their bloodthirstiness in war. In the earlier ages of the Lamanite nationality rigid chastity was observed by the men as well as the women. Indeed, it may be said that while they manifested most of the prominent vices of semi-barbarous people, they also possessed the virtues that such races, un-them; and one day they shall become a blessed people.

7. Behold, their husbands love their wives, and their wives love their husbands; and their husbands and their wives love their children; and their unbelief and their hatred towards you is because of the iniquity of their fathers; wherefore, how much better are you than they, in the sight of your great Creator?

8. O my brethren, I fear that unless ye shall repent of your sins that their skins will be whiter than yours, when ye shall be brought with them before the throne of God.

9. Wherefore, a commandment I give unto you, which is the word of God, that ye revile no more against them because of the darkness of their skins; neither shall ye revile against them because of their filthiness; but ye shall remember your own filthiness, and remember that their filthiness came because of their fathers.

10. Wherefore, ye shall remember your children, how that ye have grieved their hearts because of the example that ye have set before them; and also, remember that ye may, because of your filth-iness, bring your children unto destruction, and their sins be heaped upon your heads at the last day.

11. O my brethren, hearken unto my word; arouse the faculties of your soul; shake yourselves that ye may awake from the slumber of death; and loose yourselves from the pains of hell that ye may not become angels to the devil, to be cast into that lake of fire and brimstone which is the second death.

12. And now I, Jacob, spake many more things unto the people of Nephi, warning them against fornication and lasciviousness, and every kind of sin, telling them the awful consequences of them.

13. And a hundredth part of the proceedings of this people, which now began to be numerous, cannot be written upon these plates; but many of their proceedings are written upon the larger plates, and their wars, and their contentions, and the reigns of their kings.

14. These plates are called the plates of Jacob, and they were made by the hand of Nephi. And I make an end of speaking these words.

---

corrupted by a more luxurious mode of life, generally show. Nor would it be consistent, nor historically true, to give one general description and apply it to the whole Lamanite race, for as their numbers increased the state of society amongst them grew more complex and we read of different grades of civilization in their midst.

Notwithstanding their own vices the Nephites constantly reproached and abused their brethren, the Lamanites, because of their habits and customs. They referred to them as filthy and as loathsome, forgetting that they, too, had many faults which were to be despised and scorned. He reminds them that the dark skins of the Lamanites and their vileness were the rewards of sinful lives led by their fathers.

He gives them the commandment, which, he says, "Is the word of God, that you revile no more against them" because of these things and remember your own children that you do not bring the same destruction upon them and thereby cause that their sins be accounted against you in the great and terrible day of the Lord.

The Nephite people, in the days of Jacob, had become many. Only a part of what transpired among them could be written upon the Small Plates which were made by Nephi. Upon the Large Plates were engraved the political history of these times. That part of the Small Plates upon which Jacob wrote were called "The plates of Jacob."

## CHAPTER 4

*Jacob's teachings continued, 1-7—The Law of Moses among the Nephites, pointing them to Christ, 8-14—His rejection by the Jews foreseen, 15-18.*

### 1. Jacob's teachings continued.

1. Now behold, it came to pass that I, Jacob, having ministered much unto my people in word, (and I cannot write but a little of my words, because of the difficulty of engraving our words upon plates) and we know that the things which we write upon plates must remain;

2. But whatsoever things we write upon anything save it be upon plates must perish and vanish away; but we can write a few words upon plates, which will give our children, and also our beloved brethren, a small degree of knowledge concerning us, or concerning their fathers—

3. Now in this thing we do rejoice; and we labor diligently to engraven these words upon plates, hoping that our beloved brethren and our children will receive them with thankful hearts, and look upon them that they may learn with joy and not with sorrow, neither with contempt, concerning their first parents.

4. For, for this intent have we written these things, that they may know that we knew of Christ, and we had a hope of his glory many hundred years before his coming; and not only we ourselves had a hope of his glory, but also all the holy prophets which were before us.

5. Behold, they believed in Christ and worshiped the Father in his name, and also we worship the Father in his name. And for this intent we keep the law of Moses, it pointing our souls to him; and for this cause it is sanctified unto us for righteousness, even as it was accounted unto Abraham in the wilderness to be obedient unto the commands of God in offering up his son Isaac, which is a similitude of God and his Only Begotten Son.

6. Wherefore, we search the prophets, and we have many revelations and the spirit of prophecy; and having all these witnesses we obtain a hope, and our faith becometh unshaken, insomuch that we truly can command in the name of Jesus and the very trees obey us, or the mountains, or the waves of the sea.

7. Nevertheless, the Lord God showeth us our weakness that we may know that it is by his grace, and his great condescensions unto the children of men, that we have power to do these things.

---

VERSES 1-7. *That they may know that we knew of Christ.* Jacob, having been ordained to the Holy Priesthood by Nephi and appointed by him to a high office therein, continued to minister with much zeal among the people; teaching them by word of mouth, the wonderful things revealed to him of the glory of Christ, the

## 2. *The Law of Moses among the Nephites.*

8. Behold, great and marvelous are the works of the Lord. How unsearchable are the depths of the mysteries of him; and it is impossible that man should find out all his ways. And no man knoweth of his ways save it be revealed unto him; wherefore, brethren, despise not the revelations of God.

Messiah, whose coming was as yet, many hundreds of years away. He labored throughout all the difficulties of engraving his words upon metal plates that their children might know that their fathers knew of Christ and had a hope of his mission centuries before his birth among the children of men. Furthermore, he says that this hope and this knowledge was had by "all the holy prophets which were before us."

These prophecies and teachings were engraved upon plates of metal that they might endure and remain as an indestructible media of transmission; not to pass away and vanish as other means are apt to do.[1]

VERSE 5. *Behold, they believed in Christ.* In this verse we see clearly, that anciently, the Jews had a knowledge of Christ. The prophets of old taught and prophesied of his mission. They worshiped the Father in the name of Christ and this, the Nephites also did. The Nephites kept the law of Moses because they understood it was symbolic of the great Sacrifice that was to be made. And it prepared them to receive the blessings attendant thereon.

VERSE 6. *Wherefore, we search the prophets.* To the end that they might obtain a fuller knowledge of his glory, they searched the Scriptures to find all the prophets had written concerning him. There they found much to establish, beyond any doubt, the hope in Christ which they cherished. The knowledge they thus obtained, together with the revelations they constantly received and the spirit of prophecy that was in them, raised their faith to such a pitch of reality that they did "command in the name of Jesus and the very trees obey us, or the mountains, or the waves of the sea."

VERSE 7. *The Lord God showeth us our weakness.* In what way their weakness was made manifest to them is not stated but, nevertheless, Jacob says it was shown to them that they might know it was by the power of God and through his grace that they did these things and not by any power they, themselves, possessed.

VERSE 8. *Great and marvelous are the works of the Lord.* From the heart of Jacob there comes a glorious paean in praise of the Great Creator of earth and man. In the words of the Prophet Habakkuk (629 B.C.) we can hear him say, "I will rejoice in the Lord, I will joy in the God of my salvation." As we listen to his words we remember the Eighth Psalm of David, "O Lord, our God, how glorious is thy name in all the earth, whose majesty is rehearsed above the heavens. When I consider thy heavens, the work of thy fingers, the moon and the stars which thou hast established; what is man, that thou art mindful of him, and the son of man, that thou thinkest of him? . . . O Lord, our God, how glorious is thy name in all the earth." (Jewish Rendition) His thoughts were, undoubtedly, "I will exalt thy holy Name, I will exult in the works of thy Fingers." "How great," he says, "and marvelous are the works of the Lord." How far beyond man's understanding are his

---

[1]Reference is hereby made to the notes appended to Chapter 9, I Nephi, wherein "metal plates" as a permanent record is discussed.

9. For behold, by the power of his word man came upon the face of the earth, which earth was created by the power of his word. Wherefore, if God being able to speak and the world was, and to speak and man was created, O then, why not able to command the earth, or the workmanship of his hands upon the face of it, according to his will and pleasure?

---

gracious deeds. Those, only, to whom it is revealed, know his wondrous ways. "Wherefore, brethren," he admonished, "despise not the revelations of God." Despise means scorn, disdain, disregard, spurn, or contemn. Remember, when a truth is revealed of God, it becomes at once, a solemn obligation upon each individual. It is given, as the Apostle Peter says, for us to heed. It is not to be ignored, or in any way made inconsiderable.

VERSE 9. *Earth was created by the power of his word.* In the first part of the Book of Moses (we call it the Book of Genesis), a copy of which was in the possession of Jacob and was thus available to the Nephites, we read of the creation of earth and man. The facts there stated were familiar to all the descendants of Nephi and were used by Jacob as a proof of his further statement that if such were the case, then it is not unreasonable nor incompatible with the truth to believe that by that same power "why not able to command the earth, or the workmanship of his hands upon the face of it, according to his will and pleasure."

You will remember that in the beginning God created the heavens and the earth. The beasts of the field, the fowls of the air, and the fishes of the sea were given an abode and told to multiply and fill the earth. The Great Creator saw what he had done and pronounced it "Good." He then said, "Let us make man in our image, after our likeness." (Gen. 1:26) This was done. The knowledge of the glorious creation of man was inherited by each passing generation of Israel. It lifted them to a higher plane in their estimate of mankind. That such a belief was universal is shown when Malachi proclaimed this great truth by stating in the form of a question what was an established fact in the minds of his hearers. He asked, "Have we not all one father? hath not one God created us all?" (Mal. 2:10) The thought that they were all created in the image of God, imbued every generation of ancient Israel and sanctified before him, their prayers to him and their praise of him.

To them, he was the *"Majesty on High."*

The Nephites, whose fathers came from the Capitol City of the Jews, believed as did the Jews, in God the Father Almighty. They believed that he was the Maker and the Creator of all. They believed in a God with whom they dwelt in close relationship and one who would lead them and guide them in every experience of life. The Hebrew conception of man's relationship to God was the basis of their wisdom, and the wisdom Paul deplored, was the wisdom displayed in the pagan philosophy of Greece and Rome and of it he said that the world, by wisdom, knows not God.

This task has been left to revealed religion. It has been left to revealed religion to do that, in the attempt of which mankind has failed. It has been left to revealed religion to accomplish those things for which men have sought in all ages. Revealed religion is the Gospel of Jesus Christ. Jacob says in verse eight, "And no man knoweth of his ways save it be revealed unto him."

If you lean unto your own understanding and trust to those who are worldly wise, you may search every acre of the globe and not find it. You may follow every path of human erudition and not walk in the way of truth. A man may partake freely of all the knowledge that has accumulated since the world began, and still

10. Wherefore, brethren, seek not to counsel the Lord, but to take counsel from his hand. For behold, ye yourselves know that he counseleth in wisdom, and in justice, and in great mercy, over all his works.

---

not know that which has been revealed to even the humblest among us, "And this is life eternal, that they might know thee the only true God, and Jesus Christ whom thou hast sent." (John 17:3) Amid trial and disappointment, when his neighbors came to mock, Job stood up and said, with a voice of thunder, the reverberations of which we still hear, "For I know that my Redeemer liveth and that he shall stand at the latter day upon the earth." (Job 19:25) This differs only in the use of words from the great truth revealed through the Prophet Abinadi, "I would that ye should understand that God, himself, shall come down among the children of men, and shall redeem his people." (Mosiah 15:1) This is a great mystery revealed to the pure in heart. Learning cannot find it. The power of man cannot gain it. With money, it cannot be purchased, but it is made known to those, who, without guile, seek the Kingdom of Heaven. I have seen the golden glow of money illumine the halls of the rich. I have seen great armies, on the eve of battle, prepare to inflict their might. I have seen the learned, when they say, "I do not believe." But in the hovels of the poor, in the dwellings of the meek, in homes where toil and sorrow seem to pace the struggle to endure, I have seen the strength of faith, the power of love, the light of God's Holy Word, shine more brightly than all the riches of the world, all the learning of the ages, or all the force the armies and navies of the world can muster. These first are mysteries of God, as are prayer, forgiveness of sin, etc., and as Jacob says these mysteries "Are known only to those to whom it is revealed."

VERSE 10. *Seek not to counsel the Lord.* There are some among us who are critical of all things. "The lot of mankind," they say, "could be better." The seasons are wrong; disease, famine, pestilence, should be banished from amongst us. All is not good that seems so. Pain and perplexity come penally and punishing. They think to "check over the plans and OK the blueprints of Creation." They would advise the maker, forgetting that he created all in wisdom, and in justice and great mercy he presideth over all things.

In the Hebrew Scriptures is this wonderful statement, "The Lord by wisdom hath founded the earth; by understanding hath he established the heavens." (Proverbs 3:19) Also you will find this beautiful piece of Hebrew poetry; in it wisdom speaks, using the personal pronoun, I.

"The Lord possessed me in the beginning of his way, before his works of old.
"I was set up from everlasting, from the beginning or ever the earth was.
"When there were no depths, I was brought forth; when there were no fountains abounding with water.
"Before the mountains were settled, before the hills was I brought forth;
"While as yet he had not made the earth, nor the fields, nor the highest part of the dust of the world.
"When he prepared the heavens, was I there: when he set a compass upon the face of the depth:
"When he established the clouds above: when he strengthened the fountains of the deep:
"When he gave to the sea his decree, that the waters should not pass his commandment: when he appointed the foundation of the earth:
"Then I was by him, as one brought up with him: and I was daily his delight, rejoicing always before him." (Proverbs 8:22-30)

11. Wherefore, beloved brethren, be reconciled unto him through the atonement of Christ, his Only Begotten Son, and ye may obtain a resurrection, according to the power of the resurrection which is in Christ, and be presented as the first-fruits of Christ unto God, having faith, and obtained a good hope of glory in him before he manifesteth himself in the flesh.

12. And now, beloved, marvel not that I tell you these things; for why not speak of the atonement of Christ, and attain to a perfect knowledge of him, as to attain to the knowledge of a resurrection and the world to come?

13. Behold, my brethren, he that prophesieth, let him prophesy to the understanding of men; for the Spirit speaketh the truth and lieth not. Wherefore, it speaketh of things as they really are, and of things as they really will be; wherefore, these things are manifested unto us plainly, for the salvation of our souls. But behold, we are not witnesses alone in these things; for God also spake them unto prophets of old.

14. But behold, the Jews were a stiffnecked people; and they despised the words of plainness, and killed the prophets and sought for things that they could not understand. Wherefore, because of their blindness, which blindness came by looking beyond the mark, they must needs fall; for God hath taken away his plainness from them, and delivered unto them many things which they cannot understand, because they desired it. And because they desired it God hath done it, that they may stumble.

"Wherefore, brethren, seek not to counsel the Lord, but to take counsel from his hand."

VERSES 11-13. *He that prophesieth, let him prophesy to the understanding of men.* No prophecy of God is obscure to those who desire to know the truth. By faith it may be easily understood. It need not be added to, nor taken from. It needs no interpreter. Prophecy only knows the truth. It does not speak falsely nor foolishly. "It speaketh of things as they really are, and of things as they really will be." It "is one of the most wonderful manifestations of the Spirit upon the minds of holy men." "For the prophecy came not in old time by the will of man; but holy men of God spake as they were moved by the Holy Ghost." (II Peter 1:19)

Jacob followed his hymn of praise to the Creator whose wisdom and justice controls all, by inviting his brethren to accept the Sacrifice of his Only Begotten Son as the means that "ye may obtain a resurrection" and through Christ be presented unto God as its first fruits. That through faith, they may attain a hope of Christ's glory even before he was born.

VERSE 14. *The Jews were a stiffnecked people.* The Jews scorned the words of the holy prophets because they spoke to them in plainness, so much so that they understand every word. (1 Ne. 13:24; 14:23) Like many today they listened to eloquent speakers although they did not know what they were talking about. They preferred the things they could not understand. They killed the prophets who testified boldly to them of the wickedness that blinded them. They were carried to depths they could not fathom and to heights they could not grasp because they so wished it.

## 3. *His rejection by the Jews foreseen.*

15. And now I, Jacob, am led on by the Spirit unto prophesying; for I perceive by the workings of the Spirit which is in me, that by the stumbling of the Jews they will reject the stone upon which they might build and have safe foundation.

16. But behold, according to the scriptures, this stone shall become the great, and the last, and the only sure foundation upon which the Jews can build.

17. And now, my beloved, how is it possible that these, after having rejected the sure founda-

---

"And because they desired it God hath done it, that they may stumble." God allowed them to chastise themselves.

When Jesus began his ministry among the Jews at Jerusalem, there were many who refused to walk in the ways of the Lord and many who had forgotten the agreement their fathers had made with the Lord at Sinai. It was an agreement to be faithful to him if he would be their God.

Through iniquity, the Jews had fallen in the place they held. They had stumbled in keeping the commandments of God. Many of the ordinances and judgments they had received were abandoned; others were perverted to meet the unholy purposes of priests and kings. Their worship was fast becoming a mere form. They had ensnared themselves in the fowler's net and privally taught doctrines that robbed them of their heritage.

The Jews were quick to condemn and harsh in treatment of their neighbors. Class and class-distinction ruled their relations one with another. There were the Scribes and the Pharisees who represented the learned. There were the Sadducees who preferred the policies of Imperial Rome. There were the despised Galileans and the Samaritans, with whom the Jews seldom spoke. Each one walked in his own way and all were in pursuit of their own happiness.

Although drawn together by a common religion and bound by age-old restraints, they were torn by strife and disappointed pride. In spite of their piety and learning, crafty men interpreted the "Law" to feed the hunger of infatuation and greed. To appear more holy than others they clothed themselves in robes of righteousness. The Savior called them "hypocrites" and said to his disciples, "Take heed and beware of the leaven of the Pharisees and of the Sadducees." He likened the Pharisees to whited sepulchres: "Beautiful to look at but were full of dead men's bones." The aristocratic Sadducees did not believe in the resurrection of the dead. John the Baptist called them "a generation of vipers."

Judaism, instead of being the worship of the "True and Living God" became the "sanctuary of fools" and of those who used it as a starting place for their own peculiar notions.

VERSES 15-16. *And now I, Jacob, am led on by the spirit of prophesying.* Because of the stumbling of the Jews, in the which, they broke the covenant made by their fathers at Sinai and in the perversion of the ordinances they had received, they were brought to reject "the stone upon which they might build and have safe foundation." Jacob saw that the Jews would reject Christ and in doing so they refused to receive the stone, which according to the Scriptures "shall become the great, and the last, and the only sure foundation, upon which the Jews can build."

VERSES 17-18. *The head of their corner.* The Jews having rejected the cornerstone, which is Christ, the question is, "How can they ever build upon that sure

tion, can ever build upon it, that it may become the head of their corner?

18. Behold, my beloved brethren, I will unfold this mystery unto you; if I do not, by any means, get shaken from my firmness in the Spirit, and stumble because of my over anxiety for you.

---

and firm foundation?" Jacob, being led by the spirit of prophecy promises to unfold that *mystery*. That Christ may become the head of their corner, the *Rock* of their Salvation he will make known unless in his anxiety for his brethren he is shaken in his firmness in the spirit. In other words he asks for their faith and prayers, as we do today. That the spirit of prophecy may enlighten their minds and that they may understand what is being unrolled is his prayerful wish. He then proceeds to explain this mystery by quoting the Prophet Zenos.

## GENERAL NOTES

The knowledge these verses (3-5) impart should be remembered by us. It shows the depleted condition in which we presently find the Holy Scriptures; that is the part of them we refer to as the Old Testament. Jacob says, "All the holy prophets which were before us (about 550 years B.C.) had a hope of his glory." How many editors have deleted the mention of Christ in the Old Testament? How many interpreters have left out things pertaining to him, they cared not explain? How many writings of the holy prophets are not included in any modern version of the ancient Hebrew Scriptures? There are many. Neum prophesied that the Son of God should be crucified. Zenock, that he should be taken by the hands of wicked men and be lifted up. Zenos testified that Christ would be buried in a sepulchre and of "the three days of darkness" which should be "a sign given of his death unto those who should inhabit the isles of the sea, more especially given unto those who are of the house of Israel." (1 Ne. 19:10) The wonderful parable of the "Tame Olive Tree" which Zenos gave and which Jacob copied in full, is almost incomparable. These writings, with many others, are now left out of all Old Testament compilations. The Bible, itself, mentions some books now no longer extant; the Book of Nathan (Chron. 2:29); the Book of Enoch (Jude 14); the Book of Memorial (Ex. 17:14); the Book of Jasher (Joshua 10:13); the Book of Records (Ex. 4:15).

Jacob was a mighty preacher. He was trained in the language and the learning of his father, Lehi. Besides that, he was true to the Lord. He had the gift of prophecy which led him into many paths of righteousness. His gifts are evidenced by the fact that his brother, Nephi, engraved several of his sermons in great length upon the Small Plates. Read Chapters 6-11, 2 Nephi. the wisdom and knowledge shown, ranks them with some of the loftiest discourses ever made by the prophets of old. Moses had Aaron to speak for him. It may be that Nephi used Jacob as an instrument to teach the principles of truth to his ever-needing followers.

## CHAPTER 5

*Jacob quotes the Prophet Zenos—Allegory of the tame and the wild olive tree—Israel and the Gentiles.*

1. Behold, my brethren, do ye not remember to have read the words of the prophet Zenos, which he spake unto the house of Israel, saying:

2. Hearken, O ye house of Israel, and hear the words of me, a prophet of the Lord.

3. For behold, thus saith the Lord, I will liken thee, O house of Israel, like unto a tame olive-tree, which a man took and nourished in his vineyard; and it grew, and waxed old, and began to decay.

4. And it came to pass that the master of the vineyard went forth, and he saw that his olive-tree began to decay; and he said: I will prune it, and dig about it, and nourish it, that perhaps it may shoot forth young and tender branches, and it perish not.

5. And it came to pass that he pruned it, and digged about it, and nourished it according to his word.

6. And it came to pass that after many days it began to put forth somewhat a little, young and tender branches; but behold, the main top thereof began to perish.

7. And it came to pass that the master of the vineyard saw it, and he said unto his servant: It grieveth me that I should lose this tree; wherefore, go and pluck the branches from a wild olive-tree, and bring them hither unto me; and we will pluck off those main branches which are beginning to wither away, and we will cast them into the fire that they may be burned.

8. And behold, saith the Lord of the vineyard, I take away many of these young and tender branches, and I will graft them whithersoever I will; and it mattereth not that if it so be that the root of this tree will perish, I may preserve the fruit thereof unto myself; wherefore, I will take these young and tender branches, and I will graft them whithersoever I will.

9. Take thou the branches of the wild olive-tree, **and graft** them in, in the stead thereof;

VERSES 1-77. *Jacob quotes the Prophet Zenos.* Chapter Five of the Book of Jacob is devoted almost entirely to Jacob's recording of the prophecy of Zenos, wherein Zenos likened Israel to a tame olive tree. It is a prophetic history of the House of Israel and includes all the important events that have transpired and many that are yet to come to pass. The time encompassed by the allegory is from the covenant God made with Abraham to the Millennial reign of Christ.

First, who was Zenos? Zenos was a Hebrew prophet who labored amongst the Jews at a time which is not known to us. He is often quoted by Nephite servants of God. All we are told of his personal history is that he was slain because he testified boldly of what God had revealed to him. That he was a man greatly blessed with the spirit of prophecy is shown by the wonderful parable of the vineyard contained

and these which I have plucked off I will cast into the fire and burn them, that they may not cumber the ground of my vineyard.

10. And it came to pass that the servant of the Lord of the vineyard did according to the word of the Lord of the vineyard, and grafted in the branches of the wild olive-tree.

11. And the Lord of the vineyard caused that it should be digged about, and pruned, and nourished, saying unto his servant: It grieveth me that I should lose this tree; wherefore, that perhaps I might preserve the roots thereof that they perish not, that I might preserve them unto myself, I have done this thing.

12. Wherefore, go thy way; watch the tree, and nourish it, according to my words.

13. And these will I place in the nethermost part of my vineyard, whithersoever I will, it mattereth not unto thee; and I do it that I may preserve unto myself the natural branches of the tree; and also, that I may lay up fruit thereof against the season, unto myself; for it grieveth me that I should lose this tree and the fruit thereof.

14. And it came to pass that the Lord of the vineyard went his way, and hid the natural branches of the tame olive-tree in the nethermost parts of the vineyard, some in one and some in another, according to his will and pleasure.

15. And it came to pass that a long time passed away, and the Lord of the vineyard said unto his servant: Come, let us go down into the vineyard, that we may labor in the vineyard.

16. And it came to pass that the Lord of the vineyard, and also the servant, went down into the vineyard to labor. And it came to pass that the servant said unto his master: Behold, look here; behold the tree.

17. And it came to pass that the Lord of the vineyard looked and beheld the tree in the which the wild olive branches had been grafted; and it had sprung forth and begun to bear fruit. And he beheld that it was good; and the fruit thereof was like unto the natural fruit.

18. And he said unto the servant: Behold, the branches of the wild tree have taken hold of the moisture of the root thereof, that the root thereof hath brought

in this chapter of Jacob's Book. The prophecies of Zenos are also quoted by Nephi (1 Nephi 19:10, 12, 16), Alma (Alma 33,3, 13, 15), Amulek (Alma 34:7), Samuel, the Lamanite (Helaman 15:11), and Mormon (3 Nephi 10:16).

To obtain a proper understanding of this almost incomparable allegory, a laborious study of prophecy, history, and genealogy is entailed. In ancient times the Jews made these subjects an important part of their learning. In fact, it was the mold in which their integral lives appear to have been cast. The Prophet Nephi said, "Yea, and my soul delighteth in the words of Isaiah, for I came out of Jerusalem, and mine eyes hath beheld the things of the Jews, and I know that the Jews do understand the things of the prophets, and there is none other people that understand

forth much strength; and because of the much strength of the root thereof the wild branches have brought forth tame fruit. Now, if we had not grafted in these branches, the tree thereof would have perished. And now, behold, I shall lay up much fruit, which the tree thereof hath brought forth; and the fruit thereof I shall lay up against the season, unto mine own self.

19. And it came to pass that the Lord of the vineyard said unto the servant: Come, let us go to the nethermost part of the vineyard, and behold if the natural branches of the tree have not brought forth much fruit also, that I may lay up of the fruit thereof against the season, unto mine own self.

20. And it came to pass that they went forth whither the master had hid the natural branches of the tree, and he said unto the servant: Behold these; and he beheld the first that it had brought forth much fruit; and he beheld also that it was good. And he said unto the servant: Take of the fruit thereof, and lay it up against the season, that I may preserve it unto mine own self; for behold,

said he, this long time have I nourished it, and it hath brought forth much fruit.

21. And it came to pass that the servant said unto his master: How comest thou hither to plant this tree, or this branch of the tree? For behold, it was the poorest spot in all the land of the vineyard.

22. And the Lord of the vineyard said unto him: Counsel me not; I knew that it was a poor spot of ground; wherefore, I said unto thee, I have nourished it this long time, and thou beholdest that it hath brought forth much fruit.

23. And it came to pass that the Lord of the vineyard said unto his servant: Look hither; behold I have planted another branch of the tree also; and thou knowest that this spot of ground was poorer than the first. But behold the tree. I have nourished it this long time, and it hath brought forth much fruit; therefore, gather it, and lay it up against the season, that I may preserve it unto mine own self.

24. And it came to pass that the Lord of the vineyard said again unto his servant: Look

---

the things which were spoken unto the Jews like unto them, save it be that they are taught after the manner of the things of the Jews." (2 Nephi 25:5)

When Lehi left the Land of Jerusalem, where he had resided all his life and where his children had been reared, and partaking of the habits and the customs of the Jews, he took with him a copy of the Hebrew Scriptures, engraved upon plates of brass. Besides the writings of Moses and the prophecies of Isaiah which they contained, Lehi's son, Jacob, and other Nephite servants of God, often quoted the words of Zenos and Zenock, which were also upon these plates. The writings of these holy men are now omitted from all modern compilations of the Old Testament. Important things have been taken away from the prophets which, otherwise, would make clear many of their sayings that are now obscure.

hither, and behold another branch also, which I have planted; behold that I have nourished it also, and it hath brought forth fruit.

25. And he said unto the servant: Look hither and behold the last. Behold, this have I planted in a good spot of ground; and I have nourished it this long time, and only a part of the tree hath brought forth tame fruit, and the other part of the tree hath brought forth wild fruit; behold, I have nourished this tree like unto the others.

26. And it came to pass that the Lord of the vineyard said unto the servant: Pluck off the branches that have not brought forth good fruit, and cast them into the fire.

27. But behold, the servant said unto him: Let us prune it, and dig about it, and nourish it a little longer, that perhaps it may bring forth good fruit unto thee, that thou canst lay it up against the season.

28. And it came to pass that the Lord of the vineyard and the servant of the Lord of the vineyard did nourish all the fruit of the vineyard.

29. And it came to pass that a long time had passed away, and the Lord of the vineyard said unto his servant: Come, let us go down into the vineyard, that we may labor again in the vineyard. For behold, the time draweth near, and the end soon cometh; wherefore, I must lay up fruit against the season, unto mine own self.

30. And it came to pass that the Lord of the vineyard and the servant went down into the vineyard; and they came to the tree whose natural branches had been broken off, and the wild branches had been grafted in; and behold all sorts of fruit did cumber the tree.

31. And it came to pass that the Lord of the vineyard did taste of the fruit, every sort according to its number. And the Lord of the vineyard said: Behold, this long time have we nourished this tree, and I have laid up unto myself against the season much fruit.

32. But behold, this time it hath brought forth much fruit, and there is none of it which is good. And behold, there are all kinds of bad fruit; and it profiteth me nothing, notwithstanding all

---

In the Book of Mormon the great truths of the Gospel of Jesus Christ are made known in plainness. "For my soul delighteth in plainness; for after this manner doth the Lord God work among the children of men. For the Lord God giveth light unto the understanding; for he speaketh unto men according to their language, unto their understanding." (2 Nephi 31:3) Jacob, who, upon the death of Nephi, became the spiritual leader of the Saints in the Land of Nephi, said, "Behold my brethren, he that prophesieth, let him prophesy to the understanding of men; for the Spirit speaketh the truth and lieth not. Wherefore, it speaketh of things as they really are, and of things as they really will be; wherefore, these things are manifested unto us plainly, for the salvation of our souls." (Jacob 4:13)

No prophecy of God is obscure to those unto whom it is directed. To them its

our labor; and now it grieveth me that I should lose this tree.

33. And the Lord of the vineyard said unto the servant: What shall we do unto the tree, that I may preserve again good fruit thereof unto mine own self?

34. And the servant said unto his master: Behold, because thou didst graft in the branches of the wild olive-tree they have nourished the roots, that they are alive and they have not perished; wherefore thou beholdest that they are yet good.

35. And it came to pass that the Lord of the vineyard said unto his servant: The tree profiteth me nothing, and the roots thereof profit me nothing so long as it shall bring forth evil fruit.

36. Nevertheless, I know that the roots are good, and for mine own purpose I have preserved them; and because of their much strength they have hitherto brought forth, from the wild branches, good fruit.

37. But behold, the wild branches have grown and have overrun the roots thereof; and because that the wild branches have overcome the roots thereof it hath brought forth much evil fruit; and because that it hath brought forth so much evil fruit thou beholdest that it beginneth to perish; and it will soon become ripened, that it may be cast into the fire, except we should do something for it to preserve it.

38. And it came to pass that the Lord of the vineyard said unto his servant: Let us go down into the nethermost parts of the vineyard, and behold if the natural branches have also brought forth evil fruit.

39. And it came to pass that they went down into the nethermost parts of the vineyard. And it came to pass that they beheld that the fruit of the natural branches had become corrupt also; yea, the first and the second and also the last; and they had all become corrupt.

40. And the wild fruit of the last had overcome that part of the tree which brought forth good fruit, even that the branch had withered away and died.

41. And it came to pass that the Lord of the vineyard wept, and said unto the servant: What could I have done more for my vineyard?

42. Behold, I knew that all the

---

meaning is clear. "It need not be added to or taken from." The Apostle Peter, in his second letter to the Hebrew Christians in Asia Minor, says the apostles had not followed "cunningly devised fables" when they recounted the life of Jesus, his power and coming; for they had been eye witnesses to his majesty; they saw his glory and heard the voice from heaven, when they were with him in the holy mountain. But, he argues, if you want still more evidence of Jesus' divinity, "We have also a more sure word of prophecy; whereunto ye do well that ye take heed, as unto a light that shineth in a dark place, until the day dawn, and the day star arise in your hearts: Knowing this first, that no prophecy of the scripture is of any private interpretation. For the prophecy came not in old time by the will of man: but holy men of God spake as they were moved by the Holy Ghost." (II Peter 1:19-21) Such is the value

fruit of the vineyard, save it were these, had become corrupted. And now these which have once brought forth good fruit have also become corrupted; and now all the trees of my vineyard are good for nothing save it be to be hewn down and cast into the fire.

43. And behold this last, whose branch hath withered away, I did plant in a good spot of ground; yea, even that which was choice unto me above all other parts of the land of my vineyard.

44. And thou beheldest that I also cut down that which cumbered this spot of ground, that I might plant this tree in the stead thereof.

45. And thou beheldest that a part thereof brought forth good fruit, and a part thereof brought forth wild fruit; and because I plucked not the branches thereof and cast them into the fire, behold, they have overcome the good branch that it hath withered away.

46. And now, behold, notwithstanding all the care which we have taken of my vineyard, the trees thereof have become corrupted, that they bring forth no good fruit; and these I had hoped to preserve, to have laid up fruit thereof against the season, unto mine own self. But, behold, they have become like unto the wild olive-tree, and they are of no worth but to be hewn down and cast into the fire; and it grieveth me that I should lose them.

47. But what could I have done more in my vineyard? Have I slackened mine hand, that I have not nourished it? Nay, I have nourished it, and I have digged about it, and I have pruned it, and I have dunged it; and I have stretched forth mine hand almost all the day long, and the end draweth nigh. And it grieveth me that I should hew down all the trees of my vineyard, and cast them into the fire that they should be burned. Who is it that has corrupted my vineyard?

48. And it came to pass that the servant said unto his master: Is it not the loftiness of thy vineyard—have not the branches thereof overcome the roots which are good? And because the branches have overcome the roots thereof, behold they grew faster than the strength of the roots, taking strength unto themselves. Behold, I say, is not this the cause

---

the Apostle Peter places on the prophetic word. It is more sure, than what? Than the historical part of the Gospel, to which the apostles testified as eye witnesses. It shines as a light in a room during the dark hours, until the day breaks and the sun arises in full splendor. It is given us to heed, not to ignore. Indeed, the prophetic word is one of the most wonderful manifestations of the priesthood, caused by the operations of the Spirit upon the minds of holy men. It is the starlight for the guidance of the people of God, until the day star, the sun, comes up in glorious effulgence.

To understand and seize for one's own good, the lessons imparted in this allegory of the vineyard, it is necessary to remember it was written in the spirit of prophecy and of revelation. By that same spirit, Latter-day Saints know and proclaim its

that the trees of thy vineyard have become corrupted?

49. And it came to pass that the Lord of the vineyard said unto the servant: Let us go to and hew down the trees of the vineyard and cast them into the fire, that they shall not cumber the ground of my vineyard, for I have done all. What could I have done more for my vineyard?

50. But, behold, the servant said unto the Lord of the vineyard: Spare it a little longer.

51. And the Lord said: Yea, I will spare it a little longer, for it grieveth me that I should lose the trees of my vineyard.

52. Wherefore, let us take of the branches of these which I have planted in the nethermost parts of my vineyard, and let us graft them into the tree from whence they came; and let us pluck from the tree those branches whose fruit is most bitter, and graft in the natural branches of the tree in the stead thereof.

53. And this will I do that the tree may not perish, that, perhaps, I may preserve unto myself the roots thereof for mine own purpose.

54. And, behold, the roots of the natural branches of the tree which I planted whithersoever I would are yet alive; wherefore, that I may preserve them also for mine own purpose, I will take of the branches of this tree, and I will graft them in unto them. Yea, I will graft in unto them the branches of their mother tree, that I may preserve the roots also unto mine own self, that when they shall be sufficiently strong perhaps they may bring forth good fruit unto me, and I may yet have glory in the fruit of my vineyard.

55. And it came to pass that they took from the natural tree which had become wild, and grafted in unto the natural trees, which also had become wild.

56. And they also took of the natural trees which had become wild, and grafted into their mother tree.

57. And the Lord of the vineyard said unto the servant: Pluck not the wild branches from the trees, save it be those which are most bitter; and in them ye shall graft according to that which I have said.

58. And we will nourish again

message and hear the wonderful promise of him, whose voice is to all men, even unto the ends of the earth, "For because of my Spirit he shall know that these things are true." (Ether 4:11)

In the study of this parable and of all that is in the Book of Mormon, it is well to keep in mind that wise men, in every age of the world, have likened evil and error to night, and superstition and lack of knowledge to darkness. In contrast, they have compared truth and understanding to light. "I will be a light unto them forever . . ." is the glorious promise of the Lord to them, "that hear my words." (2 Nephi 10:14) "Who is among you that feareth the Lord, that obeyeth the voice of his servant, that walketh in darkness and hath no light?" (2 Nephi 7:10) As he watched his flock gathered about him, the Savior fondly compared himself to a

the trees of the vineyard, and we will trim up the branches thereof; and we will pluck from the trees those branches which are ripened, that must perish, and cast them into the fire.

59. And this I do that, perhaps, the roots thereof may take strength because of their goodness; and because of the change of the branches, that the good may overcome the evil.

60. And because that I have preserved the natural branches and the roots thereof, and that I have grafted in the natural branches again into their mother tree, and have preserved the roots of their mother tree, that, perhaps, the trees of my vineyard may bring forth again good fruit; and that I may have joy again in the fruit of my vineyard, and, perhaps, that I may rejoice exceedingly that I have preserved the roots and the branches of the first fruit—

61. Wherefore, go to, and call servants, that we may labor diligently with our might in the vineyard, that we may prepare the way, that I may bring forth again the natural fruit, which natural fruit is good and the most precious above all other fruit.

62. Wherefore, let us go to and labor with our might this last time, for behold the end draweth nigh, and this is for the last time that I shall prune my vineyard.

63. Graft in the branches; begin at the last that they may be first, and that the first may be last, and dig about the trees, both old and young, the first and the last; and the last and the first, that all may be nourished once again for the last time.

64. Wherefore, dig about them, and prune them, and dung them once more, for the last time, for the end draweth nigh. And if it be so that these last grafts shall grow, and bring forth the natural fruit, then shall ye prepare the way for them, that they may grow.

65. And as they begin to grow ye shall clear away the branches which bring forth bitter fruit, according to the strength of the good and the size thereof; and ye shall not clear away the bad thereof all at once, lest the roots thereof should be too strong for the graft, and the graft thereof shall perish, and I lost the trees of my vineyard.

66. For it grieveth me that I should lose the trees of my vineyard; wherefore ye shall clear away the bad according as the good shall grow, that the root and the top may be equal in strength,

---

shepherd. "I am the Good Shepherd," and with almost the same words he bid the Nephites, as he had the Jews, "Come follow me."

As men press forward in Jesus' footsteps and follow him along that path which is straight and narrow, they feel more and more "constrained to exclaim" with Isaiah, as is recorded upon the plates of brass, "O house of Jacob, come ye and let us walk in the light of the Lord." (2 Nephi 12:5. See also Isaiah 2)

And here, one should not forget the words of the ancient Hebrew Brethren, "In thy light shall we see light." (Psalm 36:9)

until the good shall overcome the bad, and the bad be hewn down and cast into the fire, that they cumber not the ground of my vineyard; and thus will I sweep away the bad out of my vineyard.

67. And the branches of the natural tree will I graft in again into the natural tree;

68. And the branches of the natural tree will I graft into the natural branches of the tree; and thus will I bring them together again, that they shall bring forth the natural fruit, and they shall be one.

69. And the bad shall be cast away, yea, even out of all the land of my vineyard; for behold, only this once will I prune my vineyard.

70. And it came to pass that the Lord of the vineyard sent his servant; and the servant went and did as the Lord had commanded him, and brought other servants; and they were few.

71. And the Lord of the vineyard said unto them: Go to, and labor in the vineyard, with your might. For behold, this is the last time that I shall nourish my vineyard; for the end is nigh at hand, and the season speedily cometh; and if ye labor with your might with me ye shall have joy in the fruit which I shall lay up unto myself against the time which will soon come.

72. And it came to pass that the servants did go and labor with their mights; and the Lord of the vineyard labored also with them; and they did obey the commandments of the Lord of the vineyard in all things.

73. And there began to be the natural fruit again in the vineyard; and the natural branches began to grow and thrive exceedingly; and the wild branches began to be plucked off and to be cast away; and they did keep the root and the top thereof equal, according to the strength thereof.

74. And thus they labored, with all diligence, according to the commandments of the Lord of the vineyard, even until the bad had been cast away out of the vineyard, and the Lord had preserved unto himself that the trees had become again the natural fruit; and they became like unto one body; and the fruits were equal; and the Lord of the vineyard had preserved unto himself the natural fruit, which was most precious unto him from the beginning.

75. And it came to pass that when the Lord of the vineyard

---

Were we to comment freely upon the events that this parable of the vineyard points to, it would make an exceeding large volume. It would be a history of many nations and peoples. It would give the reasons that we think were the cause of their rise and decay. It would be a story of man's obedience to God, or his disobedience. It would divine the future. We have already given the early history of Israel at some length and have aimed to impart knowledge concerning God's promises to our forefathers that, in them he will do his pleasure in saving his children and bringing them to the true worship of the Lamb.

saw that his fruit was good, and that his vineyard was no more corrupt, he called up his servants, and said unto them: Behold, for this last time have we nourished my vineyard; and thou beholdest that I have done according to my will; and I have preserved the natural fruit, that it is good, even like as it was in the beginning. And blessed art thou; for because ye have been diligent in laboring with me in my vineyard, and have kept my commandments, and have brought unto me again the natural fruit, that my vineyard is no more corrupted, and the bad is cast away, behold ye shall have joy with me because of the fruit of my vineyard.

76. For behold, for a long time will I lay up of the fruit of my vineyard unto mine own self against the season, which speedily cometh; and for the last time have I nourished my vineyard, and pruned it, and dug about it, and dunged it; wherefore I will lay up unto mine own self of the fruit, for a long time, according to that which I have spoken.

77. And when the time cometh that evil fruit shall again come into my vineyard, then will I cause the good and the bad to be gathered; and the good will I preserve unto myself, and the bad will I cast away into its own place. And then cometh the season and the end; and my vineyard will I cause to be burned with fire.

## CHAPTER 6

*Jacob expounds the allegory of the olive tree.—The pruning of the vineyard.*

## 1. *Jacob expounds the allegory of the olive tree.*

1. And now, behold, my brethren, as I said unto you that I would prophesy, behold, this is my prophecy—that the things which this prophet Zenos spake, concerning the house of Israel, in the which he likened them unto a tame olive-tree, must surely come to pass.

2. And the day that he shall set his hand again the second time to recover his people, is the day, yea, even the last time, that the servants of the Lord shall go forth in his power, to nourish and prune his vineyard; and after that the end soon cometh.

3. And how blessed are they

---

VERSE 1. *Must surely come to pass.* Jacob, always the mighty preacher and teacher of righteousness, herein fulfills his promise to his brethren that he would prophesy concerning the House of Israel. This is his prophecy: That all the things Zenos foretold, where, in the parable of the "tame olive-tree" he likened Israel to such a tree, "must surely come to pass." Many of the things of which he spoke have already happened. It is by that same spirit, the spirit of prophecy, that we see and recognize and understand the truths foretold in Zenos' allegory. It will not be difficult for those who have followed the history of the Jews and their neighbors as outlined in these comments, to grasp, easily, wherein many of Zenos' prophecies have been fulfilled. The others, as Jacob says, "Must surely come to pass."

VERSE 2. *The second time to recover his people.* "The Lord is mighty to save." Oftentimes he has intervened so to do. In the first place, as the chosen people of the Lord, Israel occupies an exalted position among the inhabitants of the earth. God covenanted with their father Abraham, saying, "And in thy seed shall all the nations of the earth be blessed." The blessings attending that ordination were predicated upon obedience to his commands for he ended his promise with these words, "Because thou hast obeyed my voice." Obedience was the essence of this promise, which was later renewed or confirmed by promises made to Isaac and to Jacob.

The Lord, on many occasions, rewarded Israel because of the covenant he had made with their fathers. He brought them out of Egypt. He went before them, in a pillar of cloud by day, and in a pillar of fire by night. He taught them with his own lips. He gave them laws to guide them. As a "watered garden" he cared for them.

Why? For what purpose? To what end?

To the end, "That ye may remember, and do all my commandments, and be holy unto your God. I am the Lord your God." That was early in the time that the Lord set himself to recover his people.

But they did not keep his laws. They were rebellious and, at his word, were destroyed from generation to generation. However, the Lord is long suffering, and again will send forth his servants, as was spoken by Zenos, to nourish, by his word, his people. He will give power unto his servants to prune the vineyard; that is to gather the righteous wherever they may be. The whole earth is the vineyard of our Lord and his servants will go to its uttermost parts to recover what is his. "After that the end soon cometh."

who have labored diligently in his vineyard; and how cursed are they who shall be cast out into their own place! And the world shall be burned with fire.

4. And how merciful is our God unto us, for he remembereth the house of Israel, both roots and branches; and he stretches forth his hands unto them all the day long; and they are a stiffnecked and a gainsaying people; but as many as will not harden their hearts shall be saved in the kingdom of God.

## 2. The pruning of the vineyard.

5. Wherefore, my beloved brethren, I beseech of you in words of soberness that ye would repent, and come with full purpose of heart, and cleave unto God as he cleaveth unto you. And while his arm of mercy is extended towards you in the light of the day, harden not your hearts.

6. Yea, today, if ye will hear his voice, harden not your hearts; for why will ye die?

7. For behold, after ye have been nourished by the good word of God all the day long, will ye

---

VERSE 3. *How blessed are they who have labored.* In this verse, Jacob bestows a benediction upon the servants of the Lord who have been zealous and who persevered in His service in the vineyard of our Lord. It reminds us of the words of the angel, who, in speaking for the Lord, said to Nephi, "And blessed are they who shall seek to bring forth my Zion at that day, for they shall have the gift and the power of the Holy Ghost; and if they endure unto the end they shall be lifted up at the last day, and shall be saved in the everlasting kingdom of the lamb; . . . (1 Nephi 13:37) Those who do wickedly and refuse to obey the voice of his servants "shall be cast out into their own place!" How natural it will be for the wicked to be separated from the righteous. How true it is that the wicked cannot endure the presence of the righteous man. Neither can that which is pure and holy mingle with that which is corrupt. Man, by his own actions, casts himself out; by his own deeds he renders service to God or the evil one. This is true and may be seen in church duty where a man may make of himself a mighty servant of the Lord or an impotent "hanger on." When the separation is accomplished, "The world shall be burned with fire."

VERSE 4. *He remembereth the House of Israel.* In connection with this verse let us read the words of Isaiah, as recorded in 1 Nephi 21:14. "But, behold, Zion hath said: The Lord hath forsaken me, and my Lord hath forgotten me—but he will show that he hath not." There are many assurances in Holy Writ that the Lord will remember his covenants with Israel. "The Lord hath been mindful of us; He will bless the house of Israel. He will bless them that fear the Lord, both small and great." (Jewish saying)

VERSES 5-13. *Repent . . . and cleave unto God.* In the Bible we read, "O Israel, return unto the Lord, thy God, for thou hast stumbled in thine iniquity." Likewise, Jacob implores his brethren to forsake their evil ways and hold fast to God's commandments, "as he cleaveth unto you." This was a call to repentance, and if they would repent with full purpose of heart, that includes going before the Lord in humility, he would be merciful unto them, and would hold them close

bring forth evil fruit, that ye must be hewn down and cast into the fire?

8. Behold, will ye reject these words? Will ye reject the words of the prophets; and will ye reject all the words which have been spoken concerning Christ, after so many have spoken concerning him; and deny the good word of Christ, and the power of God, and the gift of the Holy Ghost, and quench the Holy Spirit, and make a mock of the great plan of redemption, which hath been laid for you?

9. Know ye not that if ye will do these things, that the power of the redemption and the resurrection, which is in Christ, will bring you to stand with shame and awful guilt before the bar of God?

10. And according to the power of justice, for justice cannot be denied, ye must go away into that lake of fire and brimstone, whose flames are unquenchable, and whose smoke ascendeth up forever and ever, which lake of fire and brimstone is endless torment.

11. O then, my beloved brethren, repent ye, and enter in at the strait gate, and continue in the way which is narrow, until ye shall obtain eternal life.

12. O be wise; what can I say more?

13. Finally, I bid you farewell, until I shall meet you before the pleasing bar of God, which bar striketh the wicked with awful dread and fear. Amen.

---

to his bosom. He warned them that in the light they had received of God's mercy and his kindness, "Harden not your hearts." In other words, be ready, at all times, to receive, also, of his grace and his glory.

*Bring forth good fruit and not be cast into the fire.* One of the first fruits of repentance is forgiveness; upon reading further the quotation from the Bible, above referred to, the Lord says, "I will heal thy backsliding, I will love thee freely." A higher Judge than you or I has said that a tree is known by the fruit it brings forth. A good tree bringeth forth good fruit and an evil tree, evil fruit. He also says, "A man does not gather grapes of thorns nor figs of thistles." Therefore, Jacob's comment in verse seven.

Jacob asks of his brethren, why will ye refuse to believe all that has been spoken by the holy prophets concerning Christ and deny his Atoning Sacrifice? Why will ye reject the gift of the Holy Ghost and make a mockery of the plan of salvation and redemption? If you do these things, he said that *you* will be brought before the bar of God, in that day which is the day of Judgment, "and will stand with shame and awful guilt" before that Great Tribunal. And then in justice, you, having heard all these things, must go and partake of an "endless torment."

VERSE 12. *O be wise.* Jacob was familiar with the wisdom expressed by the Hebrews of old and we remember, too, "Happy is the man that findeth wisdom, and the man that getteth understanding." (Proverbs 3:13) Also, "Behold, the fear of the Lord, that is wisdom, and to depart from evil, that is understanding."

VERSE 13. *I bid you farewell.* Jacob, having borne the testimony that filled his heart; the testimony of Christ, his Atonement and saving grace, now bids farewell to his people.

## CHAPTER 7

*Sherem, denying the Christ, demands a sign and is stricken.—He confesses his sin and dies.—A reformation begins, hatred of Lamanites for Nephites.— Jacob gives the plates to his son, Enos.*

### 1. *Sherem, denying the Christ, demands a sign.*

1. And now it came to pass after some years had passed away, there came a man among the people of Nephi, whose name was Sherem.

2. And it came to pass that he began to preach among the people, and to declare unto them that there should be no Christ. And he preached many things which were flattering unto the people; and this he did that he might overthrow the doctrine of Christ.

3. And he labored diligently that he might lead away the hearts of the people, insomuch that he did lead away many hearts; and he knowing that I, Jacob, had faith in Christ who should come, he sought much opportunity that he might come unto me.

4. And he was learned, that he had a perfect knowledge of the language of the people; where-fore, he could use much flattery, and much power of speech, according to the power of the devil.

5. And he had hope to shake me from the faith, notwithstanding the many revelations and the many things which I had seen concerning these things; for I truly had seen angels, and they had ministered unto me. And also, I had heard the voice of the Lord, speaking unto me in very word, from time to time; wherefore, I could not be shaken.

6. And it came to pass that he came unto me, and on this wise did he speak unto me, saying: Brother Jacob, I have sought much opportunity that I might speak unto you; for I have heard and also know that thou goest about much, preaching that which ye call the gospel, or the doctrine of Christ.

7. And ye have led away much

VERSE 1. *A man named, Sherem.* The influence of the spirit of the world and the moral and mental condition of the Nephites at this time are forcibly depicted in the story of Sherem. This agitator appeared among the people and boldly declared that the doctrine of a divine Christ, or Messiah, was false. He was learned and eloquent, brazen and shrewd, as agents of Satan often are. In an interview with Jacob, he declared himself to be a believer in the Law of Moses, while at the same time, he denounced the doctrine of Christ as blasphemy. He understood how to hide his atheism under a mask of religion, as he knew how to gain adherents by means of flattery and I dare say so, by false promises.

Jacob refuted him and rebuked him, and when Sherem challenged Jacob to give him a sign of the power of the Holy Ghost, the prophet appealed this request to the Lord, saying, "Thy will, O Lord, be done and not mine." Immediately the blaspheming atheist was struck and fell to the earth. He had, evidently, a paralytic stroke in the sight of all present.

of this people that they pervert the right way of God, and keep not the law of Moses which is the right way; and convert the law of Moses into the worship of a being which ye say shall come many hundred years hence. And now behold, I, Sherem, declare unto you that this is blasphemy; for no man knoweth of such things; for he cannot tell of things to come. And after this manner did Sherem contend against me.

8. But behold, the Lord God poured in his Spirit into my soul, insomuch that I did confound him in all his words.

9. And I said unto him: Deniest thou the Christ who should come? And he said: If there should be a Christ, I would not deny him; but I know that there is no Christ, neither has been, nor ever will be.

10. And I said unto him: Believest thou the scriptures? And he said, Yea.

11. And I said unto him: Then ye do not understand them; for they truly testify of Christ. Behold, I say unto you that none of the prophets have written, nor

prophesied, save they have spoken concerning this Christ.

12. And this is not all—it has been made manifest unto me, for I have heard and seen; and it also has been made manifest unto me by the power of the Holy Ghost; wherefore, I know if there should be no atonement made all mankind must be lost.

13. And it came to pass that he said unto me: Show me a sign by this power of the Holy Ghost, in the which ye know so much.

14. And I said unto him: What am I that I should tempt God to show unto thee a sign in the thing which thou knowest to be true? Yet thou wilt deny it, because thou art of the devil. Nevertheless, not my will be done; but if God shall smite thee, let that be a sign unto thee that he has power, both in heaven and in earth; and also, that Christ shall come. And thy will, O Lord, be done, and not mine.

15. And it came to pass that when I, Jacob, had spoken these words, the power of the Lord came upon him, insomuch that he fell to the earth. And it came to pass that he was nourished for the space of many days.

## 2. *He confesses his sin and dies.*

16. And it came to pass that he said unto the people: Gather together on the morrow, for I shall die; wherefore, I desire to speak unto the people before I shall die.

17. And it came to pass that on the morrow the multitude were gathered together; and he spake plainly unto them and denied the things which he had taught them,

---

VERSES 16-23. *Gather together on the morrow, for I shall die.* Sherem did not recover from this "sign" of divine wrath, but before he died, he repented and confessed his error. Many heard him, believed in Christ, much to the joy of Jacob.

and confessed the Christ, and the power of the Holy Ghost, and the ministering of angels.

18. And he spake plainly unto them, that he had been deceived by the power of the devil. And he spake of hell, and of eternity, and of eternal punishment.

19. And he said: I fear lest I have committed the unpardonable sin, for I have lied unto God; for I denied the Christ, and said that I believed the scriptures; and they truly testify of him. And because I have thus lied unto God I greatly fear lest my case shall be awful; but I confess unto God.

20. And it came to pass that when he had said these words he could say no more, and he gave up the ghost.

21. And when the multitude had witnessed that he spake these things as he was about to give up the ghost, they were astonished exceedingly; insomuch that the power of God came down upon them, and they were overcome that they fell to the earth.

22. Now, this thing was pleasing unto me, Jacob, for I had requested it of my Father who was in heaven; for he had heard my cry and answered my prayer.

23. And it came to pass that peace and the love of God was restored again among the people; and they searched the scriptures, and hearkened no more to the words of this wicked man.

## 3. A reformation begins—hatred of Lamanites for the Nephites.

24. And it came to pass that many means were devised to reclaim and restore the Lamanites to the knowledge of the truth; but it all was vain, for they delighted in wars and bloodshed, and they had an eternal hatred against us, their brethren. And they sought by the power of their arms to destroy us continually.

25. Wherefore, the people of Nephi did fortify against them with their armies, and with all their might, trusting in the God and rock of their salvation; wherefore, they became as yet, conquerors of their enemies.

VERSES 24-25. *Many means were devised to restore the Lamanites.* Time now takes us to about 420 B.C. Conflict between Lamanites and Nephites had occurred as early as forty years after the exodus from Jerusalem but generally the Nephites were exceedingly prosperous in their settlement. The same is probably true of the Lamanites. Jacob says that they were in some respects, more righteous than the Nephites, notwithstanding their "filthiness and cursing," and that the Lord was merciful to them. (Jacob 3:5-7) In the year 420 B.C. the Nephites sought diligently to convert the Lamanites. They must have established missionary work among them. This, however, was, in the main, "love's labor lost." Enos, the son of Jacob, says he "saw wars between the Nephites and Lamanites in the course of my days." This was 179 years after the departure of his fathers from Judea, or 139 years from the emigration of Nephi from the settlement in the Land of Lehi, the place where he first made a home.

## 4. *Jacob gives the plates to his son, Enos.*

26. And it came to pass that I, Jacob, began to be old; and the record of this people being kept on the other plates of Nephi, wherefore, I conclude this record, declaring that I have written according to the best of my knowledge, by saying that the time passed away with us, and also our lives passed away like as it were unto us a dream, we being a lonesome and a solemn people, wanderers, cast out from Jerusalem, born in tribulation, in a wilderness, and hated of our brethren, which caused wars and contentions; wherefore, we did mourn out our days.

27. And I, Jacob, saw that I must soon go down to my grave; wherefore, I said unto my son Enos: Take these plates. And I told him the things which my brother Nephi had commanded me, and he promised obedience unto the commands. And I make an end of my writing upon these plates, which writing has been small; and to the reader I bid farewell, hoping that many of my brethren may read my words. Brethren, adieu.

---

VERSES 26-27. *And it came to pass that I, Jacob, began to be old.* Jacob now being advanced in years, delivered his records to his son, Enos, and told him of the instructions he had received from his brother, Nephi. Enos promised to carry out those instructions and so Jacob passed away.

His last days were made sad by the failure of the Nephites to convert the Lamanites and the necessity of making preparations against them to prevent wars and bloodshed. Also, by the contemplation of past experiences; the time, he says, "passed away with us, and also our lives passed away like as it were unto us a dream, we being a lonesome people, wanderers, cast out from Jerusalem, born in tribulation, in a wilderness, and hated by our brethren, which caused wars and contention; wherefore we did mourn out our days."

### JACOB

The elder of the two sons born to Lehi and Sariah (between 599 and 595 B.C.) while they were traveling in the Arabian wilderness. He was a mighty man of God and apparently, next to Nephi, the greatest and most devoted of all the sons of Lehi. When the little colony divided after the death of its patriarch, Jacob, who was yet young, followed Nephi and was ordained by him a priest to the people. Undoubtedly he received the higher priesthood or he could not have acted in the rites of the lesser priesthood, his being of the tribe of Manasseh and not of Levi. He magnified this calling with much zeal and prudence and Nephi records, at considerable length, extracts from his teachings. When Nephi died, Jacob appears to have taken charge of the spiritual concern of the people and to have presided over the church; he also became the custodian of the sacred treasures. He received many revelations and was blessed with the spirit of prophecy. So great was his faith that he could command, in the name of Jesus, and the trees, the mountains and the waves of the sea obeyed his word. For all this some of the Nephites of his day were not strong in the Lord. They gave way to the spirit of greed and lust and had to be sharply reproved by the word of the Lord through Jacob. In his day also the first anti-Christ, *Sherem,* appeared, a type of many who came after. But this presumptuous impostor was stricken by the power of God and paid the penalty of his folly with his life. Jacob had reason to rejoice in the eradication of his heresies and the return of the Nephites to sound doctrine. Jacob lived to a good old age. We have no account of the time or circumstances of his death, but before he passed away he gave the sacred records into the keeping of his son *Enos.*

## SHEREM

*Sherem.* The first of the many anti-Christ's who, at various times, appeared among the Nephites and endeavored by their teachings to lead the people from the principles of the Gospel. He appeared in the land of Nephi towards the close of the life of *Jacob,* the son of Lehi and openly taught that there would be no Christ nor necessity for atonement. He was a type of many who came after, for no matter how these apostates differed on lesser matters, they almost universally denied the coming of the Savior and taught that the faith of the Nephites in his appearing was a snare and a delusion. Sherem was a man of many words, much given to flattery and well acquainted with the language of his nation and withal very zealous in spreading his pernicious doctrines, so much so that he was successful in misleading many. Full of deceit and presumption, he contended with Jacob, denied the Christ and blasphemously called for a sign. A sign was given him. On Jacob's praying to the Lord, Sherem was smitten to the earth by the power of God and though he was nourished for many days he eventually died. The day before his death he called the people together and acknowledged his impiety and iniquity. He confessed Christ and told the people plainly that he had been deceived by the power of the devil and had lied unto God. He died with the terrible thought haunting him that he had committed the unpardonable sin. His confession and death wrought mightily among the people. Schism ceased for the time being, and the unity of the church was reestablished.

# THE BOOK OF ENOS

*The Lord's promise concerning a Nephite record to come forth
to the Lamanites—Character, condition, and wars of the two peoples.*

---

*Enos testifies of his father, a Hebrew custom, 1.—The remarkable story
of his conversion, 2-8.—States his anxiety for the welfare of his brethren and
his desire that the records should be preserved, 9-18.—He seeks for peace with
the Lamanites, 19-20.—Nephites were farmers and stockraisers, 21.—Many
prophets, Enos' own testimony and prophecies, 22-27.*

## 1. *Enos testifies of his father, a Hebrew custom.*

1. Behold, it came to pass that I, Enos, knowing my father that he was a just man—for he taught me in his language, and also in the nurture and admonition of the Lord—and blessed be the name of my God for it—

## 2. *The remarkable story of his conversion.*

2. And I will tell you of the wrestle which I had before God, before I received a remission of my sins.

3. Behold, I went to hunt beasts in the forests; and the words which I had often heard my father speak concerning eternal life, and the joy of the saints, sunk deep into my heart.

4. And my soul hungered; and I kneeled down before my Maker, and I cried unto him in mighty prayer and supplication for mine own soul; and all the day long did I cry unto him; yea, and

---

VERSE 1. You will remember that when Nephi commenced his life-story on these same plates as Enos now wrote, he, as was pointed out, paid tribute to his own parentage, Lehi and Sariah. We have shown that this was a custom amongst the Jews. (See 1 Nephi 1.) Enos, not overlooking this particularly Hebrew trait, did the same thing, and praised the Lord for the blessings he received from it. He received, at the hands of his father (Jacob) an acquaintance with those things that had been instilled in his father's heart by his grandfather, the Prophet Lehi. This included a knowledge of the language of his father which was Jewish, influenced by the mode of speech of the Egyptians. He was also brought up in the fear and the knowledge of God, being, from infancy, nurtured in his admonitions.

VERSE 2. *The wrestle I had before God.* Enos inserts in his account, a story of a struggle he had before the Lord. Not a physical but a moral and a spiritual trial at the end whereof he was assured his sins were forgiven.

VERSES 3-8. Enos was one of the most zealous servants of the Lord who ministered and prophesied to the early Nephites. As the son of Jacob, he succeeded his father in the sacred offices of priest and historian. He appears to have inherited

when the night came I did still raise my voice high that it reached the heavens.

5. And there came a voice unto me, saying: Enos, thy sins are forgiven thee, and thou shalt be blessed.

6. And I, Enos, knew that God could not lie; wherefore, my guilt was swept away.

7. And I said: Lord, how is it done?

8. And he said unto me: Because of thy faith in Christ, whom thou hast never before heard nor seen. And many years pass away before he shall manifest himself in the flesh; wherefore, go to, thy faith hath made thee whole.

### 3. States his anxiety for the welfare of his brethren.

9. Now, it came to pass that when I had heard these words I began to feel a desire for the welfare of my brethren, the Nephites; wherefore, I did pour out my whole soul unto God for them.

10. And while I was thus struggling in the spirit, behold, the voice of the Lord came into my mind again, saying: I will visit thy brethren according to their diligence in keeping my commandments. I have given unto them this land, and it is a holy land; and I curse it not save it be for the cause of iniquity; wherefore, I will visit thy brethren according as I have said; and their transgressions will I bring down with sorrow upon their own heads.

11. And after I, Enos, had heard these words, my faith began to be unshaken in the Lord; and I prayed unto him with many long strugglings for my brethren, the Lamanites.

12. And it came to pass that

his father's faith, gentleness, and devotion. Of his personal life we have no particulars but it is evident that he was a very aged man at the time of his death.

The incident Enos here records is very instructive as well as interesting. It affords us a deep insight into the purity and strength of his character. On this occasion he went in the forest to hunt but his whole soul was filled with thoughts of the prophecies and teachings of his devout father. He greatly hungered for more light regarding eternal things. In this fitting frame of mind, surrounded by the solitudes of the forest, he bowed down before the Lord and in prayers, long and fervent, sought his face. All day long he raised his voice to heaven and when night came he did not cease. At last his steadfast faith and godly yearnings prevailed. There came a heavenly voice of comfort to his heart, saying, "Enos, thy sins are forgiven thee, and thou shalt be blessed." "Lord, how is it done?" He anxiously inquired. The answer came, "Because of thy faith in Christ, whom thou hast never before heard nor seen. And many years pass away before he shall manifest himself in the flesh; wherefore, go to, thy faith hath made thee whole."

VERSES 9-18. *I began to feel a desire for the welfare of my brethren, the Nephites.* Enos continued to struggle with the Lord for promises in behalf of both Nephites and Lamanites. He received many precious assurances of things yet to be; amongst others, that the Lord would preserve the holy records and bring them forth unto the Lamanites in his own due time. Of these things Enos gladly testified to his

after I had prayed and labored with all diligence, the Lord said unto me: I will grant unto thee according to thy desires, because of thy faith.

13. And now behold, this was the desire which I desired of him —that if it should so be, that my people, the Nephites, should fall into transgressions, and by any means be destroyed, and the Lamanites should not be destroyed, that the Lord God would preserve a record of my people, the Nephites; even if it so be by the power of his holy arm, that it might be brought forth at some future day unto the Lamanites, that, perhaps, they might be brought unto salvation—

14. For at the present our strugglings were vain in restoring them to the true faith. And, they swore in their wrath that, if it were possible, they would destroy our records and us, and also all the traditions of our fathers.

15. Wherefore, I knowing that the Lord God was able to preserve our records, I cried unto him continually, for he had said unto me: Whatsoever thing ye shall ask in faith, believing that ye shall receive in the name of Christ, ye shall receive it.

16. And I had faith, and I did cry unto God that he would preserve the records; and he covenanted with me that he would bring them forth unto the Lamanites in his own due time.

17. And I, Enos, knew it would be according to the covenant which he had made; wherefore my soul did rest.

18. And the Lord said unto me: Thy fathers have also required of me this thing; and it shall be done unto them according to their faith; for their faith was like unto thine.

### 4. *He seeks for peace with the Lamanites.*

19. And now it came to pass that I, Enos, went about among the people of Nephi, prophesying of things to come, and testifying of the things which I had heard and seen.

20. And I bear record that the people of Nephi did seek diligent-

---

people, going about in their midst, prophesying of that which he had both seen and heard.

In the days of Enos the struggle still continued between Nephites and Lamanites. The latter seem to have made it the business of their lives to harass and annoy their more peaceful brethren. Their hatred was fixed. They swore in their wrath that if it were possible they would destroy the Nephites and also their records that they might no longer be compelled to listen to their warnings or be tormented by their appeals for peace and friendship.

VERSES 19-20. *People of Nephi did seek diligently.* Under his leadership, the Nephites sought diligently to make peace with the Lamanites, but, seemingly, in vain. In the almost ceaseless efforts to restore the Lamanites "unto the true faith in God" the Nephites must again have, as in the days of Jacob, established missionary work among them. Again all attempts to reclaim them failed, but instead they sank

ly to restore the Lamanites unto the true faith in God. But our labors were vain; their hatred was fixed, and they were led by their evil nature that they became wild, and ferocious, and a bloodthirsty people, full of idolatry and filthiness; feeding upon beasts of prey; dwelling in tents, and wandering about in the wilderness with a short skin girdle about their loins and their heads shaven; and their skill was in the bow, and in the cimeter, and the ax. And many of them did eat nothing save it was raw meat; and they were continually seeking to destroy us.

## 5. *Nephites were agriculturists and stock raisers.*

21. And it came to pass that the people of Nephi did till the land, and raise all manner of grain, and of fruit, and flocks of herds, and flocks of all manner of cattle of every kind, and goats, and wild goats, and also many horses.

## 6. *Many prophets, Enos's own testimony and prophecies.*

22. And there were exceeding many prophets among us. And the people were a stiffnecked people, hard to understand.
23. And there was nothing save it was exceeding harshness, preaching and prophesying of wars, and contentions, and destructions, and continually reminding them of death, and the duration of eternity, and the judgments and the power of God, and all these things—stirring them up continually to keep them in the fear of the Lord. I say there was nothing short of these things, and exceeding great plainness of speech, would keep them from going down speedily to destruction. And after this manner do I write concerning them.
24. And I saw wars between the Nephites and Lamanites in the course of my days.
25. And it came to pass that I began to be old, and an hundred

---

deeper into their savage ways, as is attested time and time again by those who refuse to serve the Lord; they become low and carnal and mean in their ways of life.

VERSE 21. *People of Nephi did till the land.* In this one paragraph we learn what the peaceful pursuits of the Nephites were. We would call them, farmers and stockmen. The picture Enos draws of the degradation into which the Lamanites had fallen at this early age is a pitiable one. On the other hand the Nephites were a rural, pastoral people, rich in grain and fruits, flocks and herds. They were industrious in their habits and committed but few offenses.

VERSES 22-27. *And there were exceeding many prophets among us.* The Nephites observed the Law of Moses but were lacking in faith, they were hard to make understand Gospel principles, they were wayward and stiffnecked. The terrors of the world had to be sounded in their ears more often than the gentler strains of Gospel invitation. They were blessed with many prophets, whose sermons, however, were harsh, threatening wars and desolation, death and destruction, to keep them on the

and seventy and nine years had passed away from the time that our father Lehi left Jerusalem.

26. And I saw that I must soon go down to my grave, having been wrought upon by the power of God that I must preach and prophesy unto this people, and declare the word according to the truth which is in Christ. And I have declared it in all my days, and have rejoiced in it above that of the world.

27. And I soon go to the place of my rest, which is with my Redeemer; for I know that in him I shall rest. And I rejoice in the day when my mortal shall put on immortality, and shall stand before him; then shall I see his face with pleasure, and he will say unto me: Come unto me, ye blessed, there is a place prepared for you in the mansions of my Father. Amen.

straight path. Enos had seen wars between the two peoples and he knew what was in store for them if they apostatized.

Jacob, as has been pointed out, was the elder of two sons born to Lehi in the Arabian wilderness between the years 600 and 590 B.C. Enos, in closing his record states that 179 years had passed since Lehi left Jerusalem. Supposing Enos was born when Jacob was thirty years old, his age when he wrote his record would then be 143 years. But we have no statement either of the time of his birth or the exact time of his death. All we know is that when he left this earth, he gave the records and the other sacred things into the hands of his son, Jarom.

Enos ends his writings with his personal testimony. He says that he has rejoiced in it all his life and that he did so above all the world and the things of the world. He says that he was wrought upon by the Spirit of God to preach and to prophesy unto this people and to declare the truth of Christ's coming among them. This he did and then he says, "I soon go to the place of my rest, which is with my Redeemer; for I know that in him I shall rest."

## GENERAL NOTES

### ENOS

A Nephite prophet, the grandson of Lehi and Sariah. Enos, if not the leading spirit of the age among his people, was undoubtedly one of the most conspicuous and zealous servants of the Lord who ministered and prophesied to the early Nephites. The son of Jacob, the priest and historian of the colony, he succeeded his father in these sacred offices and appears to have inherited his faith, gentleness and devotion. Of his personal life we have no particulars, but it is evident that he was a very aged man at the time of his departure from the scenes of mortality. His father, Jacob, was the elder of the two sons born to Lehi in the Asiatic wilderness, between the year 600 and 590 before Christ. We have no direct statement either of Enos' birth or the exact time of his death; all we know is that when he left this earth he gave the records and the sacred things associated therewith into the hands of his son, Jarom, 180 years after Lehi left Jerusalem, or 421 B.C.

# The Book of Jarom

*Jarom, son of Enos, keeps the records—The Nephites serve the Lord and are prosperous.*

---

*Jarom observes commandment of his father, Enos, to keep records that their genealogy may be preserved, 1.—Not necessary to write much because of the writings of his predecessors, 2.—Condition of Nephites and their wars and defenses against the Lamanites, 3-13.—Reason his record is small, 14-15.*

## 1. *Jarom observes commandment of his father.*

1. Now behold, I, Jarom, write a few words according to the commandment of my father, Enos, that our genealogy may be kept.

## 2. *Not necessary to write much.*

2. And as these plates are small, and as these things are written for the intent of the benefit of our brethren the Lamanites, wherefore, it must needs be that I write a little; but I shall not write the things of my prophesying, nor of my revelations. For what could I write more than my fathers have written? For have not they revealed the plan of salvation? I say unto you, Yea; and this sufficeth me.

---

VERSE 1. *I, Jarom, write . . . that our genealogy may be kept.* To keep proper and correct genealogies of all our forefathers is a vital part of the Gospel plan. Every Latter-day Saints knows that in this way we may extend to our ancestors the blessings of the Gospel and thus become saviors on Mt. Zion. The Lord has enjoined his people, in every dispensation, to keep adequate records so that his purposes, in the end, will be fulfilled. The Jews and all the other tribes of Israel were vigilant in keeping in their proper order, a record of the lineage through which they sprang. The Nephites were zealous in all efforts to do this. Lehi found upon the Plates of Brass, a genealogy of his fathers and his descendants and ever afterwards preserved this divine injunction. Jarom, therefore, that the line may not be broken, writes a "few words" according to this commandment which he had received.

VERSE 2. *These plates are small.* Because of lack of space (there not being much room left on the smaller plates to engrave all the things that had happened during the sixty years (422 to 362 B.C.) Jarom had charge of the holy things) and also because his forefathers had written many things concerning the Plan of Salvation, Jarom felt that he could add no more to what had already been placed on record. His own prophesyings and his revelations he would omit, but to keep the record in proper order he would write a little.

### 3. *Condition of the Nephites.*

3. Behold, it is expedient that much should be done among this people, because of the hardness of their hearts, and the deafness of their ears, and the blindness of their minds, and the stiffness of their necks; nevertheless, God is exceeding merciful unto them, and has not as yet swept them off from the face of the land.

4. And there are many among us who have many revelations, for they are not all stiffnecked. And as many as are not stiffnecked and have faith, have communion with the Holy Spirit, which maketh manifest unto the children of men, according to their faith.

5. And now, behold, two hundred years had passed away, and the people of Nephi had waxed strong in the land. They observed to keep the law of Moses and the sabbath day holy unto the Lord. And they profaned not; neither did they blaspheme. And the laws of the land were exceedingly strict.

6. And they were scattered upon much of the face of the land, and the Lamanites also. And they were exceeding more numerous than were they of the Nephites; and they loved murder and would drink the blood of beasts.

7. And it came to pass that they came many times against us, the Nephites, to battle. But our kings and our leaders were mighty men in the faith of the Lord; and they taught the people the ways of the Lord; wherefore, we withstood the Lamanites and swept them away out of our lands, and began to fortify our cities, or whatsoever place of our inheritance.

8. And we multiplied exceedingly, and spread upon the face of the land, and became exceeding rich in gold, and in silver, and in precious things, and in fine workmanship of wood, in buildings, and in machinery, and also in iron and copper, and brass and steel, making all manner of tools of every kind to till the ground, and weapons of war— yea, the sharp pointed arrow, and the quiver, and the dart, and the javelin, and all preparations for war.

9. And thus being prepared to meet the Lamanites, they did not

---

VERSES 3-13. . . . *ye shall prosper in the land.* The days of the Prophet Jarom saw the Nephites grow from a powerful tribe to a wealthy, though not as yet a very numerous nation. Indeed, their numbers were far from being equal to those of the wild and bloodthirsty Lamanites. The latter, like many of their descendants of today, spent their time almost exclusively in the chase of wild animals and in war; yet, notwithstanding the repeated and vigorous onslaughts of the Lamanites, the age of Jarom was to the Nephites a period of marked progress in the arts of peace.

They ceased to be entirely a pastoral people. They gave much attention to the adornment of their homes and public buildings with fine and curious work in wood and metal. Agriculture and manufacture received a new impetus by the invention of various machines, implements and tools. Their safety from successful attack by

prosper against us. But the word of the Lord was verified, which he spake unto our fathers, saying that: Inasmuch as ye will keep my commandments ye shall prosper in the land.

10. And it came to pass that the prophets of the Lord did threaten the people of Nephi, according to the word of God, that if they did not keep the commandments, but should fall into transgression, they should be destroyed from off the face of the land.

11. Wherefore, the prophets, and the priests, and the teachers, did labor diligently, exhorting with all long-suffering the people to diligence; teaching the law of Moses, and the intent for which it was given; persuading them to look forward unto the Messiah, and believe in him to come as though he already was. And after this manner did they teach them.

12. And it came to pass that by so doing they kept them from being destroyed upon the face of the land; for they did prick their hearts with the word, continually stirring them up unto repentance.

13. And it came to pass that two hundred and thirty and eight years had passed away—after the manner of wars, and contentions, and dissensions, for the space of much of the time.

### 4. Reason his record is small.

14. And I, Jarom, do not write more, for the plates are small. But behold, my brethren, ye can go to the other plates of Nephi; for behold, upon them the records of our wars are engraven, according to the writings of the kings, or those which they caused to be written.

15. And I deliver these plates into the hands of my son Omni, that they may be kept according to the commandments of my fathers.

---

the Lamanites was also measurably secured by the introduction of more perfect weapons of warfare and the development of a rude system of fortification, sufficient, however, to protect their cities and settlements from the means of attack at the command of their enemies.

Though the Nephites of this age were stiffnecked and perverse, requiring the constant warnings of prophets to keep them from backsliding, yet, the pervading tone of their society was simple and unaffected and the people were generally industrious, honest and moral. They neither blasphemed nor profaned the Holy Name of the Deity, they strictly observed the Law of Moses and kept the Sabbath Day sacred. Their prophets, priests and teachers not only instructed them in the Law of Moses but also expounded the intent for which it was given and while so doing directed their minds to the coming of Christ, the Messiah, in whom they taught the people to believe as though he had already come. That is real faith; to believe in that which is to come, as though it had already come to pass. These pointed and constant teachings preserved the Nephites from destruction by softening their hearts and bringing them to repentance when war, wealth, or pride had exerted their baneful influences.

VERSES 14-15.  *Delivers plates "to my son, Omni."*  Jarom again calls attention to the plates as being small and advises that the other plates, kept by the kings and on which they engraved or caused to be engraved a record "of the wars," are available to his brethren, the Lamanites (See v. 2) and that, therefore, he will write no more. Shortly before Jarom died he delivered the Sacred Plates to his son, Omni.

## GENERAL NOTES

### JAROM

A Nephite prophet who lived in the fourth and fifth centuries before Christ. He was the son of Enos, who was the son of Jacob, the brother of Nephi and was entrusted with the care of the plates of Nephi, which he appears to have retained 59 years, or from the 180th to the 239th year of the Nephite annals. From his record we learn that during his days many of the Nephites were a stiff-necked and hard-hearted people, among whom the prophets and priesthood labored diligently, warning them of the great evils that must ultimately result to the nation if they did not repent. Their labors were blessed with measurable success. It is pleasing to learn from Jarom's writings that the Nephite kings and leaders were mighty men in the faith of the Lord, who not only led them to victory over their earthly enemies, but also instructed them in the way of eternal salvation. The laws of the land were exceedingly strict, the law of Moses was rigorously observed, the Sabbath day was kept holy unto the Lord, and profanity and blasphemy were unknown. Under the wise and righteous administration of these kings, the Nephites spread widely over the land of Nephi, which was their home and increased greatly in numbers, though they were not nearly so numerous as the Lamanites, with whom they had several wars during the time embraced in Jarom's record. The Lamanites invaded the Nephite possessions "many times." But were driven out as often as they came. During this period the arts of peace were also encouraged and the Nephites grew exceedingly rich; it also appears to have been an epoch in which manufactures took a decided step in advance. Reference is made to progress in the working of the precious metals, in the manufacture of machinery and tools as well as of weapons of war; greater attention was paid to fine workmanship in wood and to improvements in building; altogether we may consider it a very prosperous era of this people's existence. If Jarom died in the year he delivered the plates to his son, Omni, that event took place 362 years before the advent of the Messiah.

# THE BOOK OF OMNI

## 1. Record of Omni.

1. Behold, it came to pass that I, Omni, being commanded by my father, Jarom, that I should write somewhat upon these plates, to preserve our genealogy—

2. Wherefore, in my days, I would that ye should know that I fought much with the sword to preserve my people, the Nephites, from falling into the hands of their enemies, the Lamanites. But behold, I of myself am a wicked man, and I have not kept the statutes and the command-ments of the Lord as I ought to have done.

3. And it came to pass that two hundred and seventy and six years had passed away, and we had many seasons of peace; and we had many seasons of serious war and bloodshed. Yea, and in fine, two hundred and eighty and two years had passed away, and I had kept these plates according to the commandments of my fathers; and I conferred them upon my son Amaron. And I make an end.

---

VERSES 1-3. Shortly before Jarom died he delivered the sacred plates to his son, Omni. Omni kept them for about 44 years and then handed them to his son, Amaron, who in turn transferred them to his brother, Chemish. Chemish, when his end was near, placed them in the hands of his son, Amaleki.

It is very little we know of the history of the Nephites from the death of Jarom to the time of Amaleki, a period of about 150 years. The political records of the nation were engraved on other plates, which were kept by the kings and as there was little that they felt it necessary to write beyond what Nephi and Jacob had written, their records were very short. From what little we can glean from these writings, it is evident that during this era the Nephites had frequent wars with the Lamanites in many of which they suffered severely.

The Lord permitted the Lamanites to be a constant scourge to the people of Nephi when they turned away from him and we fear the seasons were not unfrequent when they had to be reminded of their duty in this terrible way.

Omni records that he was a wicked man, who had not kept the commandments of God. But, he had, nevertheless, he says, fought for the Nephites; as if to say that the business of a warrior is not conducive to a life of righteousness. The history of his times, he sums up in one short paragraph, number 3.

## 2. *Writings of Amaron.*

4. And now I, Amaron, write the things whatsoever I write, which are few, in the book of my father.

5. Behold, it came to pass that three hundred and twenty years had passed away, and the more wicked part of the Nephites were destroyed.

6. For the Lord would not suffer, after he had led them out of the land of Jerusalem and kept and preserved them from falling into the hands of their enemies, yea, he would not suffer that the words should not be verified, which he spake unto our fathers, saying that: Inasmuch as ye will not keep my commandments ye shall not prosper in the land.

7. Wherefore, the Lord did visit them in great judgment; nevertheless, he did spare the righteous that they should not perish, but did deliver them out of the hands of their enemies.

8. And it came to pass that I did deliver the plates unto my brother Chemish.

## 3. *Testament of Chemish.*

9. Now I, Chemish, write what few things I write, in the same book with my brother; for behold, I saw the last which he wrote, that he wrote it with his own hand; and he wrote it in the day that he delivered them unto me. And after this manner we keep the records, for it is according to the commandments of our fathers. And I make an end.

## 4. *Statement made by Abinadom.*

10. Behold, I, Abinadom, am the son of Chemish. Behold, it came to pass that I saw much war and contention between my people, the Nephites, and the Lamanites; and I, with my own sword, have taken the lives of many of the Lamanites in the defence of my brethren.

11. And behold, the record of

VERSES 4-8. Amaron was the son of Omni and a descendant of Jacob, the younger brother of Nephi. He notes that 320 years after the exodus from Jerusalem, many Nephites had been slain because of their wickedness. "God," he says, "did visit them in great judgment." But he further says that the Lord did preserve the righteous and did deliver them out of the hands of their enemies. Amaron delivered the records to his brother, Chemish.

VERSE 9. Chemish testifies to the fact that his brother engraved the paragraphs credited to him, for he says that his brother wrote them, in his sight, on the day "he delivered them unto me." In this way was an unending record kept of their lineage and this was in obedience to the commands of their forefathers.

VERSES 10-11. Abinadom records that he had seen wars and contentions between Nephites and Lamanites and that he had slain many Lamanites in the defense of his people. He says, as do others, that the history of this people "is engraven upon this people is engraven upon plates which is had by the kings, according to the generations; and I know of no revelation save that which has been written, neither prophecy; wherefore, that which is sufficient is written. And I make an end.

## 5. *The record of Amaleki. God's Command to Mosiah.*

12. Behold, I am Amaleki, the son of Abinadom. Behold, I will speak unto you somewhat concerning Mosiah, who was made king over the land of Zarahemla; for behold, he being warned of the Lord that he should flee out of the land of Nephi, and as many as would hearken unto the voice of the Lord should also depart out of the land with him, into the wilderness—

13. And it came to pass that he did according as the Lord had commanded him. And they departed out of the land into the wilderness, as many as would hearken unto the voice of the Lord; and they were led by many preachings and prophesyings. And they were admonished continually by the word of God; and they were led by the power of his arm, through the wilderness, until they came down into the land which is called the land of Zarahemla.

---

plates which is had by the kings." He further says that he knows of no revelations nor prophecies that should be recorded as was commanded by the maker of the plates whereon he wrote.

VERSES 12-13. Amaleki, the son and successor of Abinadom, begins a new epoch in the history of the Nephites by relating the story of Mosiah.

But before we continue with the consideration of this branch of the House of Israel, let us examine the probable state of its "home-land," some of its physical features, its government and economy. It seems safe to assume that, to avoid the constant incursions of the warriors of the house of Laman, the Nephites had more than once forsaken their homes and retired farther northward into the wilderness. We judge this from the fact that in the days of Amaleki the land of Nephi appears to have been in or near the region we call Ecuador, a country far distant from the place where Lehi's colony first landed; and it is scarcely consistent with the narrative of the Book of Mormon to believe that Nephi and his little band, when they first separated from their brethren, made a journey of so many hundreds of miles before they established their homes. Then the very fact that the Lamanites almost immediately began to harass them in the new land which they occupied is strong evidence that their first removal was not so distant but that these enemies could, without great difficulty, reach them, a thing that would have been almost impossible if they had gone directly to the far distant region of Ecuador.

We will briefly summarize what we know of the history of the Nephites during the first three or four hundred years of their national existence.

They were governed by kings who were the direct descendants of Nephi. These kings were, as a rule, righteous men and wise rulers. The law of Moses was strictly observed and other good and just laws were enacted to regulate those matters the Mosaic law did not touch.

The Nephites multiplied greatly and also grew exceedingly rich in the wealth

## 6. *Mosiah discovers the people of Zarahemla.*

14. And they discovered a people, who were called the people of Zarahemla. Now, there was great rejoicing among the people of Zarahemla; and also Zarahemla did rejoice exceedingly, because the Lord had sent the people of Mosiah with the plates of brass which contained the record of the Jews.

15. Behold, it came to pass that Mosiah discovered that the people of Zarahemla came out from Jerusalem at the time that Zedekiah, king of Judah, was carried away captive into Babylon.

16. And they journeyed in the wilderness, and were brought by the hand of the Lord across the great waters, into the land where Mosiah discovered them; and they had dwelt there from that time forth.

17. And at the time that Mosiah discovered them, they had become exceeding numerous. Nevertheless, they had had many

---

of this world; while their artisans and mechanics were very expert in the arts and manufactures. They also spread abroad on the face of the land of Nephi and were scattered.

The Lamanites followed them from the land of their first possession and were constantly harassing them by incursions and invasions which led to numerous and bloody wars. These were sometimes very disastrous to the Nephites.

Spiritually, the Nephites had many seasons of faithfulness to God when they listened to and obeyed the words of his prophets and unfortunately, they had also many seasons of apostasy, at which times the judgments of God fell upon them; the Lamanites being often used by him as a sharp instrument to bring them to repentance and reformation.

At such a time as this, when moral and spiritual decay had undermined the righteous behavior of many of the Nephites, the Lord warned Mosiah to flee from the land of Nephi and take with him all who were willing to go. Mosiah obeyed and soon he and his followers "departed out of the land into the wilderness . . . and they were led by many preachings and prophesyings. And they were admonished continually by the word of God; and they were led by the power of his arm, through the wilderness, until they came down into the land which is called the land of Zarahemla."

Several facts are to be noted here. Zarahemla was separated from the land of Nephi by a wilderness. It occupied a lower altitude, for the travelers had to go "down" to get there. There must have been a considerable distance between the two countries, for the company was led by "many preachings and prophesyings" and it must have been a perilous journey, for they were also led by "the power of the arm of the Lord," and were admonished continually.

VERSES 14-19. All this indicates clearly a long and exacting effort, but the pilgrims were well paid for their enterprise, for finally, they discovered a new country, inhabited by a colony from Palestine. The country was called Zarahemla after its ruler by that same name.

The people there were called "the people of Zarahemla" and are now known as the *Mulekites*. The arrival of Mosiah was a joyful event, for he had, among other things, the Brass Plates from Jerusalem.

At the time of the arrival of Mosiah, the Mulekites had become exceedingly

wars and serious contentions, and had fallen by the sword from time to time; and their language had become corrupted; and they had brought no records with them; and they denied the being of their Creator; and Mosiah, nor the people of Mosiah, could understand them.

18. But it came to pass that Mosiah caused that they should be taught in his language. And it came to pass that after they were taught in the language of Mosiah, Zarahemla gave a genealogy of his fathers, according to his memory; and they are written, but not in these plates.

19. And it came to pass that the people of Zarahemla, and of Mosiah, did unite together; and Mosiah was appointed to be their king.

### 7. *Large stone brought to Mosiah.*

20. And it came to pass in the days of Mosiah, there was a large stone brought unto him with engravings on it; and he did interpret the engravings by the gift and power of God.

21. And they gave an account of one Coriantumr, and the slain of his people. And Coriantumr was discovered by the people of Zarahemla; and he dwelt with them for the space of nine moons.

22. It also spake a few words concerning his fathers. And his first parents came out from the tower, at the time the Lord con-

---

numerous, notwithstanding "wars and serious contentions."[1] Their language had been corrupted and their religion forgotten. After a while, however, the people of Mosiah and those of Zarahemla began to understand each other and united and elected Mosiah king and ruler. I think we may safely assume that both Nephites and Lamanites, during three or four centuries, had spread over an immense area, from their first two centers of population. There was no abiding place for Mosiah and his followers in the immediate vicinity of their home-land. Consequently, the Lord led them out in the wilderness.

Two geographical facts are here noted: (1) Zarahemla was separated from the Land of Nephi by a wilderness; (2) it had a lower altitude, for Mosiah "came down into the land." (v. 13) And those who would return "went up into the wilderness." (v. 27)

VERSES 20-22. In the Land of Zarahemla, Mosiah came into possession of a large stone, upon which was engraved some unknown characters. He interpreted them by the gift of God and found thereon an account of one Coriantumr and the slain of his people "whose bones were scattered in the land northward." Coriantumr had lived with the people of Zarahemla for "nine moons" and according to the engravings on said stone, the ancestors of the race of which he was the sole survivor, came from the region of the Tower of Babel. These people are known as the Jaredites. Here is another geographic fact. The land where the bones of the slain Jaredites lay scattered was north of Zarahemla.

---

[1]In view of the fact, that, in the traditions of nearly all Indians, wherever their ancestors first settled, they were the followers of others or earlier occupants, the question may be asked whether "wars" in the text indicates that the Mulekites had suffered from hostile aborigines as well as from contentions among themselves.

founded the language of the people; and the severity of the Lord fell upon them according to his judgments, which are just; and their bones lay scattered in the land northward.

## 8. *King Benjamin.*

23. Behold, I, Amaleki, was born in the days of Mosiah; and I have lived to see his death; and Benjamin, his son, reigneth in his stead.

24. And behold, I have seen, in the days of king Benjamin, a serious war and much bloodshed between the Nephites and the Lamanites. But behold, the Nephites did obtain much advantage over them; yea, insomuch that king Benjamin did drive them out of the land of Zarahemla.

## 9. *Testimony of Amaleki.*

25. And it came to pass that I began to be old; and, having no seed, and knowing king Benjamin to be a just man before the Lord, wherefore, I shall deliver up these plates unto him, exhorting all men to come unto God, the Holy One of Israel, and believe in prophesying, and in revelations, and in the ministering of angels, and in the gift of speaking with tongues, and in the gift of interpreting languages, and in all things which are good; for there is nothing which is good save it comes from the Lord; and that which is evil cometh from the devil.

26. And now, my beloved brethren, I would that ye should come unto Christ, who is the Holy One of Israel, and partake of his salvation, and the power of his redemption. Yea, come unto him, and offer your whole souls as an offering unto him, and continue in fasting and praying, and endure to the end; and as the Lord liveth ye will be saved.

---

VERSES 23-24. The historian, Amaleki, says that he (Amaleki) was born in the days of Mosiah and that he survived him. He lived through a great war between Nephites and Lamanites during the beginning of the reign of King Benjamin.[2] The Nephites drove the Lamanites out of Zarahemla.

VERSES 25-26. Knowing the plates whereon he wrote were small and that they were almost filled, nevertheless, Amaleki used a goodly portion of what was left to exhort those who should come after him to lives of goodness and purity. The personal testimony which he records is an appeal to all to come and partake of the gifts of God and through Christ, who is the Holy One of Israel, obtain salvation. The testimony of Amaleki is a sure bit of evidence pertaining to the authenticity of the Book of Mormon. For, he exhorts us only to righteousness and goodness and he says, "There is nothing which is good save it comes from the Lord."

---

[2]This war was fought in Zarahemla. Lamanites were those who sought to destroy the Nephites. Nephites were friends and adherents of that great prophet. (Jacob 1:14)

## 10. *Certain number return to land of their inheritance.*

27. And now I would speak somewhat concerning a certain number who went up into the wilderness to return to the land of Nephi; for there was a large number who were desirous to possess the land of their inheritance.

28. Wherefore, they went up into the wilderness. And their leader being a strong and mighty man, and a stiffnecked man, wherefore he caused a contention among them; and they were all slain, save fifty, in the wilderness, and they returned again to the land of Zarahemla.

29. And it came to pass that they also took others to a considerable number, and took their journey again into the wilderness.

30. And I, Amaleki, had a brother, who also went with them; and I have not since known concerning them. And I am about to lie down in my grave; and these plates are full. And I make an end of my speaking.

---

VERSES 27-30. Before Amaleki ended his account he records that many Nephites in Zarahemla desired to return to the land of Nephi, whence their forefathers came, to take possession of their inheritance, which, according to Mosaic law, always remained theirs. Accordingly, a large company was formed. The leader was a strong and a mighty man but unfit for leadership. Owing to his stubbornness, contention arose and all but a few—fifty—of their numbers perished in the wilderness. The survivors returned to Zarahemla.

Another expedition was formed. Amaleki had a brother in this company but he never heard of their experiences after their departure. (See the Record of Zeniff, Mosiah 9 *et seq.*, where the narrative shifts from the Nephites in Zarahemla to those in the original land of Nephi.)

Amaleki completed the smaller plates until there was no more room for engravings. Being without descendants, he turned them over to King Benjamin.

King Benjamin put them with the other plates that had been kept and handed down by the kings from generation to generation. The Prophet Mormon found them centuries later and finally deposited them in the Hill Cumorah. (Words of Mormon 10-11 and Mormon 6:6)

### GENERAL NOTES

Where italics are used in writing a name it indicates that a biographical sketch of that person is herewith included.

### OMNI

A Nephite prophet, son of *Jarom* and a descendant of Jacob the younger brother of Nephi. He lived in the land of Nephi and was the custodian of the plates of Nephi from the 239th to the 283rd year of the Nephite annals. He characterizes himself as a wicked man who had not kept the commandments and statutes of the Lord as he ought to have done but had been principally engaged in defending his people from constantly recurring onslaughts of the Lamanites. The history of his times he sums up in one short sentence: "And it came to pass that 276 years had passed away from the time Lehi left Jerusalem and we had many seasons of peace and we had many seasons of serious war and bloodshed." Having kept the plates according to the commandments of his fathers he conferred them upon his son *Amaron*. (B.C. 318)

## AMARON

A Nephite prophet, son of *Omni* and a descendant of Jacob, the younger brother of Nephi. He resided in the land of Nephi in the third and fourth centuries before Christ. Amaron received the plates of Nephi from his father and held them from the two hundred and eighty-third to the three hundred and twenty-first year of the Nephite annals when he transferred them to his brother *Chemish*. Owing to the increasing wickedness of the Nephite people, the Lord, during Amaron's days, visited them in great judgment so that the more wicked part were destroyed but he spared the righteous and delivered them out of the hands of their enemies. Of Amaron's private character the sacred record is silent.

## CHEMISH

The son of *Omni*, a descendant of Jacob, the son of Lehi. He received the sacred records from his brother *Amaron* in the year 280 B.C. His entire writings consist of only sixty-nine words and from them we can gather nothing regarding his private life, the history of his times, nor for how long a period he retained the plates. We must, however, suppose that his brother Amaron considered him the most suitable person on whom to impose this sacred trust and consequently believe him to have been a good man. He is ranked among the prophets by Mormon. He conferred the custody of the plates upon his son *Abinadom*.

## ABINADOM

A Nephite prophet and historian who lived in the third century before Christ. He received the plates of Nephi from his father, Chemish, who was a descendant of Jacob, the brother of Nephi, and at his death, which occurred in the days of the first Mosiah, his son Amaleki took charge of them. Either he or his son conveyed the sacred records from the land of Nephi to Zarahemla in the great migration of the Nephites under *Mosiah* but the record does not show whether he died in the land of Nephi before this movement took place or after. His record is a very short one. From it we learn that he was a warrior and had seen many wars between the Nephites and Lamanites and that in those wars he, with his own sword, had taken the lives of many of the enemy in the defense of his brethren. These disastrous wars were undoubtedly one of the causes that led to the removal of the righteous portion of the Nephites from Nephi to Zarahemla. Abinadom concludes his brief record with the following statement, "And I know of no revelation, save that which has been written, neither prophecy; wherefore, that which is sufficient is written. And I make an end."

## AMALEKI

The son of *Abinadom* and a descendant of Jacob, the son of Lehi. He was one of the custodians of the sacred records of the Nephites and was born in the days of the first Mosiah but whether in the land of Nephi or of Zarahemla does not appear. If in Nephi then he transported the plates from that land to Zarahemla in the great migration of the Nephites under Mosiah and it is quite likely that he did so, for it is he that gives the account of this vast movement. Having no children at his death he transferred the holy things of which he had charge to King Benjamin. He lived about B.C. 200.

## Mosiah I

Mosiah resided in the land of Nephi and lived there during the latter half of the third century before Christ. Whether he was originally a prophet, priest or king the historian (Amaleki) does not inform us. Most certainly he was a righteous man for the Lord made choice of him to guide the obedient Nephites from their choice country to a land that he would show them.

The causes that led the Lord to make this call upon the Nephites are not stated but some of them can be easily surmised. Among such we suggest that:

The aggressive Lamanites were constantly crowding upon them, ravaging their more remote districts, entrapping and enslaving the inhabitants of the outlying settlements, driving off their flocks and herds and keeping them in a constant state of anxiety and dread which hindered their progress and stayed the growth of the work of God. The Lord therefore led them to a land of peace.

Again, this course of events continued for so long a period, had caused much hard-heartedness and stiff-neckedness in the midst of the Nephites. Some of the people had remained righteous, some had grown very wicked. To separate these classes the Lord called the faithful and obedient to follow Mosiah to another land.

For a third reason there was a portion of the house of Israel a few hundred miles to the north entirely unknown to their Nephite brethren. These people had sunk very low in true civilization, they were so degraded that they denied the being of their Creator, they had had many wars and contentions among themselves, they had corrupted their language, had no records nor scriptures and were altogether in a deplorable condition. To save and regenerate this branch of God's covenant people Mosiah and the Nephites were led to the place where they dwelt.

The statement made by Amaleki regarding this great migration under Mosiah is brief. We are altogether left to our imagination to picture the scenes that occurred at this division of a nation. Nor can we tell how many, preferring home, kindred and friends and the endearments and associations of their native land, faltered and tarried behind, while the faithful started on their journey northward into the untrodden wilderness. Nor are we informed what afterwards became of those who allowed the allurements of the world to prevail. It is most probable that they united with the Lamanites, were absorbed into that race and like them became darkened, bloodthirsty and savage.

The Nephite evacuation of the cities built in the land of Nephi no doubt had a beneficial effect on those portions of the Lamanite race that took possession of them. They thereby became acquainted with some of the comforts and excellencies of civilization and though very slow to learn, their experience at this time laid the foundation for a slight advance of the arts of peace in their midst.

Mosiah gathered up the willing and obedient and as directed by the Lord, started on the journey. Whither they were going they understood not, only they knew that the Lord was leading them. With preachings and prophesyings they crossed the wilderness and passed down into the land of Zarahemla.

On the west bank of the River Sidon, the people of Mosiah found a populous city, of whose existence they had never before heard. Its people were a semi-civilized and irreligious race, speaking a strange language and with many habits and customs different from those of the new comers.

The meeting must have been a perplexing one to both peoples, brought face to face but unable to understand each other by reason of their different modes of speech. We often read in history of the irruption of an inferior or more barbarous race into the domains of a more highly civilized one but it is seldom, as in this case, that the superior race moves in a body, occupies the country and unites with the less enlightened people. It is probable that the first feelings of the old settlers were akin to dismay as they learned of the hosts of the invaders that were marching upon them but these feelings were soon soothed and an understanding arrived at by which the two people became one nation. We are forced to the conclusion that this arrangement could not have been effected without the direct interposition of heaven by and through which both peoples were brought to a united purpose and common understanding.

When the Nephites began to comprehend the language of their new fellow citizens they found that they were the descendants of a colony which had been led from Jerusalem by the hand of the Lord in the year that that city was destroyed by the king of Babylon (say B.C. 589. *See Mulek*). At this time their king or ruler was named *Zarahemla* (about B.C. 200). The reason assigned for their departure from the worship of the true God, their degradation and the corruption of their language was that their forefathers brought with them from their ancient home in Palestine no records or copies of the holy scriptures to guide and preserve them from error in their isolated land of adoption.

When the two races joined it was decided that Mosiah should be the king of the united people though the Nephites were then the less numerous. This arrangement probably grew out of the fact that though fewer in numbers they were the more civilized and also being worshipers of the God of Israel they would not willingly submit to be ruled by those who had no knowledge of his laws.

The education of the people of Zarahemla to the standard of the Nephites and the work of harmonizing the two races were not the task of an hour. It required much wisdom, patience and perseverance. Mosiah gave stability to the new kingdom by his own virtues and wise example, by the just laws he established and by placing the service of the Lord before all earthly consideration. It is evident that he built a temple in the new land as its existence is particularly mentioned in the days of his son, King Benjamin and as the people observed the law of Moses in the matter of sacrifices and offerings a temple would be one of their very first necessities. But to the forms, types and ceremonies of the Mosaic law were added gospel principles with a clear and definite understanding of the coming and divine work of the Messiah. Mosiah was not only a divinely inspired leader and king but he was also a seer. While reigning in Zarahemla a large engraved stone was brought to him and by the gift and power of God he translated the engravings thereon. They gave an account of the rise, fall and destruction of the great Jaredite nation from the days of its founders to the time of their last king Coriantumr, who himself was discovered by the people of Zarahemla and lived with them nine moons. When Mosiah died he was succeeded by his son Benjamin.

### ZEDEKIAH

The last king of Judea. In the first year of his reign Lehi and his family left Jerusalem. Zedekiah's name occurs eight times in the Book of Mormon, five of which are connected with Lehi's departure, the other three relate to the monarch's posterity. The killing of the sons of Zedekiah by the king of Babylon is spoken of in Helaman 8:21.

### LAND OF LEHI-NEPHI

A small division of the land of Nephi originally settled by the Nephites but after their departure it was taken possession of by the Lamanites and by them made the chief center of their government. It appears to have been simply the valley in which the City of Lehi-Nephi stood but because it at one time comprised all the territory occupied by the Nephites, whence they spread out and colonized, it is more often called the land of Nephi than the land of Lehi-Nephi; but it must not be confounded with the larger land of Nephi which grew out of it. This smaller land of Nephi is supposed to have been situated in the country now called Ecuador.

## MULEK

The infant son of Zedekiah, king of Judea, who was preserved when the rest of his brothers were slain (II Kings 25:7) by the king of Babylon. Eleven years after Lehi left Jerusalem the Lord led another colony from that city to America, among whom was Mulek, who, at that time must have been very young as his father was only 21 years old when he commenced to reign and he reigned but eleven years in Jerusalem (II Chronicles 36:11; Jeremiah 25:1). It is altogether probable that when Mulek attained a proper age he, on account of his lineage, was recognized as king or leader of the colony.

Regarding the journey of this company, all we are told in the Book of Mormon is that they came out of Jerusalem at the time that Zedekiah, king of Judea, was carried away captive into Babylon and that they journeyed in the wilderness and were brought by the hand of the Lord across the great waters. Again we are informed that they landed on the northern continent, in the land afterwards known to the Nephites as the land *Desolation* and for this reason the Nephites called North America the land of Mulek. This must not be confounded with the country immediately surrounding the city of Mulek in South America. In after years this colony migrated southward and settled on the River Sidon where their descendants were afterwards found by the Nephites.

## ZARAHEMLA

When *Mosiah I* led the more righteous portion of the Nephites northward from the land of Lehi-Nephi (about B.C. 200) he found on the west bank of the River Sidon a city inhabited by a partly civilized and irreligious people whose language he could not understand. They were ruled by a chief or king named Zarahemla. When the two races began to understand each other it was found that the people of Zarahemla were the descendants of a colony which was led by the Lord out of Jerusalem in the year when that city was destroyed by the king of Babylon (B.C. 589). After wandering in the wilderness they were brought across the great waters and landed in the southern portion of the North American continent. In after years they migrated southward to the place where they were found by Mosiah. Among the members of the original colony was *Mulek*, the youngest son of King *Zedekiah* and it is presumable that most of them were of the house of Judah.

Of the history of the colony for nearly four hundred years we know next to nothing. It is summed up in the few following words, "And at the time that Mosiah discovered them, they had become exceedingly numerous. Nevertheless, they had had many wars and serious contentions, and had fallen by the sword from time to time; and their language had become corrupted; and they had brought no records with them; and they denied the being of their Creator; and Mosiah, nor the people of Mosiah, could understand them." (Omni 1:17)

## CORIANTUMR

Coriantumr was the last of the Jaredites. We are first introduced to him as king of all the lands of the Jaredites. In his day the Prophet Ether raised his warning voice but all his words of exhortation and reproof were rejected by that rapidly decaying race.

Coriantumr, himself, was a mighty prince, well versed in the art of war, cunning, diplomatic and learned, but exceedingly corrupt. Like his people, he gave no heed to the prophecies of Ether. Troublous and terrible times followed, for the war that commenced in the first year of Ether's warnings, lasted until the nation was destroyed. This war became one of the most bloodthirsty, cruel and vindictive that ever cursed our fair planet. It was not the work of a day, it was the outgrowth of centuries of dishonor, crime and iniquity. Men's most savage passions were worked up to such an extent that every better feeling of humanity was crushed out. The women and children armed themselves for the fray with the same fiendish activity and fought with the same intense hate as the men. It was not a conflict of armies alone; it was the crushing together of a divided house that had long tottered because of internal weakness but now fell in upon itself.

Coriantumr was wounded in the last great battle of this war and when he regained consciousness, wandered forth aimlessly and alone, the last of his race. How long he thus wandered to and fro, wretched, comfortless and forlorn we know not but at last he reached the southern portion of the northern continent, thousands of miles from Ramah and there, to the great astonishment of both, he found the people of *Mulek*, who had been led by the hand of the Lord from Jerusalem. With them he spent his few remaining days and when nine moons had grown and waned he passed away to join the hosts of his people in the unknown world of spirits.

# A Closing Word

When the neighbors of Noah and those who foretold the weather, gathered about him to ridicule his efforts to save himself and his family from a flood which was to come, they joined a great throng of those who are always ready to reject the counsel of God.

"This man builds a ship where there is no water," they said. "Noah is getting old and perhaps a little mad."
"A rainstorm to flood the earth!"

*"Impossible!"*

When the brothers of Joseph sold him to some Ishmaelitish merchants going down into Africa, they did not dream that one day he would become second only to the ruler in Egypt. But when he interpreted the dreams of troubled Pharaoh, which the magicians of Pharaoh's court could not do, Joseph stored up great quantities of grain against a famine which he predicted would last for seven years.

Again the scoffers came as they had come to Noah.

"A famine in Egypt!"
"Is not the valley of the Nile the great granary of the whole earth?"
"Have our crops ever failed?"
"A famine in Egypt?"

*"Impossible!"*

Joshua led the armies of Israel. In modern warfare he would not rank as a strategist. He brought his armies to battle against the city of Jericho. One day he marched them around its walls. The second and the third day and for seven days he did the same. This must have amused the embattled people of Jericho who had heard of the strength and fierceness of Israel's hosts. To them it was strange tactics. They thought it childish strategy. Ensconced behind the bulwarks and the battlements of their great city they felt safe. I can conceive of their ignorance and infatuation as they stood upon its walls and shouted,

"Joshua take Jericho?"

*"Impossible!"*

To the skeptic who loves to carp and cavil, all things are impossible. In part let us agree. The impossible cannot happen. But, did not the flood come? Does not history record the famine in Egypt? Did not Joshua take Jericho? These things all happened, yet they were said to be impossible.

Had Noah refused to build the Ark, his family would have drowned with the wicked. Had Joseph neglected to store up grain, his parents and his brothers, who afterwards became the heads of the tribes of Israel, would have starved as would also the Egyptians. Had Joshua said, "O, what's the use?" when on the morning of the seventh day he marched his armies around the city, the Israelites and not the people of Jericho would have been destroyed.

There is a lesson, all may learn here.

These are a few instances where men chose to believe the word of God. They were benefited and blessed. History declares in the experience of six thousand years that those who refuse are destroyed.

These incidents were not accidents. They are recorded in the Hebrew Scriptures.

Are there other scriptures?

Every people have had their sacred writings. Their wise men, their poets, and their prophets have recorded their wisdom, their poetry, their prophecies. These have been preserved by their posterity. These are their scriptures. The Parsees have the *Zend Avesta;* the Hindu, the *Veda;* the Mohammedans, the *Koran;* the Jews, the *Old Testament.*

Will someone tell me, "Did the Redman of America have his?" Or will someone explain to me, "How it is that so many of the beliefs and practices of ancient Israel are to be found in the myths and saga of the American Indian? Did God speak to their wise men as he did to the great Hebrew prophets? Or, did God leave his millions of children who dwelt on the Western Hemisphere to perish in ignorance of the plan of life and salvation?"

Members of the Church of Jesus Christ of Latter-day Saints do not believe it. They believe in God the Father, Almighty, and they believe it is his "work and his glory" to bring to pass the "salvation and exaltation" of all his children, everywhere.

They believe he has spoken many times to many different peoples.

Did he speak to the ancient inhabitants of America?

The Book of Mormon testifies, "He did!"

The Book of Mormon is an inspired and revealed history of the millions of God's children who dwelt on these American continents hundreds of years ago.

It is their Scripture.

It is a *"New* Witness for God."

Its cry is Baptist-like, "Prepare ye the way of the Lord."

To those who today cry *"Impossible,"* let it be said: "Be not like the neighbors of Noah who were lost in the flood; be not like those who thought the corn of Egypt would never fail; be not like the Canaanites of Jericho who put their trust in their city's walls and saw them crumble to ruin."

Let us remember, always, "Nothing is impossible with the Lord."

Thanks be to God, the Book of Mormon is written. "It was not left to treacherous memory. It was not left to the diluting influence of oral transmission. It was not bequeathed to hearts, diseased and depraved, who might corrupt it." But it is written, and written at the very command of him who said:

"Other sheep have I which are not of this fold, them also must I bring, that there shall be one fold and one shepherd."

—P. C. R.

# INDEX

Inheritance, lands of their, 297.
Iniquity, 335.
Intemperance, 336.
Intermarriages, 165.
Intoxication, 334.
Iron, 497.
Iron Rod, 62, 84, 150.
Irreantum, 23, 173, 174, 192.
Isaac, 52, 179, 202, 466.
Isaiah, 148, 205, 208, 213, 220, 280, 323-369, 447, 448ff.
Ishmael, 22, 56, 59, 165, 170, 171, 172.
Ishmael, sons of, 260.
Islam, 417.
Isles of the sea, 203, 222, 316, 319, 412.
Israel, 74, 75, 91, 108, 134, 137, 139, 203, 252, 254, 341, 354, 413.

— J —

Jacob, son of Lehi, 23, 52, 185, 241, 252, 273, 279, 280, 321, 451, 456, 457, 472, 483, 486, 487, 489ff.
Jacob, son of Abraham, 350.
Jacob, Book of, 451.
Jacob, House of, 208, 324, 400.
Jacob, Words of, 280.
Jacobites, 455.
Jacob's Discourse, 309-11.
Jainism, 155.
Jarom, 496ff.
Javelin, 497.
Jehovah, 198, 360.
Jeremiah, 47, 49, 57.
Jerusalem, 7, 10, 30, 55, 57, 215, 218, 232, 281, 290, 323, 341, 349, 373, 376, 503.
Jesse, 358.
Jesus Christ, 10, 32, 70, 76, 79, 81, 85, 89, 93, 96, 107, 132, 147, 203, 205, 211, 218, 222, 223, 236, 241, 283, 284, 298, 312, 321, 374, 375, 376, 377, 380, 382, 383, 384, 424, 429, 445, 446, 466ff, 487, 495.
Jews, 6, 10, 30, 39, 47, 70, 74, 96, 126, 142, 203, 205, 281ff, 297, 312, 316, 372, 376, 395, 411, 413, 418, 420, 445.
John, 143.
John the Baptist, 73, 427.
John the Revelator, 141, 143.
Joseph, son of Jacob, 23, 252, 253, 255, 258, 378, 460.
Joseph, son of Lehi, 23, 185, 187, 252, 257, 273, 279, 456.
Josephites, 455.
Joy, 248, 249, 291, 301, 400.
Jubilee, year of, 381.
Judah, 323, 341, 344.
Judah, waters of, 208ff.
Judgement, 77, 107, 225, 236, 238, 273, 298, 300, 371, 446.
Justice of God, 156, 157, 301, 303, 306, 485.

— K —

Keeper, 305.
Kenosis, 82.
Kid, 422.
King, 276, 317, 452.

Kingdom, 131, 157, 225, 302, 405, 431, 459, 484.
Kingdom of God, 423.
Kingdom of the Devil, 405.
Knowledge, 300, 358, 422.

— L —

Laban, 21, 30, 33, 34, 36, 39, 274, 275, 452.
Labor, 484.
Laman, 14, 25, 26, 31, 32, 56, 111, 166, 171, 186, 258, 260, 262.
Lamanites, 111, 278, 455, 463, 488, 492, 497.
Lamb, 422.
Lamb of God, 427.
Land of Promise, 28, 45, 57, 75, 97, 122, 130, 185, 189, 232, 235, 458.
Language, 6.
Lasciviousness, 464.
Last Days, the, 373, 377, 385, 395.
Law, 303, 382, 497.
Law of Moses, 39, 46, 177, 321, 380.
Learning, 4, 386, 404.
Lebanon, 400.
Lehi, 7, 8, 9, 10, 12, 24, 25, 27, 30, 45, 46, 47, 50, 60, 69, 70, 165, 185, 189, 194, 232, 241, 252, 258, 260, 261, 273.
Lehi-Nephi, land of, 509ff.
Lemuel, 15, 26, 27, 28, 43, 56, 165, 171, 186, 260, 262.
Lemuel Valley, 27, 66.
Lemuelites, 455.
Leopard, 422.
Liahona, 165ff, 169, 187, 188, 274.
Liar, 304.
Liberty, 234.
Lie, 388.
Life eternal, 305.
Light, 175, 384, 387.
Lightnings, 107, 203, 383.
"Line upon line," 408.
Linen, 114.
Lion, 422.
Loathsome, 111, 278.
Loins, 421.
Lord, 123, 146, 222, 225, 238, 383, 384, 404.
Love, 238, 387.
Lucifer, 247.
Lusts, 226.

— M —

Machinery, 497.
Madmenah, 355.
Majesty, 325, 326.
Maker, 291, 305, 428, 491.
Malice, 386, 388, 390.
Man, 60, 80, 81.
Manasseh, 351.
Manicheism, 153.
Mansions, 495.
Marriage, 165, 390.
Mary, the mother of Jesus, 81, 82.
Mediator, 250.
Meek, 304, 400, 405, 420.
Men, 301.
Men, young, 350, 363.
Mercy, 266, 308.